CHRISTIAN
ENGLAND

Volume One in this series
CHRISTIAN ENGLAND:
ITS STORY TO THE REFORMATION

David L. Edwards

CHRISTIAN ENGLAND

VOLUME TWO
FROM THE REFORMATION TO THE EIGHTEENTH CENTURY

GRAND RAPIDS, MICHIGAN
WILLIAM B. EERDMANS PUBLISHING COMPANY

First published 1983 by William Collins Sons & Co., Ltd., Glasgow
This American edition published 1984 through special
arrangement with Collins by Wm. B. Eerdmans Publishing Company,
255 Jefferson S.E., Grand Rapids, Mich. 49503

Library of Congress Cataloging in Publication Data
(Revised for volume two)

Edwards, David Lawrence.
Christian England.

Reprint. v. 1, Originally published: New York :
Oxford University Press.
Contents: v. [1] Its story to the Reformation — v. 2.
From the Reformation to the eighteenth century.
Includes bibliographies and index.
1. England — Church history.   I. Title.
BR746.E38   1983   274.2   83-5682

ISBN 0-8028-1048-9 (v. 1)
ISBN 0-8028-1049-7 (v. 2)

To the Anglicans who are now
the cathedral and diocese
of Southwark
and to the rest of the Body of Christ
south of the Thames,
'that they may all be one'

Contents

Preface

Part One: CHRISTIANS UNDER THE TUDORS

1   PRELUDE: THE FAITH AND THE TRAGEDY   17
Two armies of martyrs.   One faith?

2   THE PROTESTANT REVOLUTION   31
The death of Henry VIII.   The Protestant wind.   The
Protestant storm.   The crisis of 1553.

3   THE CATHOLIC REACTION   58
Queen Mary's Church. John Foxe and the Protestant
victory.

4   THE ELIZABETHAN CHURCH   76
The Queen's religion.   The Established Church.
Elizabeth's first archbishop.   Jewel and Hooker.   Byrd
and Spenser.   Shakespeare's religion.

5   DEFIANT CHRISTIANS   126
The Catholic Recusants.   Popes, politics and treason.
The demands of the Puritans.   The Queen against the
Puritans.   The campaign against the Puritans.   A
hollow victory.

Part Two: A WAR BETWEEN BELIEVERS

6   THE STUART CHURCH   181
James I.   Charles I.   Four bishops.   William Laud.
John Donne.   George Herbert.   Henry Vaughan.

7   THE COUNTER-REFORMATION   224
Two Englishmen and Rome.   After the gunpowder
plot.   A Catholic holiness.

8   THE PURITAN EXPLOSION   240
Entering a new world.   The holy experiment of New
England.   The birth of religious toleration.   The
English Puritans.   A war becomes a revolution.
Executing a king.   Levellers and Ranters.   Oliver
Cromwell.

9   THE PURITAN LEGACY   300
The death of Cromwellian England.   The defeat of the
Puritans.   Richard Baxter.   John Milton.   John
Bunyan.

Part Three: RELIGION IN THE AGE OF REASON

10   THE QUAKERS   339
George Fox.   From Quakers to Friends.   Penn and
Pennsylvania.

11   A CALMER CREED   356
Wren's churches.   Two gentle spirits: Taylor and
Browne.   A rational theology.   Thomas Traherne.
Religion, magic and science.   The faith of Isaac
Newton.   Two questioners: Hobbes and Locke.   The
faith of John Dryden.   The attack on orthodoxy.   Two
voyagers: Defoe and Swift.   Bishop Butler's triumph.
Handel's triumph.

12   THIRTY YEARS OF CRISIS   427
The restored Church and Charles II.   Puritanism
becomes Dissent.   The effects of the persecution.   The
end of Popish plots.   The fall of James II.   Anglicans
as Dissenters.

13   QUIETER CHURCHES   469
A failure of comprehension.   A Tory failure.   The
Church under the Whigs.   The alliance of Church and
State.   Protestant Dissent in decline and at worship.
Catholic Dissent in obscurity and at worship.

Outline of events   510
Index   513

Preface

This book, which begins with the Reformation in the 1540s, tells the story of English Christianity through the storms of the Protestant revolution, the Catholic reaction, the Protestant and Catholic objections to the settlement made under Elizabeth I, and the Puritan explosion on both sides of the Atlantic during the seventeenth century. It ends when the dramas have died down in the eighteenth century, with a more 'reasonable' faith and a toleration of quieter Dissenting congregations – Protestant or Catholic – alongside the established Church of England. The story has, of course, previously been told in various ways, often with an authority which I cannot match. But I have tried to do justice to Roman Catholicism in victory or under persecution, and to the uncomfortably vigorous, defiant and creative varieties of Protestantism, as well as to the Church of England to which I belong; for I have attempted to write the first ecumenical history of English Christianity. I have also tried to combine some study of religion as a social or political phenomenon with an emphasis on biography and with some account of the greater writers, theological or lay, whose thought expresses or moulds an age; for I have attempted to be more comprehensive than any previous one-volume history of English religion in this period. While writing for students and general readers rather than for experts, I have tried to benefit from the researches of scholars and to provide notes which constitute a bibliography of books recommended for further reading. In the early 1980s one has the advantage of a wealth of recent literature.

Of course I have failed in all my attempts. Space is limited, as is my competence. The field to be covered is very large, for English Christianity in this period of just over two centuries was astonishingly fertile and always entangled in politics. So much of the evidence – particularly evidence about what the ordinary Englishman was thinking – is lost. So much of the surviving evidence is hard to interpret: what kind of a Christian was Shakespeare, for example? And the complexity is hard to make into a readable whole. Yet this great, often impressive, story seems to me important for all who would understand English religion, history or literature as well as for all thoughtful adherents of the English Churches which took shape in these years and eventually spread out as worldwide denominations.

In particular the story must matter to all who would encourage the present search for unity between English Christians, since a deeper, more honest and compassionate agreement about historical truth is needed almost as much as is a theological agreement or co-operation in contemporary tasks. Our common past provides many spiritual glories in which we can all take pride, although the history of Christ's Church is often a tragedy. I have written in the spirit of T. S. Eliot's *Little Gidding*:

> We cannot revive old factions
> We cannot restore old policies
> Or follow an antique drum.
> These men, and those who opposed them
> And those whom they opposed
> Accept the constitution of silence
> And are folded in a single party.
> Whatever we inherit from the fortunate
> We have taken from the defeated . . .
> We die with the dying:
> See, they depart, and we go with them.
> We are born with the dead:
> See, they return, and bring us with them.

In an earlier volume of *Christian England*, published in 1981, I told the story from the beginning to the Reformation. The project will be completed by a third volume, to appear in 1984, telling of the Evangelical and Catholic revivals, of the strengths and weaknesses of Victorian religion, of the worldwide missionary expansion, and of the impact of the First World War. I could not have read so much in preparation without the resources of the Cambridge University Library and the London Library, and the hospitality of All Souls College, Oxford, and of King's College, Cambridge, to a former Fellow. Nor could I have written and rewritten successive drafts without the patience of Miss Jean Cooper amid much other work for me while I was Dean of Norwich, the city in which I wrote this book. I am deeply grateful for the leisure which made that possible, and for the sustaining love which I experienced in Norwich Cathedral.

Southwark Cathedral   D.L.E.

Part One

CHRISTIANS UNDER THE TUDORS

CHAPTER ONE

PRELUDE: THE FAITH
AND THE TRAGEDY

TWO ARMIES OF MARTYRS

Almost three hundred English men and women were executed as Protestants in the reign of Mary I (1553–58). The first to die was John Rogers, one of the translators of the English Bible, who was executed by burning at Smithfield in London on 4 February 1555. When his widow went to clear his few belongings out of his prison cell, she found his account of his examination before some of Queen Mary's leading councillors. According to this document, there had been an argument about the authority of the Bible. 'Thou canst prove nothing by Scripture', John Rogers had been assured. 'The Scripture is dead; it must have a lively exposition.' The man thus prepared to patronize the Bible was Stephen Gardiner, Lord Chancellor of England and Bishop of Winchester, a priest-lawyer eminent in public affairs almost continuously since his days as Cardinal Wolsey's secretary. He was the lord of four palaces and of a regiment of servants; and he was presiding over this trial in the church which later became Southwark Cathedral, next to his London palace. 'No,' John Rogers had replied, 'the Scripture is alive. . . .' 'Thou wilt not burn in that gear when it cometh to the purpose,' Sir Richard Southwell had sneered. But John Rogers had recorded the conversation – or his version of it – because he had rightly been sure that his faith that the Bible was alive would be stronger than the pains of his death.

As part of a series of misjudgements which showed how little idea Queen Mary's government had of how to win a propaganda war, the preachers whom they were about to turn into martyrs were often allowed to write long letters to each other

and to the nation at large. They were even allowed to exhort
the public at some length while chained to the stake as the
faggots were being lit. And many of the executions were
bungled. The wood used was often green; the rushes were often
soggy; the gunpowder provided as a touch of charity often
failed to ignite; there were no gags to stop either 'last words' or
equally moving screams of pain. Never in English history did
preachers occupy more influential pulpits. 'Good people,' said
Rowland Taylor to his parishioners at Hadley in Suffolk, 'I
have taught you nothing but God's holy word, and those
lessons that I have taken out of God's holy book I have come
hither to seal with my blood.' And this intellectually gifted
man, who had qualified to practise as a barrister, kissed the
stake to which he was being tied for his final ordeal.

Another Protestant preacher, John Bradford, who had
toured his home county, Lancashire, trying to win the people's
hearts from Catholicism, delivered his most telling sermon as
he was being burned to death. To a young man, John Leaf, an
apprentice candlemaker, who was suffering with him, he cried
out: 'Be of good comfort, brother, for we shall have a merry
supper with the Lord this night!'

In February 1555 Bishop John Hooper was executed near
his own cathedral in Gloucester. His life had produced a
mixture of reactions in his contemporaries. He had never
settled to enjoy the beauties of the cathedral and the countryside. The diocese had been alarmed by his zeal as an inspector
of the parishes, insisting on the new Protestant worship,
inquiring fiercely into the morals of the laity, testing the clergy
on their knowledge of the Bible – with results which he went
round quoting in righteous indignation. He had disturbed the
peace. His fellow bishops had been irritated by the obstinacy
with which he refused to wear the old Catholic vestments or to
come to terms with the old Catholic sentiments. But the last
impression which he made, as he burned for almost three-
quarters of an hour, left an image more powerful than the
complaints. His martyr's agony accompanied by a sinner's
penitence was to provide the most horrific passage in John
Foxe's history of the Protestant martyrs. 'When he was black in
the mouth, and his tongue swollen that he could not speak, yet

his lips went till they were shrunk to the gums; and he did knock his breast with his hands until one of his arms fell off, and then knocked still with the other, what time the fat, water and blood dropped out at his fingers' ends, until by renewing of the fire his strength was gone and his hand did cleave fast in knocking to the iron upon his breast. So immediately bowing forwards, he yielded up his spirit.'

In October 1555, in Oxford, a white-bearded and infirm bishop, Hugh Latimer, who had been Bishop of Worcester under Henry VIII and a mighty preacher under Edward VI, was similarly exhorting his own fellow sufferer, Nicholas Ridley, who had been Bishop of London: 'Be of good comfort, Master Ridley, and play the man. We shall this day light such a candle by God's grace in England as I trust shall never be put out.' And Ridley did 'play the man' although in private notes to one another in prison both bishops had confessed to torturing fears, 'so fearful that I would creep into a mousehole'.

One of those who watched these bishops suffer (and Ridley was still alive and screaming when his legs had been burned away) was Thomas Cranmer, the scholar who had been summoned into the story by Henry VIII's decision to make him Archbishop of Canterbury because of his convenient views on the royal divorce. Eventually in March 1556 Cranmer was also burned to death in Oxford. Fear had made him unable to stand upright under the intellectual and physical pressures. He wrote out both Catholic and Protestant versions of a final speech, although he kept the Protestant version hidden in his clothes, in an agony of indecision. For a time, in recantations of increasing thoroughness, he abandoned his Protestantism as heretical; then, in disgust at the cruelty of those still resolved to burn him, he dramatically withdrew these recantations; then he confessed, when questioned as he ran to the stake, that he would have accepted the Pope had the Papists spared his life. But after all these symptoms of the confusion of a scholar under temptations and tortures, his final appeal was to the authority of 'every word and sentence taught by our Saviour Jesus Christ, his apostles and prophets in the Old and New Testament'. There his conscience came to rest, and he held steadily in the flames the hand which had signed the recantations of his Bible-based Protestant convictions. His last words were St Stephen's: 'I see heaven open and Jesus on the right hand of God.'

Many laymen were more simply courageous; six Protestants, being burned together at Colchester, clapped their hands as the flames mounted. About fifty-five women suffered the same fate. Joan Waste of Derby had been blind all her twenty-two years, but had drawn her own conclusions from the New Testament – read to her by John Hurst, who had nothing else to do since he was in prison for debt. She was now burned. Cecily Ormes, the wife of a cloth-weaver, recited a woman's song from the English Bible as she was being burned in Norwich: 'My soul doth magnify the Lord.'[1]

But these Protestants who were ready to die for what they believed about the Bible did not form the only army of martyrs to be seen in Tudor England.

More than eight hundred young Englishmen left home in order to train abroad as priests in the mission which sought to revive the Roman Catholic Church in Elizabeth's England.[2] More than a hundred of them were executed on their return, beginning with St Cuthbert Mayne at Launceston in Cornwall in 1577. Already, before this heroic acceptance of danger and death in the English mission, a small but remarkable number of priests had left Oxford, Cambridge and other comfortable posts for exile, even while the majority of Catholics were conforming to the Elizabethan establishment. One of these self-exiled scholars, Thomas Stapleton, had produced books to encourage a new pride in the Catholic past. From his pen had come the first English translation of Bede's *Ecclesiastical History of the English People*, telling the story of the conversion of the Anglo-Saxons; *The Fortress of the Faith*, a book showing that

---

[1] A modern edition of the classic account (abbreviated) is *Foxe's Book of Martyrs*, ed. G. A. Williamson (London, 1965), and a modern study is D. M. Loades, *The Oxford Martyrs* (London, 1970).

[2] See M. R. O'Connell, *Thomas Stapleton and the Counter-Reformation in England* (New Haven, Conn., 1964). H. O. Evennett, *The Spirit of the Counter-Reformation* (Cambridge, 1968), and A. D. Wright, *The Counter-Reformation in Europe* (London, 1981), are the best summaries.

Protestants needed to be converted back to the old religion; and a book praising the three martyred Thomases – St Thomas the apostle, St Thomas of Canterbury, and St Thomas More. The Catholic past had become a call to martyrdom.

'In condemning us,' said one Jesuit, Edmund Campion, to his judges before they sentenced him to death in 1581, 'you condemn all your own ancestors – all the ancient priests, bishops and kings – and that was once the glory of England, the island of saints and the most devoted child of the See of Peter. For what have we taught . . . that they did not uniformly teach?' He had been a Fellow of St John's College, Oxford, and had performed brilliantly in debates before the Queen during her state visit to the university fifteen years before; the delighted Queen had promised him her patronage. Now he had been tortured on the rack so severely that in his clumsiness 'he likened himself to an elephant'.

When he was led out to his doom it was noticed that he had no nails left. During the execution he was 'quartered'. This meant that the hangman was paid to cut him down while he was still alive, drag his bowels out while he watched, and cut his body up. Sometimes the victim was allowed to die before this final punishment for treason was inflicted; sometimes the crowd insisted on such mercy. In Campion's case a drop of blood fell from the butchery on the head of a young law student, Henry Walpole. It made him join the Jesuits – and the martyrs. Campion and Walpole were among the forty English martyrs canonized as saints in Rome in 1970.

When the hangman held up the bleeding quarters of Father Mumford Scott, 'some noticed that his knees were hardened as horn by much prayer'. A notorious Protestant sadist, Richard Topcliffe, specialized in torturing priests, and often used for this purpose his own house which was near to Westminster Abbey. When he applied this treatment to a delicate poet, St Robert Southwell, who was a Jesuit, he is said to have done so with the jeer: 'Yes, you are Christ's fellow!' At his trial Southwell said that he had been tortured ten times, 'each one worse than death'.

Laymen also showed great courage. Some were sufficiently influential, or cunning, to escape the severest penalties, but it must have required great courage for a squire who had been devoted to farming and sport, his family and his neighbourhood, perhaps as a Justice of the Peace, to refuse the oath acknowledging the Queen's ecclesiastical supremacy, and pay the heavy fines resulting from such a refusal towards the end of her reign. When in 1580 the Queen offered the ablest lawyer of the day, Edmund Plowden, the Lord Chancellorship, he replied that he found no reason to swerve from the Catholic faith in which they had both been brought up. Some less prominent lay people paid with their lives for any outspoken loyalty to Catholicism, although most escaped with a fine or a threat. We read of a farmer who, making his last journey up the ladder to the hangman's rope in Winchester, blessed his ten children with the prayer that their deaths would be no worse than his. St Margaret Clitherow, the wife of a prosperous and Protestant butcher in York, harboured Catholic priests and was arrested. In order to avoid the necessity of friends, neighbours and her own children giving evidence against her, she refused to plead and was therefore crushed to death. And the humble could be bold when they still had a chance to escape. John Rigby, a servant sent to explain that his master's daughter was too ill to appear in court, was interrogated about his own religion and, knowing that the confession might mean his death (as it did), replied that he was a Catholic. Robert Colton, a simple boy of Wisbech, when examined by the Archbishop of Canterbury and other formidable elders at Lambeth Palace, replied: 'I hear say that England hath been a Catholic Christian country a thousand years afore this queen's reign and her father's. If that were the old highway to heaven, then why should I forsake it? I have no goods to leave. I pray you give me leave to save my soul.'

Under Queen Elizabeth I about three hundred of the English sacrificed their lives in order to save their souls as Roman Catholics. And the example of their courage inspired their Church, then and for centuries to come. Before going to his brave death Edmund Campion is reported to have told the Lord Chief Justice: 'We knew that we were not lords of our own lives. To be condemned . . . is both gladness and glory to us. God lives: posterity will live: their judgement is not so liable to corruption as that of those who are now going to sentence us to death.'[3]

ONE FAITH?

Such was the witness given by two armies of martyrs, Protestant and Catholic, to the fact that England during the second half of the sixteenth century was a country where religious belief was widespread and mattered intensely. For almost a thousand years it had been Christian England, a people not entirely holy or moral but taking pride in its saints and monasteries, a scene of honour for the clergy and of genuine devotion among many of the laity. Although there had been some rebels there had been more pilgrims and many more conformists right up to the sudden storm of the Reformation in the 1530s. That storm had, however, resulted in a spectacle which remains, in Sir Maurice Powicke's words, 'one of the most mysterious things in our history'.[4] For after all the centuries when England had belonged to Catholic Christendom, there had been little intensity in the opposition to the religious or pseudo-religious innovations decreed under King Henry VIII.

It was not that Protestantism soon became popular; for years the new creed remained repulsive or virtually unknown to the conservative people inhabiting most of rural England, and even in the towns and in the more sophisticated south-east passionate Protestants often complained that they were treated as madmen. But when the monasteries and convents were invited to surrender to the agents of Henry VIII, surprisingly little resistance was offered; the northern rebellion known as the Pilgrimage of Grace was suppressed quite easily. Even when the ministers of Edward VI suppressed the whole vast

---

[3] Philip Caraman provided an anthology of vivid passages in *The Other Face: Catholic Life under Elizabeth I* (London, 1960). David Farmer included many of the forty martyrs in *The Oxford Dictionary of Saints* (1978), with bibliographies.

[4] F. M. Powicke, *The Reformation in England* (London, 1941), p. 7.

cult of prayers for the dead, and stripped the parish churches of beauty which had been accumulating for many centuries, the revolution met with little open defiance. As fresh orders came from the King's council, radically contradicting previous orders and tearing up the traditions of many centuries, the majority of the English spoke only in order to mutter a medley of old and new prayers. They lay low, their ambitions being to escape hunger and relax in the timeless rites of the family and the village. The bishops usually compromised – for example, Stephen Gardiner, who was to condemn Protestants to death under Mary I, wrote a book defending the claims of Henry VIII over the Church. Only St John Fisher, a theologian who had been given the poorest English bishopric (Rochester), and St Thomas More, a layman who had in his time been something of a liberal and something of a courtier, produced intelligent defences of Catholicism. It certainly is mysterious that so many were acquiescent during such devastating changes.

Then came another very curious development. England became a country which produced and admired martyrs. Naturally the pain of martyrdom was embraced only by a few, and the piety was not universal. There are many hints in the surviving evidence that not everyone went to church – and that not every churchgoer opened his heart to what came in through his ears. Still, after the middle of this century the revival of religious intensity was on a scale inconceivable during the humiliating decline of medieval Catholicism. Catholic or Protestant or merely national, English Christianity was now bursting with life – and ready to defy death, or at least to applaud heroes.

If we judge the situation solely by the known sales of books, we have to conclude that to Shakespeare's contemporaries the most interesting subject was religion. *A Pensive Man's Practice* by one layman, John Norden, went through more than forty editions between 1584 and 1627. And preaching mattered. Educated Elizabethan laymen developed such a taste for theology that the time was coming when the House of Commons would often spend a whole day in St Margaret's church across the street in Westminster, in order to fast, to pray and to hear immense sermons on the state of the nation. For the illiterate or semi-literate mass of the population, words spoken in the pulpit possessed an interest now hard to imagine as possible. Under Henry VIII and his three crowned children, London crowds would gather Sunday by Sunday to listen to the preacher shouting at 'Paul's Cross'. The open-air pulpit outside St Paul's Cathedral, it was the storm-centre of religious controversy. We have to guess what it felt like to live in a village where the pulpit was the only place where news from far off London could be given authoritatively, where arguments and stories illustrating them could be launched to stimulate mind and imagination, and where all life could be judged according to the values which the community at least pretended to respect. Innumerable examples have survived of women who would analyse what the preacher had said for the instruction of their children and servants; of men who would discuss sermons when they met to drink.[5]

The literature of the time often hints that scepticism developed among some of the educated. Christopher Marlowe was an 'atheist' to many of those who watched his meteoric illumination of the possibilities of the Elizabethan theatre, and somewhat later Sir Walter Ralegh, that all-round Elizabethan, was rumoured to preside over a school of atheism. But the 'atheism' was certainly not of the kind familiar in the nineteenth and twentieth centuries. It was more an individualism which failed to pay respect to the dogmas and ethics declared in the pulpits and the schoolrooms; an exuberant, Renaissance pride in life defying the conventions, not a twentieth-century humanism defying a meaningless universe. Marlowe's plays showed an imagination still deeply excited by the old Christian images of worldliness, ambition and damnation. Ralegh's *History of the World* was set within an acceptance

---

[5] Glimpses of the power of the pulpit are given in books such as J. W. Blench, *Preaching in England in the Late Fifteenth and Sixteenth Centuries* (Oxford, 1964); Millar Maclure, *The Paul's Cross Sermons 1534–1642* (Toronto, 1958); J. F. Wilson, *Pulpit in Parliament* (Princeton, N.J., 1969); *In God's Name: Examples of Preaching in England, 1534–1662*, ed. John Chandos (London, 1971); *The English Sermon 1550–1650*, ed. Martin Seymour-Smith (London, 1976).

of the Old Testament chronology and he wrote a devotional, if
finally half-sceptical, poem 'but two hours before his death' in
1618:

> Even such is Time, which takes in trust
> Our youth, our joys, and all we have,
> And pays us but with age and dust;
> Who in the dark and silent grave,
> When we have wandered all our ways,
> Shuts up the story of our days:
> And from which earth, and grave, and dust,
> The Lord shall raise me up, I trust.

He began his last speech, near the executioner, by saying that
he was going to meet God within the quarter-hour. In the next
generation Ralegh became a hero to Puritans; Oliver Cromwell, for example, loved his *History*.

The power of religion in England from about 1550 to about
1660 is agreed by all modern scholars. It is, however, controversial to claim that Catholicism and Protestantism were
essentially one religion, making for the modern student a single
field of study. In this period the most sacred rite of the medieval
Church, the Mass, was commonly denounced by Protestants
as superstitious, blasphemous and idolatrous. This was because it was believed that Roman Catholics were ensnared by
this rite into the power of wicked priests, who demanded
money for the magic of each Mass. It was also believed that
Roman Catholics thought that what the priest did in the Mass
was a fresh killing of Christ, for the bread had been changed
physically into his body. It was believed that with their talk
about the 'Sacrifice of the Mass' they denied the uniqueness of
Christ's atoning death (his 'full, perfect and sufficient sacrifice,
oblation and satisfaction for the sins of the whole world'), and
that they worshipped the bread instead of worshipping the
true, invisible Father through the one, living, eternal Christ.
Roman Catholics, on the other hand, believed that the 'Lord's
Supper' celebrated by Protestants (usually with no great
frequency) was intended to be no more than a pathetic memorial to an absent, very distant, Saviour. It did not convey
God's grace as did the blessed sacrament in Christ's true

Church. It did not plead to the father as did Calvary's propitiatory sacrifice, which was sacramentally re-enacted morning by morning in the Mass, timeless in its Latin mystery and majesty. And Roman Catholics often alleged that Protestants – whether they remembered their Saviour or forgot him – based their religion solely on their emotions, so that they ended up by being far more interested in themselves, in their ambitions and chaotically conflicting opinions, than in the Gospel entrusted to the One, Holy, Catholic and Apostolic Church along with the sacraments.

Behind the dispute about the Mass or the Lord's Supper there was, or there seemed to be, a dispute about the very meaning of reconciliation with God. As late as 1963 a distinguished Roman Catholic historian still found it necessary to assure his readers that this division was absolutely fundamental. He referred to 'the abyss that must forever separate the two religions that differ in their accounts of what reconciliation with God means, the one building upon a belief that grace is a reality in the soul, the other upon the belief that grace is no more than acceptability in God's sight'.[6]

Many similar assessments of the magnitude of the 'abyss' separating Catholic from Protestant could be quoted from the Protestant side. Indignant theologians often alleged that Roman Catholics held that man was acceptable in God's sight because of his 'works', chiefly works of piety as ordered by the Church. They also claimed that to Roman Catholics 'faith' meant not a personal, reasoned trust in the Saviour but merely believing what the Church teaches. Such credulity seemed a faith fit for dumb beasts – as was often said. 'Wherein then do we disagree?' asked Richard Hooker about the Church of England's attitude to official Roman Catholic teaching as defined by the Council of Trent. 'We disagree about the nature of the very essence of the medicine whereby Christ cureth our disease.' Many Protestants have been sure that the Bishop of Rome, so far from being the universal pastor and teacher, the representative of Christ on earth, was the great tempter and

---

[6] Philip Hughes, *The Reformation in England*, Vol. 2 (revised, London, 1963), p. 79. Hans Küng's reconciling work on *Justification* appeared in English in 1964.

corrupter, the Antichrist predicted in the last book of the Bible.

'The 'abyss' then seemed deep and wide. Indeed, it is still sometimes convenient to refer to the 'old religion' and the 'new religion', for Roman Catholicism and Protestantism have often been so called. This book is, however, written in the conviction that the talk about the gap between old and new 'religions' as an unbridgeable 'abyss' has been wrong. Since essentially there was one religion, here is the one story of English Christianity. What united these English Christians was far more significant than what separated them, although they sometimes tortured, burned or hanged each other because of their religious opinions or because of the political loyalties inextricably mixed with those opinions. Both the Catholic Mass and the Protestant Lord's Supper were, after all, attempts to do what Jesus had commanded should be done as the memorial of his self-sacrifice, making the bread mean his body and the wine mean his blood and the memory mean his life to the believing community. And both the Catholic and Protestant doctrines of 'grace' were attempts to express in broken human words the common Christian experiences – being changed deeply by the intervention of God in the soul, but still needing to trust in God's mercy as declared through Christ; living gratefully a good life, but still needing to say that no merits of one's own can finally earn the right to heaven. On both sides of the alleged 'abyss' the faith of a Christian was to be seen. It was a trust in Christ known through the Bible and the Church, a trust which resulted in the Christian 'works' of love, joy, peace, patience, kindness, goodness, fidelity, gentleness and self-control. The courage of all the martyrs was the same. So, at its heart, was their Christianity. It inspired their living and dying. If it did not inspire them to enough charity, the blame should not be placed on the gospels which define Christianity.

In 1541 eminent Catholic and Protestant theologians met at Regensburg and reached agreement on the doctrine of grace: the Christian is 'justified' by faith in God through Christ, but the faith must be made effective in love. The agreement was soon repudiated on both sides, and a hundred years later was remembered only by a few scholars. Clearly it was a mere paper agreement, unrelated to the psychological, economic and political realities which moulded societies in the days of the Reformation and Counter-Reformation. The religion which it described was divided at levels deeper than the reconciling formula – and the divisions were going to remain deep century after century. Nowhere were these divisions to go deeper than in England, the country where Parliament and the Pope acknowledged different sovereigns over long periods, and where the Roman Catholic community which had been in a position to burn Protestants was reduced by Protestant vengeance to the life or half-life of a small group, full of dilemmas and fears as well as an obstinate loyalty, on the margins of society. The examples of the martyrs were cited again and again in order to light fresh fires of bigotry and to disembowel any living hope of reconciliation. It was the central tragedy of these centuries that so much religious energy was wasted because religious labels got attached to conflicting social movements, royalist or rebellious, affluent or angry, conservative or innovating. An island people which was to have the energy to govern a quarter of mankind, to begin the modern age's industrial revolutions, and to create a more enduring empire in literature, was for many years absorbed in conflicts between Christians. Thus the development of a spiritually splendid Christian civilization was crippled by the poison of a hatred which contradicted the central teachings of the gospels, and we have only a few gestures of charity or lines of poetry as memorable symbols to show us the Christian England that might have been.

But in this book we shall not be entirely preoccupied by the disputes. We shall attempt to look beneath the divisions and to glimpse the unity of a religion as it wells up into the lives of English Christians. We shall try to catch them at prayer; listen to them singing; see their hearts breaking or lifting; find out what was the holiness they sought; go with them across the Atlantic, or into Catholic houses as exiles in Europe, or into dreams of the open road while in an English prison. We shall study some of their poetry. We shall watch the Bible coming alive to them and promising a merry supper, or we shall watch them turning back to the Catholic Church as the old highway to heaven. We shall accompany them on the journeys of Christian discipleship; on old pilgrimages made new by personal conviction, suffering and delight.

CHAPTER TWO

THE PROTESTANT REVOLUTION

THE DEATH OF HENRY VIII

On the night of 28 January 1547, in the palace in Whitehall which he had taken from Cardinal Wolsey, King Henry VIII lay dying. He had ruled England for not much less than forty years. Those around him had been frightened to warn him that the end was very near, and because of the delay in sending for a priest he had grown speechless before the arrival of the Archbishop of Canterbury, Thomas Cranmer.

When the Archbishop came, the King grasped his hand and refused to release it. Cranmer charitably understood this to be the last sign of the great monarch's trust in his Saviour. At any rate, Henry had many reasons to be grateful to an archbishop who had been so unfailingly helpful over his matrimonial problems. As the King and Cranmer held hands and death advanced, in the long gallery outside the chamber Edward Seymour, Earl of Hertford, was impatiently pacing up and down. Seymour, by birth merely a knight's son, had become the brother of Henry's third queen. That had given him his chance to display abilities which no other soldier of his day could match. He reckoned himself fully competent to discharge the office of 'Protector of the Realm' now that his nephew Edward, not ten years old, was to be king.

The obstacle was that the dying king had been empowered by an Act of Parliament to arrange the succession by will, and the latest edition of King Henry's will had made no provision for any Protector. Everything was to be decided in the young king's name by a council of twelve executors and when Edward came of age (at eighteen) he was to be fully entitled to cancel any decision reached during his minority. However, Seymour

knew that he could overcome that obstacle. He had in his
pocket the key to the safe in which this will was kept. More
important, he had beside him that night Sir William Paget, the
leading secretary of state. Seymour and Paget had made a deal.
They had agreed that the one was to be the Protector, and the
other the chief councillor, and that until the king's council had
been persuaded by Paget to accept this arrangement the death
was to be kept secret.

At three o'clock in the morning, therefore, when Henry was
safely dead, Seymour rode into a freezing night. He was
hurrying to inform King Edward of his accession to the throne
and to take him into custody. The only hitch in the plot was
that he accidentally rode off with the key to the safe, thus
delaying by a short period Paget's ability to perform his part of
the bargain. But on the Monday Seymour was back in London
with King Edward – and was acknowledged by the council as
Protector of the Realm. He soon began governing by proclamations rather than by Acts of Parliament, and reduced the
authority of the Privy Council to its lowest level in the century.
Paget felt cheated. And so, gradually, did England.

One of the reasons why Seymour was impatient during the
uncertainty surrounding King Henry's dying was patriotism.
As a general he had been ashamed of the military and financial
disasters of the last years of the reign. Determined that Mary
Queen of Scots should marry Edward VI, he was now to crush
the Scots in the battle of Pinkie and to build a network of
garrisoned forts in the vain hope of holding the conquered
country in subjection. (With a wit rarely given to peoples so
treated, the Scots called this 'the rough wooing'.) He had, too,
a soldier's contempt for civilians whose acquisitive philosophy
was too loudmouthed. He wanted things done decently; he was
to advocate justice for the poor. But this soldier did not forget
to make justice for himself his highest priority while he was
Protector of the Realm and Duke of Somerset. Even a mere
secretary could accumulate a fortune in such times – as did the
wide-awake Protector's wide-awake secretary, Sir Thomas
Thynne, who built the great house at Longleat. 'Somerset's
own behaviour towards the property of the Church', writes a
modern scholar, 'appears essentially acquisitive: it is difficult

even to dignify it with the title of a policy.'[1] Somerset House
was to rise palatially beside the Thames, replacing three
bishops' London houses and incorporating stones taken from
the cloister of St Paul's Cathedral and from a number of parish
churches. In the county of Somerset and in Wiltshire a vast
estate was to be accumulated, incorporating manors taken
from the Crown or the Church.

Thomas Cranmer was also bound to be prominent in the
reign which was beginning on that winter's night in 1547.
Right up to the moment when he finally lost consciousness, the
old king had treated his archbishop as his personal friend, to be
sheltered from any accusation. But even a king so obsessed
with himself cannot have been without a suspicion that his
friend had indeed become a Protestant – exactly as his enemies
alleged.

In 1544, looking for divine assistance in the war with France
and Scotland, Henry had commanded Cranmer to provide an
English litany (prayers sung in procession). Weaving together
material from medieval and Lutheran sources, the Archbishop
had produced a litany of great dignity, apart from a prayer for
deliverance 'from the tyranny of the Bishop of Rome and all his
detestable enormities'. Since then he had been interested
chiefly in the prospect of creating other services for an English
Prayer Book. He had studied, consulted, pondered and experimented. A turning point had been conversation with
Nicholas Ridley, then a parish priest in Kent, in 1546. Ridley
had been studying a ninth-century treatise *Of the Body and Blood
of the Lord*, by Ratramn. This independently-minded French
monk had insisted that Christ's presence in the Holy Communion was spiritual, thus offering an alternative to the more
physical doctrine of 'transubstantiation' which later became
orthodoxy. Cranmer was to recall in 1555 that 'Dr Ridley did
confer with me, and by sundry persuasions and authorities of
doctors drew me quite from my opinion'.

---

[1] Felicity Heal, *Of Prelates and Princes* (Cambridge, 1980), p. 137. This is a
detailed study of the economic and social position of the Tudor episcopate.
Sentimental pictures of Somerset as 'the good duke' have been corrected by M. L.
Bush, *The Government Policy of Somerset* (London, 1975), and D. E. Hoak, *The King's
Council in the Reign of Edward VI* (Cambridge, 1976).

The drafting of an English *Order of the Communion* had begun (with the king's permission) in August 1547. When it appeared, it was likely to reflect the theology of Ridley and Ratramn, if not the Protestantism of the great contemporary Continentals such as Luther and Calvin. Or at least it was unlikely that Cranmer would merely translate into English the Latin Mass which his king still loved. When on his deathbed Henry clutched his Archbishop's hand, he was no longer clutching conventional Catholicism. In his will he had commended his soul to the Virgin and the saints, and ordered Masses to be said for his soul's repose 'while the world shall endure'. But the hand which he clutched was to be thrust into the flames in Cranmer's last grand gesture as a Protestant martyr, not ten years later. And that hand had already begun to write an English Prayer Book.[2]

The tyrant who now lay dying had been determined not to damage his own conservative conscience, or his prospects of alliances with continental powers, by permitting Protestant heresies to be uttered openly in his realm. Under the Act for Abolishing Diversity in Opinions in 1539, it had been made a criminal offence, punishable by burning, for anyone to voice any denial of the old creed or any contempt for the old Mass. This penalty had been inflicted on a woman, Anne Askewe, in July 1546. In his harangue delivered to the House of Lords on Christmas Eve 1546 the King had warmed to his role as defender of the Catholic faith, and a too familiar treatment of the Bible by Protestants had fallen under his special displeasure. But Henry had not consistently acted in a way which would make sure of a Catholic future for the country. He had refused to include the leader of the Catholic-minded bishops, Stephen Gardiner, in the council which (as he hoped) was to govern England, explaining: 'I myself could use him, and rule him to all manner of purposes, as seemed good to me; but so shall you never do.' While the King lay dying the leading

---

[2] The standard biography is Jasper Ridley, *Thomas Cranmer* (Oxford, 1962). An earlier study, C. H. Smyth, *Cranmer and the Reformation under Edward VI*, is still valuable (reprinted London, 1973). For his thought see G. W. Bromiley, *Thomas Cranmer, Theologian* (London, 1956), and *The Works of Thomas Cranmer*, ed. G. E. Duffield (Appleford, Berks., 1964).

Catholic-minded nobleman, the old Duke of Norfolk, was in the Tower of London awaiting execution for treason. The Duke's heir, the Earl of Surrey, an arrogant young man (and a minor poet) who had been guilty of a plot to seize Prince Edward, had already been beheaded. Equally significant had been Henry's choice of a devout Protestant, Catherine Parr, who was the author of two devotional books, as the last of his six wives. Charmed by her beauty and tact, he had frustrated a plot of Bishop Gardiner to get her executed for heresy and treason. And he had entrusted the education of his heir to scholars who made no secret of their own leanings towards Protestantism. The future king's mind was being shaped by Richard Cox, the headmaster of Eton, and John Cheke, lecturer in Greek at Cambridge. Effectively, Henry VIII's legacy to England was far less clear than was the personal Catholicism reflected in his will.

Although he uttered no word to this effect that has survived, the dying king must have known that a scheme for equal councillors wielding an interim authority was doomed from the start. The country – as he of all men was aware – needed government, not a regency to be administered by a committee. He did not trouble to include in his will any provision for the appointment of new councillors to replace any who died. He must have known that a strong man would rise to the top before the new king could take over – and was likely to be, in appearance at any rate, a Protestant. But it seems that Henry had ceased to care. Grossly fat, tormented by the pain of an ulcerous leg, the tyrant who had always been so ruthlessly selfish was not interested in a future he could not control.[3]

THE PROTESTANT WIND

When Henry VIII's massive corpse had been buried in St George's Chapel, Windsor, it was inevitable that England should be swept by a Protestant wind. It was also inevitable

---

[3] The best biography is J. J. Scarisbrick, *Henry VIII* (London, 1968).

that those who achieved the overthrow of Catholicism would not fail to secure their own enrichment. It has been estimated that in the course of the reign of Edward VI Crown lands with a capital value (twenty years' rent) exceeding £400,000 were granted away, mostly to members of his council or senior government officials, and lands which were to yield much more than the £320,000 paid for them were sold off by the Crown. Most of these lands (almost a thousand manors) had come to the Crown from the suppression of the monasteries and the endowed 'chantries'. The real value of these money sums is indicated by the probability that between half and three-quarters of the parish priests lived on less than £10 a year. It was a massive transfer of power over England.[4]

The new authorities allowed the obstinately Catholic Princess Mary to make the solemn celebration of the Mass the central event in the life of her well-provided household. It was typical of their general reluctance to interfere with the private thoughts of the people or with the private practices of the gentry. They burned no one, repealing Henry's heresy laws and relaxing the laws about treason. But the main effect of the new atmosphere was to liberate Protestant propaganda, particularly in London, and this assisted Protector Somerset and his associates in their determination to transform the appearance and the public activities of the churches. For all their willingness to tolerate private Catholicism, they saw very clearly that the public position of the medieval Church must be destroyed completely. Otherwise they could not be sure of retaining the pleasant houses which they were making for themselves out of the Church's ruins.

Homilies were ordered to be read in every church, advocating mildly Protestant doctrines but waxing most eloquent on the duty of obedience. 'Where there is no right order,' the clergy were to warn the people, 'there reigneth all abuse, carnal liberty, enormity, sin and Babylonical confusion' and 'no man shall sleep in his house or bed unkilled.' These substitutes for sermons were the work of Cranmer. Injunctions were issued

---

[4] These were the estimates of W. K. Jordan, *Edward VI: The Young King* (London, 1968), pp. 103–34.

commanding every parish church to possess the whole Bible in English and a copy of the *Paraphrases of the New Testament* by Erasmus. A pulpit must be provided for preaching and no more than two candles must be lit on the altar. Parliament passed an act establishing Communion for the people in both 'kinds' (bread and wine). Commissioners were sent out to see that these orders were obeyed, and Bishop Gardiner was confined in a fairly comfortable prison for refusing to assist in their enforcement; at last his conscience as a Catholic had prevailed over his loyalty as a civil servant. Bishop Bonner of London, who at first tried to resist, was frightened into silence. Lest the Church's leaders should nurse independent ideas in the future, Parliament made it clear that bishops were not elected by the Church but were to be appointed by the King's Letters Patent, which could be withdrawn.

Next the Protestant pressure was directed against the chantries, which were abolished by Act of Parliament in 1547. Chantries had been a prominent feature of late medieval religion. Thousands of benefactors had provided for Mass to be said for the repose of their own souls and for those of their families; as we have seen, Henry VIII had done so himself. Special altars, sometimes very elaborate, had added to the beauty of cathedrals or parish churches, and some great collegiate churches had been founded on this basis. The priests serving these altars had not normally been involved in the pastoral work of a parish, but had assisted the parish priest in services and had sometimes been willing (or required) to teach boys or assist the poor. The main motive in the multiplication of the chantries had, however, reflected a genuine acceptance of the teaching of the medieval Church that time spent amid the cleansing pains of Purgatory after death could be shortened by the prayers of those still on earth, particularly by the repetition of the 'sacrifice of the Mass'. To many medieval businessmen, it seemed the greatest bargain going.

Now all this lavish investment in heaven was swept away as useless. More than 2,500 chantry priests were either persuaded to serve in the parishes, or else pensioned. Endowments worth, it has been reckoned, about £500,000 in capital value (twenty years' rent) came under the control of the Court of Augmentations of the King's Revenue. This was about a quarter of the wealth of the old monasteries. Most of these lands ended up in the hands of laymen, and one estimate is that only about £80,000-worth was left in the Crown's possession in 1553. Probably in the end the causes of education and charity gained by the transfer of wealth. England was to owe much to the immediate foundation (more accurately, the reorganization) of schools and hospitals, in many cases bearing King Edward's name, and many of the laymen now enriched felt moved to make their own gifts in due course. But the suppression of the chantries was undeniably a major change in English religion. Only a few years before 1547 it would have been resented bitterly as an act robbing ancestors, parents or dead children of all hope of Paradise. It is a measure of the rapid collapse of the old belief in Purgatory that there was now so little disturbance.[5]

Gradually the Protestant wind of change increased in force. In February 1548 the council ordered the removal of all 'images' from the churches and chapels of the whole realm. It was an order which caused some churchwardens to hide the 'idols' away in the hope of better times; the old Catholic fittings were to be found, for example, concealed in the great church at Ripon in Yorkshire in 1567. The parish churches now at last began to look more consistently Protestant, with the paintings of the saints on the walls whitewashed over, the statues of the Virgin Mary and the saints near the altars removed, the great roods in the naves dismantled, the crucifixes smashed. Although we have very little evidence as to what the average man thought about it all, probably 'the scar left on the edifice of worship was in a true sense also a scar on the faith of many thousands of humble and unlettered men'.[6]

A little later the council abolished the use of candles at Candlemas, ashes on Ash Wednesday, palms on Palm Sunday,

---

[5] See W. K. Jordan, *Edward VI: The Threshold of Power* (London, 1970), pp. 181–239, and Alan Kreider, *English Chantries: The Road to Dissolution* (Cambridge, Mass., 1979).

[6] W. K. Jordan, *Edward VI: The Young King*, p. 184. See also J. Phillips, *The Reformation of Images: The Destruction of Art in England, 1535–1660* (Berkeley, Cal., 1973).

'creeping to the cross' on Good Friday, holy bread and holy water. By September the excitement with which reformers urged on their followers, provoking conservative reactions, had grown alarmingly intense and all preaching had to be prohibited temporarily. But the authorities had no hesitation in encouraging the more learned type of Protestantism by importing theologians who, they believed, would direct the wind of change in the proper direction.

It was a bad time for the Reformation on the continent; the Catholic emperor's troops had won a resounding victory at Mühlberg. Some forty Protestant theologians arrived in England to take up ecclesiastical or university posts. Melancthon, the leading Lutheran after Luther's own death in 1546, refused to make the journey, but he sent many letters of advice in response to Cranmer's flattery – as did the Swiss reformers, Jean Calvin in Geneva and Heinrich Bullinger in Zürich. The renowned preacher of Strasburg, Martin Bucer, chose England as his place of exile, to become Regius Professor of Divinity at Cambridge. The equivalent chair at Oxford was filled by an Italian ex-monk, Pietro Martire Vermigli (Peter Martyr). In the universities scholars of this calibre could fire off lectures and sermons in Latin with some effect, although in Oxford – always the more conservative of the two universities – people in the streets shouted obscene insults at the new professor's wife. Many less distinguished refugees crossed the English Channel to become students or tradesmen. They formed a large congregation in London – the first congregation to be left free to worship in a thoroughly Protestant way, disregarding English laws and bishops. They were sustained by the sermons of John à Lasco, who also instructed the Archbishop during a long stay as his guest in Lambeth Palace; he had been a Polish nobleman and a Hungarian bishop. Thus stimulated, Cranmer dreamed of a wholly reformed Church of England as the very heart of a successful Protestant response to the Catholic revival; and of a Council of London to unite European Protestantism theologically. But Protestant unity was a doomed hope, which the reformers on the continent had already abandoned.

In March 1548, a new *Order of the Communion* was set forth by royal proclamation, inserting English devotions in the Latin Mass; these included the subsequently famous 'prayer of humble access'. The pamphlet was, however, a temporary measure. That autumn Cranmer placed drafts for a new Prayer Book before conferences of bishops and theologians held in Chertsey Abbey and Windsor Castle. The clergy in their Canterbury and York Convocations were almost certainly not consulted; some doubt on this matter arises because the King, in a letter to Princess Mary, claimed that they had been and the records of the Convocation of Canterbury were later destroyed by fire. When the final draft was annexed to an Act of Uniformity, the main debate took place in the House of Lords.

There Cranmer made a number of speeches showing that his mind was still in some confusion, but Nicholas Ridley, Bishop of Rochester since 1547, more lucidly defended the Communion service in the proposed book. On the key question, he was clear that 'bread is made by the Holy Ghost holy and remaineth bread still'. Just as 'a burning coal is more than a coal for there is fire in it', so Christ's divinity was present in the bread – but it was also present 'everywhere', while Christ's manhood was 'ever in heaven'. This doctrine, revived by the Protestant Reformers, was held to have been the teaching of the New Testament and of the Fathers of the Church until Lanfranc, Archbishop of Canterbury under William the Conqueror, had begun to work out the medieval doctrine of transubstantiation, defined by the Lateran Council of 1215. The medieval doctrine was now explicitly denied by Ridley's declaration that 'the natural substance of bread remaineth as it was before'. Against this battering Nicholas Heath, Bishop of Worcester, could only reassert what 'the people commonly called the Church' had come to believe: that in the Mass the bread became 'the body that was wounded with the spear and gushed out blood'.

Seven other bishops eventually voted with Heath, along with two lay peers, but the majority in the Lords was sufficient for the proposals, endorsed by a much larger majority in the Commons, to become law and to be enforced from Whit Sunday 1549. Clergy who refused to use it were threatened with the loss of their benefices, even with life imprisonment.

This first Book of Common Prayer was well suited to its position in an Act of Uniformity. The new aim was that 'now from henceforth all the whole Realm shall have but one use' in place of the diversity of medieval practice. Cranmer adapted much material – for example, the superb weekly 'collects' – from the Sarum Use which had become customary in Salisbury Cathedral and had already been adopted in many other churches. He was determined to replace rivals such as the 'uses' of Bangor, Hereford, Lincoln and York. Another aim was simplicity. Here Cranmer drew on the proposals of Cardinal Quinones, the reforming general of the Franciscans, who in 1535 had planned the abolition of two-thirds of the Saints' Days, but the main influence came from the many Protestants who had encouraged him to 'put away . . . our excessive multitude of ceremonies'. The ceremonies abandoned included 'unction' (anointing with holy oil) at Confirmation. The backbone of the new book was the Bible – the whole Old Testament read chapter by chapter once a year, the whole New Testament read three times a year, and the whole Psalter recited once a month, always using Coverdale's magnificent English. In place of the eight services of the medieval daily 'office' only two services were to be said daily – Mattins and Evensong, each with two biblical lessons. But as the debate in the Lords showed, the flashpoint was 'the Supper of the Lord and the Holy Communion, commonly called the Mass'.

This service had so obviously been influenced by theological essays or actual services published for use in those parts of Germany which had accepted the Reformation, for example the *Consultation* drawn up by Bucer and Melancthon for Hermann von Wied, Archbishop of Cologne, in 1542. The central prayer of the Mass in the Sarum Use survived to such an extent that the English Protestant extremist John Hooper announced that he could not receive communion if it was used. To add to the worries of Protestants, Bishop Gardiner, now imprisoned in the Tower of London, announced that he could use the book. Indeed, all the bishops except Day of Chichester gave it their approval.

However, many people suspected – and rightly – that

Cranmer's mind had already moved beyond the ambiguity of the official book to an understanding of the service which was essentially the same as that held by continental Protestants such as Bucer or Bullinger. It seemed only a matter of time before a further revision would more completely destroy the Mass of the Catholic centuries. Meanwhile this new service was entirely in English – itself a revolution after almost a thousand years of Latin. John Merbecke, a Protestant clergyman on the musical staff of St George's Chapel, Windsor, hurriedly supplied the government's printer with simple plainsong-style music to go with the new words. And on closer examination, the service was seen to be new in character. No longer was there a mention of the priest's offering of the Mass as a sacrifice on behalf of the living and the dead; no longer would he lift up to God the miraculously changed bread and wine amid the people's adoration. The whole emphasis was now on the communion of the people, receiving 'these holy mysteries as a pledge of his love and a continual remembrance of the same . . . for us to feed upon spiritually' (as it was put in an 'exhortation' introduced into the 1548–49 services). The atmosphere was to be austerely biblical. Although the scriptural readings in this Communion service were mostly retained from the Middle Ages, at Morning and Evening Prayer the 'lessons' made very few concessions to the calendar, the supreme purpose being to read the Bible through whatever the season. To Catholic-minded Englishmen, it was ominous.

The year 1549 saw another change in the appearance of the Church. Although fast days were kept (for the sake of 'the men using the trade of living by fishing in the sea', it was explained), sexual abstinence was no longer required of the clergy; all laws prohibiting the marriage of priests were ended. Here was one more blow at the old idea of the priest as a mystery-man. The parson using the new Prayer Book was not expected to mumble Latin at the altar, to 'make God' out of the bread in the Mass, to live without a woman. Instead of the Virgin in the church, there was to be a wife in the vicarage. Many parishioners must have been deeply shocked.

In the summer of 1549 a rebellion broke out in Cornwall and Devon, fanned by priests. Already, two years before, an archdeacon come to inspect the destruction of Catholic images had been murdered. The rebels now demanded the restoration of the Latin Mass and of King Henry's heresy laws; the restriction of the people's communion to Easter, and then only in the bread; the endowment of two large monasteries in each county; the return of Cardinal Reginald Pole to the country with a seat on the King's council; the withdrawal of the English Bible; and the abolition of the Prayer Book. It was alleged that the new service in English was 'like a Christmas game'. The Cornishmen claimed they did not understand English, laying themselves open to Cranmer's scornful inquiry: did they understand Latin? The rebellion spread and besieged Exeter with plans for a march on London. Its repression was a bloody business.

Sir William Paget warned Protector Somerset of the danger in which his government now stood. He had made himself unpopular among the men who administered the State by his haughtiness (only exceeded by his wife's), and his religious policy had not endeared him to the people. As Paget bravely reminded him, 'the use of the old religion is forbidden by a law and the use of the new is not yet printed in the stomachs of eleven of the twelve parts in the realm'. However, the equally conservative north remained quiet, presumably still recovering from its rebellion against Henry VIII in 1536–37. It does not seem likely that reactions to his religious policy would have severely damaged Protector Somerset, had they not coincided with risings by men made desperate by economic change.

It was an age of inflation. The main cause seems to have been the pressure of the expanding population, which appears to have doubled during the sixteenth century in England. Another cause was the expansion of the money supply: silver flowed into Europe from the Spanish mines in South America, while the rapid development of banking and other features of capitalism made it easier for those who were credit-worthy to get credit. Still another cause was the improvement of industrial technology and of agriculture, making it easier for the efficient or the fortunate to prosper and spend, while labourers found it increasingly difficult to afford food or fuel.

Such changes were making the rich richer and the poor poorer; and their symbol was the 'enclosure' of common lands, long regarded as the property of the people of the village, to provide pasture for a landowner's sheep. Most of the profits to be made out of the production of wool, for making the undyed cloth which was England's principal export, had been made before 1550, and most of the enclosures had taken place before 1500 – but it was only now, when speech was rather more free, that men dared to complain openly about the greed of the rich. The denunciation of social justice became a theme of the Protestant preachers who modelled themselves on the prophets of Israel. The most noted attack on the rich was delivered by Bishop Hugh Latimer in his sermon 'Of the Plough' at Paul's Cross in London on New Year's Day 1548. But it was not only preachers who complained. A group of lay intellectuals, the heirs of the 'Commonwealth men' who had gathered round Thomas Cromwell under Henry VIII, emerged with proposals which were the first example in English history of the imperfect science of economics being applied to the impossible art of government.[7]

Discontent became explosive. The government needed to pay for its disastrous wars, but was not willing to levy large taxes or to halt the grant or sale of Crown lands to its own members or their friends; so it issued coins containing smaller and smaller amounts of gold or silver. This debasement of the coinage began in 1544 and sank to further depths in 1547 and 1549. It shook confidence everywhere and pushed up the rate of inflation.

Protector Somerset did not know what to do. He rebuked the rich; he issued proclamations against enclosures; he opened up the royal deer park at Hampton Court; he sent a commission to investigate grievances in the Midlands; he imposed a tax on sheep. By these measures he brought little help to the poor. But he alarmed his fellow landowners. Already his prestige had suffered through the half-mad jealousy and arrogance of his brother Thomas, who had married Henry VIII's widow

---

[7] See Julian Cornwall, *The Revolt of the Peasantry in 1549* (London, 1977), and G. R. Elton, *Reform and Reformation: England 1509–58* (London, 1977), pp. 310–27.

Catherine Parr and seen her die. He had then attempted to capture the heart of the fifteen-year-old Princess Elizabeth and to persuade the King to end the protectorate. Thomas Seymour had been executed (without trial) as a traitor, but the incident had not been forgotten by the equally ruthless men who now saw Edward Seymour as a traitor to his class. And the Protector was in no position to appeal to the people over the heads of his fellow aristocrats; his own record as a landowner by no means accorded with the later legend of 'the good duke'.

A month after the Cornish rebellion against the Prayer Book, 'Kett's rebellion' broke out in Norfolk and Suffolk. These were the richest agricultural counties, the most populous and the most Protestant. Led by a man of the middle class, Robert Kett, the rebellion symbolically dismantled enclosures of common lands, effectively unnerved the gentry, and attracted about ten thousand angry people, mostly poor, to a camp overlooking Norwich. From there demands were issued, combining many grievances about rents and the grazing of rich men's sheep at the expense of peasant rights with a few requests for Protestant clergymen who would be effective preachers and pastors. One of the clergymen who came to preach under the 'Oak of Reformation' in the rebels' camp was the future Archbishop of Canterbury, Matthew Parker, and the new Prayer Book was used daily. But Parker, while enjoying this uncharacteristic adventure, seems to have taken care to warn his congregation against the sin of rebellion; and eventually, at the end of August, professional and largely German troops arrived, commanded by John Dudley, Earl of Warwick since 1547. The mercenaries butchered Kett's men, who had mistakenly supposed that the government would respond sympathetically. Totally ruthless, the Earl of Warwick was the hero of the hour with the gentry and the merchants. By October he was able to strike against the politically isolated, militarily powerless and personally unpopular Duke of Somerset. Archbishop Cranmer added his own blow. Although he had been passionately indignant against the lower-born rebels in the summer, Cranmer was now shrewd enough to see that his political ally's days of power were over, whatever the legal situation might be; and he deserted him. He presided over the council which sent Somerset to prison in the Tower of London. In the confusion there was a brief and foolish revival of the conservatives' hopes; the Mass was said again in some Oxford college chapels. Then England found itself entering a period when the junta headed by Warwick would help itself to the fruits of political victory and would stir up a fiercer storm of Protestant change.

THE PROTESTANT STORM

Because England could not afford a foreign policy Boulogne was sold off to the French, leaving only Calais as the last remnant of Henry V's empire. The government also abandoned the gestures in favour of social justice – gestures which, however futile their effect may have been, had encouraged popular resentment against landlords. There was now to be a stern discipline and the poor were to accept their lot. It has been reckoned that the price of food for a labourer's family, which had increased by half during the 1540s (after increasing by half over the period 1510–40), doubled during the 1550s. At the same time the new government began to lay the foundations of an economic recovery which would benefit the rich by restoring the value of the gold and silver in the coins; the debasement of the currency had proved too disastrous. And those who had supplanted Protector Somerset proceeded to complete the downfall of the medieval Church, the field where the richest pickings lay.

There was still no thought of religious liberty for all. An independently-minded housewife, Joan Boucher, was burned in 1550. She was heretical on the subject of the Incarnation, denying that Christ had taken the flesh of the Virgin Mary. She taunted her judges for burning her 'for a piece of flesh', reminding them that under Henry VIII they had burned Anne Askew 'for a piece of bread' although they had themselves now come to abandon the belief that in the Mass the bread was changed substantially. At the same time, in order to demonstrate further the orthodoxy of England's new rulers, a

German surgeon living in London was burned for denying the divinity of Christ.

Archbishop Cranmer approved of these burnings. He also adopted a disciplinarian's attitude when John Hooper was appointed Bishop of Gloucester but refused to wear the medieval vestments. Cranmer had him bullied and even imprisoned, to make him yield the point before he could be consecrated as a bishop. The Archbishop knew how important it was for the official English Reformation to be seen to be theologically respectable and properly dressed. He was now, however, able to make sure that the transfer of wealth to the gentry from the Church was morally respectable.

Although his dislike of the naked greed of the men now in power became obvious, so did his unwillingness even to contemplate heading a move against them. He almost entirely ceased to attend council meetings – although he successfully resisted an attempt to deprive the see of Canterbury of its surviving wealth by protesting at the prospect of 'stark beggary'.

After the formal deprivation of the imprisoned Gardiner and Turnstall, the bishoprics of Winchester and Durham were reduced to the level of a stipend thought proper by laymen who believed that they were themselves better able to resist, or at least to enjoy, wealth's temptations. There were not many clergymen as conscientious as the Dean of Durham who refused an offer of an extra £1,000 a year with promotion as Bishop of Durham, because he would not agree that two-thirds of the bishop's traditional income was to be handed over to the Crown. The new Bishop of Winchester was John Ponet, aged thirty-six. He had married a butcher's wife during her husband's lifetime, but had then divorced her and married again; and he was more obliging than the Dean of Durham over financial arrangements with the government. John Hooper, Bishop of Gloucester, was persuaded to add the work of the Bishop of Worcester to his own, thus releasing more estates for hungry laymen. Thomas Thirlby, Bishop of Westminster, was moved to Norwich, and his little diocese, created in 1540, was suppressed altogether. It seemed probable that soon all the bishops would be placed on stipends of a suitable modesty.

At the head of the invasion of the bishops' estates was John Dudley, Earl of Warwick. For many years he had been quietly rebuilding the family fortune which had seemed lost for ever when his father, Henry VII's financial agent, had been executed to appease the people in 1510. He still moved with some caution. The fallen Protector was released from prison and John Dudley's eldest son was married to one of his daughters. But when Somerset could not resist an attempt to recover his political position, he was condemned for felony (although the Lords refused to declare him guilty of treason) and 'had his head cut off upon Tower Hill between eight and nine in the morning'. So King Edward coldly recorded in his diary. The Earl of Warwick took trouble to win the young king's admiration, was elevated to the dukedom of Northumberland, and devoted himself to the acquisition of land, particularly in the north.

With the triumphant new duke as its president, the council ordered the completion of the removal from the parish churches of all the painted statues, silver plates, rich vestments and other accessories of Catholic worship. 'Idols' were to be destroyed ruthlessly, although an exception was made 'for a monument of any king, prince or nobleman or other dead person which hath not been commonly reputed or taken for a saint'. Commissioners were sent out to ensure that these temptations to superstition were sent to London for sale by the government. Enterprising churchwardens had everywhere either secreted their treasures or sold them off and applied the money to church repairs; perhaps two-thirds of the goods had disappeared in this way before the government issued its decree. But another reason for the quiet reception of the order may well have been that people saw that it was useless complaining to these noblemen, who were in no danger of being taken for saints by posterity.

Under Northumberland the council did what it could to encourage those who might fill the religious vacuum created by the old Church's fall. The new Protestantism did not have nearly enough propagandists; it seems that only about a hundred clergymen in the whole country could be trusted enough by the bishops to be licensed as preachers. But some of the preachers sponsored by the government were veritable apostles of the new religion. Bernard Gilpin toured North-umberland, preferring the worst weather because then his hearers would not be distracted by their agricultural work. Hugh Latimer preached to king and people a vision of Church and State purified and glorified. And the Protestants were now able to enforce their convictions; for example, in 1550 Nicholas Ridley began to exert his reforming authority as Bishop of London after Edmund Bonner's deprivation.[8]

Cranmer, despite his unhappiness about the Duke of North-umberland's predatory regime, seized the opportunity to pro-duce ecclesiastical reforms. He had been nursing ideas for some time. Through the turbulent summer of 1549 he was working on a new 'ordinal' or book of ordination services, which after revision was authorized by the council in March 1550. Key passages – the 'exhortation' and 'examination' in the Ordering of Priests – had been drafted by Martin Bucer. The 'minor orders' from subdeacon downwards were abol-ished. Although the Catholic orders of bishop, priest and deacon were retained from the Middle Ages (to the indignation of Bishop Hooper), the atmosphere of the new services was decidedly Protestant (to the indignation of the remaining bishops of a Catholic mind). The whole emphasis was on preaching and pastoral work, not on the priest's power to offer the 'sacrifice of the Mass'; and to drive the point home it was now ordered that the medieval stone altars in the parish churches should be replaced systematically by wooden tables. New bishops were no longer to be consecrated with the mediev-al ceremonies, putting on a mitre, a ring and gloves. In 1552 further changes were made. New bishops were no longer to be given the pastoral staff, and new priests were no longer to be given the vessels (the paten and chalice) of the Mass – although St Thomas Aquinas had taught that this formed the essential 'matter' of the sacrament of ordination, and in 1439 a pope had endorsed that teaching. What new priests of the Church of England did receive, from 1550 onwards, was a Bible.

---

[8] See Jasper Ridley, *Nicholas Ridley* (London, 1951), and A. G. Chester, *Hugh Latimer, Apostle to the English* (Philadelphia, Pa., 1954).

In July 1550 Cranmer published his only substantial exercise in theological theory: *A Defence of the True and Catholic Doctrine of the Sacrament of the Body and Blood of Christ*. It was attacked, as a denial of Catholic doctrine, in a lengthy book which Stephen Gardiner wrote that summer in a prison cell in the Tower of London – an attack to which the council replied by depriving the author both of his bishopric and of his writing materials. Since Gardiner somehow gathered materials with which to engage in a further literary controversy with the Archbishop, a more effective step was taken when the council encouraged Cranmer to edit a new and more Protestant version of the Book of Common Prayer. Writing from Geneva, Jean Calvin urged the Archbishop to make haste; 'to speak plainly, I fear that so many autumns wasted in procrastination may be followed by an eternal winter'. The lines on which revision was to proceed were laid down by Martin Bucer, who published detailed *Censura* or criticisms of the 1549 book shortly before his death. From Oxford Peter Martyr wrote in with other suggestions, most of which were accepted by the bishops.[9]

The new Prayer Book was authorized by Parliament in an Act of Uniformity passed just before Easter 1552, prescribing its use in the parish churches and imprisonment for any of the laity who absented themselves; at the third offence, imprisonment was to be for life. (In 1549 only the clergy refusing to use the new service had been punished.) It did not completely meet all Protestant demands. This was to be shown by Jean Calvin's cool judgement in January 1555 that the book of 1552 was satisfactory in the main but contained 'bearable follies'. However, in England in 1552 conservatives were horrified to see how extensive were the changes which had been made to satisfy the Protestant spokesmen.

In the Holy Communion service the revisers had altered every phrase which in 1549 had allowed men such as Gardiner to say that the doctrine of Christ's 'real presence' was taught. The old title, 'the Mass', was no longer given even as an alternative, and the old vestments were no longer to be worn.

---

[9] C. L. R. A. Hopf studied *Martin Bucer and the English Reformation* (Oxford, 1946).

At the last moment, when the book had already been passed by the bishops and Parliament and printed, the council on its own authority ordered the insertion of a 'rubric' or note which explained that the retention of the custom of kneeling at this service did not imply the recognition of any 'real and essential presence there being of Christ's natural flesh and blood'. This order by the council was made because the king had been impressed by a vehement sermon against idolatry preached by John Knox; and it greatly annoyed Cranmer. But the denial of medieval teaching was not out of keeping with Cranmer's own stately prayer that 'we, receiving these thy creatures of bread and wine . . . may be partakers of his most blessed body and blood' – not, as in the 1549 book, that the bread and the wine 'may be unto us the body and blood'. The heart of the new service was reached when the priest delivered the bread to the communicant, saying: 'Take and eat this in remembrance that Christ died for thee, and feed on him in thy heart by faith, with thanksgiving.'

Elsewhere the changes in the Prayer Book were almost equally distressing to conservatives. Familiar customs such as the 'exorcism' or expulsion of devils at Baptism and the 'signing with the cross' at Confirmation were swept away. The sick could no longer have the Body and Blood of Christ 'reserved' for them to receive privately, and when believed to be dying they could no longer be anointed with holy oil. The revised funeral service abolished prayers which implied any belief that the condition of the dead might be affected by the intercessions of the living. And the medieval vestments, which Cranmer had so recently defended against Hooper, were also abandoned. Ridley looked thoroughly Protestant when, in St Paul's Cathedral on 1 November 1552, he used the new Prayer Book for the first time.[10]

Early that year, in order to expound more fully the Protestantism behind the new Prayer Book, the council ordered

---

[10] The best survey of Cranmer's liturgical work is to be found in G. J. Cuming, *A History of Anglican Liturgy* (London, 1969). See also C. W. Dugmore, *The Mass and the English Reformers* (London, 1958), and Peter Brooks, *Thomas Cranmer's Doctrine of the Eucharist* (London, 1965).

Cranmer to produce a set of short 'articles' of belief which it proceeded to revise. Cranmer had a draft ready because for some time he had been in the habit of asking certain questions of preachers he was being asked to license, and he had been discussing the possible contents of a new statement of doctrine with fellow bishops while concentrating on the revision of worship. Eventually Forty-two Articles were authorized by a royal mandate in June 1552, requiring all clergy, all schoolmasters, and all members of the universities on taking their degrees to subscribe to them. The Articles were never submitted to any gathering of the clergy, although they were issued with the false claim that they had been 'agreed on by the Bishops and other learned and godly men, at a Synod holden in London'. Cranmer protested at this contemptuous display of lay power by the telling of a lie. His protests were disregarded.

The Articles allied the Church of England with Lutherans and Calvinists on the continent, although some of their phraseology was more gentle than were some other documents of the Reformation, and they did not seek to establish an English position about problems disputed between the Reformation's sons. The definition of the Church was all that Luther had fought for: 'the visible Church of Christ is a congregation of faithful men, in the which the pure Word of God is preached and the Sacraments be duly administered according to Christ's ordinance in all those things that of necessity are requisite to the same.' The word 'bishop' did not occur in that definition, although the next sentence did refer to the Bishops of Rome: 'the Church of Rome hath erred, not only in their living and manner of ceremonies, but also in matters of faith.' And predestination was defined in accordance with Calvin's teaching. 'Predestination to life', the article affirmed, 'is the everlasting purpose of God, whereby (before the foundations of the world were laid) he hath constantly decreed by his counsel secret to us, to deliver from curse and damnation those whom he hath chosen in Christ out of mankind, and to bring them by Christ to everlasting salvation, as vessels made to honour.' This doctrine was said to be 'full of sweet, pleasant, and unspeakable comfort to godly persons', but other articles made it clear that those *not* included in the number 'chosen in Christ

out of mankind' would never be saved. It was futile to trust in
'the merit of our own works or deservings'. A man would not be
saved because of diligence 'to frame his life according to the
light of Nature'.

This statement of doctrine, clearly the work of a committee,
has been searched for ambiguities which might permit a
Catholic interpretation; in the seventeenth century Francis
Davenport, and in the nineteenth J. H. Newman, exercised
their ingenuity in order to make out a case. But when read
dispassionately against its historical background, the document is seen as an almost total rejection of the medieval system
of the Pope's supremacy, the infallible General Council, the
sacrifice of the Mass, and so forth. Catholic doctrines taught by
Henry VIII to his obedient people were now 'a fond thing
verily invented and grounded upon no warrant of Scripture,
but rather repugnant to the Word of God'. No fewer than
eighteen of the articles attacked the Protestant extreme of
Anabaptism, however. It is clear that one important motive of
those who published such a document in the 1550s was to
assert the orthodoxy of the Church of England against the
expanding left wing of the Reformation as well as against
medieval Catholicism.

Cranmer knew perfectly well that Luther and Calvin had
inspired legislation as well as new worship and theology, and it
was his intention to accompany the doctrinal summary with a
new code of 'canons' or ecclesiastical law – a project authorized
by Parliament as long ago as 1533. Here, too, he had been
brooding and drafting for some time, and was ready when the
project was entrusted to a commission of thirty-two by Parliament in 1550. Peter Martyr was again a chief adviser. A fairly
comprehensive document, the *Reformatio Legum Ecclesiasticarum*,
was completed.

As was fitting while the memory of Henry VIII was green,
the proposed code displayed a liberal attitude towards the
dissolution of marriage. Adultery, desertion or ill-treatment
could justify a divorce, and the innocent party might remarry.
The proposed code also reflected the new practice of continental Protestantism by requiring an annual synod in every
diocese, where representatives of the laity as well as of the

clergy were to consult with the bishop. Another proposal was that the bishop should be more personally involved in the administration of discipline, instead of delegating such duties to the archdeacons and legal officials in the practice inherited from the Middle Ages. As the eager activities of Bishops Ridley and Hooper were showing at this time, the effect would be to transform the bishop's role. But here again, a main motive was to discipline the extremism of the radicals. Englishmen taking advantage of the confusion of the times to propagate new heresies, or to indulge in old vices, were to be brought before the reconstituted ecclesiastical courts, and solemnly excommunicated. An excommunicated person, the new articles reminded the people, 'ought to be taken of the whole multitude of the faithful, as an Heathen and Publican, until he be openly reconciled by penance.' Hardened heretics were to be handed over to the secular authorities for punishment, presumably death. Adulterers were to be imprisoned for life.

It was, no doubt, the prospect of restoring power to the clergy on this scale that made the council under Northumberland's leadership abandon the project of a revision of church law. The code was not published until in 1571 John Foxe brought it out unofficially, and Thomas Norton, a Puritan MP, led an abortive move to get it made official. Even then, no action was taken. Shakespeare's contemporaries had no wish to see all adulterers imprisoned for life.

THE CRISIS OF 1553

The fate of the proposed revision of church law confirmed Archbishop Cranmer's dislike of the Duke of Northumberland and his accomplices, and a more outspoken theologian, John Knox, told Northumberland to his face that he was a 'dissembler'. It does not, however, seem that any of the Protestants had any idea about how close they were to a Catholic reaction. It was generally expected that King Edward would enjoy a long life, marry and beget an heir who would be educated as a Protestant. The King, himself an increasingly well-informed and sincere Protestant, argued heatedly when attempting to dissuade his sister Mary from her insistence on attending Mass. With his piety, his white skin and his reddish hair, he looked unworldly – but he was no bookworm. He was keenly interested in sport, politics and administration. And he was imperious. During 1552 he began issuing orders which implied that he would soon become as much of a dictator as his father had been. Had he lived to the same age as his father, his reign would have lasted until 1593.

After the Christmas festivities in 1552, however, the King fell ill. At first there was no great alarm. His sister Mary visited him and they exchanged small talk. Northumberland continued to keep her informed of her brother's condition, although gradually the rumour spread that he had poisoned the King. To the doctors it became clear that the King had the disease now known as pulmonary tuberculosis – and that it would be fatal, although he was only sixteen years of age.

The danger to Protestantism was frightening. Henry VIII's will had provided for the succession of the Catholic Mary if Edward died childless. The King had himself made plans to exclude both his sisters. Mary's exclusion was to be expected because she would undo all his work, but he also excluded Elizabeth, presumably because, as an unmarried woman of twenty years and uncertain opinions, she was too unreliable. The one legal argument which he could use was that Acts of Parliament, never repealed despite Henry's will, had made both Mary and Elizabeth bastards. Perhaps intending to secure Parliamentary approval, he had prepared a 'device for the succession' in which he bequeathed the Crown first 'to the Lady Jane's heirs male'. This referred to Lady Jane Grey, the eldest daughter of Frances, Duchess of Suffolk, a daughter of Henry VIII's younger sister Mary. King Henry in his own will had paid no attention to the claim of the royal Stuarts of Scotland through descent from his elder sister, Margaret, so that King Edward had this precedent for setting aside Mary, Queen of Scots, who was a Catholic. Now, when his own death seemed near, he persuaded the Duchess of Suffolk to renounce her rights and made a simple alteration in this handwritten 'device', so that it read: 'to the Lady Jane and her heirs male'.

Lady Jane was aged sixteen, a cultured and sweet-tempered young lady, and the wife of the Duke of Northumberland's son, the Earl of Guildford. In June the King – encouraged but, it seems, not forced by Northumberland – exerted all his remaining authority to get the judges and the council to endorse his 'device' in her favour. They all knew that if the scheme miscarried it would be treason against Mary; their lives were at stake. Some of them, Cranmer included, had enough courage to protest at the change in King Henry's will. An unrepealed statute had made it treason to contravene that will and had laid it down that, unless that will were to decree otherwise, the Crown should go to the Lady Mary if Edward died without issue. But Edward insisted on his way, and it seemed treason to disobey while he was the living king. On 6 July 1553 he died.

The preparations for the reign of Queen Jane were then put into effect. Behind the plot was an army of three thousand and all the hope of a Protestant England. But the troops sent from London under Lord Robert Dudley to secure Mary found that she had been warned and had escaped. From that moment all was lost. While she remained at freedom increasing numbers rallied to her stronghold in Suffolk, Framlingham Castle. The sailors ordered to guard the East Anglian coast mutinied in her favour, and even Bishop Hooper went about urging submission to her because she was the legitimate successor. In London the councillors, for the most part sheltering in the Tower, were in mental turmoil. Collectively they had to uphold the queen they had proclaimed; individually they were preparing to abandon Jane to her fate. Sir William Petre, for example, was happy to serve as a highly efficient secretary of state through all the changes between 1544 and 1557.

To counter this instinctive royalism, Northumberland needed to display very great determination, energy and skill. Instead he went through the drama as if in a daze. For some months he had been telling his few intimate friends that he was ill, tired and depressed; and now he seemed to be more conscious of the divisions and hesitations among his fellow councillors than of the need to capture Mary at any price. On 20 July, pathetically attempting to imitate the enthusiasm of similar scenes in London the previous day, he threw his cap in the air in the market place at Cambridge and proclaimed Mary queen. Almost exactly a month later, he was executed as a traitor.

On the day before his death he took part in a Mass in the chapel of the Tower of London, explaining to the congregation: 'Truly, I profess here before you all that I have received the sacrament according to the true Catholic faith; and the plague that is upon the realm and upon us now is that we have erred from the faith these sixteen years.' It may have been an attempt to move the heart of Queen Mary. Later that day he wrote to the Earl of Arundel, a potential mediator: 'O good my lord, remember how sweet life is, and how bitter the contrary.' But both his treason and his failure had been so complete that it is difficult to believe that he seriously expected to be spared; he had himself not spared the Duke of Somerset, who in his turn had not spared his own brother. He must have known that the game was up. The probable explanation of his return to the faith of his boyhood is that as death became inescapable he thought Protestantism poor equipment for it.

Many of his fellow countrymen shared his willingness to abandon the 'new religion' at this stage. England – or enough of England to be decisive – evidently felt that a return to the religion 'which hath continued throughout all Christendom since Christ' (as Northumberland said on the scaffold) was either right in itself or, at the least, an acceptable price to pay for political and social stability under King Henry's daughter. The reign of Edward VI had been a time when preachers such as Hugh Latimer had heralded the reign of righteousness and truth. But out of the range of the preacher's visionary rhetoric, every-day life had seemed less edifying. With the churches stripped, their comforting customs prohibited, and the poor experiencing the beggary which even the bishops feared, Protestantism seemed to have done nothing but damage and 'the sordid competition of all classes for a share in ecclesiastical spoils impugned the credit both of the government and of the religious principles which the government was claiming to promote'.[11]

---

[11] A. G. Dickens, *The English Reformation* (revised London, 1967), p. 298. B. L. Beer's *Northumberland* (Kent, Ohio, 1973) added a few touches to the narrative in *Edward VI: The Threshold of Power* by another American scholar, W. K. Jordan.

CHAPTER THREE

THE CATHOLIC REACTION

QUEEN MARY'S CHURCH

Mary's reign began very hopefully, and her finest hour was in those weeks in the summer of 1553 when, at the age of thirty-seven, she gained the throne of England by courageously insisting that she had inherited it and was fully worthy of it.[1] Her strongest supporters, the agents of the emperor Charles V, had urged her to accept Queen Jane, but she knew herself and her people better. She had been admirably brave in clinging to her rights and to her religion in the reigns of her father and brother. Under Henry she had been paraded in situations designed to emphasize her inferiority to Anne Boleyn's child. Under Edward she had been bullied in repeated attempts to make her abandon the Mass which had become her chief comfort. People knew she had at length submitted to her father after Anne Boleyn's execution, accepting his supremacy over the Church in England and the unlawfulness of his marriage with her now dead mother, Catherine of Aragon; they understood that this concession had made it possible for him to appoint her as his heir should Edward die childless. But they did not hold it against her. It was almost universally believed that a daughter owed obedience to a father and a subject to a sovereign.

Now that she was herself the sovereign, she often played the role convincingly. She was interested in administration and worked long hours at it. On many occasions she knew how to dress majestically, how to behave graciously, how to make a stirring speech; we should not always see her in the light of her tragic end. She was in a number of ways her father's daughter,

---

[1] D. M. Loades, *The Reign of Mary Tudor* (London, 1979), is the best study.

and many of those who supported her against Queen Jane trusted that she would revive her father's religious policy. Until December 1554 she did exercise a supremacy over the Church while securing the repeal of the Protestant legislation passed in her brother's reign. Her coronation titles included 'Supreme Head of the Church'; a secret dispensation arrived from Rome permitting this for the time being. On later documents the ambiguous style 'etc.' was preferred, but still she exercised the supremacy. She deprived about eight hundred clergymen of their livings on the grounds that they were married and that she had decided that the Church's medieval law was to be revived, although at this time the marriage of priests was still perfectly legal by Act of Parliament. In March 1554 she deprived seven bishops of their sees and nominated seven new ones for election by their cathedral chapters (having secretly and illegally made sure of approval from Rome). Had she simply put the religious clock back to her father's time, and had she married an Englishman as proof of this patriotic Catholicism, she would probably have continued to please her people well enough – and she would have recovered much of the happiness which she had known as a little girl adored by her sometimes sentimental father.

There were, however, already signs when she became queen that she was in conscience firmly persuaded that a Catholic ought to obey the Pope in religion; that her mother, defended by the Pope, had been entirely in the right. There were also signs that the strains in her life since her father had put her mother away had inflicted deep psychological damage on her.

In July 1550 she had nearly agreed to escape from England on a ship sent over by her cousin and constant patron, the emperor Charles V. When the Emperor's agents had reached her house she had dithered at the last moment, refusing to go with them but repeating: 'What is to become of me?' Had she fled abroad then, there can be little doubt that Parliament would have felt free to overturn King Henry's will and exclude her from the succession. In the event she had decided to remain – and thus to be available for the present reversal of her fortunes, which she attributed to the direct intervention of God. But her behaviour while queen showed that in deepest

reality her heart had left England with its prejudices far
behind. She soon disclosed her determination to marry the
Emperor's son, Philip of Spain. She had been lonely for too
long. There had been only talk of marriage for her (her first
betrothal had been at the age of two, to the Dauphin of
France); she had not known what it was to be happy – or so she
said. She was pathetically thrilled to be a bride. And after all
the years during which she had relied so entirely on the
Emperor for advice and protection, she was delighted to be
marrying his son. She was marrying, moreover, a prince of
the proudly Catholic country from which her mother had
come.

The mere prospect of this Spanish match ended Mary's
honeymoon with her people. One of the leaders of a nationalist
conspiracy in January 1554 was Edward Courtenay, a Catholic aristocrat with some Plantagenet blood. He had hoped to
marry the Queen himself. Another was Lady Jane Grey's
father, the Duke of Suffolk. A future queen, Elizabeth, almost
certainly knew of the plot and would have taken advantage of it
had it succeeded. The most forceful rebel was Sir Thomas
Wyatt, a gentleman of Kent, who led an attack on London in
February. After a fortnight of uncertainty, the attack failed –
one important factor being the steadfast courage of Queen
Mary, who earlier had spoken direct to the Commons, silenc-
ing their objections to the marriage on which she had set her
heart. But inevitably the rebellion was punished, and the
executions began to create the image of 'Bloody Mary'.

In the early stages of her reign she had been so little thirsty
for the blood of Protestants that in the period 1553–55 some
eight hundred of them were allowed to leave England for
safety.[2] The exodus had included Peter Martyr from Oxford,
Bishop Ponet of Winchester, and John Knox, who under
Edward VI refused the bishopric of Rochester as being too
Papistical an office. There seems little doubt that Mary's
government would have been relieved had the most famous
Protestant leaders, Cranmer, Latimer, Hooper and Rogers,
also taken the opportunity to escape. Cranmer, for example,

---

[2] C. H. Garrett studied *The Marian Exiles* (Cambridge, 1938).

had not been imprisoned until two months after Mary's accession. He had provoked the action by an attack on the Mass as a device of Satan. Even then he had been given time to send his wife and children abroad and to have a last talk with Peter Martyr, urging him to flee. Mary had been so merciful to the conspiracy to prevent her succession that she had spared the life of Queen Jane and had taken a third of Queen Jane's council into her own; thus Sir William Paget was still a leading minister. But now in the spring of 1554, Lady Jane Grey, her husband and her father were executed like Wyatt and many others. Courtenay was exiled. Elizabeth, after a brief imprisonment, was released, having given a promise of good behaviour. For the rest of the reign the Protestant princess lay low, attending the Mass and refusing to have anything further to do with the minor protests or plots which were to punctuate her sister's reign.

Mary's marriage on 25 July 1554 in Winchester Cathedral was conducted by Bishop Gardiner, who had already officiated at the coronation. Although he had at first favoured marriage with Courtenay, Gardiner had come to accept the advantages of a firm alliance with the House of Hapsburg, clinging to the provision in the marriage treaty that Spaniards should not hold office in England. Within a year of the marriage he had written a secret memorandum for Philip, advising him how to handle the English so as to allay their suspicions but end up by ruling them. It was a document inspired by the famous book of advice to a Borgia prince by Machiavelli.[3]

Mary's long-frustrated pleasure in married life was so obvious that before long her doctors were assuring her that she was pregnant. Public rejoicings and prayers were ordered. Letters were prepared announcing the birth of the next King of England, who by the marriage treaty was to rule the Low Countries as well, with the prospect of succession to the whole Spanish empire if Philip's son by a previous marriage left no heir. Every possible domestic preparation was made in the palace at Hampton Court, and the Queen's confinement

---

[3] *A Machiavellian Treatise by Stephen Gardiner* was edited by P. S. Donaldson (Cambridge, 1975).

became the topic of a nation's talk. But the pregnancy was imaginary; modern medical opinion is that it was the result of an ovarian dropsy which caused abdominal swelling. In the end even a heartbroken Queen came to admit that there would be no child. Her private prayer book survives; the prayer before childbirth is stained with tears.

The prolonged farce angered Philip. He was eleven years Mary's junior, and was now as bored as he was embarrassed by his time among the English, whose language he could not speak. The ambitions recommended by the cynical Bishop of Winchester did not seem worth the time of a prince of Spain. In reality, since Gardiner had failed in his efforts to have Elizabeth executed, or at least excluded from the succession, the only alternative to the recognition of her as the next queen of England would be a Spanish coup. Such a move was utterly inconceivable as a piece of practical politics; so that the Bishop's Machiavellian memorandum was not so realistic, after all. Queen Mary's failure to produce a child had made her whole reign futile, and Philip was in no mood to waste more time on it. In August 1555 he cut his losses. He left England in order to attend to his responsibilities in the Netherlands – and to the young, beautiful and cheerful women to be found there. He returned for three months in the summer of 1557, solely in order to secure a declaration of war against the French and the Pope (who had excommunicated him). After that he never saw his wife again.

Plunged deeper into melancholy by the slowly apprehended truths that she was barren and that her husband had deserted her, the Queen found some consolation in the frequent comparisons made between her and Mary the mother of the Lord. Her portraits show the increasing marks on her of a sense of mission deepening into mania. She had been preserved through so many dangers in order that she might undertake a great work for God and his true Church, and she had been denied so many worldly pleasures in order that she might concentrate on her religious duties. Her white and haggard face reflected her physical, and perhaps also her mental, illness. Her staring eyes were those of a woman who could scarcely sleep but would often sob her heart out in private; and her lips became those of a publicly inflexible fanatic.

Until his death in November 1555, her Lord Chancellor was Stephen Gardiner, who thus in his old age, after five years in prison, enjoyed the power which had evaded him under his master Henry VIII. He was impatient for the full restoration of their estates to bishops, monasteries and chantries. When this was refused, he insisted more successfully on the full enforcement of the late medieval heresy laws against obstinate heretics whose wills clashed with his. The cruelty was not out of character, for it seems fair to say that Gardiner 'spoilt his abilities by ruthless arrogance, unvarying deviousness, and a relentless hatred for men who disagreed with him . . . Among the power-hungry politicians of the age he stood out as the one man who played the game invariably for keeps: none of his opponents escaped a violent death'.[4] Protestants being tried by him delighted to embarrass him by quoting his defence of Henry VIII's supremacy over the Church, particularly in his treatise *De Vera Obedientia* which was reprinted by those now in exile. Protestants also reprinted the commendation once given to that anti-papal book by Edmund Bonner, now restored as Bishop of London and very active against heretics.

Gardiner, who knew that he was hated, sometimes expressed sorrow for his violent temper but often hotly denied the charge of cruelty. He could not claim to have been completely consistent; and no doubt Queen Mary was among those who remembered how he had eloquently supported her father against her mother. His nicknames included 'Wily Winchester' and 'Doctor Doubleface'. But two consistent themes had indeed run through his life ever since his birth in the fifteenth century. He had kept the Catholic faith taught to him as a boy; he had remained faithful to that even under Edward VI. And he had served the Crown. For as long as he could under Edward VI, although he had obviously hated the Protestants in power, this highly skilled lawyer had defended himself by arguing that he was only waiting for the new king to come of age, and that until then King Henry's will was sacred. It has proved possible to write a modern biography of Wily Winches-

---

[4] G. R. Elton, *Reform and Reformation*, p. 394.

ter around the belief that 'after attaining eminence he became the devoted servitor of Church and Commonwealth'.[5]

The central figure in the full restoration of Catholicism was a prelate far less worldly than Gardiner. Cardinal Reginald Pole landed at Dover as the papal legate (ambassador) on 20 November 1554, and ten days later presided at a highly emotional ceremony reconciling England to the papacy. He had been appointed legate fifteen months before, but the Emperor had held him up in his journey since he had made no secret of his opposition to the Spanish marriage, and the English had been not at all impatient to receive him. Parliament wished to make absolutely sure that no question of the forcible restoration of church lands would arise.

Pole, unlike Gardiner, was a true aristocrat. His mother, Margaret Countess of Salisbury, had been the daughter of the Duke of Clarence, Edward IV's brother. He was also a man of deep prayer and wide culture. His time in Oxford had caused Sir Thomas More to declare him 'no less conspicuous for his virtue than for his learning'. He had gone to Italy for further study in 1521, and had returned there in 1530, since the service of Henry VIII implied in the offer of the Archbishopric of York on Cardinal Wolsey's fall was too distasteful.

He had been made a cardinal and appointed to high office in the papal states. When in 1536 Pope Paul III intended to make changes in the Vatican, Pole had been one of the reformers drawing up the programme. When the Council of Trent met to undertake reform in the winter of 1545–46, he had been one of the three cardinals presiding. When the cardinals were electing a new pope in the winter of 1549–50, he had been the Emperor's candidate and had come within one vote of the majority needed. But he had shown a cautious sympathy with moderates such as Cardinal Contarini (a fellow aristocrat), who saw the need to reform a corrupt Church. These moderates had been converted to a personal, Christ-centred religion themselves and, while loyally Catholic, did not condemn Lutheranism as totally heretical. The arrival of the French cardinals had cost Pole the papacy, but he may also have been thought too

[5] J. A. Muller, *Stephen Gardiner and the Tudor Reaction* (London, 1926), p. 301.

much the aloof English aristocrat, still a deacon not a priest. It was typical of him that he withdrew from the Council of Trent with the plea that his health had broken down under the strain. His heart had never been in the politics surrounding the papacy, and he was now glad to be recalled to an England he had not seen for almost a quarter of a century. It was a curious consequence of his response to his new vocation as a pastor among his fellow countrymen that he was at last willing to be ordained a priest – two days before his consecration as Archbishop of Canterbury, in March 1556.

During Pole's time in England, however, the former Cardinal Caraffa became Pope Paul IV. The new pope, a very stupid man, had two hatreds: for the Spaniards who had conquered his native Naples, and for reformers who for all he knew might be heretics. Both hatreds were satisfied by the insults now delivered to Philip of Spain's wife and to Pole, who was stripped of his title as papal legate to England. The title was then given to a Franciscan friar who, like the Pope, was in his eighties and totally conservative. As a member of a reforming circle under suspicion among the now triumphant guardians of ultra-orthodoxy, Pole was summoned to Rome to answer accusations of heresy before the tribunal of the Inquisition. With the support of his queen he refused to travel, and was saved from further humiliation by the long illness which led to his death. Such was the reward of his loyalty to the papacy.[6]

Why, then, was Pole described by his successor at Canterbury as the 'cannibal' of the English Church? Why did he always refuse to meet his predecessor? – thus showing considerably less courtesy than Cranmer had shown to Bishop Gardiner when at the height of his power. Why did this scholar who had risked the accusation of heresy in order to do theological justice to the Lutherans fail to take the Protestantism of his fellow countrymen seriously? And why did this spiritually-minded aristocrat who was too fastidious to be much involved in the gruesome business of burning heretics (in his own

---

[6] William Shenk, *Reginald Pole, Cardinal of England* (London, 1950), has been supplemented by David Fenlon, *Heresy and Obedience in Tridentine Italy: Cardinal Pole and the Counter-Reformation* (Cambridge, 1972).

diocese he left it to the Bishop of Dover) nevertheless allow so much energy to be diverted to that policy, so that a modern scholar can truly say that 'the Marian Church was far more concerned with the few who defied it than with the many who ignored it'?[7]

One explanation is that the Cardinal had a cosmopolitan aristocrat's contempt for the lowborn and half-educated Protestant extremists who supplied many of the victims of the purge over which he presided. Archbishop Cranmer's own attitude had not been very different. But another motive seems to have dominated the Cardinal's heart in this matter. He passionately despised Cranmer and the other bishops who had done Henry VIII's bidding. He despised them because to him Henry was not a monarch to be judged by normal standards; he was a monster. Pole had abandoned his habitual caution and good manners to say as much in the only big book he ever produced – *De Unitate Ecclesiae*, written in 1536 immediately after the shock of the executions of More and Fisher. His loathing had deepened when, pursuing revenge, Henry had executed not only the Cardinal's brother and a cousin but also his old and saintly mother. On Pole's side also, mercy had become impossible.

The desire to discredit Henry's archbishop seems to have been the reason why Cranmer was now tormented. He was held in prison, sometimes in harsh conditions, all the time from his arrest in September 1553 to his execution in March 1556. Although he had been sentenced to be hanged as a traitor, he was kept for burning as a heretic. But first his will must be broken. His mind must be confused by the arguments of theologians robust in health and with access to books; the enormity of his present offence of defying King Henry's daughter must be brought home to trouble his conscience; the prospect of great physical pain must be allowed to torture this timid scholar's imagination; and the hope of obtaining his sovereign's mercy must be sustained long enough to make him grovel. Even when at the height of his physical and intellectual powers Cranmer had turned for instruction to Henry VIII or

---

[7] D. M. Loades, *The Oxford Martyrs*, p. 148.

Nicholas Ridley, Martin Bucer or Peter Martyr; now, provided
with instructors who had the power of life or death over him, he
would be made to confess the error of his ways. But after all
these humiliations he would still not be allowed to live, because
his life of service to Henry VIII had been unforgivable. Pole's
policy was to make Cranmer repent – but still perish in agony.

Pole also possessed a returned exile's belief that nothing of
importance had happened in his absence. When he first spoke
to Parliament about his sacred mission, he promised that 'all
matters that be past' would be 'cast into the sea of forgetful-
ness'. That was received as a tactful hint that the lay owners of
the lands of the monasteries, the chantries and the bishops
were safe, and that all the clergy ordained or promoted since
the beginning of the schism would be secure in their offices. But
Pole's aloofness also implied a very arrogant dismissal of all the
religious effects of Cranmer's work and of the whole influence
of the English Bibles and the English Prayer Books. This
mistake led to a fatally inadequate response to the religious
challenge of the 1550s.

The two and a half years during which Pole was both papal
legate and Archbishop of Canterbury were too short to leave
behind more than a fragmentary impression of what was the
potential in the reconstruction of the Catholic Church. In some
ways the Cardinal was wisely cautious. On Christmas Eve
1554 he made a present to the owners of church lands by
explicitly leaving the question of their ownership to their
consciences. He also seems to have involved himself in politics
as little as he could; and he rejected repeated offers of assistance from the newly-founded Jesuit Order, preferring to rely
on loyal Englishmen.

In some other ways Pole was wisely creative. In November
1555 he summoned the bishops and clergy of the Convocations
of Canterbury and York to a national synod in London, and his
opening address blamed the evils of recent years on the
slackness of priests. In response decrees were passed dealing
with the most prominent abuses in the late medieval system.
Pastors must reside among their flocks, must live frugally,
must be chaste and charitable, must preach systematically,
and must be trained in new seminaries to be created. An

English translation of the New Testament was to be authorized, together with an official catechism to be used in teaching.
Having laid this foundation for the long overdue renewal of the
Catholic system, Pole sent commissioners to inspect the dioceses and to reform the universities.

The main problem which these inspectors faced was the
shortage of priests – or of priests willing to live as unmarried
men. It was ominous that two Spanish friars, de Soto and de
Garcina, who made themselves obnoxious at Cranmer's trial
and execution, had to be appointed as professors of Divinity
and Hebrew at Oxford. The new bishops chosen by Pole, or by
Stephen Gardiner before his arrival, were, however, chosen
well – as was to be seen when they all remained faithful to the
old religion in the next reign. Bishops were encouraged to give
a lead to the parish clergy, who were also to be heartened by an
improvement in their stipends; the Queen promised to renounce the 'first fruits' and 'tenths' which since Henry VIII's
time had gone as taxes to the Crown. Pole also gave his blessing
to the restoration of religious houses, hoping that these would
be only the first fruits of a wide recovery of the monastic life.
Amid appropriate celebrations the Benedictines returned to
Westminster Abbey, the Dominicans to Smithfield, the Franciscans to Greenwich, the Carthusians to Sheen.[8]

Pole was, however, outstanding neither as a spiritual leader
nor as an administrator. He has been criticized fairly for
concentrating too much on the legalities when the real problem
was the irreversible decline of medieval religion, shown by the
fact that of about 1,500 former monks, nuns or friars still alive
in England in the 1550s barely a hundred volunteered to staff
the restored religious houses. What England needed, if its
Catholicism was ever to be secure again, was a radical renewal
in religion. We may speculate that had Catholicism been
destined to remain established in England, Pole would have
been remembered as a transitional figure, making way for an
archbishop more typical of the ardent, energetic Catholicism of

---

[8] See David Knowles, *The Religious Orders in England*, Vol. 3 (Cambridge, 1959),
pp. 421–43, and R. H. Pogson on 'Revival and Reform in Mary Tudor's Church' in
Journal of Ecclesiastical History (London, 1974), pp. 249–65.

the Counter-Reformation. But all his schemes were doomed. So was his queen; and so was he.

Both Mary and he were ailing anyway, but their disappointments seem to have crushed any will to survive. One sign of their slackening grip was that they left five sees vacant for Elizabeth to fill, making it far easier for the changes in religion accompanying her accession to be given the prestige of legality. Queen Mary's melancholy intensified when the war with France, into which England had been dragged by Philip, resulted in the loss of the last remnant of the medieval English empire, Calais. The Cardinal's gloom deepened when the Pope, who was now his enemy, made it clear that his standing in Rome was completely lost. Both the Queen and the Cardinal were also aware that the burning of heretics had succeeded neither in attracting nor in terrorizing the English. Since January 1556 it had no longer been the practice to offer royal pardons to heretics at the stake if they would recant before the fire was lit, because of the eloquent contempt with which the offer had almost always been received. The Queen knew that she was hated by her people, and the Cardinal was not under the illusion that he was loved.

In one last cruel deception, Mary's doctors did not contradict her wild hope that the latest swelling showed that she was after all about to give birth to an heir. In fact the swollen stomach was a symptom of a dropsy which proved fatal. As the dropsy grew worse, the popular turning to Elizabeth grew more open. It was already clear that her half-sister had triumphed simply by surviving. Mary could only send her, with some jewels, a note expressing hope that she would always remain loyal to the Catholic faith.

Early in the morning of 17 November 1558, having heard a last Mass in her bedroom in her palace in Westminster, Mary died. Her will provided that her mother's body was to be brought to Westminster Abbey, to lie beside her own; in fact, Mary was to share a grave there with the triumphant Elizabeth. The news of the Queen's death was taken across the river to Cardinal Pole as he lay mortally ill in Lambeth Palace. It brought on his own last agonies.

JOHN FOXE AND THE PROTESTANT VICTORY

God knows it is not force nor might,
nor war nor warlike band,
Nor shield and spear, nor dint of sword,
that must convert the land.
It is the blood by martyrs shed,
it is that noble train,
That fight with word and not with sword,
and Christ their captain.

St Henry Walpole, the author of that poem on the execution of the Jesuit, St Edmund Campion, was willing to become a martyr himself; and his courage will impress those untouched by his verse. Hundreds of Englishmen who accepted death under Elizabeth I, in what they considered to be the defence of the Catholic faith, testified as eloquently as brave men could to the innermost reality of their religion. Of course such a religion survived Queen Mary and Cardinal Pole. It did not depend on a queen's wish to be reconciled to a pope and it could not be discredited by a pope's hostility to a cardinal – or by any other error among all the tragedies of Queen Mary's reign. The spiritual splendours of an English Catholicism loyal to Rome went back to the arrival of St Augustine in Canterbury in the sixth century and were to be increased by a great record of 'blood by martyrs shed' in the sixteenth century. We cannot be at all surprised that the bulk of the English people was slow to embrace any alternative to this faith; nor is it amazing that a remnant of the English people has always remained faithful to it. Yet it is a fact of history that the ancient glories of Roman Catholicism were in the end eclipsed in the minds of most Englishmen by the moral victory of Protestantism. And we have to ask why the new form of Christianity – an innovation which had seemed an intolerable novelty under Henry VIII, and which had been disgraced by the conduct of many who had called themselves Protestants when briefly flourishing in the reign of Edward VI – was in the end to convert the land.

It is not enough to reply that Mary was succeeded by a Protestant. As we are about to see, Elizabeth's personal position and the history of her reign were both far more complicated than that. She had to compromise. She could never have imposed a thoroughgoing Protestantism on a persistently Catholic people. For now the religious issue was becoming more important than the monarchy itself, in the eyes of some at any rate. Under Mary Protestant leaders slowly began to move away from the simple belief that the legitimate sovereign always deserved support and obedience – the belief that had been of such advantage to Mary in 1553. In exile John Ponet published *A Short Treatise of Politic Power*; it was the first book in English to say openly that a tyrant should be disobeyed, even killed, and to leave the judgement about who was a tyrant to the individual's conscience. Thus loyalty to the conscience was beginning to count for more than loyalty to the Crown, and in Elizabeth's own reign many Englishmen were to show by their lives and deaths that by the ultimate test their supreme loyalty was not to her. Such evidence demonstrates that the answer to the question 'Why did Protestantism gradually prevail?' is not to be found entirely in the personal Protestantism of an allegedly despotic Elizabeth.

The true answer can be glimpsed in the work of John Foxe. He never attained – or sought – any office in the Church higher than a canonry in Salisbury Cathedral. He wrote a big book, known familiarly as his 'Book of Martyrs'. Its full title was *Acts and Monuments of these latter and perilous days, touching matters of the Church, wherein are comprehended and described the great persecutions and horrible troubles, that have been brought and practised by the Romish prelates, specially in this Realm of England and Scotland, from the year of our Lord a thousand, unto the time now present.*

Born in 1517, Foxe became a Fellow of Magdalen College, Oxford where to the dismay of his colleagues he underwent a serious conversion and emerged a Protestant. He eventually had to leave Oxford – and England, for in 1554 he was allowed to go into exile and to earn a meagre living as a proof-reader with a printer in Switzerland. He was not the stuff of which martyrs were made, but already before he escaped from the Catholic reaction he had begun to collect materials for his book about martyrs. Some of his researches were published in Latin soon after his escape and they made known to Europe the story of the Lollards, the English heretics who had already suffered under Catholic prelates long before Martin Luther's more famous protest. A second Latin volume followed in 1559, but by now Foxe's ambition was clearer. It was to tell the story of Luther and his fellow Protestants to England, with a comprehensiveness which no previous English author had attempted. Above all, his ambition was to tell the world the story of the Englishmen who had accepted death when he had himself sought safety.

His whole life was to be given to this mission. He was not interested in ecclesiastical promotion; he disliked wearing the surplice which the Queen now ordered, but above all he disliked taking time off from his literary labours. He ruined his health by his obsession, despite his family's pleas – although he found time to befriend the poor and the troubled, as the crowd at his funeral was to show. And his insistence on writing won for him countless readers. The first English edition of his great work appeared in 1563, and an expanded edition in two volumes followed in 1570. Until his death at the age of seventy he continued to revise the work, inserting corrections or additions supplied by many correspondents. In 1571 it was ordered that every cathedral, and the dining room of every cathedral canon or superior clergyman, should possess a copy.

Foxe was convinced that the Pope was the Antichrist prophesied in the Revelation of St John the Divine. The sufferings of the medieval Lollards and of the Protestants had been the sufferings of the saints, also prophesied; Satan had been let loose for a time. Now the hour of the full vindication of the saints was drawing near, and the triumph of Queen Elizabeth was a pledge of the total victory of Christ. Meanwhile the Protestant martyrs deserved to be celebrated as the Catholic saints had been. To help this, a 'Kalendar' giving the days on which they could be remembered was added to the 1563 edition (although so ridiculed that it was later withdrawn). Protestantism was the dawning of light amid the darkness of an evil world – a world so dark that even that light could be obscured by Protestants who were unworthy. Foxe was embarrassed by Henry VIII, and openly critical of the greed shown by Protestants under Edward VI; the guilt, he maintained, had been purged only in the martyrs' flames. He deplored Protestant cruelties. He was not even willing to applaud the Elizabethan government's execution of Papists as traitors. He begged for Edmund Campion's life to be spared. He acknowledged no duty to defend the most extreme Protestants; in his index some executions were referred to as the deaths of 'Anabaptists justly condemned'. But even in relation to these extremists who were in the wrong he favoured mercy, and in the early years of Elizabeth's reign he loved to boast that 'her sword is a virgin, spotted and polluted with no drop of blood'. In 1575 'Father Foxe' (for that was the affectionate nickname which all used) was so sickened by the order to burn some Anabaptists that he petitioned the Queen: 'I befriend the lives of men since I myself am a man. . . . Would that I might be able to help the very beasts!' The very long sermon which he delivered at Paul's Cross on Good Friday 1570 fully showed that his plea was for mercy because he passionately awaited the imminent second coming of the one Judge, who had been crucified by the Church and State of his day.

The theology of Foxe was one which many Protestants shared, and as passages from his book were read or read out, or as the many woodcuts illustrating it were pondered, the theology came alive. Here – collected with an industry which was almost a martyrdom in itself – were documents which added to the authentic atmosphere. And here was a narrative so dramatic that it may have taught a lesson or two to the young William Shakespeare. Foxe treasured the conversations of the martyrs as they went through the torments to their heavenly reward; and when the evidence supplied to him failed, he was not afraid to supply remarks considered appropriate.

The result in the popular mind was to associate Catholicism with cruelty. Already under Queen Mary the suffering of the Protestants had aroused far more sympathy than had surrounded the earlier burnings of Lollards; especially towards the end of the persecution, when it had clearly failed, local officials had to be bullied by the council in London to detect heretics and to be present at their deaths, and the spectators dared to make some demonstrations of admiration and good will. But there is no evidence that the popular reaction against the burnings had been so strong that it would have brought down the government by itself. Mary's heart was broken by the loss of Philip and of Calais far more than by worry about what her subjects might be feeling. One factor was that, despite what some later historians may have imagined, England had never been filled with the stench of burning human flesh. The burnings took place mainly in the south-east, the area most influenced by continental Protestantism. No heretics at all were burned in the dioceses of Durham, Carlisle, York, Hereford and Worcester; only one each in the dioceses of Chester and Exeter; only two each in the dioceses of Lincoln and Peterborough. The effective, nationwide revulsion against the persecution seems to have come in the next reign, and supremely after the publication of Foxe's book. Roman Catholic attempts to discredit him show how devastating his propaganda was – but they were feeble and mostly in Latin.

In the sixteenth century (and later) the power of religious prejudice was such that the mere suffering of men and women would not have moved many hearts by itself. After all, the martyrs themselves did not disapprove of the death penalty for heresy. In November 1538 Cranmer, for example, associated himself with Henry VIII in condemning John Lambert to be burned for denying the real presence of Christ in the consecrated bread at the Mass. Two others who were also to be burned as Protestants, Robert Barnes and John Taylor, are known to have supported that decision at the time. But Foxe was a propagandist of rare power – and Queen Mary's government had supplied him with rare material.

It could be said that bishops such as Hooper, Latimer, Ridley and Cranmer, accepted martyrdom as a hazard of their profession, and had chosen it rather than exile. But the lay men and women who were reported to be heretics, and who then refused to save their lives by professing the Catholic faith, came out of obscurity. Some of them, when questioned about how many sacraments there were in the Catholic faith, replied that they could not remember the number – without immediately laying themselves open to the charge of being liars. Yet they were plainly not Anabaptists or other cranks. They were simple men and women who belonged to England. They died with a courage which moved their fellow laity. Cruelty against them seemed more abominable than any execution of a bishop or nobleman. In the 1580s Sir William Cecil was still using as an unanswerable debating point the story of the pregnant woman who had been burned; when she had given birth, the baby had been thrown into the fire to perish with her.

These 'great persecutions', as Foxe's title showed, had been practised against simple English folk by 'the Romish prelates'. 'Romish'! In that one category Philip of Spain and Cardinal Pole could be included despite their troubles with Rome, and the adjective summoned up all the contempt of patriotic Englishmen. And 'prelates'! In that one category Stephen Gardiner and his associates could be placed together with the bishops who had burned the Lollards, and the noun aroused all the anticlerical feelings of the age. These 'Romish prelates' had persecuted the saints since 'the year of our Lord a thousand', yet in 'the time now present' their power was crumbling away and the Reformation of the Church was moving on to the final coming of the Church's Lord. In its enlarged edition of 1570 Foxe's history stretched back to the earliest days of Christianity and to the conversion of the Roman empire through the agency of the emperor Constantine (a king born in Britain, Foxe emphasized), before reaching John Wyclif and the Lollards in Book IV and the 'dreadful and bloody regiment' of Queen Mary on page 1,567. Thus the misdeeds of the 'Romish prelates' were set by John Foxe in the context of a total interpretation of history.

Protestants willing to take part in the overthrow of the 'Romish prelates' could now tell themselves that their cause was not mere greed or heresy. It was the cause of martyrs, including English men and women as lay as they were themselves. It was the cause of God. Their time, bloody and messy as it might seem, was giving birth to the Lord Christ's glorious new age.[9]

---

[9] See J. F. Mozley, *John Foxe and His Book* (London, 1940); William Haller, *Foxe's Book of Martyrs and the Elect Nation* (London, 1963); and V. N. Elsen, *John Foxe and the Elizabethan Church* (Berkeley, Cal., 1973). The background was studied by Helen C. White, *Tudor Books of Saints and Martyrs* (Madison, Wisc., 1963). For the widespread belief that the final battle between Christ and Antichrist was imminent, see Paul Christianson, *Reformers and Babylon* (Toronto, 1978), and K. R. Firth, *The Apocalyptic Tradition in Reformation Britain* (Oxford, 1979).

CHAPTER FOUR

THE ELIZABETHAN CHURCH

THE QUEEN'S RELIGION

At the age of twenty-five, on 17 November 1558, Elizabeth knelt and recited Psalm 118 in Latin on being informed that she was Queen of England and must go to the Tower of London to prepare for her coronation. Although the psalm was a celebration of escape, she had suffered in ways which would have left many people emotionally crippled; somewhat similar experiences had deeply damaged her sister. On Palm Sunday 1554 Elizabeth had been taken to the Tower and accused of complicity in Wyatt's rebellion. She had been kept in prison for two months, and no one would have been amazed had she met a traitor's death. A copy of her letter to Mary refusing to come to court at the time of Wyatt's rebellion (because, she claimed, of ill-health) had been intercepted in the French ambassador's mail to his masters. It was not unreasonable to suspect that Elizabeth had supplied it.

In her brother's reign she had also been in peril. Thomas Seymour, Protector Somerset's over-ambitious brother, had flirted and romped with her. The incident had set tongues wagging and his head rolling after execution as a traitor. And in her father's reign, twenty-four hours before her mother's execution, the Archbishop of Canterbury had declared her a bastard. Although that archbishop had now been burned as a heretic, she always remained a whore's child in the eyes of Catholic Europe except when princes were seeking her as an ally or as a wife. Queen Mary had often pointed out the physical likeness between Elizabeth and the court musician Mark Smeaton, believed to have been one of Anne Boleyn's lovers.

All Christians were then agreed that no woman could become a priest. Some now argued with passion that no woman could be a monarch; for example, John Knox in his *First Blast of the Trumpet against the Monstrous Regiment of Women*, published in Geneva shortly before Elizabeth's accession. The exclusion of women from power was – or was said to be – the law of God. The practical difficulty of having a woman on the throne had been amply demonstrated by the disaster of Queen Matilda who had fled the country in 1148 and by the total disaster of Queen Mary. Elizabeth's probable successor was Mary Stuart, Queen of Scots, until she was executed in 1587. It was clear that Mary, although beautiful (which Elizabeth was not), was destitute of common sense, unable to rule either men or her own emotions. And it was not always clear that Elizabeth was going to be vastly more successful. Had she died in 1562 (as she nearly did, of smallpox), she would have bequeathed a chaos almost as great as the shambles she had inherited from her sister. In 1562 she named Robert Dudley Protector of the Realm in the event of her death; he was the son of the Duke of Northumerland who had been executed in 1553, and in power he would probably have been no better than his father. So slender was the thread on which depended England's peace and prosperity under this mortal queen.

But England and the world discovered that Elizabeth was one of the ablest politicians, crowned or uncrowned, in all history. Pope Sixtus V openly admired her and wished that Catholic monarchs possessed her spirit. In England the festivals of her birthday and accession replaced the medieval spectacles of the Church; it was government propaganda, of course, but it was not only that. She earned her reputation the hard way. Her experience of being accused of treason seemed only to have strengthened her will to be a survivor. The incident when she had been compromised by a teenager's flirtation had left her determined never to let her heart rule her head; and the weakness of her position as a woman alleged to be illegitimate had made her all the more resolved not only to get the better of bishops but to display to her people the 'heart of a king and of a king of England too'. Her sister's experience had not encouraged her to saddle herself with a husband, and the idea that she

was the Virgin Queen, married to her people, seems to have
been more than a poetic fancy.

Since her death the glory of the Elizabethan age has continued to be acknowledged by England and the world. It was
the moment when the English governing class and their assistants such as Shakespeare multiplied their assets by the exploitation of agriculture, industry and trade, launched their
naval and imperial conquests, and created the most splendid
literature seen in the world since the glories of Greece and
Rome. This reign was also a time when the common people
suffered much; the profits went to those to whom much had
already been given. But the only rebellion to reach London was
led by Elizabeth's ex-favourite, the Earl of Essex; and it lasted
one day.

Only a part of the explanation of the Elizabethan phenomenon lies in the extraordinary ability and industry of
William Cecil (Lord Burghley from 1571), for forty years the
Queen's principal minister. He had already held high office in
the service both of Somerset and of Northumberland under
Edward VI, and had led the councillors in their submission to
Queen Mary in 1553. Although he was a discreet Protestant
(and his wife was one emphatically), he had been allowed to
live in peace under Mary as the squire of Wimbledon. He
believed in the continuity and efficiency of government. His
eye for the practical possibility matched Elizabeth's – as did his
taste for moderation, except when treason or hostility to
England's ruler was clear. In pursuit of this agreed policy he
sometimes argued with success against some mood of Elizabeth's but he never doubted for one moment who governed
England.[1] In order to show that he was not indispensable, she
persisted in favouring his rival Robert Dudley (created Earl of
Leicester in 1564), whom he disliked and distrusted. She
refused to see him, or to receive letters from him, for four
months after the execution of Mary Queen of Scots; with royal
or feminine logic she blamed the deed on him. His work was
carried on into the next reign by his son Robert – but for five
years the Queen refused to consent to any formal appointment

---

[1] A recent study is B. W. Beckinsale, *Burghley, Tudor Statesman* (London, 1967).

of Robert Cecil to the secretaryship. She owed more to the Cecils than she acknowledged, but it was her age.[2]

One of the least expected successes of the Elizabethan age was the Church 'established' by the Act of Uniformity to which the Queen gave her assent on 8 May 1559. The Church of England has seldom been described as glorious, for it has always been the result of a compromise between Catholic and Protestant, conservative and radical; and so it was under Elizabeth I. The arrangements made for it by the Queen in Parliament in 1559 were generally expected to have a short life; 'no one really wanted the Prayer Book'.[3] In the event, however, the Queen insisted on treating the 1559 settlement as sacred, because every subsequent House of Commons in her reign would have lessened the compromise by a more Protestant emphasis unacceptable to her – and although the Elizabethan settlement was to be overthrown in the Puritan revolution of the next century, back it was to come. In the twentieth century, during the reign of Elizabeth II, the Church of England was still 'established'.

Elizabeth I took the title 'Supreme Governor of the Church'. She did not claim to be 'Supreme Head', as her father and brother had done. Even Thomas Cranmer had acknowledged that the title 'Supreme Head of the Church' most fitly belonged to Christ. Now, when it suited them, Elizabeth and her ministers could pretend that nothing was involved in the new title beyond every Christian monarch's duty to make sure that pure religion was being practised in the realm in accordance with the teachings of the Bible and the bishops. In 1569 a 'Declaration of the Queen's Proceedings' was issued in an attempt to reassure Catholics at the time of the conservative rebellion in the north. A copy survives corrected in the Queen's own hand. The declaration stressed that she had never claimed

---

[2] Introductions include Paul Johnson, *Elizabeth I: A Study in Power and Intellect* (London, 1974), and the four volumes by A. L. Rowse: *The England of Elizabeth: The Structure of Society, The Expansion of Elizabethan England, The Elizabethan Renaissance: The Life of Society* and *The Elizabethan Renaissance: The Cultural Achievement* (London, 1950–72). Wallace MacCaffrey summed up modern studies of the politics in *The Shaping of the Elizabethan Regime, 1558–72,* and *Queen Elizabeth and the Making of Policy, 1572–88* (Princeton, N.J., 1969–81).

[3] G. J. Cuming, *A History of Anglican Liturgy,* p. 131.

any right 'to define, decide or determine any article or point of the Christian faith and religion, or to change any ancient ceremony of the Church from the form before received and observed by the Catholic and Apostolic Church'. Her ecclesiastical title was defended on the ground that 'we are by God's grace the sovereign prince and queen next under God, and all the people in our realm are immediately born subjects to us and to our crown and to none else'. She was Supreme Governor of the Church as of every other English institution, but in the Church this simply involved seeing 'the laws of God and man to be duly observed' and providing that 'the Church may be governed and taught by archbishops, bishops and ministers' – duties which 'we think properly due to all Christian monarchs'.

The reality was, however, different. In 1559 the Acts of Supremacy and Uniformity were passed in defiance of solidly hostile votes by the bishops in the House of Lords, and in the knowledge that the clergy when meeting in the Convocation of Canterbury earlier in the year had shown themselves obstinately loyal to the old religion. Until the end of 1559 the Queen was unable to find bishops prepared to carry out her policy, so that she or her council governed the Church in a straightforward manner, issuing detailed injunctions to guide the clergy. When bishops were secured, they were nominated by her; Deans and Chapters elected them, but had these clergy of the cathedrals refused to do their duty they would have been outlawed, as the law made unambiguously plain. And the bishops were ordered about by her. If she sheltered behind them (as she did when convenient), it was because she had no wish to be involved in ecclesiastical controversies, not because she doubted her God-given powers. When an Archbishop of Canterbury refused to obey her, she had him placed under house arrest; and the two next archbishops were promoted because they were eager to be the Crown's agents in a campaign against those who wanted to move forward from 1559.

Clergymen had to do what she wanted, like her other subjects. When Alexander Nowell, Dean of St Paul's, was preaching in her presence on Ash Wednesday and was becoming controversial, she screamed at him: 'Leave that alone! To your text, Mr Dean! To your text! Leave that; we have heard enough of that! To your subject!' But if clergymen obeyed her they were safe, and laymen who criticized them were told firmly to leave religion to those who understood it. In 1571 she berated those MPs who had shown themselves so 'audacious, arrogant and presumptuous' as to meddle with religion and bring in ecclesiastical legislation without the prior approval of the bishops and clergy. Eighteen years later she informed the Commons that she was 'most fully and firmly settled in her conscience, by the word of God, that the estate and government of the Church of England, as it now standeth in this Reformation, may justly be compared to any church which hath been established in any Christian kingdom since the apostles' times'.[4]

It has often been assumed that her motivation in securing and defending the 1559 settlement was purely (or impurely) political, and it seems true to say that she always put first her duty to survive on the throne. But it is not necessary to deny the sincerity of her belief that her survival was a duty. All the Tudors had the knack of identifying their interests with God's and the people's. Moreover, it can be argued that she was the truest Christian in a family which always made a parade of its piety. Her attitude towards others, although usually shrewd and sometimes shrewish, was more deeply charitable than that of any other Tudor. Perhaps that reflected credit on her tutor, Roger Ascham. Although a Protestant clergyman and a learned scholar, he was far from being a fanatic; he wrote the standard book on archery, and was a great hunter (and a compulsive gambler). Although she consented to very severe punishments for real or alleged treason, it is impossible to think of her as an implacable persecutor like her sister, who executed hundreds never accused of treason. There is no reason to doubt that her agonies of mind when she had to order the death of the Duke of Norfolk or Mary Queen of Scots were genuine, although politically she had no choice. In Henry VIII's reign

---

[4] Relevant documents were collected by Claire Cross in *The Royal Supremacy in the Elizabethan Church* (London, 1969). Carl S. Mayer studied *Elizabeth I and the Religious Settlement of 1559* (St Louis, Mo., 1960).

of thirty-eight years, eighty-one heretics were burned; in Elizabeth's reign, three years longer, five.

She not only mentioned her dependence on God in public speeches (all monarchs did that); she also prayed in private and attended Morning Prayer daily. As a young woman she translated a religious poem by Queen Margaret of Navarre (*The Mirror of the Sinful Soul*) which, we are told, 'initiated a new species of English religious literature of mystical transcendence and spiritual fervour'.[5] She also translated Queen Catherine Parr's book of prayers into Latin, French and Italian. She caused a *Book of Prayers* for her household's use to be published in 1560; and she left behind her a book, only three by two inches in size, containing prayers handwritten about 1575.

Such prayers could be dismissed as literary exercises, and there is no certainty that she actually did write the most famous little poem attributed to her:

> Christ was the Word that spake it;
> He took the Bread and brake it:
> And what the Word did make it,
> That I believe, and take it.

It does not seem to have been attributed to Elizabeth before 1643, and it appeared in the 1635 edition of John Donne's poems. We do, however, possess a report of what she said to Parliament on 29 March 1585. She referred to one of her characteristics which became obscured in the legend about her – her habit of daily study. 'I suppose few, that be no professors, have read more. . . . And yet, amidst my many volumes, I hope God's book hath not been my seldomnest lectures.' She rebuked both the conservatism of the 'Romanists' and the 'new-fangledness' of others: 'I see many overbold with God almighty, making too many subtle scannings of his blessed will, as lawyers with human testaments.' And without stooping to give precise biblical references, she declared about her rejection of both the Catholic and the Protestant extremes: 'I mean to guide them both by God's holy true rule.'

---

[5] J. B. Collins, *Christian Mysticism in the Elizabethan Age* (Baltimore, Md., 1940), p. 87.

During her long, last illness Elizabeth refused to discuss politics. She was unwilling even to name her successor. When speechless, 'she took great delight in hearing prayers, and would often at the name of Jesus lift up her hands and eyes to heaven'. She died gripping Archbishop Whitgift's hand, although Bishop Goodman of Gloucester was to remember that while healthy she had been an independent Christian. 'Queen Elizabeth', he recalled, 'was wont to say she had rather speak to God herself, than to hear another speaking of God; she seldom heard sermons, but only in Lent.'[6]

THE ESTABLISHED CHURCH

In the Church which Elizabeth governed, bishops were appointed in order to execute her policies. They were not primarily hoping to be loved; and they did not all devote much time in order to administer Confirmation in the villages where most of the people lived. They were involved in politics almost to the same extent as the statesman-bishops of the Middle Ages (although only two of them were ever admitted to the Privy Council). The basic difference was that they were now expected to live and work in their own dioceses, busying themselves with local, not national, administration, treated by the council like paid magistrates useful in the management of ecclesiastical matters, sometimes also entrusted with a wider role if this was convenient. For example, they collected taxes from the clergy.[7] It was, however, a crucial defect in their

---

[6] Her piety was studied by J. P. Hedges, *The Nature of the Lion* (London, 1962). The scholarly circle to which she belonged was explored by Winthrop S. Hudson, *The Cambridge Connection and the Elizabethan Settlement of 1559* (Durham, N.C., 1980).

[7] See Ralph Houlbrooke, 'The Protestant Episcopate 1547–1603: The Pastoral Contribution', in *Church and Society in England: Henry VIII to James I*, ed. F. Heal and R. O'Day (London, 1977), pp. 78–98. This volume contains other valuable essays drawing together recent studies of local church life. Other material is in *Princes and Paupers in the English Church*, with the same editors (Leicester, 1981). Felicity Heal investigated the finances of the Elizabethan bishops in *Of Prelates and Princes*, pp. 202–327. Patrick Collinson investigated their work and much else in *The Religion of Protestants: The Church in English Society, 1559–1625* (Oxford, 1982).

position that no real attempt was made to help the bishops by reforming the church courts – a modernization which could not have been undertaken except by command of the Queen. It was her policy to use, but to curb, the power of her bishops.[8]

It is therefore possible to see the history of the Elizabethan Church of England as a series of attempts by the bishops to discipline, at the command of the Queen, all those who retained Christian convictions, whether Catholic or Protestant. It is also possible to pour scorn on the failures of these unromantic bishops to achieve even the limited objectives entrusted to them by the Queen's council. They were men without the prestige of aristocratic birth, so important in that intensely class-conscious society. (For a time the two archbishops, at Canterbury and York, were men who had been born and brought up in the same parish of St Bees on the Cumbrian coast, Edmund Grindal being a farmer's son although Edwin Sandys was a gentleman's.) Bishops were criticized if they seemed to be wealthy, and the Queen's lay favourites hastened to relieve them of their estates. At the same time they were criticized if they did not entertain the leading laity with a noble hospitality. They often felt themselves obliged to provide for their families, but when they did so they were condemned for robbing the Church. Most of these bishops, with little previous experience of parish life or of diocesan administration, possessed limited personal talents to apply to their formidable and uncertain tasks, and with administrative and legal machinery unchanged since the Middle Ages they issued orders and excommunications which the laity and even the clergy often treated with derision.

The Elizabethan Bishops of Chichester, for example, were a poor lot. The only outstanding man among them was Richard Curteys, appointed in 1570. An ardent preacher with Calvinist convictions, he was determined to hasten the progress of the Reformation in the parishes of a rural and conservative diocese. But he involved himself in unedifying disputes with many of his clergy and made the supreme mistake of summoning

---

[8] Ralph Houlbrooke studied *Church Courts and the People during the English Reformation* (Oxford, 1979).

most of the gentry of Sussex to his cathedral, where he harangued them. He seemed so troublesome that in 1578 the Privy Council suspended him from his duties. No successor was appointed until 1585, when the choice fell on an obscure clergyman aged seventy-eight who did very little in his eleven years as bishop. And the next Bishop of Chichester lived mainly in London.

The main problem of the clergy serving in Sussex under such dismally bad leadership was poverty. Although it is very difficult to be precise about money values in a period when most rectors or vicars were paid mainly in kind (in tithes), the fees being relatively unimportant, we are told that only four parishes in the whole diocese yielded an income above £30 a year, that assistant curates often had to make do on £5 a year, and that many of the clergy carried on other trades in order to support their families. Inevitably many thousands of their parishioners remained rooted in the old religion and accepted guidance from the gentry or nobility who supported priests faithful to it. At Battle Abbey, for example, an aristocratic widow who had taken over the old monastic buildings ran a well-attended chapel complete with choir and pulpit. When headway was made against this conservatism – and the evidence suggests that some headway was made in the 1580s and 1590s – this seems to have been thanks largely to the energy of the Puritan preachers. But these preachers were suspected by the authorities of Church and State, and in 1605 Archbishop Bancroft silenced and deprived the foremost ten Sussex Puritans.[9]

The history of the Elizabethan diocese of Chichester is not the Church of England at its most impressive. But two facts deserve to be remembered. The first is negative: there was no violent conflict. Not many miles of sea separated Sussex from a France which was undergoing the misery of civil war as Catholics and Protestants battled for control, yet the equivalent in Sussex of the dreadful French massacre of 1572 was the scandal over the indiscretions of Bishop Curteys. And the

---

[9] R. B. Manning examined *Religion and Society in Elizabethan Sussex* (Leicester, 1969).

second fact which should be weighed is that the Church
of England did function as the National Church in local
reality.

Probably not all the inhabitants of any town or village could
be found in church at service time. Those who were 'Romanists' or 'Recusants' out of loyalty to the old religion absented
themselves. The really poor do not seem to have been expected
to attend, and the really careless could be found at home or in
the ale house, although the churchwardens were supposed to
fine them twelve pence for each Sunday's absence. But all the
evidence suggests that the great majority of England's parish
priests remained at their posts under Elizabeth as they had
done, however the storms of religious change blew, under her
father, brother and sister. There certainly was a shortage of
clergy at the beginning of the reign; in 1559 fewer than half of
the parishes in the diocese of Canterbury had a resident
clergyman, and the experiment of using lay readers or 'lectors'
to take the services had to be attempted. But mass ordinations
of new priests dealt with that emergency and it is clear that,
whoever the priest was, he was needed. For the parish church
remained the centre of social life, under the Tudors as in the
Middle Ages.

It had no rival. Its bell summoned one and all. The Sunday
assembly for Morning Prayer was the time to catch up with the
news and gossip and perhaps also to absorb some edification.
After service there would be sports in the churchyard. Christenings, weddings and funerals were the turning points in
private lives; and the whole community's year was given its
pattern by the festivities of Christmastide after the preparation
of Advent, the drama of Easter following Lent, the May Day
dancing to greet the spring in the churchyard, the 'church ale'
at Whitsuntide in the churchyard or if wet in the church, the
autumn harvest festivities which often returned to the churchyard for more merriment, the autumnal remembrances of All
Saints and All Souls (although the authorities battled against
the 'superstition' of prayers for the dead). The provision made
by the Book of Common Prayer for Mattins and Evensong, or
Morning and Evening Prayer, to be said daily in every parish
church seldom seems to have been put into effect; but if the

parish priest was conscientious he would say the litany in church every Wednesday and Friday morning, interceding for all in trouble.

The allocation of pews in the church was a matter of great interest and often of contention, since it marked a family's social status. The humiliation of sinners was also a matter of interest, and took place in church. Fornicators and adulterers were supposed to do penance in a white sheet before all the congregation during Morning Prayer on three successive Sundays, after the sentence by the court of the archdeacon or the bishop. (A month before his death William Shakespeare was relieved to learn that his son-in-law, Thomas Quinney, who had fathered a bastard, was to be spared this public humiliation and allowed to do penance in the bishop's chapel.) The whole congregation could meet to discuss parish affairs, although in many parishes, especially in towns, this touch of democracy was being replaced by a committee of the leading parishioners known as the 'vestry'. The unpaid churchwardens, elected for the year at Easter, were responsible not only for the maintenance of the church, churchyard and any 'church house', but also for a great variety of other business – the relief of the poor, the punishment of rogues and the upkeep of almshouses, roads, bridges and ponds, either by themselves or in collaboration with other officials. The schoolmaster, licensed by the bishop, often taught in the church; the trainbands (militia) kept their weapons there: the local magistrates often administered justice there. It might have many, many other uses, being in effect the village hall. And everyone, except suicides, was buried in the church or churchyard.[10]

In every parish church the Prayer Book of 1559 was used Sunday by Sunday. Morning Prayer and Litany formed the chief service, with Evening Prayer early in the afternoon, and Holy Communion perhaps once a month (but in many country parishes neither Evening Prayer nor Holy Communion would

---

[10] See A. Tindal Hart, *The Country Clergy in Elizabethan and Stuart Times* (London, 1958), and *The Man in the Pew, 1558–1660* (London, 1966). Many glimpses of parish life were provided by J. S. Purvis, *Tudor Parish Documents of the Diocese of York* (Cambridge, 1948), and W. K. Jordan, *The Charities of Rural England, 1480–1660* (London, 1961).

be held so often). By being used, the Prayer Book's beauty slowly found its way into the affections of the people – and the clergy. It was a sign of the times that towards the end of Elizabeth's reign the pressures brought to bear by bishops and archdeacons were resulting in a higher standard of maintenance in the church buildings. The demoralizing effects of the many orders to destroy superstitious images seem to have been largely overcome, and on Sundays parishioners saw a more or less decent substitute for the vanished glories of the Middle Ages. In innumerable parishes the church was repaired, often with the aid of a 'church rate', a tax levied by the churchwardens on all householders. It was often whitewashed, adorned with scriptural texts, strewn with straw or rushes to make kneeling easier, and given one new touch of colour – the royal arms. As in the Middle Ages, the chancel might well be in a worse state of repair than the nave, for the chancel was the responsibility of the 'rector' or 'parson' (the two terms were interchangeable, lesser clergy being called the 'vicar' or 'curate'). But bishops and archdeacons, when they conducted their 'visitations' in the medieval style, often made complaints designed to secure action from the rector. There was often a similar problem about the repair of the rectory, parsonage or vicarage, for which the clergyman was personally responsible.

Although Elizabethan England saw no great church building – were not its richest men's huge country houses the new cathedrals of the cult of Mammon? – these changes in the medieval parish church made it a suitable little theatre for the performance of the Prayer Book services.

Most of the services were not accompanied by sermons. A special licence was needed before a clergyman was allowed to expound the Bible's message in his own words, and over many areas for many years such licences were few. Many of the licensed preachers when they did arrive were enthusiastic Puritans, hostile to the remnants of Popery in the Prayer Book. But the bishops persisted in hoping that 'godly preachers' would persuade the people to love and use the authorized services. The steady hope of the Queen and her council (particularly of William Cecil, who was Chancellor of Cambridge University) was that the universities would persuade enough young men of the merits of the religious establishment, so that they would become preachers. And slowly such hopes were to a considerable extent fulfilled. The Church of England became an institution in which graduates were content to be employed. It was a quiet but major change. At the beginning of Elizabeth's reign the medieval pattern was still taken for granted and few graduates were to be found serving parishes. 'The non-resident clergy were university-educated, and socially, geographically and economically quite mobile: the parochial clergy were of local origin and modest education, and had little prospect of further preferment. ... Yet the post-Reformation Church was committed to the task of reforming its clergy and finding well-educated and vocationally suitable men to fill its parishes, even down to the poorest rectories and vicarages, many of which were currently standing vacant.'[11] And this ideal was translated into practice to a surprising extent.

The official religion of Elizabethan England was enforced by the Justices of the Peace (unpaid magistrates) alongside the bishops and archdeacons. Probably many of the laity conformed because no alternative seemed open; and they were often bored stiff as they sat in churches which were cold and smelly (from the dead), listening to a parson droning on with the stereotyped worship ordered in an Act of Parliament, hearing homilies and other official hand-outs read from the pulpit. Men and women sat separately, and the atmosphere must have been rather like a school's. The churchwardens preserved discipline, reporting cases of brawling to their own superiors. Since the day of popular hymns had not yet come, the only opportunity to sing together was provided by the *Book of Psalms* in metre by Sternhold, Hopkins and others (1560) and by its Puritan rivals. No one could call the Elizabethan Church entertaining. But it made a people which had been Catholic for many centuries vociferously Protestant.

---

[11] Rosemary O'Day, *The English Clergy: The Emergence and Consolidation of a Profession 1558–1642* (Leicester, 1979), p. 6. M. H. Curtis studied this change from another angle in *Oxford and Cambridge in Transition 1558–1642* (Oxford, 1959).

ELIZABETH'S FIRST ARCHBISHOP

Matthew Parker, whom Elizabeth chose as her first Archbishop of Canterbury, was consecrated a bishop by four others – William Barlow, Bishop of St David's under Henry VIII; John Hodgkin, who had been Suffragan Bishop of Bedford in the same reign; John Scory, Bishop of Chichester under Edward VI; and Miles Coverdale, Bishop of Exeter 1551–55. They used a service which had been authorized by Parliament along with the Prayer Book of 1552. By an oversight no 'ordinal' (book of ordination services) had been authorized in the 1559 Act of Uniformity, but the Crown claimed the power to supply this defect. The ceremony took place in the chapel of Lambeth Palace, early on the morning of 17 December 1559.

Anglicans have claimed that this was a valid consecration – an important claim, since Archbishop Parker was to consecrate other bishops and was thus to embody the Anglican assertion of continuity with the Catholic Church of the Middle Ages. The Roman Catholic authorities have not agreed with that claim – and the invalidity of the proceedings that December morning was one of the reasons given by Pope Leo XIII in 1897 for declaring Anglican ordinations 'absolutely null and utterly void'. It is not our duty to enter such controversies, but we may observe that not one of the bishops serving in Queen Mary's reign was willing to lend a hand in making Matthew Parker Archbishop of Canterbury, despite the government's many blandishments or threats; and the Pope was never consulted. It was an affair very different from the consecration of Cardinal Pole to be Archbishop of Canterbury. It was also very different from the consecration of Thomas Cranmer in St Stephen's chapel in the palace of Westminster in March 1535 – a ceremony performed by the Bishops of Lincoln, Exeter and St Asaph according to the Catholic rites on the basis of letters or 'bulls' issued in Rome by the Pope.

By choosing Matthew Parker for Canterbury and arranging at least a superficial continuity between him and his predecessors, Elizabeth's government demonstrated that its policy was to be Protestantism without disruption. Protestantism there had to be, but the government had to avoid giving needless offence to Catholics and quietly dropped Archbishop Cranmer's opinion that the Crown could simply appoint a bishop. The Queen wanted to reign in peace. And as her archbishop she had chosen a man of peace.

Parker was fifty-five when chosen. Most of his life had been spent in places of piety and study. He had been Dean of Stoke-by-Clare (a college suppressed in 1548), then Dean of Lincoln and Master of Corpus Christi College, Cambridge. Under Queen Mary he had been deprived of his posts but allowed to live in what he called 'delightful literary leisure'. He retired to his native Norfolk and spent the time turning the psalms into doggerel verse and writing a book – not published until 1567 – which preached what he practised: marriage for the clergy. The fact that he was so firmly married (after an engagement of seven years) might have been expected to damn him in Elizabeth's eyes, and his relationship with her never seems to have been close, although he had come into contact with her back in the 1530s during a brief spell as chaplain to her mother. It is unlikely that he was seriously attracted by the worldly side of the archbishopric. The Queen expected him to live in state like a nobleman and he did so; but he was at heart a scholarly and domestic gentleman. Whether or not the Queen actually insulted Mrs Parker quite so crudely as gossip maintained, the gossip showed the risks he was running.[12] In 1559 he found one excuse after another why he could not leave the university, and when the excuses ran out he did not answer letters. In 1535 Cranmer had also been slow to accept Canterbury (he rightly insisted on this at his trial), but had already allowed himself to become involved in the political service of Henry VIII. Parker's preference for the quiet of a study and a home in Cambridge probably went deeper.

The Queen's ministers persisted in urging him to accept the order, and there is no evidence that anyone else was ever in mind for Canterbury, although rumours circulated. The ex-

---

[12] The Queen was reported to have taken her leave after a feast thus: 'And you, *Madam* I may not call you, and *Mistress* I am ashamed to call you, so I know not what to call you, but yet I do thank you.' This anecdote was first printed in 1607.

planation seems to be that, although a careful administrator, Parker had no awkward theories of his own other than his conviction that any Protestant, lay or ordained, was entitled to be married. He was not a reformer likely to give trouble to a Tudor. Queen Mary let him live. Queen Elizabeth knew that he would never do more than complain in private. The test of this came when in a moment of temperament during 1561, she ordered the exclusion of clergymen's wives from cathedrals and colleges. Parker wrote to William Cecil that he was 'in horror to hear such words'. In order to carry out the Queen's policy while shielding her reputation he had been content to incur 'foul reports' from her Catholic or Protestant enemies, and now he was rewarded with this decree, which had left him 'neither joy of house, land or name'. But, confining his protest to this letter, he stayed put – as did the wives, for Elizabeth occasionally knew better than to insist on her way.

On other questions the Supreme Governor was, however, inflexible, and this meant that poor Parker had to issue and enforce his *Advertisements* of 1565 telling the clergy what clothes to wear. Being a sixteenth-century woman, the Queen knew that how a clergyman looked showed his position in society and in religion. Parker would probably have been indifferent to such details if left to himself, and was aggrieved when the Queen refused to acknowledge her personal responsibility for her orders, leaving him to bear all the Puritans' counter-attacks and 'foul reports'. He wore a worried look and a drooping moustache, as his portraits show – but of course he was prepared also to wear the clothes which his sovereign had commanded. He told others to obey the Queen because the vice that most angered him was disobedience. Both Catholic and Protestant dissenters 'have one mark to shoot at', he once reminded Cecil, 'plain disobedience; some of simplicity, some of wiliness and stubbornness'. When he had sacrificed the scholarly quiet of Cambridge in order to serve the Church of England at the Queen's command, he saw no reason why Puritans or Romanists should refuse to abandon their preferences in the trivialities of church life once the Queen had made her wishes plain. He was deeply persuaded that God's blessing rested on England under Elizabeth. 'Where Almighty God is so much English as he is,' he once asked Cecil, 'should we not requite his mercy with some earnesty to prefer his honour and true religion?'

This scholarly archbishop's gentle goodness – which he called his 'cowardice' when feeling depressed – did something to commend the Queen's policy. She rebuked him for being too mild with those who wished to obey the Bible and the Bible only. He showed where his own heart lay by supervising a new translation of the Bible (the Bishops' Bible of 1568, revised in 1572), with 'no bitter notes upon any text'. But he was also gracious to the Catholic bishops surviving from the previous reign and left by the government half-imprisoned in his house; and he must have pleased many conservatives by his labours as patron and as editor in the printing of the works of medieval chroniclers, and by his supervision of a history of all the Archbishops of Canterbury. A short life of himself, the seventieth archbishop, was prepared for publication after his death. He took a special pride in the privileges of the great church of Canterbury but asserted that Christianity had flourished long before the landing of the first archbishop, who had suffered the handicap of being sent from Rome. Joseph of Arimathea had headed the missionary band sent from France by the apostle Philip in A.D. 63, and the Christian King Lucius had in the first Christian century exercised a supremacy over the Church not unlike Elizabeth's. Honouring another king, in 1574 he had Asser's *Life of Alfred* printed in type specially made to represent the original Anglo-Saxon.

He died the next year. He left a rich collection of ancient manuscripts and printed books to Corpus Christi College, Cambridge, where he had been happiest. With characteristic caution, he invited the master of another Cambridge college (Caius) to inspect the collection each year; if six manuscripts were missing, he was to be entitled to take the whole of the rest of the library with him to his own college. The Cambridge treasure, rescued from the dispersal of the monastic libraries and from many other sources, was priceless evidence about Christian England's heritage, now preserved – at least in part – through the storm of the Reformation. One item was a splendid copy of the gospels sent from Rome to St Augustine, Canterbury's first archbishop.[13]

JEWEL AND HOOKER

John Jewel had a stronger appetite for controversy than Matthew Parker could ever develop. His learning was as great as Parker's, and it lay in fields immediately useful to the government.

While an Oxford don in the 1540s, he wrote an *Oratio contra Rhetoricum*. An academic piece, it attacked rhetoric with all the skill of a scholar steeped in Latin literature, especially the oratory of Cicero. It was natural that in the crucial early days of Elizabethan England a scholar so eloquent found himself talking incessantly. He was a Protestant spokesman at the theological disputation held to advertise the new queen's intentions in Westminster Abbey in March 1559. Four months later he was nominated Bishop of Salisbury, to serve on a royal commission to enforce the new settlement in the western counties, destroying altars, statues, paintings and the other symbols of Catholicism. In November he was back in London, preaching with high drama at Paul's Cross. This became famous as his 'Challenge Sermon'. Only 'if any learned man of all our adversaries, or if all the learned men that be alive, be able to bring any one sufficient sentence out of any old Catholic doctor or father, or out of any old General Council, or out of the Holy Scriptures of God, or any one example of the primitive Church whereby it may be clearly and plainly proved, that there was any private Mass in the whole world at that time, for the space of six hundred years after Christ', would Jewel subscribe to the doctrine taught by the Pope. Similarly he challenged Roman Catholic teachings about the Pope being the universal head of the Church; about the bread and wine of the sacrament being 'really, substantially' Christ's body and blood; about the frequent restrictions of communion to the

---

[13] See V. J. K. Brook, *A Life of Archbishop Parker* (Oxford, 1962).

priest alone and the invariable denial of the cup to the laity; about the 'worship' of images in churches; about the refusal to allow lay people to read the Bible in their own language. All these doctrines or practices were, he claimed, innovations like the practice of the private Mass.

In 1561, at Cecil's request, he wrote a letter in Latin defending the government from the rumour that England was in chaos because of the government's religious innovations. This letter was sent over to be printed in Paris without naming any author; Cecil wished to conceal the fact that the author was a highly placed official of the Church being defended. Next year, again at Cecil's request, the ever-ready bishop completed a longer *Apologia*, again in Latin because it was directed to the educated public of Europe. The whole purpose was to make the Elizabethan settlement of English religion theologically respectable in a Christendom where John Calvin still lived (until 1564), and where the chief event was the re-assembly of the reforming Council of Trent without Protestant participation (in 1562).

Jewel's *Apologia* aroused the admiration of leading Protestants and the contempt of learned Catholics. Within England translations were quickly prepared (the best being volunteered by a scholarly Protestant otherwise known to history as the mother of Sir Francis Bacon), but conservatives were by no means silenced. What can perhaps be agreed upon now is the fact that Jewel was no mean debater. In order to divert attention from the confusion in England resulting from the latest of the religious revolutions of the 1550s, he dwelt positively upon the clergy's united obedience to the queen and negatively on the variety to be found within the Catholic tradition (for example, in the multiplicity of the orders of monks, nuns, friars and canons). In order to justify the supremacy of the queen over the Church of England, he cited the role played by Christian emperors and kings from Constantine onwards. He stressed, too, the damage done by the alternative: the claim of the Bishops of Rome to universal jurisdiction. He minimized the New Testament passages referring to St Peter and the passages in the Church's Fathers referring to the popes of Rome, and made a more successful attempt to show that

neither Christ nor the apostles nor any other of the undivided
Church's acknowledged teachers had ever expressed any
approval in advance of the claims of the medieval papacy. That
was his negative achievement: a debater's achievement. Positively, he advocated the equality of bishops in the Catholic
Church, with only a vague primacy of honour granted to
archbishops such as the pope.

The confident tone of Bishop Jewel as the official apologist
for the Elizabethan Church of England is interesting since in
the previous reign he had behaved far more timidly. In Oxford
he had functioned as a minor official during the trials of Ridley
and Cranmer. Frightened by their fates, he had signed 'articles' of the Roman Catholic faith – seizing the pen and trying
to make a joke of it: 'What, have you a mind to see how well I
can write?' Only when warned that he was himself about to be
arrested for heresy, and no doubt burned like Ridley and
Cranmer, had he escaped to Germany, confessing his cowardice to the English Protestants already in exile. This unhappy
incident had been recalled when as Bishop of Salisbury he had
deprived Thomas Harding of a canonry in Salisbury Cathedral. The two men had gone to the same grammar school (at
Barnstaple in Devon) and had been contemporaries at Oxford.
But Harding had become a Protestant after graduating – and
had urged Jewel to remain boldly faithful to the Protestant
cause. Later Harding had returned to the Catholic fold, but his
contempt for Jewel's cowardice had no doubt remained. We
cannot wonder that having been expelled from Salisbury
Cathedral, the now steadfastly Catholic Thomas Harding
devoted a part of his exile to writing very rudely about Bishop
John Jewel.

We need not accept Harding's estimate of his former friend,
however. A different estimate suggests itself when we read
Jewel on the Bible: 'Here is to be seen the triumph of God, the
Lord of lords and the King of kings: how he hath made the
name of his Son triumph over principalities and powers, and
over the whole world. Here is a paradise full of delights; no
tongue is able to speak of them, they are so many; no heart is
able to conceive them, they be so great. Here is a shop, wherein
is set out the wisdom and knowledge, the power, the judge-

ments, and mercies of God. Which way soever we look, we see the works of his hands; his works of creation, and preservation of all things; his works of severe justice upon the wicked, and of gracious redemption to the believer. If we desire pleasant music or excellent harmony, it speaketh unto us the words of the Father . . .'[14]

Jewel, we may conclude, became a deeply convinced Protestant. But we know also that while officially defending the Elizabethan Church he came near to resignation because he did not regard the 1559 settlement as Protestant enough; and in his official defence, he avoided the deep questions. Was the settlement of 1559 to be only the beginning of a much more radical transformation of the English Church, as Jewel and those who with him had gone into exile from Queen Mary's England certainly wished? If so, was there any prospect of maintaining national unity or of restoring it? How should the new despotism which England had found necessary (or at least acceptable) be reconciled with a medieval tradition where the powers of monarchs, although substantial and essential, had been only one element in the complex feudal system? How could the position of the English Crown be reconciled with the international traditions both of Catholicism and of Protestantism? And what precisely was the status of the Church of England's bishops? How could bishops govern the Catholic Church when many fervent Protestants disliked the very name of 'bishop', and when the Queen insisted on instructing them in their duties? How could an international council of bishops be held if it had to be summoned by monarchs who were often at war with each other? If social conditions had changed during the sixteenth century, could it not be agreed that they had changed from age to age previously – and if so, was it possible to agree on standards by which the legitimacy of religious developments could be judged? Was the papacy allowed to evolve as England had evolved? Could the Church

---

[14] Quoted in P. E. Hughes, *The Theology of the English Reformers* (London, 1965), p. 43. See W. M. Southgate, *John Jewel and the Problem of Doctrinal Authority* (Cambridge, Mass., 1962), and J. E. Booty, *John Jewel as Apologist of the Church of England* (London, 1963).

evolve, or did the New Testament provide a perpetually authoritative pattern? Granted that the pattern laid down for England in 1559 could not be found in the New Testament, was it still right to enforce it?

Jewel died when he was not yet fifty, but he had defined the lines on which the spokesmen of the Church of England were to defend themselves from Roman Catholic claims over more than a hundred years. In 1610 Archbishop Bancroft ordered that a copy of 'Jewel's Apology' should be placed in every parish church in England.

Richard Hooker took up this defence of the Church of England but conducted it at a higher level and directed it mainly against Protestant objections. He was in an intimately personal sense Jewel's successor, for Jewel undertook to be his patron when he was a boy doing well at the grammar school at Exeter, and secured for him a place at his old college in Oxford. For sixteen years Hooker remained in this college; among other tasks he taught logic (basically Aristotle's) and Hebrew. Then he was appointed to the key pulpit among London's lawyers, as Master of the Temple – although he had the embarrassment that the defeated candidate for the post, Walter Travers, stayed on as assistant or 'Reader' and preached every Sunday afternoon to a larger congregation, contradicting what had been said in the morning. Travers was a Puritan and the controversy with him, however irritating, stimulated the Oxford scholar into beginning his masterpiece, *Of the Laws of Ecclesiastical Polity*. He accepted appointments to two country parishes – one near Salisbury, the other near Canterbury – in order to concentrate on what he had come to see as his life's work. The first four parts or 'books', having been submitted to Archbishop Whitgift and to the all-seeing Lord Burghley, were published in 1593, followed by a fifth four years later. This fifth book, by far the longest and most controversial, was a detailed defence of the customs of the Church of England, dedicated to Whitgift.

Hooker died in 1600, like Jewel not yet fifty years of age and like him worn out; as his biographer Isaak Walton put it, 'it is thought he hastened his own death by giving life to his books'. But writing in 1664 Walton also quoted what Pope Clement

VIII was reported to have said, when Thomas Stapleton had read Hooker's first book to him: 'There is no learning that this man hath not searched into: nothing so hard for his understanding. . . . His books will get reverence by age; for there is in them such seeds of eternity, that if the rest be like this, they shall last till the last fire shall consume all learning.'

The difficulties which Hooker faced were those which Jewel had evaded. They were reflected in the delays which postponed the publication of the remaining three parts of his great work, left by him almost complete. The sixth and eighth books were first printed in 1648, and the seventh followed in 1662. Both in the seventeenth century and later there were speculations that other hands had tampered with the manuscript to suit their own wishes. It has aroused suspicion that the seventh book, praising the power of bishops with far more enthusiasm than can be found in Hooker's earlier writings, was given to the world by Bishop John Gauden, at a time when bishops had just been restored along with Charles II and when this particular bishop was claiming his rewards (first the bishopric of Exeter, then that of Worcester) for having compiled or forged *Eikon Basilike*, the book of prayers attributed to the martyred king, Charles I. Those modern scholars who accept these post-humously published books as authentic (at least in the main) still point out that the problems tackled in them were not small. Was the 'right of kings' divine, or did it ultimately derive from the people under God? Had Members of Parliament the right to change the religious legislation of 1559? Had bishops the right to govern the Church – a right derived not from the Church or from any earthly monarch but from Christ himself? It seems understandable if, after wrestling with such conundrums and trying to keep intact his loyalty to a queen determined to govern MPs and bishops alike, Hooker felt exhausted before a premature death.

Some of the character of his *magnum opus* was shaped by his work as a university teacher. He appealed repeatedly to the authority in philosophy of Aristotle, 'the most judicious philosopher whose eye scarce anything did escape which was to be found in the bosom of nature'. He also appealed to the Old Testament, where kings clearly ruled priests. So his specialist knowledge of logic and Hebrew encouraged him to argue that it was reasonable for Elizabeth I to be Supreme Governor of the Church of England – and for the English to obey orders issued by her authority in ecclesiastical affairs. But his mind had to range far beyond his Oxford preoccupations, for now he had to defend such a position against the whole tendency of the Reformation since Jean Calvin's triumphant return to Geneva in 1541: the tendency to rely on the New Testament as the only real authority for Christians. He had to argue that what was at stake in the detailed controversies between the Elizabethan government and the Calvinist extremists was nothing less than the question of whether or not the Christians' God blessed the creative progress of human reasoning and the peaceful ordering of human society. He was an advocate of civilization.

He approached the controversies of the time about matters such as clergymen's robes through a leisurely exposition of the Eternal Law, the Celestial Law (for angels and other invisible spirits), the Law of Reason which guides the conscience, the laws commanded by the Scriptures and the laws decreed by the nations to order human affairs where the Scriptures had not spoken decisively.

This last category of law – 'positive' or 'municipal' law – is, Hooker grants, alterable, to suit changing circumstances. It also needs to be sanctioned by the agreement of the whole people to live under a form of government, which need not be a monarchy. But 'without order there is no living in public society'. So there can be no right for the individual to prefer his private judgement to the law of the State within the government's proper sphere; even when the government trespassed beyond its power sphere, and the subject feels morally obliged to offer a passive resistance, there can be no right to rebel. And here Hooker came to the crux of the matter. Calvinists such as his rival Walter Travers had, he argued, no right to defy the orders of Queen Elizabeth and her ministers in ecclesiastical affairs. The matters in dispute (clergymen's robes, for example) had not been regulated by the Scriptures. Therefore in a Christian country such matters properly belonged to the sphere of the government.

Hooker rejected the Protestant tradition which pitted

68345.

Church against State as 'two kingdoms'. He preferred to compare Church and State with two sides of a triangle. The Church ought always, everywhere, to be working for a day when its membership would be identical with the State's; and that day had long ago arrived in England, where 'there is not any man a member of the commonwealth, which is not also of the Church of England'. And any government ought to be working for the 'good life' of its subjects, as Aristotle had said; God had not ordained kings 'to fat up men like hogs'. And for Hooker, the Protestant tradition which confined the Church to the straitjacket of the New Testament was wrong. The Church had been perfectly right to develop (on this, Hooker was clearer than Jewel); to bring into its worship the glories of the world such as architecture and music; to endow the clergy with tithes or with a bishop's wealth, and to give some of them high authority; to elaborate a theology based on reason as well as on the Scriptures.

The immediate influence of such argumentation should not be exaggerated. Twelve hundred copies of the 1593 edition were printed and were not sold out until 1606. The old-fashioned reliance on Aristotle and the Church Fathers limited Hooker's appeal even among the intellectuals. The first words of his Preface show his sombre mood. 'Though for no other cause, yet for this; that posterity may know we have not loosely through silence permitted things to pass away as in a dream, there shall be for men's information extant thus much concerning the present state of the Church of God established among us, and their careful endeavour which would have upheld the same.' And the first words of his first book were similar, showing that he knew that he was unlikely to be popular, whereas 'he that goeth about to persuade a multitude, that they are not so well governed as they ought to be, shall never want attentive and favourable hearers'. The same sharp tone marks his comments surviving in the margin of a copy of an anonymous pamphlet attempting to reply to him (*A Christian Letter of Certain English Protestants*, 1599). His real influence came in the seventeenth century, and it lay among those Anglicans who wanted reassurance that the Elizabethan settlement which they had inherited was defensible spiritually and intellectually as well as politically. Thus James I, according to Walton, 'never did mention him but with the epithet of the learned, or judicious, or reverend, or venerable Mr Hooker'; and Charles I recommended a study of Hooker to his scholarly daughter, Elizabeth. His learning and holiness helped this continuing prestige. His opinions may not have been always to the liking of James or Charles; in private papers which have survived he clearly denied the divine right of kings. But they knew he was a theologian in the great tradition. And later Anglicans have found very congenial Hooker's balance of the claims of Scripture, tradition and reason in an atmosphere of quiet legality and piety.

'Of law', wrote Hooker when he lifted his eyes above the controversies of his age, 'there can be no less acknowledged, than that her seat is the bosom of God, her voice the harmony of the world, all things in heaven and earth do her homage, the very least as feeling her care, and the greatest as not exempted from her power, but angels and men and creatures of what condition so ever, though each in different sort and manner, yet all with uniform consent, admiring her as the mother of their peace and joy.' And Izaak Walton could record that, as he lay dying in his rectory in Kent, Richard Hooker 'was meditating the number and nature of angels, and their blessed obedience and order, without which peace could not be in heaven; and oh that it might be so on earth!'[15]

BYRD AND SPENSER

The Queen gave her direct patronage to two laymen whose genius was profoundly religious but whose convictions were very different. William Byrd's greatest music was a lament for the tragedy overwhelming an England which had been part of

---

[15] Recent studies include J. S. Marshall, *Hooker and the Anglican Tradition* (Sewanee, Tenn., 1963); *Studies in Richard Hooker*, ed. W. Speed Hill (Cleveland, Ohio, 1972); R. K. Faulkner, *Richard Hooker and the Politics of a Christian England* (Berkeley, Cal, 1981).

Catholic Christendom; yet he enjoyed the Queen's favour. So did Edmund Spenser, whose poetry celebrated the new day of imperial Protestantism. Together, Byrd and Spenser enable us to glimpse what it meant to the souls of men that the Elizabethan Church claimed to be in some sense Catholic while being predominantly Protestant.

William Byrd was the pupil and intimate friend of Thomas Tallis, whose personal religion is difficult to penetrate. Tallis was organist of Waltham Abbey in Essex in the 1530s. After the abbey's suppression he continued to compose settings for the old words of worship, but became a Gentleman of the Chapel Royal in 1540. He retained the favour of successive monarchs until his death in 1585, and set the new Prayer Book to music which is still being used daily in Anglican cathedrals in the twentieth century. He was buried in the Chapel Royal at Greenwich, and the form of his will suggests that he died an Anglican.

Of Byrd's religion we know more. Having become organist of Lincoln Cathedral when barely twenty years old, he joined the staff of the Chapel Royal in 1570 and was always favoured by the Queen. She granted him and Tallis jointly the monopoly of music-printing for twenty-one years – a grant which was profitable in a country so devoted to music-making. They collaborated in a collection of sacred songs dedicated to her in 1575. But from the 1580s onwards Byrd's name appeared on many lists of Recusants known to be loyal to Rome, although he seems to have been excused the normal fines. This conversion – or was it an unbroken loyalty to Rome? – had a profound influence on him. He still provided fine music to accompany the Prayer Book services in the Chapel Royal, but from 1593 onwards his main home was in the Essex village of Stondon Massey. During thirty years of quiet there, he poured his genius into volumes of sacred songs often Catholic in their sources, into a hundred Latin motets to accompany the Mass (his *Gradualia*, issued in 1605–07), and into three Latin Masses for three, four and five voices. Much of this music was dedicated to peers of known Papist convictions. It belonged clearly to the renewal of Catholicism in the Counter-Reformation. The Council of Trent had forbidden the use of music for the

Mass which was based on every-day songs or which was irreverently florid. In his dedication of the *Gradualia* Byrd said that the music had suggested itself while he was meditating on the texts; so he was composing restrained religious music just as the council had desired. He was doing in England what his equal in polyphonic composition, Palestrina, was doing in Rome itself. Deliberately he refrained from the repetition of secular or religious music already in stock; the composition must be free, personal, his own worship. And he refused to spin out the words of the Mass as an excuse for elaborate musical passages showing his talents or the choir's; the music must serve the sacred words.

When we hear the lamentations of Jeremiah over the desolation of Jerusalem set to this music, we can, however, hear something more than the exposition of the text. We can hear a Catholic Englishman's nostalgia for the glories of the devastated shrines of his own nation. And when Byrd pours out splendid praise for Easter or All Saints, he implies a tribute to the enduring faith of his suffering fellow Catholics. For all the austere intensity of his devotion, he is self-revealing.

Yet Elizabeth's Chapel Royal had room for this musician who was in love with God and with the Catholic past. In 1586 he was a guest in the same house as two newly arrived Jesuit priests, William Weston and Robert Southwell. Probably they sang a Mass together. Weston proudly noted in his journal that Byrd had 'sacrificed everything' for his religion, but that was not accurate. Elizabeth did not require many sacrifices from men such as William Byrd who, while genuinely feeling religious nostalgia, were willing to accept her political authority. She also protected Thomas Morley, another distinguished composer who was on the staff of her Chapel Royal, and Sebastian Westcote, the organist of St Paul's Cathedral. Like Byrd, they both openly adhered to the old religion. Their music-making was a sound which echoed her policy of tolerating peaceful conservatives.[16]

[16] See Edmund Fellowes, *William Byrd* (revised, Oxford, 1948), and Peter Le Huray, *Music and the Reformation in England, 1549–1660* (London, 1967), pp. 227–46. Joseph Kerman has studied *The Masses and Motets of William Byrd* (London, 1981).

The son of a modest home in London, born probably in 1552, Edmund Spenser was given his chance by the new Merchant Taylors' School. He was a student in a Cambridge dominated by the debate about Calvinism and its consequences. Accepting the prevailing Protestantism, he was determined to become a great poet. After a brief spell as the Bishop of Rochester's secretary he made his name by his *Shepherd's Calendar* (1579). It was undeniably a clever poem, but a young man's. Most dangerously, it was too clever in its allusions to the triangular relationship between the Earl of Leicester (who had become his chief patron), his countess and his queen. It was also indiscreet in his praise of a good shepherd called 'Agrin', since Archbishop Grindal was at that moment in disgrace with the Queen. Nor was the oblique reference to Grindal solemn enough to flatter an elderly archbishop. Spenser used the Greek legend about an eagle dropping an oyster on the white head of old Aeschylus in the belief that it was a piece of chalk. This may have seemed a learned and witty reference, but Grindal no doubt remembered that according to the legend the eagle's mistake had caused the death of Aeschylus. The clever young poet was rewarded by an appointment as secretary to the Lord Deputy in distant (and not at all witty) Ireland.

England's colonial war against the Irish could scarcely have been more degrading, but Spenser gained a large estate and leisure; he grew to love the countryside as much as he disliked and feared the natives. His leisure was devoted to a great poem, *The Faerie Queene*, and in 1590 he visited the court in order to present the Queen with the first half. Elizabeth encouraged him with a handsome pension and he went back to Ireland to complete this project and other writing. He also made a second marriage; his love for Elizabeth Boyle produced some marvellous sonnets. But his home at Kilcolman in Munster was wrecked in the rebellion of 1598 and, returning with official letters to the court in Westminster, he died, shattered. He was buried in Westminster Abbey near the grave of Geoffrey Chaucer, whose work in the creation of English as a poet's language he had pondered, imitated and taken to 'glory' (a key word for him).

His masterpiece has been variously judged. C. S. Lewis, who loved it, though it 'perhaps the most difficult poem in English'. He found special difficulty in getting at its author's religion. In the end he concluded that 'the religion that underlies the form of the poet's imagination is simply the worship of the "glad Creator" '. He quoted Spenser's own confession in his *View of the Present State of Ireland*: 'Little have I to say of religion. . . . Myself have not been much conversant in that calling'.[17] Lewis regarded Spenser's poetry as essentially a celebration of created life – its orderliness, its bounty. And it is obviously true that Spenser was by profession a civil servant not a theologian, and by vocation a sensuous poet rather than an original philosopher. His cold-blooded view of Ireland was that the English conquest needed to be completed with determination, and his view of poetry was that it was an incantation in elaborately ceremonious and pictorial – although also learned – language, which lured the reader able to understand it into an enchanted dream very different from the realities of Ireland. His religion encouraged both this colonialism (since the English were extending Christian civilization) and this escapism (since heroic poetry was an adornment of the civilization being propagated among 'savages' with sword and fire). But surely we have no need to doubt that there was a layman's Protestantism at the centre of Spenser's attempt 'to fashion a gentleman or noble person in virtuous and gentle discipline'. In another modern critic's judgement, *The Faerie Queene* is 'above all a Christian work, founded upon an unquestioning acceptance of the primary relation of creature to Creator, and of the need of men to live in the light of, and by the help of, God's grace. Book I, the most openly Christian and doctrinal, a sort of Pilgrim's Progress through the fallen world of error, doubt, sin, temptation and evil, the book about the achieving of truth and holiness, is the crucial book . . . the most successful, the most unified and the most perfect in its structure and in the relationship in it of structure to purpose and message.'[18]

The Christian pilgrim in this Book I is the Red Cross Knight

---

[17] C. S. Lewis, *Spenser's Images of Life* (Cambridge, 1967), p. 140.
[18] Peter Bayley, *Edmund Spenser: Prince of Poets* (London, 1971), p. 124.

('Saint George of merry England'). He comes to grief except when guided by a fair lady, Una, who represents Truth. He is healed of his sins by personified virtues in the House of Holiness, given baptism in the well of life, and strengthened by Communion as he receives balm from the tree of life. Such passages correspond with the explicitly Christian (if unoriginal) content of Spenser's hymns *To Heavenly Love* and *To Heavenly Beauty*. To doubt that here a Protestant stated his own ideals for the future of England is like doubting that a nostalgic Catholic let his heart's beat be heard in William Byrd's Latin church music.

'*The Faerie Queene*', concludes the author of an elaborate study of its many allegories, 'is a book of religious inspiration and moral instruction, comparable in its purpose with the Revelation of St John and the *Divine Comedy* of Dante' – and partly indebted to those inexhaustible sources.[19] As such it had a great impact on the élite which was able to read it, so that it helped to create a new type of English gentleman, as well-read as he was well-born, as courtly as he was brave, as Protestant as he was patriotic. Surely Spenser, no less than Byrd, should be remembered if we think that the Church which Elizabeth governed had no soul.[20]

SHAKESPEARE'S RELIGION

Coleridge wrote of 'the greatest genius that perhaps human nature has yet produced, our *myriad-minded* Shakespeare'. There has been widespread agreement with such an assessment – and few would doubt that Shakespeare had a personal religion. But there has been less agreement about what his religion was.[21] It has been claimed that at heart he was a

---

[19] J. E. Hankins, *Source and Meaning in Spenser's Allegory* (Oxford, 1971), p. 298.
[20] Fritz Caspari studied the emergence of the new ideal in *Humanism and the Social Order in Tudor England* (Chicago, Ill., 1954).
[21] The facts were set out by Samuel Schoenbaum in *William Shakespeare: A Compact Documentary Life* (Oxford, 1977), and the gossip and speculations by the same cool scholar in *Shakespeare's Lives* (Oxford, 1970). Introductions to the work include M. C. Bradbrook, *Shakespeare: The Poet in His World* (London, 1978). Kenneth Muir surveyed *The Sources of Shakespeare's Plays* (London, 1977).

Roman Catholic.[22] Simon Hunt, one of the five schoolmasters in charge of the boy's education, may have been the Simon Hunt who became a Jesuit in 1578. Another of his teachers, John Cottom, left Stratford-upon-Avon in 1581 to become a firm Recusant in his native Lancashire, and had a brother who was a priest executed along with Edmund Campion. No doubt a number of the Shakespeares' neighbours were also of the old religion, and it has been suggested that the boy's own father was. We know that John Shakespeare was prominent in the commercial and public life of Stratford until 1576. He rose to the position of bailiff, the equivalent of mayor, and as such must have taken the oath acknowledging the Queen's supremacy over the Church. But he ceased to attend council meetings, and for a period also the parish church. When Campion and his fellow Jesuit Persons were in the neighbourhood in 1580 they distributed copies of a Catholic profession of faith compiled by St Charles Borromeo in Milan, and it is said that a copy was found in 1757 in the tiles of the roof of the house in Henley Street where William Shakespeare was born. And more than half a century after William Shakespeare's death, Richard Davies, the rector of a nearby village, made a short note: 'He died a Papist.'

However, by far the most probable explanation of John Shakespeare's withdrawal from public life is the reason given by the justices of the peace for his absence from church in 1592: 'for fear of process of debt'. We know that he had good cause to be afraid of some 'process' being started by irate creditors if he appeared on public occasions; he sold off pieces of land and was let off contributions to the relief of the poor. He was never fined or reported as a Recusant. The copy of the Catholic statement which he is said to have endorsed (but no signature of his has survived) has disappeared. The scholar Edmond Malone, who saw it, was in the end convinced that it could not be genuine. And even if John Shakespeare did for a time find consolation in the old religion, it does not follow that his son copied him – or copied his Roman Catholic schoolmasters. When in 1585 William Shakespeare abandoned Stratford, it was not to train

---

[22] As by Peter Milward, *Shakespeare's Religious Background* (London, 1973).

as a priest: he left his father to house his wife Anne and their
three young children, and he went (perhaps not directly) to
learn and earn in London.

The evidence that in his maturity he was a conforming
member of the Church of England is strong. His name is absent
from all known lists of Recusants – unlike his friend and rival,
Ben Jonson – and instead he appears in contexts which show
that he was acceptable to the clergy. For example, in 1614 the
Stratford corporation supplied him with a quart of sack and a
quart of claret to help him entertain a visiting preacher.
Perhaps he thought of his guest as Costard thought of the
curate in *Love's Labour's Lost*: 'a foolish mild man, an honest
man, look you, but soon dashed . . . a marvellous good neighbour, faith, and a very good bowler.' Far more important as
evidence are the many echoes in the plays of the church
services which he began attending when John Bretchgirdle
baptized him on 26 April 1564. A. L. Rowse has summed up
the evidence of the plays. 'Of all Shakespeare's "sources" the
Bible and the Prayer Book come first and are the most constant. Altogether there were definite allusions to forty-two
books of the Bible, including the Apocrypha . . . Phrases from
Morning and Evening Prayer are constantly echoed . . . There
are similar phrases and echoes from all the services, from
Baptism and Holy Matrimony – references to which are
numerous – the Commination service and the Churching of
Women. He had attended them all many times . . . He was an
orthodox, conforming member of the Church into which he
had been baptized, in which he was brought up and married, in
which his children were reared and in whose arms he at length
was buried . . . Above all, it was the psalms, Sunday by Sunday
at Morning and Evening Prayer, that made a life-long impression on him . . . It is impossible to exaggerate the importance of
this grounding in childhood.'[23]

Shakespeare made his will on 25 March 1616, 'in perfect
health and memory, God be praised'. It had the regular

---

[23] A. L. Rowse, *William Shakespeare* (London, 1963), pp. 41–7, is based on
Richmond Noble's full study of *Shakespeare's Biblical Knowledge and Use of the Book of
Common Prayer* (London, 1935).

Protestant introduction (ignoring the Virgin and the saints): 'I commend my soul into the hands of God my Creator, hoping and assuredly believing through the only merits of Jesus Christ my Saviour to be made partaker of life everlasting.' He asked to be buried in his parish church, and when he had died on 23 April, St George's Day, all that was mortal of him was put beneath a gravestone. This stone was inscribed with a curious message to the sexton who would normally have felt free to get rid of old bones:

> Good friend, for Jesu's sake forbear
> To dig the dust enclosed here . . .

But of course neither of these formal farewell utterances is conclusive evidence of a man's personal religion. It is possible to work through the plays collecting rather more eloquent passages which may testify to an acceptance of the conventional religion of his time. Thus we can take note of Isabella's creed in *Measure for Measure*:

> Why, all the souls that were were forfeit once
> And he that might the vantage best have took
> Found out the remedy.

But it is also possible to go through the plays collecting passages which suggest that Shakespeare's philosophy was the 'mixed and muddled scepticism of the Renaissance'.[24] Or we may suppose that the final 'message' of the plays is Macbeth's:

> Life's but a walking shadow: a poor player,
> That struts and frets his hour upon the stage
> And then is heard no more: it is a tale
> Told by an idiot, full of sound and fury,
> Signifying nothing.

The truth, however, seems to be that the plays express many philosophies, for their author was a dramatist not a philosopher. 'The play's the thing' – as he proved by neglecting to prepare his own plays for the printer.[25]

---

[24] T. S. Eliot, *Selected Essays* (London, 1932), p. 117.
[25] J. W. Leaver summed up the scholarly debate on 'Shakespeare and the Ideas of His Time' in *Shakespeare Survey 29* (Cambridge, 1976), pp. 79–91.

In the first scene of *Hamlet*, when the ghost has just disappeared, Marcellus agrees with Horatio that 'it faded on the crowing of the cock'. Then he reminds him of what 'some say' – that in the season

> Wherein our Saviour's birth is celebrated,
> The bird of dawning singeth all night long:
> And then, they say, no spirit can walk abroad . . .

Horatio replies:

> So have I heard and do in part believe it.

And almost all students of the plays would agree that while the dramatist often uses medieval superstitions still popular in his time, that does not disclose what he himself wholly believes.

This reserved attitude did not result from some quirk in this particular dramatist's temperament. Nor was it produced by some moral failure on his part. 'He sacrifices virtue to convenience', wrote Samuel Johnson, 'and is so much more careful to please than to instruct, that he seems to write without any moral purpose.' But it was taken for granted in Shakespeare's time that the drama of the London stage was not intended to instruct the public in Christian theology or morals. Direct instruction had been given by the old medieval drama under the Church's sponsorship, and such 'miracle' and 'morality' plays were still sometimes performed in Elizabethan England. But Shakespeare never used the Bible as the source of a whole play, as he used Hall's or Holinshed's chronicles of England or North's *Plutarch* for the Roman plays. He provided no play to mark an event in the life of the Church; the nearest he came to that was when he provided entertainments for the royal family which coincided with Christian festivals. Although many moral axioms are spoken by the characters he put on the stage, he did not write in order to commend the Church's moral teaching. His drama was Renaissance drama, directly modelled on Latin classics rather than on medieval Christian examples, investigating human rather than divine mysteries. When Francis Meres, a young clergyman, was praising his work in 1598, he called him 'honey-tongued' like Ovid, and 'most excellent' for comedies like Plautus and for tragedies like Seneca. The London stage in Shakespeare's day was not so offensive to the godly as it later became (so that the Puritans closed it down entirely in 1642) – but it was already the last place in the world where anyone expected to hear the Church's creed expounded directly.[26]

To find Shakespeare's religion, if by that we mean his view of ultimate reality, it is not enough to notice the belief or disbelief expressed in a few lines in a play. We have to look at the whole pattern of his work.

He made his name by *Henry VI* and *Richard III*, by light comedies, and by revising a spectacular tragedy by Thomas Kyd. The only serious theme which emerges from his early plays – and which runs right through his work to the end – is the majesty and responsibility of kingship. Curiously enough the only manuscript which has survived in his handwriting, 127 lines of an early play about Sir Thomas More, puts into More's mouth this conventional Tudor sentiment:

> For to the king God hath his office lent
> Of dread, of justice, power and command . . .

But the main impression left by this apprentice's work is of exuberant, if superficial, facility. By 1592 Robert Greene, a bitterly envious author near death, was attacking the upstart dramatist's conceit.

However, in 1592 tragedy came very near in real life. The plague closed down the London theatres and claimed many Londoners. Next year Christopher Marlowe, a dramatist whose achievement had until then been far greater than Shakespeare's, was killed in a tavern brawl; later Shakespeare was to salute him as the 'dead shepherd'. Had Shakespeare died in the plague, no commanding height would have been occupied by his name in the history of England. But from these plague years come the sonnets, almost certainly written to be read in private by his patron, Henry Wriothesley, Earl of

---

[26] See R. M. Frye, *Shakespeare and Christian Doctrine* (Princeton, N.J., 1963), qualified by some of the essays collected in G. Wilson Knight's *Shakespeare and Religion* (London, 1967).

Southampton, to whom two longer poems were dedicated when published in 1593–4. The sonnets record an inner turmoil. A young poet is gripped by all the existential questions which afflict any exceptionally insecure, sensitive and articulate youth: the remorseless passing of time, the frailty of beauty, the nearness of failure and death, the 'expense of spirit' which he deplores even while he yields to his sexual appetite. The fascinating but humiliating centre of his life is his infatuation with the mistress whom he has to share with his patron. 'Love's not Time's fool' is for such a man still a question. In the end no Christian answers are propounded, although Sonnet 108 casually mentions that the poet says his prayers daily.

After the plague, the eight golden years 1594–1601 saw Shakespeare at work with stupendous energy and originality. He purchased a shareholding in his company, the Lord Chamberlain's Men, presumably with Southampton's help, and that was the making of his fortune. For this company he wrote more and greater history plays, including *King John*, on the surface a routine 'No Popery' play but including the Bastard's profound realism; *Richard II*, which brought Henry Bolingbroke, a man of affairs, to take the country over from an incompetent ruler, but introduced deep musings by the doomed Richard; and *Henry V*, allowing the common soldiers to speak for themselves before they die. There was *Henry IV*, combining history with the more-than-man-sized creation of a comic hero, Falstaff; and *Julius Caesar*, combining history with the near-achievement of a tragic hero, Brutus. There was *The Merchant of Venice*, piercing the character of the Jew: 'If you prick us, do we not bleed?' There was *Romeo and Juliet*, turning someone else's dreary poem into ecstasy. And there was *Twelfth Night*, a celebration of the freedom, vigour and wit of women as well as their beauty – in an age so far from feminism that these parts had to be acted by boys. It seems to have been written in eight days for performance before the Queen in the great hall of Whitehall Palace on 6 January 1601. 'The play is done,' sang Robert Armin playing Feste, alone on the stage at the end,

And we'll strive to please you every day.

But after that not even Shakespeare could produce more plays
which would 'please'. He could not take the comedy of love
further than he had done in *Twelfth Night*.

So he achieved the diagnosis of the human agony in the great
tragedies. We naturally ask what in his life inspired the change
of mood, but there is almost no evidence. The situation behind
the sonnets is fairly clear; but we lack the key to unlock the
tragedies.

In 1599 *Henry V* had included a reference to Essex's depar-
ture for Ireland, with Southampton in the expeditionary force
which, it was hoped, would win another Agincourt. It was the
mess that Essex made of this campaign (including the promotion of Southampton in defiance of the Queen) that set in
motion the train of events leading to his crazy insurrection in
February 1601. The rebellion led to Essex being executed and
Southampton being imprisoned until the Queen's death.
Shakespeare was himself implicated, however remotely. Shortly before their act of folly a number of Essex's supporters put on
a performance of *Richard II*, and the point about Richard's
deposition was not lost on Elizabeth. 'I am Richard II, know ye
not that?' she remarked to William Lambarde when he was
showing her some archives. The performance of this play was
investigated at Essex's trial. Was this, then, the catastrophe for
which we are looking? The sonnets had protested an unalterable love for Southampton. It can be assumed that
Shakespeare was to some extent always loyal to his former
patron; he was conspicuously not among the poets who paid
tributes to the Queen immediately after her death, and in
Hamlet the pompous old bore Polonius, whose death occurs so
unceremoniously, seems to be a skit on the recently dead Lord
Burghley, whom the Essex-Southampton circle always regarded as an enemy. It has been suggested that *The Phoenix and
the Turtle*, published not long after the collapse of the rebellion
in 1601, is a lament for Essex and his friends: 'truth and beauty
buried be'. It is also possible that the career of Essex –
impetuous but inconsistent, glamorous but in the end almost
mad – contributed to the character of Hamlet. But it is unlikely
that the poet, now famous and well-off, was profoundly de-
jected by the follies and fates of aristocrats. It seems more

probable that he disapproved of their rebellion – as he certainly condemned rebellion in principle. The publication of the sonnets suggests that by 1609 (at the latest) any emotional relationship there may have been with Southampton belonged to the past, but there is no evidence, and little probability, that the Earl had ever admitted John Shakespeare's son to a truly intimate friendship.

Was there a sufficient disaster in the poet's private life? Had he written *King Lear* immediately after the death of his only son, Hamnet, in 1596, we might have had our answer. But he did not; and we are left to find the innocence of Hamnet reflected in young Arthur in *King John*, a play probably written that winter. Instead of collapsing, William Shakespeare secured recognition as a gentleman from the heralds and bought the grandest house in Stratford. Although Hamnet's twin Judith seems to have caused him anxiety – she was not married until she was thirty-one, and then unsatisfactorily – he was consoled by his eldest child, Susanna, who married a scholarly doctor. The tragedies include eloquent expressions of loneliness, and are full of disgust at sex; although such moods were already present in the sonnets, common sense suggests that their increase had something to do with his unsatisfactory marriage with an illiterate woman eight years older than he was. But there was no final breach between him and Anne. It is probable that he had provided for her handsomely before making his will, since had he not done so the law would have compelled him to leave his widow one third of his property – more than the 'second best bed' specially mentioned (perhaps for sentimental reasons) in that much-discussed document. In brief, we have no evidence of a dramatic catastrophe in his private life to account for the mood of the great tragedies of the 1600s.

It has accordingly been suggested that the main driving force behind the tragedies was the ambition to excel in that field, reckoned the chief challenge to any dramatist, when he was at the height of his powers and prosperity.[27] Yet it seems

---

[27] This was the argument of the 1934 lecture by C. J. Sisson on 'The Mythical Sorrows of Shakespeare' reprinted in *Studies in Shakespeare*, ed. Peter Alexander (Oxford, 1964), pp. 9–32.

worth repeating the chief themes of the plays, not in order to attempt any addition to the piles of literary criticism under which this mountain range of genius has been covered but solely in order that we may remember that the work done in this mysterious period had a unity.

Hamlet was an already familiar plot, handled in a play now lost by Thomas Kyd or one of his imitators; but into the simple plot of a delay in taking revenge Shakespeare poured poetry and genius when he got to work in 1600–01 (we know the date because of a number of contemporary references). Indeed, he permanently expanded the self-consciousness of the educated Englishman. It was an achievement which can be appreciated by comparing it with the crude contemporary psychology of 'humours'. The hero of *Hamlet* is an inexhaustibly ambiguous anti-hero. Driven forward by a traditional sense of duty and by courage (however fitful), capable of ruthlessness, he is a man like a god, the beauty of the world, the paragon of animals; yet he is also too clever to be guided by tradition, a man paralysed by self-analysis, sickened by a cynical weariness with existence, terrified of death, the quintessence of dust. By his own complexity which holds him back from the decisive action, he brings disaster to many – including the woman he loves, and himself. His life's achievement is simply to show what he is.

After *Hamlet* Shakespeare, it seems, tried to turn back to histories and comedies. But *Troilus and Cressida* could not be another celebration of love (as in Chaucer's poem of the same title) or of heroism (as in Chapman's 1598 translation of Homer's *Iliad*, dedicated to Essex). Around the unfaithfulness of Cressida is shown a chaos of sordid lust and pointless conflicts. As Thersites exclaims: 'lechery, lechery; still wars and lechery; nothing else holds fashion: a burning devil take them!' That verdict would be a valid comment on most of the characters in *All's Well that Ends Well* and *Measure for Measure*. Both plays became 'problem plays' – for the 'bed-tricks', the ensnaring of Bertram and the exposure of Angelo in a sex-mad world, were not truly comic themes. It was clear that the next masterpiece had to be a more straightforward tragedy. And it came. On All Saints' Day 1604 the royal court saw *Othello*, the first of three tragedies which were studies in pride.

Othello's killing of Desdemona is brought about by the sheer evil of Iago's suggestions to her husband. But the subtler tragedy concerns what is killed within Othello (whereas the Italian novel from which the plot came showed no interest at all in Othello's character). His nobility is killed by his pride. His pride is the reason why Iago can inflame his jealousy; his pride makes him his wife's implacable judge; and even when Emilia in her own dying speech has so terribly condemned him, his farewell speech is full of pride turned into self-pity.

Timon of Athens seems to have been a tragedy abandoned by its author while still in draft. It was not acted in his lifetime. The most obvious theme is the ingratitude of Timon's friends, but the subtler plot is that Timon has looked to his friends only for the confirmation of his pride. That flaw is what in the end makes him a hater of mankind; he lives like a beast and dies mysteriously alone by the salt sea. Another of the tragedies, *Coriolanus*, did receive performances – and it, too, was a study in the bitter fruits of pride. The Roman people's pride makes them ungrateful to Coriolanus, while his own pride makes him turn against his city. But neither the despairing Athenian nor the coldly arrogant Roman general has ever really fascinated an audience. What happens to a hater of men does not much affect men.

By their failures these two sequels to *Othello* show that not even this genius could be a genius always, able to grip an audience's profound attention and sympathy. But two transcendent plays were acted at court in 1606 – in the summer, when the King of Denmark was on a state visit, *Macbeth*; on the day after Christmas, *King Lear*.

At its simplest *Macbeth* was an entertainment provided by the company called the King's Men and written by a dramatist who had walked in scarlet to the coronation of King James I. It was a comment on the gunpowder plot of Guy Fawkes and others in the previous year. It condemned the murder of Duncan, and featured Banquo who was an ancestor of James; and it condemned witches, for whose reality James had argued in a book. But beneath this surface can be found layer upon

layer of meditation about the corruption of a well-rewarded
hero by an ungrateful and pitiless ambition incarnate in his
wife, leading him into treachery, solitude, darkness and hell. Is
it a total corruption? Here is the deepest fascination of *Macbeth*:
the audience is brought to pity this 'dead butcher and his
fiend-like queen'.

On its surface *Lear*, like *Macbeth*, shows that it is wrong to be
disloyal to a king. But because Shakespeare added so much
to the plot about the ungrateful daughters (taken from someone
else's *King Leir*), he was able to present the whole world of
human evil. It is evil to be proud – and Lear is himself full of
flattered self-will. Then pride breeds misery. But the escape
from evil begins when Lear, instead of pitying himself as
Timon always does, pities other people. In *Hamlet*, *Othello* and
Macbeth there had been many Christian images, and above all
there had been the affirmation of the control of life by the divine
justice and providence, but the Britain of *Lear* was pre-
Christian. In the earlier tragedies some relief had been added
at the end by the reaffirmation of the life of Athens or Rome,
Denmark or Scotland, but *Lear* showed how trivial any political hope would be in comparison with the pitiable fate of man,
the 'poor, bare fork'd animal' stretched out 'upon the rack of
this tough world'.

'Who is it that can tell me who I am?' asks Lear in the first
act. The human condition is now seen through godless eyes:

> Thou know'st the first time that we smell the air
> We wawl and cry. I will preach to thee: mark . . .
> When we are born, we cry that we are come
> To this great stage of fools.

Or if there are gods, they are evil:

> As flies to wanton boys, are we to the gods;
> They kill us for their sport.

Where human life begins is the place of corruption:

> But to the girdle do the gods inherit,
> Beneath is all the fiends';
> There's hell, there's darkness, there's the sulphurous pit,
> Burning, scalding, stench, consumption.

Only one morality can be expected after such a start:

> Humanity must perforce prey on itself
> Like monsters of the deep.

And only one end is to be expected:

> Men must endure
> Their going hence, even as their coming hither.

And it is the supreme tribute to *Lear* that, although it has perhaps the most improbable of all Shakespeare's plots, we feel for a time that here is the truth about life:

> The weight of this sad time we must obey,
> Speak what we feel, not what we ought to say.

How obsessive in all this work of the 1600s, despite the great variety of the plots taken from so many sources, is the theme that pride corrupts and causes ingratitude and treachery, and how profoundly sour is the attitude to sex! It is difficult to believe that this insistent message about arrogance and lust – a message coming from a distance far beyond the convention of tragic drama that pride comes before a fall, a message which had to be voiced even when Shakespeare was trying to write a comedy – was produced solely by a dramatist's professional skill. It seems more likely that at some date some event or events which we shall never know about worked on, and almost broke, his heart and mind. This need not have been at the time when the tragedies were written: emotional shock can be delayed in its effects. It is also possible, it seems, that the tragedies brought relief and healing to their own author – as to many other sad people. He saw the condition of the rest of humanity more fully than had been possible for him at the time of his self-absorbed, self-pitying sonnets. And some medicine for his own hurt was found in his compassion for fellow creatures. Lear's eyes were opened when he saw the 'poor naked wretches' on the heath in the storm. Are we to believe that he who was about to create Ophelia was not moved when a young woman was found drowned in a stream near Stratford shortly before Christmas 1579? Her name was Katherine Hamlett. Or that he who was about to create Cordelia as King

Lear's one loving daughter was not moved when the youngest
daughter of old Sir Brian Annesley resisted her sisters' attempt
to get him declared insane? Her name was Cordell.

After the great tragedies we enter the final period, when
Shakespeare's output gives some signals of exhaustion. His
death on what is believed to have been his fifty-second birthday
(although the date of his birth is uncertain) seems to have come
when the play of his life was felt to be over. But before the end
came, his work showed his peace.

It is possible to argue that the new happiness was, like the
previous dark period, solely a response to the demands of the
theatre. Plays were now most profitable if written for performance by candlelight, either at court or indoors in private
theatres such as the Blackfriars, used by Shakespeare's company from 1609 onwards. Plays should therefore be accompanied by stately music and dancing which would be snobbish
reminders of more expensive dramatic entertainments, the
'masques' which King James and Queen Anne loved; and with
a general message that all was well with the world, they should
be aimed at an audience able to afford the Blackfriars seats. A
sophisticated specimen of this style was *The Two Noble Kinsmen*,
a play of 1613 mainly by John Fletcher, with some scenes by
the old master. But again we should look at the unity of the
serious work in this period and ask whether it shows anything
of Shakespeare's heart.

The key figure is now a girl, lost and restored – but with that
girl is recovered a whole world previously abandoned in
disgust. This girl is 'all fire and air', as Cleopatra hopes to be –
but the fire is less smoky, the air purer, than in that supreme
tale of the mid-life crisis, *Anthony and Cleopatra* (which may have
been written as early as the year of *Macbeth* and *Lear*). In the
three acts which Shakespeare seems to have contributed to
Pericles, Prince of Tyre, Marina ends her father's despairing grief.
In *Cymbeline* Imogen's loving loveliness as she comes to her
marriage with Posthumus is at the heart of the final mood of
peace. In *The Winter's Tale* Perdita is restored to her father
along with his wife, Hermione. In *The Tempest* Miranda's
marriage is the centre-piece of the general reconciliation and
deliverance on the magic island.

It is possible that this enchanting girl emerged in Shakespeare's mind out of his sources; but it does not seem very likely. Behind the girl did he see his daughter Susanna, the 'good Mistress Hall' described on her tombstone of 1649 as being 'wise unto salvation'? Or was it some other woman who consoled him for his less than fulfilling marriage, or some transfiguration of many women in the memory? Or was he deeply reconciled to his wife? We do not know. But it can be said that 'what is here asserted, under the guise of the play's poetic symbolism, is nothing less than a concept of spiritual resurrection . . . a re-integrated and regenerated humanity.'[28] For it seems clear – not so much from anything anyone says in a play as from the unity of the themes of this final period – that the dramatist had himself come to share Hermione's creed:

> If powers divine
> Behold our human actions, as they do,
> I doubt not then but increase shall make
> False accusation blush, and tyranny
> Tremble at patience.

The healing which is celebrated in this final period is partly the slow work of nature. Many passages in *The Tempest* say or sing that. The flowers of an English summer, the sheep-shearing feast, the jokes of countrymen – all these fill the sixteen-year gap at the centre of *The Winter's Tale*. But *Lear* is by itself sufficient to show the ugly face of nature, so that if the questions of the tragedies are to receive answers bringing peace, there must be a supernatural reality which is benevolent.

Caliban, whose previous remarks have shown that he takes a definitely unromantic view of nature, exits with:

> I'll be wise hereafter,
> And seek for grace.

At another turning point Miranda, confronting a gang of villains, declares:

---

[28] Derek Traversi, *Shakespeare: The Last Phase* (London, 1954), p. 40. See also Frances Yates, *Shakespeare's Last Plays: A New Approach* (London, 1975).

> O wonder!
> How many goodly creatures are there here!
> How beauteous mankind is! O brave new world
> That has such people in't!

Her father sensibly comments, ' 'Tis new *to thee*'. The cruel and
cowardly old world has been transformed in a woman's mind
by the action of what at the end of *Macbeth* is called 'the grace
of Grace'; by what Ferdinand now proceeds to call 'immortal
Providence'; by the gods whom Gonzalo thanks,

> For it is you that have chalk'd the way
> Which brought us hither.

And Prospero in his epilogue pulls the play together:

> And my ending is despair,
> Unless I be reliev'd by prayer,
> Which pierces so that it assaults
> Mercy itself and frees all faults.
> As you from crimes would pardon'd be
> Let your indulgence set me free.

None of these plays names the Christians' God, and although
some critics have loved to spot the 'Christ figure' in them,
actually the redeemer is a girl assisted by magic. It may
therefore seem sentimental to suggest that the end of Shakespeare's spiritual journey brought an acceptance of the Christians' God in a spirit of forgiveness fully Christian and accompanied by the assurance of the 'brave new world' of Easter.
Certainly any such suggestion ought to acknowledge that on
the stage for which Shakespeare wrote any preaching was
expected to be very oblique. But even in the 'problem plays',
where apparently the spirit of comedy was entirely poisoned by
cynicism, the themes of innocence, forgiveness and reconciliation had been heard and there had been glimpses of the
restoration of order in society (as in nature), so that it is
inaccurate to say that these poems show that Shakespeare then
'believed in nothing'. Not for nothing did the very title of
Measure for Measure come from the Sermon on the Mount. And
already in the tragedies there was power in good as well as in
evil. This is, after all, what one would expect. As has often been

pointed out, the origins lie in the Ancient Greek rites of purification, for the least that happens in true tragedy is that the audience is first taken out of its own concerns by a new terror and is then purified by the new emotion of pity. But something else often happens in tragedy, if through its medium the good is distinguished more sharply than before from the evil – even if good and evil mix, as mix they must, in the vulnerable hero. At the end, the good is seen to possess a power mysteriously present in those apparently damned – and secure beyond the worst than can happen. Tragedy, while impossible if the triumph of the good seems assured, is equally impossible if the triumph of the good is also impossible.

A cautious scholar has accordingly observed that 'there is a sense in which *King Lear* can be regarded as a Christian play. We are asked to imagine a world in which there is no knowledge of Christian teaching, in which there is a savage struggle for survival, in which men like ravenous fishes feed on one another; and we are driven to realize that man needs neither wealth, nor power, but patience, fortitude, love and mutual forgiveness.'[29] At the beginning of the twentieth century – a century when *Lear* has often seemed contemporary – one of the greatest of all commentators on Shakespeare pointed out that at the end Lear's sight is 'so purged with scalding tears that it sees at last how power and place and all things in the world are vanity except love'.[30]

Before Cordelia dies, Lear says it himself:

> We two alone will sing like birds i' th' cage:
> When thou dost ask me blessing, I'll kneel down
> And ask of thee forgiveness: so we'll live,
> And pray, and sing, and tell old tales, and laugh
> At gilded butterflies: and hear (poor rogues)
> Talk of court news, and we'll talk with them too,

---

[29] Kenneth Muir, *Shakespeare's Tragic Sequence* (London, 1972), p. 139. See also W. R. Elton, *King Lear and the Gods* (San Marino, Cal., 1960), and Ivor Morris, *Shakespeare's God: The Role of Religion in the Tragedies* (London, 1972).

[30] A. C. Bradley, *Shakespearean Tragedy* (revised, London, 1905), p. 285. John Bayley, *Shakespeare and Tragedy* (London, 1981), avoided Bradley's moralism but could not entirely dissent from this conclusion.

Who loses, and who wins; who's in, who's out;
And take upon's the mystery of things,
As if we were God's spies: and we'll wear out
In a wall'd prison, packs and sects of great ones,
That ebb and flow by th' moon . . .
Upon such sacrifices, my Cordelia,
The gods themselves throw incense.

In *Lear* the contradiction of faith in God by the facts of life
seems to be so severe that Christianity is not going to be 'what
we feel'. The birth of the hope of a resurrection 'which does
redeem all sorrows' is aborted. With Cordelia's dead body in
his arms, Lear knows that this answer is given to Albany's
prayer for her, 'The gods defend her':

Never, never, never, never, never!

But an explicitly Christian mood fills every corner of the last
play which Shakespeare wrote – with, it seems, some assistance from John Fletcher.

Like *The Tempest, Henry VIII* is a ceremonious play; because a
gun was fired during a performance in June 1613 (possibly the
first performance), the Globe was burned down. The characters cannot be reconciled – Tudor history was too well known
for that. But they can be brought together in Shakespeare's
glorifying mind. The London mob is infinitely more genial
than the mob in *Coriolanus*. The pure woman in this play is
Queen Catherine, long-suffering and morally triumphant in
her meekness as she looks forward to death. Clergymen are
seen in a kinder light than surrounds them in any other play.
Even the proud Wolsey becomes human and moving in his
repentance. Cranmer is portrayed as a humble Christian,
but at the baptism of the future Queen Elizabeth he is filled
with the spirit of prophecy: 'heaven now bids me . . .' Shakespeare had in 1608 watched his only granddaughter being
baptized Elizabeth, and he was now writing at a time when the
nation was rejoicing over the Protestant marriage of Princess
Elizabeth. At the close of his life the greatest of all the
Elizabethans – and of all the English – added his tribute to his
dead queen:

She shall be lov'd and fear'd; her own shall bless her;
Her foes shake like a field of beaten corn . . .
God shall be truly known; and those about her
From her shall read the perfect ways of honour,
And by those claim their greatness, not by blood.

CHAPTER FIVE

DEFIANT CHRISTIANS

THE CATHOLIC
RECUSANTS

The story of the Recusants who refused to attend their parish
churches under Elizabeth I out of loyalty to the old religion of
Pope and Mass constitutes a tragedy to which perhaps only the
genius we have been studying could do justice. Roger Dibdale,
a priest executed in 1586, had been at school with William
Shakespeare. There is, however, no evidence that Shakespeare
was specially interested in the subject. His plays show a
fascination with national monarchy, not with the papacy; with
England, not with the Catholic Church. It appears that he took
the conventional view that a Recusant was, at least potentially,
a mere traitor to his sovereign; that inside the cloak of piety was
the dagger of a Macbeth. Whatever may have been his share in
the writing of *Sir Thomas More*, the play showed no interest in
the religious issue behind the death of that martyr. And there
seems to be a contemptuous reference to the Jesuit missionaries
who were martyrs under Elizabeth in Sonnet 124:

> . . . the fools of time,
> Which die for goodness, who have lived for crime.

But the Roman Catholic community in Shakespeare's England
contributed its share of heroes to the national heritage.[1]
William Allen, for instance, who was made a cardinal in 1587
and appointed Archbishop of Malines shortly before his death,
had as much ability and dedication as most Archbishops of

---

[1] Recent studies were summed up by Adrian Morey, *The Catholic Subjects of
Elizabeth I* (London, 1978), and Peter Holmes, *Resistance and Compromise* (Cambridge, 1982).

Canterbury. Brought up in Lancashire, he taught in Oxford until 1563, for the last four years privately. After five wandering years during which he was ordained a Catholic priest in Malines, he settled down as the head of a new college in the new university at Douai in Flanders. There he pioneered the training of English priests: astonishingly, no one had ever attempted this systematically before 1568. By this step, taken on his own initiative, he made it possible for the Catholic laity of England to be served by a new generation of priests faithful to the religion taught in Rome.

At first he seems to have intended merely a training in devotion and theology for men who would be ready to answer the call when Catholicism was officially re-established, but before long he realized that the urgent need was for missionaries who would work as well as wait. Beginning in 1574, Allen sent to England not mere propaganda but men to live and to die. His finances were never far from disaster; he relied first on a Spanish subsidy and, when anti-English feelings among the citizens of Douai forced him to move his college to Rheims (1578–93), on a grant from the Duke of Guise. His human material was often unsatisfactory, as callow youths came over from England with confused religious opinions. By a regime of devout austerity and excellent teaching (he had Oxford and Cambridge professors on his staff) he made them into priests. Most were trained for a mission of constant discomfort and tension, riding from house to house with a one-in-two chance of arrest and a one-in-seven chance of execution, braving a certainty which to many a Tudor Englishman was probably as worrying as the risk of a painful death: official condemnation and popular execration as traitors. Before long Allen's extraordinary seminary was so attractive that it became too small, and eager recruits had to be sent for training elsewhere.

He accompanied his teaching by a stream of publications. Some of these books his former pupils could recommend to simple inquirers; others they could rely on as answers to their highly placed enemies. Before he died in 1594 his last message to the priests whom he had trained was a final warning that Catholics were on no account to be allowed to worship with Protestants. But, he added, those who did so 'for mere fear or saving their family, wife and children from ruin' were to be treated with 'great compassion and mercifulness'. It was an instruction typical of his combination of courageous idealism with humane friendliness. He boasted that his college, for all its strictness, did not need written rules.

After Allen's death the oversight of the English mission was mainly in the hands of Robert Persons (or Parsons), who had already been his ally in the foundation of colleges for the overflow of students. This successor's task was the harder since the hopes with which the older man had pioneered had not been fulfilled. Just before Persons died in 1610 John Donne bitterly attacked his influence in *Pseudo-Martyr*, a 400-page onslaught, followed by a satire in learned Latin translated as *Ignatius his Conclave*. (The conclave addressed by the founder of the Jesuits takes place in hell, and includes a proposal to send these missionaries on a mission to the moon.) Donne's own family had 'endured and suffered in their persons and fortunes', as many others had done, at the call of this man who fascinated some, repelled others and baffled most. In his preface to *Pseudo-Martyr*, Donne recalled how impressed he had once been 'by Persons, who by nature had a power and superiority over my will'.

At every stage of his adult life Persons made enemies, Catholic as well as Protestant. Some claimed that because he was a Somerset blacksmith's son he could not get on with his colleagues while he was a Fellow of Balliol College, Oxford. Whatever may have been the truth there, he committed himself to Roman Catholicism in the 1570s and became a Jesuit. The Society of Jesus had been founded by St Ignatius Loyola and given its constitution by the Pope in 1540; as the spearhead of the Counter-Reformation it was at the Pope's disposal in Rome itself, or in India or China or across the Atlantic or on the spiritual battlefields of the struggle for Europe. Persons was always disappointed that there were not enough recruits to form an English 'province' in the Jesuit order (that was not to come until 1623), but he gradually took over control of the English College in Rome, founded 1576–79, becoming rector in 1587. Disappointed also by the laxity which he observed in Rome and by the general lack of heroism which he discovered among English Catholics during his return to the country in 1580–81, he put his hopes in a new generation. In 1582 he persuaded the Duke of Guise to found the school for boys which, when moved to St Omer and placed under the control of the Jesuits, became the pioneer of Roman Catholic education for the English.[2]

Persons was sensitive to the human cost of the English mission; the walls of the chapel in the English College at Rome were painted with scenes showing priests being tortured and executed. But his answer was to go on dreaming. Among his unpublished papers was a *Memorial for the Reformation of England*, envisaging the future: a Council of Reformation was to appoint bishops and parish priests of good character and to remove those who proved disappointing. Church lands were to be recovered and seminaries, schools and hospitals financed out of them. England was to be given a third archbishopric (at Bristol) and a third university (at Durham). Meanwhile another answer to the realities awaiting the Jesuits in Elizabethan England was to set Persons' hopes on diplomatic intrigue and military force. He knew how to gain the ear of Philip of Spain and how to delude him into believing that Elizabeth could be overthrown with ease. Like Allen, Persons was a prolific writer. He was more prolific than wise, but one of his books, *The Christian Exercise appertaining to Resolution* (1584), became a best-seller and, in a censored version edited by a Puritan named Bunny, was used by many Protestants who shared his conviction that being a Christian meant being uncomfortable. In the next century a greater Puritan, Richard Baxter, used to say that his soul had been awakened by reading an old, torn copy of 'Bunny's *Resolution*' when a boy of fifteen.[3]

Persons wrote the first biography of St Edmund Campion and always kept on his person a portion of the rope which had

---

[2] See A. C. F. Beales, *Education under Penalty* (London, 1963).

[3] There is a memoir in *Letters and Memorials of Father Robert Persons*, Vol. 1, ed. L. Hicks (London, 1942), and see Bernard Basset in *The English Jesuits* (London, 1967), pp. 55–96. Martin Haile wrote about Allen as *An Elizabethan Cardinal* (London, 1914). T. H. Clancy studied *Papist Pamphleteers: The Allen-Persons Party and the Political Thought of the Counter-Reformation in England* (Chicago, Ill., 1964).

bound Campion to the scaffold. This famous Jesuit martyr made his way on foot to Rome in 1573, leaving behind a career of the highest promise at Oxford. He was happy teaching in the Jesuit college at Prague until sent on the order's first mission to England, in 1580 with Persons as leader. His existing reputation, his eloquence and his gift for friendship all contributed greatly to the mission's impact in stirring up the ardour of priests surviving from Queen Mary's time and in reaching families who were to send many sons to serve the mission in later years. Perhaps what made the biggest impression was his courage, for despite his disguise this gifted young man was convinced that he was going to this death. 'I cannot long escape the hands of the heretics,' he reported to the distant general of the Jesuit order, 'the enemies have so many eyes, so many tongues, so many scouts and crafts. I am in apparel very ridiculous; I often change it and my name also. I read letters sometimes myself that in the first front tell news that Campion is taken, which, noised in every place where I come, so filleth my ears with the sound thereof that fear itself hath taken away all fear.' With a strange fatalism he wrote an open letter to the Privy Council; when published from a secret press at Stonor Park, it became known as his 'brag'. He challenged not only the councillors but also the theologians of the universities to debate. He sounded confident, but he knew that he was going to a cruel death. Although 'racked with your torments . . . we have made a league – all the Jesuits of the world, whose succession and multitude must over-reach all the practices of England – cheerfully to carry the cross you shall lay upon us.' The death he had expected he met bravely during 1581.[4]

The priests who followed Campion in the English mission were a varied lot of men. Some were far more cunning; for example, Richard Holtby, 'a little man with a reddish beard' who was the leading priest in the north. Between his return to his native Yorkshire in 1591 and his peaceful death in 1640,

---

[4] Evelyn Waugh wrote a short study of *Edmund Campion* (London, 1935), relying largely on the biography by Richard Simpson (1867). E. E. Reynolds, *Campion and Parsons* (London, 1980), was better researched.

this Jesuit was never once arrested. Others were the opposite of cautious; for example, Thurstan Hunt, who organized the many Recusants of Lancashire. He was arrested in 1600 while attempting to rescue a fellow priest from captivity, and during his own imprisonment he wrote to the Queen to accuse the Bishop of Chester of wishing to see the Earl of Essex crowned king.

Naturally we know most of the men who, like Campion, could be eloquent on paper. Many hearts, particularly young men's hearts, must have been touched by the gallant courage of the Jesuit missioners of the 1590s in the Midlands and the south, John Gerard and William Weston; they were imprisoned but not executed. Both men were able journalists, and almost four hundred years later it is difficult to read their autobiographies with an unthrilled or unmoved heart. Scarcely less remarkable is the story of Henry Garnet. A shrewd and prudent man, he succeeded Weston as the superior of the Jesuits within England in 1586. He remained at this very difficult and dangerous post of leadership for twenty years. If he lacked the glamour of Persons, Campion, Gerard and Weston, he may be said to have achieved more solidly pastoral work. But in 1606 he was arrested and tortured. Already deeply depressed by his duty of attending many public executions of his fellow Jesuits, he seems to have broken down under twenty-two 'examinations' before his trial. One factor was his own confusion of mind once he had become vaguely aware of the gunpowder plot against James I and Parliament. 'I was very much distempered and could never sleep quietly afterwards, but sometimes prayed to God that it should not take effect', he told his judges. Later he cried passionately but uselessly: 'I would to God I had never known of the powder treason!'

After twenty years of discretion, Henry Garnet had been caught up in the treasonable and murderous plots of laymen who were great fools. And all that he could now do, in their defence and his own, was to equivocate – thus earning for himself a place in *Macbeth*. 'An equivocator . . . who committed treason enough for God's sake, yet could not equivocate to heaven', sneers the Porter in Act II. But he died with dignity and his nephew, St Thomas Garnet, now banished, had the courage to return next year to England and to death.[5]

One of the Jesuits, St Robert Southwell, wrote English poetry of enduring quality during the six years while he was a hunted mission priest (1586–92). During the three years which he spent in solitary confinement, undergoing torture and awaiting execution, he was not allowed writing materials. When his prayer book or 'breviary' was recovered, its only clue to this poet's mind was a row of pricks under the name of Jesus.

Of course we admire priests who undertook a mission where the penalties were so terrible. Lord Mountjoy, who was to conquer Ireland for Elizabeth, exclaimed when he had just witnessed the execution of Robert Southwell: 'I cannot answer for his religion, but I wish to God that my soul may be with his.' Seeking an explanation of their heroism, we notice that many of them fell under the influence of Allen or Persons, and above all under the psychological pressure of the month spent in the first experience of the *Spiritual Exercises* of St Ignatius Loyola at an impressionable age. Robert Southwell, for example, was sent from his father's manor house in Norfolk to be trained at Douai in 1576 when about fifteen years old. Evidence survives that the young man had to battle with ardent natural longings before he became the complete Jesuit. But he entered the order at the age of seventeen, and was sent to Rome. There he became so fluent in Italian that he had to relearn English before he could return on his doomed mission. Above all, he became thoroughly practised in the *Spiritual Exercises* and in the rest of the discipline of the Counter-Reformation. Hour by hour in Rome, he learned to meditate in the manner which was later to shape his poems. Memory, understanding and will were all made to concentrate on one point, preferably a point in the life of Christ but possibly another point in Catholic doctrine. All one's attention was, like sunlight, concentrated until

---

[5] Philip Caraman, a Jesuit author with many gifts, translated and edited the autobiographies of *John Gerard* and *William Weston*, and also wrote about *Henry Garnet* (London, 1951–57). Modern histories of *The Jesuits* have been provided by David Mitchell and Hugh Aveling (London, 1980–81); Aveling's is better. Henry More's history published in Latin in 1660 was edited by Francis Edwards as *The English Jesuits* (London, 1981).

the point burst into flames. Here was a discipline which was to be of great significance for English poetry as well as for English prayer.[6]

Another potent source of inspiration was opened up when among Englishmen who still accepted the Pope's authority the Bible began to be given the place which had been denied to it throughout the Middle Ages. The first English version of the Bible ever to receive a Roman Catholic blessing was compiled abroad, for use in the training of priests for the English mission. It was printed at Rheims in 1582 (the New Testament only) and at Douai in 1609–10 (including the Old Testament). It was mainly the work of Gregory Martin. Starved of funds, based on the Latin Vulgate version not on the Hebrew or Greek, inventing half-Latin words in order to avoid English which the Protestants had taken over, prefaced by a feeble attempt to defend the previous refusal to give the laity a Bible they could understand, it had many defects which Protestants delighted to point out. But it did what it was meant to do. It aroused devotion; it inspired martyrdom.

POPES, POLITICS AND TREASON

Why did Englishmen of that spiritual quality have to live in the shadow of the executioner's scaffold?

In 1570 the involvement of Roman Catholicism in Elizabethan politics came to a head when a layman, John Felton, fastened to the gates of the Bishop of London's palace a 'bull' from Pope Pius V excommunicating and deposing the Queen. He had obtained a copy through an Italian banker living in London, Roberto Ridolfi. Felton was promptly arrested and executed, but his was not the only life lost through this bull, known from its first Latin words as *Regnans in excelsis*.

An outright declaration of war against the Elizabethan

---

[6] See Louis Martz, *The Poetry of Meditation* (New Haven, Conn., 1954); Christopher Devlin, *The Life of Robert Southwell, Poet and Martyr* (London, 1956); Joseph D. Scallon, *The Poetry of Robert Southwell, S. J.* (Salzburg, 1975).

government, *Regnans in excelsis* went so far as to say that the Queen had claimed to be 'Supreme Head' of the Church and that the papacy had never recognized her right to her throne – two claims which were historically inaccurate. Although there was no explicit command to rebel, or invitation to foreign powers to invade, much was implied by the bull's excommunication of all who obeyed the Queen's 'orders, mandates and laws'. Much was implied, too, by the encouragement given by papal diplomats to potential invaders. It was a document more controversial than any subsequent political move by a pope. Within fifteen years of its publication Pope Gregory XIII had felt obliged to explain that no Catholic need rebel against Elizabeth, 'things being as they are', and an eminent English Jesuit, Cardinal Robert Bellarmine, had publicly emphasized that a pope's power to depose a wicked prince was not effective unless the people concurred, thus beginning the retreat from the 'plenitude of power' claimed by the medieval papacy. Indeed, while the bull has never been explicitly disowned in Rome, in practice popes and their agents have been so far from continuing to act in the spirit of 1570 that they have laid themselves open to the charge of failing to denounce wicked rulers out of fear of doing damage to Roman Catholic interests narrowly interpreted. It is one of the many paradoxes in the history of papal Rome that the authority which declared war against Elizabeth I never excommunicated Adolf Hitler.

Regnans in excelsis created an intolerable strain in the conscience of any Englishman who wished to be at the same time a Catholic and a patriot. But it should be seen against its background. Ridolfi had been instrumental in arranging an engagement to marry between the leading English aristocrat of conservative inclinations, the Duke of Norfolk, and Mary, Queen of Scots, who had a clearer right than anyone else to inherit the throne from the still unmarried Elizabeth. In 1569 the atmosphere of conspiracy had exploded in the rebellion of the two northern earls, Northumberland and Westmorland, many of whose supporters had been poor and innocently devout Catholics. The rebellion had failed. The evidence suggests that the not very intelligent aristocrats leading it had set it off prematurely and without realistic objectives. The Earl of

Leicester, who had been involved on the periphery, had betrayed the plot to Cecil, the Duke of Norfolk had been imprisoned, and a summons to London had made the earls panic. Most of the Catholic gentry in the north had either supported the government or held aloof. But without waiting for the news of the rebels' fate to reach him, Pope Pius determined to relieve those who attempted to overthrow the Protestant government from any fear of having committed a sin. His chief motive was not political. Although in *Regnans in excelsis* he claimed to be 'ruler over all peoples and kingdoms', he was in practice an austerely living, very hardworking, Dominican friar, nicknamed 'Brother Woodenshoes' at the time and later canonized as a saint. He had been Grand Inquisitor and was interested chiefly in questions of belief and conscience. He made no effort to bring his bull to the English government's attention, beyond asking for it to be displayed in ports where English seamen would notice it. He neither consulted, nor officially informed, the Catholic monarchs who would have been expected to pay for any invasion of England in treasure and blood.

These monarchs were not pleased. Philip of Spain disapproved of the indiscretion of the Roman Pope even more than he had disapproved of the indiscretion of the English rebels. He had been interested in England chiefly as an ally against France, and he had shared the hope of the first of the Counter-Reformation Pope, Pius IV (1559–65), that some arrangement could be reached with the formidable Elizabeth. At the beginning of her reign there had even been some talk that he might marry her. Another Catholic monarch, the emperor Maximilian, openly begged the Pope to withdraw the bull, and in 1572–73 both Spain and France agreed not to press the claims of Mary, Queen of Scots to the throne of England. It was only gradually – and largely because English soldiers and sailors made themselves such a nuisance fighting Spaniards in the Netherlands and at sea – that Philip felt sufficiently provoked to take advantage of the papal condemnation of Elizabeth and to begin 'the enterprise of England' with its climax in the Armada of 1588.

St Pius V was not much aware of the likely political consequences of his bull in 1570. But he was aware of one need – the need to act dramatically if the Counter-Reformation was to influence England, for during the 1560s the government's fairly lenient policy had been bringing about a slow weakening of the old ties. Those who at least occasionally attended their parish churches while adhering to the old religion in their hearts were known as 'Church Papists', and although they had effectively deterred the Queen from making the Church of England militantly Protestant it had been anyone's guess how long they or their families would remain 'Papists' in any real sense. For this reason the conformity of the 'Church Papists' had been formally condemned by committees of theologians in Rome and at the Council of Trent in 1562, and by Pius V in 1566. An unknown number of priests who had served under Mary had by now become chaplains to the gentry, or had simply retired or gone underground, and these had enabled an unknown number of laity to hear Mass from time to time, but such a ministry had not amounted to a fully alternative Church – or to a permanent arrangement. Lady Magdalen, Viscountess Montague, a widow who had once been a maid of honour at the court of Queen Mary, in her country house continuously kept the most rigorous devotional diet of that period right up to her death in 1608; she housed three chaplains, and hearing three Masses a day was only a part of her nun-like routine.[7] But she was quite exceptional. A modern study of the laity as a whole up to 1573 is reasonably called 'The Dormant Years'.[8] So a resurrection was essential; and this Pope Pius knew.

However, when we have done all that we can to understand the motivation behind *Regnans in excelsis*, we may still conclude that it was a mistake. Without this papal interference the resurrection of Roman Catholicism in England would have been easier and larger.

A simple indignation that the Pope had invited Englishmen to commit treason was now the theme of government propaganda. It was also the theme of the Act of 1571 which made it treason for anyone to bring a papal bull into the country or to

---

[7] See *An Elizabethan Recusant House*, ed. A. C. Southern (London, 1950).

[8] W. R. Trimble, *The Catholic Laity in Elizabethan England* (Cambridge, Mass., 1964), pp. 8–68.

reconcile anyone to Rome on the basis of such a bull. Ten years later another Act of Parliament made a traitor's death the penalty for withdrawing the Queen's subjects from their 'natural obedience' – and made a year's imprisonment with a large fine the penalty for attendance at Mass.

A pamphlet distributed by William Cecil in 1583 defended the 'execution of justice' – meaning the executions of priests which began in 1577.[9] And when brave men persisted in obeying the Pope rather than the Queen, 'justice' was made still more severe. In 1585 it was made treason to be, or to assist, a seminary-trained priest in England. In 1593 'popish recusants' were forbidden to move more than five miles from their homes. The fines for refusal to attend the parish church became a fearsome deterrent: £20 a month, laid down in the 1581 Act, was a fine which only the richest could bear, although in practice its imposition was selective and spasmodic. Usually the real threat was that a Recusant might be imprisoned and all his property confiscated for inability to pay the fine, leaving his family to starve.

The ruthlessness which the Elizabethan government now displayed surprised Elizabeth herself. The new policy of terror, sending about three hundred Roman Catholics to their deaths, was in striking contrast with the mildness of the treatment meted out during the 1560s to priests and bishops who retained their religion from Queen Mary's reign. Fewer than two hundred parish priests had been deprived of their livings. Not one bishop had been executed. Even that much-hated persecutor, Edmund Bonner, had not met anything like the death he had inflicted on Protestants. Nicholas Heath, Archbishop of York and Lord Chancellor, had served on the Queen's council until January 1559 but had then bravely attacked her claim to supremacy over the Church in the House of Lords, which had meant a period in the Tower of London. In the end Heath had been allowed to retire with dignity to his estate in Surrey, where he died in 1579. John Feckenham, the Dean of St Paul's

---

[9] R. M. Kingdom edited William Cecil's *The Execution of Justice in England*, with William Allen's reply *A True, Sincere and Modest Defence of English Catholics* (Ithaca, N.Y., 1965).

who had volunteered to serve under Mary as the last Abbot of Westminster, lived until 1584 and although he was imprisoned because of his loyalty to the old religion the conditions of his imprisonment were not harsh.

The stern new policy of the 1570s also differed from the treatment of the laity in the 1560s. Although an Act of 1563 had made it a very serious crime (punishable by the total confiscation of property on the first offence and by death on the second) to refuse to take the oath acknowledging the Queen's supremacy over the Church, the enforcement of that law had not been pursued vigorously.

It is at least possible to believe that if from 1570 onwards the priests had confined themselves to the advocacy of the very powerful and attractive religion of the Counter-Reformation, without getting entangled in politics, the government would not have inflicted savage penalties on them and their converts. In his 1583 pamphlet Cecil felt obliged to make the idiotic claim that the warders 'whose office it is to handle the rack' were 'specially charged to use it in as charitable a manner as such a thing might be'. It is tempting to speculate about the influence that might have been secured by a generation of priests trained in the newly confident theology of the Counter-Reformation, inspired to minister to laity who found no food for their souls in the new-fangled Protestantism, openly supported by the many old-fashioned gentlemen who still retained great influence and patronage in the countryside, on good terms with the many old-fashioned clergy who had accepted posts in the Church of England, led by chief pastors who were allowed to stay alive, and in general treated no worse by the government than were the extreme Protestants who would have been their rivals.[10]

As it was, the seminary-trained priests sent into England from 1574 onwards had to labour under the most fearful of handicaps and paid horrific penalties for their devotion to the

---

[10] An impression of the strength of the Roman Catholic case may be gained from A. C. Southern, *Elizabethan Recusant Prose* (London, 1950); and the strength of the religious, rather than political, support was shown by Arnold Pritchard, *Catholic Loyalism in Elizabethan England* (London, 1979).

papacy which had issued *Regnans in excelsis*. The courage of the martyrs alleged to be traitors attracted some, but the resurrection of Roman Catholicism would probably have been far stronger had it not been identified with treason. At any rate, that was the conviction of an exceptionally well-informed and thoughtful observer: William Gifford, an Englishman who went into exile and became Archbishop of Rheims. He passionately believed that the whole policy of Pius V, William Allen and Robert Persons had been a tragic mistake.

The difficulties were familiar to Allen and Persons, as is shown by their surviving private correspondence if not by their morale-raising publications. But their awareness of the difficulties in converting their fellow countrymen one by one only led them deeper into the support of actions designed to make England Catholic by another act of state such as the succession of Queen Mary in 1553. Deeds such as the murder of the Dutch Protestant leader, William, Prince of Orange, in 1584 gave them no qualms – although in England it brought about an atmosphere of hysteria and an immense 'association' to defend the Queen. Pope Pius V encouraged the plot of Roberto Ridolfi for the restoration of Catholicism by the seizure of Elizabeth – the plot which cost the Duke of Norfolk his life. Pope Gregory XIII encouraged other plots to murder Elizabeth and ordered a *Te Deum* to be sung in thanksgiving when French Protestants were massacred. Why, then, should Allen or Persons hesitate? They were enthusiastic about the papally blessed rising in Ireland in 1579–80 and the Duke of Guise's abortive plots of 1581–83. Had Spanish troops landed off the Armada in 1588 they would have distributed a pamphlet against the Queen written by Persons in virulently personal terms – and, in the event, published by a gleeful Cecil. Had those troops occupied England, the Pope would have become the country's feudal overlord, as in the days of King John – an arrangement insisted on by Sixtus V in return for his cash. Had England been conquered then or later, Allen and Persons would have fully shared the delight of other Englishmen who indulged in exiles' dreams.[11]

---

[11] See A. H. Loomis, *The Spanish Elizabethans* (New York, 1963).

Men on the rack before execution, or facing financial ruin for themselves and their families, had to be rather more careful in their thoughts about the morality of treason. Many times Englishmen loyal to the Pope were being examined by authorities who had been unable to prove any treasonable act. (Jesuits, for example, were under strict orders not to talk about politics while in England.) They were then asked what they would do if the Pope were to send over an army to bring the kingdom back to its Catholic allegiance. They often tried evasion. Edmund Campion (who was to be executed under a medieval statute against traitors) replied that the question could be debated in the universities but did not concern him; his last words were a prayer for 'your queen and my queen'. John Gerard would say only that he would act as a true Catholic and a true subject. Others refused to answer at all. But privately Gerard confessed that a straightforward answer must be disloyal to the Pope or the Queen, and thus damage soul or body. It was called the 'bloody question', and Sir Francis Walsingham would sometimes attend the examination of priests in order to give himself the pleasure of asking it.

Naturally many hoped that a question so terrible would somehow go away. In 1585 four rich gentlemen of the old school and the old religion – Sir Thomas Tresham, Lord Vaux, Sir William Catesbury and Sir John Arundell – petitioned the Queen to the effect that while a gentleman's chaplain would feel in conscience bound to advise against attendance at the parish church a gentleman should be allowed to vouch for his own patriotic loyalty and that of his chaplain. But the Recusant from Sussex who managed to present this petition to the Queen in her garden at Greenwich died in prison, and his brother was executed. Sir Thomas Tresham, the leading petitioner and the leading landowner in Northamptonshire, was a man so sincerely patriotic that he begged to be allowed to enlist in the armed forces at the time of Armada, when almost seventy; 'an ancient and true servant unto her majesty', as the Queen's council itself was willing to declare in 1598. But he spent most of the years 1581–96 in prison, and when he died in 1605 was deep in debt because the fines had been a drain even on his finances.

Some criticism of the papacy surfaced even among Roman Catholic priests in England. Towards the end of Elizabeth's reign arrested priests who did not seem particularly dangerous were sent to concentration camps in Wisbech and Framlingham castles in East Anglia. Their imprisonment was not harsh. When William Weston arrived in 1594 and attempted to impose his idea of discipline, particularly disapproving of morris dancing and a hobbyhorse at Christmas, dissension arose. Similar quarrels rent the English College in Rome before the Jesuit triumph there. But the most scandalous controversy surrounded *A Conference about the Next Succession to the Crown of England*, a book of 1594 inspired by Persons. This discussed who should be the Catholic successor to Elizabeth, making it clear that the decision lay with Parliament guided by the Pope; and the clear implication was that Philip II's daughter Isabella was best suited. A publication so foolish brought to a head the dissatisfaction of many English Catholics with the Jesuits. In 1598 a group of priests begged Rome for the appointment of an English bishop. Instead the Pope appointed an 'archpriest', George Blackwell, who allied himself with the Jesuits. In response the anti-Jesuit opposition went to surprising lengths both in appealing to the Pope and in allying itself with the government; and Elizabeth's most able bishop, Richard Bancroft, much enjoyed himself stirring up the public controversy between Papists. Behind the clash of personalities and the pamphlet war lay the serious question, whether it was spiritually essential for faithful Catholics to expose themselves and their families to such punishments by a complete refusal to have anything to do with the Church of England, and by a complete acceptance of the Jesuit advocacy of the papacy's political claims.

Early in 1603, shortly before the Queen's death, thirteen priests put their names to a 'protestation' which sought to reassure both sides about the loyalties of patriotic Catholics. 'As we are most ready to spend our blood in the defence of her majesty and our country,' they declared, 'so we will rather lose our lives than infringe the lawful authority of Christ's Catholic Church.' But two of those who signed this protestation were soon to be executed for refusing the oath of allegiance required by the Queen's successor.

Naturally it is impossible for historians to be sure how effective the English mission was on the basis laid down in *Regnans in excelsis*. The contemporary literature about the mission, although prolific, is ambiguous. Most of it was written in order to edify and encourage fellow Catholics. It had a tale to tell of the gratitude of thousands who rejoiced to be able once again to receive the absolution of their sins and the sacrament of the Body of Christ from a Catholic priest risking his life to save their souls. But the same literature shows that the Catholics whom these priests served included not a few who were willing to betray them. It seems to have been rare for a priest to land without the government being tipped off both by its spies abroad and by informers at home, and many arrests were made in the midst of congregations to which only known Catholics would have been admitted.

By 1600 there seem to have been only about three hundred Roman Catholic priests in the country, including a dozen or so Jesuits. This contrasted with the figure of about ten thousand clergy of the Church of England. The returns made by the Anglican parish priests to their bishops in 1603 reported a total of 8,590 Recusants, and a modern authority reckons that even including Roman Catholics who were children under the age of sixteen, those who had avoided being reported, and those who escaped any penalty by attending their parish churches, the whole Roman Catholic community in the country was under forty thousand, as compared with an Anglican communicant population of two and a half millions.[12] The records of fines by the government for Recusancy in the period 1593–1600 contain only about five thousand names, most of them in Yorkshire, Lancashire and Cheshire. Cheshire was often said to be riddled with Popery, yet examination of the surviving records leads to the surprising conclusion that 'in the whole of the reign of Elizabeth I only 302 Recusants can be identified with any certainty' – in a population around 64,000. An attempt at a

---

[12] John Bossy, *The English Catholic Community 1570–1850* (London, 1976), pp. 191–3.

thorough census of Recusants in Yorkshire in 1604 produced 3,500 in a population of more than three hundred thousand. In Lancashire the proportion of actual Recusants (not necessarily reported to the authorities) was far greater, since in that isolated county Protestantism had never really taken root outside the Manchester and Blackburn areas. It would have been extremely difficult for a Bishop of Chester or an Earl of Derby to enforce the religious laws, even with more activity than was displayed. William Cecil kept a map of Lancashire in his office, but could not solve the problem. It was typical that of the eight hundred Recusants 'presented' at the assizes of 1592, only eleven appear to have been forced to pay fines. At the assizes in 1630 almost 3,500 were reported, out of a population of about a hundred thousand. Outside Lancashire the statistics, although obviously always incomplete, suggest that the average Englishman with Catholic leanings was not prepared to accept the cause of the papacy as defined in and after 1570 and thus to defy Elizabeth's determined government.[13]

'The history of Elizabethan Catholicism', it has been said, 'is a progress from inertia to inertia in three generations.'[14] As its Roman Catholic author has acknowledged, that epigram was too gloomy; but another Roman Catholic historian has written accurately that when the century ended English Catholics were 'only too well aware that their community was disorderly, devoid of central authority, sharply divided, and an object of mockery to both Roman officials and English Protestant administrators.'[15]

---

[13] See K. R. Wark, *Elizabethan Recusancy in Cheshire* (Manchester, 1971); Hugh Aveling, *Northern Catholics: The Catholic Recusants of the North Riding of Yorkshire* (London, 1966); Christopher Haigh, *Reformation and Resistance in Tudor Lancashire* (Cambridge, 1975).

[14] See John Bossy, 'The Character of Elizabethan Catholicism' in *The Crisis in Europe, 1560–1660*, ed. T. Aston (London, 1965), pp. 223–46.

[15] Hugh Aveling, *The Handle and the Axe: The Catholic Recusants in England from Reformation to Emancipation* (London, 1976), pp. 71–2.

THE DEMANDS OF THE PURITANS

The Protestant critics of the Elizabethan establishment were called 'Precisians' or 'Puritans'.[16] The latter word, coming into use in the 1560s, had the future before it. Indeed, Puritanism came to wield so great an influence in America as well as in England that historians have been eager to debate the question: who should be called a Puritan in these early, formative years? It has been tempting to define this 'ism' as a system in contrast with Anglicanism.[17] However, the Elizabethans did not often think in terms of theological systems. Of course the systematic theology of Jean Calvin was vastly influential.[18] But if the Elizabethan Puritans were Calvinists so was their archenemy, Archbishop Whitgift. No rigid party line was taken by those who wanted further progress in the English Reformation, and they were not all radicals in rebellion against the Establishment. Many clergymen and laymen who were prominent and comfortable in the universities, among rich merchants, in the great houses of the countryside or at court, were Puritans.[19] 'The common factor', writes a scholar who has supplied a useful analysis of the many modern definitions of Puritanism, 'is not so much a "Puritan spirit" as a dislike of the *status quo*. There was considerable agreement about what ought to be swept away but much less agreement about what to put in its place.'[20] All that can be done by historians aware of the confusion of the very lively debate is to make a list of changes desired by many of those who with varying degrees of

---

[16] The standard modern study is Patrick Collinson, *The Elizabethan Puritan Movement* (London, 1967), and documents have been collected by H. C. Porter in *Puritanism in Tudor England* (London, 1970).

[17] As in J. F. H. New, *Anglican and Puritan: The Basis of Their Opposition, 1558–1640* (London, 1964).

[18] The best study of the man is now T. H. L. Parker, *John Calvin* (London, 1975), and a recent study of his theological influence in England is R. T. Kendall, *Calvin and English Calvinism to 1649* (Oxford, 1980).

[19] This was demonstrated by C. K. and K. George, *The Protestant Mind of the English Reformation* (Princeton, N.J., 1961), and Peter Lake, *Moderate Puritans and the Elizabethan Church* (Cambridge, 1982).

[20] Patrick McGrath, *Papists and Puritans under Elizabeth I* (London, 1967), p. 46. See also Basil Hall's essay on 'Puritanism: The Problem of Definition' in *Studies in Church History*, Vol. 2, ed. G. J. Cuming (London, 1965), pp. 283–96.

moderation wanted what Milton was to call the 'reforming of Reformation itself'.[21]

Many Puritans objected to conventional features of the Baptism service. They were uneasy when the priest used the sign of the cross on the infant's forehead; it reminded them of the tricks of a pagan magician. They also disliked the custom by which godparents were chosen more for social than for theological reasons, while the natural parents were not featured. (In the Middle Ages infants had almost always been baptized when their mothers were still confined to bed.) They wanted the emphasis to be more clearly on the parents' faith as justifying the practice of infant baptism (if it could be justified: 'Anabaptists' thought not) – although with the parents could be associated godparents who were themselves godly Christians. Finally they objected to midwives and other women baptizing privately infants thought to be in danger of death. This custom seemed to ignore the fact that the infant had already been predestined by God to heaven or hell, without waiting for baptism.

Such objections to the Prayer Book's arrangements for Baptism already implied the whole 'reforming of Reformation'. For Puritans, religion should be based not on human wishes but on God's agreement with those on whom his favour rested (his 'covenant of grace'); not on social conventions but on personal faith; not on superstitious customs but on the Holy Bible. The Church was understood not as the whole baptized English people but as the gathering around the Bible of the 'elect' – those elected by God – who might be few. A Prayer Book suitable for such a Church ought to be based entirely on the Bible, more particularly on the Bible read with Calvinist eyes, not on Cranmer's eclectic gathering of treasures from all the centuries. To show what was needed a *Book of the Form of Common Prayers* was published in the mid-1580s, based on Calvin's work in Geneva thirty years before. The Bible was understood not as literature from which the Church selected passages at its own discretion, but as God's own self-revelation

---

[21] There are 630 entries in *Religious Controversies of the Elizabethan Age*, ed. Peter Milward (London, 1977), a survey of printed sources.

to his people, completely authoritative. Incidentally, the Bible did not include the books known as the Apocrypha; these books were rejected by the Jewish rabbis in their first century but were used in Roman Catholic and Eastern Orthodox services. Puritans had their own preferred version of the Bible, and it was not the Bishops' Bible sponsored by Archbishop Parker in 1565. It was the Geneva Bible completed in 1560 by a group of exiles led by William Whittingham – a translation scholarly in its rendering of the Hebrew and Greek, adorned with many prefaces and notes, clear in its printing (in Roman type – the only Roman thing about it), sized compactly and sold inexpensively. Less than a month after Parker's death in 1575 a licence was issued for the printing of the Geneva Bible in England, and its popularity can be illustrated from Shakespeare's plays. Although he was no Puritan (he quoted from the Apocrypha), his plays show that he took to using the Geneva Bible in the mid-1590s.

Other demands applied the Puritan insistence on a Bible-based Church to successive stages of the Christian life. It was not thought necessary that a bishop should confirm a child before admission to Holy Communion; the one essential qualification for communicating was personal faith. The service was regarded as 'the Lord's Supper' where the faithful should sit around a table (not a stone altar). The service was not a sacrifice offered to God by a priest; it was a reminder to the whole congregation of Christ's all-sufficient sacrifice on Calvary. Kneeling to receive the sacrament was rejected because it was thought to suggest the worship of the bread and wine. So, too, the wearing of medieval vestments (the white surplice or the coloured chasuble or cope), the lighting of candles, the veneration of crucifixes and respect for the images of saints were all thought to imply the acceptance of medieval priestcraft and superstition; and the rejection of these practices was passionate. Standing for the creed, bowing to the altar or at the name of Jesus, even taking one's hat off because one was a man in church – all these medieval customs smacked of idolatry. The same austerity extended to weddings and burials. It seemed unnecessary, or worse, for a bride to have a ring put on her finger and for her to be blessed by a priest; marriage was a contract not a sacrament, and the vital moment was the betrothal. And when a body was buried 'in sure and certain hope of the resurrection to eternal life', Puritans protested that the prospect of heaven for the mass of mankind was far from sure.

Similarly there seemed no need to celebrate Christmas, which was not dated in the Bible. About forty other 'feasts' on weekdays interrupted work. Almost as much damage to an economy which depended on hard labour might be inflicted by about a hundred 'fasts' in the Church's traditional calendar. On the other hand, the strict observance of Sunday could be derived from the biblical laws about the Sabbath and could be additionally justified as providing a much needed regular rest-day for those who obeyed the biblical commandment to toil. And there seemed no need to perpetuate the customs by which the medieval Church had given special responsibilities to laymen in the provision of music. Puritans tended to dislike skilled choirs, bell-ringing and organ-playing. The music they welcomed was congregational psalm-singing, with the psalms newly translated and rhymed and often sung to popular ballad tunes. That was music which the faithful could offer without expert leadership.[22]

There was a place for leaders in a Protestant Church, but it was a place very different from the priesthood of the Middle Ages. A minister – who might perhaps be called a 'priest' although the word 'presbyter' was certainly less misleading – was useful to his fellow Christians if he was expert in the Bible and able to expound it. Preaching was not therefore of secondary importance to taking services or visiting parishioners or conducting administration, as priests and their inspecting bishops had assumed for centuries. On the contrary, public and continual preaching of God's word was 'the ordinary mean and instrument of the salvation of mankind'. So Archbishop Grindal, in many ways a Puritan, once informed the Queen – whose own view was that three or four preachers in a county,

---

[22] The social implications of the Puritan demands were explored by Christopher Hill, *Society and Puritanism in Pre-Revolutionary England* (London, 1964).

all that had existed in her father's time or in the early years of her own reign, were quite enough.[23]

All Protestants agreed in principle that it was essential to support a preaching ministry, but here, too, Puritans tended to disapprove of arrangements inherited from the Middle Ages. One problem was that the 'tithes', which in theory guaranteed a tenth of the produce to the pastor of the parish, had sometimes been commuted for cash which with inflation declined in real value. With many forms of production and trade – sheep-farming, market-gardening, clothes-making, mining, shop-keeping in general – a cash settlement in lieu of tithes was almost inevitable, and offered endless scope for disagreement about what was fair. Another problem was that the 'great tithes' or 'rector's tithes' – a tenth of the corn, hay and wood – could be separated from the 'small tithes'. In perhaps a third of the parishes they had belonged to monasteries in the 1520s, leaving a small income to the vicar or chaplain who did the work. Now with the monasteries gone, these 'great tithes' had often descended to laymen; Shakespeare bought the right to tithes in Stratford. Or they might have been granted to bishops by the Crown in exchange for estates. It seems that of about 9,250 'livings' (churches with incomes attached to them), by 1603 about 3,850 were parishes where the rector's share of the tithes had been 'impropriated' to laymen. Richard Hooker estimated that the Church lost £126,000 a year in this way at a time when vicars could be expected to live on £10 or less a year. Yet another problem was that the incomes of many parishes could not sustain resident clergymen, or at least not clergymen with a graduate's sense of what an adequate income was. During the 1580s Archbishop Whitgift guessed that half the 'livings' in England were worth less than £10 a year, and that of some 8,800 parishes (the figure was an underestimate) 'there are not six hundred sufficient for learned men.'

Puritan preachers tended to regard all these arrangements as abuses. It was, however, not easy to suggest solutions. Many Puritan parishioners shared the general reluctance to pay tithes, let alone increase them. Some Puritan gentlemen re-

---

[23] See A. F. Herr, *The Elizabethan Sermon* (Philadelphia, Penn., 1940).

tained or bought up the 'great' tithes with the plea that it gave them the right to appoint a godly vicar. And some Puritan graduate preachers were not above collecting 'pluralities' – incomes derived from more than one parish.[24]

Puritans did not feel committed to the maintenance of the medieval system by which the Church was governed by bishops. It was a matter of convenience; episcopacy (government by bishops) might be desirable in one place or period and not in another. In the early years of Elizabeth's reign some clergymen who would later have been classified as Puritans became bishops, and the system seems to have been generally accepted in the hope that the bishops would be reformers – although it was ominous that some highly honoured Protestants refused to accept prominent posts in the restored system, among them being Bishop Miles Coverdale and John Foxe. Later, particularly when bishops were seen as disciplinarians hired by the government against Puritans, criticism of the system hardened.

Overlarge dioceses were a target of criticism. Church courts, little changed since medieval days and staffed by laymen who tended to be anti-Puritan, were particularly condemned. There was indignation about the fact that because of the frustration of Cranmer's efforts the 'canon' law of the Church had never been revised. It was also thought to be scandalous that the penalty of excommunication, described so solemnly in the New Testament, was often imposed for relatively minor offences against the Church's antiquated laws and courts, and was so little regarded that many of the excommunicated never troubled to have the penalty revoked. Discipline seemed to Puritans to be an essential mark of a healthy Church. One way of securing it was to appoint some of the faithful laymen of the parish to be 'elders' with authority for 'spiritual rule'. Another solution was to gather the faithful preachers in an area for mutual correction and edification, in what came to be known as a 'conference', 'classis' or 'presbytery'. Over these local meetings could arise provincial and national 'synods' to decide

---

[24] See Christopher Hill, *Economic Problems of the Church from Archbishop Whitgift to the Long Parliament* (Oxford, 1956) and E. J. Evans, *Contentious Tithe* (London, 1976).

the larger questions, and the bishops could safely disappear. The whole system of Church courts should, however, be controlled by a clear and up-to-date 'Book of Discipline'. A key text was Matthew 18:17: 'tell the church'. Sins and doubts were to be reported to bodies equipped and eager to deal with them – to bodies with a clear authority to excommunicate sinners, however arrogant. Most shocking of all Puritan beliefs in the eyes of the authorities was the conviction that even a monarch was subject to this spiritual discipline exercised by God's elect.

Preferring to regard all preachers as equal in status, Puritans tended to dislike the surviving pomp of bishops – or any other reminder that the bishops of the Church of England were continuous with the bishops of the Middle Ages. But they had to face the fact that not all clergy were equally faithful. Since many rectors, vicars or curates were unable or unwilling to preach as Puritans wished, and were obliged to comply with the bishop's regulations, lay Puritans increasingly gave their loyalty and their money to 'lecturers' or other unbeneficed clergy. These lecturers could be appointed by those who paid them and they could preach acceptably in the parish churches, if necessary outside the normal times for services.[25] The only alternative to letting off steam through this safety-valve seemed to be the explosion of 'Separatism' – separating oneself entirely from the Church of England. But in Tudor times this remedy appealed to only a few. The hope of the rest was that, given time, the Church would be reformed in accordance with demands which seemed so clearly in keeping with the Scriptures and with the conscience of the educated public.

Many of these demands of the Puritans were trifles, as they were often reminded by their critics. That was one of the factors delaying a confrontation or separation. But matters of dress, or fashions in furniture, or styles of music, or ways of enjoying holidays, or methods of supervision have often been flashpoints in quarrels between Christians; and there was a

---

[25] See P. S. Seaver, *The Puritan Lectureships: The Politics of Religious Dissent 1560–1640* (Stanford, Cal., 1970).

basic controversy here. Puritans wanted the Church of England not only to *be* a Reformed Church but also to look thoroughly like one. It should be seen to be a sister church of those Calvinists who were at the time offering heroic battle against the revival of Popery on the Continent – fighting against great odds in the Netherlands, or being massacred in France. To be Reformed seemed to those who were so the clear consequence of obedience to the Bible; and Puritans claimed to subscribe not to any theological movement but simply to the Bible.

Throughout Elizabeth's reign the majority of the House of Commons wanted – or could be led by the more articulate MPs to want – 'further Reformation' along these lines. The same was true of the majority of the Privy Council. When the Catholic theologians who had had their time under Queen Mary had fled or come to terms, Oxford and Cambridge heard very little except lectures of which Puritans approved. The educated clergy who were licensed as preachers by the bishops seem almost all to have been thorough-going Protestants, although they chose to obey the bishops rather than the Puritan extremists over trivial matters such as dress. In 1563 when the Convocation of Canterbury debated six Puritan proposals (for example, that kneeling at the Holy Communion should be voluntary), the motion in favour of them failed by only one vote (59–58) when proxies had been called. That gathering of the clergy did adopt the Thirty-Nine Articles of Religion, based on the Forty-Two Articles of 1553 and therefore embodying many phrases dear to Lutherans or Calvinists on the continent while preserving a certain caution. Article 29, 'Of the Wicked which eat not the Body of Christ', was so firmly Protestant that the articles were published by the government without it. In 1563 the Convocation added, for use in popular instruction, a catechism reflecting the Calvinism of the Dean of St Paul's who drafted it (Alexander Nowell). Eventually in 1571 the Thirty-Nine Articles, with Article 29 restored, received Parliamentary ratification. Undeterred by the government's caution, Puritans went on hoping for official support for their cause, and the next year two brilliantly eloquent and aggressive propagandists in their early twenties, John Field and Thomas Wilcox, issued an *Admonition to Parliament* urging MPs to hasten the day of radical reform.[26]

Many Puritans were convinced that the government's resistance to 'further Reformation' was unprincipled. The Queen irritated them by her unwillingness to identify herself wholly with the Reformation even when the Pope's claim to depose her had shown beyond dispute that she was at war with Roman Catholicism. Puritans were of course very reluctant to seem to be traitors like the Papists; when John Stubbe issued a tract warning the Queen against marrying a Papist (*The Discovery of a Gaping Gulf*) and had the hand responsible cut off, he waved his hat with the other, shouting: 'God save the Queen!' Yet their impatience sometimes boiled over, and turned into indignation when the Queen appeared to be persecuting them because of their obedience to God. Her only motive seemed to be a cowardice inspired by worldliness.

THE QUEEN
AGAINST THE PURITANS

On three dramatic occasions we can hear Puritans speaking their minds about Queen Elizabeth I.

On 20 June 1567 seven Protestant Londoners accused of absenting themselves from their parish churches were examined by the Bishop of London (Grindal), the Lord Mayor and others. When they objected to the uniform which the Queen commanded for the clergy, the Lord Mayor told them to think of it as being like the wearing of civic robes in local government: how else could an alderman be recognized? 'The Queen hath not established these garments and things for any holiness' sake or religion, but only for a civil order and comeliness.' Even the theologians admitted that the clothes were comparatively unimportant, 'indifferent'. But these defenders of the Queen's policy were rebuked by John Smith:

---

[26] The Convocation of 1563 was put in its historical context by W. P. Haugaard, *Elizabeth and the English Reformation* (Cambridge, 1968).

'How can you prove that indifferent, which is abominable?' While the Protestant laymen quoted biblical texts at them, the official theologians fell back on the authority of the Queen to end an argument which was getting out of hand. 'Have we not a godly prince? Answer, is she evil?' So Bishop Grindal demanded; and Thomas Bowland bravely replied, 'No: but the servants of God are persecuted under her.'

On 25 February 1570 a famous Puritan preacher and writer who was then chaplain at the Tower of London preached a long sermon before the Queen. Edward Dering took Elizabeth through the Bible, pointing out what godly princes had done for the pure worship of God. The tour ended with plain speaking about the Church of England. 'I would lead you first to your benefices.' Then he mentioned all the charges there could be on the income of a parish priest before it reached the priest. 'Look after this upon your patrons. And lo, some are selling their benefices, some farming them, some keep them for their children, some give them to boys, some to servingmen, a very few seek after learned pastors. And yet you shall see more abominations than these. Look upon your ministry, and there are some of one occupation, some of another . . . some ruffians, some hawkers and hunters, some dicers and carders, some blind guides and cannot see, some dumb dogs and will not bark. And yet a thousand more iniquities have now covered the priesthood. And yet you, in the meanwhile that all these whoredoms are committed, you at whose hands God will require it, you sit still and are careless.'

On 8 February 1576 Peter Wentworth, who represented Tregoney in Cornwall, dared to attack the Queen in the House of Commons, beginning his carefully written speech: 'Sweet indeed is the name of liberty.' Resisting Puritan pressures, the Queen had told the previous Parliament not to touch Bills about religion unless these had first been 'considered or liked' by the clergy. Wentworth protested: 'It was as much as to say: Sirs, ye shall not deal in God's causes . . . God, even the great and mighty God, whose name is the Lord of Hosts, great in counsel and infinite in thought, and who is the only good director of all hearts, was the last session shut out of doors.' Wentworth was sent to the Tower of London for this brave outburst. Although soon released, he was to die there in 1597 at the age of seventy-three, having given further offence.[27]

Why, then, did Elizabeth – so often admired for her statesmanship, so proud to 'count the glory of my crown, that I have reigned with your loves' – pursue a policy which alienated so many of the clerical and lay leaders of the Church she was pledged to protect? And why did she so divide the Protestant forces when the Papists were doing their utmost to dethrone her?

It is probable that the best clue to an answer is neither ecclesiastical nor theological. Despite outbursts against married clergymen and their wives, Elizabeth had no ambition to teach Christian doctrine. Although she admired her father, unlike her brother and sister she did not inherit his taste for the personal supervision of theology; and unlike her successor James I she did not enjoy discussing the subject. She dismissed arguments about doctrine as 'a dream of fools or enthusiasts', the speculations of theologians as 'ropes of sand or sea-slime leading to the moon'. Nor did Elizabeth have any appetite for ecclesiastical administration. Even her imperious father had for a time been glad to delegate the supervision of church life to Thomas Cromwell, and her opinionated sister had developed 'Commissioners Ecclesiastical' to attend to the details of the restoration of Catholicism. Elizabeth went further in the delegation of her powers as Supreme Governor. She allowed her Ecclesiastical Commissioners' powers and staff to develop mightily, so that they became known as the 'High Commission'. The commission for the province of Canterbury became a very important tribunal; Archbishop Whitgift once said that without it ecclesiastical law would have been a 'carcass without a soul'. It attracted business away from the old courts of the archbishops and bishops because it was prompt and efficient; and unlike the old church courts it could punish by fines and imprisonment. Common lawyers often objected to the High Commission's methods, since suspects could be put on oath to answer questions truthfully without being warned about the

[27] These explosions are recorded in *Elizabethan Puritanism*, documents edited by L. J. Trinterud (New York, 1971).

questions or confronted by their accusers or defended by a lawyer or presumed innocent until judged guilty by a jury. This '*ex officio* oath' seemed disgracefully un-English. Suspects judged guilty by those who had questioned them found it virtually impossible to appeal elsewhere. Nevertheless the Queen raised no objection, because while being unwilling to give her personal attention to such trifles she needed a machine so formidable against those who opposed her central policy.[28]

This central policy was conservative, partly because in her view the Puritan demands constituted a political danger. John Knox himself admitted that his relations with Elizabeth had been ruined by his attack on the 'monstrous regiment of women', and although he found his sphere in Scotland when the Queen had forbidden him to enter her kingdom, it is probable that his rejection of the idea of a woman as sovereign on biblical grounds was thought by her to be typical of his co-religionists. Certainly she was often ready to believe the worst about the loyalty of her Puritan subjects. A record survives of a conversation in 1585 when she attacked a group of bishops for failing to discipline ministers who 'preach what they list . . . to the breach of unity'. Such men, she said, were 'curious and busy fellows' whose preaching 'tendeth only to popularity'.

However, she must have known, right from the time of her triumphant entry into London as queen, that the Protestants were not a real threat to her throne. They supported her because they had no alternative monarch to nominate and a republic was inconceivable. These preachers, however irritating they might be, were not likely to become traitors in a time when only Elizabeth's life stood between them and a Catholic reaction under Mary, Queen of Scots. It therefore seems clear that the decisive factor in the Queen's ecclesiastical conservatism was her knowledge that to capitulate to all the Protestant demands would be to alienate the mass of her subjects. She was determined to woo Catholic-minded Englishmen into loyalty,

---

[28] See R. G. Usher, *The Rise and Fall of the High Commission* (revised, Oxford, 1968).

just as she was prepared to flirt with Catholic princes for political purposes; and it maddened her when Puritans nearly frustrated her.

She knew that the Catholicism of a thousand years could not be eradicated overnight. In 1564 the government ordered the bishops to assess the degree of support which the Justices of the Peace would give to its religious policy, for on them law and order in the countryside depended. The bishops reported that although 431 were favourable 157 JPs were hostile, and 264 indifferent or neutral: a reliable majority of ten at a time when for five years the national government had clearly favoured Protestantism. In 1561 Professor Nicholas Sander of Oxford assured Cardinal Morone that among the ordinary people the Protestants were a tiny majority: 'not so many as one in a hundred of the English is infected'. Whatever may have been the accuracy of such assessments, it is significant that as late as 1571 the Queen vetoed a proposal by Parliament that everyone should be required to receive communion in the Church of England at least once a year. She saw the need to adjust the National Church over which she was Supreme Governor to this reality of the nation's conservatism. She did not want to persecute Catholic-minded Englishmen until this was made to seem politically essential by a pope's claim to depose her. If, as Sir Francis Bacon observed, the Queen did not wish to 'make windows into men's hearts and secret thoughts', one reason was that she knew she would find there a religion still more conservative than her own. And she did not want to repel Catholic-minded Englishmen from attending their parish churches by making those churches too obviously Protestant. In this caution she was more realistic than was her indispensable William Cecil, or Sir Francis Walsingham (despite the invaluable efficiency of his work against plotting Papists). She knew better than her great aristocratic friends, the brothers who were Earls of Leicester and Warwick, and Francis Russell, Earl of Bedford. All these men thought it safe to be known as patrons of the Puritans. The Queen did not.

Her continuing and mounting indignation against the Puritans in the 1590s requires another explanation, for a fierce patriotism surrounded the defeat of the Spanish Armada of 1588 and its successors in 1596 and 1597. The English government could at last feel more relaxed about the possibility of a rebellion in which foreign invaders could have allied themselves with native religious conservatism to bring about a regime acceptable to the Pope; yet the war against the Jesuits and the 'seminary priests' went on relentlessly and, on the whole, successfully. It may well seem that in the 1590s Elizabeth could have afforded to make concessions to the Puritans without anxiety about the Church of England being made to look dangerously Protestant. Instead, she chose to accept the theory that the Puritans had joined the Papists as conspirators threatening the government.

The explanation seems to be that she was an old woman, irritated by her critics; resentful of their obstinate defiance as perhaps only a Tudor monarch could be; determined to use the new strength of her position to teach them the consequences of disobedience; and anyway too old and too bored to begin a period of religious reconstruction. And she had reason to think that public opinion was with her as she gave way to her prejudices. Ordinary Englishmen disliked the Puritans as killjoys and it is probable that Malvolio in *Twelfth Night* was understood as a caricature. Towards the end of her reign even the House of Commons, while still firmly Protestant, had lost heart for the defence of these too-earnest clergymen against the Queen's bishops. Elizabeth was by now a living legend, the Gloriana on whose behalf God had blown his winds against the fleets of Spain; and not many men were eager to incur her majestic rebukes or less majestic tantrums. But there was another factor operating in the 1590s. Precisely by making sure that the Puritans would see the bishops as their enemies, the Queen had made it certain that they would dream of a Presbyterian system without any bishops – and precisely by treating the Puritans always as her own enemies, Elizabeth had done all that she could to tempt them to treason. This she must have known and it must have made her very uneasy, although there is no real evidence that any Puritans yielded to the temptation. Sir John Neale has described this as 'the strangest paradox of her reign': 'Her Puritan fanatics had no more obstinate opponent; she, in turn, had no more devoted worshippers'.[29]

THE CAMPAIGN AGAINST
THE PURITANS

Detailed investigation of Elizabeth's first Parliament, meeting in January 1559, has shown how strong was the Protestant element in it, as in all its successors.[30] Some of the most influential men in the Commons were just back from exile; others had been dominated by Protestant-minded grandees such as Francis Russell, Earl of Bedford; around all shone the glow cast on Protestantism by the recent martyrdoms. Possibly the Queen would have been content at this early stage to secure Parliamentary recognition of her succession to the throne and of her supremacy over the Church. She had no wish to alienate Catholics, who were strong in the House of Lords. But she also knew that if she was to secure the loyalty she needed, she had to please Protestants. Accordingly the Parliamentary session was prolonged beyond Easter, and when the Act of Uniformity was forced through the Lords it reimposed the Prayer Book of 1552, not the more Catholic version of 1549.

All that the Queen and other conservatives could secure lay in the insistence that it must be an English, not a continental, book, and in four comparatively minor changes to the 1552 book. It was agreed to omit from the Litany a prayer for deliverance from 'the tyranny of the Bishop of Rome and all his detestable enormities'. The 'black rubric' which had been added by the council in 1552 was now abandoned and an additional phrase at the moment of communion was brought back from 1549; these two changes encouraged those who believed that Christ really was present, that the Body and Blood of Christ really were given, in the sacrament. And a new

---

[29] *Essays in Elizabethan History* (London, 1958), p. 124.
[30] Sir John Neale wrote the classic study of *Elizabeth I and her Parliaments* (2 vols., London, 1953–59). But more recent research has questioned his version of events in 1559; see, e.g., D. M. Loades, *The Reign of Mary Tudor*, p. 462.

order was made that the clergy should wear again the vestments which had been worn 'in the second year of the reign of
King Edward VI' (1547–48) at least until the Queen issued
'further orders'. This suggested that the coloured copes and
chasubles, as well as the white surplices, would become normal
– a development which, however, did not occur until the
nineteenth century.

However, although not all the details of the 1559 settlement
were to her liking, and although it was widely believed that this
settlement was only a temporary compromise, the Queen
clung obstinately to it throughout her reign – with the result
that, despite a few further modifications during the seventeenth century, essentially the 1559 book remained the standard of worship in the Church of England until the 1920s. The
only modifications which the Queen allowed were all in a
Catholic direction. During the 1560s a Latin Prayer Book was
published for use in cathedrals and colleges containing various
Catholic features, and a calendar restoring the main Saints'
Days was added to the English Prayer Book. In the 'Vestiarian
controversy' of the 1560s the Queen took a calculated risk in
insisting that all the clergy, including Protestant theologians
who were fighting the strong Catholicism of Oxford, should
wear surplices as tokens of their obedience to her. Archbishop
Parker was driven by her to issue strict *Advertisements* or
regulations to this effect. Had the Oxford Protestants resisted
in the spirit of the martyrs under Mary, Elizabeth would surely
have been in deep trouble in the propaganda war. The two
most prominently unsurpliced Protestants were Laurence
Humphrey, President of Magdalen College, and Thomas
Sampson, Dean of Christ Church. They were disciplined – but
the gamble paid off, for they gave no trouble. Humphrey
conformed and ended up as Dean of Gloucester; and Sampson,
although he never wore a surplice, accepted a canonry at St
Paul's Cathedral.

The Queen, however, did not really get on with clergymen.
She could not flirt with them, she seldom troubled to charm
them, and even the bishops who owed their positions to her
favour were probably not much attached to her person while
she plundered their estates and handed down brutal instruc-

tions. And she had few clergymen from whom to choose bishops to her taste.

It was ominous for her that when James Pilkington had refused the bishopric of Winchester on the terms she offered he still had to be made Bishop of Durham, owing to a shortage of other plausible candidates. He once expressed his unenthusiastic attitude towards the Supreme Governor: 'We are under authority and can innovate nothing without the Queen; nor can we alter the laws; the only thing left for our choice is, whether we will bear these things, or break the peace of the Church.' The Queen had to employ the learned John Jewel, Bishop of Salisbury, as her chief religious propagandist although he was contemplating resignation in 1560, after his first year in office, since he did not share her own liking for surplices and for the rest of what he called the 'scenic apparatus of divine worship'.

She had to authorize the appointment of the strongly Protestant Edmund Grindal to the key diocese of London (where he naturally failed to discipline the Puritans as she wished) before moving him to York (where he was more at home attempting to discipline the many Papists after the failure of their 1569 revolt) and finally to Canterbury (on William Cecil's strong recommendation). 'We who are now bishops,' Grindal once explained to the Swiss theological critic Bullinger, 'on our first return, and before we entered our ministry, contended long and earnestly for the removal of those things that have occasioned the present dispute; but as we were unable to prevail, either with the Queen or with Parliament, we judged it best, after a consultation on the subject, not to desert our churches for the sake of a few ceremonies, and those not unlawful in themselves, especially since the pure doctrine of the Gospel remained in all its integrity and freedom.'

That was not exactly enthusiasm for the Church of England as by law established; and the poor personal quality of two of Grindal's successors in London also showed how difficult it was for the government to find bishops both acceptable and reliable. John Aylmer was a hot-tempered and bitter man, soured by fourteen years as Archdeacon of London. Richard Fletcher, formerly the Queen's handsome favourite at court, was suspended soon after his appointment to London because he suddenly married a widow – and the youth and uncertain morals of his bride caused additional scandal. He was restored to office but died next year while 'taking tobacco in his chair'. He is best remembered as the father of John Fletcher, Shakespeare's collaborator.

Edwin Sandys, appointed successively to Worcester, London and York, was another bishop whose character did little to commend the government to Puritans. His temper was as hot as Aylmer's, quarrels surrounded him, and he enriched his family at the Church's expense. A great story went round that he had been discovered in bed with an innkeeper's wife. Although he may well have been the victim of a plot, he foolishly tried to silence his accusers with money. He was, however, something of a Puritan at heart, stating in his will made in 1588 that although he accepted 'certain rites and ceremonies' as having been 'by political constitution authorized among us', he hoped that they would be 'disused little by little'. All Grindal's successors at York were definite Protestants until Richard Neile in 1632. The attitude of Matthew Hutton, the gentle scholar who was archbishop 1595–1606, showed how out of sympathy with the Queen such men were. 'The Puritans, whose fantastical zeal I mislike,' he once wrote, 'though they differ in ceremonies and accidents, yet they agree with us in the substance of religion.'[31]

This very strong current of opinion in favour of Puritan principles was brought to a head in December 1576 when Edmund Grindal, who had been Archbishop of Canterbury for about a year, was ordered by the Queen to suppress 'prophesyings' – the name given to informal gatherings of preachers for study and discussion of the Bible. Elizabeth feared treason, but Grindal (who had consulted his fellow bishops) defended the right of patriotic preachers to educate themselves for their pulpit work. He therefore refused to obey and offered his resignation. For good measure, he asked the Queen to leave church business to the bishops and even went

[31] Quoted in R. A. Marchant, *The Puritans and the Church Courts in the Diocese of York 1560–1642* (London, 1960), p. 23.

so far as to write: 'Remember, Madam, that you are a mortal creature.'

It was one of the bravest letters in the history of England. Its author was a man whose boyhood had been passed among the Lakes and whose young manhood was spent as a disciple of the martyr Ridley. While in exile under Queen Mary he had gathered reports about the Protestant martyrs and had shared them with John Foxe. A modern historian prejudiced against him wrote about this letter: 'his weakness of character flew to obstinacy'.[32] But so far from being weak or obstinate, Grindal had won the respect of many churchmen by his behaviour as a bishop since 1559, and great expectations surrounded his move to Canterbury. Nor had he disappointed his admirers by his first moves. Knowing how unsatisfactory was the administration of ecclesiastical law, he waded into reform. He sacrificed what might have been a great Primacy by his defiance of the Queen, for her fury was intense. She wanted Grindal to be deprived of his office, but since he refused to go quietly Elizabeth had to be restrained; her advisers dreaded the scandal. He never again performed the administrative functions of an archbishop, except in a few cases where the Queen's ministers gave him specific orders. He was kept under house arrest in Lambeth Palace. He went blind and, broken in spirit and health, died in 1583 while arrangements were at last in hand for his resignation.[33]

In Grindal's successor, John Whitgift, the Queen had a man after her own heart. He had driven Professor Thomas Cartwright from Cambridge when that provocative theologian had caused a sensation in the spring of 1570 by lecturing on the Acts of the Apostles. Cartwright had declared that the Church of England ought to be reformed so that it was more like the Church to be found in those Acts and in the continental centres of Protestantism; bishops, he had urged, should have purely spiritual functions, not jurisdictions. In response Whitgift,

---

[32] This misjudgement by W. H. Frere is to be found in *A Dictionary of English Church History*, ed. S. L. Ollard (revised, London, 1948), p. 261.

[33] Patrick Collinson's biography of *Archbishop Grindal* (London, 1980), not only brought this forgotten hero back to life but also illuminated his times.

who was then Master of Trinity College, had secured new
statutes for the university from the Queen, greatly strengthening the authority of the heads of the colleges. Cartwright had
been forced to live abroad, so as to taste the paradise about
which he had lectured. And when radical young Puritans had
published their *Admonition to Parliament* in 1572, Whitgift's
scholarship and eloquence had been valuable to those in
charge of Church and State. He had replied at length to their
manifesto – only to have Cartwright leaping heavily to their
defence with a *Second Admonition*.[34]

All that distinguished service against troublesome Puritans
the Queen, no doubt, remembered gratefully. The Puritans
remembered other things. Whitgift first came into contact with
national politics in 1565 – when he identified himself with the
Puritans. He then signed a letter to Cecil begging him to
protect those in Cambridge whose consciences forbade them to
wear surplices. Puritans also noted that thirty years later
Whitgift was still in agreement with resident Cambridge
theologians about the foundations of Calvinist orthodoxy, to be
upheld in all the university's teaching. He issued the 'Lambeth
Articles' to this effect – only to be compelled by the Queen to
say that they were unofficial. When as Archbishop of Canterbury Whitgift enforced the Queen's policy against the Puritans, including the insistence on surplices, he seemed a mere
time-server. And the records certainly suggest that Whitgift
had in a sense been bought. He enjoyed several other sources of
income, including the Deanery of Lincoln, while Master of
Trinity College, and when he became a bishop he was given
financial advantages which the Queen did not allow to any of
his colleagues. The records also show that while he was at
Cambridge the teacher with the most influence over him was
Alexander Perne, the Master of Peterhouse, who had persuaded his own conscience to conform to the ecclesiastical
policies of no fewer than four Tudor monarchs. Whitgift was
the Queen's man, her 'little black husband' as she called him;
and the Puritans, for all their own loyalty to her, were con-

---

[34] See D. J. McGinn, *The Admonition Controversy* (New Brunswick, N.J., 1949).

vinced that this was the only reason why he resisted their Bible-based demands.[35]

He received the full backing of the Queen and her council for most of his time as archbishop. For example, when in the Parliament of 1587 a Bill was produced to substitute the Geneva service book for the Book of Common Prayer it was confiscated, with dire threats to its sponsor. However, when Whitgift marked his arrival as Archbishop of Canterbury in 1583 by insisting that all the clergy of the Church of England should swear their acceptance of three 'articles' representing the policy of his royal mistress, he had to bow to protests which were shared by many on the Queen's council. One of those articles was virtually non-controversial among Protestants at that time: it acknowledged the royal supremacy over the Church. But the other articles insisted not only that the Thirty-Nine Articles (which contained some points which some Puritans disputed) were 'agreeable' to the Word of God but also that the Book of Common Prayer contained 'nothing contrary' to the Word of God (precisely the claim that many rejected). Eventually Whitgift had to agree that the new oath was to be demanded only of men who were being ordained or admitted into new benefices as rectors, vicars or cathedral clergy.

When as a member of the Ecclesiastical Commission he probed too deeply into the opinions of Puritans being examined, William Cecil protested: 'I think the Inquisitors of Spain use not so many questions to comprehend and trap their preys.' The most influential Elizabethan official was here appealing to the Queen's own principle that windows were not to be opened into men's souls, to check her campaign against the Puritans. The Parliaments meeting in 1584 and 1585 were far less polite as members fulminated against the persecution of godly preachers. And the new archbishop, although he defended himself at length, had to moderate his enthusiasm.[36] In

---

[35] For a far more sympathetic assessment see V. J. K. Brook, *John Whitgift and the English Church* (London, 1957).

[36] The correspondence between Burghley and Whitgift is printed in Claire Cross, *The Royal Supremacy and the Elizabethan Church*, pp. 199–205.

1585 his old enemy, Thomas Cartwright, returned to England under the protection of Cecil and of the Earl of Leicester, who appointed him master of the hospital he controlled in Warwick. And another sign of the vitality of Puritanism during these years was the foundation in 1587 of Emmanuel College, Cambridge, by the Chancellor of the Exchequer, Sir Walter Mildmay, in order to train Protestant preachers under a strict discipline.

In the 1590s the campaign against the Puritans continued, however. The great men who had protected them – Bedford, Leicester, Walsingham, William Cecil – died. Robert Cecil took over much of the administration, but the main influence over the Queen was exercised by Sir Christopher Hatton, the Lord Chancellor, who led the flattering cult of the 'Virgin Queen'. Hatton had none of William Cecil's sympathy with Puritan ideals. On the contrary, he encouraged one of his chaplains to concentrate his abundant energies on a systematic campaign against the Puritans. His name was Richard Bancroft.

In 1587 this able canon of Westminster Abbey was appointed to the High Commission and became its driving power. Strangely gifted as a detective, he tracked down the secret printing press which in 1588–89 had been pouring out anti-establishment pamphlets written violently and very readably by one 'Martin Marprelate' – but even he could not prove who 'Marprelate' really was.[37] Himself also gifted as a propagandist, he launched a savage personal attack on the Puritan leaders in a Paul's Cross sermon which immediately became famous in 1589. Having gathered a mass of evidence and shaped it to his own purposes, he claimed that the Puritans were occupying politically *Dangerous Positions* – the short title of a widely circulated pamphlet written by him in 1593. In 1597 this detective and pamphleteer was given the key position of Bishop of London, and he used it to intensify his crusade.[38]

---

[37] D. J. McGinn argued for John Penry in *John Penry and the Marprelate Controversy* (New Brunswick, N.J., 1966), and Leland Carlson for Job Throkmorton in *Martin Marprelate, Gentleman* (San Marino, Cal., 1981).

[38] See S. B. Babbage, *Puritanism and Richard Bancroft* (London, 1962).

Bancroft met no one among the Puritans to match him, for in 1588 their ablest organizer and journalist, John Field, died. With his base in London Field had been in effect General Secretary to the Puritan movement, keeping groups in touch with each other, maintaining morale but all the time seeing that the movement kept within the law. The committee which advised him had included Laurence Thomson, secretary to Sir Francis Walsingham; thus the committee had been able to keep in touch with the activities of the Queen's council itself. Field's death was a double disaster since letters found in his study were now quoted (perhaps out of context) to prove that what he had been holding together was a treasonable conspiracy. Thomas Cartwright and eight other prominent leaders were arrested in 1590 and brought before two courts, the High Commission and the Star Chamber. For a time their case looked bad, particularly when fanatics, one proclaiming himself the Messiah, announced that they would deliver them from prison. But in the end they were delivered by the lawyers. The Attorney General advised William Cecil that their conduct had not been illegal, and since they threatened to appeal to the Queen's council they were eventually released. For the rest of his life Cartwright kept out of trouble, although he never abandoned his convictions. He spent seven years on the island of Guernsey, which although an English possession was far from any bishop. Returning home to Warwick as an invalid, he died soon after the queen who had over the years frustrated him.[39]

Another Puritan leader in decline was Richard Hooker's rival Walter Travers, although his *Book of Discipline*, written in Latin in Geneva, remained the classic statement of the Presbyterian proposals for church government after its translation into English by Cartwright. For a time he was in the household of William Cecil as tutor to his son Robert, and it was thanks to Cecil's influence that he preached every Sunday afternoon to the lawyers of the Temple. But his refusal to be ordained by a bishop cost him the Mastership there and eventually he agreed

[39] See A. F. Scott Peason, *Thomas Cartwright and Elizabethan Puritanism* (Cambridge, 1928).

to leave the English scene, becoming the first Provost of Trinity College, Dublin.[40]

With giants such as Field, Cartwright and Travers out of the way, the smaller fry among the Puritans could be patronized witheringly or punished savagely. Whitgift, summoning some clergymen from Sussex, subjected them to a fireside chat in Lambeth and assured them that they were but 'boys' in comparison with 'us'. 'You are not called to rule in this Church of England,' he reminded them. More terrible treatment was meted out to three other clergymen: Henry Barrow, John Greenwood and John Penry were all hanged in 1593. In the same year an 'Act to Retain the Queen's Subjects in Obedience' was passed as part of a campaign to terrify Puritans as well as Papists. Under such pressures, the high spirits which had marked the 'Martin Marprelate' pamphlets disappeared, and the brave few who did form 'Separatist' congregations saw little future for their ideals in England. In 1582 Robert Browne, aptly nicknamed 'Troublechurch Browne', had escaped from Norwich to the Netherlands, to publish there his *Treatise of Reformation without Tarrying for Any* and to work it out in the shape of a pure congregation. But the congregation had split up in personal quarrels and he had crept back to England – to become the rector of a country parish until his death in 1633 (although he then died in Northampton gaol, for he had again attracted attention as a troublemaker). It is not surprising that Browne's name was now popularly used with contempt. 'Policy I hate,' declared Sir Andrew Aguecheek in *Twelfth Night*: 'I had as lief be a Brownist as a politician.'

A more substantial history followed the acceptance by Francis Johnson of a call to become pastor of Puritan 'Separatists' in London in 1592; a permanent congregation gathered around his preaching and his administration of Baptism and Lord's Supper. They used no set forms of prayer; John Greenwood informed the bishop examining him that even to repeat the Lord's Prayer was 'superstitious babbling'. But Johnson's congregation proved permanent only because it migrated first to Amsterdam and then to the new colony of Virginia. And it

---

[40] See S. J. Knox, *Walter Travers, Paragon of Elizabethan Puritanism* (London, 1962).

did not remain united; it split in Amsterdam on the issue of whether authority was to lie in the whole congregation or (as Johnson wanted) in the minister and a small group of elders. Another controversy was stirred up among the exiles in Amsterdam when an over-enthusiastic Cambridge theologian, John Smyth, argued that the minister must translate the lessons from the Hebrew or the Greek extempore, since no printed version in England was sufficiently inspired. Smyth baptized himself in order to show not only how futile had been his own earlier baptism as an infant, but also how difficult it was to find another minister worthy to perform this role. Eventually, however, before his premature death, he resolved to 'put an end to all controversies and questions about the outward Church and ceremonies with all men'; he would 'spend my time in the main matters wherein consisteth salvation'. Such were some of the problems surrounding the obscure Elizabethan birth of the Free Church tradition which was eventually to include many millions of Christians throughout the English-speaking world.[41]

Meanwhile in the Established Church few young graduates felt tempted to leave for the wilderness along with Browne, Johnson or Smyth – and although many of the clergy were Puritans at heart a new generation grew up who were to be the founders of the more definitely High Church movement, attaching much importance to the bishop's sacred functions. A modern student of this period has argued that the 'scornful condemnation of the late Elizabethan Church as a position born of compromise, timorously defended, and maintained only because the political exigencies admitted no deeper commitment, cannot stand in the face of the piety, learning and loyalty that flowered in the first generation of men whose religious experience was wholly within the life of Elizabethan Anglicanism. Bilson, Field, Mason, Hall, Morton, Montague, Overall, Andrewes, Laud – here is a numbering of the stars in the firmament of the early Stuart Church. Yet all came to manhood in the days of Whitgift's defence of the establishment against the Puritan challenge. The light that they shed over the

---

first years of the seventeenth century was a brilliance reflected from the Elizabethan sunset'.[42]

It was by now the generally agreed Puritan policy to await the Queen's death and her replacement by a more 'godly' successor from a securely Protestant Scotland. When James VI eventually did ride south as King James I of England, he was greeted by carefully organized Puritan petitions, and showed that he was impressed by calling a conference at Hampton Court to discuss grievances. It is difficult to be sure exactly what took place there. William Barlow, Bishop of Lincoln, compiled the official report of the proceedings in answer to Puritan claims of victory, but his report, too, was full of bias. The most probable interpretation of the evidence suggests that John Rainolds, a much respected scholar who had been Dean of Lincoln and before that Richard Hooker's tutor at Oxford, was virtually the only Puritan who spoke up in the conversation.

As voiced by Rainolds, the requests were moderate – in contrast with the far-reaching plots which had been attributed to the Puritans by Richard Bancroft. He seems to have asked that the Church of England should no longer insist on the use of the sign of the cross in Baptism, on a child needing to be confirmed by a bishop before receiving the Holy Communion, on kneeling at the Communion, and on the wearing of the surplice at Morning and Evening Prayer. The Apocrypha should no longer be read as part of the Bible, and the form of 'subscription' to the Prayer Book and the Articles by clergymen should be changed. That was scarcely a revolution. But this scholar's moderation made little impression on a sarcastic king; Whitgift and Bancroft, who had been alarmed lest James should regard the constitution of the Church of England as a debating topic, need not have worried. The sound of men voicing theological opinions not his own was bound to madden James. Although when he had slept and recovered his temper the new king did make conciliatory promises, the only positive result of the conference was an agreement to collaborate on minor changes in the Prayer Book and on a new English version of the Bible.

---

[42] P. M. Dawley, *John Whitgift and the Reformation* (London, 1955), p. 193.

Basically, it seems, James accepted Elizabeth's own mistaken belief that some or many of the English Puritans were intent on the destruction of the monarchy, so that it was fortunate that when they appeared at Hampton Court they seemed to be, after all, only a small and contemptible group of troublemakers, who could quite easily be browbeaten. In a letter of 1590, written in anger when Penry and other preachers had fled to Scotland, the great Queen had warned him: 'Here is risen, both in your realm and mine, a sect of perilous consequence, such as would have no kings but a presbytery.' His own famous explosion at the end of a tiring day of arguments with Rainolds at Hampton Court in January was: 'Then Jack and Tom and Will and Dick shall meet, and at their pleasure censure me and my council and all our proceedings . . . Dr Rainolds, till you find that I grow lazy, let that alone . . . No bishop, no king . . . I will make them conform themselves or I will harry them out of this land or else do worse.'[43]

A HOLLOW VICTORY

In the short run, therefore, the Queen triumphed in her anti-Puritan campaign. And her triumph has often been applauded by those who would say with Sir Andrew Aguecheek that a Puritan deserved to be beaten 'like a dog'. ('Thy exquisite reason, dear knight?' asks Sir Toby Belch, to whom Sir Andrew replies: 'I have no exquisite reason for it, but I have reason good enough.') A relatively restrained modern scholar has recorded his impression that 'the foundations of Puritanism lay in hatred; in hatred of the natural world, hatred of its social institutions and hatred of human nature. Puritans insisted on the complete depravity of man and refused to place any confidence whatever in his rational and in his natural faculties. And yet, automatically, this desire of self-abasement

---

[43] M. H. Curtis reconstructed 'The Hampton Court Conference and its Aftermath' in *History* (London, 1961), pp. 1–6, with an emphasis which may exaggerate the King's disagreements with the bishops.

generated, as it was being indulged in, its very opposite: an arrogant pride. The Puritan who felt that he was one of the elect could indeed ride roughshod over all cautious objections and doubts, for he knew with certainty what the divine truth was. . . . This outlook naturally foreshadowed one of the most rigid systems of moralism human experience has ever known. The Puritan would condemn any pursuit of pleasure that was not orientated towards the super-natural.'[44] If all this is true, then the wise man of Elizabeth's reign was not John Field, the Puritans' General Secretary, but his son Nathan – who became a chorister in the Chapel Royal, an actor and a great lover of other men's wives.

But it seems reasonable to conclude that in the long run the damage which English Christianity sustained through Elizabeth's triumph was substantial. Considerable numbers of parish priests (how many we do not know) were forced to resign because they refused to promise to wear the surplice and to obey the other anti-Puritan regulations. Those who remained felt that their Protestant queen and their own bishops were deeply prejudiced against them despite all their piety and patriotism. Their discouragement must have been a real loss to the Church's pastoral effectiveness.

One example will be sufficient. Richard Greenham was a Puritan scholar of Cambridge who in 1570 became rector of Dry Drayton, a village not far away. Without seeking fame he became famous for the austerity of his life, his devotion to his parishioners and the vigour and frequency of his sermons. Students from Cambridge, and visitors from far and wide, sought him out and learned holiness and much else from him. But in 1588 Greenham left the parish, disappointed; he had, he said, converted only one family in almost twenty years. After that, he relied on the support of Puritan laymen in London. The Church of England under Elizabeth I was not so rich in manpower that it could neglect such a preacher and pastor with impunity. It may be observed that Greenham was not actually deprived of his parish. This was because he avoided controversy whenever he could – and because his bishop was

---

[44] Peter Munz, *The Place of Hooker in the History of Thought*, pp. 37–8.

Richard Cox. This veteran Bishop of Ely, who in younger days as a Headmaster of Eton had acquired a disciplinarian's fame, was indignant when Puritan defiance seemed to show a basic lack of patriotism (in exile under Mary, he had been indignant when the worship offered in Frankfurt was insufficiently patriotic). But he was not going to end work such as Greenham's because of a missing surplice (he had not been prepared to fight for surplices in Frankfurt). Nor was he himself prepared to obey the Queen in all things. He refused to minister in her chapel while it contained a crucifix; he refused to transfer the Bishop of Ely's house in London to Sir Christopher Hatton; and he refused to consider her prejudices when at the age of seventy he wanted to marry a widow. Richard Greenham wrote a letter to Cox in which he pleaded that his only interest lay 'in preaching Christ crucified unto myself and country people'; and the bishop was impressed.

For more than seventeen years after Cox's death the diocese of Ely was left without a bishop while the income went to the Crown. The see of Oxford was left vacant from 1559 to 1604, apart from inglorious bishops who briefly occupied it in the years 1567–68 and 1589–92. It was widely agreed that Elizabeth's enthusiasm for moving bishops from diocese to diocese was not unconnected with the custom which brought the 'first fruits' (more or less the first year's income in the new post) to the Crown. In contrast with this official plunder of the Church, the Puritans loved the Church to the point of self-sacrifice. Thomas Cartwright so loved his work for the Church that from student days he spent only five hours a night in bed. The clergy of this persuasion devoted themselves to frequent preaching, a duty understood to involve a close study of the Bible before expounding it at length, as well as much earnest private discussion of its message with parishioners and with neighbouring clergy. Out of their own purses Puritan laymen supported a 'shadow church' on a considerable scale in order to provide lecturers or assistant curates who would discharge a preacher's duty, thus interpreted, when the priest who received the parish's tithes was (at least to Puritan ears) 'dumb'.

It is unfair to see Puritanism through the eyes of its enemies – eyes always quick to spot any tendency to treason. Fortunately the minute book of the *classis* (conference) of about twenty Puritan clergymen in the Dedham district of Essex between 1582 and 1589 has been preserved. It does not record long discussions about the national government in Church or State, and we need not suppose that such discussions took place secretly. The whole emphasis is local and moral; there are ministers urging each other to do their duty as they see it. In fact they exercise over each other the kind of oversight which would in the Victorian Age and later come from an active bishop or archdeacon, and the earnest self-examination of these Christian ministers may fairly be said to be filling a vacuum left by the lack of leadership from the Church's official hierarchy.[45]

There have also been careful studies of how the Puritans actually worshipped or wished to worship. One scholar has explained how it came to be that the Puritans complained about the shortness as well as about the impersonal formality of an official Prayer Book service; their own worship combined a reverence for the Scriptures with a relevance to the conditions of the worshippers, and they often enjoyed it greatly. It was 'characterized by purity, simplicity and spirituality. It attempted to recreate the Pentecostal fervour and expectation of the Apostolic Church. Where it failed, it was only because spiritual earnestness could not be maintained on such a high plane of worship.'[46] And there have been studies of what the Puritans actually taught or wished to teach.[47] These studies have shown that the idea that they invented a 'Protestant ethic' which encouraged the competitive ruthlessness of capitalism has little historical foundation. It is true that many successful businessmen found their personal religion through the Puritan preachers. Repeating the commonplaces of Christian morality, these preachers promised God's blessing on the virtues of

---

[45] See *The Presbyterian Movement in the Reign of Queen Elizabeth as illustrated by the Minute Book . . .*, ed. R. G. Usher (London, 1905).

[46] Horton Davis, *The Worship of the English Puritans* (London, 1948), p. 259. This scholar developed the theme against a wide background in *Worship and Theology in England: From Cranmer to Hooker, 1534–1603* (Princeton, N.J., 1970).

[47] For example, E. G. Irvonwy Morgan, *The Godly Preachers of the Elizabethan Church* (London, 1965).

thrift, sobriety, chastity and industry; and they added a new Protestant emphasis on the dignity of a man's work or 'calling' in the world. But it is not true that a radically new social morality is found in Puritan sermons and books. Almost everything a Puritan preacher said about society in his day would have been said by the preaching friars in a medieval town.

Equally false is the idea that it was the habit of Puritan preachers to dwell gloomily on the doctrine of 'double pre-destination', which taught that God had from eternity pre-destined one fixed number (small) to heaven and another (much larger) number to the everlasting torments of hell. The eternal context of man's brief mortal life was always in the background of Puritan thinking, and the account of eternity given in the Calvinist tradition impressed the Puritans deeply because it seemed to be based on the Bible. But 'Calvinism' was understood differently by different Calvinists, and after an attempt to impose theological uniformity English theologians were in practice allowed a certain degree of freedom. When in the mid-1590s Professor Peter Baro, a refugee from France, and William Barrett, a young college chaplain, introduced liberal doctrines into Cambridge they were forced to resign; for they taught that Christ had died in order to make possible the salvation of all men, not merely of the predestined few. Their teaching shocked orthodox Calvinists because it gave some place to the freedom of the human will and to the importance of 'works' in salvation (and in fact young Barrett went abroad to become a Roman Catholic layman). That, however, did not prevent Baro's leading English disciple, John Overall, from being elected a professor in Cambridge and then moving to London as Dean of St Paul's.

It was generally agreed that the mysteries debated by such liberals with the strict Calvinists in the universities should be handled delicately, if at all, in the parishes. These were 'deep points'. The plain message to the parishes was that those who responded to the preaching were destined for the joys of salvation. In fact, Puritan preaching as it reached the parishes was virtually indistinguishable from a repetition of the New Testament – stern but not grim in its morality, awestruck but not despairing in its estimate of man's condition under the justice of God. When Puritans were exceptionally holy, their holiness seems to have been basically like the holiness of the saints in any age of Christianity. They condemned themselves rather than others, and they prayed for strength to love and serve God and neighbour. One of the leading Puritan theologians of the Elizabethan age was William Whitaker, Master of St John's College, Cambridge. His most important book was a *Disputation of Holy Scripture*, advocating the authority of the Bible against the Jesuit, Cardinal Bellarmine. Two of his sons became missionaries, expounding the Bible in Virginia during the years 1611–24. Such lives showed the main thrust of Elizabethan Puritanism.[48]

William Perkins became a Fellow of Christ's College, Cambridge, in 1584 and died in 1602. He was the author of a wide range of books of 'practical divinity' based on the Bible, such as expositions of the Lord's Prayer and the Apostles' Creed or a *Treatise of Vocations* which encouraged laymen to think of their jobs as God-given. His first 'rule' was that 'every person of every degree, state, sex, or condition, without exception, must have some particular and personal calling to walk in'; and although 'every man must judge that particular calling in which God hath placed him to be the best of all callings for him', yet 'a particular calling must give place to the general calling of a Christian when they cannot both stand together'. In England his reputation became such that between 1608 and 1635 his collected works, totalling over 2,500 pages, reached eight printings. His influence crossed the Atlantic with the Puritan emigrants. A modern scholar has said: 'Anyone who reads the writings of early New Englanders learns that Perkins was indeed a towering figure in Puritan eyes. Nor were English and American divines alone in their veneration for him. His works were translated into many languages and circulated in all Reformed communities; he was one of the outstanding pulpit orators of the day, and the seventeenth century, Catho-

---

[48] See Gordon Wakefield, *Puritan Devotion* (London, 1957). The thoughts of two clergymen are revealed in *Two Elizabethan Puritan Diaries*, ed. M. M. Knappen (Chicago, 1933), and those of a lady in Yorkshire who combined the lives of a housewife and a hermit in *The Diary of Lady Margaret Holtby*, ed. D. M. Meads (London, 1930).

lics as well as Protestant, ranked him with Calvin.'[49]

Perkins was the opposite of vague in his fundamental beliefs; his *Golden Chain* of 1591 brought together the teachings of Jean Calvin and of continental Calvinists such as Theodore Beza. He made, in fact, a rigid chain of the predestination theories – but this was not the main message which he entrusted to the young men sent from the university to preach to the English people. The main message was the Gospel as given in the New Testament long before Calvin. Sensitive readers of his systematic theology might be appalled by the thought that if they were not among the 'elect' predestined to heaven they were 'reprobates' given a temporary 'taste' of faith or morality only to be plunged with the accursed into hell, since 'God hath determined to reject certain men unto eternal destruction and misery and that to the praise of his justice'. But his main purpose was positive and pastoral. It was that preachers should assure believers that they were saved and ought to give thanks by good lives. He propounded 'a form of reasoning or practical syllogism':

> Everyone that believes is the child of God:
> But I do believe:
> Therefore I am the child of God.

He once wrote down 'the Order and Sum of the sacred and only method of Preaching':

1. To read the text distinctly out of the canonical Scriptures.

2. To give the sense and understanding of it, being read, by the Scripture itself.

3. To collect a few and profitable points of doctrine out of the natural sense.

4. To apply (if he have the gift) the doctrines rightly collected, to the life and manners of men in a simple and plain speech.[50]

---

[49] Perry Miller, *Errand into the Wilderness* (Cambridge, Mass., 1956), p. 57. See *The Work of William Perkins*, ed. Ian Breward (Abingdon, Berks., 1970), and the study of his thought in R. T. Kendall, *Calvin and English Calvinism to 1649*.

[50] Quoted in H. C. Porter, *Reformation and Reaction in Tudor Cambridge* (Cambridge, 1958), p. 225. See also his chapter on 'The Theology of William Perkins'.

What the Puritans wanted most was to revive religion. With all their limitations (they had no appreciation of visual beauty, or of poetry outside the Bible, or of Shakespeare's 'cakes and ale'), they argued boldly and persistently for the reformation of life in obedience to the New Testament and for the completion of the renewal of the medieval Church by a scriptural holiness. M. M. Knappen, a great authority, reckoned that of the quarter of Elizabeth's subjects who held firm opinions on religious questions, more than half were Puritans, because that was the most powerful brand of Christian idealism.[51] It was an Elizabethan tragedy that this noble contribution was branded as treason, creating agonies of conscience for laymen who wished to combine piety with patriotism, and thrusting sincere and brave religious leaders out into the wilderness. Church and State alike were impoverished when Puritan preachers were given an official treatment scarcely less hostile than the total rejection of the Roman Catholic missionaries. The identification of Roman Catholicism with treason was the error of popes, we may conclude; but the alienation of the Puritans was the error of the Queen.[52]

Puritanism, it is true, could not be stamped out. But despite the high and influential quality of many of the clergy and laity who adhered to it, it was not officially encouraged to enrich the quiet work of the Church of England in normal villages and towns. Nor, despite the high culture of some individual Puritans, was this movement allowed to become an integral part of the stupendous flowering of civilization in Elizabethan and Stuart England. Instead, the Puritan movement against which Elizabeth I had campaigned found other outlets. It encouraged the slow birth of an English-speaking republic on the other side of the Atlantic. In seventeenth-century England, it inspired events which ended in a violently destructive revolution.

---

[51] See M. M. Knappen, *Tudor Puritanism: A Chapter in the History of Idealism* (Chicago, Ill., 1939).

[52] The roughly similar dilemmas of the two groups in opposition were analysed by Elliot Rose in *Cases of Conscience: Alternatives Open to Recusants and Puritans under Elizabeth I and James I* (Cambridge, 1974).

Part Two

A WAR BETWEEN BELIEVERS

CHAPTER SIX

THE STUART CHURCH

JAMES I

Both James I and Charles I were believing members of the Church of England – the father a learned theologian, the son a martyr in some sense. And the deep interest which they both took in religion was typical of an age when the energies of Englishmen were expressed more creatively in religion than in any other sphere. The Stuarts ruled a country which was in the main authentically and enthusiastically religious. It was, however, less influenced by the New Testament in the matter of Christians loving each other, and no small part of the blame for a situation which led to civil war must rest on the two kings who made all-embracing claims to be responsible for their people's welfare. Through laziness in the father, and through blindness followed by obstinacy in the son, the kings failed to take the Puritan element in English Christianity with the seriousness which it deserved.[1]

A modern biographer has remarked that James 'took the Church of England to his heart in a long rapturous embrace that lasted for the rest of his life'.[2] The bishops of the Established Church, well schooled by Elizabeth, were submissive to a monarch – and James had been one since his coronation soon after his first birthday. The leading bishops, Whitgift and

---

[1] A useful collection of illustrative extracts is *Politics, Religion and Literature in the Seventeenth Century*, ed. William Lamont and Sybil Oldfield (London, 1975). Introductions to the politics include J. P. Kenyon, *Stuart England* (London, 1978), and Barry Coward, *The Stuart Age* (London, 1980).

[2] D. Harris Willson, *King James VI and I* (London, 1956), p. 197. Caroline Bingham, *James I of England* (London, 1981), is another good biography. Peter Milward, *The Religious Controversies of the Jacobean Age* (London, 1978), is a survey of the printed sources.

Bancroft, assured him that the old queen had been perfectly right to link the Puritans with those Presbyterian preachers who had bored him, and tried to dominate him, ever since John Knox had preached his coronation sermon. One of the many delights in becoming king of the far richer kingdom to the south was deliverance from those sermons, and James had not the least intention of suffering under English pulpits.

Now he would do the teaching. In an exhortation to his eldest son Henry written in 1598 (*Basilikon Doron*), he had mocked 'the preposterous humility of the proud Puritans, claiming to their parity and crying "We are all but vile worms", and yet who will judge and give law to their king but will be judged nor controlled by none.' James boasted about the lessons he taught to the Puritans at the Hampton Court conference of 1604: 'I peppered them soundly.' He preferred to have bishops not because they were princes of the Church but because they were deferential to his own mastery of 'kingcraft'. They would, he trusted, make others share their sense of his importance; that was why he had created three bishops for Scotland in 1610. He also liked bishops because most of them were learned in theology, where he was no less expert. He had himself been thoroughly trained as a scholar by his tutor George Buchanan, and he kept up bookish habits throughout his life. Nothing pleased him more than to have a bishop or potential bishop standing beside his chair while he dined, serving up quotations from the Bible and the Fathers which supported the royal doctrines. In this enjoyment of the company of leading clergymen, he was unlike Elizabeth. He was also unlike her in his respect for their interests. James warmly approved of a law of 1604 which forbade the bishops to alienate the estates of their sees. They were not even to transfer them to the Crown. The King wanted his bishops to enjoy their rights and to feel at ease, as he did.

He rightly expected his grateful bishops not to blench at his conceit, which was monumental ('If you will consider the attributes of God,' he informed Parliament in 1610, 'you shall see how they agree in the person of a king'); or at his table manners, which were disgusting; or at his homosexuality, which became blatant; or at the extravagant and often inebriated disorder of his court; or at his passion for hunting, which meant that his attention to politics was intermittent. These fellow theologians would surely either applaud or not notice. He also expected them to share his rejection of interference by the popes.

In theory he was willing to acknowledge some primacy in the religious position of the Bishop of Rome, but in practice Roman Catholicism meant to him the religion of his mother and of those who wished to assassinate him. His mother had arranged for his father's murder and had been nothing but a nuisance to him before her execution (which he secretly approved). He took the identification of Roman Catholicism with terrorism seriously; his clothes were specially padded and he hated to see a drawn sword. While King of England he wrote – or at any rate claimed the authorship of – four books defending the God-given rights of kings against the political pretensions of mere popes; and he hurt his Roman Catholic subjects more directly by approving the execution of seventeen of them. He had imbibed to the full the Calvinism of his education, and to prove his orthodoxy he had Edward Wightman, a draper who had denied the divinity of Christ, burned in 1612 – the last Englishman to suffer death for heresy. He personally briefed the English delegates sent to the international reaffirmation of Calvinist orthodoxy at the synod of Dort (Dordrecht) in 1618. He had previously given strict instructions to his ambassador to curtail the posthumous influence of Professor Jacob Harmensz of Leyden. The professor was to be important in English history because his Latinized name Arminius was given to an international movement, Arminianism.[3]

What the King really liked was the Calvinism of a bishop such as James Montague of Winchester (the editor of his collected works), or Toby Matthew of York, or Vaughan of London, or Davenant of Salisbury. It was the kind of Calvinism that taught that, among all God's elect, a king was particularly chosen for the blessings of the God who was not

---

[3] See Carl Bangs, *Arminius* (Nashville, Tenn., 1974); R. T. Kendall, *Calvin and English Calvinism to 1649*, pp. 141–64; *Reform and Reformation*, ed. Derek Baker (Oxford, 1979), pp. 195–243.

decisively interested in morality. In religion James (the 'British Solomon') was the nation's schoolmaster, but not usually a censorious one. He genially promoted a few bishops who were at least crypto-Arminians, such as Richard Neile of Durham. His teaching about witchcraft showed his general approach. In Scotland he had been fascinated by the subject and had written a treatise on *Demonology*, but in England he found that educated men laughed and he grew bored.[4] Almost forty years of plot and counter-plot in Scotland had made him thankful to be alive, so that his general attitude was 'live and let live' (excluding the deer). His motto was 'Blessed are the peacemakers', and he once wrote: 'I did ever hold persecution as one of the infallible notes of a false church.'

His relaxed attitude extended to family affairs and to foreign affairs, between which there was a good deal of overlap. He had married a Danish princess when he had needed an ally back in 1589, but he allowed her to find her own peace in the Roman Catholic faith while he comforted himself with the affections of handsome young men. Although he was delighted when his beautiful daughter Elizabeth married the Elector Palatine, a firm Protestant, and so became the 'queen of hearts', he was determined to establish and strengthen peace with Catholic Spain, consummating it if possible by a marriage alliance for his son. This meant that he did not share the enthusiasm of many of his subjects, including MPs, for intervention on the Protestant side when the Thirty Years' War started. The war began in earnest with the Catholic victories over his son-in-law, temporarily King of Bohemia, in 1619–20, but English Protestant passions were not allowed to lead to sustained action. To the indignation of the Puritans, the much-loved Elizabeth was left in exile and poverty in The Hague. Her royal father sent much sympathy – but little else.

At home the King's love of peace – and also of himself as the maker of peace – gave rise to the episode of the *Declaration of Sports*. This was ordered to be read in all churches in 1618, and was a treatise approving healthy exercise on a Sunday after-

---

[4] See Christina Larner in *The Reign of James VI and I*, ed. A. G. R. Smith (London, 1975), pp. 74–90.

noon. This royal defence of football, wrestling, archery, morris dances, Maypoles, Whitsun ales and so forth had several advantages in the eyes of the British Solomon. It pleased his people by his gracious patronage of their recreations; it kept them out of the alehouses where they might grumble about his government; it exercised them as potential soldiers available for any wars into which he might be forced; and it asserted his authority over those Puritans who preferred the people to spend Sunday afternoon reading the Bible, a book not always sound in its attitude to monarchs. But when he found that many of the clergy and some of the bishops strongly objected to his declaration, he withdrew it and so restored theological peace.

His permanent religious achievement was his sponsorship of the Authorized or King James Version of the Bible, published in 1611.

At the Hampton Court conference he agreed both with Puritan criticisms of the inaccuracies of the Bishops' Bible, and with the bishops' attack on the controversial notes and new words (such as *congregation* instead of the old *church*) in the Geneva Bible. Having thus made peace with all his fellow scholars, he announced a project which was to be the chief glory of his reign. There was to be a translation on which all could agree. No time was lost in appointing fifty-four translators to compare the Bishops' Bible and the rival English versions with the original Hebrew and Greek. These translators included some Puritan scholars, among them John Rainolds who had taken the lead at Hampton Court. Guided by 'rules' given to them in the King's name, they worked in six companies, at Oxford, Cambridge and Westminster, with a central committee and two final revisers (Bishops Bilson and Miles Smith). They had all the scholarship of the age at their command – and, fortunately for their self-confidence, did not realize how defective were the New Testament manuscripts on which their translation was based, or how incomplete was their mastery of Hebrew. Enough of the work of the early English translators, Tyndale and Coverdale, survived to give the 1611 version its tone of an already old-fashioned majesty, but the result went far beyond the light revision of the Bishops' Bible which was the original plan.

The acceptance of the new Bible took time. For many years even bishops as scholarly, and as deferential to royal opinions, as Lancelot Andrewes and William Laud continued to use the familiar Geneva Bible when preaching. Wisely, the King did not force the issue. The Bible which became famous as the 'Authorized Version' was in fact never authorized in any exclusive sense. Such a step might have aroused opposition for which the King had no taste. The way chosen was more effective: the King's Printer published the new version in a large (folio) edition suitable for use in churches, and no earlier translation was reprinted in that size. Read in churches with less and less competition, the new Bible gradually made its way into people's loyalties by the force of its language and by the quality of its scholarship with its multi-layered authorship. The language was not everyday; there was no equivalent here of Shakespeare's comic crowd scenes. Indeed, it was sometimes not clear; St Paul's theology as translated here can never have been entirely and immediately plain to all churchgoers. But the biblical themes of grace and glory were presented with a dignity worthy of the great declamations in Shakespearean drama and the stories were told with a powerful simplicity. Popular appreciation of the achievement meant that the excitement with which the first English versions had been received was renewed and prolonged, and the effects did not begin to fade out of the consciousness of the English-speaking peoples until the twentieth century. The dedication to the king of this 'King James Version' (the American term) was well deserved – although its fulsomeness was in contrast with the restraint of the Bible when speaking about God.[5]

That was a major contribution to the religion of the English, but historians have asked: could there have been more?

The new translation of the Bible might have been accompanied by a new settlement of the Church. It would surely not have been impossible for a king equipped to understand the issues involved to insist that the Church of England should be more fully reformed, or at least made more welcoming to

---

[5] See David Daiches, *The King James Version of the English Bible* (Chicago, Ill., 1941), and T. R. Henn, *The Bible as Literature* (London, 1970).

reformers. Even the dispute with Rome would have been made less destructive had there been a systematic attempt to win the loyalty of Roman Catholics who were willing to be loyal (like James's own wife). But this self-advertising king was no statesman. Robert Cecil, his chief minister until 1612, was treated like a useful dog and nicknamed 'the Beagle'. Archbishop Bancroft who served alongside him was, like Cecil, a highly competent administrator – and he had a policy, to build up the Church of England efficiently but narrowly. James, however, failed to appoint a successor to Bancroft who would continue that policy. The truth was that James, for all his pride in his mastery of 'kingcraft', had learned that trade in a country where the bureaucracy was primitive in comparison with that of England. He had grown accustomed to purchasing the support of potential troublemakers by titles and pensions, and he had never seen any need to appoint ministers capable of forming and executing a longterm policy. Survival had been his purpose, and bribery had been his method. His failures to appoint bishops who would make an impression as the agents of a coherent and farsighted policy only illustrated his general approach to 'kingcraft'. He appointed bishops to whom he took a fancy, or who were recommended to him by laymen whom he wished to please.[6]

A modern scholar has sadly commented on the results. 'The story of the first decade of James I's reign, Cecil's decade,' writes Professor Joel Hurstfield, 'is in Church as in State the story of solutions glimpsed and opportunities missed. No one in that brief interval of promise had sufficient of either the will or the power to solve the problems which for half a century had pressed for a solution: namely to broaden the Church sufficiently to meet the reasonable demands of the moderate Puritans and to broaden the state sufficiently to meet the reasonable demands of the moderate Catholics.'[7]

---

[6] Two instructive essays are by H. R. Trevor-Roper in his *Historical Essays* (London, 1957), pp. 139–45, and by Arthur P. Kautz in *Early Stuart Studies*, ed. H. S. Reinmuth (Minneapolis, Minn., 1970), pp. 152–79. But Patrick Collinson has sympathetically portrayed the Jacobean Church in his *The Religion of Protestants*.

[7] Joel Hurstfield, *Freedom, Corruption and Government* (London, 1973), p. 101.

CHARLES I

Although Charles I – whose reign began in 1625 – resembled his father in his attachment to the Church of England and its bishops, he did not favour orthodox Calvinists. His taste for Arminians needs some explaining, since the new king, essentially an aesthete, had none of his father's academic interest in theology.

Theologically Arminianism was defined by the 'Remonstrance' published by the Dutch supporters of the provocative Professor Harmensz in 1610, the year after his death. It maintained five points – that God has decreed the salvation of all who believe in Christ, that Christ died 'for all' but that only believers enjoy forgiveness of sins, that man must be regenerated by the Holy Spirit, that grace is 'not irresistible', and that perseverance is granted through 'the assistance of the grace of the Holy Spirit'. This creed aroused a very fierce controversy, for at each of these points the emphasis seemed to be on the possibility that any man might actively respond to the love of God declared in Christ's death, his will only being assisted by the Holy Spirit if he was willing to receive such assistance – and there was not a corresponding emphasis on the decree that some were eternally elect and others eternally damned whatever their own merits.

Summing up the orthodox reaction, the Synod of Dordrecht (Dort) proclaimed the five points of Calvinism, popularly recalled by the acrostic TULIP – total depravity, unconditional election, limited atonement (Christ died for the elect only), irresistible grace (saving the elect), the perseverance of the elect (only) until they safely reach heaven. Thus in orthodox Calvinism the sovereignty of God was reasserted against man's free will. In its practical consequences Arminianism had not originally been royalist; it had been the religion of self-confident businessmen critical of Prince Maurice and that had been the main reason why James I had been so much against it. John Milton, who was to argue that it had been right to execute King Charles, was an Arminian. But Arminianism appealed to Charles in his optimism at the beginning of his reign. It seemed a fit religion for a happy kingdom at peace (whereas in the Netherlands the narrow, angry, creed of orthodox Calvinism was still needed as a fighting creed against Spain). Above all, it appealed because of what William Laud and other churchmen who won influence over the new king told him. To them, Arminianism offered a suitable inspiration for a working partnership of kings and priests against Puritan troublemakers. To believe in free will as a theological theory meant to accept the King's will in practice. That was why, as George Morley (a future Bishop of Winchester) quipped, the answer to 'What do the Arminians hold?' was that they held all the best bishoprics and deaneries in the kingdom.[8]

Such importance had been attached to Charles's adherence to the Church of England that his Roman Catholic mother had not been allowed to bring him up. Like his father he had therefore starved of affection in his childhood; in his falsetto voice with a Scots accent, he always stammered badly. Like his father he had formed his first intimate, life-giving, friendship with a man. For James the liberator of the emotions had been Esmé Stuart, Duke of Lennox, in the 1580s; for 'Baby Charles' (as his father always called him) it was George Villiers, Duke of Buckingham, his beloved 'Steenie', in the 1620s. Both dukes flattered their royal friends with talk of the absolute powers of the Spanish and French monarchies. But Charles was never infatuated physically by any man; on the contrary, it would appear that he had for long avoided starting a friendship with Buckingham because he had disapproved of his own father's intimate relationship with him. After the shock of the murder of Buckingham in 1628 he never again gave his full friendship to any man, or did much to win any man's love; at court or in prison, he treated all men as his servants. Instead he fell fully in love with Henrietta Maria, his French Catholic queen whom he had married for political reasons four years before.

Together these two little people (the King was only five and a half feet tall and his Queen came up to his shoulder) were at the centre of the England of the 1630s.[9] Children were born

---

[8] In the 1630s Arminianism began to be tolerated even in the Netherlands. See A. W. Harrison, *Arminianism* (London, 1936), and Douglas Nobbs, *Theocracy and Toleration* (Cambridge, 1938).

[9] The best biographies are Pauline Gregg, *Charles I* (London, 1981), and Elizabeth Hamilton, *Henrietta Maria* (London, 1976).

from 1629 onwards, and the court which revolved around their
exemplary family life was thoroughly respectable but also full
of polite amusements. The courtiers were still supplied with
food and drink on a sumptuous scale, but there was none of the
gross vulgarity which James had enjoyed. Nor were theological
disputations to be heard; Charles disliked arguments of any
sort. Instead there was heavy and discriminating expenditure
on art of the highest quality. Contemplating the silent beauty
of a painting, a king could find reassurance. He could also find
it in rituals. Stately acts of worship, masques and banquets
became the court's routine, and something of their spirit seems
to be perpetually in the air of the chapel of St James's Palace,
the Banqueting House in Whitehall and the Queen's House in
Greenwich – the surviving masterpieces which Inigo Jones
achieved in his service of Stuart magnificence. Never has the
English monarchy shown better taste.

Seldom has it been so cut off from the people. Its sophisticated luxury contrasted with the real poverty of many of the
English, particularly many in London – but the court did not
even appeal to those who might have been its allies because
they, too, were privileged. The nobility and gentry (the
bishops, too) were discouraged from attendance at court unless
they had definite business there, and the King and Queen did
not tour round other great people's houses. Queen Elizabeth
had known how to capture the heart of a casually met visitor
with a joke; but now King Charles passed through his
courtiers, smiling distantly. His very love of beauty alienated
him from his subjects, since there were so few English artists
whom he could employ. Tensions arose both because of his
acceptance of his wife's French Catholic priests (despite early
explosions and later grumbles) – and because of his own
Anglican piety. He was religious in a style very different from
the Puritanism which animated large and growing numbers of
his subjects. His father, for all his glaring faults, seems to have
been more genuinely popular. James had often been adroit at
handling individuals. He had thoroughly sympathized with
other people's sexual and financial appetites, had been amused
to see his guests' rich clothes covered with cream puddings,
and had been delighted when ladies of the court, acting in

masques, had rolled about drunk. Were they not all humanly depraved together? Yet the Puritan preachers had consoled themselves with the belief that their strange monarch was, like them, a Calvinist theologian. The coldly correct Charles was far more isolated. It is revealing that he refused to bow to the storm which burst when he reissued his father's *Declaration of Sports*. What was at stake for him was not that people should enjoy themselves, but that he should be obeyed. Until he was dead he was not widely loved.

This isolation of the King from ordinary men's feelings encouraged many in the country to suspect that Popery, or something close to it, flourished at court, but those with some inside knowledge knew that the King was satisfied with the Arminian version of Protestantism. It was a sign of things to come that the Duke of Buckingham, when he chaired a public debate on the topic of predestination at York House in February 1626, showed that his own (not very profound) opinions were Arminian. In the very first year of his reign Charles, with Buckingham's encouragement, sheltered an Arminian clergyman, Richard Montague, when the Commons had committed him to prison as the author of provocative (and, it was alleged, Papist) pamphlets. Three years later Montague was made Bishop of Chichester; the news of Buckingham's murder reached the bishops when they were assembled for this consecration. The King tried to dampen the controversy by reissuing the Thirty-Nine Articles with a declaration insisting on their 'literal and grammatical sense'. It was the royal will that disputes about predestination going beyond the Articles were to be 'shut up in God's promises'. But orthodox Calvinists were not going to be shut up, for they were convinced that Arminianism was not merely a heresy within Protestantism. A more dramatic conviction was voiced when the Commons debated religion in January 1629. Francis Rous, a bold Cornish MP, then announced: 'An Arminian is the spawn of a Papist.' When Parliament at last met again, in 1640, John Pym had high on the list of grievances 'innovations in religion'.[10]

---

[10] The course of this theological revolution was charted by Nicholas Tyacke in *The Origins of the Civil War*, ed. Conrad Russell (London, 1973), pp. 119–43.

The civil war broke out after a chain of events which began with the King's attempt to impose on Scotland the Church of England's standards of beauty and order as these were interpreted by the Arminian clergy. His father had also nursed the ambition to unite his two kingdoms of England and Scotland religiously, but had been too shrewd – or too lazy – to do much about it. James had imposed bishops on the Scots in 1610, but these had been little more than chairmen of the ministers' presbyteries and they had not been ordained priests before being consecrated bishops. Seeking more power for these agents of his, James had visited Scotland in 1617, but he had taken no effective steps to impose his wishes when the Scots, virtually as one man, rejected them. Charles had already received warning of the Protestant nationalism of his northern subjects by the criticisms they had offered loudly when he had staged a pompous coronation in Edinburgh in 1633 and had appointed bishops to high political office, but he was undeterred. Encouraged by Laud and by these Scottish bishops, he conceived the totally unrealistic policy of imposing on the Church of Scotland (without consulting its General Assembly) a Prayer Book almost identical with the Book of Common Prayer of the Church of England. This was the work of Scotsmen and it used the word 'presbyter' not 'priest', but was in some other details less Protestant. The Communion service represented a partial return to the 1549 Prayer Book.[11]

Riots in Edinburgh rapidly led to the signing of a National Covenant to resist the bishops and their Papistical book to the death, and so Charles had the 'First Bishops' War' on his hands. Without the authority of Parliament to raise taxes, he could not equip an effective expeditionary force. Instead he made the situation worse by soliciting gifts from those who wished to be reckoned his friends, and by sending north a civilian army of militiamen. This army promptly made a truce with the Scots. The foolish Prayer Book was withdrawn, but Charles was unwilling to accept the further humiliation of making a final settlement with the lay-dominated assembly of

---

[11] Gordon Donaldson studied *The Making of the Scottish Prayer Book of 1637* (Edinburgh, 1954).

the Church of Scotland, abandoning his bishops as well as his Prayer Book.

At length a rich and blunt Yorkshireman, Thomas Wentworth, was called home from his seven years as the brutally effective administrator of Ireland and created Earl of Strafford and Lieutenant-General. His advice was taken. An army must be raised against the rebellious Scots; therefore taxes must be raised; therefore, after eleven years without one, a parliament must be summoned. It met on 17 April 1640.[12]

To see why the House of Commons – now at last given its opportunity – was bound to want to reform the Church, we must look at some English bishops.

FOUR BISHOPS

In Richard Bancroft James had inherited one of the ablest administrators in the whole history of the Church of England, and one who had proved his energy and skill as the right-hand man of Archbishop Whitgift in the campaign against the Elizabethan Puritans. It seemed inevitable that he should be appointed Archbishop of Canterbury as Whitgift's successor in December 1604.

Shortly before that appointment a new set of ecclesiastical laws or canons had been passed by the clergy in the Convocation of Canterbury and ordered by the King to be 'diligently observed . . . by all our loving subjects.' The key canon was 36, repeating the insistence of Whitgift in 1583 that all clergy should solemnly swear that the Prayer Book contained nothing contrary to the Word of God in the Bible. But there were 141 of these canons, codifying Tudor and earlier regulations; and in a series of visitations of his own diocese and many others, Bancroft embarked on a strenuous campaign to enforce them. Recruiting and encouraging competent lawyers and other

---

[12] Dame Veronica Wedgwood told the story of these years brilliantly in her *The King's Peace, 1637–41* (London, 1955), although some of her judgements have been revised in later scholarship.

staff, he proved that this medieval weapon of the visitation could still be wielded to good effect as various kinds of sinners or nonconformists were punished or rebuked – and as a check was made of their subsequent behaviour. And for the first time since the 1530s there was insistence on keeping proper records both in the ecclesiastical courts and in the parish churches.

Bancroft had the wisdom to advise that clergy who would conform to the Prayer Book in practice, but who could not swallow Canon 36, should be left alone. In the end, out of some ten thousand clergy only about ninety were deprived of their parishes for their open refusal to conform – and about a fifth of these seem to have been reinstated on promising obedience.[13]

One reason why most of the clergy were co-operative was that it was widely known that Bancroft had set his heart on raising their incomes. It was the Archbishop's old-fashioned ideal that a resident pastor should receive a full tenth of all the produce of his parish. Under his impetus the High Commission at the centre, and the revived diocesan courts at the circumference, began a long process of rescinding various arrangements which had in effect reduced the Elizabethan clergy to the economic status of servants. Payments customary in the Middle Ages, such as tithes on mining operations, had been waived; the agricultural tithes had been commuted for cash which fell in value; many tithes had been alienated to laymen. All these battles were fought again under Bancroft. At the same time adjacent parishes, individually too small to support a clergyman, were merged. There were still many 'pluralities', but these cases where one man was incumbent of more than one parish were at least to be licensed formally by the bishops. The glebe (the priest's own land) was exempt from tax, to help the poorer clergy. More frequent preaching by the clergy after training and licensing was encouraged. In the House of Lords in 1610 Bancroft even put forward a scheme for a national fund to buy out all the lay rectors' rights in the parishes, and to restore all the tithes to the clergy who did the

---

[13] This was the conclusion of S. B. Babbage, *Puritanism and Richard Bancroft*, pp. 217–19. R. G. Usher, *The Reconstruction of the English Church* (2 vols, New York, 1910), is still useful.

work. It was all part of a detailed plan to restore the clergy's tithes as literally one tenth of the national product.[14]

Many laymen naturally took fright at the prospect of the bishops recovering their disciplinary powers and clergymen recovering their economic status. There were protests in Parliament at any idea that canons such as those of 1604, agreed to only by the clergy, could be imposed on the laity. Spurred on by Sir Edward Coke who was Chief Justice until abruptly dismissed by the King in 1616, the judges attacked the right of the ecclesiastical courts, particularly the High Commission, to function with this new vigour. Defending towns and industries from taxation by the Church, they also declared that the clergy had no right to tithes 'of such things whereof the gain comes by the labour of man', except where a custom to the contrary could be proved. James was pleased to arbitrate between the enraged judges and the ecclesiastical lawyers, but characteristically did little more than to declare a truce. Despite hopes which had been raised both by the Puritans at the Hampton Court conference and by the Puritans' arch-enemy Bancroft, the parish clergy were left with no hope of any major improvement in their financial position. The complacent view of most of the laity was, it seems, that reform was desirable but impossible.

Bancroft's theology was considerably less energetic than his administration. He seems to have been a mild Calvinist. Although he was always talking about discipline, he had no religious vision of the Church with which to compete against the vision of the Puritan preachers. He also lacked an ideology with which to fight against the gentry whose vision was of an England where laymen prospered. An ecclesiastic who did have such a religious vision was Lancelot Andrewes, widely regarded – and, it was reported, recommended by the bishops to the King – as the natural successor to Bancroft at Canterbury in 1610.

Andrewes was the most admired preacher of his age, summoned to edify King James year after year on the great festivals of the Church. His learning and sanctity expressed themselves

---

[14] See Christopher Hill, *Economic Problems of the Church*, pp. 246–7.

not only in the pulpit but also in private; his notebook of devotions and intercessions, *Preces Privatae*, has been treasured by discerning Anglicans ever since its publication in 1648, long after his death. He is said to have mastered fifteen modern and six ancient languages, and his skill as a translator is preserved in the Old Testament of the 1611 version. He seemed destined to make the Church of England the spiritual leader of Europe – as those who wished to flatter James often claimed it already was. He was also an efficient administrator. From the Deanery of Westminster he was promoted to be a bishop, first of Chichester and then of Ely.

James, however, did not offer him Canterbury on Bancroft's death, moving him instead to Winchester in 1618. The reason, it seems, was that the high churchmanship of Andrewes worried the laity, including the King. In his own chapel the Bishop used candles and incense. What if this meant that he hankered after a return to the medieval status of the clergy? It seemed alarming that he had refused to be made a bishop under Elizabeth because he was unwilling to drive a financial bargain. While he claimed that he was no Arminian heretic, he also refused to repeat the great Calvinist slogans. James did not make him leader of the English delegation to the Calvinists' Synod of Dort – or Archbishop of Canterbury.

We should not make a martyr out of Andrewes. He was one of those who in 1613 voted at the King's behest in favour of the divorce of Frances Howard (on the ground that her husband was impotent towards her – but not towards other women) in order that she might be free to marry the King's favourite Robert Carr (later made Earl of Somerset). When in attendance on the Privy Council or in the House of Lords, he often kept silence. Secretly he recorded his penitence in the tear-stained notebook of *Preces Privatae*, and he prayed: 'Deliver me from making gods of kings.' Yet in the pulpit his prose was 'not inferior to that of any sermons in the language, unless it be some of Newman's', in the judgement of T. S. Eliot.[15]

---

[15] See T. S. Eliot, *For Lancelot Andrewes* (London, 1928); Maurice F. Reidy, *Bishop Lancelot Andrewes, Jacobean Court Preacher* (Chicago, Ill., 1955); Paul A. Welsby, *Lancelot Andrewes* (London, 1958).

The man preferred for Canterbury in 1610 was far less complex. George Abbot was an Oxford theologian who combined moderate Calvinism with a firm belief in the royal supremacy – exactly the mixture that the King most relished.

He had made his mark in 1608 when he had accompanied the Earl of Dunbar, as his chaplain, on a mission from King James to seek to persuade the General Assembly of the Church of Scotland of the merits of government by bishops. The Scots had remained suspicious of bishops, but the King had been grateful to his emissaries for their efforts. Abbot therefore found himself being enthroned as Bishop of Lichfield and Coventry in December 1609, and as Bishop of London in February 1610. A year later his appointment as Archbishop of Canterbury was announced, when he had nearly given up hope because of the death of the Earl of Dunbar. According to his secretary George Calvert, the King gave Abbot a revealing explanation: 'It is neither the respect of his learning, his wisdom, nor his sincerity (although he is well persuaded that there is none of them wanting in him) that hath made him prefer him before the rest of his fellows, but merely the recommendation of his faithful servant Dunbar that is dead, whose suit [plea] on behalf of the bishop he cannot forget, nor will not suffer [allow] to lose his intention.' To add to his favour, the King made George Abbot's brother Robert (theologically his twin) Bishop of Salisbury.

Abbot was far less interested than Bancroft in ecclesiastical administration, and his appointment made sure that there would no longer be a firm hand on the helm. He did not set eyes on Canterbury Cathedral until he had been archbishop for four years. But surprisingly, he retained something of a Calvinist conscience. In the Howard divorce case of 1613, when Andrewes did what he was told, Abbot braved the wrath of the King; he kept on repeating that he was meant to be a judge, that he must abide by the law laid down in the Bible. He kept the archbishopric, but his relationship with the King was far cooler than before.

It was while relaxing after consecrating the new chapel of Bramshill House near Reading in July 1621 that Abbot met disaster. To his horror he found that a clumsy shot from his cross-bow had killed a deerkeeper. Characteristically the King reassured him about the accident and a royal commission absolved him from guilt. The incident, however, made the Archbishop a 'man of blood' and two rising churchmen, John Williams and William Laud, then awaiting consecration as bishops, refused to be touched by hands so stained. The reason which Lancelot Andrewes gave for leniency to Abbot was unheroic: 'Brethren, be not too busy to condemn any for Uncanonicals according to the strictness thereof, lest we render ourselves in the same condition.'

For the rest of his life the homicide discredited the Archbishop. His advocacy of war to help the Protestants in Germany, and of an end to the plans for a marriage treaty with Spain, irritated the old King without making him a hero to the Puritans. After the death of James Abbot angered the new King by refusing to license the printing of an adulatory sermon by a Northampton clergyman, one Robert Sibthorpe. 'Where the word of the King is, there is power,' the preacher had declared, 'and who may say to him, "What doest thou?" ' King Charles certainly felt able to ask that question of Archbishop Abbot, who was suspended from his duties for a year. Even when he had been restored, there was no power in his words. Everyone knew that the King was merely waiting for the death of the morose old Calvinist – who had killed a man – in order to make William Laud archbishop.[16]

Had Abbot resigned or been deprived immediately after the homicide, John Williams might have been promoted to Canterbury. As he smugly wrote to the Duke of Buckingham at that juncture, 'His Majesty hath promised me one of the best places in this Church.' The fear of that appointment may have reconciled Andrewes to the prospect of Abbot being restored to his functions as archbishop, since Andrewes was one of the many Englishmen who disapproved of Williams as a Welsh rogue.

When John Williams lay dying in 1650, he wished that he could be 'assured that by my preaching I had converted one soul to God.' But he still looked back proudly over his career: 'I

---

[16] See Paul A. Welsby, *George Abbot: The Unwanted Archbishop* (London, 1962).

have passed through many places of honour and trust both in Church and State, more than any of my order in England the seventy years before.' After a spell as secretary to the Lord Chancellor, he had attracted the favour of King James. He was a handsome bachelor, a brilliant conversationalist, a man for peace and pleasure. When the Deanery of Westminster fell vacant in 1620, he seemed thoroughly suitable. More surprisingly, he also seemed suitable for an additional job when next year Francis Bacon was dismissed for corruption from the post of Lord Chancellor or 'Lord Keeper of the Great Seal'. To be sure, Williams was not a lawyer – but he was, he declared, eager to study the law, and the not-too-legal-sounding title of 'Lord Keeper' could be used. To be sure, he was not yet a bishop – but he could be made Bishop of Lincoln, and promptly was so made, without resigning as Dean of Westminster. With Abbot in disgrace, it was Bishop Williams who talked devoutly in Latin with the dying King James, who closed the eyes of his corpse, and who preached a funeral sermon never surpassed in the records of flattery. But his basic cynicism about the Church is to be seen in the advice he had given to James when his son-in-law, Frederick, had been driven out by the conquering Catholics. He had not advocated military aid or the admission of ordinary refugees from the Palatinate or Bohemia, but he had acknowledged that provision had to be made for Frederick's two sons, Prince Rupert and Prince Maurice. He had proposed that they should be placed in the bishoprics of Durham and Winchester. A sermon of his survives as an exercise in the interpretation of the passage in the gospels where it is pointed out that those who wear soft clothing live in kings' houses (whereas St John the Baptist lived in the desert). John Williams approved of this factual observation and felt no hesitation in wearing soft clothing; the rebuke delivered in the Bible, he explained, was directed at those who wore richer dress than was appropriate to their station in life.

On the death of his royal patron Bishop Williams could not hope to retain power. He had already shocked the new King by his worldliness, and he soon caused fresh displeasure by making an attempt to mediate between Charles and the House of Commons. Deprived of his high political office, he retired to live as Bishop of Lincoln. He still lived in a high style, rebuilding the bishop's palace at Buckden, educating noblemen's sons as his pages, keeping open house to visiting peers and occasionally going south to his Westminster Deanery (always to be ordered back to his diocese by the implacable King). Eventually in 1637 the indignation at the King's court exploded. Williams was condemned on trumped-up charges, deprived of almost all his wealth, and imprisoned in the Tower.

Four years later a frightened Charles, at last acknowledging his abilities, made him Archbishop of York. Had Williams been put in charge of affairs in the 1630s, his very lack of principle would presumably have helped to prevent a head-on confrontation between the King and the Puritans. He was a consistent compromiser. After Strafford's trial he advised the King to sacrifice his fallen servant to the executioner's axe, and during the civil war he advised him to make terms with Parliament – exactly the advice he had tendered at the beginning of the reign. He retired to North Wales for the duration of the war. At first he organized the area's defence in the King's interest, but later he accepted and assisted the Parliamentary victory, so that the Royalists despised him as a turncoat.

What really interested him was, it seems, prosperity – his own but also other people's, spending the money on supporting education as well as food and drink, houses and gardens. As a motive it was not magnificent, but it may have been in the nation's interests as well as his own that he had the shrewdness to see that Puritanism had to be humoured if the nation's wealth was to be preserved and increased. Although personally the opposite of every ideal which the Puritans held, he knew the strength of their creed. That was why he urged and practised compromise, and why when he had lived to see England and Wales torn apart by civil war he died in despair.[17]

---

[17] B. D. Roberts provided a sympathetic biography called *Mitre and Musket* (London, 1938).

WILLIAM LAUD

William Laud was the tenth child born in a modest home which was also a small clothing factory, in Reading. All through his life he knew that men made jokes behind his back about his lowly origins, and it gave him an inferiority complex. But he knew that he had greatness in him – and that others did not. He once came out with the devastating truth about King Charles: 'a mild and gracious prince who knew not how to be, or be made, great.'

Although he became a competent scholar at Oxford, his only substantial publication was his *Conference with Fisher the Jesuit*, designed to impress the Duke of Buckingham's mother with the Church of England's claims. To him, administration was sacred. His real contribution to Oxford was made as chancellor of the university from 1629; he was a great organizer of other men's studies, a great censor of other men's conduct, dress and haircuts. He loved to dwell on the God-given powers of kings and bishops, who together must govern Church and State. 'The King is the sun. He draws some vapours, some support, some supply, from us.' Similarly, a bishop is the successor of the apostles, deriving his authority from Christ himself. A bishop's power, Laud said at his trial, is exercised only with the King's permission; but the power itself is 'by divine apostolical right and unalterable'.

Laud was obviously a man born to be a bishop. But how was he to become one? Men did not like him. He was too inhuman, with none of the Welsh gusto for life which John Williams displayed. With a tendency to correct all those around him went a tendency to lose his temper. 'A little red-faced man' was how one socially superior enemy described him. He had to find a patron, and the necessity was such that as chaplain to the Earl of Devon he officiated at the Earl's marriage with Lady Rich, who had been divorced for adultery with him. He thus sacrificed his conscience to his ambition – although he always kept the day of the wedding, St Stephen's Day, as a fast. Later he attached himself to Buckingham, and still displayed a high ambition; as he recorded in his journal during 1625, 'In my sleep it seemed to me that the Duke of Buckingham got into my

bed, where he showed me much love'. It was a dream, however, and in reality he received relatively minor promotion –
Dean of Gloucester, Bishop of St David's, Bishop of Bath and
Wells. King James analysed his character acutely: 'He hath a
restless spirit and cannot see when matters are well, but loves
to toss and change and bring things to a pitch of reformation
floating in his own brain.' In his worried dreams he saw his
rival John Williams, nine years his junior, outstripping him.
That is one key to the character of William Laud: a man with
an itch to govern and reform other people, he was not able to be
a martinet with sufficient scope until he was made Bishop of
London at the age of fifty-five – and even then he had to wait
another five years for Canterbury on Abbot's death. He had
grown impatient.

Another key is his high Anglican churchmanship. Those
who believed that this amounted to an inner conviction of the
truth of Roman Catholicism did not begin to understand his
psychology. When in August 1633 he was given to understand
that he might hope to be a cardinal if he became a Roman
Catholic, he replied that 'somewhat dwelt within me, which
would not suffer [allow] that, till Rome were other than it is.'
His Catholicism was purely English. It was a reaction against a
long experience of the general acceptance of disorder in English churches. When in Gloucester Cathedral he had moved
the Communion table to the east end and put a rail around it,
his bishop had sworn never to set foot in the cathedral again.
During the trial of one of his opponents who accused him of
superstition (William Prynne), Laud flashed out: ' 'Tis superstition nowadays for any man to come with more reverence into
a church than a tinker and his bitch come into an ale-house.'
He had grown embittered by the contempt in which most men
held his own clerical profession. It was a contempt which, he
had to admit, often seemed to be justified. Several of the
bishops appointed by James I showed little evidence of theological or spiritual interests: the convivial poet, Corbett, for
example. One of the richest deans, Newton of Durham, was not
ordained and never saw his cathedral. But Laud hated all this
sordid confusion. Against it, his task was to wield his commission from the King and a bishop's Christ-given authority.

When at last he was appointed Archbishop of Canterbury in 1633, he wrote to Strafford: 'They which have gotten so much power in and over the Church will not let go their hold.' For a moment he was dismayed by the size of the task. But in alliance with a king far more reliable than James he showed himself determined to continue and complete Richard Bancroft's efficient, if narrow, policies. He, too, codified the Church's law, although to enact new canons he had to wait until 1640 (when the clergy could be summoned to meet in Convocation along-side Parliament). He imitated Bancroft's example of devotion to discipline and kept up pressure on other bishops to imitate him. He made full use of Bancroft's instrument, the High Commission, and above all of the older court of Star Chamber, to impose fines and other penalties on those who resisted. From his king he received stronger support than Bancroft had enjoyed; in 1638 Charles plainly told the judges to attempt no interference in the working of the ecclesiastical courts without the Archbishop's licence. Laud pursued Bancroft's policy of attempting to extract proper incomes for the clergy out of the laity, meanwhile defying any squire who attempted to cheat his parson. He secured the suppression of a group of London Puritans (the 'Feoffees for Impropriations') who were found to be buying up the rector's tithes in parishes and using them for the benefit of their favoured ministers; and he did his utmost to end the Puritan patronage of 'lecturers' in the parishes by insisting on the rights of bishops. No man was to be ordained merely to be a lecturer, and no existing clergyman was to become or remain one without the bishop's licence.

Such a reassertion of a bishop's authority caused widespread alarm among Puritans who under George Abbot had forgotten what it felt like to be harried. No more than Bancroft did Laud suspend large numbers of clergy from their duties because of their nonconformity; there were fewer than a hundred such cases in the whole of England during his time as archbishop. Nor was Laud exceptionally savage in voting for the physical mutilation of the authorities' boldest critics. Although we are shocked that he could record complacently in his diary the whipping, ear-cropping, nose-slitting and ten-year imprison-ment of a fellow theologian, Dr Alexander Leighton, who had written a book against the bishops, it is fair to remember that the Puritans were to show themselves stern censors and executioners when in power.

Laud, despite his enemies' propaganda, did not admire tyranny. Indeed, he once told Lord Saye and Sele that 'my very soul abominates' Calvinism – 'for it makes God, the God of all mercy, to be the most fierce and unreasonable tyrant in the world.' However, he certainly made many enemies. The clamour of the 1640s for the removal of the bishops and their whole system, 'root and branch', showed how deeply the Puritans had become alarmed by the activities of this meddlesome archbishop and of fellow Arminians such as Richard Neile (successively at Lincoln, Durham, Winchester and York) or Matthew Wren (who followed Francis White, also an Arminian, both at Norwich and at Ely). As early as 1625 Laud had drawn up a list of the prominent clergy for the Duke of Buckingham, branding his enemies 'P' for Puritan and his friends 'O' for 'Orthodox' – as if Calvinism had not been the Church of England's orthodoxy ever since Elizabeth's day. Now many preachers were afraid that 'true religion' would soon be banished from Laud's church.

Their alarm was shared by many gentlemen (including some MPs who were to take the King's side in the civil war). They feared that the claims of the clergy for more tithes, if supported by the King, might at length lead to some action being taken at the expense of the laity – a prospect which everyone thought had been banished for ever at the time of the Reformation. There seemed to be a threat to many lay possessions in the movement of opinion expressed by one Norfolk squire, Sir Henry Spelman, who on religious grounds publicly attacked the possession of tithes by laymen – and who was compiling an unpublishable book showing the fates of laymen who had taken over the ownership of lands rightly belonging to the monasteries. It seemed ominous that Laud sided against the gentry, in favour of the common people, in several local disputes brought before one of the royal courts or commissions on which he sat. He thought it the noblest part of the work of the King's council to defend the people against the 'private ends' of rich men; and when he was taken from Lambeth

Palace to prison in March 1641, after his impeachment by the Commons for high treason, his diary recorded his pride that 'hundreds of my poor neighbours stood there and prayed for my safety.' Thus he encouraged the gentry to fear that Church and King were lining up against them.[18]

As his power and ambition increased, Laud sent many agents to hold visitations on his behalf – even in Lincoln Cathedral, despite legal action by Bishop Williams. He took almost as keen an interest in the ecclesiastical affairs of the province of York, of Scotland and of Ireland, as in his own province of Canterbury. He made what efforts he could to curb the religious deviations of the English settlers in the Netherlands or America. And especially after the Earl of Portland's death in 1635, Laud's influence also penetrated many political affairs; he once claimed that 'a bishop may preach the Gospel more publicly and to far greater edification in a court of judicature, or at a council-table, where great men are met together to draw things to an issue, than many preachers . . .' He used this pulpit. More than anyone else he seems to have inspired the flow of detailed orders to magistrates about the relief of the poor and other local duties. The climax of his influence came in 1636, when at his suggestion the King appointed Bishop Juxon of London as Lord Treasurer. The clear implication was that only a clergyman would be sufficiently honest. 'No churchman had it since Henry VIII's time,' Laud wrote in his diary. 'I pray God to bless him to carry it so that the Church may have honour and the King and the State contentment by it. And now if the Church will not hold up themselves under God, I can do no more.'

All these activities, wise or foolish, sprang not only out of personal ambition but also out of a genuine love of the Church of England. While he was Bishop of London Laud achieved the restoration of St Paul's Cathedral, where the spire had been destroyed by lightning in 1561 and where the fabric had been visibly decaying for centuries; and to the repaired Gothic cathedral was added a giant classical portico by Inigo Jones, the gift of the King. While Archbishop of Canterbury Laud led

---

[18] See Christopher Hill, *Economic Problems of the Church*, pp. 245–447.

a campaign to get the surplice worn decently as the clerical uniform; to get the holy table fenced off and reverenced as a sacred altar; to get men's heads bowed humbly at the name of Jesus. When he was brought to trial in 1644 after three years in prison, he defended his record with such dignity and acuteness that the impeachment for treason had to be dropped and a simple Bill of Attainder introduced. When he was about to be executed in January 1645, he repeated the essence of his self-defence: 'I was born and baptized in the bosom of the Church of England established by law. In that profession I have lived; and in that I come now to die.' At greater leisure he had held up his proud vision of his Church during his learned argument with the Jesuit Fisher in 1622. 'To believe the Scripture and the Creeds, to believe these in the sense of the ancient primitive Church, to receive the four great General Councils, to believe all points of doctrine generally received as fundamental in the Church of Christ, is a faith in which to live and die cannot but give salvation.' Basically this pride in the Church of England was what was puzzling about William Laud. It would have been puzzling and alarming to many, even if he had taken more trouble to conciliate those who disliked his autocratic manner.

'We begin to live here in the Church Triumphant', wrote James Howell in 1635. Next summer the King visited Oxford, partly to see the newly completed Canterbury Quadrangle in St John's College where Laud had been President. If Laud had been capable of enjoyment, he would have enjoyed this festivity at the peak of his power. As it was, he confided to his diary his pleasure that after the feast which he had provided for the court only two spoons had disappeared.[19]

What judgement is fair on these bishops?

In Bancroft and Laud the Church of England possessed administrators who worked tirelessly for its welfare, narrowly conceived; yet their policy was not in the Church's long-term interests. They were so proudly allied with the monarchy, and

---

[19] See H. R. Trevor-Roper, *Archbishop Laud* (with a new Preface, London, 1962), and E. C. E. Bourne's case for the defence, *The Anglicanism of William Laud* (London, 1947).

so provocatively full of the sense of a bishop's power, as to arouse hatred. Their activism, their insistence on uniformity, increased the likelihood that both kings and bishops would be pulled down by the vengeance of the Puritans whom they had alienated. The pity was that among the bishops only Bancroft and Laud were major figures who combined firm ambitions for the Church along with the royal favour. In Lancelot Andrewes the Church of England possessed a theologian greater in intellectual and spiritual stature than any of the archbishops – but he was incapable of working out a policy, for he depended on the corrupting James.

None of these bishops can by himself explain why the Church of England now commanded the devotion of its members to an extent not seen under Elizabeth I. To learn why, we must turn to three great poets.

JOHN DONNE

John Donne, Dean of St Paul's, wept while he preached in memory of Magdalen, Lady Danvers, one Sunday in 1627. She had been his friend for more than twenty years and by her first marriage was the mother of his fellow poet, George Herbert. That sermon's themes were to remain at the centre of all that he said until he preached the morbidly magnificent 'Death's Duel' shortly before his own death. He spoke of her devout life: she had said Morning and Evening Prayer daily with her family; and of her death-bed, 'as quiet as her grave'; and of her lovely body: 'that body which now, whilst I speak, is mouldering and crumbling into less and less dust, and so hath some motion, though no life'; and of her resurrection: 'that body at last shall have her last expectation satisfied, and dwell bodily, with that Righteousness, in these new Heavens and new Earth, for ever, and ever, and ever, and infinite, and super-infinite evers.'

Death is the theme which always makes Donne the preacher live. For much of the time, a twentieth-century reader can study his sermons without finding them powerful. Many of these words are Latin; clearly the Vulgate Bible in Latin is the version which has formed the preacher's mind. The theology or morality being conveyed, although with touches of Calvinism as in its insistence on God's choice of the elect, often seems to be essentially medieval, and behind the Middle Ages lie the Fathers such as Augustine or Tertullian, here imitated both in substance and in style. His friend Henry King, later Bishop of Chichester, recalled how Donne 'three days before his death delivered into my hands those excellent sermons of his now made public . . . together with which (as his best legacy) he gave me all his sermon-notes, and his other papers, containing an extract of near fifteen hundred authors.' In those discourses – so arduously prepared by a week's work, learned by heart so as to be delivered not read, and polished up further for the printer – the biblical text was expounded in a tradition which had been thought appropriate when addressing well-educated Englishmen over a thousand years.

Inevitably a modern public has altered in its expectations of a sermon and in its powers of endurance, but Donne's sermons still come alive when they approach death, 'the most inglorious and contemptible vilification, the most deadly and peremptory nullification of man, that we can consider.' He kept his hearers awake by images as alarming as the plague which often surrounded them in London. 'The Holy Ghost', he maintained, 'is an eloquent author, a vehement and an abundant author, but yet not luxuriant'; and that was his own style as he tolled the bell for those who, like himself, were about to die. 'All our life is but a going out to the place of execution, to death', he once pointed out. 'Now was there ever any man seen to sleep in the cart . . .?'

It is strange that Donne's style should have been called 'metaphysical'. Samuel Johnson popularized the description in the eighteenth century, but it surely ought to have been abandoned by later critics who have been, on the whole, more enthusiastic. Intellectual Donne always was. He despised the escapism of previous English poets (such as Spenser) into the ordered prettiness of a dream world. He always preferred to stimulate thought by hinting at the logic in some extraordinary association of images drawn from daily life (he wrote a poem about the flea crawling on his mistress). As has been observed, in true metaphysical poetry 'the intellectual parallel, or the recondite image, expresses awareness of a world in which the separate and apparently unrelated parts strangely echo one another.'[20] And Donne as he made these associations was often 'witty', pouring out paradoxes which combine the colloquial with the florid, the familiar with the audacious, the passionate with the learned. In his solemn 'Hymn to God the Father', set to music and often sung as an anthem in St Paul's Cathedral in his presence, he met his God with a pun ('thou hast done'). But he was never 'metaphysical' in the sense of being superior to physical reality. The great Samuel Johnson (who believed that genuine 'intercourse between God and the human soul' could not be the material of poetry) was completely wrong to say of the 'metaphysical poets' that 'to show their learning was their whole endeavour'. Answering the charge that he was always simply an egotist, Dame Helen Gardner has rightly claimed that 'the feeling that the subject is greater than the treatment, and the poem more important than the poet, goes well with the religious sense of the importance of the given'; and answering the charge that he was too intellectual, T. S. Eliot made his famous observation that 'a thought to Donne was an experience; it modified his sensibility.'[21]

In Donne's poetry, as in all 'metaphysical' poetry, three essential paradoxes are always present – the poet is acutely self-conscious, yet the poem does matter more; the poet is witty, yet never remote from important reality (Donne wrote of 'the feeling brain and the naked thinking heart'); the tone is conversational, but the imagery is unconventional because a strenuous effort is being made to experience and to communicate a new revelation of reality. It is, indeed, clear that Donne felt that writing poetry was like making love. He believed in love's disclosure of eternity:

> Love, all alike, no season knows, nor clime,
> Nor hours, days, months, which are the rags of time.

---

[20] Joan Bennett, *Five Metaphysical Poets* (Cambridge, 1964), p. 76.
[21] Helen Gardner, *Religion and Literature* (London, 1971), p. 193; T. S. Eliot, *Selected Essays*, pp. 281–91.

But love must take flesh:

> Love's mysteries in souls do grow,
> But yet the body is his book.

For such a man, although he wrote much about souls, complete joy could never be disembodied. The actual body which the worms have eaten, leaving behind only dust, must be raised. When he prepares for his own death, he compares with map-makers the doctors poring over his body; for his present body, which may soon die, is only a feeble representation of the body he will discover when he has died ('A Hymn to God, my God, in my Sickness'). So this preacher of the resurrection can celebrate the final glory of a woman's body with a rapture no less physical than the ecstasy of Jack Donne the erotic poet:

> Licence my roving hands and let them go,
> Before, behind, between, above, below . . .
> To teach thee, I am naked first; why then,
> What need'st thou have more covering than a man?

A vividly imagined resurrection, triumphing over a vividly imagined death 'for super-infinite evers' is what awakens us; and we ask what life had given the preacher such a Gospel.

John Donne (1572–1631) was an Elizabethan man-about-town who became a preacher only in his forties. Through his mother he was descended from a leading Recusant family. Sir Thomas More was his great-grand-uncle, and, when John was only two years old, a grand-uncle had been hanged as a priest. Two of his uncles, both Oxford scholars of great promise, had passed their lives as exiled Jesuits. He had been unable to take a degree because it would have meant taking the oath about the Queen and the Church. His brother Henry had died of fever in prison when he was twenty-four; he had been sheltering a priest. John Donne had all that motivation to master intellectually the whole field in dispute, with results to be seen in his anti-Jesuit book of 1610, *Pseudo-Martyr*. At the end of the book he recalled how 'I have been ever kept awake in a meditation of martyrdom, by being derived from such a stock and race.' His intensely visual imagination always did belong to the same world as the *Spiritual Exercises* of the Jesuits, where the pains of hell and the pleasures of heaven were to be savoured sensually.

The passion with which he turned to experiments with women, and to experiments in verse celebrating his conquests, was keenly felt. Being (as he put it) 'love's martyr' was for him an alternative to the life and death of a Recusant. It was a worldly path; had he been obeying the morality instilled into him as a boy he would have remained a Roman Catholic. Love for him did not mean sighs about a lack of communication with the beloved, as had almost always been the posture of previous poets of love. It meant sex. But he still used his brain. Even when propelled into a girl's bed by simple lust he remained the self-conscious intellectual: his love poetry never portrays the girl but always examines his own experience. And a part of his brain, the part surviving from his boyhood, told him that all this was emptiness. During the very years when he could sincerely write 'I can love both fair and brown', he was seriously struggling to see what was at the top of the mountain obscured by the clouds of religious controversy:

> On a huge hill
> Cragged and steep, Truth stands, and he that will
> Reach her about must, and about must go.

And sexual intercourse could itself be thought about in religious terms:

> We die and rise the same, and prove
> Mysterious by this love.

In the end, he explored sex most fully through a marriage contracted in defiance of the conventions. He sailed as a gentleman-adventurer with Essex and Ralegh in their expeditions of 1596–97 during the war against Spain, and with this proof of his patriotic manliness entered the service of the Lord Keeper, Sir Thomas Egerton. By then he must have conformed to the Church of England. He seemed all set for a rich career when he fell in love with a niece of the wife of Sir Thomas, and married her secretly although she was still a minor. Sir Thomas dismissed him, and thirteen years of poverty followed. Letters and poems survive which show how unheroically he could fawn in his efforts to obtain employment. A book on suicide (not published until 1644) is other evidence of his depression, increased by much illness; 'Whensoever any affliction assails me methinks I have the keys of my prison in mine own hand and no remedy presents itself so soon to my heart as mine own sword.'

These years were, however, not wasted. His suffering gave him a sympathy lacking in the egotistical poems of his youth. His marriage with Ann was an education in fidelity and gave him many consolations: 'We had not one another at so cheap a rate that we should ever be weary of one another,' he reminded her after thirteen years of marriage. It may be said that she converted him to true love, in contrast with the cynicism of some of the early love-poems too closely modelled on the morals as well as the poetry of Romans such as Ovid. And *The Divine Poems* show that this deepening love of a faithful woman helped him to grow in the love of God. J. B. Leishman rightly draws attention to 'a continuous progress in seriousness, and even in devotional religiousness, co-existing, in a manner that many modern readers may find baffling and even, at times, disconcerting, with an unregenerate wit and worldliness and willingness to flatter the great'.[22]

In the damp study of a cottage at Mitcham, surrounded by squalling children, he became one of the most learned theologians of his age. He considered death itself in a learned way: the book on suicide was as scholarly as *Pseudo-Martyr*. When as early as 1607 he was urged by a friend who had just become Dean of Gloucester to become a priest in the Church of England, he refused because he felt unworthy. He knew that his reputation was as the author of poems which were pornographic by the standards of the day: 'some irregularities of my life have been so visible to some men . . .' But in 1612 he wrote to the King's favourite, the Earl of Somerset: 'I have resolved to make my profession divinity.' Three years later he finally was ordained, because he was persuaded by James I; he said so on the epitaph which he composed for his own grave. The King had steadily refused to place him as a civil servant; instead he had made promises about prospects in the Church. As Donne

---

[22] J. B. Leishman, *The Monarch of Wit* (London, 1951), p. 268.

was later to preach: 'When I asked perchance a stone, he gave me bread; when I asked perchance a scorpion, he gave me a fish.'

When in the pulpit he denounced sins he knew what he was talking about, and most members of the congregation knew that he knew. When he preached at court he addressed men who relished – or knew of – the witty gusto of his love poems, passed from hand to hand in manuscript. When he addressed the lawyers of Lincoln's Inn, as he did almost every week in the period 1616–21, he spoke to men some of whom had enjoyed the 1590s with him. 'Forgive me my crying sins, and my whispering sins,' he once pleaded in the pulpit, 'sins of uncharitable hate, and sins of unchaste love.' He valued preaching because it enabled him to communicate the Gospel of forgiveness to others. 'What a coronation is our taking of orders,' he said, 'and what an inthronization is the coming up into a pulpit, where God invests his servants with his ordinance . . . *woe be unto thee if thou do not preach*, and then enables him to preach peace, mercy, consolation, to the whole congregation!' But his prayer was all the more infectious for being still frankly a penitent's, even an amateur's, prayer: 'a memory of yesterday's pleasures, a fear of tomorrow's dangers, a straw under my knee, a noise in mine ear, a light in mine eye, an anything, a nothing, a fancy, a Chimera in my brain, troubles my prayer.' His faith was all the more touching because, as he confessed in his 'Hymn to God the Father' (written when he had nearly died of fever),

> I have a sin of fear, that when I have spun
> My last thread, I shall perish on the shore.

He knew how to preach to fellow sinners from the brink of eternity, from the presence of the holy and immortal God; 'all knowledge that begins not and ends not with his glory is but a giddy, but a vertiginous circle, but an elaborate and exquisite ignorance.' But the sense of sinful egotism, of sensual frailty, of guilt (in, for example, the *Devotions* which he wrote during a convalescence) went so deep that he knew that for himself the coming of God into a human life must be as physical as sex:

> Batter my heart, three-person'd God; for you
> As yet but knock, breathe, shine and seek to mend;

That I may rise, and stand, o'erthrow me, and bend
Your force, to break, blow, burn and make me new . . .
Take me to you, imprison me, for I
Except you enthrall me, never shall be free,
Nor ever chaste, except you ravish me.

What finally turned his mind to God was, it seems, not his ordination in 1615 but the death of his wife two years later. He grieved so intensely that he seemed 'crucified'. She was aged thirty-three and she died of exhaustion, a week after giving birth to her twelfth child, still-born. He drew the conclusion not that it had been wrong to inflict so many pregnancies on her but that it was always foolish to hope that any earthly happiness could be more than fleeting. Her death was the price he had to pay for the granting of his prayer:

I turn my back to thee, but to receive
Corrections, till thy mercies bid thee leave.
O think me worth thine anger, punish me,
Burn off my rusts, and my deformity,
Restore thine image, so much, by thy grace,
That thou may'st know me, and I'll turn my face.

It was only when he had fully turned his face to God after burying Ann that he saw the true pattern of his previous life. He was never totally ashamed of that life; he kept a portrait of himself as a melancholy young lover in his Deanery and bequeathed it to a friend in his will. For his whole life, he now saw, had been God's wooing of him. His days had not been destitute of achievement – and, as he once declaimed, 'to have something to do, to do it, and then to rejoice in having done it, to embrace a calling, to perform the duties of that calling, to joy and rest in the peaceful testimony of having done so; this is Christianly done, Christ did it; angelically done, angels do it; godly done, God does it.' But his real achievement had been to gain his convictions about the 'providence and goodness' of God and the resurrection to come. So he assured a friend shortly before his death, adding: 'I am therefore full of inexpressible joy and shall die in peace.'

All that discovery had to be made before John Donne could stand in the pulpit of St Paul's Cathedral on the evening of

Christmas Day 1624 and speak about a monarch more bounti-
ful than James VI of Scotland and I of England. 'If some king
of the earth have so large an extent of dominion, in north and
south, as that he hath winter and summer together in his
dominions, so large an extent east and west as that he hath day
and night together in his dominions, much more hath God
joined mercy and judgement together. He brought light of
darkness, not out of a lesser light; he can bring thy summer out
of winter though thou have no spring. Though in the ways of
fortune, or understanding, or conscience, thou have been
benighted till now, wintered and frozen, clouded and eclipsed,
damped and benumbed, smothered and stupefied till now,
now God comes to thee, not as in the dawning of the day, not as
in the bud of spring, but as the sun at noon to illustrate all
shadows, as the sheaves in harvest to fill all penuries. All
occasions invite his mercies, and all times are his seasons.'[23]

GEORGE HERBERT

Donne sent a copy of his personal seal with a poem to George
Herbert; and the other poet, then twenty years his junior,
repaid the compliment with three Latin epigrams. It is, however, clear that Herbert's own poetry was deeply indebted to
Donne and that their friendship went far deeper than this, their
only recorded exchange. We know that they were fellow guests
in a Chelsea house in 1625, when George Herbert was staying
with his mother and John Donne was escaping from the
plague.

In many ways Herbert resembled Donne. He remembered
his ambition for an active life:

---

[23] R. C. Bald assembled the facts in *John Donne : A Life* (Oxford, 1970). *John Donne: Essays in Celebration*, ed. A. J. Smith (London, 1972), and John Carey, *John Donne: Life, Mind and Art* (London, 1981), are the best of the voluminous criticism, although Professor Carey fails to prove his case that Donne's preaching was 'resolute self-deception'.

> Whereas my birth and spirit rather took
> > The way that takes the town,
> Thou didst betray me to a ling'ring book,
> > And wrap me in a gown.

'The Pearl' recalls at greater length the lures of the ways of learning, honour and pleasure; and like Donne, Herbert could use his learning to flatter King James. The two men's hesitations over a priest's life were also similar:

> Now I am here, what thou wilt do with me
> None of my books will show.

And in the end Herbert used the same 'witty' style in devotion to the Christ of Easter:

> Awake, my lute, and struggle for thy part
> > With all thy art:
> The cross taught all wood to resound his name
> > Who bore the same;
> His stretched sinews taught all strings what key
> Is best to celebrate this most high day.

But Herbert's life and poetry were far more than imitations of Donne. His mother was not a Recusant but a rich and accomplished lady, Donne's patron. Whereas Cambridge took much persuading to award Donne an honorary doctorate despite the King's command, that university delighted to honour George Herbert, who was so outstanding in his classical scholarship that he was appointed to lecture on the classics and to compose official letters and addresses as Public Orator. In contrast with Donne's notoriety as a poet of profligacy, Herbert from an early age accepted his devout mother's guidance. He sent two sonnets to her avowing his dedication to sacred poetry while he was an undergraduate; as early as 1618 he described theology as 'the platform of my future life'; and he made a respectable match for Jane, the daughter of a proud Wiltshire family, when he was aged thirty-six. In the second half of the 1620s Herbert ceased to live in Cambridge, and, like Donne before 1615, nursed hopes of employment in the service of the State; but being so well connected, he did not need to stoop to Donne's level by begging for favour or money. In 1624 he was a Member of Parliament. The decisive question of Donne's life concerned the nature of love, and when he married he did not hesitate to throw away ambition for love. In contrast, the struggle for Herbert was against ambition, and it was the slow conquest of ambition that was the making of him as a saint and as a poet. He became famous because he renounced fame.

It shows the difference between the two men that Herbert was eventually willing to embrace the life of a country parson – whereas Donne, while drawing the incomes of rectories in Kent and Bedfordshire, went on living in or near London with no qualms of conscience. Once Herbert had made his great decision he adopted a preaching style much simpler than Donne's, without any allusion to the learning of his Cambridge years (or so we are told – no sermons by him have survived). He became every inch the priest, the mediator between God and the parish, the devoted pastor who reminded his people of man's calling to be 'the world's high priest'.

With the difference in the characters and the sermons of the two men went a difference as poets. It is not that Herbert was really as spontaneous as he can appear. A manuscript discovered in 1874 shows his poetry growing and being revised, the process almost certainly beginning well before his ordination. The real difference in the two men's art was that Herbert was a natural believer, while Donne was a natural sceptic. It is because Herbert has the supreme capacity to articulate faith that the editor of an anthology such as *The New Oxford Book of Christian Verse* (1981) finds himself testing poems by this question: 'Does it deserve to appear between the same covers as Herbert's "The Collar" or his "Church-monuments"?'

In Herbert's poems of struggle the lament is not for the loss of faith but for the temporary loss of religious emotion due to worldliness:

> But as I rav'd and grew more fierce and wild
>> At every word,
> Methoughts I heard one calling, *Child!*
> And I replied, *My Lord.*

The acceptance of 'my Lord' is ultimately inevitable because his invitation was understood long ago. Herbert's life was in the poem given the place of honour at the end of *The Temple*:

> Love made me welcome; yet my soul drew back,
>   Guilty of dust and sin.
> But quick-ey'd Love, observing me grow slack
>   From my first entrance in,
> Drew near to me, sweetly questioning
>   If I lack'd anything . . .

With all Herbert's delight in beauty went a religious hunger which nothing in this world could satisfy:

> Sweet spring, full of sweet days and roses,
> A box where sweets compacted lie;
> My music shows ye have your closes,
>   And all must die.

> Only a sweet and virtuous soul,
> Like season'd timber, never gives;
> But though the whole world turn to coal,
>   Then chiefly lives.

The joy found in his life and celebrated in his poems finds a very clear centre in the person of Christ, as in his long poem 'The Sacrifice'. It was his habit to speak of 'Jesus my Master'. And this joy provides the 'elixir' which redeems the most obscure drudgery:

> Who sweeps a room as for thy laws
> Makes that and th' action fine.

It makes the Church 'shout' with psalms and makes the poet forget any 'tempests' so effectively that we do not know exactly why he waited until 1630 before becoming a priest:

> And now in age I bud again,
> After so many deaths I live and write;
>   I once more smell the dew and rain,
> And relish versing: O, my only Light,
>   It cannot be
>   That I am he
> On whom thy tempests fell all night.

Herbert was a parish priest for less than three years. He did not live in poverty; his will showed that he employed six domestic servants and two assistant curates. But before his death in 1633 he found time to add to, and revise, *The Temple*; to repair his church and rectory; to educate three orphaned nieces in his home; to overcome various illnesses; and to befriend his three hundred parishioners. His energy also led him to write notes about the duties of a country parson, it seems mainly in order to bring into focus his meditations about his duties. This little book published in 1652 as *A Priest to the Temple*. 'A pastor,' it began, 'is the deputy of Christ for the reducing of man to the obedience of God'; indeed, 'the country parson is in God's stead to his parish.' 'The country parson is exceeding exact in his life, being holy . . .'; indeed, 'the country parson's library is a holy life.' But the pastor must commend his authority by a holiness which country folk can understand, 'because country people live hardly, and therefore as feeling their own sweat.' So the priest needs temperance, prayerfulness, humility, hospitality and courtesy. And his charity must be practical: 'the country parson desires to be all to his parish, not only a pastor but a lawyer also, and a physician.' It was a revolutionary vision of the work of a country priest – work which all through English history had not been thought fit for a gentleman. The little book was, as he said, only 'a mark to aim at'; but it encouraged many others to have the same aim.

In real life Herbert was by no means the Laudian portrayed by Izaak Walton when he published a short *Life* of him in 1670. His patron was Laud's rival, John Williams, and he never fell out with his own brother Edward (Lord Herbert of Cherbury), who was definitely unorthodox in his religious thought. When examining *The Temple*, the Vice-Chancellor of Cambridge was startled to find how enthusiastic about the Puritan migration to America Herbert had remained despite his disappointment over the first colony in Virginia:

> Religion stands on tip-toe in our land,
> Ready to pass to the American strand.

But Herbert was certainly as devoted to the Church of England as ever Laud was. To him it was 'the mean' between the 'painted shrines' of Rome and the disorder of Protestantism:

> But, dearest Mother, what those miss,
> The mean, thy praise and glory is,
>   And long may be.

Blessed be God, whose love it was
To double-moat thee with his grace,
    And none but thee.

In two of his most famous poems, he recorded what he felt
when at worship in the Church of England:

Church-bells beyond the stars heard, the soul's blood,
The land of spices; something understood.

Come, my Way, my Truth, my Life . . .
Come, my Light, my Feast, my Strength . . .
Come, my Joy, my Love, my Heart. . . .[24]

One of his closest friends, Nicholas Ferrar, had George Herbert's poems prepared for publication in his manor house at
Little Gidding near Cambridge. Ferrar was disappointed over
the Virginian colony, in which he had invested heavily. At
Little Gidding a mixed community of men and women, his
family and friends, lived somewhat like a monastery (the
'Arminian nunnery' was how it was denounced in a Puritan
pamphlet) – reciting the whole Psalter once a day in hourly
services to which different groups came, praying also through
the night, practising crafts, visiting the sick and the poor.
Ferrar died in 1637 and the community was dissolved in 1646.
It was a curious experiment. Ferrar was a deacon not a priest,
so that the Eucharist was never at the centre of this community's life; and it was too dependent on his wealth. But Little
Gidding had brought the monastic ideal back to the Church of
England, just as George Herbert's own experiment at
Bremerton had brought back the highest idealism of the parish
priest.[25]

---

[24] Studies include Rosemond Tuve, *A Reading of George Herbert* (London, 1952);
Margaret Bottrall, *George Herbert* (London, 1954); Joseph H. Summers, *George
Herbert: His Religion and His Art* (London, 1954); Helen Verdler, *The Poetry of George
Herbert* (Cambridge, Mass., 1975); Amy M. Charles, *A Life of George Herbert* (Ithaca,
N.Y., 1977); Kenneth Mason, *George Herbert, Priest and Poet* (Oxford, 1980).

[25] See A. L. Maycock, *Nicholas Ferrar of Little Gidding* (London, 1938); *The Ferrar
Papers*, ed. B. Blackstone (Cambridge, 1938); *Conversations at Little Gidding*, ed. A. M.
Williams (Cambridge, 1970).

HENRY VAUGHAN

Henry Vaughan paid George Herbert the tribute of very close imitation – in technique, in images, in direct quotations, even in his titles. In his Preface to the second part of *Silex Scintillans*, dated 1654, he paid him another tribute by writing about the stream of 'idle or sensual' poems produced by worldly 'wits' and adding this: 'the first that with any effectual success attempted a diversion of this foul and overflowing stream was the blessed man, Mr George Herbert, whose holy life and verse gained many pious converts (of whom I am the least).'

What Vaughan seems to mean is that Herbert's poetry helped him to see that his own direct apprehension of God in the beauty of nature could be connected with traditional Christianity. He was not always orthodox; he was influenced by the seventeenth-century revival of interest in the ancient 'Hermetic' books with their occult lore. Fascinated by the promise of the transformation of matter through alchemy, and by the prospect of the deification of man through the knowledge of God, both he and his twin brother Thomas (a clergyman) wrote or translated books in this esoteric tradition. But he also developed the ability to be conventionally devout like Herbert. His mysticism was in the end not 'nature-mysticism', meaning pantheism; it was the discovery of the Church's God. Indeed, the great poetry about nature arose simultaneously with the experience of a conversion to a full Christian faith – and died down as the excitement of the religious conversion faded. Vaughan seems to have found a quiet happiness by work as a translator 'in his sickness and retirement' and by practising as a country doctor, but his poetic silence from the enlarged *Silex Scintillans* in 1655 to his death in 1695 was broken only by one not very impressive book, in 1678.

We know very little for certain about the decisive years of his life, but in 1673 he told John Aubrey that his ambitions as a student of law in London had been 'wholly frustrated' by the 'sudden eruption' of the civil war. It seems that his health was damaged by his service in the Royalist army. He saw friends killed and their cause defeated, and about 1645 he crept back to the very lovely and remote valley of the Usk in Breconshire where he had been a boy and where his father was still a small landowner. There, in 1646–47, he prepared two volumes of inferior verse, feebly imitating Donne. In 1648 he was grief-stricken by a brother's death.

All this heartbreak was his making as a great poet. It caused him to cry when not yet thirty years of age:

> They are all gone into the world of light!
>   And I alone sit ling'ring here . . .
> I see them walking in an air of glory,
>   Whose light doth trample on my days:
> My days, which are at best but dull and hoary,
>   Mere glimmering and decays . . .
>
> Dear, beauteous death! the Jewel of the Just,
>   Shining nowhere, but in the dark . . .

But as the 1640s turned into the 1650s he gained the sense that the dead were, after all, alive and near:

> But these all night,
> Like candles, shed
> Their beams and light
> Us into bed.
> They are – indeed – our pillar fires
>   Seen as we go;
> They are that City's shining spires
>   We travel to.

Above all, he gained the sense that God was alive and near. The return of spring in the familiar valley brought back memories of the blessedness of childhood, but also hinted at a future with 'bright shoots of everlastingness'. In his 'Regeneration' he was another young Moses, awestruck by the burning bush:

> The unthrift sun shot vital gold,
>   A thousand pieces;
> And heaven its azure did unfold
>   Chequer'd with snowy fleeces;
> The air was all in spice,
>   And every bush
> A garland wore; thus fed my eyes,
>   But all the ear lay hush.

After all his misery he had found the God worshipped by nature:

> O joys! infinite sweetness! with what flowers,
> And shoots of glory, my soul breaks, and buds! . . .
>> The rising winds,
>> And falling springs,
>> Birds, beasts, all things
> Adore him in their kinds.
>> Thus all is hurl'd
> In sacred hymns and order, the great chime
> And symphony of nature. Prayer is
>> The world in tune . . .

This is the God in whom is 'a deep but dazzling darkness', the God who is great beyond all human imagination:

> I saw Eternity the other night,
> Like a great Ring of pure and endless light,
>> And calm, as it was bright;
> And round beneath it, Time, in hours, days, years,
>> Driven by the spheres,
> Like a vast shadow moved; in which the world
> And all her train were hurl'd . . .

But this God is also the God of the Bible, the God of the Church, the God who saves men who need salvation, the God who in the poem just quoted offers another ring, the bridegroom's ring for his bride. He is the God who comes in Christ:

> He is thy gracious friend
>> And (O my soul awake!)
> Did in pure love descend
>> To die here for thy sake.
> If thou canst get but thither,
>> There grows the flower of peace,
> The rose that cannot wither,
>> Thy fortress, and thy ease.
> Leave then thy foolish ranges;
>> For none can thee secure,
> But One who never changes,
>> Thy God, thy life, thy cure.[26]

---

[26] Studies include E. C. Pettet, *Of Paradise and Light* (Cambridge, 1960); R. A. Durr, *On the Mystical Poetry of Henry Vaughan* (Cambridge, Mass., 1962); F. E. Hutchinson, *Henry Vaughan: A Life and Interpretation* (revised, Oxford, 1971).

CHAPTER SEVEN

THE COUNTER-REFORMATION

TWO ENGLISHMEN AND ROME

Many Englishmen could not feel that the Church of England was a fully satisfactory home for the new vitality of Christian faith and dedication in the first half of the seventeenth century. The Church depended too obviously on the personal whims of the Stuart kings, as in the previous half-century it had depended on the personality of Elizabeth I. That, as we have seen, was the fatal defect in the teaching and the work of its ablest bishops. The Established Church did not attract enough idealists to match the heroism of Recusants and Puritans. Even Donne and Herbert were slow to respond. It did not offer a clear creed or a strong discipline, despite royal proclamations ordering strict adherence to the Prayer Book and the 'literal' acceptance of the Thirty-Nine Articles. While its leaders disagreed quietly or openly about the precise mixture of Catholicism and Calvinism that might be held by theologians, its laity often went their own ways. It was a sign of lay laxity that in the middle of the 1650s Henry Vaughan married his deceased wife's sister, contrary to the Church's rules. In an age of ardent faith the Church of England often seemed out of place. It gave a dismaying impression of being a ramshackle department of the State, riddled with abuses, incoherent in its spiritual life, unable to command men's deepest loyalties despite the Laudian rally and the raptures of Donne, Herbert and Vaughan.

Two lives help to show the appeal of the Roman Catholic Counter-Reformation.

When made Bishop of Gloucester at the age of forty-three, Godfrey Goodman hoped for promotion to a wealthier see and when such a see presented itself in the shape of Hereford in 1633 he was so confident that he had secured it that he packed his furniture – only to have to unpack. To his friends he now 'showed his discontentment'. In 1636 he got in touch with Panzani the papal agent to the royal court, who reported to Rome: 'The Bishop of Gloucester . . . says the Divine Office according to the Roman Breviary and reads the Martyrology daily . . . He wanted to have an Italian priest in his house, who would be prepared to live with him *incognito* . . .' But the authorities in Rome were cautious, since Goodman was not willing to abandon his bishopric. To a friend at this time he said that 'the religion of England is more remiss than that of Rome, but Catholic it is'. He refused to subscribe to Laud's new canons, presumably because they included an attack on the 'gross superstition of Popery', but his temporary imprisonment for this offence did not save him from being impeached for treason together with the other bishops. He spent much of 1642 in the Tower near Laud's cell – although they never spoke. On his release he fled, like John Williams, back to his native Wales. The manuscript of the *Church History* which was to have been his *magnum opus* was destroyed in the pillaging of his home. At length he grew intolerably bored and in 1652 removed himself to a house in the churchyard of St Margaret's, Westminster, where he was to be buried. Although he had been forced to sell most of his books 'to buy bread', before his death in 1656 he was able to write, and to get published, a defence of Christian orthodoxy.

The confusion of his life was not completely cleared up by his will. He could not make a simple announcement that he died a Roman Catholic. He declared instead that he died, as he had lived, believing 'all the doctrine of God's Holy Catholic and Apostolic Church, whereof I do acknowledge the Church of Rome to be the Mother Church; and I do verily believe that no other Church hath any salvation in it, but only so far as it concurs with the faith of the Church of Rome.'[1]

It is in a few poems of Richard Crashaw that we can see most vividly what the Counter-Reformation had to contribute to the spiritual life of England. This poet was the son of a London clergyman who was a strong Puritan, and it was presumably in

---

[1] Geoffrey Soden provided a biography of *Godfrey Goodman* (London, 1953).

his father's collection of Papist books that the boy came across the religion to which he was to yield his allegiance. For long the young man was satisfied, or at least made do, with the Church of England's version of Catholicism. The two Cambridge colleges where he was a scholar (Pembroke) and a fellow (Peterhouse) were centres of Laudian or Anglo-Catholic piety and learning. In his time two famous high churchmen, Matthew Wren and John Cosin, occupied the post of Master of Peterhouse and busied themselves with Catholicizing the worship and appearance of the college chapel. Crashaw was given charge of Little St Mary's, the parish church adjacent to the college, and in that beautiful shrine would meditate and write poems. Some of these poems were tributes to George Herbert and the Little Gidding community.

So he might have lived out his days. But in 1643, when he was just over thirty years old, Cromwell's troops sacked those Cambridge colleges which they regarded as nurseries of Popish superstition. The priest-poet was convinced that he would never live to see the pleasantness of Anglican devotion restored. He resigned his posts in Cambridge and accepted the Roman Catholic faith which his previous teaching and poetry had only approached. He fled abroad and published his largest collection of poems, *Steps to the Temple* (a deliberate echo of Herbert), partly in order to attract a patron; he was destitute. For a time he was at the exiled Queen's court in Paris, and for a time in attendance on a cardinal in Rome. Finally he was granted a modest position as one of the priests who looked after the pilgrims to the Holy House at Loreto (which was believed to be the Virgin's home, transported by angels from Nazareth). And there after a few months he died, in 1649.

His most original poems show a joyful, even intoxicated, surrender to the spirit of the Counter-Reformation and to all the imagery most characteristic of Baroque architecture and painting. In them as in a Jesuit church in Rome, we are pounded by the restless vigour of the new hunger for faith and holiness, a hunger felt with all the senses; the insistence that because they are so intensely human even saints can sin again and again and be forgiven (two favourite figures are St Peter and St Mary Magdalen); the conviction that penitent saints can be penetrated and deeply ravished by the divine love (the comparison between prayer and sex is very frequent and very elaborate); the praise of heroic commitment and energy in devotion, preaching and charity; the proud delight both in the growing triumph of the one true Church and in the assured glories of heaven. It is a religion of weeping, longing, suffering and fighting. 'Is she a flaming fountain or a weeping fire?' Crashaw asks at one point, and his poetry is full of floods, flames, wounds and swords – until it ends in the blinding splendour of a supernatural light.

Contemplating a picture of St Teresa being pierced by the dart of God's love, Crashaw is excited into an ecstasy in his address to the saint:

> O thou undaunted daughter of desires!
> By all thy dower of lights and fires;
> By all the eagle in thee, all the dove;
> By all thy lives and deaths of love;
> By thy large draughts of intellectual day,
> And by thy thirsts of love more large than they;
> By all thy brim-fill'd bowls of fierce desire,
> By thy last morning's draught of liquid fire;
> By the full kingdom of that final kiss
> That seized thy parting soul, and seal'd thee His ...

And the contemplation of the Nativity arouses a similar, although quieter, passion of wonder:

> Welcome, all wonders in one sight!
>   Eternity shut in a span.
> Summer in winter. Day in night.
>   Heaven in earth, and God in man.
> Great little one! whose all-embracing birth
>   Lifts earth to heaven, stoops heav'n to earth.
>
> To thee, meek majesty! soft King
>   Of simple graces and sweet loves,
> Each of us his lamb will bring,
>   Each his pair of silver doves
> Till burnt at last in fire of thy fair eyes,
>   Our selves become our own best sacrifice.[2]

---

[2] Studies of *Richard Crashaw* include those by Austin Warren and R. C. Wallerstein (London, 1957–59).

AFTER THE
GUNPOWDER PLOT

We have now to ask a prosaic question. Unlike Goodman or Crashaw, most Englishmen could not read books about the great Catholic tradition which had been vibrantly renewed in the Counter-Reformation. For them, what were the chances of discovering and inhabiting this old but new world of the spirit?

At first the death of Elizabeth held out hope to the Recusants. James I wanted, and obtained, peace with Spain. His queen, Anne, had become a Roman Catholic in Scotland during the 1590s and although she was no Crashaw heroine, she gave hints; she always refused to communicate with the Church of England. In 1603 old Sigebert Buckley, formerly a monk of Westminster Abbey, marked the new mood by renewing his religious vows – thus putting himself in a position (or so he claimed) to transmit all the rights of the Benedictines of medieval England to the monks of a new generation. In May 1603 the new mood of leniency began to benefit the laity, whose Recusancy fines were no longer collected, and in the same mood the King restored the earldom of Arundel to young Philip Howard, who had been brought up a strict Recusant, and created another of the Howards Earl of Northampton. In Rome Pope Clement nursed hopes of the King's conversion.

But the mood did not last. During the next winter the government, irritated that the Recusants had not rallied more decisively in gratitude, began enforcing the Elizabethan statutes again. The desperate reply of some Recusants, led by Robert Catesby, was the famous gunpowder plot. Some of them had been involved in Essex's rebellion against Elizabeth and their folly was demonstrated anew when one of them warned his brother-in-law (Lord Mounteagle) to stay away from the formal opening of Parliament on 5 November 1605. During the night of 4–5 November Guy Fawkes, a soldier of fortune from Yorkshire, was found with thirty-six barrels of gunpowder in a cellar beneath the House of Lords.

No gesture by Recusant hotheads could have been better calculated to alienate the King, who was always terrified of assassination (particularly murder by gunpowder, which had killed his father). And no move could have done more to discredit Roman Catholicism in the country at large. Jesuits had been half-heartedly aware of the plot and now paid the price, but it was equally convenient that no aristocrat was even remotely involved apart from the Earl of Northumberland, who was sent to the Tower. Had Fawkes let off his gunpowder, he and the other conspirators would still have found it extremely difficult to produce a monarchy and government to their liking. In the event, all that exploded was public opinion, thrilled by the drama and furious at an attempt which had nearly plunged the country into chaos. When in 1610 the news arrived of the murder of the King of France by a Catholic fanatic, there was a further outburst of English Protestant anger – and of shame among the English Recusants. It was this news from France that finally made Ben Jonson renounce his Roman Catholicism. Year by year Guy Fawkes and his plot were commemorated up and down England by processions, bonfires and anti-Papist oratory; an official service of thanksgiving for the nation's deliverance was authorized for use in churches until 1859. Indeed, the propaganda victory which the plotters handed on a plate to the goverment was so immense that the suggestion has been made that the government must have inspired the whole plot from first to last. No evidence has been produced to prove this interpretation, which seems improbable. It is more likely that some time before the arrest of Guy Fawkes the plot had been betrayed to the government by informers; there were many of these in the ranks of the Recusants (Ben Jonson was one of them). It seems just possible that the warning to Mounteagle was intended by a conspirator as a signal to others that they had been betrayed, although Guy Fawkes was left to his fate.[3]

After this disaster hope eventually revived – but in a way dangerous to any long-term popular revival of Roman Catholicism. For the hope that Recusants would be tolerated was now bound up with the expectation that the government would be forced to make concessions at home in the interests of its policy

---

[3] See Joel Hurstfield's reconstruction in *Early Stuart Studies*, ed. H. S. Reinmuth, pp. 95–121, and B. N. De Luna, *Jonson's Romish Plot* (Oxford, 1967).

of peace with the Catholic powers; and most Englishmen condemned that appeasing policy as unpatriotic. The Recusants who stood to gain by it were distrusted all the more.

In 1612 Henry, Prince of Wales, who had been popularly regarded as a young Elizabethan hero, died unmarried. Six years later Sir Walter Ralegh was executed to appease Spain. For thirteen years from 1613 the King hoped to see his next son and heir, Charles, married to a princess from Spain. For ten years from 1618 the chief minister was the Duke of Buckingham, whose wife, mother and two brothers were all known to be Roman Catholics (although the wife publicly conformed to Anglicanism). This period was ended by the Spaniards' refusal to release their princess and by the murder of Buckingham, but Protestant hostility was further inflamed when Charles did marry a French princess. Bowing to public opinion, the government reneged on the secret clause in the marriage treaty which promised toleration to the English Recusants. The permission to Henrietta Maria to import her own priests who were to officiate in her own chapels could not be withdrawn, however, and Puritans grew frantic when they thought of the Englishmen exposed to the moral danger of the Mass at court. During the first unhappy period of his marriage Charles fully shared his subjects' prejudices.

Although Charles I never deviated from the Church which had crowned and anointed him, there certainly were strong Roman Catholic influences at his court. In the mid-1630s they received a focus in the two papal agents, Gregorio Panzani and George Conn, with whom Bishop Goodman was in touch. Some aristocratic ladies were openly converted, and some prominent ministers – Portland, the Lord Treasurer, for example, or Cottington, the Chancellor of the Exchequer, or Sir Francis Windebank, the joint Secretary of State – were Roman Catholics at heart while not willing to suffer as Recusants. By 1640 almost a quarter of the House of Lords adhered to the old religion. But it was especially among men eminent in the arts that the Counter-Reformation made its appeal. The aesthetic activity which gave immortal beauty to the court of Charles I was steeped in the Catholic culture of Flanders or Italy. This connection was symbolized by the knighthoods conferred on

Rubens and his pupil, Van Dyck, painters who lavished their genius on the royal family, but the biggest *coup* came early: the purchase of the very rich art collection of the Dukes of Mantua. The dominant architect and masque-designer, Inigo Jones, was a Roman Catholic, as was the leading dramatist, James Shirley. John Bull was so indiscreet that he had to leave the Chapel Royal to become the organist of Antwerp Cathedral. As we observe the extent of this invasion by the colour, the elegance and the passionate prayer of the Counter-Reformation then so vigorous in Europe, we cannot wonder that many Puritans were alarmed.[4]

In the country as opposed to the court in this period, the position of the Recusants is hard to determine accurately. A Roman Catholic historian was surely right to suggest that probably 'the most contented and peaceful period which the harassed Catholics were to enjoy between the outbreak of the Elizabethan repression and the last years of the eighteenth century was that space of a generation lasting from the middle of the reign of James I to the outbreak of the civil war in 1642.'[5] And certainly there survive from these years moving examples of the faithfulness of English men and women to the Catholic Church despite all the penalties and temptations.[6] Although he had abandoned them, and had denounced their leaders, John Donne knew these Papists. 'Men and brethren,' he told his congregation in St Paul's in 1629, 'I am a Papist, that is, I will fast and pray as much as any Papist, and enable myself for the service of God as seriously, as sedulously, as laboriously, as any Papist.'

However, despite such heroism it seems probable that in England as a whole the Roman Catholic Church – defined as the community of those who habitually resorted to priests for baptism, confession and the Mass – was not large. An historian who has examined the records with detailed care estimates this community's strength at forty thousand in 1603 and no more than sixty thousand in 1641–42, when there was intense

---

[4] See Gordon Albion, *Charles I and the Court of Rome* (London, 1935).
[5] David Mathew, *Catholicism in England* (revised, London, 1948), p. 77.
[6] Philip Caraman edited an anthology of extracts called *The Years of Siege* (London, 1966).

activity to make a count of Recusants. An earlier historian thought that the number of two hundred thousand in 1641 was well-established and half a million possible. Another earlier estimate was 'about 320,000 to 360,000'.[7] The lowest estimate is probably the most accurate, although the higher figures suggest why there were so many Puritan fears, voiced loudly in the Parliaments of 1625–29, that Papists were everywhere. One indication of the failure of the community to grow on the ground was that priests quite often found themselves condemned either to unemployment or penury. In the 1630s the Jesuits reported to Rome that their priests in England, between a hundred and 180 in number, were each averaging between four and five converts a year. It was not very encouraging.

The Roman Catholic community's growth was so limited because the government's policy was cleverly designed to prevent that growth. There was a combination of severity with indulgence. Under James I and Charles I gentlemen who had priests to stay as guests or permanent lodgers were seldom penalized for it. The number of executions dropped (1607–10, eight; 1611–18, nine; 1619–25, none). In the fifteen years before the recall of Parliament in 1640, not a single Roman Catholic was executed apart from a priest, Edward Arrowsmith, and a labourer, Richard Herst, who suffered in Lancaster before the King's pardon could reach them. Thus the glamour of martyrdom ceased to surround the English mission. On the contrary, there were many temptations to laymen with Catholic hearts but worldly ambitions to conform to the religious establishment. An Earl of Arundel led the way. Such men knew that a compromise would be rewarded by cash in a period when great houses built by the most fortunate, and manor houses rebuilt spaciously by many others, told the tale: local influence still helped the accumulation and legal defence of estates, and influence at court was still the golden key to many lucrative offices and privileges out of which land could be bought, houses raised and families founded.

---

[7] John Bossy, *The English Catholic Community 1570–1850*, pp. 186–8; Bryan Magee, *The English Recusants* (London, 1938), pp. 94–112; M. J. Havran, *The Catholics in Caroline England* (Stanford, Cal., 1962), p. 83.

The evidence suggests that among the gentry the number of compromising 'Church Papists' was considerably larger than the number who stayed at home and, in relative poverty, obeyed the advice of the priests that Catholics must never worship with Protestants. It also seems that many of the Church Papists became as licentious or corrupt as their friends or competitors, so that they were further disinclined to confess their sins to a priest. And even if a gentleman did not go as far as this, he could still obtain exemption from the Recusancy fines at the price of behaviour which would be good in the government's eyes. In the end almost every Roman Catholic in England had to compromise – for the churches or churchyards controlled by the Anglican clergy were the only legal places for burial. The coffin of a Recusant squire would be brought into church silently and the parson would, if co-operative, read the Prayer Book service when the mourners had left. Corpses of lesser status, brought to the churchyard, might not escape greater insults.

But the government's policy was in some ways severe. Recusants wishing to clear their names of treachery had to take the 1606 Oath of Allegiance, renouncing not only the political claims of the papacy but also (in the opinion of many priests) all respect for the Pope. The first half of the oath denied a pope's right to depose a king or 'to authorize any foreign prince to invade or annoy him', and corresponded with many a patriotic Catholic's conscience. But the second half was deliberately offensive, abhorring the doctrine that kings deposed by popes may be 'deposed or murdered' by their subjects as not only 'damnable' but also 'impious and heretical'. The oath was intended to divide Roman Catholics, and it did. George Blackwell, the archpriest of the English mission, took the oath and was promptly deposed. The Pope denounced it and faithful Recusant laity accepted his ruling, however reluctantly. For more than a decade controversy about the Pope and the oath raged; Robert Persons and the great Cardinal Bellarmine wrote on one side, James I, Bishop Lancelot Andrewes and John Donne on the other. And executions of priests continued until 1616, when they were abandoned for the sake of reconciliation with Spain. Recusancy fines remained in theory very severe and could be imposed particularly on people whose economic position was middling, so that they were rich enough to pay without being so rich that they had bought exemptions from the officials.

The most devastating consequence of the government's patronizing attitude – not often making a martyr, but never recognizing the right of Roman Catholics to live in public as patriotic Englishmen – was that the community was demoralized by the absence of known and accepted leadership. The Tudor state had succeeded in deposing, exiling or executing all who traditionally would have been the Catholic authorities. No Englishman exercised the normal jurisdiction of a bishop of the Counter-Reformation until William Bishop in 1623. The arrival of a more formidable bishop, Richard Smith, in 1625, was part of the government's brief agreement to tolerate Henrietta Maria's fellow Catholics. His position was that of 'vicar apostolic' representing Rome and this position was more authoritative than that of the 'archpriests' of earlier years in the English mission, but he was so tactless in asserting a bishop's authority after this long gap that six years later Rome reminded him of where the power was meant to lie by a large curtailment of his jurisdiction. In anger Smith fled to France but refused to resign as England's Catholic bishop; he did not die until 1655. He left behind him a 'chapter' of priests whose authority was denied in Rome. Since no bishop was there to unite them, the Jesuits, the 'religious' and the 'secular' priests conducted bitter arguments in public. When the ecclesiastical leadership was so confused, the real authority was wielded by the nobleman or gentleman in whose house a priest was living – and among whose tenants or dependent neighbours could be found any congregation. It is not surprising that not much teaching or originality or spiritual dignity came from priests who were in effect chaplains liable to dismissal by the squire at a moment's notice. Nor is it surprising that the effect of evangelism was limited when the deployment of the clergy was decided by the availability of a gentleman's house to serve as a base.

A CATHOLIC HOLINESS

Had the Roman Catholic community in England been free to live its own life under its natural leaders, its history would presumably have been both more prosperous and more edifying. What might have been can be seen in an amazing fact: no fewer than five thousand English men or women entered religious houses on the continent during the first forty years of the seventeenth century. For example, the English Franciscan order was revived in a small convent in Douai in 1617. The contrast was very great with the mood of the sixteenth century, where specially in England this religious life had seemed finally overthrown and discredited; writing about 1580, the Recusant poet Robert Southwell had noted that in England, Germany and elsewhere the names of 'monk' and 'scoundrel' had the same meaning for most people. We might have expected English religion to have been changed on a large scale as a result of this large-scale renewal of monastic idealism. Instead, we find that the revival produced only fragmentary teaching, doomed to result either in neglect or in controversy. The English harvest of the Counter-Reformation was disappointing in quality.

The spiritual writer of this period most used by later Roman Catholics was Augustine (born David) Baker. The story of his early life can be pieced together from the autobiographical passages included in a commentary on a medieval treatise on prayer (Walter Hilton's *Cloud of Unknowing*) which he wrote in 1629. It is the story of a young Welsh lawyer who embraced the Roman Catholic faith as a result of his own studies accompanied by his own prayers. He was one of the first recruits made when the Benedictine order was revived in England under James I. Sent to Italy for training as a monk, his prayers became arid, his heart became homesick and he returned home. Back in England he tried again and became a priest. But he was, as he recalled, only a 'tepid' priest, who supported himself by resuming the work of a lawyer in London. It was in 1620 that he finally committed himself to the concentration on lonely mortification and mystical prayer (sometimes for eleven hours in a day) which lasted until his death in 1641. At first he was chaplain to a Recusant family in Devon; then, at last beginning the Benedictine community life, he spent nine years as spiritual director to the new little community of English nuns in Cambrai. Finally he was transferred to a convent in Douai for five years. But by now his health was feeble and his constant stress on mortification had become melancholy; and once again he was unbearably homesick. In 1683 he returned to London, to die of the plague. He left behind many writings about the spiritual life, and a selection from these (itself some five hundred pages long) was published by a disciple, Serenus Cressy, in 1657 under the title *Sancta Sophia*. This book did something to secure for him the audience he had never found before his death.[8]

Another Benedictine monk, John Barnes, was more interested in the age around him. He attempted to build a theological bridge between Catholicism and Protestantism, but was thought to be mad and taken to a Roman prison. The most creative theologian among the English Roman Catholics of this (or the next) century was Thomas White. Not for nothing was he the contemporary of the French genius, René Descartes. As interested in experimental science as in experimental prayer, he saw the need of the Counter-Reformation to modernize its theology to match its devotion. He wrote some forty books, but as 'Blacklaw' and under other pseudonyms. None of them had much effect. Like Augustine Baker after 1638, he found himself leading an independent gentleman's life – and like John Barnes he was thought to be mad by most of his co-religionists if they were aware of his existence. He spent thirty years exiled in Holland, returning to London to die in obscurity in 1676.

Another spiritual writer produced by the English Catholic community in this period, and one with a greater influence in the short term (although today he is largely forgotten), was Benet of Canfield. His *Rule of Perfection*, printed in eight languages from 1610 onwards, expounded a spirituality typical

---

[8] *Memorials of Father Baker* were edited by R. H. Connolly and J. McCann (London, 1933). Critical assessments include those by David Knowles, *The English Mystical Tradition* (London, 1961), pp. 178–87, and David Lunn, *The English Benedictines* (London, 1980), pp. 197–219.

of the Counter-Reformation. The one essential point is the total surrender of the will to God, in conformity with the crucified Christ. To do 'from the sole motive of pleasing God all that one is aware that God desires, commands, counsels and inspires' – that is perfection, and the Christian is called to it, first through active obedience, then through the superior contemplative life.

This teaching had such influence that it has aroused criticism from two very different viewpoints. In 1689 the *Rule of Perfection* was put on the Roman index of books prohibited to Catholics, two years after the papal condemnation of 'quietism'. Quietism was a tendency found in French spiritual writers and alleged to exaggerate the extent to which the perfect soul should be quietly passive. The danger seen in Rome was that Catholics might be encouraged to disregard intellectual and moral activity in accordance with the Church's down-to-earth dogmas. In 1941 Aldous Huxley published a very different criticism. He pointed out that Benet's most famous disciple was another Capuchin (Franciscan) friar, Père Joseph, whose *Introduction to the Spiritual Life* was full of his influence. This barefoot follower of St Francis, noted for the austerity of his life and the many ecstasies of his prayers, was the ruthless adviser and assistant of Cardinal Richelieu in persecuting the French Protestants, in crushing all others thought to oppose the French monarch, and in stirring up the Thirty Years War (in alliance with the Swedes, who were Protestants). Huxley enquired whether the mysticism taught by Benet to Joseph was itself to blame, and developed a criticism made at the time by Augustine Baker: that Benet insisted that meditation on Christ's cross must be continued even when the soul was becoming perfect, instead of the abandonment of all images. Huxley suggested that Benet's encouragement of thought about suffering instead of calm and complete 'absorption in the ultimate reality' may have encouraged Père Joseph to inflict suffering both on himself and on other people, believing that this was the will of God.[9]

---

[9] See R. A. Knox on Quietism in *Enthusiasm* (Oxford, 1950), pp. 231–355, and Aldous Huxley, *Grey Eminence: A Study in Religion and Politics* (London, 1941).

A more generous verdict would say that Benet's teaching
about the contemplation and imitation of Christ was in a great
tradition and should not be blamed for the cruelties of contemporary politicians, but that something was lost because this
powerful teacher never did a spell of pastoral work in his own
country. Benet, by birth William Fitch, abandoned England
soon after his conversion to Roman Catholicism while a dissolute student of law in 1585. His *Rule of Perfection* seems to have
been completed before his thirtieth birthday in 1592, during
his training in the Franciscan order in France and Italy. It was
a book full of the ardour of a young convert who was very
conscious of the glories of French Catholicism and of the price
he had paid for his own surrender to the will of God. Sent on a
mission to England in 1599, he was soon arrested and in 1602
expelled back to France, having written another book, *The
Christian Knight*, during his captivity. These two books showed
a splendid and astonishing maturity in the ways of contemplative prayer, and an impressive ability to summon fellow Catholics to heroism, but they did not have a great deal to say to, or
about, those who had little wish to become perfect Christian
knights. This was mainly because the author had given up
mixing with such people; from his conversion to his death (in
1610) he lived among the élite. Had Benet lived and listened
more among his own people, he could surely have been
expected to develop a more compassionate understanding of
the ordinary man or woman. Here, in his élitism, was the fatal
defect in his teaching. It was, we may judge, the simple
blindness of Père Joseph to the people's suffering, not the
Christ-centredness of his advanced mysticism, that betrayed
this near-saint into doing work which most ordinary people
would reckon demonic.[10]

The leading Englishwoman devoted to the old religion in
this period was Mary Ward, who had the bold plan of founding
an Institute of the Blessed Virgin Mary for women, modelled

---

[10] Henri Bremond, *A Literary History of Religious Thought in France*, Vol. 2 (English
translation, London, 1930), pp. 112–44, offered a rather puzzled discussion of the
spirituality of the two friars, Benet and Joseph. The only full study is Optat de
Veghel, *Benoit de Canfield* (Rome, 1949).

on the Jesuit order. After some years with the Poor Clares (the women Franciscans) she established her own little community with a school for girls at Omer in Flanders in 1609. But her further idea that women should move about the world in pastoral and teaching work horrified the ecclesiastical authorities when she went to Rome to seek approval for it in 1629. Her experiment was suppressed and she herself was imprisoned. She eventually managed to found modified communities of her Institute in Rome itself, and London and Yorkshire in the period 1639–42, but such was the suspicion with which she was still surrounded, right up to her death in 1645, that this highly promising order barely survived. Its rules did not receive papal approval until 1703. It seems fair to say that with Mary Ward's vision the post-1570 Roman Catholic community in England 'had been offered the opportunity of a second wind, which could have carried its phase of primitive expansion on through the seventeenth century. In rejecting it, it registered its determination to play safe, and missed the boat for a couple of generations'.[11]

All these were independently-minded radicals, impatient for holiness, who would have been a trial to any pastor charged with the care of them, but in this they were typical of a much wider English enthusiasm for religion in this period. Their particular tragedy was that they never found an adequate base for their ideals, so that their energies burned out on alien soil or in futile controversy. Most of their fellow countrymen regarded such 'Papists' as eccentrics who for wicked or inexplicable reasons had chosen to be identified with traitors such as Guy Fawkes. The pity of it all, the loss of English religion, can be felt when we reflect that the seventeenth century included 'a second Protestant Reformation, and a second Catholic Counter-Reformation, both more vigorous and more passionate than their sixteenth-century counterparts.'[12] Yet England's Counter-Reformation did not create a new world of spirituality to match the world of the Puritans.

---

[11] John Bossy, *op.cit.*, p. 282. Margaret Oliver provided a biography of *Mary Ward* (London, 1960).

[12] Hugh Aveling, *The Handle and the Axe*, p. 75.

CHAPTER EIGHT

THE PURITAN EXPLOSION

ENTERING A NEW WORLD

The passionate energy of many Englishmen refused to accept conformity under the control of England's bishops – or poverty under the pressure of England's over-population. They had to find freedom abroad.

It is reckoned that over twenty thousand Englishmen went to live on the continent in the years 1620–40. As we have seen, many were Recusants who found the Counter-Reformation in full force in their places of refuge. But there were also thousands of militant Protestants who chose to live in the Netherlands. There conditions would not be too disappointing if they could find jobs and form a little community around a favourite preacher. Some, however, could not adjust themselves to the Netherlands. There was a shortage of suitable employment. Life in a Dutch town, although acceptably Protestant, could also be disturbingly sophisticated and, by the standards of the English countryside, dissolute. These refugees, patriots even in exile, were alarmed by the thought that their children would probably be absorbed into the Dutch population. They longed for a country where a man might feed his family by his own honest labour on the land or in a village, and where he might obey the 'ordinances of God' – all the time speaking English. The major outlet for Protestants wishing to emigrate therefore became America.

The perils were obvious. The little ships crossing the Atlantic were tossed by storms and ravaged by diseases, and the usually miserable voyage took a minimum of five weeks. The 'Indians' might be cruelly hostile to the intruders; clearing the land of trees and stones was backbreaking work; starvation was the penalty if crops could not be grown in time; and should these perils be survived, epidemics swept through the primitive settlements in the wilderness. But there were attractions. John Donne had heard the Elizabethan talk about the harvest of the sea off Newfoundland, and speculation about other riches, and so had found a new metaphor for sex:

> O my America! my New-found-land,
> My Kingdom, safeliest when with one man manned . . .

In 1609 he applied in vain for the secretaryship of the new colony of Virginia. (Had he sailed for America then, his ship would have been shipwrecked on the Bermudas – the adventure which gave Shakespeare material for *The Tempest*.)

In 1622 Dean Donne became a member of the council of the Virginia Company and delivered the sermon before the company's annual feast. The evening was designed to advertise the company, and that year the Dean had to use all his eloquence 'to keep the wheel in due motion' after the meagre returns on the investment to date, and after the 'flood of blood' when the colonists had been massacred by the Indians. He told his congregation not to be disheartened by the losses but to concentrate on the evangelism of the Indians: 'You shall have much this island, which is but as the suburbs of the old world, a bridge, a gallery to the new; to join all to that world that shall never grow old, the kingdom of heaven.'

This colony with which John Donne was thus identified was not dominated by men wishing to escape from the Church of England. A clergyman, Robert Hunt, arrived with the first colonists who founded Virginia in 1607. One of their earliest acts was to fell trees to make rough walls and benches for a church, with an old sail as the roof. More than two-thirds of that congregation died of famine and disease during the first year and it often seemed as if the little settlement in Chesapeake Bay was doomed, as earlier tiny colonies on the American coast sponsored by Sir Humphrey Gilbert and Sir Walter Ralegh had been in the 1580s. But for the sake of morale among the settlers Thomas Dale, who arrived as governor in 1611, insisted that everyone should attend Morning and Evening Prayer daily, and the same emphasis on the struggling colony's religious dimension ran through the propaganda put out in

support of Virginia – for example, in the books and maps of
Captain John Smith, the adventurer who gave New England
its name.

There was a period when it seemed that it would be easy to
make the Indians friendly and Christian. Pocahontas, the
daughter of the local chief – a girl who (the story went) had
earlier saved John Smith's life – was instructed in the faith of
the Church of England by a Puritan chaplain, Alexander
Whitaker. She was baptized Rebecca, married to an Englishman, and paraded at the court of James I before her rapid
death. But on Good Friday 1622 Indians massacred some three
hundred of the white men, not without provocation. Despite
John Donne's eloquence in London that November, the missionary idealism of the colony went up in smoke – like the
tobacco which had become its chief worldly asset; and the
Dean's sermon proved to be the last in the series extolling
the company as a missionary society. One result of this
weakening in religious motivation was to expose the company
further to the attacks of those who thought they could manage
its affairs better than Sir Edwin Sandys and his associates (who
included Shakespeare's patron, the Earl of Southampton).
George Herbert's stepfather and Nicholas Ferrar his closest
friend took the lead in trying to persuade the House of Commons to come to the rescue, but James I forbade discussion.
Eventually, in July 1624, the company's charter was revoked.[1]

The colony in Virginia survived as a cluster of tobacco
plantations under the direct control of the government. But
more powerful motives were needed if there was to be colonization on a larger scale – and in practice that meant that Puritan
motives were needed.[2] It is in the story of the Puritans in New
England that we find the main fulfilment of the vision of the
English-speaking world, as set out in the prophecy of Samuel
Daniel:

---

[1] See Louis B. Wright, *Religion and Empire: The Alliance between Religion and
Commerce in English Expansion, 1558–1625* (Chapel Hill, N.C., 1943).

[2] Two books by American scholars are illuminating: Wallace Notestein, *The
English People on the Eve of Colonization, 1603–30* (New York, 1954), and Carl
Brindenbaugh, *Vexed and Troubled Englishmen, 1590–1642* (New York, 1968).

And who in time knows whither we may vent
The treasure of our tongue, to what strange shores
This gain of our best glory shall be sent,
T' inrich unknowing nations with our stores,
What worlds in th' yet unformed Occident
May come refin'd with th' accents that are ours?

Puritan motives were shared by most of the 'Pilgrim Fathers' – the passengers, a little over a hundred in number, who landed from the *Mayflower* on the rocky coast of Massachusetts Bay in November 1620. It had been agreed with a suspicious government (and with their backers, led by Thomas Western, a London merchant) that they should settle in Virginia; it seems to have been due to a navigational error that they ended up hundreds of miles to the north. Anyway the need to establish a 'civil body politic' from scratch when there was some talk of mutiny forced these Pilgrim Fathers to make a solemn 'compact' on the *Mayflower* before they landed; and the need to base this 'compact' on religion (for no other basis seemed conceivable to seventeenth-century Englishmen) emphasized the religious origins of their adventure.

Those origins lay in a meeting for Puritan worship in Scrooby, an obscure village just off the Great North Road, about halfway between London and Scotland. The preacher to this little congregation was John Robinson, who encouraged it to emigrate with him to Leyden in the Netherlands. He might have undertaken the further move to America, but the majority of the congregation had persuaded him to stay in Leyden with them. In his farewell to those leaving he had urged them to accept other pastors, since 'the Lord hath more truth and light yet to break forth out of his holy Word'. According to notes made of this sermon (no full manuscript has survived), he also looked forward to a further Reformation beyond the achievements of Luther and Calvin, as well as beyond the practices of the Church of England. It is, however, clear that those who joined the *Mayflower* had no intention of embarking on theological adventures. Although the group from Leyden made up only a third of the Pilgrim Fathers (thirty-five, with sixty-six 'strangers'), it was successful in imposing the ideology they had learned. When half of the pilgrims had survived the winter and had gathered in a harvest, their thanksgiving feast was accompanied by prayer in the established Puritan style. However, for the most part they did not, it seems, regard themselves as being for ever separated from the Church of England, since they trusted that the biblical basis of their purer understanding of the Church would soon be acknowledged by the authorities at home. As Francis Higginson put it when he led a little company joining them: 'We will not say ... "Farewell, Babylon!" "Farewell, Rome!" but we will say, "Farewell, dear England! Farewell, the Church of God in England, and the Christian friends there! We do not go to New England as separatists from the Church of England; though we cannot but separate from the corruptions in it; but we go to practise the positive part of church reformation, and propagate the Gospel in America!" '

East Anglian Puritans dominated the New England Company, which received a grant of territory and sent three hundred colonists with two clergymen to Salem in Massachusetts in 1628–29. In 1630 they were joined by a larger party, led by John Winthrop, an able lawyer. By birth and by his own nature Winthrop was a leader of men; before sailing for the new world, he had been lord of the manor at Groton and a Justice of the Peace. But his legal career in London seemed to be blocked – as he could not help thinking, because he was a Puritan. His motives become clear in the paper which he drew up listing 'reasons for justifying the undertakers of the intended plantation in New England'.

The first two reasons were religious – to spread the Gospel (and incidentally 'to raise a bulwark against the kingdom of Anti-Christ which the Jesuits labour to rear up in these parts'), and to provide 'tabernacles and food' in the wilderness to which the true Church could flee from the 'desolation' and 'general calamity' of Protestantism in Europe. Winthrop then recited the economic woes of England amid the depressions of 1619–24 and 1629–31 caused by over-population and inflation. 'This land grows weary of its inhabitants, so as man who is the most precious of all creatures is here more vile and base than the earth we tread upon, and of less price than a horse or a sheep ... Many men spending as much labour and cost to recover or keep sometimes an acre or two of land as would procure them many hundred as good or better in another country . . . No man's estate will suffice to keep sail with his equals.' It is clear from Winthrop's tone that he expected the response to come not from the really poor but from farmers and tradesmen who, to speak in a secular style, wanted to better themselves.

The same memorandum supplied three convenient answers to the objection that 'we have no warrant to enter upon that land which hath been so long possessed by others'. 'If we leave them sufficient for their use, we may lawfully take the rest'; 'we shall come in with the good leave of the natives'; 'God hath consumed the natives with a great plague in those parts so there be few inhabitants left.' The only real objection to the adventure was seen to be that 'it is attended with many and great difficulties'. But to that Winthrop gave the robust answer: 'So is every good action.' This was the leader who, preaching to his fellow passengers on the *Arabella* in mid-Atlantic in the spring of 1630 declared: 'We shall be as a city upon a hill, the eyes of all people are upon us.'[3]

THE HOLY EXPERIMENT OF NEW ENGLAND

New England's preachers preached a strong Gospel in their wooden churches erected on soil never before touched by man's implements.[4] The theology which supported their message can be seen in one of their favourite textbooks, *The Marrow of Sacred Divinity*. Its author was William Ames, a Cambridge theologian who because of his Puritan convictions had become a refugee in the Netherlands. Ames accompanied his exposition of his faith by a major work on moral problems, which became almost equally authoritative in New England, and shortly before he died he was making plans to cross the Atlantic.[5]

---

[3] *The Puritan Tradition in America*, ed. A. T. Vaughan (New York, 1972), pp. 26–35. Another valuable collection of documents is *The Puritans*, ed. Perry Miller and F. H. Johnson (New York, 1963). See also Edmund S. Morgan, *The Puritan Dilemma: The Story of John Winthrop* (Boston, Mass., 1958).

[4] See David D. Hall, *The Faithful Shepherd: A History of the New England Ministry in the Seventeenth Century* (Chapel Hill, N.C., 1972).

[5] See K. L. Sprunger, *The Learned Dr William Ames* (Urbana, Ill., 1972).

Such Puritan doctrine has been called a 'federal' theology because, within an orthodox Calvinist framework, its stress was on the 'federal' covenant or agreement between the Creator and the believer. It taught that the God who granted this covenant to the elect was reasonable and reliable; that he had made his character well known in a clear revelation; and that he summoned the believer to study his revelation and to reason clearly about it and about the world which it illuminated. Nothing about the Puritans in New England is more impressive than the speed with which they established a college: Harvard College, founded in Cambridge, Massachusetts, by the appropriation of half the infant colony's taxes as early as 1636. The college was necessary in order to make these Puritans' sons reasonable, reliable and sound preachers of the Gospel. Its official theology was Calvinism as defined in *The Marrow*, to be studied every Saturday morning. To these New Englanders a college was almost as indispensable as was the congregation itself – defined by Ames as 'a society of believers joined together in a special bond for the continual exercise of the communion of saints among themselves'; as Christians covenanting with each other on the basis of God's covenant with them.

A few 'Praying Indians' were allowed to graduate at Harvard College. Their presence was a reminder that a professed purpose of the migration to New England was missionary; the cry of the Macedonians to St Paul, 'Come over and help us', appeared on the official seal of Massachusetts. As late as 1646, disturbed because very little missionary work had yet been achieved, John Eliot preached the first Puritan sermon in a Red Indian language. Three years later the first English missionary society was formed to support his work. In 1662 he brought out the whole of the Bible in the Algonquian language, an astonishing feat of translation; it was the first Bible to be printed in North America. The rationale of this missionary work, in Calvinist eyes, was that it was unsafe to assume that the heathen did not include any of God's elect who would be saved for ever by responding with faith on hearing the Gospel. But on the whole, the function of the American Indians was to provide land, willingly or unwillingly, for those on whom

God's covenanted favour rested, like the Canaanites whose role in Old Testament theology was modest.[6]

Some Christian villages were formed for these 'Praying Indians'; the first, for Mohicans, was granted land in 1651. But the 'holy experiment' pursued in the Puritan settlers' own towns and villages became incomparably more important than any missionary work among America's original inhabitants, for the hope was always that the success of this experiment would teach the whole of Christendom what true Christianity was. The experiment needed to be thoroughly and conspicuously holy and, although this may seem paradoxical in view of the Calvinist insistence on the faith of the elect, New England's emphasis on law was very pronounced. The rationale was that without obedience to God's law the saints could not prove their gratitude for their election – and the sinners would be even more thoroughly damned than they were already. The ideal society, as conceived by these Puritans, was one which was strictly regulated by magistrates enforcing the Ten Commandments and their consequences as interpreted by the best preachers. The stress on keeping the divine law in a holy life was so strong among the Puritans of New England that at times it almost abandoned the insistence in Calvinist orthodoxy on God's freedom to choose to favour the wicked. A modern historian observes that a typical New England preacher 'comes perilously close to the greatest danger that covenant theology creates: failing to maintain the distinction between works and grace.'[7] In view of the alarm raised by the Puritans about Arminianism in England, this development in America is curious.

When John Winthrop's little fleet took the largest party of Puritans yet seen in the new world to Massachusetts Bay in 1630, the most precious item in the cargo was this company's

---

[6] See A. T. Vaughan, *New England Frontier: Puritans and Indians, 1620–1675* (Boston, Mass., 1965), and Francis Jennings, *The Invasion of America* (Chapel Hill, N.C., 1975). C. W. Kellaway studied the history of the earliest missionary society in *The New England Company* (London, 1961).

[7] Everett Emerson, *Puritanism in America 1620–1750* (Boston, Mass., 1977), p. 59. Larzer Ziff, *Puritanism in America* (New York, 1973), also supplements Perry Miller's classic study of *The New England Mind* (2 vols, Cambridge, Mass., 1939–53).

royal charter. Although Charles I had not intended his covenant with a group of Puritans to be excessively gracious, his
clerks had omitted to specify that the charter declaring his
grace should be kept safely for possible revision in London.
The charter was also unexpectedly and accidentally gracious
in that it allowed those crossing the Atlantic to purchase so
many shares in the venture that by law they effectively controlled it. As had never been the case in Virginia, their 'holy
experiment' was their own.

These legal circumstances meant that strong-minded magistrates in the new colony could order its affairs in accordance
with the exhortations of strong-minded preachers. The Pilgrim
Fathers in the Plymouth area were, it is true, somewhat
suspicious of the clergymen (other than John Robinson, whom
they had left behind in the Netherlands). Their early services
in America were taken by an 'elder', William Brewster, and
even when professional preachers arrived power was kept
firmly in the hands of laymen such as William Bradford, the
governor of Plymouth for almost thirty years. In the larger
Massachusetts Bay colony the preachers were never magistrates themselves. But the preachers often gave the magistrates
direct advice from the pulpit, most publicly in the annual
'election sermon'. Preachers as spiritually powerful as John
Cotton or Thomas Hooker (both of whom arrived in 1633
with established reputations) had therefore great political
influence.[8] And when a primitive electoral system was established in 1631, it was decided that only those who had been
co-opted as church members, taking the Lord's Supper once a
month and walking in the way of righteousness, were to have
votes.

Some twenty thousand men and women were willing to
leave England during the 1630s to join a colony so constituted,
and they could not be stopped by the Lords Commissioners
for Plantations, a body set up by the King in 1632 with
Archbishop Laud in the chair. There was a sense in which they

---

[8] There are studies of *John Cotton* by Larzer Ziff (Princeton, N.J., 1962) and
Everett Emerson (New York, 1965), and of *Thomas Hooker* by George Williams
(Cambridge, Mass., 1975) and Frank Shuffelton (Princeton, N.J., 1977).

joined a monastery, like many of the Recusants fleeing in these years to the continent. John Cotton, writing about 1637, reported a procedure for the admission of new church members which would not have brought discredit to a monastery. First candidates were asked questions such as these. 'How it pleased God to work in them to bring them home to Christ? Whether the law had convinced them of sin? How the Lord had won them to deny themselves and their own righteousness and to rely on the righteousness of Christ?' The account which candidates gave of themselves had to be supported both by a public confession, of perhaps fifteen minutes, and by recommendations from existing members. Only then were candidates allowed to 'enter a holy covenant with God and with them', being assured in return that 'we likewise will walk towards you in all brotherly love and holy watchfulness'.

When the numbers of full church members who had been willing to undergo this procedure became too small an element in the colony to be plausible as its electorate, it was decided that men who were respectable Christians but not able or willing to pass all the tests for church membership could be given the vote, making use of the concept of the 'half-way covenant'. But the religious purity of the little commonwealth between the wilderness and the ocean was still thought by its leadership to be the main justification for its existence. Towards the end of his long governorship John Bradford grew weary and somewhat disillusioned with the Plymouth settlement, and ceased to record its history in order to find time to learn Hebrew, but in his history he had already summed up the lesson which he rightly believed would be drawn from the pioneering days. 'May and ought not the children of these fathers rightly say, "Our fathers were Englishmen which came over this great ocean, and were ready to perish in the wilderness, but they cried unto the Lord, and he heard their voice and looked upon their adversity"?'[9] The new Israel, rescued from all the perils of this exodus to America, had a duty to build the city of God in the wilderness – a very clear duty, although they

---

[9] The best edition is William Bradford, *Of Plymouth Plantation*, ed. S. E. Morison (New York, 1952).

knew that they were sinners. 'Sir,' someone said to Thomas Hooker, the dying pastor, in 1647, 'you are going to receive the reward of all your labours.' Hooker had built up, and dominated, the new settlement at Hartford in Connecticut. But he now replied: 'Brother, I am going to receive mercy.' When Edward Johnson came to write his *History of New England* (1654), however, his theme was expressed in his sub-title: *The Wonderworking Providence of Zion's Saviour in America*. Their experience while labouring to establish a Christian civilization in the wilderness across an ocean had confirmed their belief in miracles.

Early in the eighteenth century spokesmen for the orthodox Puritanism of New England still looked back and around with pride. Despite all the sins to be expected from human nature, the 'holy experiment' had been blessed. In his immense work entitled *Magnalia Christi Americana* (1702), Cotton Mather had no hesitation in announcing that a new chapter in church history had been opened by men such as his grandfather, John Cotton: 'I write the wonders of the Christian religion,' he proclaimed, 'flying from the depravations of Europe to the American strand.' Frequently the preachers compared the colonists with the Ancient Israelites who had cried to the Lord in the wilderness, had been given a good land, had been guilty of backsliding, but had returned to the Lord, at least partially and temporarily.

In 1646–48 a synod summoned to define Massachusetts orthodoxy stated its doctrine in keeping with the Westminster Confession recently drawn up by English Calvinist divines, and its discipline on the basis of the covenant freely entered into by church members but supported by the 'helpful' magistrates. At the same time as the construction of this 'Cambridge Platform' dealing with church life, 'Laws and Liberties' codified and developed the colony's earlier legislation with a theological introduction and a strong peppering of biblical references. Although in practice the laws of Massachusetts were based more on English common law than on the Old Testament, death was the penalty for idolatry, blasphemy or adultery. A son 'of sixteen years of age which will not obey the voice of his father or the voice of his mother' was to be put to death in accordance with Exodus 21:17. A man drunk was fined ten shillings; a man smoking in public one shilling. In 1639 a Boston shopkeeper narrowly escaped excommunication and was subjected to a heavy fine because he had overcharged his customers. In his sermon on the occasion John Cotton explicitly denounced the suggestion 'that a man might sell as dear as he can and buy as cheap as he can'. It was to such conditions that preachers looked back nostalgically in days when the colony had grown more worldly, when Puritans had become Yankees. Increase Mather asked in 1679: 'Where was there ever a place so like unto new Jerusalem as New England hath been?'[10]

THE BIRTH OF RELIGIOUS TOLERATION

Taking leave of the Pilgrim Fathers, John Robinson had prophesied that 'new light' would come to the Puritans in America. He would have been astonished had he known that later generations would praise the pilgrims who became settlers chiefly for their discovery of the idea of religious toleration. It was a slow discovery for, as we have often observed, Puritanism was not naturally tolerant. At first when the problem of religious diversity arose, the solution seemed to be to begin a new settlement where the rebellious form of Christianity could become the official religion. Then the American adventure became a more courageous recognition that the white light of the Christian Gospel was made up of many colours.

Even in Massachusetts, a colony planned to be uniform, there were independent spirits. Thomas Hooker was a preacher whose bent was more mystical than legal; one of his books was entitled *The Soul's Possession of Christ* (1638). He was given permission to lead a fresh exodus, to found the colony of Connecticut; and in Connecticut although the elected governor was to be 'always a member of some approved congregation', those electing him need not always be full church members themselves. Another preacher, Roger Williams, had

---

[10] See D. B. Rutman, *Winthrop's Boston: Portrait of a Puritan Town, 1630–49* (Chapel Hill, N.C., 1965).

been in a series of disputes with the Massachusetts authorities since landing in 1631. In January 1636 he was warned by Governor Winthrop that he was about to be shipped back to England. Instead he stumbled out of Salem into a snowstorm, was sheltered by some Indians, and went on to found a settlement at Providence. This eventually grew into the colony of Rhode Island, the first American colony to base itself permanently upon 'soul liberty', the guaranteed toleration of all Christians. As early as 1637 Mrs Anne Hutchinson, with her husband and her eleven children, was banished from Massachusetts for claiming direct 'revelations' from God. These revelations supported her enthusiasm for her interpretation of the message of her favourite preacher, John Cotton; what John Cotton really thought about his embarrassing admirer is not so clear. She found a temporary refuge on Rhode Island before moving on to more pioneering (and to death in one of the Indians' periodic massacres of the Dutch colonists to the north of Manhattan). Many others found freedom in Rhode Island, including Baptists, as the old 'Anabaptists' who denied the validity of infant baptism were coming to be called; and the colony received a royal charter on this broad basis in 1663. Thus gradually within a new colony it was admitted that dissenters who claimed 'soul liberty' did not need to found yet another new colony.[11]

Roger Williams had been trained at Cambridge as a Calvinist of impeccable orthodoxy, and he never abandoned that central belief. He was not a democrat; he was a Calvinist, a theocrat. But he had two revolutionary ideas. The first was that an English king had no right to dispose of the lands of the Indians to English colonists. The second was that the magistrates had no right to use worldly weapons to enforce laws about religion; for example, they had no right to punish any who broke the Sabbath calm of Sunday. Such malefactors ought to be left to the punishment of their own consciences. To Williams, Christ was not a pillar of the Puritan establishment, or of any other form of Christendom; he was a 'beggar's brat laid in a manger and a gallow's bird'. To follow Christ meant

---

[11] See Emery Battis, *Saints and Sectaries* (Chapel Hill, N.C., 1962).

the way of the cross – as Williams had himself felt when he had given up his legal career (where he had enjoyed the direct patronage of the formidable Sir Edward Coke) to become a minister of Christ, and when he had then given up a career in the Church of England in order to minister in the American wilderness.

Williams was no slack liberal. Those who took that narrow way must be thoroughly converted before taking it; one of his pamphlets was entitled *Christenings Make Not Christians*. Thus the Christian Church must be radically different from any political society; God's people and Caesar's must be separate. John Winthrop (who retained much bemused good will towards this amazing radical) understood him as teaching that a man should not pray with his wife unless he could be sure that she had been converted. It was essentially because those who followed Christ truly must be free and few that Williams rejected indignantly any suggestion that men might be compelled to conform outwardly in matters of religion. He returned to England in 1643 in order to urge his policy of toleration on Parliament, writing a long pamphlet which in its very title called 'persecution for cause of conscience' a 'bloody' teaching – only to have the book burned by the common hangman. Back in New England a pamphlet from John Cotton asserted that the so-called 'bloody' doctrine was in fact fully Christian; it had been 'washed in the blood of the lamb'.

In the course of his life (and he was about eighty years old when he died) Williams grew sceptical about the merits even of Christian organizations, however small. Although he often talked with Indians about Christ – 'God was pleased to give me a painful, patient spirit to lodge with them in their filthy, smoky holes' – he never tried to form an Indian congregation. He became a small landowner and opened a trading post, although he did not sell alcohol or guns to his beloved Indians as rival traders did; instead, he wrote the first book in English explaining the 'language of America'. He took a full part in the young life of the colony, even if it meant bearing arms against the Indians when to his great sorrow they turned against the settlers in 1675–76 ('King Philip's war') and burned his house and papers, reducing him to poverty. Much of his energy went into theological controversy against a new sect, the Quakers, but he never consented to any persecution of them. He made no attempt to build up a congregation of his fellow whites around his preaching, as men such as John Cotton – once his neighbour when they were both Church of England clergymen in Lincolnshire – had done so successfully. To follow Christ must mean to be a seeker, to the end. In the year before his death in 1683 he wrote to the governor of Massachusetts: 'Eternity (O eternity!) is our business.'[12]

This separation of Church and State was to save the life of American Christianity when the religious enthusiasm of the first days in New England was becoming a burden to the majority of the colonists – and when the diversity of the religious foundations of the various colonies was becoming a problem along the long path to co-operation and union. Even in Massachusetts when a new royal charter was issued in 1691 the religious qualification for voting disappeared. In the Connecticut valley churches, Samuel Stobbard was teaching that Christians should be admitted to the Lord's Supper even if they had not been able to convince the existing church members that they had been soundly converted. The profession of Christian faith and a good life were all that was required; 'all professors walking blamelessly are visible saints'. In 1700 this clergyman actually published such liberal notions. A year earlier, a church had been founded in Boston itself where admission to Baptism and Communion was left to the discretion of the minister, not to the votes of the congregation.

Meanwhile another experiment showed how wide was to be the liberty offered by America. Sir George Calvert renounced high office under James I in order to become a Roman Catholic in 1624. He was compensated by an Irish peerage as Lord Baltimore – and, under Charles I, by the grant of a huge tract of land around Chesapeake Bay to the north of Virginia. Both Baltimore and his royal master dreamed of solving the problem

---

[12] Recent studies include Edmund S. Morgan, *Roger Williams: The Church and the State* (New York, 1967); John Garrett, *Roger Williams, Witness beyond Christendom* (New York, 1970); W. Clark Gilpin, *The Millenarian Piety of Roger Williams* (Chicago, Ill., 1979).

of the Recusants by persuading them to migrate. On his death his son Cecil modified the project in order to make it pay, and in the hope that it would be more acceptable to New England's Puritans: it was to include Anglicans, although Roman Catholic and other Trinitarian Christians were to be free to practise their religion privately. In 1634 a boat carrying two Jesuit priests (as 'gentlemen adventurers') and sixteen Roman Catholic families, along with some two hundred other people, arrived in the fertile upper reaches of Chesapeake Bay to begin the new colony, Maryland – so named after Queen Henrietta Maria. The 'Act of Toleration' adopted in 1649 (at Baltimore's insistence after various internal conflicts) was the Christian world's most formal affirmation to that date of the principle of religious liberty. However, even then offences such as the denial of the divinity of Christ remained punishable by death, and gradually the Anglican influence in Maryland so prevailed that in 1702 the Church of England was established.[13]

That is why Rhode Island, although slightly younger than Maryland, is honoured as the first colony to make permanent an experiment which against all expectations became possible as Christianity entered the new world across the Atlantic: the clear separation of Church and State within a society still fundamentally Christian.

THE ENGLISH PURITANS

The influence of Puritanism ran underground while Charles I and Archbishop Laud governed England, but that did not stop the influence being powerful. The force that created New England could not be impotent in the colonists' home country.

We can see it in the career of John Preston – or rather, in his refusal to embrace a career if it meant any disloyalty to his main vocation, which was to be a pastor and preacher. The son of a Northamptonshire farmer, Preston won honours at Cam-

---

[13] T. O. Hanley examined *Their Rights and Liberties: The Beginnings of Religious and Political Freedom in Maryland* (Westminster, Md., 1959).

bridge; a memory survives of him reading St Thomas Aquinas 'as the barber cut his hair, and when any fell upon the place he read, he would not lay down his book but blow it off'. He specialized in the philosophy of Aristotle and studied medicine. Then the direction of his life was changed by a sermon by John Cotton; for the rest of that life, he stayed every summer in Cotton's vicarage. In Cambridge he became a winning teacher and trainer of young Puritans and Master of Emmanuel College. He was also summoned to succeed John Donne as the preacher to the lawyers of Lincoln's Inn. As he moved between Cambridge and London, many future MPs came under his influence as he had come under John Cotton's.

In 1621 he was given the key post of chaplain to the most powerful young man in the kingdom, Prince Charles, under the patronage of the reigning favourite, the Duke of Buckingham. When the old king died, Preston was the third man in the carriage which bore Charles and Buckingham away to being their joint ascendancy; and when John Williams was dismissed as Lord Keeper, Buckingham offered to obtain the post for him. Preston consulted his friends and rejected the offer. When not long afterwards the King and the Duke came out in favour of Arminianism, Preston broke with them. His closest friend was William Fiennes, Lord Saye and Sele – a man who was to exercise great influence among Puritan MPs in the 1640s. Preston would presumably have had a rather similar influence, had he not died of consumption a month after Buckingham's murder. He was little more than forty years old and had burned himself out.[14]

For many movements, such a leader's unwillingness to assume political office, his later breach with the king and the king's favourite, and his premature death, would all have been disasters. English Puritanism, however, had learned by the time of Preston's death not to depend on royal favour or on any one man's leadership. Its lay leaders were deprived of a national platform by the decision of the King to govern without

---

[14] See Irvonwy Morgan, *Prince Charles's Puritan Chaplain* (London, 1957); and Christopher Hill, *Puritanism and Revolution* (London, 1958), pp. 239–74.

Parliament, and its clerical leaders were deprived of prestigious offices. But that did not alter the attractiveness of Puritanism.

The sons of the gentry were taking themselves with a new seriousness. That was shown by their ambitions in the House of Commons and their wish to be educated at the universities or at the 'inns of court' where lawyers were trained. It was also shown by the earnest conviction of many of them that life was about something more important than careers, properties, families and sports. To such men Puritanism held out an invitation. Many older men rich in piety were rich in worldly possessions. Several Puritan earls revealed themselves fully in the 1640s – most notably Bedford, whose central influence was cut short by death, Warwick, who commanded the navy on Parliament's behalf, his son-in-law Manchester, the Major General of the army of the Eastern Association in East Anglia, and Essex, the Lord General of the Parliamentary army. The frequent meetings of the backers of the Massachusetts Bay Company, or the supporters of the shorter-lived Providence Island colony in the Caribbean, saw English as well as transatlantic affairs discussed by Puritan gentlemen.

Although the Puritans' favourite preachers were not now bishops, deans or professors, and were harassed by Archbishop Laud, they could still be heard – and read, for Laud's censorship did very little to stop the flood of edifying books by the best-known Puritan preachers, all linked with John Preston and with each other. A man such as John Dod, although silenced by James I after a nineteen-year ministry in one parish, was rescued by a Puritan squire who gave him another parish, in Northamptonshire (where John Preston was buried). Many thousands of readers delighted to find Dod's incisive and often witty preaching on the printed page, and he probably exercised as much influence as any bishop before his death in 1645 at the age of ninety. We have noticed that John Preston was converted by John Cotton; but the preacher who converted John Cotton, Richard Sibbes, was as influential as Preston (his intimate friend) among Cambridge students and London lawyers. Preston's leading disciple, Thomas Goodwin, was another prince of the Puritan pulpit. Goodwin could look back to his conversion, through a sermon at a funeral on the afternoon of Monday, 2 October 1620. Exiled under Laud, he never ceased to be influential and lived to become a leading theologian at Oxford.

Clergymen such as these were morally the leaders of their profession; and it was a profession that was full of men dissatisfied with the existing system and alienated from the official leadership. In this period when religion fascinated almost all thinking men, and when the universities were pouring out more graduates than ever before, the number of posts within the official Church able to support graduate preachers in the style they expected was limited, almost to the extent already seen under Elizabeth. This does not seem to have been a time of widespread poverty in the rectories. With rising prices of corn, rectors entitled to a tenth of the parish's harvest could do well. But many graduates with a good opinion of themselves failed to find patrons to appoint them to rectories. Some 3,800 vicars often found that because the 'great' tithes of corn were the property of a rector or (more likely) a layman, their own families must suffer. A lectureship in a town church might well be more attractive, and there the appointment was usually made by Puritan laymen.[15]

The decisive factor in the spread of Puritanism was, however, not any preacher's financial discontent. It was the transforming effect which a Puritan in the pulpit or in conversation could have on an individual who could be brought to believe that from eternity God had predestined him to heaven. Thomas Hooker, who wrote several books analysing the process of conversion, summed up 'the soul's preparation for Christ': 'to believe is the hardest thing that a man is put to under heaven.' But the effect of belief, once that light had dawned, was a readiness to receive a glorious salvation, and with salvation the gift of the Holy Spirit, producing all the harvest of a godly life. Although a preacher could be an invaluable guide in that life, the decisions had all to be taken by the individual, as he or she read the Scriptures with the aid of

---

[15] These were the conclusions drawn by Rosemary O'Day in *The English Clergy: The Emergence and Consolidation of a Profession, 1558–1642*.

the Spirit. Conversion with these results formed the theme of innumerable sermons preached at funerals and subsequently printed, and of many autobiographies.[16]

The great emphasis on the converted layman's experience explains why Puritanism was able to flourish in places where there was no dominant layman and no distinguished preacher of this persuasion. If need be, all that was really needed was a Christian believer, able to take family prayers in the approved style and to exhort his neighbours.[17] Probably it did Puritan gentlemen – and clergymen – no real harm that their exclusion from the seats of power in the 1630s threw them back on Bible study, prayer and private morality. The vast majority never crossed the Atlantic, but many seem to have become pilgrims in spirit.[18]

When they won their political victory in England, they inaugurated a new age. That age was called 'the Puritan revolution' by S. R. Gardiner, the historian whose many-volumed narrative of it (begun in 1863, continued by Sir Charles Firth and brought to completion by another disciple in 1955) has never been surpassed for richness of detail. In twentieth-century historical work the name has gone out of fashion, and that is understandable. The word 'revolution' – borrowed from astronomy and indicating a cyclical, not linear, pattern in events – was very seldom applied to English events at the time. It was a French historian, Guizot, who compared the 1640s with the French Revolution in a book of 1826. A century and a half later, few historians were eager to repeat the comparison. And if it was a revolution, was it Puritan? John Pym, speaking in the Parliament of 1621, rejected 'that odious and factious name of Puritans'. Almost twenty years later another MP, Sir Benjamin Rudyard, was still fuming about the

---

[16] The same theme ran through Geoffrey Nuttall, *The Holy Spirit in Puritan Faith and Experience* (Oxford, 1946); Gordon Wakefield, *Puritan Devotion* (London, 1957); Owen Watkins, *The Puritan Experience* (London, 1972).

[17] This was brought out by R. C. Richardson, *Puritanism in North-west England* (Manchester, 1972).

[18] Classic studies are by William Haller: *The Rise of Puritanism* (New York, 1938) and *Liberty and Reformation in the Puritan Revolution* (New York, 1955). Recent studies include Christopher Hill, *Society and Puritanism in Pre-Revolutionary England* (London, 1964), and Perez Zagorin, *The Court and the Country* (London, 1969).

imprecise nickname. 'Whosoever squares his actions by any rule, divine or human, is a Puritan. Whosoever would be governed by the King's laws, he is a Puritan.' So we need to remember that the men going to Parliament in 1640 had no idea of launching a revolution and little sense of belonging to a single, cohesive Puritan movement. However, it remains true that the train of events begun in 1640 became revolutionary. It is also true that this result would have been impossible without the energy and self-confidence given to Englishmen by the kind of Protestantism that came to be classified as Puritanism. And these truths deserve careful analysis because this civil war was such a traumatic crisis in English history.

In our own materialistic age it has naturally been difficult for historians to believe that any brand of the Christian religion could once have wielded compelling authority. It has been suggested instead that the key factor was the economic rise of the gentry, determined to sweep away the outdated feudal monarchy and aristocracy – an interpretation which fits in well with the Marxist analysis of the long, unhappy prelude to the rise of the proletariat. The counter-suggestion has been made that in that age of inflation many of the 'mere' gentry were not rising but falling, so that they looked with envy and hatred on the few who were favoured by the Court with profitable offices, grants of monopolies in certain trades or other support. Savage controversies about the gentry's rise or fall have raged in academic journals.[19]

Such debates between scholars were not a complete waste of time. They acknowledged the truth that great movements in society do not get started solely by speeches in Parliament or by sermons in the pulpit, so that religion, like politics, must be studied in its proper context, the total life of a society. Recent controversies have also stimulated much useful research into the financial affairs of hundreds of men who occupied leading positions in the civil war, and into the life of the counties far from London. But continuing research has shown how mis-

---

[19] See the extracts collected by Laurence Stone in *Social Change and Revolution in England* (London, 1965), with R. K. Richardson, *The Debate on the English Revolution* (London, 1977).

leading it can be to categorize the men who were to divide in 1642, and how much caution should be exercised when generalizing about economic trends in the 1630s. It seems to be generally true that the seventeenth century brought to the fortunate a growing profitability, in towns and countryside alike. But those who successfully exploited their estates, or other capital, had to be unusually efficient, resolute or lucky. Gentlemen who started with the same advantage as the fortunate declined because they could not compete, and one historian has ventured the opinion that the majority of the gentry 'may just have endured'.

Some generalizations about changing trends affecting the gentry and the merchants are obviously true: the monarchy could no longer obtain enough revenue to rule without parliamentary taxation; the peerage could no longer exert a military discipline over vast districts in alliance with the Crown; some or many landowners and merchants who were to be able to influence Parliament had felt seriously frustrated or threatened by the policies of the Stuart kings; towns rather than rural areas, the more developed south and east rather than the relatively backward north and west, tended to side with Parliament when war came. But it does not follow that being a 'mere' gentleman or a 'mere' merchant without influence at Court compelled one into rebellion in order to rescue one's economic interests. Lord Digby spoke in the Commons in 1641 about 'the liberty, the property of the subject fundamentally subverted' – but ended up an ardent Royalist. Many impoverished gentlemen declared for the King. The enthusiastic supporters of Parliament included some who had held profitable offices from the King. Among them was John Pym, the first great organizer of the Parliamentary war effort. John Hutchinson, who commanded the garrison of Nottingham in the Parliamentary interest, had attempted to buy an office of profit in the court of Star Chamber as late as 1649.[20] The supporters of Parliament included many landowners who had been doing well during the eleven years of 'tyranny'.

---

[20] His widow Lucy wrote a classic biography: *Memoirs of the Life of Colonel Hutchinson*, ed. James Sutherland (Oxford, 1973).

Research into the private affairs of MPs has found little difference in the prosperity of the estates of those who took the one side or the other. Research into their elections has shown that if the election was contested (which was unusual) the issues tended to be local not national. The merchants of London were divided; when the King was feasted by the Lord Mayor in November 1641 his position seemed secure, and it needed drastic change in the composition of the Common Council during the next month to make the City of London Milton's 'mansion house of liberty'. In the counties, there were many attempts to make neutral zones and there was much reluctance to serve outside the county. And as the horror of civil war engulfed the homes of the gentlemen of England, it was not unknown for father and son, or for brothers, to take different sides. Sir Edmund Verney, the King's standard-bearer, was wretched to learn that his eldest son, Ralph, had sided with Parliament; and John Milton's brother Christopher was a Royalist.[21]

It seems, then, that among men with possessions, economic grievances or ambitions were often less decisive than were convictions about how England ought to be governed, and in particular about how religion ought to be established in a Christian country. This cannot be a surprise to anyone who reflects how terrible a step it was for English gentlemen to renew the medieval civil wars. The convictions of reasoning men who thought this step necessary were often clothed in religious terminology, and since this was an age of flourishing religious faith, we are under no obligation to regard either side as hypocritical.

On the Royalist side the convictions were no less real for not being sanctimoniously eloquent. (Sir Jacob Astley's prayer before the battle at Edgehill has become famous: 'Lord, thou

---

[21] Studies which have built up this picture include D. Brunton and D. H. Pennington, *Members of the Long Parliament* (London, 1953), supplemented by M. F. Keeler, *The Long Parliament 1640–41: A Biographical Study* (Philadelphia, Pa., 1954); G. E. Aylmer, *The King's Servants* (London, 1961); Valerie Pearl, *London and the Outbreak of the Puritan Revolution* (Oxford, 1961), supplemented by Robert Ashton, *The City and the Court 1603–43* (London, 1979); David Underdown, *Pride's Purge* (London, 1971); J. S. Morrill, *The Revolt of the Provinces* (London, 1976).

knowest how busy I must be this day. If I forget thee, do not thou forget me . . . March on, boys!') The convictions of James I about the divine right of kings were now made more glamorous because the King was a fastidiously clean-living son of the Church of England (if almost more futile, since the King lacked his father's low cunning). According to Royalist beliefs at their extreme, a king was anointed in order to rule and it was the simple duty of his subjects to obey him. On the scaffold, a few minutes before his execution, Charles I declared that the people's freedom 'consists in having of government'. He did not mean 'having share in government, that is nothing pertaining to them'; 'a subject and a sovereign are clean different things.'

There was, however, a subtler form of Royalism, expressed by moderate Royalists such as Edward Hyde (later Earl of Clarendon) and in some moods or for some purposes by the King himself. At his trial Charles was surprisingly eloquent. He argued that most Englishmen were on his side, because they accepted his anointing by God to be their king as the best guarantee of the continuation of the mixture of laws and liberties which they had inherited from their ancestors. He was defending the achievements of many generations in the life of a generally happy and prosperous people. After this flagrant rebellion against England's monarchy which had been continuous since Anglo-Saxon days, no doubt many other ancient institutions would suffer a similar fate. So, claimed the King, 'it is not my case alone, it is the freedom and the liberty of the people of England' – against 'power without law'. He was 'the Martyr of the People'. And such appeals to conservative instincts touched the hearts of many thousands, drawn from all ranks of society, who were willing to sacrifice savings and lives for the King in the civil war.[22]

In opposition to the Royalist creed or creeds, Puritan religion gave rise to an ideology which appealed in somewhat the same way as a later revolutionary movement such as Marxism. It was a religion based on the Bible as squarely as Communism was to be based on the teachings of Marx, Lenin, Stalin or

[22] Dame Veronica Wedgwood has told the story of *The Trial of Charles I* (London, 1964.

Mao. Those who argued about politics on this basis constantly employed scriptural texts applauding the overthrow of wicked kings or wicked priests or wicked rich men and hailing the birth of a new age of righteousness. It was the conviction of those who in the end took Parliament's side that a new age could indeed dawn for England, and should dawn, because England deserved better than to be governed by kings such as Charles Stuart, ministers such as Buckingham or Strafford, and bishops such as Laud. An elected Parliament was morally entitled to decide through taxation what was to be the scope of the government's activity and through legislation what was to be the direction of the government's policy in vital matters such as religion.

As yet there was no thought of total freedom for all, but there certainly was the conviction that many Englishmen had definite 'liberties', political and religious, which had been flouted – and that Parliament had the power and the duty to assert these rights. The driving force behind this conviction can be discerned even in Ben Jonson's presentation of Zeal-of-the-Land Busy in *Bartholomew Fair* (1614). It was a pride in England fostered by a faith in England's proper religion, the religion of the Bible, the religion which promised the coming of the kingdom of God. The Bible announced the great dignity of men and women after salvation by Christ; and Puritans were sure that they, together with many of their fellow Englishmen, had been saved, becoming 'God's people', deserving God's kingdom. Meanwhile the 'saints' chosen by God must pray, watch and struggle for the great day; the imagery of spiritual warfare was constantly used. In 1643 Stephen Marshall, the preacher who was called 'the trumpet', reminded other Englishmen of the promise in the Revelation of St John the Divine that Christ and his saints would reign for a thousand years. It was the promise of the millennium, and 'we have the whole army of Protestant interpreters agreeing on the general scope and meaning of it'.[23]

---

[23] See William Shenk, *The Concern for Social Justice in the Puritan Revolution* (London, 1948), and Michael Walzer, *The Revolution of the Saints* (London, 1966). Much can be learned from W. P. Holden, *Anti-Puritan Satire, 1572–1642* (New Haven, Conn., 1954).

But the saints of Puritan England were for the most part patient in awaiting the fulfilment of the divine promises, and were not agreed as to what form it should take in the government of the country when power was in their hands. This was because the visionary and dynamic utopianism of the Puritan sermon was almost always accompanied among the Puritan gentry by a conservative social philosophy. The promised kingdom would be revealed in God's time. It was not for mortal men to insist on knowing its date or its form. They must do their duty in the circumstances appointed by God – which for practical purposes meant, in their allotted place in the social order. So St Paul had taught: converted slaves must still accept slavery.[24]

Elizabethan and Stuart government propagandists often compared Puritanism with Popery because it was alleged to preach disobedience, but in fact English Puritanism never produced a preacher able either to depose a monarch or to ignite resistance by his claim to have the power of deposition. Being based so solidly on the Bible, Puritans always had to reckon with the very texts to which the Royalists appealed – texts urging obedience to kings, reverence for apostles and elders, the general acceptance of one's lot in life. Jean Calvin had himself given great weight to those texts and had been extremely reluctant to countenance any disorder. As much as Richard Hooker was that Puritan pundit, William Perkins, sure that in general 'orderly comeliness is part of the goodness of a thing' and that in particular 'as a king by his laws brings his people in order, and keeps them in subjection, so Christ by his word, and the preaching of it, as it were by a mighty army, draws his elect into his kingdom, and fashions them all to all holy obedience.' As we have just seen, Calvinism exported to America had erected a regime which was in many ways repressive in its insistence on 'holy obedience'. In England the

---

[24] The character of Puritanism as a search for spiritual liberty was well brought out by John S. Coolidge, *The Pauline Renaissance in England: Puritanism and the Bible* (Oxford, 1970). J. Sears McGee, *The Godly Man in Stuart England* (New Haven, Conn., 1976), similarly moved away from analysis in terms of Marxism, while stressing the Puritan dynamism in contrast with the official Church's constant plea for peace and charity.

very discipline on which the Puritan prided himself – discipline
in private prayer and public worship, in chastity and sobriety,
in honest toil – was extended to disciplined obedience to 'the
magistrate', the 'powers that be' ordained by God as part of his
stern response to the Fall of Adam. William Perkins, when he
had boldly declared that when 'Christ is all' there is 'neither
father nor mother, neither master, mistress, maid nor servant,
nor husband nor wife, nor lord, nor subject, nor inferior',
would always go on to remind his fellow Elizabethans that
social distinctions had not yet been·eliminated. This warning
was endlessly repeated by Puritan preachers under the Stuarts.
The Puritan movement included peers, rich aldermen in the
cities and many gentlemen who controlled the countryside as
deputy lieutenants, sheriffs or Justices of the Peace. In their
eyes, Puritanism was an eminently respectable religion.

The case of William Prynne is fairly typical. A lawyer gifted
both with moral courage and the power of invective, he wrote
the best known warning against the doctrines of Laudians
(*Anti-Arminianism*, 1629) and had his ears cropped on the
orders of Laud and other judges for later, very outspoken,
attacks on the bishops and on the Queen's participation in
allegedly lewd plays. But he was so disillusioned by the moral
disorder caused by the civil war that he moved in revulsion to
oppose Cromwell vociferously, and to take part in Royalist
plots. Before he died in 1669 he made a future Archbishop of
Canterbury (Tillotson) his literary executor. The sincere concern of this unattractively abusive and long-winded lawyer was
the moral purification of himself and his contemporaries.[25]

Opposition to the policies of Laud, Strafford and the others
who had been the King's ministers in the 1630s was morally
possible – indeed, imperative – for Puritan MPs; but as events
unfolded they showed that the Puritans in Parliament had no
agreed alternative programme. Did they want to keep bishops
divested of power as in the primitive Church, or to give power
to presbyteries of preachers as in Scotland, or to allow each
congregation to be independent as in Massachusetts? Puritans

---

[25] W. M. Lamont studied *Marginal Prynne* (London, 1963). The ambiguity of *The
Christian Polity of John Calvin* was brought out in Harro Höpfl's study (Cambridge,
1982).

were not agreed in an ecclesiastical policy, any more than they were agreed on what kind of constitutional, limited, monarchy they wanted. This was because the only political conviction that united them was the conviction of an opposition – and of a mostly conservative one. The Petition of Right presented by the Commons to an indignant king in 1628 had behind it the legal conservatism with which Sir Edward Coke had defied King James. In the 1640s there was again much talk about Magna Carta and about an English freedom older than the 'Norman yoke'. The extension of the tax of 'ship money' to inland shires in time of peace was an innovation in 1634, although upheld by a majority of the judges when a very rich gentleman, John Hampden, refused to pay it. Behind Hampden were rich men who had already refused to pay and had been let off – and even after the judgement against Hampden the sheriffs told to collect ship money often found themselves unable to enforce the order. Almost as much indignation was caused by the enforcement of outmoded payments to the king under feudal laws. In the 1630s these, too, seemed to be an innovation, to be resisted. But the opposition's loudest complaint was about innovations in religion, in particular about the Arminian theological revolution which seemed to be changing the face of the Church of England. The defence of the Protestant establishment was a cause which bestowed a halo on the not very heroic figure of a gentleman who refused to pay ship money or a feudal fee.

The opposition to the King's ministers in Parliament was, it is clear, a split within the English governing class – a split which most gentlemen did not wish to see become a revolution. Of the 493 members elected to the 'Long Parliament' in the autumn of 1640, fewer than a hundred seem to have expressed 'Court' rather than 'Country' views in the early stages. But it did not follow that the House of Commons was full of ardent revolutionaries. Those who managed the business of the House often complained that members were absent, indulging in the amusements of London or in their more interesting duties at home; and among members who did attend to the business, there was no unanimity. In November 1641 the Grand Remonstrance setting out the grievances of the Commons passed by only eleven votes (159 to 148). More than fifty MPs served in the King's army, and more than a hundred others in the assembly which he summoned to Oxford in 1644–45. The House of Commons remaining in Westminster included about the same number. In 1645–46 244 new members were elected, all pledged to support the 'Parliamentary' cause, but another decisive vote on the last day of 1646 found 105 voting for the prohibition of all preaching by laymen, 57 against. No fewer than 231 MPs had to be excluded by the soldiers in 'Pride's Purge' in December 1648 before the King's execution could be secured; of the remaining MPs, some 250 in all, only about sixty sat regularly because they were prepared to co-operate with the army. Less than half of that sixty finally approved of the King's execution.

The picture emerging from modern research seems, therefore, to support the older picture of the opposition to the ministers of King Charles as a conservative affair given a limited amount of courage by Puritanism.[26] But this split within the governing class was not the only kind of hostility which confronted the King's ministers. There was another kind of Puritanism, or at least of Protestantism, and it was far more revolutionary.

London was the centre of this extremist movement. Naturally, London preachers tended to be the most eloquent and the most excited. And already in politically quieter days London had witnessed a minor religious revolution: the permanent establishment of congregations which were defiantly separate from the Church of England.

There were three dozen of these 'separatist' churches in existence by 1646. The earliest was a group around a Nottinghamshire squire, Thomas Helwys, who had gone into exile rather than conform – and who in 1612 dared to return to

---

[26] Recent studies include Robert Ashton, *The English Civil War: Conservatism and Revolution, 1603–49* (London, 1978); Anthony Fletcher, *The Outbreak of the English Civil War* (London, 1981); and the 1973 volume already recommended: *The Origins of the Civil War*, ed. Conrad Russell. Some of the theoretical background was sketched by W. M. Lamont, *Godly Rule: Politics and Religion 1603–60* (London, 1969), and David Little, *Religion, Order and Law: A Study in Pre-Revolutionary England* (Oxford, 1970).

England. He also dared to publish a pamphlet dedicated to the King and pleading that 'the King is a mortal man and not God: therefore hath no power over the immortal souls of his subjects, to make laws and ordinances for them, and to set spiritual laws over them.' This plea for religious liberty (the first of its kind in English) landed him in prison. Another group was founded when a few laymen in a house in Southwark joined hands in a ring with a clergyman, Henry Jacob, who had dared to return from exile in 1616. They all believed that only adult baptism was valid, but these early Baptists were not Calvinists, for they rejected the doctrine that Christ had died only to save the 'elect'. Their creed was to become known as the 'General Baptist' position. But during the 1630s 'Particular Baptist' congregations were formed. These not only confined baptism to adults but also confined salvation to the elect. The first pastor of such a congregation was John Spilsbury, a cobbler by trade. Radicalism in religion began to include the belief that a congregation could get along without paying for a full-time pastor. And such radicalism in religion might encourage radicalism in politics.[27]

Whether or not preachers fanned its revolutionary spirit, by 1640 a large element in the London mob was spoiling for a fight with the authorities. It often staged demonstrations, beginning with one to welcome William Prynne on his release from prison. For months on end the mob did all it could to intimidate the Parliament sitting in Westminster. The howls of the angry people were probably decisive in making Lords and Commons press for the execution of Strafford and the imprisonment of Laud. Cries of 'Justice! Justice! Justice!' drowned hesitations. At various later turning-points in the plot the Parliamentary stage at Westminster was invaded by the mob. Cries for 'Bread!' often mingled with 'Justice!' – for the mob was a ragged army which the hunger and fear of so many in the countryside had brought together in London. 'The population of London and its suburbs may have numbered as many as 450,000 at this time', we are told. 'It . . . was by very

---

[27] These London separatist churches were studied by Murray Tolmie, *The Triumph of the Saints* (Cambridge, 1977).

far [the] largest urban area, no other town in the country
having more than 25,000 inhabitants. London contained the
most massive concentration of poor people in the whole kingdom, and a very high proportion of its population consisted of
recent immigrants from the provinces. Crowded together in
the slums, they shed many of the traditions of deference into
which they had been born in their villages . . . London had
grown too fast for its machinery of government, with the forces
of repression at its disposal, to be able very easily to control its
population and maintain order; but it had not grown too
quickly for rumours and ideas to spread quickly over the whole
area.'[28]

The most readily believed of these rumours was the tale that
the King's ministers were about to bring in a large army of
murdering Papists – from Ireland, from France, from Spain,
from heaven knew where. The fear of a return of Popery was
the most conspicuous feature of the Grand Remonstrance, and
we cannot wonder, for the Pope was often being preached
about as Antichrist. The accusation that he had plotted to
introduce an army from Ireland was what destroyed Strafford.
Laud's Arminian theology was probably not much understood
by the London mob; but the rumour was that the bishops were
friends of the Papists, allies of Antichrist. Fifteen thousand
signatures were collected for the petition from London to
Parliament in December 1640 calling for the abolition of the
whole system of bishops, 'root and branch'. The mob had
made the Papists the scapegoats for its own unhappiness and
insecurity, and therefore it was out to get the bishops.[29]

The time-absorbing concentration of Londoners on the
political excitements of 1640–42 increased the difficulties of
production and trade – particularly in the cloth industry,
which was depressed anyway. It was not long before the
common people of lesser towns began to set up their own cries
for justice and bread, and to voice their own fears that some-

---

[28] Brian Manning, *The English People and the English Revolution, 1640–49* (London,
1976), p. 71.
[29] The popular hatred which lumped Roman Catholics and Church of England
bishops together has been studied by Christopher Hill in *Antichrist in Seventeenth-
century England* (London, 1971).

how the Papists were to blame. Thousands of signatures were collected for petitions to Parliament demanding that something should be done – a concerted movement without precedent in English history. At the same time ominous riots occurred in some rural areas. The pressure of overpopulation which had influenced thousands of the most adventurous to start farming the virgin soil of North America also meant that the untilled land of England became more important. Many obscure country folk had supported themselves from the 'waste' lands (for example, from the reeds and the fowls of the Fens) and were hostile to the 'improvement' of these lands (for example, the drainage of the Fens) since it meant that in future they would have to pay rents. At the same time inflation meant that ambitious landlords were raising their rents and reducing the perquisites of their labourers – and all this in an age when the prices of staple foodstuffs steadily mounted. The evidence suggests that the 1630s had been years of misery for many thousands of obscure English families. Inevitably many peasants began rejoicing when stories reached them that the King, the lords and the gentlemen were at each other's throats in London. Hearing that Bishop John Williams was unlikely to reappear in his great house at Buckden, local women drove their cows into the newly extended park and, when a magistrate rebuked them, 'only answered him with contemptuous words'. Elsewhere violence as well as insults expressed the pent-up indignation of the peasantry. Puritanism, which had been basically a religion of gentlemen and merchants who admired preachers, was involved in one (and, it seems, only one) way. It was easy to cry that the landlords were open or concealed Papists – the very cry which some of these landlords in Parliament were setting up against the bishops.

There was no organized peasants' revolt, because there was no national leadership and no common cry apart from the hysterical fear of Popery. But the demonstrations in London and the riots in the countryside were like the first drops in a new storm. Alarm about disorder seems to have been an important factor in moving considerable numbers of the propertied, including MPs, to view the King's cause with much more sympathy. But Parliament needed soldiers to fight for it, was prepared to pay them, and drew them largely from the ranks of those who had suffered in the recent economic changes; and then revolution came nearer. In the army those soldiers might hear Puritan chaplains telling them that their strengths were greater, and their lives more precious, than those of the Royalist gentlemen, the Lord's enemies, whom they had to fight to the death. Some of the low-born soldiers might be made officers, so great were the necessities of war. As Oliver Cromwell wrote to the Suffolk county committee in 1643: 'I had rather have a plain russet-coated captain that knows what he fights for, and loves what he knows, than that which you call a gentleman and is nothing else.'

As the war fought with Puritan slogans proceeded, it became what the noblemen and gentlemen meeting in Parliament had never intended: a revolution.

A WAR BECOMES A REVOLUTION

In the 'Short Parliament' which met in April 1640 the attitudes which were to bring a foolish king to his execution were all displayed.[30] Although he claimed such great powers for anointed kings, he did not take the trouble to work out, or present, a coherent policy. Instead he got the Lord Keeper to ask for taxes and was surprised when the House of Commons, organized by John Pym, insisted on the redress of grievances before it would vote a supply of taxes. In reply he turned for help to the House of Lords and then, alleging that some MPs were in league with the rebellious Scots, abruptly dismissed Parliament.

Such actions were characteristic. Charles always relied on his counsellors – among whom the most disastrous (because the most ignorant) was his French queen – but he liked to play one counsellor off against another. In that way he hoped to show who was master. He did not pursue a consistent policy in

---

[30] The best narrative of the civil war remains C. V. Wedgwood, *The King's War 1641–47* (London, 1958). The best analysis is Ivan Roots, *The Great Rebellion, 1642–60* (London, 1966).

dealing with opposition because it was hard for him to believe in his heart that the opposition could exist. When he made gestures of co-operation with the gentry (in 1640 he offered to abandon the collection of ship money in exchange for some approved system of revenue raising), he did not make his gestures large enough. Charles never allowed a strong moderate party to form around him, although such a party could have controlled the Commons at any date before December 1648. On the other hand, he was always too much of a patriot to obtain the large subsidies from France or Spain which alone could have enabled him to finance his court, army and civil service without needing the good will of the Commons. He was never even able to make up his mind between France or Spain. All that he did in this field was to write letters, ineffectively asking for help and damaging his reputation when the letters became known in England. At almost every juncture he intrigued amateurishly, hoping to divide his enemies (as in his plea to the peers in 1640) but often succeeding only in alienating them all still further. Then his anger that a king should have to stoop to such devices would flare up and he would take hasty action intended to end the problem once and for all; action which usually misfired. In his own eyes and in the eyes of his followers, the King behaved almost always as a Christian gentleman. The one major error which Charles admitted was a moral error: he allowed himself to be released by Strafford from his own oath that his minister should not suffer in life or estate. Charles came to believe that, because of this sin, God had allowed him to be defeated by traitors and brought to execution. Otherwise the King's tone was one of injured innocence. Yet his enemies came to regard him as a 'man of blood' whose own blood should be shed, because the succession of futile tricks by which he attempted to divide and rule his subjects had cost those subjects dear and needed to be brought to an end by the axe.

For long Archbishop Laud and his supporters seem to have been blind to the danger to the Church of England in its reliance on a king who was such an inept politician. In the spring of 1640 this, too, was demonstrated. The Convocation of the clergy continued to sit after the dissolution of Parliament, in defiance of constitutional precedent. It voted the King a small sum of money, infuriating the dispersed MPs without substantially helping the King. And it accepted from Laud and the clergy a new set of canons, further alienating the Puritans. These canons ordered that bearing arms against a king 'on any pretext whatsoever' should always be held sinful, and that a sermon in praise of the divine right of kings should be preached in every church once a quarter. Another imposed on the clergy an oath of loyalty to the government of the Church by 'archbishops, bishops, archdeacons, deans, *et cetera*'. Many Puritans chose to believe that *et cetera* might include the Pope, although the oath went on to reject 'the usurpations and superstitions of the See of Rome'.

Twelve peers presented a petition for another parliament, but what made the summons of the 'Long Parliament' inevitable in November 1640 was another invasion by the Scots, who had to be bought off. This parliament lasted for so long because it insisted on the King's consent to an Act providing that it should never be dissolved without its own consent. In its initial stages Parliament was so largely united because its policy was conservative: to punish Strafford and Laud for their innovations and to prevent their repetition. Even when Strafford's impeachment for 'endeavouring to subvert the fundamental laws' had to be abandoned in response to his brilliant self-defence, the Act of Attainder which finally brought him to the block was supported by a majority in the Commons so large, and by a majority in the Lords so surprising, that the King added his own consent. Then a rapid series of measures demolished the apparatus on which Strafford and Laud had relied. A parliament must meet for at least fifty days every three years. Non-parliamentary taxes and the grants of commercial monopolies to royal favourites were declared illegal. The courts of Star Chamber and High Commission were abolished.

It seems perfectly possible that the King could now have established a moderate administration in England supported by bishops with strictly limited powers, had he been so determined. In the summer of 1641 he visited Scotland, set up a government consisting of his former enemies, and had the satisfaction of seeing the Scottish army in England disbanded. But he took no major steps to secure the loyalty of prominent English moderates; and in May 1641 he lost by death from smallpox an aristocrat much admired by Puritans, the Earl of Bedford, who given a chance would have become a reforming Lord Treasurer with his associate, John Pym, as Chancellor of the Exchequer.

A fresh crisis arose in October 1641, when the Irish Catholics seized the opportunity to rebel – for the Commons, having reason to distrust the King, insisted on control of the expeditionary force for which they were prepared to pay. Another result of the Irish rebellion was to enflame the anti-Papist emotions of the London mob; the fire seems to have been fanned by John Pym. That December the London apprentices occupied themselves by preventing the bishops from taking their seats in the House of Lords, shouting 'No bishops!' and 'No Popish lords!' At the suggestion of John Williams (now the Church's leading figure, with Laud in prison), the bishops replied by claiming that the proceedings of the Lords in their absence were invalid – a reply which greatly embarrassed those in Parliament who had been struggling for the survival of the bishops, their revenues and their remaining political powers. A dozen bishops were promptly impeached and sent off to the Tower. Their permanent exclusion from Parliament became inevitable when the King failed to carry off a counter-*coup*, the arrest of his five leading enemies in the Commons on charges of subverting the 'fundamental laws'.

The whole future of the bishops, and of much else, now depended on the outcome of the propaganda war which opened at the beginning of 1642. The King left the capital and moved around the country, having enlisted Edward Hyde as his chief propagandist and having agreed to Hyde's moderate constitutionalism as the line to be taken. The Commons – increasingly under the dominance of John Pym, who had escaped arrest – did not believe that the King seriously intended concessions. They strengthened their hold on the unpaid militia or 'trained bands' in London and the counties, and made sure of the navy. They appealed to their supporters to gather horses and arms, and thus encouraged the King to take the advice of the militants who gathered round him to compete with the moderates. On 22 August 1642 he raised his standard at Nottingham. Soon afterwards he issued a manifesto to his supporters: 'You shall meet with no enemies but traitors, most of them Brownists, Anabaptists and Atheists; such who desire to destroy both Church and State . . .'

Although both sides had appealed to arms in the belief that the issue would be settled in a matter of months, none of the early battles in the civil war decided much. For a few weeks it seemed possible that the Royalists would simply march into London – but London defended itself, and then sent its men to relieve a city under a more prolonged siege, Gloucester. The first decisive move was the Solemn League and Covenant entered into by Parliament with the Scots in St Margaret's church, Westminster, a year after the war's outbreak. Parliament, led by Pym, bought this military support by a promise to establish a new system of church government, uniform in all three kingdoms of England, Scotland and Ireland, 'according to the Word of God and the example of the best reformed Churches'. This treaty was decisive because the prospect of an army from the north stiffened Parliament's supporters in the field to resist the Royalist forces who had previously seemed likely to prevail – and because the price paid showed the political determination of the Parliamentary leadership. Pym was willing to run the risk of relying on the Scots, rather than run the risk of relying on the King; and when he died of cancer in December 1643 he was succeeded in the leadership not by more moderate but more extreme men. Oliver St John the lawyer who was an implacable prosecutor, Harry Vane who had returned from New England with a stern mission, Oliver Cromwell the soldier – such men were resolved to win the war against the King whatever instruments they had to use. On the Royalist side one of the leading moderates, Lord Falkland, died on the battlefield of Newbury, and the King's ear was increasingly filled with the advice of professional soldiers such as his nephew Prince Rupert, promising a military solution to his problems.

Parliament's abolition of the jurisdiction of bishops and archdeacons, and of cathedral deans and chapters, came in

January 1643. It was a step which had to be taken in order to satisfy both the consciences and the pockets of those now fighting for Parliament. Estates of bishops and cathedrals, sold off during the 1640s to those favoured by Parliament, raised over a million pounds, mostly spent on the war.

Recommendations about the positive reform of the Church were entrusted to a conference of 121 theologians, with thirty lay assessors, by an ordinance issued by Parliament in June 1643. As a gesture four bishops were included together with five doctors of divinity prepared to defend them; but this group made practically no contribution. The initiative was taken and held by Calvinist Presbyterians who talked the same theological language as the Scots, together with some 'Independents' who talked the same language as the English soldiers. This 'Westminster Assembly' met that summer in Westminster Abbey, moving when the autumn came to the Jerusalem Chamber where a fireplace offered some comfort. We may take a brief holiday from the civil war by considering the outcome. The main contribution which the conference made to the history of the Christian world was contained in its statement of Calvinist doctrine, the Westminster Confession, intended to provide a theological basis for agreement between the English and the Scots. Completed before the end of 1646, this document was approved by the General Assembly of the Church of Scotland in 1647 and by the English Parliament the following year. It was followed by two documents intended for the instruction of the laity – the Longer and Shorter Catechisms, largely drafted by the vicar of Boston in Lincolnshire, Anthony Tuckney. These, too, were officially adopted in Scotland and England. By the time that Tuckney died in 1670 he had seen his work rejected by government and theologians alike in England; yet Scotland remained faithful to it, the Westminster Confession continued to be a 'standard of faith' among all orthodox Presbyterians, and the Shorter Catechism was to teach many generations of the children of Presbyterian and other parents. The position adopted in response to the disputes caused by Arminianism was an affirmation of God's predestinating decree to save a 'certain and definite' number of angels and men 'without any foresight of faith or good works, or perseverance in either of them'. When some acknowledgement of 'second causes' in an individual's salvation was added in the teaching given by this Westminster Assembly, it was less emphatic. But the main lesson which was to be remembered by the young, from the Shorter Catechism of 1647, was the definition of the 'chief end of man': 'to glorify God and to enjoy him for ever'.[31]

Meanwhile the civil war in England was not enjoyable. Whether the Scots were going to prevail with their insistence on a Presbyterian church government, or Independents such as John Milton were going to persuade the English that 'new presbyter' would be little better than 'old priest', what was clear after the treaty with the Scots was that the Elizabethan settlement of English religion was at an end. And it was beginning to seem possible that the whole Elizabethan order of society might be among the victims of an increasingly bitter war. In August 1643 a crowd of women with white ribbons in their hats demonstrated outside the House of Commons, crying 'Peace!' The only result was that one of them was killed, along with two men looking on, as the demonstration was violently dispersed.

In 1644 the Scots arrived and, combining with Oliver Cromwell's troops from East Anglia, defeated Prince Rupert on Marston Moor on 2 July. To turn that victory into the complete defeat of the King, it now seemed essential to signalize the end of the old religious order by executing old William Laud on 2 January 1645. In the same month a new *Directory of Public Worship* compiled by the Puritan divines of the Westminster Assembly was substituted for the old Book of Common Prayer as the national standard intended to be observed in the parishes. Although this directory permitted a considerable variety, a rigid discipline marked the reorganization of the

---

[31] Narratives were compiled by B. B. Warfield, *The Westminster Assembly and its Work* (London, 1931), and S. W. Carruthers, *The Everyday Work of the Westminster Assembly* (Philadelphia, Pa., 1943). R. T. Kendall, *Calvin and English Calvinism to 1649*, pp. 185–208, concluded that there was 'complete fundamental harmony' in theology, although he disagreed with Warfield over the extent of the influence of Calvin. He argued that the Westminster divines owed more to Beza or to his English exponent, William Perkins, as modified by Ames.

military forces on which Parliament depended. This decisive period of retraining saw the birth of the 'New Model Army' which was to bring victory. The final move in the reorganization was to exclude the three earls, Essex, Manchester and Warwick, from command. Cromwell had moved the 'Self-Denying Ordinance' which compelled peers or MPs to resign their commissions, but since the House of Lords insisted on an amendment which made re-appointment possible, and since he seemed indispensable, he ended up as Lieutenant-General; Sir Thomas Fairfax, a professional soldier, remained his superior.

The great military fact of 1645 was the triumph of the New Model Army. Deploying superior numbers and discipline, and sending in its cavalry under Cromwell, it routed the Royalists at Naseby near Leicester. Not long afterwards Prince Rupert surrendered Bristol, to his royal uncle's fury. The King's only hope now lay in enlisting in his cause an army from outside England. His previous intrigues with this motive, documented in papers captured at Naseby, hardened opinion against him when printed as *The King's Cabinet Opened*; but he clung to the hope. At the end of April 1646 he slipped out of Oxford (which had been his wartime headquarters) and at Southwell gave himself up to the surprised Scots. He was counting on their instinctive loyalty to their sovereign. He was also counting on their suspicion of the New Model Army.

Most of the remaining members of the House of Commons shared the King's hope of a rally of the conservative forces. Oliver Cromwell had accused the Earl of Manchester of not really wanting to see the King defeated, but the Earl had replied with accusations far more damaging in the eyes of most MPs. Cromwell was alleged to have said that he wanted 'to live to see never a nobleman in England' and that he was ready to fight for religious liberty even if it meant drawing his sword against the Scots. Now after Naseby Cromwell sent the Speaker of the House of Commons a letter which did something to bear out the Earl's accusations. 'Honest men served you faithfully in this action,' he wrote. 'Sir, they are trusty. I beseech you in the name of God not to discourage them . . . He that ventures his life for the liberty of his country, I wish he trust God for the liberty of his conscience, and you for the liberty he fights for.'

When the Commons printed the letter they suppressed that last sentence, but it was a fact that the soldiers of the New Model Army, although recruited to be defenders of the Presbyterian MPs and the allies of the Presbyterian Scots, had not been subjected to any theological test. 'The State in choosing men,' Cromwell had declared, 'takes no notice of their opinions.' In practice the soldiers held a wide variety of opinions and were disturbingly willing to demand liberty for them. A fortnight after the battle of Marston Moor the attack on religious persecution had been launched in the book by Roger Williams, but that plea from an eccentric New England preacher had led to an outcry among the respectable; of course Christian England must be uniform – on a Presbyterian, if not an Anglican, basis. After the New Model Army's triumph at Naseby, John Lilburne's pamphlet claiming religious liberty as *England's Birthright* could not be howled down so readily. Even in the House of Commons some MPs who were elders in Presbyterian churches were now tending to vote with Independents such as Cromwell because they feared the tyranny of a Presbyterian Church established on a national scale. The majority of MPs had no wish to see any preacher's tyranny; in March 1646 they agreed to the establishment of presbyteries all over England, but only after insisting that anyone excommunicated would have the right to appeal to a parliamentary committee. Even less, however, did they wish to see Cromwell's soldiers dictating terms which seemed likely to destroy the whole stability of Church and State. A book of 1646 by Thomas Edwards catalogued the heresies which seemed to be poisoning and destroying the very life of Christian England. It was a long catalogue, and it was called *Gangraena*. MPs were among those who read it with horror.[32]

While the gentlemen in Parliament nursed these fears of anarchy, the people in the country seem to have been domin-

---

[32] See George Yule, *The Independents in the English Civil War* (Cambridge, 1958), and J. R. McCormack, *Revolutionary Politics in the Long Parliament* (Cambridge, Mass., 1973).

ated by the simple desire to see the conflict ended, the armies disbanded, trade restored and taxation lowered. The small armies which had fought the civil war had not done a great deal of physical damage, but they certainly had interrupted both commerce and agriculture. And to sustain the war, Parliament had taxed the country far more heavily than any Stuart king had ever attempted. The new excise duty on beer or tobacco was particularly unpopular. It seemed the right time for the settlement with the King which Parliament had always claimed to be seeking; and it was reasonable to calculate that an agreement could be reached by taking two steps – the King making an alliance with the Scots, and Parliament preferring this alliance to the greater risks of radical government by soldiers and religious leadership by heretics.

The essential preliminary was, however, that the King should accept the support of the Scots on their terms, even if it meant accepting Presbyterianism for the time being. When he made himself their prisoner, the Scots naturally thought that this was his intention. From France his queen urged him to abandon the Anglican bishops; to her they were not true Catholic bishops – and he could, of course, always go back on the gesture once he had regained power. Day after day, Presbyterians argued with the King by speech or writing, attempting to persuade him to sign the covenant against Popery and prelacy. He persistently refused. Instead of making this tactical alliance with his gaolers, he attempted to negotiate once again with Parliament; but here, too, he refused to yield on the vital point of abdicating control of the armed forces for twenty years. He told Henrietta Maria that they must not 'stir one jot' from the authority to which their son was heir – and that of the two possible concessions, the renunciation of the bishops would be the more dangerous to the monarchy, 'for people are governed by pulpits more than the sword'. His cause, he later added, was 'the cause of every king in Christendom'. Eventually the Scots preferred to reach an agreement with Parliament, which at least had money to pay them off, rather than with the bewilderingly obstinate king. Charles was therefore entrusted to the mercies of his English subjects.

EXECUTING A KING

The King had virtually signed his own death warrant when he refused to abandon the bishops in order to purchase the support of the Scots, at a time when he could continue to rely reasonably on the support of the moderates who still constituted the majority in Parliament. That is his best claim to the title of martyr. And perhaps subconsciously he now began a journey towards martyrdom – as that very different martyr, Thomas Becket, had done when laying down his life against a king almost six hundred years before. But just as the future St Thomas of Canterbury had complicated his later reputation by arrogant, perverse and argumentative behaviour almost till the moment when he had allowed the knights to strike him down in his own cathedral, so the future King Charles the Martyr now conducted himself in a way that was less than saintly. He plotted almost until the day when he gave his flawless last performance in the icy sunshine on the scaffold outside the Banqueting House in Whitehall. Indeed, the King probably did believe that, being endowed by God with the authority and wisdom monopolized by kings, he could divide his enemies and appeal to the still loyal hearts of his people. More than once he made the request to be allowed back to London. If only he could return to the capital where he had been crowned and anointed, surely he would return to an invincible popularity. In fact he was brought back to die – but even during his trial the emotion dominant in him was indignant, incredulous surprise that the judges appointed by what was left of the House of Commons actually were sentencing a king to death.

As spring turned into summer in 1647 he was kept in custody by Parliament at Holdenby House in Northamptonshire. He watched with pleasure the tensions growing between the MPs and the soldiers. Parliament blundered badly by refusing (at first) to pay the soldiers' arrears of pay and to assure them of pardon for any offences during the war. 'Agitators' were chosen to get something done about the soldiers' demands. One of the things they did was to send Cornet Joyce to take the King to Hampton Court; when Charles asked him for his commission, this junior officer simply pointed to the troops behind him. But the King still did not feel doomed, for as confusion mounted the army was seen to be split not only from Parliament but also within itself.

Fairfax, Cromwell and most of the other senior officers – the 'grandees' as they were called – were at this stage prepared to reach a compromise. Cromwell kept repeating that they must have a king; 'no men could enjoy their lives and estates quietly without the king had his rights.' On one occasion he even called Charles 'the uprightest and most conscientious man of his three kingdoms'. When Cromwell had changed his mind and had brought Charles to trial, Fairfax's wife was to shout in the King's defence. 'Not half the people,' she protested, wanted the trial. But in that summer of 1647 many of the rank and file of the army had no such tender feelings about the monarchy. They knew only that a new age was dawning. The King had been defeated and a thrilling opportunity had arrived to pull down others who had denied 'the people's just rights and liberties'. A declaration of the army, claiming those rights, boasted: 'We were not a mere mercenary army . . . but called forth and conjured by the several declarations of Parliament . . . against all particular parties or interests whatsoever.' And now, as the agitator of Fairfax's own regiment blurted out, there was 'no visible authority in the kingdom but the power and force of the sword'.

That summer the Levellers put about many radical ideas, although they were divided. Some wanted no more than the sovereignty of Parliament – a Parliament to be elected by all adult males who were not servants, alms-takers or Royalists (which would have excluded two-thirds of Englishmen). Others wanted one man, one vote (excluding only supporters of the King) leading to a radical redistribution of wealth, with communes to take over the agriculture from the feudal manors and the privately owned farms. On two points all Levellers were agreed. The King must be stripped of all his powers. The clergy must be stripped of the security of their right to tithes.[33]

---

[33] Recent studies include H. N. Brailsford, *The Levellers and the English Revolution* (London, 1961); C. B. Macpherson, *The Political Theory of Possessive Individualism* (Oxford, 1962), chapter 3; G. E. Aylmer, *The Levellers in the English Revolution* (London, 1975).

The army slowly marched on London and, once there, was in a position to impose its will. But in the autumn of 1647 it was very uncertain what its will was. The parish church of Putney was the scene of long debates as soldiers, all appealing to divine guidance and quoting rival texts of Scripture, stumbled towards formulating the political theories of Right and Left in response to the 'Agreement of the People' drawn up by the Levellers. Cromwell played an uncertain role for much of the time throughout these months of intoxicating confusion. He tended to back his fellow soldiers against his fellow MPs and had no wish to see Presbyterianism enforced, but he also expressed horror at the suggestion that men who had 'no interest but the interest of breathing' might have votes. In the Putney debates, he pleaded for compromise and unity. Colonel Thomas Rainborough displayed and urged more courage; not for nothing was he the brother-in-law of Governor Winthrop of Massachusetts. 'I do think the poorest man in England is not at all bound in a strict sense to that government that he hath not had a voice to put himself under.' And he boasted: 'When I leap I shall take so much of God with me, and so much of just and right with me, as I shall jump sure.'[34]

In the end it was Cromwell who jumped decisively. He persuaded the confused debaters in the Putney church that the agitators ought to return to the regiments. The reason given was that the agitators would then be better able to gather the soldiers' opinions in preparation for a fuller debate, but in fact a different policy towards the Levellers was becoming clear in Cromwell's mind. 'Break them,' he told his fellow officers, 'or they will break you.' When some of the troops demonstrated by sticking the slogan 'England's Freedom, Soldiers' Rights' in their hats, the General cut down the mutiny with his own sword.

Charles also attempted to jump, but once again he tried to be too clever, jumping in too many directions. For some time he seemed to be moving towards the worried generals and the

---

[34] See A. S. P. Woodhouse, *Puritanism and Liberty, Being the Army Debates 1647–49* (London, 1938); Leo F. Solt, *Saints in Arms: Puritanism and Democracy in Cromwell's Army* (Stanford, Cal., 1959); A. L. Morton, *Freedom in Arms* (London, 1975).

moderate MPs. He escaped from the soldiers' custody in Hampton Court (almost certainly with Cromwell's connivance) and took refuge in the Isle of Wight (which was commanded by Cromwell's cousin). From the greater security of Carisbrooke Castle he made – or seemed to make – handsome offers to the English moderates: he would renounce the control of the armed forces for his lifetime and the bishops for an experimental period of three years. But he dangled similar baits before the Scots, and refused his assent when MPs translated his bargaining offers into actual bills. His double-dealing was now apparent, and in January 1648 the Commons voted to hold no more negotiations with him. All now depended on what the Scots would do to support the Royalists, and in the spring and summer of 1648 a second civil war flared up.

It turned out that the King had jumped into the fire. The second civil war was widespread but short-lived. The decisive action was Cromwell's defeat of the invaders from Scotland at Preston. Even now the pressures for a settlement were such that many MPs were soon again trying to come to terms with the King (and again refusing to settle the arrears of the soldiers' pay); and a few of the army officers, including Fairfax the General, still shared the hope of a compromise. But other officers encouraged Colonel Pride, who was in command of the troops guarding Parliament, to exclude most of the MPs as traitors to 'the cause'. Pride's Purge, on 6 December, was accepted by Cromwell, although he had not initiated it. The officers now controlling the 'Rump Parliament' were increasingly dominated by Cromwell's personality – and determined, as Cromwell now was, to end the King's plots once and for all, before they cost more English lives. On the first day of January 1649 the Commons set up a special court to try Charles Stuart for treason in making war against Parliament and the kingdom. The refusal by the Lords to participate in an act so lacking in precedent was swept aside. Pushed by events which he called 'providences', Cromwell was jumping into a republic.

In the long run Cromwell was not wise to arrange for the King's execution, because the monarchy still occupied a unique place in the feelings, if not in the reasonings, of most Englishmen – and the dignity of the King as the end approached was the peak moment in the 'kingcraft' of the Stuart dynasty. The condemned man made sure that his famous last injunction to Bishop Juxon, 'Remember!', would be obeyed. The last words which he heard on 30 January 1649, from the executioner, were 'Your Majesty'. A great deep groan went up from the crowd when they saw his head severed. It is not much of an exaggeration to say that a shudder went through all Europe as the news spread. A book of prayers and meditations compiled by a clergyman, almost certainly John Gauden, was attributed to Charles and provided an edifying portrait of 'his Sacred Majesty in his Sufferings and Solitude'. Despite its Greek title *Eikon Basilike* (which was probably given in order to confuse the censors), it was a rapid and steady best-seller. In the long run, therefore, the King's execution added invaluably to the mystique of the monarchy. Again a comparison may be made with Thomas Becket's martyrdom – which did more for the Church than his life had ever done.

LEVELLERS AND RANTERS

In the practical politics of 1649 the Royalist cause seemed to be buried along with the King's corpse, taken to lie in a vault beside Henry VIII in St George's Chapel, Windsor, as snow fell. The reason why Charles had had to wait four hours in the Banqueting House before his execution was that it had suddenly been remembered that it was necessary for the Rump Parliament to pass an act forbidding the proclamation of a new king; but the precaution was probably not necessary, for the dead king's heir was a powerless, poverty-stricken exile. At home Royalists, stunned by the regicide, had to pay large fines or see their estates confiscated. Crown lands and church lands were sold off, and the triumphant officers enjoyed the financial fruits of victory. The House of Lords was formally abolished in March, and the monarchy followed two months later. In theory, all the sovereignty now resided in the House of Commons. In practice, however, the average sitting consisted of some eighty MPs, looking nervously over their shoulders to see what the army was thinking.

Further excited by this removal of old landmarks, the Levellers poured proposals into the soldiers' ears and pamphlets into the public debate. When a young trooper was shot for disobedience, his London funeral became a great demonstration in their favour, with their sea-green colours everywhere. A wider mutiny broke out in the army. This shocked Cromwell into resolute action again. He and Fairfax kept the loyalty of their own regiments and of enough other soldiers to end the disturbance, and when some of the mutineers fled he surprised them at Burford on Sunday 13 May. He killed some, imprisoned the rest in a church, and then publicly shot the ringleaders. A grateful Oxford University – so recently the Royalist headquarters – awarded the generals honorary doctorates and the City of London gave them a banquet.

Cromwell knew, however, that the struggle was not yet over, for Leveller propaganda could not be stopped by a few bullets or banquets. The distress of the people was too real; 1649 was a year when bad harvests, high taxation and the general dislocation caused by the war had reduced many English families to the misery which welcomes revolutionary talk. In London 'Honest John' Lilburne made himself conspicuous both as a radical pamphleteer against 'England's new chains' and as a prisoner in the Tower, and a jury failed to agree with the furious MPs that he was guilty of treason.[35] Still more dramatically, the 'True Levellers' set up a commune on St George's Hill near Kingston-upon-Thames. Because they began to cultivate the ground in a way that was supposed to encourage Communism all over England, they were nicknamed 'the Diggers'. Although the experiment collapsed, what was not so quickly forgotten was the eloquence of its leader, Gerrard Winstanley, pleading that once private property was abolished Christ would rise in his 'sons and daughters', the free English.[36]

---

[35] See Pauline Gregg, *Free-born John: A Biography of John Lilburne* (London, 1961).

[36] See *The Law of Freedom and Other Writings by Gerrard Winstanley*, ed. Christopher Hill (London, 1973), and T. Wilson Hayes, *Winstanley the Digger* (Cambridge, Mass., 1979).

In many parts of England in this revolutionary year 1649 there was an outburst of crude democracy in free speech and free behaviour. Back in 1646 *Gangraena* by Thomas Edwards had catalogued 199 heresies. Now there were more. The most vociferous of the radicals were known as 'the Ranters' – publicly deriding all the sacred conventions of Church and State, praising the people's wisdom along with the people's pleasures of sex, beer and tobacco, demanding the people's liberation, questioning the existence of God along with the privileges of the gentry. A typical incident occurred in the churchyard of Walton-upon-Thames. A soldier announced to the congregation, as it left after the Sunday afternoon service, that the Sabbath, the tithes, the ministers and the magistrates had all been abolished. He then produced a Bible, 'Here is a book you have in great veneration . . . but I must tell you, it is abolished. It containeth beggarly elements, milk for babes. But now Christ is in glory amongst us.' And taking the candle from his lantern, he set fire to the Bible. Parliament reacted by a Blasphemy Act, imposing a lifelong exile for a second offence.[37]

Alarmed by such extremists, the men in power were unwilling to disturb the social order further by destroying all the structure of the parishes or all the security of the clergy. Tithes were therefore still collected to support lay rectors or ordained ministers, and gentlemen who had not been branded as Royalists continued to be lay rectors or patrons of the parishes, appointing the ministers. The ecclesiastical rights of 'delinquent' gentry were taken over by county committees and those of the Crown reverted to individual congregations. In practice clergymen with a wide variety of opinions, including Anglican opinions or non-Calvinist Protestant opinions, were left free to preach. The only national authority was a committee of ministers and laymen given power to eject unsuitable ministers and schoolmasters. There was no General Assembly supervising the religion of England on the model provided by the General Assembly of the Church of Scotland, and the *Directory of Worship* which Parliament had accepted in 1645 had left much

---

[37] The best study is A. L. Morton, *The World of the Ranters* (London, 1970).

freedom in the hands of parish ministers. In brief, the tidy Presbyterian system which had been the aim of the majority when Parliament had made its Solemn League and Covenant with the Scots in 1643 did not exist in England six years later. Although the bishops had been reduced to obscurity and poverty, although the Westminster Assembly of divines had been able to reach a complete theological agreement about orthodox Calvinism, it had not proved possible to establish a Calvinist system of church government with a uniformity which would have satisfied Calvin's logical mind. Discipline remained less conspicuous than variety. England remained a land of compromises, with many remnants of the old order of squire and parson surviving alongside the radical ideas of the revolutionary movements.

OLIVER CROMWELL

At the head of the victorious English army was Oliver Cromwell. Even while surrounded by his troops or immersed in the affairs of the State he was essentially a solitary man, especially after the death of his friend, fellow soldier and son-in-law, Henry Ireton, in 1651.[38] Although the Royalists naturally accused him of consistent, ruthless and unlimited ambition, it would be fairer to call him an opportunist, responding to emergencies. A remark which he is said to have made to the French ambassador in July 1647 seems to have been honest in its mixture of uncertainty and a willingness to accept promotion: 'None rises so high as he who knows not wither he is going.'

The Royalists also associated him personally with the vandalism despoiling church buildings, and in the twentieth

---

[38] Biographies include Robert S. Paul, *The Lord Protector: Religion and Politics in the Life of Oliver Cromwell* (London, 1955), and Antonia Fraser, *Cromwell Our Chief of Men* (London, 1973). Maurice Ashley, *Oliver Cromwell and His World* (London, 1972), is splendidly illustrated. Assessments were collected as *Cromwell: A Profile*, ed. Ivan Roots (London, 1973).

century it is still being said about many a church that 'Cromwell stabled his horses here'. It is true that no evidence suggests that Anglican doctrine or worship ever appealed to him. On the other hand, he was no vandal – and no Presbyterian. Nor does he seem to have been completely an Independent, believing as a matter of theological principle in the independence of each local congregation. So far as we know he never formally joined a local congregation. He was thoroughly a layman. His respect for preaching was far from being unlimited; he secured the right of a national committee controlled by him to supervise all 'public preachers'. There is no evidence that he habitually consulted any clergyman about what to do while a farmer, while a soldier or while Lord Protector.[39] Throughout his life his religious views seem to have been very much his own. He wrestled for himself with the Scriptures and with the evidence of events. In political success, above all in military victory (he was never defeated), he found evidence of God's approval and grew ecstatic. A letter to his daughter Bridget in 1646 expressed some sympathy with the new sect of the Seekers, but showed that he was too conscious of his own vocation to success to join that group. 'To be a seeker is to be of the best sect next to a finder, and such a one shall every faithful, humble seeker be at the end.'

Born in 1599, he was in many ways an Elizabethan; his mother, wife and favourite daughter were all called Elizabeth, and when in power he was enthusiastic about the 'Western Design' to fight Spain for the riches of America. He belonged to the backbone of Elizabethan England, the class that had provided the magistrates; he found several cousins sitting alongside him in the Parliament of 1628. Most of the fairly modest (and fluctuating) wealth of his family was based on lands which were or which had been church lands, his biggest asset at the end of the 1630s being the right to farm estates left to Ely Cathedral. Basically he owed such education as he had to Huntingdon Grammar School and its Puritan schoolmaster, Thomas Beard, author of *The Theatre of God's Judgements*, a little book about 'the admirable judgements of God upon the trans-

---

[39] See Geoffrey Nuttall in *The Puritan Spirit* (London, 1967), pp. 130–40.

gressors of his commandments'. Apart from this schooling, we know only of one year at Cambridge, possibly followed by some time studying law. He was not at all a glamorous figure; a Royalist MP has left a description of him aged forty-one, dressed in an ill-fitting plain cloth suit with specks of blood on his neck-band. The only clue from his early years that his personality was exceptional is provided by evidence that he underwent a nervous breakdown and a profound spiritual conversion at the end of the 1620s; there survives a note by a distinguished London physician whom he consulted, to the effect that he was 'extremely melancholy'. But with the life-long tendency to melancholia and self-doubt when inactive went a rare, almost manic, determination to act once his mind had cleared. Reports of the 1630s prove that he could be impetuous in his interventions in local politics. They also suggest that he seriously considered selling up and going to New England. He whispered to his neighbour in the Commons that had the Grand Remonstrance passed he certainly would have emigrated in 1641. And so there came the day in January 1644 when, having lived for some years in a house close by Ely Cathedral, brooding over his sins and the people's, he suddenly arrived in the cathedral and furiously drove out its surprised congregation.

His reputation became the reputation of a brilliant General. It remains mysterious just how, when already in his forties, he learned and communicated outstanding skills as a trainer and commander of the cavalry, the pikemen and the musketeers that conquered their King – although it is true that most of the officers on the King's side shared his own lack of previous military experience. What is clear is that the key was discipline, made possible by appealing to a morale inspired by religion. On the Royalist side Prince Rupert's cavalry scattered after a charge; their instinct was to plunder. On the Parliamentary side Cromwell's cavalry remained under orders, for their General had learned the lesson of the first, indecisive battle at Edgehill. Talking over the battle with his cousin John Hampden, Cromwell wondered how the 'base and mean fellows' on their side could ever 'encounter gentlemen that have honour and courage and resolution in them'. The answer came to him: 'You must get men of spirit.' He meant the Puritan spirit. The regiment which he raised for the Eastern Association in 1643 surprised contemporaries by the punishments which the soldiers accepted for drunkenness and swearing, but the whole point was that the soldiers knew why this discipline was necessary. Only men who were not the traditional soldiery, brutal and licentious, could have the self-respect required to remain disciplined in defeat or victory.

As the war proceeded Cromwell increasingly regarded it as a crusade. 'Religion was not the thing at first contested for,' he reflected, 'but God brought it to that issue at last . . . and at last proved that which was most dear to us.' And he seemed to become more and more flexible in his attitude to the religion in which his men believed, on the one condition that it would make them crusaders. At an early stage he had invited an eminently respectable clergyman, Richard Baxter, to be chaplain to his own regiment of 'Ironsides'. Baxter had refused, and when visiting the New Model Army after its victory at Naseby had been horrified by developments. Most of the soldiers seemed 'honest, sober, orthodox men', but about a twentieth were 'proud, self-conceited, hot-headed Sectaries' – and it was the minority that Cromwell seemed to favour, since by its 'heat and activity' it was 'the soul of the army'. Baxter heard with great alarm declarations 'sometimes for State Democracy and sometimes for Church Democracy': the one seemed as bad as the other. Now time would have to tell whether the majority of soldiers would insist on democracy or would support a conservative regime headed by the General who had emerged because, as he frequently claimed, God's hand was mysteriously on him.

A sense of being a man of destiny, God's avenging instrument, was strong in Cromwell as he led the various moves needed in 1649–51 to crush attempts to put Charles II on his father's throne. First he commanded the army in Ireland through a campaign disgraced by atrocities which have never been forgotten. Then, disregarding the resignation of Fairfax who refused to take an oath of loyalty to the republic, he turned against Charles and the Scots. Charles had made the firm alliance which his father had rejected by signing the covenant against bishops, but the concession was now in vain. Cromwell, after making his famous plea to the Scots, 'in the bowels of Christ', to think it possible that they might be mistaken, defeated them at Dunbar and occupied Edinburgh – showing more mercy than in Ireland, since the Scots were not Papists. When an unenthusiastic Charles kept some Scottish supporters and accompanied an army of them in a hopeless march south, the war-weary English failed to rise and Cromwell caught up with the outnumbered invaders. Another famous victory at Worcester (on 3 September 1651) was received with widespread thanksgiving as the 'crowning mercy'. All that the shattered Royalists could do was to organize Charles's romantic escape back into exile.

Cromwell's army had shouted 'The Lord of Hosts!' at Dunbar. It now looked for its reward – and for a reward more solid than a demobilization which would leave power in the hands of the Rump Parliament. Cromwell, too, wondered what the future held for him, at a time when Milton was hailing him in a sonnet as 'our chief of men'. One autumn evening in 1652 he had a conversation with Bulstrode Whitelocke, strolling in St James's Park in Westminster. Cromwell was thinking aloud and groping his way forward as he often did until the moment came when God's providence called him into a display of military strength; and Whitelocke later recalled their talk – perhaps not with a perfect memory, for he wrote it down when Cromwell was dead and in disgrace and he was surviving as a shrewd, conservative lawyer.[40] According to this account, the General observed that MPs were 'engrossing all places of honour and profit to themselves and their friends' and so providing 'ground for people to open their mouths against them'. Yet they had been 'acknowledged the supreme power'. What was the solution? Cromwell knew that most of the English preferred a government 'with something of monarchical in it'. So 'what if a man should take it upon him to be king?'

---

[40] Whitelocke was portrayed by Ruth Spalding as *The Improbable Puritan* (London, 1975).

Whitelocke dismissed the daydream of King Oliver – 'the remedy would be worse than the disease' – and proposed instead that he should make an arrangement with the defeated but legitimate Charles II, 'to secure yourself and your friends and their fortunes'. Instead, on 20 April 1653, Cromwell acted with far less cynicism. He dismissed the Rump Parliament and dissolved the council which in its name had governed, or failed to govern, the country; and he set about establishing a Cromwellian regime in its place.

A nominated assembly was summoned: Cromwell's fear of free elections told its own tale. Nicknamed the 'Barebones Parliament' (after a member, Praise-God Barbone), it embarked on a comprehensive programme to reform the law, the revenues and other aspects of the nation's life. However, it showed itself to be almost equally divided on a crucial question. The radicals kept voicing the Levellers' demand for the abolition of tithes – a step which would have made the small farmers richer and the ministers entirely dependent on their congregations. The conservatives drew back, and not only because many laymen were still receiving tithes. Rather than accept the prospect of anarchy in religion and of financial loss to the gentry, these conservatives handed their power back to Cromwell; presumably they had been assured in advance that the offer would not be rejected. The maintenance of tithes had become a symbol of the need to maintain law and order in Church and State.

Before the end of 1653 the General had been installed as Lord Protector. The first written constitution in English history (the 'Instrument of Government') gave him great powers provided that he pursued a policy approved of by the Council of State, in effect a military junta. A minor role – mainly one of confirming the ordinances to be issued by this council – was allotted to a single-chamber parliament, to be elected once every three years by the propertied rather than by the people as a whole. Those who had acted against Parliament at any time since January 1641 were to be denied votes. From a strictly parliamentary point of view, this was a considerable anticlimax after the rhetoric of Pym and many others in the early 1640s.

On the basis of an army of thirty thousand men rather than any paper constitution, Cromwell governed a Commonwealth uniting England, Wales, Scotland and Ireland. He and his fellow officers pursued an aggressive foreign policy with some success – the first rulers of England to do so since the death of Henry V. The fleet commanded by Robert Blake distinguished itself and Jamaica was occupied. Thus the naval and imperial themes which were to dominate English history were announced and consecrated by anti-Spanish Protestantism (except that it was also necessary to fight a trading war against the Dutch). At home the regime kept the people quiet by treason laws which threatened the death penalty for anyone denying the supreme authority of the Lord Protector and the Parliament. There was a police and spy system, considerably the most efficient ever to be seen in England, with the country divided into eleven areas under major-generals. Equally relevant to Cromwell's success, however, was a general policy of non-interference with those who stayed quiet.

The ineffectiveness of the Royalist conspiracies supplied the most important commentary on this regime. Only minor problems were caused by minor indiscretions. Some of the less intelligent major-generals tried to enforce Puritan morals. Nationwide, there were the even more foolish official prohibitions of church weddings and the Christmas festivities – orders which were widely defied. The main problem was that stability depended on control by the army and, within the army, on control by a general with Cromwell's prestige.

Anglicans and Roman Catholics were lumped together in a way that would have amazed the Elizabethans, and their treatment showed the same combination of firmness with tolerance. The use of the Prayer Book was forbidden in 1655, the year of the main Royalist insurrection, but this stern measure was soon accompanied by a reassurance: 'His Highness doth declare that towards such of the said persons as have . . . given . . . a real testimony of their godliness and good affection to the present government, so much tenderness shall be used as may consist with the safety and good of the nation.' In other words, it was hinted that except when Royalists were troublemakers Cromwell would connive at the use of the

Prayer Book. And there is much evidence that Anglican services were held discreetly up and down the country, especially baptisms, weddings and funerals. John Evelyn's diary shows both that this Anglican gentleman regularly attended the non-Anglican services in his parish church, and that he could always find Prayer Book services to attend in London when he so wished. Although marriage before a civil magistrate had been made compulsory in 1653, the Lord Protector's own daughter Mary was married (to Lord Fauconberg) in the chapel of Hampton Court according to the old service. James Ussher, the moderate who had been Archbishop of Armagh and a saintly scholar respected by all, received a Prayer Book funeral in Westminster Abbey.[41]

In relation to Roman Catholics the old legislation remained in force, and under it a priest aged seventy was executed in 1654. The law was toughened in 1657, under the excitement of the war with Spain. But the local enforcement of fines for recusancy was even more patchy than it had been under Elizabeth or Charles I. Cromwell was content to leave it so; the French ambassador was one of the many who were reminded that the Lord Protector opposed all persecution of those who remained quiet in politics. Indeed, in 1655 Cromwell went so far as to arrange for the return of some Jews to London, ending the prohibition imposed in 1290.

Presbyterians, Independents and Baptists all ministered in the old parishes and were sustained by the old tithes; 'though a man be of any of those three judgements,' said Cromwell, 'if he have the root of the matter in him he may be admitted.' An attempt was made to tackle the perennial problem of the poverty of the clergy remaining in the parishes by supporting the lower-paid ministers out of some of the lands which had once belonged to the bishops and the cathedrals. Many priests who had been ordained by bishops, and who had never inwardly acquired the Puritan 'root of the matter', were also allowed to carry on their work. They 'lay low', as one vicar put it. Many used the new fashions in worship on Sundays while sticking to the old services for baptisms, weddings and funer-

---

[41] R. Buick Knox studied *James Ussher, Archbishop of Armagh* (Cardiff, 1967).

als. Although this was a period when many congregations discovered with considerable excitement and joy that they were at last free and able to be the Christian Church in the style advocated by the Puritans, in more than two-thirds of England's parishes there was no change of minister under the Commonwealth.[42]

Among the preachers who flourished under this regime were men who were by any standards Christians completely dedicated to their ministry.[43] In 1654 two ordinances made the control of other preachers stricter. The task of examining candidates for the parish pulpits was now entrusted to a strong national committee of ministers and laymen – the 'Triers' or 'Commissioners for the Approbation of Public Preachers'. Unfortunately most of the records of their work were lost when they were suppressed, but a candid critic, Richard Baxter, paid them a compliment. 'To give them their due,' he later wrote, 'they did abundance of good to the Church. They saved many a congregation from ignorant, ungodly, drunken teachers.' In each county a local committee handled the task of ejecting unsatisfactory ministers. Like the national committee which had been functioning before 1654, these 'Ejectors' could be ruthless. Many ugly stories were told of violence used when evicting clergy and their families for loyalty to the Prayer Book, although in theory if they went quietly they were promised a fifth of the next incumbent's income. It has been estimated that between 1643 and 1660 about seven hundred and fifty posts of dignity in the old Church of England (from bishoprics to minor canonries in the cathedrals) were suppressed, that some eight hundred Anglicans were expelled from the universities, and that almost 2,500 parishes were 'sequestered' because their incumbents were 'delinquents'. Beyond doubt there was suffering, but there were many factors which complicated the

---

[42] See Geoffrey Nuttall, *Visible Saints: the Congregational Way 1640–1660* (Oxford, 1957). On the patchy establishment of the Presbyterian system in the country, nothing has yet replaced W. A. Shaw, *A History of the English Church during the Civil Wars and under the Commonwealth* (2 vols, London, 1900).

[43] Examples may be found in two biographies: R. P. Stearns, *The Strenuous Puritan: Hugh Peter* (Urbana, Ill., 1954), and V. de Sola Pinto, *Peter Sterry* (Cambridge, 1934).

picture – two or more of the superior posts had often been held
by one man; some of those ejected later made their peace with
the regime and were given fresh posts; and some who suffered
had been unsatisfactory as pastors.[44]

In their triumph the Puritans were, of course, determined to
show that the looseness of the organization of the National
Church did not extend to any laxity in upholding orthodox
Christianity against any who might take advantage of the
disturbed times. When an ex-soldier, James Nayler, caused a
scandal by re-enacting Christ's entry into Jerusalem by a ride
into Bristol, the Commons debated and condemned the blasphemy. Cromwell protested against the savage punishment
(which was not authorized under the Instrument of Government), but he was powerless to stop it; and he was not able to
do more than express a private sympathy with the Quakers, a
popular anti-clerical movement in which Nayler was a leading
figure. More than once he allowed their remaining leader,
George Fox, to hold earnest conversation with him. His dislike
of religious persecution – 'I had rather that Mahometanism
were permitted among us than that one of God's children
should be persecuted' – remained from the convictions with
which the New Model Army had been prepared to fight King
and Parliament alike.

Little else of the idealism remained. He assured a Quaker,
John Rogers, that tithes to support the clergy were not anti-
Christian – only to be rebuked: 'You were once of another
mind'. And it was true that he had changed. As he told his first
Parliament, 'a nobleman, a gentleman, a yeoman: that is a
good interest of the nation and a great one. The magistracy of
the nation, was it not almost trampled underfoot, under
despite and contempt by men of Levelling principles?' Now
under the Lord Protector the traditional social system was
protected; and if tithes had to be kept for this reason, Cromwell
would pay the price. Looking back over his life, he once said: 'I
did out of necessity undertake that business, not so much out of

---

[44] John Walker's *Attempt towards Recovering an Account of the Numbers and Sufferings of
the Clergy of the Church of England* was published in 1714 and corrected by A. G.
Matthews, *Walker Revised* (Oxford, 1948).

a hope of doing any good, as out of a desire to prevent mischief and evil.' That was more than a passing mood of depression. As one of the best of his modern biographers has put it, after 1653 'he was a tired, disillusioned old man, still confident that he enjoyed a special relationship with God, but with few positive ideas left, on the defensive. He no longer hoped to realize the rule of God's people in England: he saw himself as a constable whose task was to prevent Englishmen from flying at one another's throats. He was forced back upon the support of an army purged of radicals, an army which in the last resort had to be paid by taxes collected from the propertied class, the natural rulers of the countryside. The Revolution was over.'[45]

---

[45] Christopher Hill, *God's Englishman* (London, 1970), p. 143. The ferment of radical ideas during the English revolution was surveyed by Christopher Hill, *The World Turned Upside Down* (London, 1972).

CHAPTER NINE

THE PURITAN LEGACY

THE DEATH OF
CROMWELLIAN ENGLAND

While Oliver Cromwell lived, his system of government in Church and State seemed secure. Many shared Cromwell's own opinion that all that the exiled Charles Stuart cared for was 'a shoulder of mutton and a whore'. In comparison, the Lord Protector was a giant among men – and he could control the army. The chief interest lay in the question whether Cromwell would, or would not, accept the title of king. The crown was urged on him by many MPs who wanted that additional return to legality. In the end he refused, deterred chiefly by the opposition within the army. Colonel Pride, who had once purged the old Commons, organized an officers' petition against any idea of a new king. But the Lord Protector did accept a new constitution which gave him more power over the council – and a second installation, a ceremony which came close to a coronation. He created a second chamber in Parliament, and urged the Commons to be less niggardly in voting taxes; he maintained a dignified court and his friends became known as the 'Court' party. It was in many ways like the old times of the Stuarts.

What the Lord Protector could not produce was an able son – and in that, too, he resembled several crowned kings of England. He quarrelled with John Lambert, who had become his closest military and political associate but had been one of the leaders of the opposition to the crowning. Lambert's dismissal left no successor more obvious than Richard Cromwell, a diffident young man nicknamed 'Tumbledown Dick', whose sole claim was being the oldest son. That showed the fatal weakness in the whole regime of a semi-monarchy which in reality depended on one general's hold on the army. Although the Royalists seemed to be in complete disarray, probably many Englishmen knew in their hearts that the legitmate monarchy's restoration was inevitable. This thought may well have been deep in the minds first of the soldiers, and then of Cromwell himself, when they acknowledged the impossibility of taking over the throne as Henry IV had taken it over from Richard II or Henry VII from Richard III.

The Lord Protector died on 3 September 1658. Towards the end of his great life he had grown manifestly exhausted although not yet sixty years old, and it was a sign of his exhaustion that he took no sensible action about his succession. To assume that his oldest son would inherit his position, as he seems to have done although there was no clear arrangement, was as unrealistic as Henry VIII's will had been back in 1547. England remained a republic and therefore in some sense a democracy; yet it was invited to accept as its Lord Protector, with powers greater than those of Charles I, a man who lacked the sacred mystique of hereditary kingship and whose own abilities were not impressive. In 1658 as in 1547, what England needed was government.

Trying to assert his authority over the generals, the new Lord Protector appealed to the soldiers – who refused to rescue him. A similar refusal came from Puritan ministers such as John Owen, who had once been among Oliver Cromwell's favourites and a preacher of sermons to Parliament announcing that God was doing great things through the triumphs of the godly.[1] Idealistic pamphleteers such as Richard Baxter and John Milton announced that the time had come to establish a government based on wisdom, but some force seemed necessary since disruptive ideals were also being voiced in this open debate. Revolutionary visionaries such as the Fifth Monarchy Men who had emerged back in 1652 as the heirs of the Levellers prophesied that the 'fifth monarchy' of the seventh chapter of the Book of Daniel was about to come to pass in England, bringing in the rule of King Jesus and the

---

[1] A biography of Owen has been provided by Peter Toon, *God's Statesman* (Exeter, Devon, 1971).

saints. Private property would be among the institutions destroyed as the world was made new.[2]

After the dissolution of the pathetic new Lord Protector's
even more pathetic Parliament it seemed possible that the
army might reimpose its rule, brushing aside the idealists and
revolutionaries. The trouble was that after all the changes
since 1640 the officers were left with no very clear idea as to
what they wanted. Two of the generals (Harrison and Overton) were Fifth Monarchy men. Others who had done well for
themselves seem to have begun reckoning with the rewards
that might accompany the inevitability of a Stuart, rather than
a heavenly, king. The rank and file were worried most about
the uncertainty of their pay. An army so divided had the power
but not the will. The vacuum was filled temporarily by the
return of some hundred and twenty members of the old Rump
Parliament, to whom Richard Cromwell handed in his resignation. He had his reward: after twenty years in obscure exile, he
was to be permitted to return to live out his days as a quiet
country gentleman until 1712. But this resurrected Parliament
could not control the army any more than Richard Cromwell
could. On the contrary, some army officers, among whom
John Lambert was the most active, were plainly determined
to establish 'sword government' – a prospect which other
officers found dismaying. Suddenly the Puritan movement,
which had seemed invincible while Oliver Cromwell lived,
was visibly disintegrating. The prophecy of the old Royalist,
Sir Jacob Astley, was coming true: 'You have now done your
work, and may go play, unless you will fall out amongst your-
selves.'

Once again, as divided MPs and confused soldiers struggled
for the government of England, both sides sought the support
of an army from Scotland – only this time the army was
commanded by George Monck, once a Royalist, latterly Oliver
Cromwell's trusted and very effective agent, a man who was
every inch a professional soldier and who included in his
professionalism convictions that soldiers ought to be paid well
but ought not to form governments. Monck commanded an

---

[2] See B. S. Capp, *The Fifth Monarchy Men* (London, 1972).

army that had done very well out of the Cromwellian conquest of Scotland, was paid regularly, and was loyal to him personally. He seemed just the man to rescue the conservative counter-revolution from the disorder into which it had been reduced by his master's death.

At the end of 1659 Monck's army crossed into England. On his arrival in London he made only one objective clear: the readmission of conservative MPs who had been excluded by Pride's Purge back in 1648. Then another aim emerged: the Long Parliament must vote for its own dissolution and for the election of a more representative 'convention'. This objective was achieved when the Parliament which had first met in 1640 dissolved itself on 16 March 1660. Before dispersing MPs showed their hopes of the future by also voting for the introduction of the full Presbyterian system in the Church. Such a prospect also appealed to many merchants in the City of London, who meanwhile were backing Monck against less constitutionally-minded soldiers such as Lambert. But Royalists were allowed to stand in the elections, and in his exile at Breda Charles strengthened their cause (although he angered hotheads) by issuing a vague but conciliatory declaration, drafted by Edward Hyde. If he was restored to his throne, the King promised a general pardon and religious toleration pending a permanent settlement by Parliament. Parliament was also to answer the key question of whose estates were to be restored. On the same day (1 May) that it formally received this declaration, the new House of Commons voted that 'the government is, and ought to be, by King, Lords and Commons'. By the end of that month Charles had been proclaimed king, had landed at Dover, and amid a rapturous welcome had entered London.

The Cromwellian counter-revolution had not, after all, outlasted Oliver Cromwell. Needing a monarchy and failing to find it in a Cromwellian dynasty, propertied men such as General Monck or the MPs turned back to the legitimate king. Only he could provide the stability they most wanted. Many hoped that much of the Cromwellian achievement would be preserved – that, for example, bishops (if there had to be bishops) would never again wield the powers of William Laud.

Presbyterian preachers were prominent in the welcome given to Charles in May 1660 and heard with pleasure his praises of the Bible. But stringent terms had not been imposed on the new king, because no one, not even General Monck, had the power or the will to impose them. With Oliver Cromwell dead, there could be no guarantee of a political future for militant Puritanism. The Lord of Hosts who had given them so many victories, from Marston Moor to Worcester, in Ireland, in Scotland and at sea, had not given the Puritans strength or unity of purpose under the pressures released by the great General's death. 'The Lord', said Major-General Fleetwood in 1658, 'has spit in our faces.'[3]

THE DEFEAT OF THE PURITANS

For about a year after the restoration of the king the outcome for English religion was uncertain. It was a period when the decisions were being made not by battles or riots but by negotiations between a few men in London. The bulk of the country seems simply to have waited, relieved that the threat of anarchy was over, willing to accept any settlement to be imposed, provided only that it was not Popery. Fortunately we have the daily journal of Ralph Josselin, the vicar of the village of Earl's Colne in Essex from 1641 to 1683, to remind us that all through these crises what really mattered to the average man was health or sickness or death affecting his family and neighbours, or sun or rain creating the harvest, with the hope of heaven as the great consolation. Josselin was a devout Christian who brooded over the Bible's promises of the Kingdom of God. And he was no fool. Having been the first clergyman in Essex to swear loyalty to the Commonwealth, at this stage he was noting that his fellow Englishmen were 'looking more to Charles Stuart out of love to themselves, not him'. His awareness of current affairs must have been exceptional; he even dreamed about politics. But the preoccupations of his diary

---

3 Recent studies include *The Interregnum: The Quest for a Settlement*, edited by G. E. Aylmer (London, 1972), and Maurice Ashley, *General Monck* (London, 1977).

were naturally and properly local, and often he would write in thanksgiving about his affairs: 'God was good to me.'[4]

No one in 1660 could be sure what the King's power would be in practice. Men had preferred him to Richard Cromwell because his hereditary right put him in an infinitely stronger position; so 1660 saw the restoration of a monarchy with a history of executive power stretching back through medieval to Anglo-Saxon days, and it was a restoration without conditions other than the imprecise promises in the royal exile's declaration 'given . . . at our court at Breda . . . in the twelfth year of our reign'. The King's own brother, James, was to show when he came to reign that he expected an unquestioning obedience to be given by his subjects as a religious duty. On the other hand, the Commons' agreement with the Lords on 1 May 1660, that 'according to the ancient and fundamental laws of this kingdom the Government is, and ought to be, by King, Lords and Commons' deserved to be analysed for its inclusion of Parliament as well as King in 'the Government'. In practice a body of MPs known to history as the Cavalier Parliament of 1661–79 was to have a mind of its own, although vociferously loyal to the monarchy in principle. It was to reject the leadership offered by the King's ministers and to secure their dismissal – and it was never to allow the King enough money with which to govern without Parliament. After 1660 there was no real intention of going back behind 1640, and Charles II recognized this even if his stupid brother James did not. He knew that the only way in which he could fight free of having to humour the Commons was the degradation involved in receiving subsidies from France. Although this was hidden from many eyes in 1660, the religious policy that was to prevail was the policy which commended itself to the House of Commons.

Equally uncertain was the motivation of the restored King in his new dialogue with the Commons. In public Charles II professed to be devoted to his father's Church – as did his brother and heir until he ceased to receive Holy Communion as an Anglican in 1672. During their exile their quarrels with

---

[1] Alan Macfarlane reconstructed *The Family Life of Ralph Josselin* (Cambridge, 1970) and edited *The Diary of Ralph Josselin* (Oxford, 1976).

their Roman Catholic mother had strengthened the impression
of a sound English churchmanship. No doubt most Englishmen took it for granted that in religion Charles would be the
royal martyr's son, at least formally. But those who knew him
knew that the Church of England meant little to him religiously. He was a worldly womanizer (as was James at this stage).
Unlike his father he had been willing to take the Presbyterians'
Solemn League and Covenant and he owed his restoration to
Presbyterian soldiers and merchants, not to any Cavalier
uprising. It seemed perfectly possible that it would be his
policy to conciliate the Presbyterians, either by including them
in the National Church or by insisting on the 'liberty to tender
consciences' promised in the Declaration of Breda. It also
seemed likely that he would attempt to secure better terms for
the Roman Catholics, many of whom had supported his father
in the civil war. His decision to marry a Roman Catholic
princess, as his father had done, caused no surprise; there were
very few Protestant princesses available. There were, indeed,
rumours in the early 1660s that in exile Charles had become a
Roman Catholic himself, and a law had to be passed making it
treason to repeat the story. The King's personal religion
remained something of an enigma, until on his deathbed he
was received into the Roman Catholic Church.

But in 1660 it was not even certain what would be the
attitude of the leaders of the Church of England. During the
Commonwealth Anglican leadership had been divided and, on
the whole, ineffective.

'I secure myself the same way as the tortoise doth, by not
going out of my shell' had been the confession of a comparatively brave bishop, Brian Duppa of Salisbury. He had been
typical. The most respectable advocate of buying safety by
judicious compromise had been Professor Robert Sanderson of
Oxford. Although ejected from Oxford, he had advised his
fellow Anglicans not to obtrude their loyalty to monarchy,
episcopacy or the Book of Common Prayer to the extent of
provoking retaliation. He had retained the respect of many,
and at the Restoration was made Bishop of Lincoln although in
his seventies. Indeed, Izaak Walton thought so highly of him
that he added a *Life* to his studies of Anglican heroes such as

Hooker, Donne and Herbert. Even more caution had been displayed by the senior bishop, William Juxon, who had served Charles I as Bishop of London and Lord Treasurer, and had attended him on the scaffold. Under the Commonwealth he had retreated to his manor house in Gloucestershire and had devoted himself to prayer and hunting. He and his fellow bishops had not consecrated any successors after 1644, although loyally Anglican Royalists abroad were indignant at the risk being run. The result was that in the twenty-seven English and Welsh dioceses, by 1660 only ten bishops survived, mostly in their seventies. Bishop Skinner of Oxford was the only one of them who had openly expressed a willingness to ordain priests under the Commonwealth.

When Charles II exchanged pious remarks with Presbyterian ministers on his return to London, it therefore seemed possible that government of the Church by bishops would be forgotten. After all, the estates confiscated from the bishops and their cathedrals were now in lay hands. No one thought of restoring their formerly vast estates to the monasteries. Why revive the power and wealth of the bishops?

The theologian who had rallied Anglicans less willing to compromise with the Puritan rulers of England had been Henry Hammond, a learned scholar who before the war had been an exemplary parish priest. A man of outstanding holiness, he was extensively consulted in problems of conscience, and during the 1650s spread his views by writing more than twenty-five books. He always advised steadfast courage, although he was no fanatic in his attitude to non-Anglicans. There were others like him, who quietly did their duty and urged others to do the same – John Pearson, for example, who in 1659 completed an *Exposition of the Creed* based on lectures in a London church, a treatise which had great influence for two centuries; or Richard Allestree, an Oxford Scholar who almost certainly was the author of a very influential book for the laity on *The Whole Duty of Man*. Another scholar, Herbert Thorndike, wrote a book published in 1659 under the gloomy title *An Epilogue to the Tragedy of the Church of England*; it turned out to be a prologue to the triumph. But Henry Hammond was the spiritual leader in this circle, and it was a real tragedy for the

Church of England that he died prematurely, shortly before the Restoration.[5]

In the end the leadership went to those Anglicans who, like Hammond, had refused to compromise while their Church was under persecution (or at least under a cloud). This was partly because some of them had found refuge as chaplains to gentlemen whose sons became devoted to them and who were to sit in the Commons after the Restoration. But some of the most steadfast Anglicans went into exile and there did battle against Roman Catholic influences while also refusing to be classified as simply Protestant. One of the exiles was a Yorkshireman, Joseph Bramhall, who had become Archbishop of Armagh and who during the 1650s published massive defences of Anglican orthodoxy against the claims of Rome as well as against the scepticism of Thomas Hobbes. Another was John Cosin, so well-known as a defender of the faith while Anglican chaplain in the household of Queen Henrietta Maria in Paris that he was made Bishop of Durham in 1660, winning a further reputation as an energetic disciplinarian before his death in 1672. Cosin was, by Anglican standards, a High Churchman, who in the 1620s had been in trouble for ritualism offensive to Protestants and who in the 1630s had presided over the Cambridge college chapel where Richard Crashaw loved to worship; but when his own son became a Roman Catholic like Crashaw, Cosin disinherited him. While so many had compromised Cosin had been unyielding, and now had the reward which sometimes goes to the obstinate.

If the character of the leadership of the Church of England was uncertain in 1660, still less was it clear how many of the clergy and laity who had accepted the loosely organized National Church of the Commonwealth would now accept the bishops and the Prayer Book – or how much the bishops and the Prayer Book could be changed in order to accommodate the Puritan element. Not long after his return home the King was persuaded to appoint a dozen Puritan divines as his chaplains. Three of them – Richard Baxter, Edmund Calamy

---

[5] J. W. Packer studied Hammond's life and work in *The Transformation of Anglicanism, 1643–60* (Manchester, 1969).

and Edward Reynolds – were even offered diocesan bishoprics. Baxter and Calamy refused, because it was clear to them that the old Anglican system would be insufficiently changed; but Reynolds agreed to become Bishop of Norwich and wrote the General Thanksgiving added to the Prayer Book in 1662. And even after their refusals, Baxter and Calamy went on hoping that the authorities of the Church of England, who had compromised so often in the past, would now compromise with them.

The situation was clarified in the spring of 1661 by the elections to the Commons, which produced MPs thirsting for revenge on defeated rebels. The effects of the ecclesiastical appointments made by the King, advised by Edward Hyde now Earl of Clarendon, were decisive. About seven hundred ministers had been ejected in order to make way for Royalists who had been expelled under the Commonwealth, although there was as yet no insistence on ordination by a bishop. Appointments to bishoprics and cathedrals conveyed the message that the restored Crown would reward those who had been loyal to it through the Great Rebellion. The most effective of the new bishops were Gilbert Sheldon at London (from 1663 at Canterbury) and George Morley at Worcester (from 1662 at Winchester), and neither of them intended to go any distance to meet Puritan demands. Sheldon had been ejected from the Wardenship of All Souls College, Oxford, and after a brief imprisonment had lived quietly in the Midlands, collaborating with Hammond in giving advice and where possible relief to the ejected clergy. He celebrated the return of the King by giving the beautiful Sheldonian Theatre to his university. Morley, although he seems to have retained many of the Calvinist beliefs of an earlier Anglican age, had been a Wiltshire rector before the war and had done more than anyone else to keep the Anglican exiles in harmony and good heart. Both Sheldon and Morley were masterful men of business, pure in their own lives but in tune with the cocksure MPs of the Cavalier Parliament. Such men were eager to restore their Church, not to alter it.

A gathering of bishops and Puritans met in Sheldon's lodgings at the King's command. The motives of the Anglican authorities in this 'Savoy Conference' have been variously interpreted. It is quite possible that the King and Clarendon genuinely wanted an agreement along the lines of the declaration which they had issued from Worcester House (Clarendon's residence) the previous October: a declaration which had promised to make episcopacy more pastoral (by appointing suffragan or assistant bishops, for example) and the Prayer Book more acceptable to the Puritans. It can be argued that it was the royal policy to be more generously statesmanlike than the Royalists.[6] But it is also possible to conclude that the real initiative lay all the time with the strictly Anglican and fervently Royalist churchmen, since the King did not show enough interest in religion to risk unpopularity for its sake. The consistent loyalty to the Church of England which Clarendon liked to claim, as he looked back on his life as an old man in the 1670s, may have been sincere in the 1660s, so that any appearance of a willingness to compromise was then always insincere.[7]

Richard Baxter blamed the arrogance of the bishops in the Savoy Conference and their Cavalier backers in the Commons: 'We spoke to the deaf.' But the facts were far more complicated, including a genuine reluctance on the part of the King and the wise Clarendon to see Parliament passing an Act of Uniformity which they knew would cause great trouble if enforced. There is evidence that the government's pressure was exerted against the legislation which appealed to the vindictive Cavaliers, and it is certain that when that pressure failed the alternative policy was pursued of issuing an 'indulgence' on the royal authority until the King had to admit defeat. It seems probable that the bishops would have secured the King's favour had they been able to buy peace by a few acceptable concessions. But Baxter and his fellow Puritans did not help. Baxter was far too talkative; he did not concentrate on pressing home a few demands. And his fellow Puritans, although they reluctantly accepted him as their chief spokes-

---

[6] This was argued by George Abernathy, *The English Presbyterians and the Stuart Restoration* (Philadelphia, Pa., 1965).

[7] Robert S. Bosher interpreted *The Making of the Restoration Settlement* as 'the influence of the Laudians' (London, 1951).

man in the Savoy Conference, were too divided to agree on a single, simple policy which might have been successful. Some seem to have wanted places in a modified Church of England (the policy of 'comprehension', although the word did not become familiar before the end of the 1660s). They were not really interested in a mere 'toleration', especially not in the toleration of Papists. Others were far more radical, wanting 'toleration' for Protestant congregations gathered outside any National Church and if need be even for the Roman Catholics. The split had been obvious in Oliver Cromwell's day and it was not going to be healed overnight.

Finally, the changes in the Church of England agreed to by the bishops and by the clergy in a joint meeting of the Convocations of Canterbury and York, and accepted by King and Parliament, were modest. The most important changes were negative. The courts of Star Chamber and High Commission, on which William Laud had depended, were suppressed. This meant that the bishops once again had to rely on the creaking machinery of the diocesan courts. The canons of 1640 were declared illegal. This meant that the only law of the Church of England was now the out-of-date code of 1604. By an unwritten agreement between Clarendon and Sheldon, the claim of the Convocations to tax the clergy was abandoned. The result was that the Convocations need not meet at all; they were to be effectively suppressed from 1664 to 1689 and during most of the next century and a half. Although the Prayer Book of 1662 was the work of the Convocations, the Commons agreed to accept this work, without debate, by a majority of only six and insisted on its right to debate any future changes. If Laudianism is to be understood as an attempt to reaffirm the power of the clergy, we must say that the Restoration was by no means a Laudian triumph. On the contrary, it can be better understood as the climax of a process continuous since the 1530s: the triumph of the laity.[8]

But these changes were made in order to serve the worldly interest of laymen prepared to accept the clergy's religious

---

[8] This was the sub-title of Claire Cross's study of *Church and People, 1450–1660* (London, 1976).

ministrations, not in order to satisfy Puritan consciences. In the end Puritans were also disappointed by the changes in the Prayer Book, some six hundred in number but mostly minor. Some generally acceptable prayers were added and it was pointed out that a new service of 'Baptism of such as are of Riper Years' would be useful when dealing with 'Natives in our Plantations'. Forms of prayer for use at sea showed awareness of the newly revealed destiny of the Protestant island. The general tone of the revisions was cautious ('which' was retained in the Lord's Prayer although it was changed to 'who' elsewhere), and some churchmen who wanted a greater enrichment were almost as disappointed as the Puritans. But the Catholic tendency of the restored Church was apparent in touches such as the provisions for blessing the water at Baptism and for manual acts by the priests when consecrating the bread and the wine in the Holy Communion. A note that baptized children dying before committing a sin were 'undoubtedly saved' seemed to signify the rejection of the Calvinist doctrine of predestination.[9]

The Act of Uniformity incorporating this revised Prayer Book came into force on St Bartholomew's Day, 24 August 1662. Not all the parishes whose ministers had to accept it or depart had by then received copies of the new book, but the nature of the Restoration Settlement was clear to all: it was a crushing defeat for those who advocated the 'comprehension' of Puritans by allowing ministers much freedom (as Baxter, for example, urged) or at least by making optional the ceremonies such as signing with the cross at Baptism to which there had been Puritan objections since Elizabethan times. The critics of the new book were referred to in its preface as 'men of factious, peevish and perverse spirits' unlikely to be 'satisfied with any thing that can be done in this kind by any other than themselves'. More than four hundred of the ministers who objected to the Restoration settlement had been ordained by bishops, but all understood the intention behind the new book's insistence that only episcopally ordained priests should celebrate

---

[9] The long discussion leading to the revision was well summarized by G. J. Cuming, *A History of Anglican Liturgy*, pp. 149–67.

Holy Communion. Richard Baxter gave the lead by an early announcement that he could no longer preach in the Church of England. With impressive courage 936 ministers, with their families, left the security of their rectories or vicarages on or before St Bartholomew's Day – before the tithes for the year were collected at Michaelmas. They received no compensation. In all, some 1,760 ministers were expelled from their parishes for their Puritan convictions in 1660–62.[10]

There was still to be wide diversity over the country in local Anglican attitudes to those who would not conform. Some parish churches were still used for services not in the Prayer Book, and some ministers not acceptable to bishops stayed on as private chaplains to Puritan gentlemen and noblemen. In his Essex parish Ralph Josselin did not wear a white surplice until 1680. But nationally there was to be a cleavage between 'Church' and 'Dissent'. Although there were still to be schemes to bring the ejected ministers, their succesors and their followers back into the National Church, no such plan was to achieve success during the next three centuries.[11]

However, the greatest legacy of the Puritan movement was a spiritual achievement which was to be embodied in imperishable literature and to become the heritage of the whole English-speaking world.

RICHARD BAXTER

The legacy of English Puritanism to the nation and to the world, surviving the Restoration, is to be seen in the work of three authors of outstanding significance: Richard Baxter who

---

[10] A. G. Matthews, *Calamy Revised* (Oxford, 1934), is the standard study of the Great Ejection. It scrutinized the lists published by Edmund Calamy in 1702–27.

[11] The best studies of the results of the Restoration Settlement are by Anne Whiteman and E. C. Ratcliff in *From Uniformity to Unity*, ed. Geoffrey Nuttall and Owen Chadwick (London, 1962), and by I. M. Green in *The Re-establishment of the Church of England* (Oxford, 1977). Joan Thirsk edited a collection of documents and comments, *The Restoration* (London, 1976).

lived until 1691, John Milton who lived until 1674, and John
Bunyan who lived until 1688.

Baxter, although he never held a post higher than the parish
of Kidderminster, may be reckoned the most truly eminent
English churchman of his century. He wrote almost a hundred
and fifty books; one of them, his *Christian Directory*, contained
over a million words. In them he dealt with almost all the
problems in morality and church life. It was the heartache of
his own life that the work he loved, the work of preacher and
pastor in a parish, was closed to him in 1661 because he could
not accept the 'new prelatical way', which meant the control of
parish ministers by diocesan bishops, and uniformity of
worship in every parish by the enforcement of the Book of
Common Prayer. For the next thirty years his influence was
mainly that of a writer, although he so ardently wished to
preach that in order to do so despite the official prohibition he
was ready to face spells of imprisonment. He was also ready
to accept the forced sale of two libraries which he had
collected.

By the example of his persistent courage as much as by his
writing, Baxter became the first patriarch of the denominations emerging out of the disintegration of Puritanism. In 1672
he registered himself simply as 'a mere Nonconformist', for he
refused to adopt the narrower position of a Presbyterian or
Congregationalist or Baptist; and in 1689 he was able to look
back over the whole struggle in his history of *The English
Nonconformity as under King Charles II and King James II*. But he
would have been delighted to become a Conformist, if only the
Church of England would allow more power to its parish clergy
to run their own parishes and to compose their own services,
and meanwhile he thought of himself as a 'nonconforming
churchman'. He attended many Prayer Book services devoutly
and when he conducted Nonconformist worship did so at times
which did not clash with the services in parish churches. He
became a spiritually great man, speaking out of the Puritan
tradition to the whole of the large Nonconformist element in
later English life; speaking also to the coming Evangelicalism
within the Church of England from which he never finally
separated himself.

He faced many handicaps. Physically he was not strong; his autobiography refers to many ailments.[12] His daily pain seems to have made him irritable, but he had another handicap: because his parents had thought it unnecessary for him to go to a university, he always had the independence of the man who was self-taught and without the experience of arguing with equals while young. He had little tact; he did not know how to make friends among the great or how to use them to further his own schemes. When Oliver Cromwell had treated him to one of his long monologues about recent English history, Baxter simply asked what had been wrong with the ancient monarchy. When Richard Cromwell was plainly doomed, Baxter dedicated his *Holy Commonwealth* to him. When the ancient monarchy was restored, and the bishops were full of themselves, Baxter was no less full of his own experiences, opinions and demands. When Charles II tried to secure toleration for all, this perpetually awkward theologian resisted the attempt on the ground that it would benefit Papists and heretics. On the other hand, he refused to subscribe to the conventional view that the Pope was Antichrist. A man so unco-operative was, it is clear, not suited for the bishopric of Hereford, offered to him when Clarendon as the King's chief minister was still trying to rally all moderates. But for all his independence he was a consistent advocate of moderation, and although no diplomat he was superbly well-equipped to be the pastor of his own parish and the author of his own books.

The ideals which inspired his work at Kidderminster were immortalized in *The Reformed Pastor* (1656). It was a ministry over nineteen years from 1641, apart from five years away when he felt obliged to preach to the troops on the Parliamentary side. He tried to keep his parish isolated from the Presbyterian and Independent (or Congregational) movements; and he was always sure that the majority of the English shared this wish. On the one hand, he had no desire to see the full Presbyterian system established in accordance with the Solemn League and Covenant. The leading laymen in the

---

[12] Conveniently abridged in Everyman's Library (London, 1931), *Reliquae Baxterianae* was printed in full in 1696 and 1829.

Kidderminster church were called 'deacons' or 'seniors', not Calvin's 'elders'; and he refused to accept Calvin's creed that some people were predestined by God to damnation. On the other hand, he was not a full Independent. He was highly critical of the Savoy Declaration which John Owen and other Independents published in 1659. He approved of the State controlling the National Church. He thought that Richard Hooker had made too many concessions to democracy, and dismissed the work of the Levellers as an 'abundance of wild pamphlets as changeable as the moon'. He saw society as a large family under one father, and his insistence on social stability was almost medieval.[13]

He believed strongly that congregations ought to be grouped in a spiritual family. In the 1650s he took the lead in the Worcestershire Association, a voluntary group of churches where the most important power was the right to excommunicate any sinner. No church in the group would receive a person thus punished. He was quite prepared to see a bishop presiding over such an association, and it would not trouble him if this bishop were to be appointed by the King. He had been ordained by the Bishop of Worcester before the war (certainly as a deacon, almost certainly also as a priest), and he always allowed a place for bishops in the Church. He intensely admired the moderate Archbishop Ussher, and would have liked most the fulfilment of Ussher's dream of every minister in pastoral charge of a market town becoming a bishop and gathering for regular conferences the other parish ministers in the neighbourhood.

What interested Baxter, we may conclude, was neither the Presbyterian nor the Independent nor the 'prelatical' theory, but what he regarded as the central working reality of church life: the parish church as a family, strengthened by a family-like local association. 'A particular church of Christ's institution by his apostles', he wrote, 'is a sacred society consisting of one or more pastors and a capable number of Christian neighbours consociate by Christ's appointment and their own

---

[13] His conservatism in relation to his contemporaries was brought out by R. L. Schlatter, *Social Ideas of Religious Leaders, 1660–88* (Oxford, 1940).

consent for personal communion in God's public worship and holy living.'

His convictions about church order on the national level were less clear. 'It is better,' he wrote, 'that men should be disorderly saved than orderly damned; and that the Church be disorderly preserved than orderly destroyed.' It was only in the period 1676–84 that he despaired of seeing a national church order which he could accept, and towards the end of his life his optimism returned. But he leaves the impression of not being greatly bothered about details at the national level. The saying of Peter Meiderlin was one of his favourite quotations: 'Unity in things necessary, liberty in things unnecessary, and charity in all.' The key to the life of the 'sacred society' was the parish, and the key to the parish was discipline administered by the pastor.

In Kidderminster he refused to give Holy Communion to those who would not accept the church's discipline; accordingly the communicants were always a minority among the adult parishioners, some six hundred out of 1,800. Baxter did not hesitate to say that he must 'take my people for my children' – just as the magistrate must govern 'the rabble'. An example of his self-confidence came during the Savoy Conference with the bishops in 1661. Challenged to say what deviations from the Prayer Book should be permitted, Baxter went away and after a fortnight's work produced a whole alternative Prayer Book, his *Reformed Liturgy*. But in the parish, he insisted, the minister must give himself utterly to the welfare of his parishioners. Baxter saw families for an hour at a time in his house during seven hours each week, and his two assistant ministers visited other folk systematically in their own homes. The conversation was not light; it was about faith and morals. And while some of his parishioners resented their pastor's attentions, all must have known that he was zealous to defend their interests. For five or six years he acted as a doctor in Kidderminster. The last treatise that he wrote – in 1699, not long before his death – was *The Poor Husbandman's Advocate to Rich Racking Landlords*. And those around him at every stage of his life must have known that he was no hireling. At Kidderminster all through the 1650s he let the ineffective former vicar, George Dance, stay in the vicarage and draw part of the income. Later on he offered to work as Dance's honorary curate (in vain), and it was his boast that he never in his life accepted a fee for a sermon.

Through many years when Puritanism was under persecution, Baxter maintained these ideals. At the heart of his wordy – sometimes too wordy – testimony there always was a devotional ardour so genuine that many, including many Anglican churchmen, were outraged when in 1685 Judge Jeffreys abused him coarsely during one of his trials. The 'holy angels bright' of his most famous hymn did not seem far off. His hope that the Church of England might so relax its own plan of discipline as to find a place for him was doomed to disappointment, but when imprisoned in 1686 this astonishing old man occupied himself with a fresh study of the Revelation of St John the Divine, leading to a fresh conviction that it was right to have a National Church under a Christian King while they awaited the rule of the saints under King Jesus.

Before he died he seems to have sensed clearly enough that there would be room for his Nonconformist ideals – for the Bible at the centre of the local congregation – in the continuing life of England outside the established National Church. Looking back he was sure that it had been God's work to mock the ambition of Cromwell and to destroy the pride of militant Puritanism by the restoration of Charles II ('and without one bloody nose!') – although it had left 'the poor Church of Christ, the sober, sound, religious part', crucified. His conclusion was that 'Christians must imitate Christ, and suffer with him' – a conclusion confirmed by 'the observation of God's dealing with the Church in every age'; for everywhere in history could be seen 'his befooling them that have dreamed of glorious times'. With such words he could part with his own dreams at Kidderminster – dreams in which perhaps he, too, had been ambitious and proud. But Richard Baxter could also look forward with a sober hope. 'God will have other generations to succeed us,' he once wrote, 'let us thank him that we have had our time . . . The Gospel dieth not when I die: the Church dieth not: the praises of God die not: the world dieth not: and perhaps it shall grow better, and those prayers shall be answered which seemed lost: yea, and it may be that some of the seed that I have sown shall spring up to some benefit of the dark unpeaceable world when I am dead.'[14]

JOHN MILTON

Baxter's hope was to some extent fulfilled, but a greater immortality of reputation has surrounded John Milton, as a poet acknowledged by almost all to be second only to Shakespeare – whom he addressed in 1630 as 'the great heir of Fame'. Writing in 1940, at a time when it was fashionable to denigrate him in comparison with Donne, Lord David Cecil claimed that Milton 'did not live by faith, scorned hope, and was indisposed to charity'; but he admitted that Milton remained 'the greatest of English poets who have made religion their subject'.[15]

His education may be said to have been continuous from some time before his entry into St Paul's School in London, in or about 1605, right up to 1639, when he returned home from his Italian tour and moved back to London, to begin teaching his nephew and his nation. He was one of the best-educated Englishmen of his day, and one of his best prose writings was *Of Education* (1644), with its plea that some at least of his contemporaries might be instructed in part at least of the immense syllabus which he had covered ('as ever in my great Task-master's eye'). He owed this preparation to his father, a businessman of substance and an amateur musician of distinction. The father's wealth and encouragement enabled the son to set out to become a great poet, although a Latin poem *Ad Patrem* shows that the father grew impatient as year after year went by without the son earning his living.

A very strenuous course of reading occupied John Milton up

---

[14] The best biography is by Geoffrey Nuttall (London, 1965). R. L. Schlatter studied *Richard Baxter and Puritan Politics* (Brunswick, N.J., 1957), and A. H. Wood his ecclesiology in *Church Unity without Uniformity* (London, 1963). See also William Lamont, *Richard Baxter and the Millennium* (London, 1979).

[15] *Oxford Book of Christian Verse* (Oxford, 1940), p. xxi.

to his thirtieth year, with the result that his prose or poetry was full, perhaps too full, of allusions to classical literature and to the seventeenth century's culture in general. He was the master of many languages, and wrote Latin as easily as English (sometimes confusing the two languages, critics have complained). After the age of twelve he rarely went to bed before midnight, so devoted was he to his candle-lit books; which was why he went totally blind when little over forty. He was nicknamed 'the Lady' while an undergraduate, being a prig as well as a goodlooker. He grew out of much of his youthful faith; for instance, although his favourite tutor, Thomas Young, was to be the author of a book on Sabbath-keeping and a leading Presbyterian, Milton became so convinced of the individual's ability to worship God in solitude that Sabbaths were not needed and presbyters not wanted. Once he had put aside all thought of being ordained he dared to be independent in basic theology, as Baxter did not. 'Custom without truth', he once wrote, 'is but agedness of error.' He also dared to say that ministers of the Gospel should be a few itinerant preachers, dependent on people's alms, like the apostles in the New Testament. But it was Puritanism – regarded always as the release of religious liberty and virtue, never as the overthrow of the traditional social order – that gave Milton the inspiration for his life's task: 'To leave something so written to aftertimes, as they should not willingly let die.'

From the years of preparation came poems of rare promise. An English paraphrase of Psalm 136, written when he was fifteen, has become a familiar hymn: 'Let us with a gladsome mind . . .' A Latin poem on the death of Bishop Lancelot Andrewes, written two years later, concluded with the first of his many literary visions of heaven. His first grand English poem, *On the Morning of Christ's Nativity*, written at Christmas 1629, imagined the Bethlehem which had already inspired countless English songs, and did so with a young exuberance and with many quaintly charming touches, but it lacked the passionate devotion to Christ of Richard Crashaw; the offering brought by Milton was one of clever metres and abundant 'conceits', sometimes reminiscent of Donne although without his impact. Before the next Easter he had attempted, and had abandoned, a poem on Christ's crucifixion – a theme which, in fact, he never handled at any length. Far more successful was the pair of poems, *L'Allegro* and *Il Pensoroso*, celebrating the delights of innocent 'mirth' and studious 'melancholy' amid rural beauty and classical scholarship. The latter poem ended with all heaven brought before the poet's eyes by the combination of architecture and music in Anglican worship, presumably in the great chapel of King's College, Cambridge. It is an odd passage to find in John Milton, although his father had been a chorister at Christ Church, Oxford. A masque performed at Ludlow Castle in 1634, *Comus*, offered similarly exalted praises of piety and virginity. But among all these poems of the 1630s only *Lycidas* had the power which we think of as Miltonic; and it was powerful because it gave the poet an opportunity to tell the world about himself.

Lycidas was a lament for Edward King, a young graduate of Milton's Cambridge college (Christ's), drowned in a shipwreck in 1637. It seems that Milton had scarcely known King, but the death of a contemporary stirred him to ask whether all human ambition was futile. That was his own question, for

> Fame is the spur that the clear spirit doth raise
> (That last infirmity of noble mind)
> To scorn delights, and live laborious days . . .

And the fact that King had been a candidate for ordination in Laud's Church gave an excuse for the poet to curse the clergy:

> Blind mouths! that scarce themselves know how to hold
> A sheep-hook, or have learned aught else the least
> That to the faithful herdman's art belongs! . . .
> The hungry sheep look up, and are not fed,
> But swoln with wind, and the rank mist they draw,
> Rot inwardly, and foul contagion spread.

This assessment of the Church of England was put into the mouth of St Peter, who was also made to comment on the menace of Popery and on the promise of reform:

> Besides what the grim wolf with privy paw
> Daily devours apace, and nothing said;
> But that two-handed engine at the door
> Stands ready to smite once, and smite no more.

Exactly what the 'two-handed engine' would be, *Lycidas* did
not make clear. But Milton's next great outburst is to be found
in his five pamphlets against the bishops. As his own power
was about to be taken away Laud had commissioned one of his
more scholarly and saintly colleagues, Joseph Hall, to write a
book advocating the 'divine right' of the bishops to govern the
Church. Hall lived to see his own cathedral (at Norwich)
invaded by a mob which tore out more or less everything that
could be moved.[16] Scarcely less violent was the theological
controversy caused by his book, although he was a sound
Calvinist and therefore not a thorough Laudian. To the debate
Milton contributed with a pent-up energy rather like the
Norwich mob's.

He rejected all the compromising proposals of moderates
such as Archbishop Ussher and Richard Baxter, who pleaded
that episcopacy might be saved by being 'reduced'. He wrote
with bitter contempt, tearing down the false scholarship which
had found prelacy within the New Testament and demolishing
any claim on behalf of the religion which the prelates had
supervised. As he wrote, it began to seem that only this
prelatical system which the parliamentary engine could so
easily smite stood between England and the fulfilment of the
Reformation. Was not an age of glory beginning in the 1640s?
'Then', wrote Milton at the end of *Reformation in England*,
'amidst the hymns and hallelujahs of saints, some one may
perhaps be heard offering at high strains in new and lofty
measures to sing and celebrate thy divine mercies and marvellous judgements in this land thoughout all ages.' Milton meant
to be that 'one', the poet of what he called 'the jubilee and
resurrection of the state'. He saw why he had been prepared for
his task – for he saw Christ waiting to claim his Kingdom. In
another anti-episcopal pamphlet he prayed: 'Come forth out of
thy royal chambers, O Prince of all the kings of the earth! Put
on the visible robes of thy imperial majesty, take up that
unlimited sceptre which thy Almighty Father hath bequeathed
thee; for now the voice of thy bride calls thee, and all creatures
sigh to be renewed.'

---

[16] F. L. Huntley portrayed *Bishop Joseph Hall* (Cambridge, 1979).

Milton is next to be found using his great learning and powers of invective in pleading for a law to permit divorce on the ground of incompatibility. His own disastrous marriage to Mary Powell spurred him on. She was the young daughter of a Royalist squire who owed money to his father, and Milton – so complete in his literary education, so lacking in experience of life – seems to have married her within a month of their first meeting. The reason is plain in *Paradise Lost*, where the poet who had celebrated chastity in *Comus* now rejoiced that Eve did not refuse the 'rites mysterious of connubial love',

> Whatever hypocrites austerely talk
> Of purity and place and innocence,
> Defaming as impure what God declares
> Pure, and commands to some, leaves free to all.
> Our Maker bids increase; who bids abstain
> But our destroyer, foe to God and man?

Eve, of course, had no right to refuse – for in *Samson Agonistes* Milton made it plain:

> Therefore God's universal law
> Gave to the man despotic power
> Over his female in due awe,
> Not from that right to part an hour,
> Smile she or lour . . .

Milton's young bride, however, soon ran away – only to return with her family when the Royalist cause was finally ruined. There was some reconciliation; she gave Milton daughters. But the blow which the marriage inflicted on the poet's pride drove him into public controversy on the topic of divorce, then generally believed to be forbidden to Christians by Christ's own words.

The controversy is significant because it showed Milton exalting the individual's conscience. Milton pleaded that the permission of divorce in the law of Moses still stood. In public he hinted – and in private he argued – that the Old Testament's permission of many wives to the patriarchs was relevant to Christians. When a shocked Presbyterian preacher denounced one of his pamphlets in a sermon to the House of

Commons, demanding the suppression of such subversive
literature, Milton published his *Areopagitica*, pleading for the
abolition of licensing in advance of publication (although he
did not suggest that Popish or other authors of 'that which is
impious or evil absolutely, either against faith or manners'
should escape punishment). He was still on fire with optimism
about the capacity of the English to achieve virtue by their free
struggles for the truth. 'Lords and commons of England!
consider what nation it is whereof ye are, and whereof ye are
the governors: a nation not slow and dull, but of a quick
ingenious and piercing spirit; acute to invent, subtle and
sinewy to discourse, not beneath the reach of any point the
highest that human capacity could soar to.' In other words, he
trusted that the English (with the known exceptions of his wife
and her family) resembled Milton himself.

The refusal of the Commons to listen to him on this dangerous topic seems to have begun Milton's disillusionment with
parliaments, but it would of course be wrong to think that a
mind so strong could be swayed by personal grudges alone
(particularly since death brought Milton release from his first
wife and her tribe in 1652). Milton genuinely despised what
was left of the Long Parliament, thought it incapable of
governing, and believed that its policy of imposing Presbyterianism on the country was utterly wrong.

Still more did he despise the sentimentality which idolized a
living king and turned an executed one into a martyr. He
admired Cromwell, who (he maintained) had won victory over
his own passions before winning any battle in the war. He was
proud to be appointed Secretary for Foreign Tongues to the
Council of State, and doubly proud to be commissioned to
defend King Charles's execution. To the writing of his *Eikono-
klastes* (1649) he brought the full power of his harsh joy that
there was now no bishop and no king. To the writing of his
Defensio pro Populo Anglicano (1651) he sacrificed the remnants
of his eyesight. The fact that the majority of the English people
regretted regicide did not trouble him, any more than did the
fact that Cromwell did not dare to summon a freely elected
Parliament. The time seemed to have come for government by
the virtuous and for freedom of worship for all who accepted

that government. Only slowly did he acknowledge that what he had written in his *Nativity* ode about the coming 'age of gold' was still true:

> But wisest Fate says no,
> This must not yet be so.

After 1655 Milton drew a pension rather than a salary from the government, and was again left free to work largely on his own. At first the loss of his sight was a profound shock:

> When I consider how my light is spent,
> Ere half my days, in this dark world and wide,
> And that one talent which is death to hide
> Lodged with me useless . . .

And his loneliness became the more intense when his second wife, Katherine, and the daughter born to them both died in 1658. In his grief he wrote his most moving poem:

> Methought I saw my late espoused saint . . .
> Came vested all in white, pure as her mind.
> Her face was veiled, yet to my fancied sight
> Love, sweetness, goodness, in her person shined . . .
> I waked, she fled, and day brought back my night.

When Cromwell (to whom he was never, it seems, personally close) died in the next year, and when it turned out that the political hopes of Puritanism had died with him, the blind poet for a time feared the hideous execution inflicted on traitors, before influential friends secured his safety. But he was spared; presumably his blindness was an argument in persuading the authorities not to hang the poet writing *Paradise Lost*, on the ground that he had already written high treason against Charles I. And that blindness, his bereavement and his political disillusionment all turned out to be indispensable factors in the fulfilment of the ambition to stand alongside Chaucer, Spenser and Shakespeare as a poet: the ambition which had been laid aside in 1640. He used to lie in bed, particularly in the winter months, until in the morning his daughters (with many grumbles, we gather) and other assistants would come to 'milk' him of the forty-odd lines he had composed in his mind. Perhaps half of those lines would be allowed to remain when the draft was read back to him. His third wife was a good cook

who controlled his daughters and any visitors. So the conditions for serious work were created. And the collapse of his
political hopes made this always serious, always essentially
solitary, genius ask with a new creative passion what were the
values he thought eternal.

For a long time he had been fascinated by the early history of
Britain. He had thought that it might be his vocation to write
an epic poem on King Arthur, a deliverer only matched by
Cromwell. He did some work, instead, on a *History of Britain* to
the Norman Conquest; and in the 1660s he completed it – only
now, a prominent theme was a lament that the British had not
proved worthy of freedom when the Roman yoke was removed.
For a long time his religion had been obstinately his own. Now
he began to collect texts from the Bible with his own comments,
in Latin, knowing that his heresies could not be published
while either Puritans or Royalists held power. In fact, *De
Doctrina Christiana*, which he seems to have gone on compiling
until his death, was not discovered and prepared for the printer
until 1823. For the time being, all that it could do was to clear
his own mind. The long-delayed epic poem to which he gave
himself could not be openly treacherous or heretical; but it
could take a theme which was safe because scriptural. And it
could tell an audience 'fit though few' what he had learned
from the public and private achievements and tragedies which
he had now experienced.

Paradise Lost (1667) and its sequel *Paradise Regained* (1671)
were, of course, primarily narratives, expanded from the bare
biblical text by the splendour of a poet's imaginative genius.
The music of their words has been enjoyed by very many
readers who have cared little for politics or theology; and being
on the surface biblical, they got past the censors in the reign of
Charles II. But like everything else of any real power that
Milton ever wrote, they are also a very proud man's autobiography. Here, he knew, was his last, supreme chance of
self-expression

> though fall'n on evil days,
> On evil days though fall'n, and evil tongues;
> In darkness, and with dangers compassed round,
> And solitude; yet not alone . . .

There is something of the excitement of the civil war in the account of the war in heaven in those books of *Paradise Lost* which were written while Cromwell was still alive. There is something of Milton's marriages in his portraiture of Adam and Eve and of Samson and Delila. The woman is subordinate (of course) and the first sinner (of course) – but the man loves her, in Adam's case enough to choose her rather than God. There is something of the poet's contempt for Stuart kings in his praise of Christ's rejection of the trappings of monarchy in *Paradise Regained*. There is also something of his contempt for Laudian prelates and priests in his description of the Philistines' religion in *Samson Agonistes* (a poem published in 1671 but written ten years or more earlier). The prayer of joy in nature which Adam and Eve offer ('unmeditated', the poet insists) in the middle of Book V of *Paradise Lost* seems to be Milton at his most positive and most impressive. And is there not a further self-revelation? Milton has such a reputation for cold arrogance that readers might expect him to appear in these poems as God. It was, however, one of the many curiosities of his religion that his God was not lovable and we must look elsewhere for the appearance of the poet, who certainly loved himself.

Some of Satan's speeches inciting the angels to rebellion against the divine tyrant, or defying God's revenging wrath, do sound rather like Milton. Plainly the poet enjoyed and admired Satan's 'courage never to submit or yield'. Indeed, William Blake suggested that 'the reason Milton wrote in fetters when he wrote of angels and God, and at liberty when of devils and hell, is because he was a true poet and of the Devil's party without knowing it.' But it is perverse to conclude that the mature Milton approved of Satan's rebellion when his whole theme was the calm acceptance of God's will. Most scholars are agreed that Milton identified himself mostly with the Son of God and with Samson (who was regarded as a precursor of Christ in the standard Puritan expositions of the Bible).

We readily understand how easy it was for Milton to speak through Samson, the blind hero who had once defended his people against the oppressor and who was now about to take vengeance on all his triumphant enemies as he died. It becomes easier for us to appreciate the personal link between the poet and the Son of God when we learn from *De Doctrina Christiana* that Milton believed that the Son of God was inferior to God.

In Milton's mature belief, God did not create the world 'out of nothing' as orthodoxy claimed. Instead, the primal chaos out of which the ordered world was created itself originated from God. The distinction may seem subtle, but it served to suggest that matter was in some sense divine. And God created not a fresh immortal soul for each new human being, but the one Adam, one body into which he breathed life or soul. Eve was made out of Adam, and all their descendants owed their souls as well as their bodies to sexual reproduction. God was therefore released from the 'servile' and risky work of soul-making. He was left free to uphold the ordinary course of nature or history, while men and women, made in the normal course of events, made their own destinies without any decisive initiative, interference or assistance from God. The advantage of this theology was that, although it made God out to be static, remote and remorseless, it freed him from the blame which is liable to attach to an Almighty Father who is believed to be willing to perform some miracles to rescue some people on some occasions. Only thus, Milton believed, could he 'justify the ways of God to man'.[17]

The Son of God did the work of creation in Milton's scheme, since God himself must not be involved. But Milton was an 'Arian' (after Arius, who died in c.336), in that he believed that the Son had been begotten by the Father within time, not as orthodoxy asserted 'before all worlds'. Although Milton accepted the orthodox anti-Arian statement that the Father and the Son were of one being (he translated the Greek *ousia* by the Latin *substantia*), he denied that they were of one essence (*essentia*). In the Father's address to the Son in Book III of *Paradise Lost*, the highest compliment which the former can pay to the latter is:

---

[17] A modern atheist can therefore commend Milton up to a point. See William Empson, *Milton's God* (London, 1961).

Both God and man, Son both of God and man.

And when the angels hymn Jesus at the end of *Paradise Regained*, the praise is no higher:

The Son of God, with God-like force endued.

These abstruse and obscure points of theology encouraged the practical belief that men could imitate Christ and thus become sons of God themselves. It was also important that Milton was an Arminian, like the hated Laud. His rejection of Calvin's teaching that some were predestined to damnation is most famous because of his description of the fallen angels who

> reason high
> Of providence, foreknowledge, will and fate,
> Fixed fate, free will, foreknowledge absolute,
> And found no end, in wand'ring mazes lost.

But the point is that no true Calvinist could have been so contemptuous of such talk, the normal reasoning expected from the most trusted theologians. Milton's rejection of 'fixed fate' meant that he could combine praise of the moral virtue of the 'saints' with a moral condemnation of those who, exercising their own free wills, rejected God's call. Thus the Father declares in *Paradise Lost*:

> Some I have chosen of peculiar grace
> Elect above the rest; so is my will.
> The rest shall hear me call, and oft be warned
> Their sinful state, and to appease betimes
> Th' incensèd Deity, while offered grace
> Invites . . .

For to Milton all men were free, 'sufficient to have stood, though free to fall'.

After Adam's fall his heirs are still free to respond to the promptings of conscience:

> And I will place within them as a guide
> My umpire, Conscience, whom if they will hear,
> Light after light well us'd they shall attain,
> And to the end persisting, safe arrive.

What was essential was that men, aided by God's grace, should cultivate the heroic virtues. That was why in Milton's poem Paradise, having being lost when Adam chose to love Eve rather than obey God, was regained when the Son of God heroically chose to obey God during his temptations in the wilderness. Milton, although he could sound orthodox enough about the Saviour's work and the Saviour's grace, never found occasion to write at any length about any atonement achieved by the crucifixion. He also made nothing important depend on Christ's resurrection. Indeed, he believed that even for the Christian saint after death 'the soul as well as the body sleeps until the day of resurrection'. This was 'Mortalism', leaving to the individual only the hope of resurrection at the end of the world. Heaven and hell, to say nothing of Dante's purgatory, thus receded from Milton's immediate concern. He still accepted the final judgement by God, but it seems probable that he thought of heaven and hell as being only states of mind, at least until that judgement – agreeing at this point with Satan:

> The mind is its own place, and in itself
> Can make a heav'n of hell, a hell of heav'n.

For practical purposes his mature religion austerely taught obedience to God in this life.

It was an attitude not essentially different from a Stoic or Muslim submission to fate; and it was an attitude perfectly possible for all the virtuous who were masters of themselves. Such a religion falls short of the love of the Father, of the Saviour and of the sinner as practised and advocated by the Christian saints. But not far short – as Adam shows when he concludes *Paradise Lost*:

> Henceforth I learn that to obey is best,
> And love with fear the only God, to walk
> As in his presence, ever to observe
> His providence, and on him sole depend. . . .

Moreover, Milton seems to have known, in some moods at any rate, what was lacking. In the poem the Angel congratulates

Adam on attaining the 'sum of wisdom' but warns him that in order to possess 'a paradise within thee' he must add

> Deeds to thy knowledge answerable, add faith,
> Add virtue, patience, temperance, add love,
> By name to come called charity, the soul
> Of all the rest . . .

What, then, of politics? Milton's final verdict on the Puritan Revolution resembled Richard Baxter's: the Commonwealth had been betrayed by the unheroic weakness of its own citizens. There had been a time when 'by the general instinct of holy and devout men, as they daily and solemnly express their thoughts, God is decreeing to begin some new and great period in his Church, even to the reforming of Reformation itself; what does he then but reveal himself to his servants, and as his manner is, first to his Englishmen?' So he had enthused in *Areopagitica*. But already in 1648 he showed his regret that the war had done such damage and had left such power in the army's hands. In his sonnet to General Fairfax he asked:

> For what can war but endless war still breed
> Till truth and right from violence be freed?

After the war Parliament had refused to rise to the central challenge of the 1640s, which was to give religious liberty to all, so that all might learn for themselves how to be heroic. The people had also been to blame – by refusing to achieve the heroism open to them, which was submission to the divinely decreed social order. And even Cromwell had been at fault in the 1650s, when unlike Christ he had unheroically yielded to the temptation to grab political power.

Amid the confusion of 1659 Milton published one of his last pamphlets, *The Ready and Easy Way to Establish a Free Commonwealth*. His way involved forgetting the very name of Parliament, all thought of popular direct elections, and all government by a 'single person'. Instead there was to be an assembly in each county guided by 'the nobility and chief gentry', if virtuous. There was also to be a General Council for the whole Commonwealth, elected for life by those with property; in a complicated scheme successive elections were envisaged in

order to winnow out electors or candidates not possessed of
sufficient virtue or sufficient property. And there was to be a
Council of State, with no Lord Protector. The poet cannot have
been entirely surprised when this 'ready and easy way' was
disregarded by the politicians and the soldiers, so that the
restoration of the king and the bishops became inevitable. He
never again dictated thoughts directly about politics, so far as
we know; his only publication in this field during his lifetime
was in 1673, a pamphlet advocating the toleration of Protestants but emphatically not of Papists.

After 1660 the resurrection of the Puritan Revolution
seemed to be as remote as the hope of heaven. But meanwhile it
was open to men to reform and discipline themselves. If it was
God's will, there might one day be a revolution ruled by saints,
an England fit for heroes. And meanwhile the poet could find
his rest, in a death accepted heroically. Samson says of himself:

> I was no private but a person raised
> With strength sufficient and command from heaven
> To free my country . . .

And after his death it is declared of him:

> Nothing is here for tears, nothing to wail
> Or knock the breast, no weakness, no contempt,
> Dispraise, or blame; nothing but well and fair,
> And what may quiet us in a death so noble.

As for the 'Good Old Cause' of the Puritan Revolution:

> All is best, though we oft doubt,
> What th' unsearchable dispose
> Of Highest Wisdom brings about,
> And ever best found in the close . . .
> His servants he, with new acquist
> Of true experience from this great event,
> With peace and consolation hath dismissed,
> And calm of mind, all passion spent.[18]

---

[18] Christopher Hill, *Milton and the Puritan Revolution* (London, 1977), puts the life
against its background and lists many other studies. E. M. W. Tillyard, *Milton*
(revised London, 1966), and Hugh Richmond, *The Christian Revolutionary: John
Milton* (Berkeley, Cal., 1974), were usefully concise. C. S. Lewis assessed Milton as

JOHN BUNYAN

Two of John Bunyan's books will always be of supreme interest to anyone who would understand English religion. He was a preacher and pastor, born in 1628 and called to full-time service by his Bedford church in 1671. Tearing himself away from his wife and blind daughter (he compared that with 'the pulling of the flesh from my bones'), he accepted imprisonment for twelve years, with a second period to follow, rather than undertake not to preach. His imprisonment was not always severe; there is evidence that he was allowed to spend many nights at home and to go to London. He often preached to Nonconformist congregations while technically a prisoner. But he spent enough time in prison to suffer some privations – and to become a great writer. He came to believe that his imprisonment had been within God's providence because it had given him what his normal life would never have provided – the incentive and the time to write. And he wrote with a success which he naïvely celebrated. By the time of his death in 1688 (he had caught a chill on a journey undertaken in order to reconcile a father and a son) he was famous. His most outstanding gift was an extraordinary ability to recreate everyday English scenes and conversations, and to make them the symbols and dramas of the Puritans' spiritual world.

He was never a cool professional in religion. His autobiography, *Grace Abounding to the Chief of Sinners*, told of the tempests of self-accusation, religious doubt and existential despair which made year after year of his young life miserable. And he was never a literary gentleman. It was not only that he was innocent of Latin. Although he quoted the Bible so freely, his own prose was remarkably unlike the stately Authorized Version's. It captured on paper the colloquial speech of the day and was inspired by popular literature – fairy stories and cheap

'overwhelmingly Christian' in *A Preface to Paradise Lost* (Oxford, 1942), and C. A. Patrides presented him as a substantially orthodox Protestant in *Milton and the Christian Tradition* (Oxford, 1966), but see Arthur Sewell, *A Study in Milton's Christian Doctrine* (Oxford, 1939), and N. T. Burns, *Christian Moralism from Tyndale to Milton* (Cambridge, Mass., 1972). J. S. Hill, *John Milton: Poet, Priest and Prophet* (London, 1979), studied Milton's profound belief that he had been called by God – a vocation not ended by disaster.

novels. This often confused and barely educated man wrote for the people as he preached to the people, from the heart to the heart, with a mission which never separated him from them. English Nonconformity was to consist of millions like him.

Richard Baxter's wife was well-off, which was why he was able to spend his last thirty years as a writer. John Milton's rich father enabled the poet to spend his first thirty years as a student. But John Bunyan earned his living as a wandering tinker or odd-job-man, like his father. His idea of education was to thank God that he was able to read the two books which his first wife's father had left her when he died, *The Plain Man's Pathway to Heaven* and *The Practice of Piety*, 'though we came together as poor as poor might be (not having so much household stuff as a dish or a spoon betwixt us both)'. And he was never captured by middle-class conventions. He once wrote a book about a businessman whose acquisitiveness had the energy which some twentieth-century writers have suggested was given to the prospering bourgeoisie by Calvinism. Although it has been described as the first English novel, it is virtually unreadable because its central character was damned hopelessly from the start. It was called *Mr Badman*.

Two books of his have become classics. *Grace Abounding* (1666) is the direct story of how an ignorant but very introspective young man, psychologically (it would seem) sometimes depressive and sometimes manic, felt the threats and promises of the English Bible rolling over his soul like waves which almost drowned him. While playing tipcat on Elstow village green he heard a voice: 'Wilt thou leave thy sins and go to heaven, or have thy sins and go to hell?' 'One morning as I did lie in bed, I was, as at other times, most fiercely assaulted with this temptation, *To sell and part with Christ*; the wicked suggestion still running in my mind, *Sell him, sell him, sell him, sell him, sell him*, as fast as a man could speak.' 'The glory of the holiness of God did at this time break me to pieces.'

The Pilgrim's Progress (in two parts published in 1678–84) told basically the same story, but projected it into a journey such as would be taken by a tinker through the English countryside – with an anvil on his back which to the imagination became the burden of sin; sometimes admitted into the

'House Beautiful' and many humbler homes but spending far more time outdoors; falling in with many different companions on the road; finding that the road easily became a quagmire, the Slough of Despond; being rather frightened at Vanity Fair but needed to go there because he needed the work. The memory of the freedom of the road no doubt often came back to Bunyan while he slept in prison. That lies behind the famous opening: 'As I walked through the wilderness of this world, I lighted upon a certain place where there was a den, and laid me down in that place to sleep: and, as I slept, I dreamed a dream.'

The book was true to life in so many subtle ways. The action is somewhat repetitive and more than one of the sermons by which Christian is instructed hints that the preacher has fallen into an unexciting routine. But the adventure is provided by life itself, for it is impossible for Christian to tell what lies ahead. ' "Do you see yonder wicket-gate?" The man said, "No". Then said the other, "Do you see yonder shining light?" He said, "I think I do." ' It is also impossible for Christian to be secure until the end; even when Doubting Castle and the Valley of the Shadow of Death have been left behind, it is seen that there is 'a way to Hell even from the gates of Heaven, as well as from the City of Destruction'. And it is impossible for anyone who comes after to duplicate the same experiences exactly. For others the way may be harder; Christian's companion, Faithful, is put to death in Vanity Fair. But his own wife and four sons, who take Christian's road in the second part of the *Progress*, find the going much easier and have time for music and dancing during their pilgrimage (or, as Ronald Knox called it, their 'walking tour'). The only guidance which every pilgrim could and should follow is indicated by Mr Standfast when he looks back: 'I have loved to hear my Lord spoken of, and wherever I have seen the print of his shoe in the earth, there I have coveted to set my foot too.' But even for Mr Standfast, the heroic virtue of proud John Milton is impossible. Like the other pilgrims, Mr Standfast still needs a Saviour long after his conversion.

The church in Bedford to which Bunyan belonged was founded by eleven working men in 1650; it was one of the fruits of Cromwell's policy of toleration for Protestant 'separatists'.

It has usually been called a Baptist church, but it was described as Congregational when it applied for a licence under
the King's Declaration of Indulgence in 1672. Certainly it was
far removed from all the accusations of immorality and general
rebelliousness which had brought scandal to the Continental
Anabaptist movement in the sixteenth century. Respectable
housewives such as Christiana felt at home there. It was
possible to become a member of this congregation, a 'saint',
without having been baptized as an adult – or at all. Baptism is
not decisive in the *Progress*. Although Bunyan is known from his
other books to have adhered much more closely to Calvin's
scheme of salvation than did Milton, he was not rigid. The
Progress is true to life in that it gives no sense that its characters
lack the freedom to go forward or fall back. And the will of God
is that they should go forward; 'the last words of Mr Honest
were, *Grace reigns*'.

There was a future for the Puritan religion taught by John
Bunyan: the Nonconformist future in England, the Evangelical
movement among Anglicans, the missionary work around the
world. Fanfares of fame have sounded for this imprisoned
odd-job-man, as the trumpets sounded for Mr Valiant-for-
truth when he had crossed the river of death, leaving his sword
'to him that shall succeed me in my pilgrimage.'[19]

---

[19] There is no really good biography, but see W. Y. Tindall, *John Bunyan:
Mechanick Preacher* (New York, 1934); Monica Furlong, *Puritan's Progress* (London,
1975); *Bunyan: The Pilgrim's Progress*, ed. Roger Sharrock (London, 1976).

Part Three

RELIGION IN
THE AGE OF REASON

CHAPTER TEN

THE QUAKERS

GEORGE FOX

George Fox began to preach in Nottinghamshire in 1647, the year when Charles I was defeated and the victorious army awaited the reconstruction of English society. A congregation was formed at Mansfield under his influence in the following year; and one incident, typical of many, helps to explain the magnetism of the man. Having interrupted a preacher in church, Fox was lynched by a mob and beaten with clubs until he fell unconscious. On regaining consciousness, 'I lay a little still, and the power of the Lord sprang through me, and the eternal refreshings refreshed me, that I stood up again in the eternal power of God and stretched out my arms amongst them all, and said again with a loud voice, "Strike again, here is my arms and my head and my cheeks".'

He was a lion among men, but his courage was not the most rare of his characteristics. 'He was of an innocent life,' wrote William Penn, 'no busy-body, nor self-seeker, neither touchy nor critical; what fell from him was very inoffensive, if not very edifying. So meek, contented, modest, easy, steady, tender, it was a pleasure to be in his company. He exercised no authority but over evil, and that everywhere and in all, but with love, compassion, and long-suffering, a most merciful man, as ready to forgive as unapt to take or give an offence.' And Fox himself pointed to the heart of his joy: 'I saw that there was an ocean of darkness and death, but an infinite ocean of light and love, which flowed over the ocean of darkness.' The ferment of radical religious ideas also produced groups such as the Seekers, who worshipped in silence rather than use words which had ceased to be authentic; the Ranters and Levellers, who rejected society's conventions rather than deny the Christ in every man; or the Fifth Monarchy Men who pressed forward impatiently into the reign of King Jesus. But the personality of George Fox provides a large part of the answer to the question: why did the Quakers survive when all these other groups were forgotten?

Born in a Leicestershire village in 1624, he was the son of a devout weaver nicknamed Righteous Christer. But the normal pieties of family and village did not satisfy the boy. He left home early and ceased to attend church. When 'towards nineteen years of age' and working as a shoemaker, he became convinced that he was called to be a pilgrim, literally – and alone. As he lay sleepless one night after leaving a beer-party in disgust, he saw 'young people go together into vanity and old people into the earth; and thou must forsake all, both young and old, and keep out of all, and be as a stranger unto all.' Three years or more of wandering and seeking followed. He consulted clergymen, and found that 'to be bred at Oxford or Cambridge was not enough to make a man fit to be a minister of Christ'. He consulted 'separatist' preachers and found that they, too, could not satisfy him. But his search was rewarded. 'When all my hope in them and in all men were gone, so that I had nothing outwardly to help me, nor could tell what to do, then, Oh then, I heard a voice which said, "There is one, even Christ Jesus, that can speak to thy condition", and when I heard it my heart did leap for joy.'

Charismatic excitement marked the meetings which he addressed. As he put it, 'now was I come up in the spirit through the flaming sword into the paradise of God. All things were new, and all the creation gave another smell unto me than before . . .' He bade a Derby magistrate tremble at the word of the Lord in 1650, and the magistrate's nickname for his movement stuck: they were 'Quakers', although Fox wanted them to be called 'Children of the Light'. Men and women (whose equality was itself revolutionary) joyfully surrendered themselves to ecstasies which sober churchmen had not expected to meet outside the pages of the Acts of the Apostles. Fox claimed that there were many healing miracles, although most of these claims were suppressed when his *Journal* was printed. The Quakers met in each other's homes and often denounced the priests of the steeple-houses. (Fox used the term 'priests' of all the clergymen, and called all churches 'steeple-houses'.) They saw no point in continuing the sacraments of Baptism and Holy Communion since the age of the spirit had arrived.

Not even the Bible retained its accustomed authority. With a thrill of excitement Margaret Fell heard George Fox exclaim in Ulverston parish church: 'You will say, "Christ saith this, and the apostles say this" – *but what canst thou say?*' That kind of question shocked not only the bishops but also Roger Williams, Richard Baxter and John Bunyan, all of whom were stirred to write against the Quakers. But many were glad to hear it asked and confident that they could answer it. John Lilburne, for instance, read Quaker books when he was imprisoned in Dover Castle in 1650, after his latest defiance of the political authorities. He was soon writing that he had 'really and substantially found that which my soul many years hath sought diligently after'. So he knew peace before he died, aged forty-two.

The customs of the Quakers outside their meetings drew further attention – sometimes fascinated, often hostile. They refused to use the pagan names of days or months; Sunday was the First Day, January the First Month. Fearing hypocrisy, they refused to wear any finery, to join most of the normal amusements, to use any titles, to remove their hats when addressing others, or to call anyone by the courtly 'you' instead of the plain, old-fashioned 'thou'. They were also convinced that the Sermon on the Mount forbade them to take any oaths, to participate in any violence, or to wear weapons. On several dramatic occasions they appeared in outlandish clothing, or in no clothing at all, as prophets in public places, 'for a sign'.

Their leaders were constantly on the move, often forced to sleep out of doors, often imprisoned, often surrounded by outbreaks of hysteria; and under such a strain they sometimes acted hysterically. George Fox walked barefoot up and down Lichfield crying 'Woe unto the bloody city!' To Fox's intense alarm, James Nayler allowed a little group of muddy women to chant 'Hosanna' and 'Holy, Holy, Holy' as he rode through Wells and Glastonbury and into Bristol in the rain one October day in 1656; he had just finished a long spell of fasting and prayer in Exeter jail. But the main impression left by the early Quaker leaders is not of hysteria.

Marmaduke Stephenson was not unique in his cold courage: 'In the beginning of the year 1655,' he recalled when he found himself in Boston prison in Massachusetts not five years later, 'I was at the plough in the east parts of Yorkshire . . . and as I walked after the plough I was filled with the love and presence of the living God which did ravish my heart when I felt it . . . And the word of the Lord came to me in a still small voice which I did hear perfectly, saying to me in the secret of my heart and conscience, *I have ordained thee a prophet unto the nations.*' In 1658 he felt a call to go to the island of Barbados, leaving 'my dear and loving wife and tender children', and while he was there he heard that 'New England had made a law to put the servants of the Living God to death'. This seemed to him an excellent reason why he should proceed to Massachusetts and refuse to leave it; and he was hanged.

Even James Nayler was not a mere hysteric. A ploughman who had served in the New Model Army for nine years (mostly as a quartermaster), he became an eloquent mystic whose best-known book was called *The Lamb's War*. His fatal mistake, the ride into Bristol, seems to have occurred because at that time, after his imprisonment and its mystical raptures, he was scarcely conscious of the everyday world. His body, like his reputation, never fully recovered from his punishment for that blasphemy; while he was walking home from London to Yorkshire he was beaten up by robbers and soon died. But the spirit in which he died showed that he was not unworthy to speak of the spiritual war being led by the non-violent Lamb. 'There is a spirit which I feel,' he wrote, 'that delights to do no evil nor to avenge any wrong, but delights to endure all things in hope to enjoy its own in the end. Its hope is to outlive all wrath and contention and to weary out all exultation and cruelty and whatever is of a nature contrary to itself. It sees to the end of all temptations. As it bears no evil in itself, so it conceives none in thoughts to any other. If it be betrayed, it bears it, for its ground and spring is the mercies and forgiveness of God.'[1]

---

[1] See Geoffrey Nuttall, *James Nayler: A Fresh Approach* (London, 1954).

George Fox, although like Nayler lacking in formal education, dictated a *Journal* recording his life to 1676. Published
three years after his death in 1691, it took its place among the
classics of English religion.[2] To call it literature would be
inaccurate, but there is no denying its power to recreate
physical and emotional dramas with words of strength and a
simple dignity. More unusual still was Fox's organizing capacity. In the crisis caused by the indiscretion of the ride into
Bristol, Fox had no hesitation in rejecting Nayler as a heretic.
Nor did he hesitate to set up a system which would make sure
that there would be no more Naylers. When Nayler offered him
a kiss of reconciliation, Fox once felt guided to hold out his foot.
He organized special meetings for counties or groups of counties, with a national meeting at Skipton in 1660. He was a
cobbler, with leather breeches and a white (undyed) hat; but
he somehow became the first Englishman to lead a nationwide
denomination – meaning by 'denomination' a religious body
not aspiring to be the National Church.

His vision crossed the seas. As early as 1652, as he looked
down from Pendle Hill across Lancashire to the sea, 'the Lord
let me see a top of the hill in what places he had a great people
to be gathered'. Believing that Friends were called to 'walk
cheerfully over the world, answering that of God in every one'
(as he put it in 1656), he became the most internationally-
minded man England had produced for many years. In 1671–
73 he was in Barbados, Jamaica, Virginia and New England,
declaring on his return: 'We can challenge all the world'. With
his encouragement Quaker missionaries went not only to New
England but also to the Netherlands, to Germany and to the
East, announcing the 'Kingdom of Jesus' like the biblical
apostles. George Robinson testified in Jerusalem. Mary Fisher
lectured the Sultan. When he courteously asked what she
thought of the Prophet of Islam, she replied that he had been a
true prophet if what he spoke was from God: a verdict to which
the Sultan could not take exception. In the East only the
authorities in Rome violently resented this form of evangelism,

---

[2] *The Journal of George Fox* was edited by J. L. Nickalls (Cambridge, 1952), and
George Fox's Book of Miracles by H. J. Cadbury (Cambridge, 1948).

and one Quaker, John Luffe, was hanged there. George Fox
sent a letter to the Emperor of China 'from the People of God in
England, in English called Quakers'. 'Friends,' he announced,
'there is a Power above all Powers, and this Power is making
itself manifest.'

This explosion of religious energy created stirs in many
places but had the most lasting consequences in Yorkshire, the
Lake counties and other northern areas of England. There
medieval Catholicism had at last died down but no Protestant
minister had made much impact – often because the still
medieval parish system left him with too big a district. In so far
as Fox had a home and his movement a base, from 1652
onwards this was Swarthmoor Hall in Lancashire; in 1669 he
married Margaret Fell, the widow of its owner. However, he
was never a man to settle down to the life of a squire. Of their
twenty-one years of married life – years of mutual devotion – he
and his Margaret passed little more than five in each other's
company. He was not a squire but an apostle, imprisoned nine
times; and because of its uncluttered directness the movement
which he led appealed to many countrymen in the backward
southwest and to the working class in England's largest cities,
London and Bristol. It is not surprising that after the rising of
Fifth Monarchy Men in London in 1661 the Cavalier gentry
assembled in Parliament rushed through a special Act to
suppress the Quakers. Locally magistrates assumed that these
eccentrics were revolutionaries and threw thousands of them
into prison where hundreds of them died of gaol fever. But all
the evidence confirms the Quakers' own claim that religious,
rather than political, energy had been awakened. And there is
no shortage of printed evidence about the motives of this
movement founded by George Fox. It has been reckoned that a
new Quaker book or pamphlet appeared every week from the
first tracts of 1652 to the end of the seventeenth century.[3]

---

[3] W. C. Braithwaite studied *The Beginnings of Quakerism* (revised, Cambridge,
1955) and Hugh Barbour *The Quakers in Puritan England* (New Haven, Conn., 1964).
Early Quaker Writings were edited by Hugh Barbour and A. O. Roberts (Grand
Rapids, Mich., 1973). There is no good biography of George Fox, but the discussion
by Michael Watts in *The Dissenters*, Vol. 1 (Oxford, 1978), pp. 179–212, is of special
value.

FROM QUAKERS TO FRIENDS

In the great persecution of 1662–72 (which was less severe in the period 1665–70), and under many further sufferings prolonged until the Toleration Act of 1689, the Quakers were conspicuous for their courage. They deliberately left the doors of the houses where they met for worship unlocked. If the meeting was surrounded by an insulting mob, it carried on; if its members were arrested, they resumed their worship in prison. If the meeting house was pulled down, Quakers would still be found on the spot the next First Day; and if no adult Quakers were out of prison, it was not unknown for the children to assemble. A Quaker meeting needed no preacher; it did not even need a Bible; the 'inner light', it was claimed, was the guide. The Spirit in their midst seemed to grow stronger as the persecutors put themselves more and more in the wrong in the eyes of ordinary Christians. Much evidence suggests that although at the beginning of the persecution the movement was regarded as ridiculous or as alarming, by the 1670s the Quakers had won a respect which they have never forfeited in England. 'They go like lambs without any resistance', wrote a baffled Samuel Pepys in his diary. 'I would to God they would either conform, or be more wise, and not be catched.'

The most difficult problem came to be not how to survive persecution but how to survive prosperity.

One great strength of the Quakers under persecution was their tight organization; in this, too, they resembled the early Christians. They encouraged powerful leadership by treating the leaders and other ministers (who were 'recorded', not appointed or paid) as men or women inspired by God. They 'watched over' each other's moral progress. They were in each other's company as often as possible, and recognized each other by their strange customs even when they did not already know each other by name. They founded schools to educate each other's children. They supported each other very generously when in trouble. From 1667 onwards Fox systematically organized Monthly Meetings which decided policy in matters great or small. A national meeting held in London at Christmas 1668 became the London Yearly Meeting – at a time when the Church of England itself possessed no comparable national forum. The 'Meeting for Sufferings' was a committee which from 1676 onwards kept a nationwide check on the English Quakers' troubles. It retained its central role (and its name) when the persecution had died down, and devoted much of its time to the teething troubles of the Quaker settlements in America. But with this organizational strength, problems grew.

Even Fox did not escape fierce criticism from some Quakers who resented the masterfulness of his personality. The mutual care of Quakers could also be resented. It might seem to be intolerable prying into each other's affairs, especially when 'elders' were appointed to lead the meetings (a custom made nationwide in 1727). Their uniform could itself be criticized, especially as people realized that the costume originally adopted as plain everyday wear now seemed merely outdated and queer. Quaker children thus garbed were tormented by cries of 'Quack! Quack!' in the streets. Moreover, the well-to-do adults' dress was often tailor-made and rather expensive. The schools, founded on a large scale from 1750 onwards, could be attacked because they kept young Quakers in a hothouse atmosphere, with the inevitable rebellions. And the growing moral pressure of the meetings to 'keep in the unity' could be contrasted with the earlier days when the message had appealed as an encouragement of the individual to 'keep your feet upon the top of the mountains and sound deep to the witness of God in every man' (as Fox wrote in 1660). It is the judgement of more than one Quaker scholar that 'by 1800 the Society of Friends had become a rigid institution, subject to the very institutional faults against which the early Friends had carried out their costly struggle.'[4]

Another great strength of the early Quakers lay in their 'convincement' that the Truth within was nothing less than the Christ within. In the early days there seemed no need to be theological about this. A man such as George Fox simply assumed that what was true must be Christian. Although he was a sturdy individualist and no great reader of other men's

---

[4] Harold Loukes, *The Quaker Contribution* (London, 1965), p. 66.

books, it was said that if the Bible had been lost it could have been recovered from his dictation. But inevitably many Quakers, particularly the more educated, became anxious to dissociate the movement from extremists, such as the Ranters who were frankly heretical. John Perrot refused to remove his hat when another Quaker was offering prayer to God in a meeting, and this 'hat heresy' had to be pursued when it was carried to the West Indies and New England. The problem was how to do battle against such heresies when there was no official creed, and when almost all the evangelists ('public Friends' was their title) had no theological training.

Robert Barclay, a Scot who became a Quaker in 1666, published a substantial *Apologia* in Latin ten years later. He remained enough of a Calvinist to teach very firmly that the 'inner light' was an 'inward and immediate revelation' of Christ, the saving Light of the World. In essence this was the old Puritan orthodoxy about the work of the Holy Spirit. Barclay was fascinated by a mystical sentence which he heard at the first Quaker meeting he attended: 'In stillness there is fullness; in fullness there is nothingness; in nothingness there are all things.' But he stressed that every Quaker meeting must end with only one 'sense of the meeting' – and that this sense must subordinate all things to Christ. Even during the seventeenth century this synthesis was under strain; George Keith, who had worked with Barclay, caused trouble among the Americans by organizing a movement known as the 'Christian Quakers' and ended up being ordained by the Bishop of London. The Quaker reliance on 'the Light of Christ within men without anything else' was, he kept on declaring on his return to America, insufficient; and he stirred up controversy until his death in 1716. Thereafter the controversy slumbered, but it caused serious divisions in the Quakers' ranks when it came out into the open in the 1820s and 1830s. The theological question, once raised after the strong simplicity of the first days, could not be suppressed.

The early Quakers were as untouched by wealth as they were by theology, But they were hard-working and honest. They came from social groups unaffected by aristocratic values, and it was from such groups that England's manufacturers and tradesmen were working their way into prosperity. By 'watching over' each other they to a large extent enforced the rigorous moral standards which Richard Baxter (for instance) demanded in his books. Quaker traders or bankers could be trusted; Quaker employers might even be loved. And honest toil was rewarded. Before the seventeenth century had ended there were rich Quakers, especially in London. Even the average Quaker was found to be reliable, and therefore eminently employable. Much was gained – but something was lost in comparison with the 1650s, when under George Fox's charismatic leadership poor men and women, the Children of Light, had challenged the 'world's people' to be spiritually rich.

PENN AND PENNSYLVANIA

The new respectability of the Quakers was associated with the personality of William Penn. The son of the admiral who had conquered Jamaica for Cromwell before becoming a distinguished servant of Charles II, he first heard Quaker preaching when a lad of twelve. As an undergraduate at Christ Church, Oxford, he was enough of a rebel against the Anglicans in control to prefer the teaching of John Owen, the ex-dean; and he was asked to leave. Not even travel as a young aristocrat in France and Italy, or residence as a young landowner in Ireland, could get the Quaker challenge out of his mind. He openly became a Quaker himself. Having publicly attacked the doctrines of the Church of England, he was imprisoned in the Tower of London, and there wrote a devotional classic: *No Cross, No Crown*. On his acquittal by a jury which refused to be intimidated, he was recognized as the best-educated and the most socially prominent Quaker. He often talked in that capacity with Charles II and James II.

Both kings admired him personally, in addition to their gratitude to his father. In 1681 Charles granted him extensive lands south of New England and New Jersey, and north of Maryland and Virginia. They had been won from the Dutch, who had never made much of 'New Netherland'. This tract was empty, apart from a few Dutchmen, Swedes and Finns together with Indian tribesmen who were declining in vigour; and, once cultivated, it would be fertile. The reason given for the grant (made when all efforts had failed to find a purchaser) was that the Crown was in debt to old Admiral Penn. It seems clear, however, the King hoped that William Penn would lead his fellow Quakers far away across the Atlantic, for he disliked having his peace troubled by their persecution as much as he disliked having his vices denounced by their prophecies. The idea of emigration had also occurred to Penn, who had already managed the purchase of lands on which to settle Quakers in New Jersey. The new 'province' was named Pennsylvania by the King; Penn had wanted to call it New Wales, and perhaps Charles was teasing him by insisting on the grandiloquent name, to be compared with the settlements of Carolina in the south. Penn spent only two periods there – periods of less than two years each, separated by fifteen years – but he made sure that his ideas were stamped on the growth of Pennsylvania.

From the first he insisted on liberty of conscience for all; on the promise that (in the words of the 1701 Charter of Privileges) no one should 'at any time be compelled to frequent or maintain any religious worship, place or ministry whatever, contrary to his, or her, mind.' He insisted, too, on friendly relations and fair bargains with the Indians. Benjamin West's painting of William Penn's treaty with the Indians under the great elm at Shackamaxon is familiar to many Americans (although there is no contemporary record of such a treaty). Penn welcomed George Fox's exhortation: 'Let your light shine among the Indians, and the Blacks and the Whites, that ye may answer the truth in them.'

Early Pennsylvania knew a remarkable measure of democracy. Penn drew up a *Frame of Government* which gave restricted power to himself as proprietor and governor, and much to an elected council of seventy-two. The council was to propose laws to an annual General Assembly of some two hundred, elected by all freemen with property. It was by no means a society of strict equality. Power lay with the council, the nucleus of Pennsylvania's future aristocracy. Penn owned a

few Negro slaves, as did some other early settlers, and there
were many 'bond servants' – immigrants who had bound
themselves to their masters, usually for five years, in exchange
for their transatlantic fares. But the Quakers practised a
remarkable degree of brotherhood. There is truth in the claim
made for Pennsylvania before about 1740 that 'this life was an
artistic creation as beautiful in its simplicity and proportion as
was the architecture of its meeting houses'.[5] In this strange
colony, the proprietor himself had a book printed under the
title *England's Liberties* (1682) which contained not only his
patent from the Crown but also Magna Carta. And the
brotherhood was not exclusively Quaker. The first Quakers
arriving were given no privileges over the other Europeans
already in the area. Philadelphia was planned with its streets
like a chess-board; the houses varied in handsomeness and
their owners varied in wealth, but all must fit into the ordered
pattern of the City of Brotherly Love.

However, the establishment of Pennsylvania, promising as it
was, involved William Penn in problems which had never
burdened George Fox; and although he used others – including
men who were not Quakers – as his deputies, he could not
escape his responsibilities. Indeed, his correspondence often
shows an irritated, even secular, tone as he insisted on his
political and financial rights as proprietor. This 'Lord of the
Soil' attempted to exercise over Pennsylvania a power which
he denied to the kings in England. It is surprising neither that
such claims were resisted nor that the opposition was led by
two Welshmen, Thomas and David Lloyd. There were bitter
disputes over land, rights and status among the settlers and
between them and neighbouring colonies. There were crimes,
and the criminals had to be punished – even hanged; in 1718
Pennsylvania adopted the same death penalties as England.
There were threats from the French, and a promise that the
Quakers would contribute to their own military defence was
made a condition of the renewal of Penn's grant. For years the
pacifism of the Pennsylvania Quakers was preserved by
equivocations; in 1745, when they voted money for 'grain', the

[5] R. H. Bainton, *Friends for 300 Years* (New York, 1952), p. 184.

governor interpreted this as including gunpowder. There were quarrels with the Indians; although Penn in his lifetime could insist on the 'peaceable kingdom' and later Quakers obstinately clung to this vision, conflicts and massacres eventually led to the Indian war of 1756. Recognizing that military action was now inescapable, but being unwilling to participate in it, most of the Quakers then resigned from the General Assembly of Pennsylvania. This perfectionist withdrawal from government and war came fifty-five years after Penn's last visit to his province.

He lived to see the Quakers accepting some compromise in England. Although never willing to give evidence in criminal cases or to serve on juries, they solved the problem which they had created by being unwilling to take the Oath of Allegiance as well as lesser oaths, by now agreeing to the formula, 'I do declare in the presence of Almighty God, the Witness of the truth of what I say'. Penn was controversially involved in politics as a result of his friendship with James II; to the indignation of Anglicans, he accepted James's Declaration of Indulgence protecting the Roman Catholics. Although he also accepted that monarch's overthrow, he was more than once arrested on suspicion of treason after the revolution of 1688 – and it seems likely that he was aware of some of the plots of the Jacobites, even if only on the fringes. The unhappiness of his latter years was increased by a financial dispute with the heirs of the man on whom he had relied to handle his properties, by debts which caused his imprisonment for almost a year, and eventually by a stroke which deprived him of rationality. It seems clear that these miseries were caused chiefly by overwork, since he struggled to minister to the whole Quaker movement as George Fox's spiritual successor, while also being burdened by many more worldly responsibilities. He kept his mental powers long enough to write the movement's first history (*The Rise and Progress of the People Called Quakers*, 1694), and an eloquent defence of its principles (*Primitive Christianity*, 1696); but before his stroke in 1712 he must have sensed that there had been a decline in the spiritual power of the religious movement whose leadership he had inherited from George Fox. He died in 1718.

A factor in the Quakers' decline in England was the absorption of so many of them in the practical labours necessary to till the soil, to build the settlements, to expand the commerce and generally to run colonial America. Even at the time some English Quakers were worried about the psychological effects of the transatlantic migration – although the enthusiasm with which others corresponded with the new colonies, or crossed the Atlantic to visit them, was more pronounced. The American Quakers could not spare the energy needed to develop a new world of spiritual and intellectual life. Their schools were good and distinctive, and many individual Quakers who became leaders of commerce were well-educated; William Penn's secretary, James Logan, lived to become one of the most accomplished scholars, scientists and men of affairs in eighteenth-century America. But Rufus Jones, who wrote the first systematic account of the Quakers in the American colonies, lamented the lack of higher education on specifically Quaker foundations. It contributed, he believed, to the dearth of leaders of thought after Penn's death. 'The absence of constructive leaders, the later tendency to withdraw from civic tasks, the relaxing of the idea of reshaping the world, which this history reveals, were due, in the main, to the lack of expansive education.'[6]

Philadelphia, however, rapidly became the largest city in North America. It was the centre of a triangular commerce with England and the West Indies, but it was also a cultural centre lively enough to attract young Benjamin Franklin away from Boston and to respond to his many initiatives and inventions. One way in which it earned its wealth was that it was the first example of the ethnic mix which was to become one of the proudest achievements of the United States. Not

---

[6] Rufus M. Jones, *The Quakers in the American Colonies* (New York and London, 1911), p. xxvii. More recent studies include Frederic B. Tolles, *Meeting House and Counting House* (Chapel Hill, N.C., 1948), and *Quakers and the Atlantic Culture* (New York, 1960), and Geoffrey B. Nash, *Quakers and Politics: Pennsylvania 1681–1726* (Princeton, N.J., 1968). Catherine Peare, *William Penn* (Philadelphia, Pa., 1957), is the best biography, and Mary Maples Dunn, *William Penn: Politics and Conscience*, and Melvin B. Endy, *William Penn and Early Quakerism* (Princeton, N.J., 1967–73), are the best studies of his thought.

only Quakers found refuge in Pennsylvania. Strict Baptists came from far off Wales, with Protestant Huguenots as refugees from France, and persecuted Roman Catholics from nearby Maryland. Even Jews came, although they could not hold public office. Large numbers of Germans came from the Rhineland, importing 'Pennsylvania Dutch' (which remained a language in use for many years) and much jolly folk art. Most of these were either Lutheran or Reformed in religion, but the Mennonites and the Amish among them resembled the English Quakers. Many Scotch-Irish came from Ulster and pioneered in the wilderness inland. On this frontier they were able to find a reward for their energy, and a freedom for their Presbyterian faith, which had not been available in Ireland. With its satellite colonies, New Jersey and Delaware, Pennsylvania became a wonder; and the prosperity of its peacefully mixed population advertised the principles of democracy and religious liberty. Its success (despite many internal controversies) was the decisive model which inspired the shaping of republican independence. The Declaration of Independence read out to the cheering crowd in the yard of State House in Philadelphia on 8 July 1776, to the accompaniment of the ringing of the Liberty Bell, had been drafted by a Virginian – but Jefferson seems to have had his chance since Benjamin Franklin was too busy devising a new constitution for Pennsylvania itself. And certainly no eighteenth-century American, not even Franklin or Jefferson or Washington, left a sweeter memory behind him than the Quaker John Woolman, whose *Journal* shows that in his gentle way he was the friend of slaves, the friend of Indians and the friend of God.

It seems to be impossible to be accurate about the number of Quakers in eighteenth-century England. One Quaker historian guessed that numbers dropped from some sixty thousand in 1680 to only thirty-two thousand in 1800; another, that numbers remained steady at around fifty thousand. What we do know is that the records of local meetings often mention disappointment that there were few conversions or 'convincements' of outsiders. The majority of Quakers were brought into the society by their parents, although many brothers or sisters refused to join them. Quakerism, which had begun as a

world-wide movement, was becoming an hereditary sect, pic-
turesque rather than explosive. Yet the same change won for
the sect an acceptance, even a popularity. A typical leader was
Penn's successor, George Whitehead. As the best historian of
the origins of the Society of Friends wrote, Whitehead 'was
now the leading survivor of the First Publishers of Truth, and
would guide the policy of the Society for the next quarter of a
century. He was the embodiment of worthy and drab respectability, devoid of genius, and of little humour, but industrious
and politic, one who had achieved so much for Quakerism that
he no longer sought fresh adventures or inspired new
enthusiasms.'[7]

Three verdicts may be considered as we try to assess the first
hundred years of this extraordinary society which George Fox
founded. A distinguished American historian has lamented
that 'their self-righteousness and their rigidity' made the
Quakers a sect in America, even in Pennsylvania itself. He
argues that their unconventional, energetic, practical religion
could have inspired the people of the emerging United States
far more widely – if only the Quakers had been more willing to
compromise on inessentials. To him 'this is the story of one of
the greatest lost opportunities in all American history'.[8] An
English historian might be tempted to use similar words about
the limited numbers of the English Quakers. But to Ronald
Knox, George Fox's enthusiastic perfectionism was so clearly
doomed from the start that even the dull survival of the small
Society of Friends was a marvel. 'What survived was', he
commented, 'a band of well-to-do reformers, distinguished by
their wide influence and active benevolence, but numbering
only a handful of adherents among the multitudes on whom
they had compassion. Among all the daydreams which flitted
through the mind of George Fox as he travelled about the roads

---

[7] W. C. Braithwaite, *The Second Period of Quakerism* (revised, Cambridge, 1961),
pp. 177–8. See also Arnold Lloyd, *Quaker Social History 1669–1738* (London, 1950),
and Richard T. Vann, *The Social Development of English Quakerism 1655–1755* (Cambridge, Mass., 1969).

[8] Daniel J. Boorstin, *The Americans: The Colonial Experience* (New York, 1958),
pp. 33–69.

of England, none, surely, was stranger than this.'[9] And even that tribute did not do full justice to the astonishing facts; perhaps Knox, a firm and distinguished Roman Catholic, had to be too cautious.

'To maintain the Christian quality in the world of business and of domestic life, and to maintain it without pretensions or hypocrisy,' wrote G. M. Trevelyan, 'was the great achievement of these extraordinary people . . . The Puritan pot had boiled over, with much heat and fury; when it had cooled and been poured away, this precious sediment was left at the bottom.'[10]

[9] R. A. Knox, *Enthusiasm*, p. 168.
[10] G. M. Trevelyan, *English Social History* (London, 1942), p. 267.

CHAPTER ELEVEN

A CALMER CREED

WREN'S CHURCHES

The churches designed by Sir Christopher Wren after the Great Fire of London in 1666 were built at a time when the vice and squalor of much of the city continued to be obvious; and they were consecrated in an Anglican faith which was not yet completely secure, Protestant Dissent and Roman Catholicism being both still formidable challengers. But Wren's churches were the temples of a faith far less troubled than the religion of the English had been since the Middle Ages. The God to be worshipped in them was a God of order, of reason, of light; a God with whom well-behaved, reasonable, enlightened Englishmen felt at home. To understand their spirit is to understand much about the calmer creed of England, 1660–1760.

From the beginning Wren belonged to the governing class both by birth and by recognized ability. His father was Dean of Windsor under Charles I. His uncle was Bishop of Ely. In his youth he was entrusted with a personal message from Oliver Cromwell to his uncle: the old man could leave prison in the Tower of London. The invitation was rejected, because it would have involved accepting Cromwell's 'detestable tyranny'. Thus Christopher Wren inherited an impeccable position as a Royalist son of the Church of England. He also inherited a taste and talent for architecture (and for mathematics) from his highly cultivated father. At Oxford he caught the infection of science as an intellectual passion. His first posts were professorships of astronomy in Gresham's College, London, and at Oxford; and he was for many years active in the work of the Royal Society. While still in his twenties he was entrusted with the design of the Sheldonian Theatre at Oxford and the chapel of Pembroke College, Cambridge, and promised appointment as Surveyor General of the Royal Works when a vacancy occurred. Although his architecture was inspired by the Palladian buildings which were the last, lovely flowering of the Renaissance in Italy, he did not think it necessary to go to Italy. He spent half a year in France, but the rest he got from books. He was an English gentleman.

He was dismissed from his office under the Crown in 1717 after accusations that his assistants were fraudulent and incompetent. But by then he was in his eighties – and had done as much as anyone in history to glorify the English monarchy by noble extensions to the palaces at Kensington and Hampton Court, and by the great Royal Hospitals built for soldiers in Chelsea and for sailors at Greenwich. Had there been money available, yet more majestic buildings would have arisen: he prepared designs for a vast mausoleum for Charles I as part of a remodelling of Windsor Castle, for a palace and parliament house arising where fire had destroyed Whitehall Palace in 1696. Had the citizens of London been willing to accept his radical plan after the Great Fire of 1666, the huddled, stinking city of medieval and Tudor days would have been rebuilt on magnificently rational lines, with an embankment lining up great houses by the Thames and with splendid public buildings and paved squares giving drama to the long, straight streets.

As it was, support was not forthcoming for this imaginative scheme, or for any other of Wren's boldest ideas in the secular sphere. It was as a church architect that he won his enduring triumphs – because his style perfectly matched the feeling of London merchants that they, too, were becoming triumphant and should give thanks.

He built more than fifty churches for London after the Great Fire, and above their very cleverly varied steeples and towers rose one of the greatest buildings of the European Renaissance: St Paul's Cathedral. And he left his mark on other churches. He built a church dedicated to St James (under James II) in the newly developed area of Piccadilly, for instance, and, still working in his old age, rescued from decay the fabric of Westminster Abbey, adding for Westminster School a handsome dormitory block in the nearby garden. He had been a schoolboy at Westminster. Surviving plans show that if Wren had had his way, the abbey would have been crowned by a steeple or even a dome.

When he became London's leading architect 'Old St Paul's' was still standing, as the world's biggest church apart from St Peter's, Rome. Wren admired the gigantic classical portico added by Inigo Jones to the west end, and urged the replacement of the remnants of the spire on the decayed tower by a new dome, surmounted by a pineapple some seventy feet high. That problem was solved by the Great Fire in September 1666, although even then it took some time for the authorities to realize that the great black ruin of the medieval cathedral must be demolished totally.

Apart from the consummate mastery of the final design executed in Portland stone and marble, and the superb quality of the craftsmanship of most of the furnishings, what is most striking about the rebuilding of St Paul's is the determination of Parliament, and of the nation as a whole, to have a cathedral which would dominate London, whatever the expense. Within Wren's lifetime the work seems to have cost about £850,000, some two-thirds of the annual sum allowed by Parliament for the upkeep of the monarchy and government when Charles II was at the height of his power. While part of the cost was met by nationwide appeals for gifts, more than £800,000 came from a tax on coal entering London voted in 1670. Wren's city churches were financed from the same source, although there was no willingness to finance his visions of a royal palace. No one leader seems to have been decisive in securing the adoption of this boldly expensive plan. Gilbert Sheldon was then Archbishop of Canterbury, and William Sancroft, who was to follow him at Canterbury, was Dean of St Paul's; and both were able and active men. But the decision seems to have been more or less spontaneous. No alternative was really thinkable, although the obscure Bishop of London (Henchman) wrote a gloomy paper entitled 'Nine considerations against building a new cathedral'.

Wren deployed both genius and great patience in devising architecture which would respond to this unique challenge: the

creation of a cathedral when it had been assumed that the age
of cathedrals was over. The preliminary plans already broke
away from any idea of rebuilding in the 'Gothic' style (the word
was already in general use to refer vaguely to the architecture
of the Middle Ages after the Normans). But at the beginning of
his active involvement in the project for a cathedral – an
involvement which covered more than thirty-five years – Wren
had modest dimensions in mind. His first plan has been called
'box-like'. Then his imagination blazed and he produced the
far bolder plan known as the 'great model' because it was taken
seriously enough to be translated into a wooden model. That
plan still envisaged the cathedral as a larger parish church.
The whole point about Wren's churches was that they were
Protestant: the sermon mattered more than any sacrament,
and the aim was to seat the congregation within fifty feet of the
preacher. Wren imagined a larger congregation assembled
around the pulpit in the cathedral but seized the opportunity to
place over them a dome described as 'coloss and beautiful'.
The only concession which he made to conservatism was to
propose a large Corinthian portico, replacing the one by Inigo
Jones and joined to the symmetrical hall under the great dome
by a narthex including a lesser dome. The plan was in the end
abandoned because the clergy insisted on a long choir where
the daily services of Morning and Evening Prayer could be
sung. They also wanted most of the congregation to be able to
see the altar, which would have been tucked away in one of the
short arms of the 'Greek cross' plan in Wren's model. And they
wanted aisles as in the Middle Ages, although there were at
this time no processions to move round them.

Wren wept when his plan was rejected, but he went on to
produce a feeble plan in order to get the work started by a royal
warrant in 1675. As the work proceeded this plan was somehow transmuted into magnificence. Although less original
than the earlier 'great model', in the end this substitute
managed to satisfy both those who used the cathedral for
religious activities and the larger number who looked on it as
the massive centre-piece in London's skyline, assisted by the
fact that the portico on top of Ludgate Hill remained as one of
the concessions to conservatism. Through many years Wren's

close supervision continued; it was his practice to visit the site each Saturday. There were complaints about the delay and in 1697 Parliament decreed that half his salary should be kept until the work was complete; he had to petition for the arrears in 1711. But the main reason for the delay which cost him dear was his insistence on perfection. For his idea of what a cathedral, or a parish church, ought to be was very clear.

In Wren's churches the element of religious mystery was lacking. In medieval churches coloured glass illustrating the stories of the Bible and the saints kept out any sight of the surroundings, but Wren wanted clear glass, to unite the church with the world. The altar was not magnified to suggest separation from sinners. There were no candle-lit chapels or embroidered banners or painted statues to add tenderness and consolation, as in a medieval church. There were no dramatic paintings or carvings of the agonized Saviour, the blissful Mother or the swooning saint, as in the Baroque churches of Rome. For Wren, a church was not a refuge into which a mother could slip quietly in order to pour out prayers about a child. It was a meeting place for solid citizens who were growing accustomed to comfort in their own homes and who wanted to thank their divine benefactor. They met in order to recite the beautiful, legally authorized, words of the Book of Common Prayer and in order to hear a preacher who would remind them of the reasons why they should be grateful and in other ways dutiful.

While in church they were to be impressed by the sober beauty above them, but even in the cathedral Wren's architecture had its domestic elements. It showed off the carpentry of Grinling Gibbons or the ironwork of Jean Tijou – work which would have been admired in any drawing room or garden. Its restraint can be compared with the more dramatic work at Blenheim Palace and elsewhere of Wren's successors at the head of the architectural profession, Nicholas Hawksmoor (his pupil and assistant) and Sir John Vanbrugh (who came to architecture through soldiering, play-writing and scene-painting). And Wren's philosophy was not only domestic; it was very cautiously democratic. When commissioners were appointed in 1711 to build fifty new churches for London and

Westminster, and he was one of them, he advocated building churches near the homes of 'the better sort', even though the sites would be more expensive. But he added: 'a church should not be so fill'd with pews, but that the poor may have room enough to stand and sit in the alleys, for to them equally is the Gospel preach'd.'[1]

TWO GENTLE SPIRITS: TAYLOR AND BROWNE

Two of the most attractive Anglicans in the middle of the seventeenth century, Jeremy Taylor and Thomas Browne, wrote very beautiful prose – but they showed by the ambiguity of their arguments how necessary it was becoming for thinking Englishmen to find a new intellectual basis for religious belief.

Taylor became one of the most learned scholars and most distinguished writers in a great literary age; Coleridge later ranked him near Shakespeare and Milton. His father was a barber in Cambridge, and in that city he received his education. While an undergraduate he was sufficiently influenced by High Church clergymen for him to become one himself, attracting the patronage of Archbishop Laud. He was made a chaplain both to the Archbishop and to the King. His first book was *Of the Sacred Order and Offices of Episcopacy, by Divine Institution, Apostolic Tradition and Catholic Practice* (1642). He bravely dedicated another book, an attack on the work of the Westminster Assembly, to Charles I shortly after the King's execution. At the Restoration he was made a bishop in Northern Ireland and as such enforced the Act of Uniformity, expelling Presbyterian ministers from their parishes. His last books were treatises of which Laud and Charles I would have approved. He asserted the Catholic character of the Church he served in *The Worthy Communicant* and *A Discourse on Confirmation*,

---

[1] Wren's 'Thoughts on Churches' are in Martin S. Briggs, *Wren the Incomparable* (London, 1953), pp. 135–8. The second centenary of his death encouraged the publication of twenty volumes by the Wren Society. On that basis there are good biographies by Bryan Little and Harold F. Hutchinson (London, 1975–76). Additional material of interest is to be found in *A History of St Paul's Cathedral*, ed. W. R. Matthews and W. M. Atkins (London, 1957).

and defended it with vigour in *A Dissuasive from Popery to the People of Ireland*. His largest work, *Ductor Dubitantum*, was a conservative discussion of Christian ethics. Strongly Royalist, it was completed just in time to be dedicated to the restored king in 1660, when 'worthily to accept of our prosperity is all our business'.

Yet Taylor was not trusted by the conservative Archbishop Sheldon, who frustrated his hopes of an English bishopric and who described him when he heard of his death in 1667 as 'a man of dangerous temper, apt to break into extravagances'. The two men had begun their uneasy relationship when Gilbert Sheldon had been Warden of All Souls College, Oxford, and Taylor a poor young man from Cambridge who had been appointed to a fellowship against the college statutes which insisted on an Oxford education. But basically the problem was psychological. Taylor incurred suspicion not because he was deliberately heretical but because of the delicacy of his generously humane and cultured mind, reflected in a style which set out to commend faith and prayer by the beauty of holiness. It was reported that while he was a bishop he bought up all the unsold copies of his *Liberty of Prophesying* and burned them – but that plea for toleration, published in 1647, could not be forgotten. The civil war which he had witnessed had appalled him. 'If persons be Christians in their lives and . . . if they acknowledge the eternal Son of God for their Master and their Lord', he had asked, in 1647, 'why then should I hate such persons whom God loves and who love God?' He had urged Englishmen to bury their quarrels – 'to cling to the creed of the Apostles; and in all other things an honest endeavour to find out what truth we can.' Charles I had let his displeasure be known.

After this unpopular plea for liberty, Taylor turned to the writing of devotional literature. It was his real contribution to a troubled age. He was sheltered after the war by the hospitality of the Earl of Carbery in the great house of Golden Grove in Wales; and he was heartened by the encouragement of the young countess, on whose premature death he preached the most beautiful of a very lovely series of sermons. He wrote *The Rules and Exercises of Holy Living* for her, with *Holy Dying* as a sequel printed just in time for her funeral. For a wider public he wrote *The Great Exemplar*, the first life of Christ in English. It was not in any way a critical work, but it quietly glowed like a Nativity by an old master.

In these books he broke right away from the old monastic tradition. Some of the most wonderful passages were on marriage (which, 'like the useful bee, builds a house and gathers sweetness from every flower . . . and is that state of good things to which God hath designed the present constitution of the world') and on children ('their stammering, their little angers, their innocence, their imperfections, their necessities, are so many little emanations of joy and comfort to him that delights in their persons and society'). When such teaching was scrutinized by the orthodox, Taylor's God resembled a loving father to an extent that alarmed. Presumably this God would never willingly doom any of his children to the everlasting torments of hell, or condemn them for any offence except their own conduct. He would never decide one of his children's eternal destiny by seeing whether or not that child repeated a theological formula on his deathbed. Not only was Taylor an Arminian; he seemed to be reducing the Gospel to morality. So critics asked: was Christ *only* the 'great exemplar' and not the Saviour and the perfect sacrifice for sin? Some three centuries later the criticism was still being offered that 'Christianity is, for Jeremy Taylor, an enterprise only for those capable of helping themselves'.[2] The unorthodoxy alleged to poison the wine of Jeremy Taylor's devotional prose is said to have contributed to a disastrous emphasis in later Anglicanism on works, not faith. In the 1650s Gilbert Sheldon was one of the clergy who wrote to beg Taylor to withdraw or to keep silent. He received an unrepentant reply. 'You are a happy person, private and unharmed; my folly and forwardness hath wrought my trouble; but yet there was zeal in it, and I thought there was much reason, and I am sure I intended piously, and there are very many that do still think so.'

Taylor, who wrote exquisitely about the dawning sun or the falling rose, or the marks of the tide on the beach, or the shining

---

[2] C. F. Allison, *The Rise of Moralism* (London, 1966), p. 80.

of light on water, could never conceive how in such a beautiful world anyone could be an atheist. 'To see rare effects and no cause; an excellent government and no prince; a motion without an immovable; a circle without a centre; a time without eternity; a second without a first . . . these things are so against philosophy and natural reason, that he must be a beast in his understanding. This is the atheist: *the fool hath said in his heart, there is no God.*' So Taylor preached – but he never dealt with the religious problems suggested by those aspects of nature which do not make pleasant illustrations for sermons. If he had done so, he might have expressed some sympathy with the atheist; and he might have run into more trouble for doing so.[3]

In this age of many controversies another author with a magic style, Sir Thomas Browne, shared Jeremy Taylor's unwillingness to reduce the richness of life to any single system of dogmas.

In the mid-1630s he wrote down some of his musings about the 'religion of a physician' and what he had written was printed in 1642 without his permission as *Religio Medici*. Denounced by both Catholic and Protestant stalwarts, Browne replied that 'I have no genius to disputes in religion'. He then issued an authorized version of the book, and went on musing as he practised medicine in Norwich. He had no desire to overturn the old order, social or spiritual, which gave security to simple folk. Indeed, he shared many of the popular beliefs. The world of spirits seemed very real to him, as to his patients. 'I have ever believed, and do now know, that there are witches; they that doubt of these, do not only deny them, but spirits.' It was always his conviction that time mattered less than eternity, that the created world was a mere 'parenthesis in eternity'. But his study of medicine had taught him the beginnings of a scientific approach. He was insatiable in his desire to probe popular superstitions, to collect curiosities, to conduct

---

[3] See C. J. Stranks, *The Life and Writings of Jeremy Taylor* (London, 1952); H. Trevor Hughes, *The Piety of Jeremy Taylor* (London, 1960); F. L. Huntley, *Jeremy Taylor and the Great Rebellion* (Ann Arbor, Mich., 1970). H. R. McAdoo studied *The Structure of Caroline Moral Theology* (London, 1949).

experiments. 'The world was made to be inhabited by beasts', he wrote, 'but studied and contemplated by man; 'tis the debt of our reason we owe to God, and the homage we pay for not being beasts.'

This devout doctor reconciled the two worlds of religion and science by urging modesty on one and all. To him human life was perpetually surrounded by the mystery of death – a mystery which was impenetrable. When a collection of ancient funeral urns was discovered in a field, he felt inspired to assemble all that he could discover about burial customs. His thought (or feeling) was a tissue of many languages and civilizations, united only by the charm of his personality as he moved so gently among his grateful patients and among the dead who interested him equally. But he did not apologize for any confusion. He believed that the world of religion was as important as the world of science; that, however, there were two worlds, to be reconciled only in eternity; that before he dies man is 'that great and true Amphibium whose nature is disposed to live not only like other creatures in divers elements but in divided and distinguished worlds.'[4]

A RATIONAL THEOLOGY

To some, the time seemed to have arrived for a simpler religion. The doctrines which Jeremy Taylor could preach with an enchanting beauty seemed to others merely old and dangerous battle-cries. The ghosts of the Middle Ages who still haunted Sir Thomas Browne's mind looked to others thoroughly dead. It seemed far better to go straight to the Bible, interpreted in the light of the individual's reason and conscience. What was advocated has been called 'rational theology' but here was no shallow rationalism; the new, deeply

---

[4] See Joan Bennett, *Sir Thomas Browne* (Cambridge, 1962), and *Sir Thomas Browne: The Major Works*, ed. C. A. Patrides (Harmondsworth, Middx, 1977). Another whimsical writer whose prose was an enchanting contrast with the violence around him was the historian, Thomas Fuller. Sir William Addison studied *Worthy Dr Fuller* (London, 1951).

spiritual, creed was a kind of Quakerism for sober and educated Church of England people. The work of the theologians
who pioneered in this way deserves to be remembered, for it
was courageous work. In the whole history of Christianity,
there had been no exact precedent for its attempt to reconcile
religion and reason.

The danger which many Christians sensed was, of course,
that the educated individual might when interpreting the Bible
destroy all the power of the Gospel. Lord Herbert of Cherbury,
in his book *De Veritate* issued discreetly in Latin and in Paris in
1624, had listed five religious ideas common to all men in all
places. He had claimed that, in comparison with these, the
revelations claimed by priests were at best uncertain. The five
ideas were: (1) that God exists, (2) that he ought to be
worshipped, (3) that virtue is the chief part of worship, (4) that
there should be repentance for vices and crimes, and (5) that
there are rewards and punishments after this life. These were
not offensive ideas but it had been left to Lord Herbert's
brother, George, to make poetry out of a more heartfelt and
popular religion.[5]

Two other pioneers of this tradition had found rest in a
religion less cold than Lord Herbert's.

In 1628 William Chillingworth, a newly elected Fellow of
Trinity College, Oxford, and a godson of Archbishop Laud,
was temporarily persuaded by the arguments of Jesuits. He
abandoned Oxford and went to be trained as a Recusant priest
at Douai. 'I reconciled myself to the Church of Rome', he later
explained, 'because I thought myself to have sufficient reason
to believe that there was, and must be always in the world,
some Church that could not err; and consequently, seeing all
other Churches disclaimed this privilege of not being subject to
error, the Church of Rome must be that Church which cannot
err.' But he did not stay long in Douai. Laud claimed that 'my
letters brought him back'. Actually, he was influenced by his
own disillusionment and took some time to recover any conviction on any religious topic. His integrity was shown when he

---

[5] S. R. D. Beford, *The Defence of Truth: Herbert of Cherbury and the Seventeenth Century*
(Manchester, 1979).

refused to take up the offer of an income in the Church of England. He found a refuge in the library of the manor house at Great Tew near Oxford, the home of the liberal Lucius Carey, Viscount Falkland. There he wrote *The Religion of Protestants, a Safe Way to Salvation*, published in 1637.

The book is best remembered for its affirmation that 'the Bible, the Bible only' was the religion of Protestants. If that had been all its argument, it would have been one of many Puritan treatises. But it made a point of rejecting Calvinism, defending instead a few 'fundamental truths' to be found in Scripture's 'plain places'. Chillingworth had not reached the conclusion that Calvin could not err. Instead, he now viewed Roman Catholicism as a possible way to salvation – if a less safe one, because of the arrogance of its claim to infallibility. All divisions between Christians were regretted, because they were divisions within the Church; but schismatics, heretics, even heathen Turks, could all find that their good lives led them to salvation. This strange book condemned all persecution.

When the civil war broke out Chillingworth was very distressed: 'war is not the way of Jesus Christ'. But he joined the Royalist army as a chaplain. His friend Lord Falkland exposed himself to the musket-fire and was killed early in the war, not unwillingly; the hopes of the Great Tew circle seemed to be already dead. Chillingworth was taken prisoner in January 1644 and soon fell mortally sick. He was nursed by a fellow clergyman, Francis Cheynell, who being an ardent Calvinist hoped that he would live to repent of his heresies. When the patient had disappointed his nurse, his body was buried in the cloister of Chichester Cathedral. Cheynell threw a copy of *The Religion of Protestants* on top of it, 'that thou mayest rot with thy author'.[6]

A number of other able young men, searching for a way of peace, had shared the liberal hospitality and hopes of Lord Falkland at Great Tew. The only middle-aged theologian among them was John Hales. Born in 1584, he lived until 1656.

---

[6] See Robert Orr, *Reason and Authority: The Thought of William Chillingworth* (Oxford, 1967).

He, too, suffered. As a promising Oxford scholar he took part
in the Calvinist Synod of Dort in 1618 and because of what he
saw there – the mixture of tough politics with useless speculation and theological hatred – 'bade John Calvin goodnight'.
Back in England he happily resumed the obscurity of a Fellow
of Eton College, visiting Oxford to discharge his duties as
Professor of Greek. He told Edward Hyde that he was glad to
have few duties as a preacher, since he preferred to keep his
opinions to himself. The pamphlets that he did write pleaded
for Christian modesty and reunion, arguing that 'it hath been
the common disease of Christians from the beginning, not to
content ourselves with that measure of faith, which God and
the Scriptures have expressly afforded us'. Hales amassed a
great library and spent most of his days using it, but had to sell
it, apart from a few devotional books, when he was ejected from
his post in 1649. He forbade any bell-ringing when he was
buried in Eton churchyard, 'as in my life I have done the
Church no service'. But he had, in fact, done a service which he
thus described: 'the pursuit of truth hath been my only care
ever since I first understood the meaning of the word'. And
when in 1659 *The Golden Remains of Ever-memorable Mr John Hales
of Eton College* was published, the book showed that he was able
to teach a simple but fervent religion, close to Chillingworth's.[7]

Both Chillingworth and Hales were rumoured to be 'Socinians'. The word, derived from an Italian named Sozzini who
died in Poland in 1604, suggested the denial of the divinity of
Christ and the Holy Spirit. In fact, neither Chillingworth nor
Hales advocated that heresy, and even Sozzini had been
cautious. He had approved of the adoration of Christ, who
possessed a *divinitas* of function although not the *deitas* of the
divine nature. It was only when the followers of Sozzini had
finally been expelled from Poland in the 1650s, as the Counter-
Reformation revived Catholicism, that a defiantly heretical
minority movement, Unitarianism, emerged into the open. In
England the first Unitarian theology was published in a
pamphlet of 1647 giving twelve arguments against the divinity
of the Holy Spirit. Its author was a Gloucester schoolmaster,

---

[7] J. H. Elson studied *John Hales of Eton* (New York, 1948).

John Biddle, who followed it up with some even more provocative statements about Christ. Banished to the Scilly Isles, on
his release he insisted on returning to London and continuing
his propaganda. He was thrown into jail and died of fever there
in 1662. At the time his attacks on the doctrine of the Trinity
seemed outrageous. The tendency of almost all those who
wanted to simplify and rationalize Christianity was much less
controversial: it was the insistence on 'the Bible only', interpreted reasonably.[8]

A considerable group of reasonable theologians, the 'Cambridge Platonists', rejected the harshness of Calvinism without
involving themselves in Lord Herbert's aristocratic contempt
for popular religion or in any denial of basic Christian doctrines such as the Trinity.

Their approach was epitomized when the most public figure
among them, Benjamin Whichcote, replied to a warning from
the strong Calvinist who had taught him as an undergraduate.
The warning was that in his preaching there was too much
emphasis on reason. Whichcote replied: 'I oppose not rational
to spiritual, for spiritual is most rational.' His favourite text
was one of the proverbs in the Old Testament (20:27): 'the
spirit of a man is the candle of the Lord.' He was convinced that
no unreasonable theology could be true; 'to go against reason is
to go against God'. Reasoning about faith was a necessary
discipline; 'we should doubt and deliberate, before we resolve
and determine.' No previous theologian had possessed a name
big enough to silence debate; 'believe things rather than men.'
But others could share his own reasoned certainty about the
essentials of Christianity, especially since 'the moral part of
religion lies in a good mind and a good life; all else is about
religion.' The greatest essential was love; 'universal charity is a
thing final in religion.' His own life was infectiously happy. 'In
the use of reason and the exercise of virtue,' he said, 'we enjoy
God.'

He had no wish to quarrel with anyone. Appointed Provost
of King's College, Cambridge, by Parliament in 1644, he

---

[8] H. J. MacLachlan surveyed *Socinianism in Seventeenth Century England* (Oxford, 1951).

remained on good terms with his ejected predecessor by
allowing him half the income. Ejected in his turn at the
Restoration, he found a happy outlet as a London preacher.
His message was about a reality where Church and Dissent,
beauty and goodness, happiness and holiness, could all combine in a calm assurance; and it was spread by his example, not
by a fully developed theological system. He was a Platonist in
the sense that he belonged to the great tradition which had
derived from the Greek philosopher encouragement to believe
that the reasoning soul of man could apprehend eternal truth.
Every glimpse of goodness or beauty was a glimpse of that
truth; 'the judgement of right is the reason of our minds
perceiving the Reason of things.'

His ablest disciple in Cambridge, John Smith, died in 1652
while still in his thirties, leaving behind him ten 'discourses'
preached in his college chapel. Smith spoke of man's soul as
'something really distinct from his body, of an indivisible
nature'; and of Christ 'not only as a particular person, but as a
Divine principle in holy souls.' The work was taken up by
another of Whichcote's Cambridge friends, in whose house he
died: Ralph Cudworth, Master of Christ's College, 1654–88.
But Cudworth's two shapelessly vast books, on *The True
Intellectual System of the Universe* and *Eternal and Immutable Morality*, were, and have remained, virtually unreadable. They tried
to deal with everything: and it was too much. So cool was the
reception given to *The True Intellectual System* that Cudworth
never wrote the second volume which he had planned and was
discouraged from completing his treatise on morality, which
remained in manuscript for almost half a century after his
death.

Cudworth's importance in the history of English religion is
that he took the trouble to assemble his over-large intellectual
system because he was the first theologian to take the challenge
of atheism seriously. His example encouraged others, especially when his work was abridged and updated by Thomas Wise
in 1706. Cudworth attempted to answer fourteen possible
grounds of atheism, including these: 'No man can have an idea
of conception of God . . . Everything that is must have been
from eternity . . . God is not visibly extended, therefore he is

not . . . To suppose an Incorporeal Mind to be the original of
all things is nothing else but to make the abstract notion of a
mere accident to be the First Cause . . . Mind stemmed from
the chance arrangement of atoms . . . Reason is only human,
and related to flesh and bones: therefore there can be no divine
intelligence presiding overall. All living beings are concretions
of atoms liable to death and dissolution . . . The world is so ill
made that God could not be responsible for it in all its
imperfections. All in human affairs is chaos and confusion:
Providence is defective.'[9]

Henry More was the best-known author of this group which
saw that the real challenge to Christianity was now sheer
unbelief, not any of the issues being debated and fought over by
the leaders of England's churches during and after the civil
war. 'The age we live in', he wrote, 'is a searching, inquisitive,
rational and philosophical age.' His father, a strong Calvinist,
read Spenser to him as a boy; he shared the same tutor as
Milton; he plunged deep into the received learning of his time;
but in his introduction to his collected works he recalled how
all his studies had 'ended in nothing . . . in mere scepticism'.
What he needed more than learning was 'simplicity of mind'.
From 1639 to 1687 he lived quietly and happily in Cambridge,
expounding the Gospel of simplicity in many volumes.

He wrote poetry and much prose, including an *Explanation of
the Grand Mystery of Godliness* as big as Cudworth's tomes. He
was the first Englishman to consider at any length the philosophy of René Descartes, although he lost his first enthusiasm for
the Frenchman when he came to realize the danger of Carte-
sianism's stress on the material and the mechanical to the
religious view of the world as held in the Platonic tradition. He
could not be expected to agree with the unmystical teaching of
Descartes, who called the soul a 'thinking substance'.

He said of his arguments against atheism: 'I borrowed them
not from books but fetch'd them from . . . indelible ideas of the
soul of man.' He wrote about the pure vision of God in
childhood. And he thought that all learning ought to be
dedicated to the recovery of that vision. 'Ethics are defined to

---

[9] See J. A. Passmore, *Ralph Cudworth: An Interpretation* (Cambridge, 1951).

be the art of living well and happily' and 'happiness is that pleasure which the mind takes in from a sense of virtue.' The greatest happiness is taken in the supreme virtue, the soul's love of God. ' 'Tis by this the soul relisheth what is simply the best; thither it tends, and in that alone it hath joy and triumph. Hence we are instructed how to set God before our eyes; to love him above all; to adhere to him as the supremest good; to consider him as the perfection of all reason, of all beauty, of all love; how all was made by his power, and that all is upheld by his providence. Hence also the soul is taught how to affect and admire the creation, and all the parcels of it . . .'[10]

THOMAS TRAHERNE

Cudworth and More were thoroughly academic, and they overloaded their arguments with quotations from other writers ancient or modern. Cambridge libraries were their downfall. But it is clear that many of their less intellectual contemporaries were feeling their way towards a simpler religion and a rational theology.

That tendency accounts for the vast influence of John Tillotson, who went on from his curate's place in Benjamin Whichcote's church to become Dean of St Paul's in 1689 and Archbishop of Canterbury two years later. He wished for a generous latitude in the interpretation of the Church of England's requirements. Such a position was known abusively as 'Latitudinarianism'. One of its exponents, Edward Stillingfleet, Tillotson's predecessor as Dean of St Paul's, was Bishop of Worcester for ten years from 1689. Another, Simon Patrick,

---

[10] See Aharon Lichtenstein, *Henry More: The Rational Theology of a Cambridge Platonist* (London, 1962). The movement has been studied by F. J. Powicke, *The Cambridge Platonists* (London, 1926); W. C. de Pauley, *The Candle of the Lord* (London, 1937); Ernst Cassirer, *The Platonic Renaissance in England* (London, 1953); R. L. Colie, *Light and Enlightenment* (Cambridge, 1957). Two anthologies of *The Cambridge Platonists* have been edited by C. A. Patrides (London, 1969) and G. A. Cragg (New York, 1980). For links with earlier thinkers, see H. R. McAdoo, *The Spirit of Anglicanism* (London, 1965).

was Bishop of Chichester and of Ely. All three scholarly moderates had been at Cambridge under the Commonwealth.

Tillotson had accompanied Richard Baxter to the Savoy Conference as a Presbyterian, and to the end of his days he sought to include Presbyterians in the National Church. More successfully, he wanted to include all who would respond to his plain, rational style of preaching. It was a style totally different from the 'conceits' of Andrewes, Donne and Taylor. Another liberal bishop, Gilbert Burnet of Salisbury, wrote of Tillotson: 'he was not only the best preacher of the age but seemed to have brought preaching to perfection; his sermons were so well heard and liked that all the nation proposed him as a pattern.' A modern historian of preaching warns us, however, that 'it is frankly impossible to convey a true idea of Tillotson's achievement by the quotation of occasional passages, for his manner at its best is only gauged by the perusal of a complete sermon, such as the great sermon against atheism preached in 1664, entitled *The Wisdom of being Religious*. Only so can his architectonic ability in designing a sermon, the propriety of his examples, and the uniform dignity yet simplicity of his diction be fully appreciated.'[11]

Tillotson's sermons, so greatly admired by his age, would strike almost all twentieth-century readers as intolerably moralizing and platitudinous. That, however, is itself an explanation of their appeal to hearers bored or disgusted with theological controversy. And we can study the new search for a simpler religion in the work of a man who, although obscure in his own time and only thirty-seven when he died, possessed genius.

Thomas Traherne, after graduating at Oxford, returned there for some years of intense research. Unfortunately his field was controversy against Roman Catholicism, the resultant book being *Roman Forgeries* (1673). His next major project was *Christian Ethics*. He quoted St Thomas Aquinas at length and seems to have planned to be almost as comprehensive as Jeremy Taylor and Richard Baxter were in their tomes, but he

---

[11] W. Fraser Mitchell, *English Pulpit Oratory from Andrewes to Tillotson* (London, 1932), p. 337. A more recent study is L. G. Locke, *Tillotson* (Copenhagen, 1954).

was trying to make the key idea 'felicity', like Henry More. When he died in 1674 this project was incomplete. And that was substantially all that was known about him when in 1895 two notebooks were bought for a few pence from a barrow in a London street. One combined extracts from other authors with some original poems; the other contained more than five hundred short prose passages. Eventually it was noticed that the poetry was similar to that in *A Serious and Pathetical Contemplation of the Mercies of God*, a little work by an anonymous author who had been 'private chaplain to Sir Orlando Bridgman'. The chaplain's name was identified; his *Christian Ethics* was resurrected; and a printed passage of verse by him was found to be identical with one in the manuscripts. Thomas Traherne's two notebooks were then published, in 1903–08. It was instantly agreed that the volume of short prose passages, entitled in seventeenth-century handwriting *Centuries of Meditation*, was gold.

The life now revealed was a life spent in seeking to recapture 'felicity'. Traherne was the son of a Hereford cobbler who died when the boy was young, leaving him to be brought up by his uncle, a prosperous but very worldly innkeeper. Glimpses of glory in childhood were never forgotten. 'I was a little stranger which at my entrance into the world was saluted and surrounded with innumerable joys . . . The corn was orient and immortal wheat, which never should be reaped, nor was ever sown. I thought it had stood from everlasting to everlasting. The dust and stones of the street were as precious as gold. The gates were at first the end of the world. The green trees when I saw them first through one of the gates transported and ravished me, their sweetness and unusual beauty made my heart to leap and almost mad with ecstasy . . . The men! O what venerable and reverend creatures did the aged seem! Immortal Cherubims! And young men glittering and sparkling angels, and maids strange Seraphic pieces of life and beauty! Boys and girls tumbling in the street, and playing, were moving jewels. I knew not that they were born or should die. But all things abided eternally as they were in their proper places. Eternity was manifest in the light of the day, and some thing infinite behind everything appeared: which talked with my expectation and moved my desire. The city seemed to stand in Eden, or to be built in heaven. The streets were mine, the temple was mine, the people were mine, their clothes and gold and silver were mine, as much as their sparkling eyes, fair skins and ruddy faces. The skies were mine and so were the sun and moon and stars, and all the world was mine, and I the only spectator and enjoyer of it.'

Traherne was reflecting on childhood after the experience of adolescence and adulthood – on the raw material which reason, later on, had to make into religion. 'My knowledge was divine. I knew by intuition those things which since my apostasy I collected again by the highest reason. My very ignorance was advantageous. I seemed as one brought into the estate of innocence. All things were spotless and pure and glorious: yet and infinitely mine, and joyful and precious. I knew not that there were any sins, or complaints, or laws. I dreamed not of poverties, contentions or vices. All tears and quarrels were hidden from mine eyes. Everything was at rest, free and immortal . . .'

He knew what had destroyed childhood's glory. 'Once I remember (I think I was about four years old, when) I thus reasoned with myself, sitting in a little obscure room in my father's poor house. If there be a God certainly he must be infinite in goodness . . . He must do most glorious things and give us infinite riches. How comes it to pass therefore that I am so poor?'

He had fought his way out of poverty to Oxford and to life – only to find that all life conspired to destroy 'the first light which shined in my infancy'. In the Hereford inn he experienced 'rude, vulgar and worthless things that like so many loads of earth and dung did overhelm and bury it.' At the university he was impressed by the treasures of knowledge: 'I saw that logic, ethics, physics, metaphysics, geometry, astronomy, poesy, medicine, grammar, music, rhetoric, all kinds of arts, trades and mechanisms that adorned the world pertained to felicity.' But even Oxford disappointed: 'there was never a tutor that did professly teach felicity.'

He recovered 'felicity' when he returned to the Herefordshire countryside. He was made rector of the little village of

Credenhill, four miles from the cathedral city, in 1657. After a spell back in Oxford for further study, he gave himself to what the country had to give him. 'When I came unto the country, and being seated among silent trees and meads and hills had all my time in mine own hands, I resolved to spend it all, whatever it cost me, in search of happiness, and to satiate that burning thirst which nature had enkindled in me from my youth.' But he did not identify nature with God. He knew too well that nature's moods varied like his own – and left behind a classic description of the mood to be familiar to the twentieth century as anxiety, *angst*. 'Another time, in a lowering and sad evening, being alone in the field, when all things were dead and quiet, a certain want and horror fell upon me, beyond imagination. The unprofitableness and silence of the place dissatisfied me, its wideness terrified me, from the utmost ends of the earth fears surrounded me . . . I was a weak and little child, and had forgotten that there was a man alive in the earth.'

He knew that he needed both his Creator and the people who were his fellow creatures. The experience of utter loneliness that sad evening 'taught me that I was concerned in all the world: and that in the remotest borders the causes of peace delight me, and the beauties of the earth when seen were made to entertain me: that I was made to hold a communion with the secrets of divine providence in all the world . . .: that the presence of cities, temples and kingdoms ought to sustain me, and that to be alone in the world was to be desolate and miserable. The comfort of houses and friends, and the clear assurance of treasures everywhere, God's care and love, his goodness, wisdom and power, his presence and watchfulness in all the ends of the earth, were my strength and assurance for ever . . .'

In 1667 he accepted an invitation to join the household of Sir Orlando Bridgman, then Lord Keeper. As things turned out, the move was not so useful to a career as it must have seemed from the invitation. Sir Orlando was dismissed when he refused to affix the great seal of the realm to Charles II's Declaration of Indulgence in 1672; he protested that it would benefit the Papists. But Traherne had clearly been willing to live amid the physical and moral squalor of Restoration London in order that he might enjoy and serve his age to the full. In 1660 he had hastened to obtain ordination by a bishop, although previously he had been equally happy to obtain certificates of reliability from noted Puritan preachers in order that he might accept the offer of the rectory at Credenhill. It seems that he began writing his meditations while at Credenhill as a gift to a devout neighbour, Mrs Susanna Hopton, but continued adding to them while he was Sir Orlando's chaplain and left them uncompleted when he died, soon after his fallen patron.

His purpose was to encourage Susanna Hopton to be a joyful Christian. 'Remember always that thou art about a magnificent work', he urged her. His particular theme was that she would find felicity, as he had done, by loving all nature and all people because God had given everything and everyone to her to be enjoyed through love. 'You will never enjoy the world aright, till you see how a sand exhibiteth the wisdom and power of God: and prize in every thing the service which they do you, by manifesting his glory and goodness to your soul. . . . Your enjoyment of the world is never right, till every morning you awake in heaven: see yourself in your Father's palace: and look upon the skies and the earth and the air as celestial joys. . . . You will never enjoy the world aright, till the sea itself floweth in your veins, till you are clothed with the heavens, and crowned with the stars: and perceive yourself to be the sole heir of the whole world: and more then so, because men are in it who are every one sole heirs as well as you. . . . Till your spirit filleth the whole world, and the stars are your jewels, till you are as familiar with the ways of God in all ages as with your walk and table: till you are intimately acquainted with that shady nothing out of which the world was made: till you love all men so as to desire their happiness with a thirst equal to the zeal of your own: till you delight in God for being good to all: you will never enjoy the world.'

The criticism has been made that he never seems to have undergone the dark night of the soul, to have been purged so painfully that the death of the old self made possible a new life of union with God. Certainly he does not record such experience in the material which we now possess. It would, however,

be unfair to condemn him as a thoughtless optimist or naïve
nature-worshipper. He experienced many evils during his
short life. He did not choose to tell Susanna Hopton about
them; he was her pastor. But it is clear that when a fully mature
man he was full of wondering gratitude that the glory of his
childhood had been so largely restored to him. He marvelled,
but not arrogantly, that 'all ages are present in my soul, and all
kingdoms, and God blessed for ever. And thus Jesus Christ is
seen in me and dwelleth in me, when I believe upon him. And
thus all saints are in me, and I in them. And thus all angels and
the eternity and infinity of God are in me evermore.'[12]

RELIGION, MAGIC AND SCIENCE

In Elizabethan England the triangular relationship of religion,
magic and science had been different: there had been only a
thin partition between magic and science. The Church was
officially the enemy of magic, and scientists were afraid that
this would make it their enemy too. To reassure a Christian
society, Elizabethans interested in science emphasized that the
new discoveries – the astronomy of Copernicus, for example –
had only increased their awe as men surrounded by the
marvels of creation. They also stressed the practical utility:
more knowledge of the stars assisted navigation. But the
problem remained that science seemed essentially dangerous,
foolish and irreligious because, like magic, it seemed out of the
ordinary. The leading scientist of Elizabethan England, Dr
John Dee, was an alchemist trying to transmute baser metals
into gold – and the Queen's favourite astrologer. His library
and laboratory were wrecked by a mob in 1583. After the death
of his royal patron he was left to die in poverty and to be
satirized in Ben Jonson's play of 1610, The Alchemist.[13]

---

[12] Traherne's Centuries, Poems and Thanksgivings were edited by H. M. Margiliouth
(2 vols, Oxford, 1958). See also Gladys Wade, Thomas Traherne (Princeton, N.J.,
1944), and K. W. Salter, Thomas Traherne: Mystic and Poet (London, 1964).
[13] Recent studies include Paul H. Hocher, Science and Religion in Elizabethan
England (New York, 1969), and Frances Yates, The Occult Philosophy in the Elizabethan
Age (London, 1979).

Modern students are of course inclined to take Dee's side because of his courageous curiosity about nature and the possibility of gaining power to change it, if only into gold. If Dee is called a magician, we think of the benevolent Prospero in *The Tempest*. However, the fact seems to be that science was regarded by many Elizabethans and their successors as one vast trick, like magic. Magic was a very widespread cult, encouraged by the general unsettlement of the times but also by the end of the authority of the medieval Church. Medieval archdeacons had been stern in punishing 'sorcery', but medieval parish priests had been obligingly ready to exorcize evil spirits by their own incantations and to secure divine blessings by their intercessions – and medieval religion in general had offered plenty of officially authorized scope to the miracle-seekers and to the hysterical. In many ways, therefore, the Church had controlled the always vigorous market for magic in the Middle Ages. Now, in an England deprived of the supernatural powers which had been generally believed to be at the disposal of the medieval Church, any disaster could be blamed on magic, although many people were ready enough to use 'white' magic for their own convenience; and any woman who seemed mentally ill or merely eccentric to her neighbours could be gossiped about as a witch and perhaps eventually terrified or tortured into a confession. Popular fears were whipped up by the spread of the late medieval belief that witches had made a pact with the Devil – a belief to which Christopher Marlowe's play, *Dr Faustus*, was a witness at the end of 1580s. Despite protests against this popular nonsense by educated men such as Reginald Scot (whose *Discovery of Witchcraft* in 1584 discovered that it did not exist), Parliament pandered to the people by the fierce anti-witchcraft statute of 1604. It seems that about a thousand 'witches', mostly women, suffered death in England in the disgraceful century and a half which ended with the execution of Alice Molland at Exeter in 1685. In New England the belief was powerful for a rather longer period; a score of men and women suffered execution after the witchcraft scare in the Massachusetts village of Salem in 1692.

One reason for the progress of science in Restoration

England was that magic was then rapidly ceasing to be taken seriously by the public. Of course the belief lingered on. In the 1640s a professional witch-hunter, Matthew Hopkins, conducted a campaign which brought about two hundred women to their deaths, and such a memory was not easily forgotten. In a less harmful ritual of ancient tradition, Charles II 'touched' many thousands of his grateful subjects who were the victims of 'the king's evil', scrofula, caused by infected milk. Even the great Sir Isaac Newton, who became virtually the dictator of the new intellectual world of science, secretly dabbled in experiments in alchemy. But an historian who has investigated the very long story of battles between the Church and the 'cunning' men or 'wise' women who wielded a rival power in the villages concludes that 'the real change in attitude seems to have come with the Restoration of the Anglican Church after 1660. The inquiries after charmers and sorcerers which had been so prominent a feature of visitation articles before the civil war now silently disappeared from the list of matters on which the bishops and archdeacons normally sought information from their flock.'[14]

It might be expected that religion would decline rapidly along with magic. The two activities have not been unconnected. A large part of the hold of the Church on the mind of the Middle Ages had been due to credulity about the supernatural powers possessed by the Church's officials and sacraments, and a large part of the attack on ceremonies left over from the Middle Ages in the Book of Common Prayer had been inspired by the Puritans' conviction that Popery was merely superstitious; so that after 1600 a spread of disbelief in the Puritans' gospel itself, or in the godly preachers of the established Church of England, might be expected to be as fast as the spread of disbelief in magic. And in the long run this may have been the pattern in the profound secularization of modern England, still proceeding in the twentieth century and still beyond an objective historian's complete understanding. But

---

[14] Keith Thomas, *Religion and the Decline of Magic* (revised, Harmondsworth, Middx, 1971), p. 309. Alan Macfarlane studied *Witchcraft in Tudor and Stuart England* with special reference to Essex (London, 1970).

what actually happened in the seventeenth century was that the pioneers of science were almost unanimously anxious to make it clear that they had no quarrel with the Bible. Their attitude was that the medieval Church, in so far as it had been magical, had been less than Christian. Christianity was the true religion, revealed by the God who had long ago created nature and who had recently guided the scientists to discover their kind of truth about nature. It was the duty of intelligent men to accept both the Gospel and the natural laws confirmed or discovered by science, for both were the gifts of the one Creator.

There were many causes for the slow move of educated opinion out of the world of magic and into the world of science seen as contrary to magic. But it was the special work of two Englishmen to advocate the 'new philosophy' by reassuring Christians: Francis Bacon, Lord Chancellor under James I, and John Wilkins, Bishop of Chester under Charles II. Neither man was a major scientist in his own right. William Harvey, the great medical researcher, told John Aubrey that Bacon wrote philosophy 'like a Lord Chancellor', and it could have been said that Wilkins was as scientific as a bishop could be. But Wilkins, who was twelve years old when Bacon died in 1625, did more than any other Englishman of the seventeenth century to organize and popularize science along the lines for which Bacon had pleaded.

Born in 1561, Bacon saw that the many technical advances made in his lifetime could be assembled and developed in such a way as to create a far more rational and a far richer society. To this end he was prepared to sacrifice the medieval world-view with its strange combination of Aristotle, the Platonists, the Bible and popular mythology, but so far from thinking it necessary to sacrifice the Christian religion to science he claimed that religion and science could flourish in two compartments. The only condition was that the 'book of God's words' should be separated from nature, which was the 'book of God's works'; so that both theologians and scientists should be warned 'that they do not unwisely mingle or confound these learnings together'. To Bacon, religious truth was revealed by God and therefore not a fit subject for investigation. It was like the rules of games such as chess, to be 'received as they are and not disputed; but how to play a skilful and winning game is scientific and rational.' Everything except religion could and should be examined afresh, for the finding out of the true nature of all things 'whereby God might have the more glory in the workmanship of them, and men the more fruit in the use of them'. There should be no respect for the *idola* of conventional belief about the world; the Latin word, although usually translated 'idols', meant 'phantoms'. Noting how many were the causes of irrationality, Bacon distinguished between the *idola* of the tribe, the market place, the cave and the theatre. His whole call was to men to move out of this world of illusions into reality, but he never denied that the Christian religion had revealed God as the supreme reality. 'When the mind of man works upon nature, the creatures of God, it is limited thereby, but if it works upon itself or upon too small a part of material things, it spins out laborious webs of learning.' By limiting its material to the separate self-revelations of God in nature and the Bible, the human mind could achieve understanding of what was real.

That was the programme – but there was always something unreal about the idea of Francis Bacon as a scientist.

James I – who was a shrewd observer of his fellow men when not too drunk or too conceited to notice – appointed him Lord Chancellor for a time, but thought him capable of 'great volumes' rather than great deeds. Queen Elizabeth had given much the same reason when refusing him the political office for which he craved. William Cecil had encouraged his ambition to be a statesman in succession to his father, Sir Nicholas Bacon, since Cecil and old Sir Nicholas had married sisters; but it had not been auspicious when the young man, petitioning for a post in the civil service, had assured Elizabeth's chief minister that his real interest was in acquiring an income in order to be able to study, since he had taken 'all knowledge' as his province. Francis Bacon was not cut out to be a statesman – and, for all his genius as a visionary and as a writer, never had the time or aptitude to excel in the two arts which were vitally necessary before his hopes of a science-based society could be fulfilled. He never mastered either the art of making practical

experiments like any workman, or the art of persuading practical men to collaborate so that by their experiments they
helped each other. During the last journey of his life he made
an experiment which caused a fatal chill. He had the coach
stopped in order that a dead chicken might be stuffed with
snow; he was pondering the effects of refrigeration. But he had
founded no experimental, co-operative school of Baconians
before he died.[15]

John Wilkins gained much by being born far more humbly
than Francis Bacon. He was the son of an Oxford goldsmith,
and throughout his life not only enjoyed discussing other men's
technical experiments but also experimented himself. While he
was a bishop he dissected a dolphin, and when he lay dying in
1672 he announced that he was 'prepared for the great experiment'. He was equally enthusiastic in his writing about recent
discoveries and in his personal relations with other scientists,
professional or amateur. Perhaps he inherited his mastery of
these arts of popularity from his grandfather, the moderate
Puritan preacher and saint, John Dod.

Before he began a literary clergyman's career as chaplain to
successive noblemen, he made his mark with a book about the
moon, written in his spare hours as an Oxford tutor. He was
sure that the moon was inhabited and hopeful that it would one
day be reached by a 'flying chariot'. The publication of another
work of popular science, *Mathematical Magic* (which prophesied
submarines), coincided with his appointment as Warden of
Wadham College, Oxford, in 1648. At no stage of his life does
he seem to have held strong doctrinal or political views, so that
he was now as ready to accept Cromwell's ascendancy as he
was to be to accept Charles II in 1660. Indeed, he was willing
to marry the Lord Protector's sister Robina, although under
Charles II he ungraciously claimed that the marriage had been
forced on him. In a Puritan-dominated Oxford he persuaded
his colleagues to make the college noted for its food, its music
and its garden. In the garden was a hollow statue. Hiding in it,

---

[15] See Benjamin Farrington, *The Philosophy of Francis Bacon* (Liverpool, 1964),
and for the background Richard Westfall, *Religion and Science in Seventeenth Century
England* (New Haven, Conn., 1958).

he spoke, with what he hoped was an angelic voice, to a colleague who was walking about wrapped in meditation: 'Ashwell, go preach the Gospel in Virginia.' But he could speak more seriously; his time at Oxford was also remarkable for his ability to attract and encourage young scientists, including Christopher Wren. He did not introduce science into Oxford. The university had recently made distinguished contributions to medicine and to mathematics (then specially prized because of its use in the art of navigation). But he was able to get scientists to work happily together; a set of agreed rules survives for the Oxford Experimental Science Club in 1651. The contribution made by his personal magnetism was seen when this Oxford group disintegrated on his brief move to Cambridge as Master of Trinity College.

His position as Oliver Cromwell's brother-in-law was a definite embarrassment in the next reign, and he lost his Cambridge post. But he made no difficulties about accepting king or bishops, wanting to enlist the king as a patron of science and wanting to be a bishop himself in order to promote the causes dear to him. At Oxford members of the science club had been forbidden to mention religion, and Wilkins now still struggled both to protect science from rival dogmas and to enlarge the Established Church so as to 'comprehend' Protestant dissenters. He negotiated both with Cromwell's old chaplain, John Owen, and with Cromwell's old critic, Richard Baxter, in the hope of agreeing on a scheme full of compromises, but in the end failed to reach agreement and only made himself unpopular with the victorious Cavalier MPs and with stiff churchmen such as Archbishop Sheldon. He was financed by a variety of ecclesiastical posts, but his main life was in London before he was made Bishop of Chester in 1668. As chairman or secretary he played the key role in the formation of the Royal Society for the encouragement of science.

The society's first meetings in 1660 were held in Gresham's College, which had been founded by a legacy left by the financier Sir Thomas Gresham in 1579. It had always been a centre for some scientific activity, and under the Commonwealth there had been other encouragement given to technical experiments in London, for the Puritans in their time of power showed something of a Baconian interest in 'utility' for the benefit of commerce. Another influence favourable to the birth of the Royal Society had been the whole Puritan rejection of the medieval world-view with its cult of miracles and its blessing on superstitions. A theologian such as John Preston may have inadvertently assisted science by his declaration that outside the pages of the Bible 'God alters no law of nature'. But clearly a very strong motive was a simple interest in the experiments themselves, as they opened up the possibility of rewriting the whole of science with many profitable spinoffs. This delight was increased by the contrast between the rational peace of the charmed circle of experimental science and the bitter conflicts in religion and politics. It was a time when many felt 'the vanity of dogmatizing': that was the title of a book of 1661 by Joseph Glanvill, openly attacking the Ancient Greek philosophy still being taught in English universities and refraining from any long defence of the importance of dogmatic theology (although Glanvill defended belief in witchcraft).[16] And another factor was contact with the genial enthusiasm of John Wilkins, whose Oxford friends, now meeting in London, formed the core of the working Fellows of the Royal Society.

Wilkins had by this stage become chiefly an administrator, but he did have an intellectual passion for the simplification and rationalization of language, so that men could communicate without bewildering, insulting or excommunicating each other. He tried to work out the principles of a new universal language and (more usefully) himself gave an example of using plain English when speaking in or out of the pulpit. This example was picked up by his son-in-law Archbishop Tillotson, who edited for the press after his death his book on *The Principles and Duties of Natural Religion*. For the time being John Wilkins was defeated in ecclesiastical politics; the passions of intolerance were too powerful in an age when a more typical churchman was Bishop Seth Ward, once professor of astronomy in Oxford, now a fierce persecutor of the Dissenters. But the contribution which he made to the rise of science in England placed him not far from Lord Chancellor Bacon. And

---

[16] See J. I. Cope, *Joseph Glanvill, Anglican Apologist* (St Louis, Mo., 1956).

Bacon was – as Thomas Sprat, later Bishop of Rochester, declared in his *History of the Royal Society* (1667) – the 'one great man who had the imagination of the whole enterprise'.[17]

THE FAITH OF ISAAC NEWTON

Alexander Pope's famous epitaph shows his reputation:

Nature and Nature's laws lay hid in night,
God said, *Let Newton be!*, and all was Light.

Pope exaggerated, because science had made many advances before the publication of Isaac Newton's *Philosophiae Naturalis Principia Mathematica* in 1687. But Newton's mathematical genius has seldom if ever been equalled. Essentially what he did was to offer a convincing mathematical explanation of gravity, the force which kept the planets in their courses around the sun and which determined many natural movements on this planet; and he explained the composition of white light. After all the talk of semi-scientists such as the Elizabethan Dee about the mysteries of the stars and their effects on the earth, after all the half-light of medieval and Renaissance learning, that was the decisive burst of the light of science, although it could be followed up in many ways – as in the researches of other Fellows of the Royal Society, of which Newton was elected President each year from 1703 until his death aged eighty-five in 1727. Whilst an undergraduate William Wordsworth had rooms only a few yards away from the chapel of Trinity College, Cambridge:

---

[17] See Barbara Shapiro, *John Wilkins* (Berkeley, Cal., 1969). There has been controversy about the contributions made by different religious groups to science. Christopher Hill, *The Intellectual Origins of the English Revolution* (Oxford, 1965), stressed the Puritan contribution, but see Margery Purver, *The Royal Society: Concept and Creation* (London, 1967), and the further debate in *The Intellectual Revolution of the Seventeenth Century*, ed. Charles Webster (London, 1974). Charles Webster has provided a masterly account of 'science, medicine and reform, 1626–60' in *The Great Instauration* (London, 1975), and Michael Hunter a judicious survey of *Science and Society in Restoration England* (Cambridge, 1981).

The antechapel where the statue stood
Of Newton with his prism and silent face,
The marble index of a mind for ever
Voyaging through strange seas of thought alone.

Newton cared nothing for poetry's claim to illuminate the mysteries of the human heart, and almost as little for technology as improving the material lot of man; and because of these defects his influence was to be subjected to famous onslaughts by William Blake during the 'Romantic' revival. But he would not have been greatly disturbed by Blake, an avowed enemy of the Established Church. Newton was far more concerned to stay out of trouble with the Church and to demonstrate that his science supported true religion. He learned more than mathematics from his predecessor in the Cambridge professorship, Isaac Barrow, a distinguished theologian. He himself wrote a great deal of theology, but left almost all of it unpublished (although, it seems, prepared for the press) because the theology moved far beyond Barrow's safe position. His successor as professor of mathematics, William Whiston, and his scientific assistant, Samuel Clarke, both got themselves involved in bitter controversies with the orthodox clergy. Whiston founded a Society for the Restoration of Primitive Christianity. The more cautious Newton kept his reputation as a churchman well enough to be knighted by Queen Anne, made Master of the Mint, lionized by intellectual London and buried in Westminster Abbey. He was not going to expose himself as a heretic; it was enough for him that, watching the apple fall in the garden of Woolsthorpe in Lincolnshire, he had suddenly seen the force which kept God and man, earth and sun, moon and star in a beautiful order. And he understood the gravitational force which was to keep Church and State stable during the eighteenth century.

The noble vision of the Creator which he reached is summed up in a short passage in the *Principia* which Whiston translated. 'This Being governs all things, not as a Soul of the World, but as Lord of the Universe; and upon account of his dominion he is stiled Lord God, supreme over all. . . . The supreme God is an eternal, infinite, absolutely perfect Being, but a Being how perfect soever without dominion is not Lord God. For we say

my God . . . but we do not say my Eternal . . . my Infinite . . .
my Perfect . . . for these terms have no relation to servants.'
Beyond doubt Newton, although often either fiercely quarrelsome or coldly arrogant in his dealings with other men,
regarded himself as a servant of God. His private papers
clearly record his profound humility as he contemplated the
work of the Lord God who created matter and life (which were
sharply distinguished) and who kept them in order. It was only
to be expected that when according to his system the courses
of the planets needed occasional adjustments he relied on
God to do the adjusting. Leibniz said that this made God a
bungling watchmaker, but Newton never understood the
criticism.

Equally humble was his approach to the Bible. There he
found God's own promises about the future, for history was to
be brought fully under the 'dominion' of the orderly Creator.
He was fascinated by the biblical prophecies and happily spent
many months working out their chronology. His passionate
intellectual curiosity was applied to many problems in these
biblical studies, but never did he deviate from his belief that the
Bible was, from cover to cover, the Word of God. He accepted
the miracle stories of the Bible as the records of God's past
interferences in history; after all, God also adjusted the courses
of the planets from time to time. God's interferences had
ceased, however, apart from those repairs to the planetary
system. He told John Locke that 'miracles of good credit
continued in the Church for about two or three hundred years.'
He accepted Christ's death as a sacrifice to the Father, and also
his resurrection, although most of the teaching of Christ
seemed to be no more than the confirmation of the natural
religion already known to all rational men. The biblical
prophecies commanded his attention because they seemed to
be predictions that in the future God would resume his widespread interventions in the course of nature and in the world's
history.

Newton's theological beliefs seem to have been close to those
developed in public by later Christian heretics but he was
content to leave further explorations in religion, as in science,
to the future. This proud genius wrote to his nephew: 'To

myself I seem to have been only a boy playing on the seashore, and diverting myself in now and then finding a smoother pebble or a prettier shell than ordinary, while the great ocean of truth lay all undiscovered before me.'[18]

Around Newton many lesser lights were thrown on nature by scientists, and were believed to reveal 'the wisdom of God manifested in the works of the creation'. This phrase was used as the title of a book by John Ray in 1691. It epitomized the attitude of a considerable movement. Robert Boyle, the father of chemistry in England, was the author of *The Christian Virtuoso* (1690); and he endowed annual lectures to be delivered in a London church, confuting atheism by science. He regarded the human eye as a wonder which was particularly useful in proving the creation by a benevolent God, but the Boyle lecturers ranged far and wide over nature in the same cause. This was the approach of John Ray, who is honoured as the father of scientific botany in England. He retired from Cambridge in order to pursue detailed scientific studies and to write a series of 'physico-theological discourses' tackling problems such as the relationship between the opening chapters of the Bible and seventeenth-century knowledge. The existence of fossils which seemed older than the time allowed by the Bible for the world's history was one of the few features of nature which gave him some temporary difficulty.

Writers such as these cheerfully disregarded Bacon's warning not to mingle theology with science – and their punishment came when, in later generations, they were laughed at both by scientists and by religious believers. But their assurance shows how little tension was thought to exist between the new science and the Christian faith, in the age which would come to be remembered as the age of Newton. The light of knowledge had shone into the darkness of magic. It was appropriate that one of the three Members of Parliament who sponsored the repeal of

---

[18] Recent studies include Frank E. Manuel, *The Religion of Isaac Newton* (Oxford, 1974) and *A Portrait of Isaac Newton* (London, 1980); Margaret C. Jacob, *The Newtonians and the English Revolution, 1689–1720* (Hassocks, Sussex, 1976); Richard Westfall, *Never at Rest: A Biography of Isaac Newton* (Cambridge, 1981).

the Witchcraft Act in 1736 was John Conduitt. He greatly admired Sir Isaac Newton, whose niece he had married.[19]

TWO QUESTIONERS:
HOBBES AND LOCKE

In 1679 Thomas Hobbes died. He had been born in a Gloucestershire vicarage – prematurely, when his mother heard of the approach of the Spanish Armada. He had lived to see the sharp decline, if not the total fall, of the world of magic in which his father's parishioners had believed; and his own writings were part of the propaganda against belief in witches, fairies and ghosts. He had often talked with Francis Bacon in the early 1620s, had been intoxicated by his discoveries of geometry and mathematics, and had tried to get elected to the Royal Society in the 1660s, but was repeatedly refused, it seems more because of his reputation as an atheist than because of his limitations as a scientist. He had learned how to write well by his deep studies of the Greek classics and had formed the ambition to clear up the mysteries of politics and religion by writing English with a geometric or mathematical precision. All the superstitions which Shakespeare, for example, put into people's mouths without any evident disapproval were condemned by Hobbes. Reality was substituted, reality being thus defined: 'external objects cause conceptions, and conceptions appetite or fear, which are the first unperceived beginnings of our actions.' Using this approach to England, his *Leviathan* (1651) provoked thought and argument long after he was dead. Charles II said that the Church trained young clergymen by putting them on to answer Hobbes as dogs were exercised by being encouraged to bait a bear. For much of the eighteenth century clergymen thought that all English infidels able to read were at heart Hobbists. This genius asked questions which could not be answered merely by making Christianity a simpler religion, or by showing that the Fellows of the Royal Society managed to be Christians even if somewhat unorthodox.

---

[19] See Mitchell Fisher, *Robert Boyle, Devout Naturalist* (Philadelphia, Pa., 1945), and Charles Raven, *John Ray, Naturalist* (Cambridge, 1942).

Before the civil wars Hobbes earned his living as a secretary to rich gentlemen, mainly two Earls of Devonshire. *Leviathan* was written in exile in Paris when its author's mind was preoccupied by the need to end the miseries inflicted on England by the wars. Its great plea was for obedience to the sovereign, but it totally abandoned the Cavalier talk about the divine right of kings. God entrusted complete authority to whichever government had power – and the people consented because owing to their selfishness the only alternative was anarchy. When in their shared exile Clarendon asked him why he had written a book which justified any government in power Hobbes, half-joking, blurted out: 'The truth is, I have a mind to go home'; and not long after completing *Leviathan* he went to live in London under the Commonwealth. But we have no need to doubt the intellectual integrity of the main argument: the necessity of sovereignty. Nor need we doubt the horror with which Hobbes viewed Roman Catholicism as an enemy of the English state ('the ghost of the deceased Roman empire, sitting crowned upon the grave thereof'). Nor need we question his hatred of Protestant enthusiasm as an enemy of the social order. This basically political reaction to the harm done by religion inspired his denunciation of the 'kingdom of darkness' ruled by priests and preachers. It is, however, far more difficult to tell what Hobbes did actually believe in religiously. Friends such as John Aubrey presented him to the public as a kind, humorous churchgoer, and Hobbes often said that he was no atheist. His advice was that 'it is with the mysteries of our religion as with wholesome pills for the sick; which swallowed whole, have the virtue to cure; but chewed up, are for the most part cast up again without effect.' More than half of *Leviathan* dealt with the religious topics and showed a mastery of the Bible.

He did not let the Bible master him. He speculated about the origins of religion. Did it arise out of a foolish belief in ghosts? He noted the contemporary English Christian use of the phrase 'God the Holy Ghost'. Did it arise out of the absence of science, out of 'ignorance of causes'? He noted that 'this perpetual fear, always accompanying mankind in the ignorance of causes, as it were in the dark, must needs have for object something.' Did it arise out of 'devotion to what men fear'? Or out of the human inability to take 'things casual' for what they were? Hobbes concluded that religion was 'fear of power invisible, feigned by the mind, or imagined from tales publicly allowed.' He hastily added that 'when the power imagined is truly such as we imagine', the seventeenth century had 'true religion'. He added, too, that the 'wise and learned interpretation' of the Scriptures could guide men without running the risks of 'enthusiasm or supernatural inspiration'. But for practical purposes what was decisive in religion – as in law, or in life in general – was not the Scriptures but what the sovereign willed. The individual certainly had no right to force his views on others. If a man told others that God spoke to him in a dream, this 'is no more than to say he dreamed that God spoke to him'. Prophecy, like miracles, had long ago ceased.

About the Church as an institution, Hobbes could be more cheerfully and openly destructive. He defined a church as 'a company of men professing Christian religion, united in the person of one sovereign, at whose command they ought to assemble, and without whose authority they ought not to assemble.' Faith in the heavenly Christ and 'obedience to laws' were all that was necessary to salvation, and it was right to have faith in Christ because of who he was. Faith, Hobbes explained, is the kind of assent to a proposition which derives its reasons 'not from the proposition itself but from the person propounding'; it is assent which 'grows not from any confidence of our own, but from another man's knowledge'. But the sole concern of Christ was with heaven, and the sole message of the first Christians was 'that Jesus was the Christ, that is to say the King that was to save them and reign over them eternally in the world to come.' Such a Gospel could never give trouble to a sovereign.[20]

For many years English authors competed with each other to produce angry and contemptuous reasons for rejecting

---

[20] The best introductions are Richard Peters, *Hobbes* (Harmondsworth, Middx, 1956), and F. C. Hood, *The Divine Politics of Thomas Hobbes* (Oxford, 1964). For the debate about him see S. I. Mintz, *The Hunting of Leviathan* (Cambridge, 1962), and John Bowle, *Hobbes and His Critics* (London, 1969).

Hobbes. But there came a time when a new generation took up his questions more calmly. Belief in the divine right of kings was still powerful, but in politics the most influential viewpoint in the long run was that which John Locke expressed classically: because all the people who mattered had agreed only to a limited contract with the government, the power of the sovereign – the monarchy or the executive – must be subject to Parliament and to the laws made by Parliament. And in religion also, the questions which Hobbes asked were debated more freely when the censorship of printing was relaxed in the 1690s. Adventurous theologians were then no longer afraid to publish books which they had not previously submitted to the Archbishop of Canterbury or the Bishop of London, although it remained possible to prosecute them for seditious or blasphemous libel. The result was a flood of publications probing the character and status of the Christian religion. Francis Bacon had taught, probably with his tongue in his cheek, that 'we are obliged to believe the word of God, though our reason be shocked by it'; that, indeed, 'the more absurd and incredible any divine mystery is, the greater honour we do to God in believing it.' Such a caution still prevailed largely among the clergy – but not among laymen who followed the current debate.

Much of that debate was a commentary on the thought of John Locke, for 'it was Locke's appointed task to work up into a system all the assumptions about God, Nature and Man which, as the seventeenth-century storm clouds blew off, seemed to most men to stand firm and unquestionable in the light of common day'.[21]

John Locke was a widely accomplished layman, from 1667 until he fled to Holland in 1683 the secretary of an active politician, the Earl of Shaftesbury. He was himself no troublemaker. He published his writings on religion anonymously and always denied that their intention was Socinian or in any other way heretical. He was so anxious to dissociate himself from Hobbes that he took to pretending that he had never read him properly. Although after his return from exile he found himself

---

[21] Basil Willey, *The Seventeenth-century Background* (London, 1934), p. 267.

highly honoured, the chief interest of his last years became writing a book on St Paul. He died in an armchair in 1704, having spent that day listening to psalms being read to him by his closest friend, Ralph Cudworth's daughter Damaris. But clergymen wrote against him. The two most prominent were Edward Stillingfleet, the Latitudinarian bishop, who thought that here latitude had been extended too far, and John Edwards, almost the sole surviving representative of the once dominant school of Cambridge Calvinism. And they were right to see in Locke's thought a challenge to every old orthodoxy.

In *An Essay concerning Human Understanding*, finished on the last day of 1686 and published just before Christmas 1689, he made a proposal. Its effect would be to banish many theological propositions from the intellectual world, as decisively as James II was exiled from England on account of his Roman Catholicism, between the writing of the book and its publication. For Locke confined the category of 'propositions according to reason' with a strictness which began the English emphasis on empiricism. Such propositions, he wrote, are those 'whose truth we can discover by examining and tracing those ideas we have from sensation and reflection, and by natural deduction find to be true or probable'. Among such truths was the existence of God. 'We more certainly know that there is a God, than that there is anything else without us.' But 'contrary to reason are such propositions as are inconsistent with, or irreconcilable to, our clear and distinct ideas'; an example he gave was the polytheist's belief that there is more than one god. Locke's own claim for his work was modest. He was, he wrote, not one of the 'master builders' such as 'the incomparable Mr Newton'. It was for him 'ambition enough to be employed as an under-labourer in clearing the ground a little and removing some of the rubbish that lies in the way to knowledge.' But to theologians Locke seemed a remarkable 'under-labourer', in that he condemned ideas not derived from the sense, or from rational reflection on the evidence of the senses, as 'rubbish'.

At first Locke's views on theology seemed significant chiefly because, by showing how difficult it was to reach an understanding of religious matters that could be reckoned true knowledge, he helped to show how nonsensical it was to try to compel men by force into holding religious beliefs. Thoughts in favour of religious liberty which had been maturing in his mind through the troubled 1680s were conveniently ready to be published in defence of the Toleration Act of 1689. *A Letter concerning Toleration* was written during his exile in the Netherlands and published, anonymously and at first in Latin, in 1689. It was followed by two more *Letters* replying to its argument that civil government ought to be confined to securing men's lives, liberty, health and possessions, leaving the salvation of souls to religious bodies whose only sanction should be excommunication. Locke was cautious when drawing conclusions for England from this grand principle. He never welcomed liberty for Roman Catholics because he regarded them as the agents of a foreign power. He also refused to draw the conclusion that atheists should be given liberty as equal citizens. In the constitution which he helped to draft for the American 'province' of Carolina (in which his employer, the Earl of Shaftesbury, had the largest financial interest), the matter was made plain: 'No man shall be permitted to be a freeman of Carolina, or have any estate or habitation in it, who does not acknowledge a God and that God is publicly to be worshipped.' One reason was that only those who believed in rewards and punishments after death were thought fit to be trusted to make oaths and agreements. But with these important qualifications, Locke argued impressively for religious toleration as a consequence of the very nature of true religion. And he did so at a time when most English Christians wanted to be persuaded about such a solution to the nation's conflicts but had been taught to abhor the idea of toleration as an insult to Christianity.

In the new atmosphere of tolerance which he lived to see, there was a free debate about the hallowed doctrine of the ancient faith, both in conversation among those who frequented taverns or the new coffee-shops, and in print as the intellectuals or the ambitious hastened to persuade or insult each other in pamphlets and books.

Locke, somewhat like Hobbes, allowed room for doctrines which were 'above reason' rather than contrary to it; an example he gave was the doctrine of the resurrection of the dead. Faith in such doctrines was a 'firm assent of the mind . . . regulated . . . upon good reason'. Faith was distinguished from reason because it was not deduced from ideas got by the use of the senses or of reflection; but it was legitimate if it was assent made 'upon the credit of the proposer, as coming from God in some extraordinary way of communication. This way of discovering truths to men we call *revelation*.' When Jesus Christ proposed his doctrines, he was credit-worthy because of the 'outward signs': predictions of his coming were fulfilled, and miracles, supremely his own resurrection, were performed. On this basis it was reasonable to believe him. On any basis less reasonable, the acceptance of the teaching of Jesus would be wrong. 'Whatever God hath revealed is certainly true; no doubt can be made of it . . . but whether it be a divine revelation or no, reason must judge.'

Locke's own reason, and the reason of his age, refused to approve of the Calvinist interpretation of the New Testament; that was dismissed without much argument. But a more liberal interpretation could also be dismissed as not genuine revelation. Locke grew to be critical of the Cambridge Platonists. They had taught that every child was born with some ideas already innate before any education could be made from the evidence of the senses; and they had been confident of the ability of the mind to understand eternal substances. To Henry More, man's reason could become a 'divine sagacity'. Now Platonism, and other forms of metaphysics, seemed to be doomed if the only appeal allowed was to 'the ideas we have from sensation and reflection' supplemented by the plain teaching of Jesus.

What, then, was Christianity?

An essay on *The Reasonableness of Christianity as Delivered in the Scriptures*, which Locke published anonymously in 1695, reduced the religion in order to make it reasonable but claimed that this reduction was no more than a return to the New Testament. The essential faith was to believe that Jesus of Nazareth was the Messiah because of the prophecies and miracles. To those who so believed, God 'proposed' the forgiveness of sins 'for his Son's sake, because they gave themselves up to him, to be his subjects'; but men still needed sincerely to obey the laws of the kingdom which they had entered, for otherwise 'they were but the greater rebels'. The laws of this kingdom of the Messiah were old laws, arising from God's eternal nature, but it made all the difference that the Messiah commanded them. 'There is not, I think, any of the duties of morality which he has not, somewhere or other, by himself and his apostles, inculcated over and over again to his followers in express terms.' This 'morality' was superior to 'the attempts of philosophers before Our Saviour's time' because their systems fell short of 'the perfection of a true and complete morality'; but the main difference was now that Christians had a Legislator who taught morality with an authority and a simplicity which 'the bulk of mankind' could understand. 'The writers and wranglers in religion fill it with niceties, and dress it up with notions' – but 'the greatest part of mankind have no leisure for learning and logic, and superfine distinctions of the schools. Where the hand is used to the plough and spade, the head is seldom elevated to sublime motions, or exercised in mysterious reasonings. 'Tis well if men of that rank (to say nothing of the other sex) can comprehend plain propositions.'

Plain propositions, made reasonable because they had first been proposed by the Messiah who fulfilled the prophecies and performed the miracles, constituted the Christianity which John Locke recommended to his fellow Englishmen. It was a creed different from the creed of the Catholic centuries and from the religion held by his father, a Puritan lawyer in Somerset; but in Locke's own eyes, it was more truly biblical than Popery or Calvinism had ever been. Determined to die in peace, he left it to others to quarrel with the Church.[22]

---

[22] The best biography is Maurice Cranston, *John Locke* (London, 1957). See also *John Locke: Problems and Perspectives*, ed. J. W. Yolton (Cambridge, 1969). Paul Hazard's classic study of the intellectual crisis in which Locke figured prominently was translated as *The European Mind, 1680–1715* (London, 1953).

THE FAITH OF JOHN DRYDEN

But John Locke did not provide the only answer available to thinking Englishmen. The greatest poet of the age, John Dryden, became a Roman Catholic sometime in 1685 or 1686. In keeping with his conviction that literature should be only distantly related to the emotions, he left behind no account of his conversion and the psychology of it remains something of an enigma. He was said to have changed his religious beliefs in order to keep his appointments at court now that the King was a Roman Catholic, but it does not seem that James II was then insisting on such changes. There is this evidence of the convert's sincerity: he did not alter his beliefs again. Rather than take the oath to the Protestant William and Mary when James II had fled, he resigned as Poet Laureate and Historiographer Royal and accepted some real disabilities and humiliations as a Papist. We need not doubt that he was always a man of honour, a man who chose Roman Catholicism because he had come to believe that it was true.

Dryden wrote two long religious poems, one before and one after his conversion. *Religio Laici or a Layman's Faith* came in 1682 when he was at the height of his powers as a Tory satirist, and he acknowledged that from him 'the handling of so serious a subject wou'd not be expected'. The poem showed a close attention to current theology, but also a sturdily lay approach. Despite advice to be more cautious, he retained a criticism of St Athanasius for teaching that the heathen must be damned. He also criticized the Church of England's own clergy for neglect of their duties. The theology expounded was the standard Anglicanism of the time. A preface attacked the Papists 'because they have kept the Scripture from us, what they cou'd; and have reserv'd to themselves the right of interpreting what they have deliver'd under the pretence of infallibility.' In particular they were rebuked for their defence of 'king-killing'. The Puritans and their Dissenting heirs, now called 'the Fanatics', were dismissed with a more complete contempt. Perhaps Dryden was here reacting against being much preached at in his boyhood: his father was a Puritan and a justice of the peace in Cromwellian England. He wrote: 'If spiritual pride, venom, violence, contempt of superiors and slander had been made the marks of orthodox belief, the presbytery and the rest of our schismatics which are their spawn were always the most visible Church in the Christian world.'

Proudly distancing himself from such enthusiasts, Dryden declared that he was one 'naturally inclined to scepticism in philosophy'. Much has been read into this admission by some modern commentators. But he advocated a religion which partly accepted the obvious truths of Christianity and partly conformed to the laws of the State:

> Faith is not built on disquisitions vain;
> The things we *must* believe, are few and plain:
> But since men *will* believe more than they need,
> And every man will make himself a creed,
> In doubtful questions 'tis the safest way
> To learn what unsuspected ancients say:
> For 'tis not likely we shou'd higher soar
> In search of heaven, than all the Church before . . .
> And after hearing what our Church can say,
> If still our reason runs another way
> That private reason 'tis more just to curb
> Than by disputes the public peace disturb.
> For points obscure are of small use to learn:
> But common quiet is mankind's concern.

Five years after this defence of the Church of England in *Religio Laici*, he published *The Hind and the Panther*. It was a longer poem and far more interesting. Although still confined within the golden cage of the 'heroic couplet' and still addressed to a mainly Anglican readership which would understand scholarly references, it showed that his conversion to Roman Catholicism had brought John Dryden more maturity, calm, charitableness and sense of devotion. (How wrong was Macaulay, with his Victorian superiority, to say that 'Dryden knew little and cared little about religion'!) His argument was that the Church of Rome had the best claim to have preserved the revelation entrusted by the Saviour to the ancient, undivided Church. The Church of England taught 'nonsense' because of too many compromises, but the two Churches still had much in common, in particular a common cause against ignorant and intolerant Protestant fanatics:

> O happy regions, Italy and Spain,
> Which never did those monsters entertain!
> The Wolf, the Bear, the Boar can there advance
> No native claim of just inheritance.

And this poem of 1687, although written by a convert who might have been expected to praise all attempts to convert England, hinted broadly at a continuing dislike of Jesuit influence and of any kind of provocative extremism; Dryden combined his loyalty to the papacy, as he had combined his loyalty to the Church of England, with a noticeable amount of anticlericalism.

The preface commended the poem to the reader as a plea for toleration, and the very first line presented the Roman Catholic Church not as an aggressor but as 'a milk white hind, immortal and unchang'd'. The Church of England was depicted as a panther, but even in this image, which might have been deeply offensive, there was some tact:

> The Panther sure the noblest, next the Hind,
> And fairest creature of the spotted kind;
> Oh, could her in-born stains be wash'd away
> She were too good to be a beast of prey! . . .
> Her wild belief in ev'ry wave is tossed,
> But sure no church can better morals boast.
> True to her king her principles are found;
> Oh that her practice were but half so sound! . . .
> Thus is the Panther neither lov'd nor fear'd,
> A mere mock queen of a divided herd.

A year before his death in 1700, Dryden wrote *The Good Parson* – about an Anglican, an astonishing tribute from one who had been so definitely anticlerical. Already in 1687 his poem ended with the Church of England still open to persuasion, although not exactly alert to it:

> Thus did the gentle Hind her fable end,
> Nor would the Panther blame it, nor commend;
> But with affected yawnings at the close,
> Seem'd to require her natural repose.

Concluding *The Hind and the Panther*, the poet was grateful for his own knowledge that God had provided an 'unerring guide', a Church with authority. Here was a conviction that only the old religion, the unchanged faith of Catholic Christendom, could give a man peace of soul amid all the debates and conflicts of the age. Here was a layman's confidence, a calm faith, in God, which would survive King James's or the Jesuits' antics:

> Thy throne is darkness in th' abyss of light,
> A blaze of glory that forbids the sight;
> O teach me to believe thee thus conceal'd,
> And search no further than thy self reveal'd;
> But her alone for my director take
> Whom thou hast promis'd never to forsake![23]

THE ATTACK ON ORTHODOXY

In the eighteenth century John Dryden's fears that Protestantism would result in an intolerable chaos of opinions seemed to be justified. One of the vocal 'Free Thinkers' was Anthony Collins, a well-to-do squire who as a young man won the aged Locke's friendship; his *Discourse of Freethinking* (1713) popularized the word. In *A Discourse of the Grounds and Reasons of the Christian Religion* (1724) Collins examined the Old Testament in order to show that its prophecies had not been literal predictions of the coming of Jesus; and he outlined further criticism of traditional Christian apologetics.

Three years later a Cambridge don who was so eccentric as perhaps to be of unsound mind began publishing *Discourses on the Miracles of Our Saviour*. In these discourses Thomas Woolston treated the story of the resurrection of Jesus as 'the most notorious and monstrous imposture, that ever was put on

---

[23] Philip Harth, *Contexts of Dryden's Thought* (Chicago, Ill., 1968), answered the charge that the poet was either a deep sceptic or a time-server. The best treatment is to be found in C. Douglas Atkins, *The Faith of John Dryden* (Lexington, Ken., 1980). For the intellectual life of the community which Dryden joined, see T. H. Clancy, *English Catholic Books, 1641–1700* (Chicago, Ill., 1974).

mankind'. He was imprisoned, but when a London preacher, Thomas Sherlock, defended the apostles' credibility he did so by imagining a trial where the most persuasive arguments were used by the counsel for the Apostles. His *Trial of the Witnesses of the Resurrection of Jesus* (1729) attracted and convinced many readers. But this clever book showed the Church being obliged to defend its teaching on territory which had hitherto been regarded as very much its own possession. And even when the resurrection of Jesus was still granted to be true and miraculous, other writers arose to affirm that the age of miracles in the Church had ceased with the deaths of the apostles – and to hint that its existence before that date was by no means as certain as the Church's tradition maintained.

If prophecies and miracles as proofs of the Messiahship of Jesus were open to such criticisms, what of the plain message which Locke had presented as the teaching of the Messiah? Here the attack on orthodoxy, so far from being silenced, came to a climax.

In 1690 a book by the Rector of Exeter College, Oxford, on *The Naked Gospel*, was burned and its author driven out by a furious Bishop of Exeter because the Gospel had been interpreted (or so it seemed) as a denial of the Church's creeds. Six years later John Toland, an Irishman in reaction against a Roman Catholic upbringing, published anonymously a book based on the independent reading and reflection which he had managed while studying at Edinburgh and Oxford. It was called *Christianity not Mysterious* and flatly denied that there could be any religious truths 'above reason'.

Jesus, Toland claimed, had taught nothing so absurd as 'the Gibberish of your Divinity Schools'. On the contrary, he had made the truth 'easy and obvious to the meanest capacities'. The complications had been introduced by 'priestcraft' from 'pagan mystic rites' and similar sources. This early publication did not suggest very clearly what was the truth about God, but Toland did not cease to develop and to write. He invented the term 'pantheist' in 1705 in order to equate God with the universe, and later published a Prayer Book based on this creed. He also wrote controversially in defence of Milton and in criticism of the New Testament narratives. His patrons included the third Earl of Shaftesbury (who had once been Locke's pupil and was now a philosopher in his own right). They did not include Locke, who was embarrassed by the Irishman's crudity while indignant at the storm with which the orthodox responded.

During Toland's lifetime a much more serious theologian questioned the orthodox doctrine of the Trinity. Hitherto this had been unthinkable for a priest of the Church of England. Indeed, whether inclining more to Catholicism or to Calvinism the Church had gloried in its claim to be impeccably orthodox, teaching the same faith as the Bible and an undivided Church. It was assumed that there was one continuous orthodoxy despite various heretical corruptions, and a characteristic Anglican contribution had been the work of George Bull, a learned parish priest who ended up as Bishop of St David's. In one major work Bull attempted to show that the teaching of the New Testament on the relationship between faith and works was a harmonious whole; in another, that the Fathers of the Church before the Council of Nicaea already held the same Trinitarian beliefs that the Council was to proclaim. But in 1712 Samuel Clarke, Rector of St James, Piccadilly, caused a sensation by his *Scripture-Doctrine of the Trinity*, examining 1,251 texts and concluding that there was in the Bible no single doctrine, let alone one which was orthodox as Nicaea was to define orthodoxy. While the author refrained from any clearly heretical conclusion, he suggested independence and indicated sympathy with some Unitarian objections to the Nicene definition. That tendency was what Anthony Collins had in mind when he observed that no one had doubted the existence of God until Dr Clarke had undertaken to demonstrate it.

This courageous book mattered because it was written by the leading philosophical theologian of the day – a brilliant man who was Isaac Newton's favourite pupil and was offered the Mastership of the Mint on Newton's death. While in his twenties Clarke had published Boyle Lectures, *A Discourse Concerning the Being and Attributes of God, the Obligations of Natural Religion, and the Truth and Certainty of the Christian Revelation*. That book had made his reputation, and it had been an orthodox reputation. Clarke had attacked Hobbes and the Dutch pan-

theist Spinoza, and although he had shown an understanding
of Deist objections to orthodox Christianity he had not surrendered to them. Such a thinker might well have become a
famous leader of the Church of England. Instead in the 1720s
he let it be known that he could not subscribe to the Thirty-
Nine Articles and when Sir Robert Walpole tried to make him
a bishop even that all-powerful minister had to withdraw.[24]

The severity of the new challenges was made plain by
Matthew Tindal – who, however, managed to retain his
fellowship at All Souls College, Oxford, from 1678 to his death
in 1733. He first appeared before a large public with a book of
1706, *The Rights of the Christian Church asserted against the Romish
and all Other Priests who claim an Independent Power over it*. The title
would have delighted the old Puritans, but Tindal left few of
the Church's doctrines standing by the time he had finished
asserting its rights. What was allowed to survive was no more
than reason could demonstrate and the State could approve as
being good for morality. In 1730 Tindal made his rejection of
the Church's tradition still clearer by issuing *Christianity as Old
as the Creation, or the Gospel a Republication of the Religion of Nature*.
His argument was that 'the religion of nature is absolutely
perfect; revelation can neither add to, nor take away from, its
perfection.' It was then not possible for a Fellow of All Souls to
say outright that Christianity was false; but it could be said
that every reasonable man agreed with what it really was, and
that Jesus had had a happy knack of telling memorable stories
to illustrate the world's philosophical commonplaces.[25]

Tindal was a 'Deist' (although he called himself a 'Christian
Deist'). That is: it seemed obvious to him that mankind as a
whole believed in one orderly, benevolent God, or would have
believed in him had priests not corrupted the original innocence. It seemed obvious, too, that what had always been

---

[24] James Ferguson studied *The Philosophy of Dr Samuel Clarke and its Critics* (New
York, 1974), and Robert Sullivan, *John Toland and the Deist Controversy* (Cambridge,
1982).
[25] Extracts from this whole debate, and comments on it, were provided in
Religious Thought of the Eighteenth Century, ed. J. M. Creed and J. S. Boys Smith
(Cambridge, 1934). See also R. N. Stranberg, *Religious Liberalism in Eighteenth-century
England* (Oxford, 1954), and John Redwood, *Reason, Ridicule and Religion: The Age of
Enlightenment in England 1660–1750*, quoting many pamphlets (London, 1976).

presented as the distinctively Christian doctrines about God deserved to be forgotten now that the nature of religion was at last understood in an enlightened age. Surely the old picture of man as a sinner in danger of hell should be abandoned. It was no more credible than the old Christian insistence that, for men to be saved, the true God needed to be revealed by Christ. Not all Deists stopped there. Some dared to ask openly: in the new age of enlightenment, although all sensible men agreed with morality in theory, were they not right to sacrifice it to the higher laws of profit and pleasure? And although all sensible men believed in God, was it not true that God did not matter much, being powerless to influence either the individual or the march of history.

In 1714 a London doctor, Bernard de Manderville, published *The Fable of the Bees*, complacent about 'private vices' since the expenditure which these stimulated caused 'public benefits'. In the second edition he attacked churchmen for educating the children of the poor in the new charity schools; it was not a public benefit to put ideas into such heads. Later he issued a plea for the approval and licensing of brothels. Such books were only the tips of an iceberg of talk, for in many taverns and private dining rooms Restoration and eighteenth-century men tended to admire and debauch each other, now that the restraints of Puritan discipline had been removed. It remained only to remove the Puritan theory of man.

We have no need to trace the long process by which the dark picture of man bequeathed by Augustine of Hippo and developed by Calvin of Geneva was ridiculed and widely forgotten, but can note as a sign of the times that the philosophy of the third Earl of Shaftesbury affirmed the importance of man's moral and aesthetic senses apart from religion. In a widely influential book of 1738 on *The Scripture-Doctrine of Original Sin*, a Presbyterian minister, John Taylor, expounded the view that Augustine and Calvin had not even done justice to the men who wrote the Bible. The Bible itself, as Taylor read it, did not teach that Adam's guilt had been transmitted to all his descendants. If men were naturally corrupt, Taylor concluded, they were not morally responsible. He totally rejected the Calvinist belief that amid a general corruption a few had been predestined to salvation. It was his conviction that the Law in the Old Testament attached its penalties to individual's actual sins – for which Christ made Atonement, thus saving from eternal extinction all those sinners who repented and desired to partake of the 'grace' offered universally. 'Pray consider seriously,' he wrote, 'what a God he must be who can be displeased with and can curse his innocent creatures even before they have a being. Is this thy God, O Christian?'

As G. R. Cragg has said about the decline of Calvinism among Englishmen after 1600, 'seldom has a reversal of fortune been so complete. Within fifty years Calvinism in England fell from a position of immense authority to obscurity and insignificance . . . Calvinism had a magnificent opportunity, and for a brief period wielded wider powers than its popular support would probably have warranted. It prepared its own undoing; it failed to use its great advantages so as to win the sympathies of ordinary Englishmen.' And with the decline of belief in Calvinist gloom about the moral and spiritual condition of the average Englishman went a decline of belief in hell, so far as we can judge from what we know about sermons and popular reactions to them. A densely populated hell now seemed not terrifying but ridiculously unreasonable. For not only John Taylor rejected Calvinism with its claim that God had decreed in advance of any human actions the everlasting punishment of the majority of the human race. The most influential Anglican preacher of the age, Archbishop John Tillotson, made a quiet comment. 'That,' he said, 'is that which no good man could do.'[26]

TWO VOYAGERS:
DEFOE AND SWIFT

While he was Queen Anne's chief minister from 1710 to 1714, Robert Harley employed two journalists of genius: Daniel Defoe and Jonathan Swift.[27] Defoe, who was able to commend

---

[26] G. R. Cragg, *From Puritanism to the Age of Reason* (Cambridge, 1950), pp. 30, 34. D. P. Walker has studied *The Decline of Hell* (London, 1964).

[27] See J. A. Downie, *Robert Harley and the Press* (Cambridge, 1979).

himself to almost any circle because he was so full of unaffected admiration for his fellow men's lives and achievements, was sent all over the country to make propaganda by conversation as well as by writing. For all this work he was paid. Swift, in contrast, remained a writer and in what he wrote did not conceal his contempt for most of his fellow men (although to the few whom he admitted into friendship, he was wonderfully loyal: he was to be loyal after Harley's fall and imprisonment). He was too proud to accept any ordinary fee for his journalism although he hoped for a bishopric. And in the contrasting personalities of the two great journalists, Defoe and Swift, lay the origins of two very different convictions about English Christianity in the eighteenth century.

Born in or about 1660, Daniel Defoe was the son of a Puritan and was sent to one of the new 'academies' of the Dissenters in the hope that he would become a preacher. No one has ever been able to unravel all his often unsuccessful business enterprises, or to count up his literary output, but always he was a preacher – in a sense. Although many of his fellow Dissenters thought him insufficiently sober and honest, he risked and incurred severe punishment for his savagely ironical pamphlet in their defence, *The Shortest Way with Dissenters* (the shortest way being to hang the preachers and exile the congregations). Swift, in contrast, was born in 1667 in an impoverished Cavalier family. He was proud to be an Anglican clergyman; 'gentlemen' was one of his favourite words. He despised tradesmen and Dissenters. He particularly despised Defoe.

Both men wrote famous fiction which took advantage of the popularity of books about voyages. Defoe's *Robinson Crusoe* (1719) was based partly on the experiences of a sailor, Alexander Selkirk, who was shipwrecked on an uninhabited island in 1704 and came back to tell the tale five years later. But even this novel was a vehicle for a Dissenter's message, spelled out in a sequel consisting of moral essays, *The Serious Reflections of Robinson Crusoe*. It seems that the hero's name was suggested by the author's admiration for Timothy Cruso, a Dissenting preacher; but mainly the message was implicit in the matter-of-fact story itself, an eighteenth-century version of the Puritan spiritual diary. The hero helped himself – and assessed everything and everyone in economic terms. He preserved his morality through almost thirty years on his island, instructed the basically noble savage, Friday, in the Christian religion, and was assisted in his self-help by an approving God. In the world now opening up to the industrious middle classes of England, nothing seemed impossible to the determined individual. Defoe's *Tour*, published in 1724, showed Crusoe-like enterprise transforming Great Britain and, as he almost always thought, improving it – and he rejoiced to see men and women improving themselves in the process. As a lively novel of 1722 made clear, in this new society even respectability was not an impossible goal for a whore, if she was Moll Flanders. Over the seas lay many lands presenting still greater opportunities for profit and for mission. Defoe's God-fearing but self-helping Englishman was voyaging into the world, both to exploit it and to instruct it.[28]

Swift had a vastly more complicated purpose in mind when he published *Gulliver's Travels* in 1726. He attacked the prominence given by Defoe to commercial enterprise. When he realized the consequences for Ireland of economic exploitation by the English, he did not hesitate to say so – with a wrath which made Defoe's Dissent seem like a tea party. But he was not really interested in any isolated individual such as a shipwrecked sailor. To him the essential problem was man in society. The individual had to relate to others, and in order to do so had to come to terms with, and to control, the brutal power of the irrational passions of his animal nature. And while Defoe liked stories to have happy endings, Swift found no answer to his problem.

Lemuel Gulliver is sent on voyages to contrasting lands – Lilliput, where the inhabitants are six inches high, and correspondingly ridiculous, and Brobdingnag, where the gigantic inhabitants feel themselves in a position to assess the English as 'the most pernicious race of little odious vermin that nature ever suffered to crawl upon the surface of the earth'. He visits Laputa, a land where the men are mad about science and the

---

[28] See G. A. Starr, *Defoe and Spiritual Autobiography* (Princeton, N.J., 1965), and Peter Earle, *The World of Defoe* (London, 1976).

women are mad about visitors more interesting and more useful than the scientists. Finally he finds himself in a land ruled by the Houyhnhnms, horses whose 'grand maxim is to cultivate reason and to be wholly governed by it', but also peopled by the ugly, irrational, totally undignified, man-like Yahoos. The energy and brilliance of the imagination which conceived these various fantastic beings, and the half-convincing straightforwardness of the narratives about them, provide the explanation why *Gulliver's Travels* was instantly placed near the top of English prose and has retained much of its popularity ever since. As a children's book the first half has even rivalled *Crusoe*. But in writing the book Swift's 'chief end' was, as he put it, 'to vex the world rather than divert it' – for just beneath the surface were the great questions. What is man, so great or so small depending on circumstances and on the ambiguities of his own flawed nature? Do your disputes matter more than the dwarfs' squabbles? Are the beauties which arouse your greed or lust really more attractive than the colossal bodies, with their blemishes and stinks, which terrified and horrified Gulliver in the land of the giants? How helpful in the real challenges confronting man is your science? Are the people whom you profess to love really more admirable than the Yahoos?

Gulliver's Travels referred to the disputes between Catholics and Protestants: 'It is computed that eleven thousand persons have, at several times, suffered death, rather than to submit to break their eggs at the smaller end.' Wars costing many millions of lives have been fought over differences in opinion, 'for instance, whether *flesh* be *bread*, or *bread* be *flesh*; whether the juice of a certain berry be *blood* or *wine*; whether whistling be a *vice* or *virtue*; whether it is better to *kiss a post*, or *throw it in the fire*; what is the best colour for a *coat*, whether *black*, *white*, *red* or *grey* and whether it should be *long* or *short*, *narrow* or *wide*, *dirty* or *clean*, with many more.' And a similar tone marked the references to English politics in the age of Sir Robert Walpole. Among the Lilliputian dwarfs, Flimnap the Treasurer kept his high position by dancing on the tight-rope, and other ministers were awarded coloured silken threads for their lesser skills in acrobatics. Swift asked: are your much vaunted and well rewarded religious and political activities really more than that?

For half a century he took his place among his fellow men as a priest. Those sermons which have survived are severely plain and moral. His first major satire, *A Tale of a Tub*, was written soon after he became a clergyman in 1694 and was based on the theological reading which he had had to undertake in order to be ordained. Its mockery of 'Peter' was the old Anglican attack on the Papal claims; the doctrine of transubstantiation is reduced to Peter serving up a brown penny loaf as mutton. Its fiercer contempt for the coarser 'Jack' was the new Anglican hatred of the Presbyterian followers of Jean Calvin and their even more fanatical allies. Its hero was 'Martin', so named because Anglicanism seemed to stand close to Martin Luther, although in the mind of Swift its appeal was far more rational than Evangelical.

Swift's *Argument against Abolishing Christianity*, written in 1708, was his first minor masterpiece of prose irony. Its serious message was that 'real Christianity' had been 'for some time wholly laid aside by general consent, as utterly inconsistent with all our present schemes of wealth or power.' For men who pursued wealth, power or wit after a rejection of rational Christianity as defined by 'Martin', Swift had only contempt. Had the current attacks on Christianity not given them a suitable subject, he wrote, the 'Free-Thinkers' of the time would have had nothing to 'divert their spleen from falling on each other, or on themselves'. It is therefore possible to present Swift as in religion and politics the perpetual Cavalier, who 'loved authority more dearly than anything else'.[29]

Much evidence has survived about his life as Dean of St Patrick's in Dublin, between his arrival to take up residence in the mood of an exile in 1714 until he was deprived of speech and reason by a stroke in 1742. Most of his activities were examples of the conduct hoped for from an eighteenth-century clergyman. As he devoutly attended daily services, officiated at

---

[29] Nigel Dennis, *Jonathan Swift: A Short Character* (New York, 1964), p. 30. A study of the religious background of *A Tale of a Tub* was made by Philip Harth in *Swift and Anglican Rationalism* (Chicago, Ill., 1961).

a weekly Communion (the only such service in Dublin), preached once a month and administered the cathedral's affairs, he showed a rare devotion to duty. He allocated a third of his income to charities; he left almost all of what he saved to found a lunatic asylum. He wrote with such passion in defence of the Irish poor against exploitation that he became a popular hero, cheered in the streets. He also keenly defended the interests of fellow clergymen less privileged than he became. He first made himself known to the London politicians when the Irish clergy sent him over to argue for a reduction of their taxes; in the end he was successful by persuading Harley. Dean Swift, in the end undeniably the cleverest and most famous man in his Ireland, was in many ways an advertisement for 'real Christianity'.[30]

But he never wrote a theological or devotional masterpiece, or found much time in his later years to read other men's efforts in the religious field. His *Letter to a Young Gentleman lately entered into Holy Orders* (1721) was almost entirely taken up with warnings against preachers' affectations. He gave advice as a stylist; his own style is summed up by his advice that 'when a man's thoughts are clear, the properest words will generally offer themselves first, and his own judgement will direct him in what order to place them, so as they may be best understood.' He warned the young gentleman against attempting 'to explain the mysteries of the Christian religion'. 'If you explain them, they are mysteries no longer; if you fail, you have laboured to no purpose.' It was not that Swift was at heart an atheist or an agnostic: 'no gentleman of a liberal education, and regular in his morals, did ever profess himself a Free-Thinker.' But it seemed 'most reasonable and safe . . . upon solemn days to deliver the doctrine as the Church holds it, and confirm it by Scripture.' That did not suggest that his own thoughts on theology were clear.

Thoughts on Religion, published after his death, pointed dis-

---

[30] Louis A. Landa studied *Swift and the Church of Ireland* (Oxford, 1954). Ricardo Quintana, *The Mind and Art of Jonathan Swift* (Gloucester, Mass., 1965), decisively showed that Swift's motivation was Christian. See also Peter Steele, *Jonathan Swift: Preacher and Jester* (Oxford, 1978).

creetly to some uncertainty as to what would happen were the mysteries of Christianity to be explained. On the one hand, it was Swift's maxim that 'I am in all opinions to believe according to my own impartial reason'. On the other hand, reason might not always confirm conventional beliefs and 'the want of belief is a defect that ought to be concealed when it cannot be overcome'. The latter thought was worked out with evident sincerity. 'I am not answerable to God for the doubts that arise in my own breast, since they are the consequences of that reason which he hath planted in me, if I take care to conceal those doubts from others, if I use my best endeavours to subdue them, and if they have no influence on the conduct of my life.'

Swift's variety of rationalism was compatible with this conservatism, and he explained why. 'Liberty of conscience, properly speaking, is no more than the liberty of possessing our own thoughts and opinions, which every man enjoys without fear of the magistrate; but how far he shall publicly act in pursuance of those opinions, is to be regulated by the laws of the country.' That was where he parted from Defoe. He said of his profession: 'I look upon myself, in the capacity of a clergyman, to be one appointed by Providence for defending a post assigned me, and for gaining over as many enemies as I can.' But he never fully explained whether or not he was prepared to defend all the usual Christian doctrines – a remarkable silence in a clergyman so eloquent. About 'Christ's divinity' he wrote this: 'in a country already Christian, to bring so fundamental a point of faith into debate, can have no consequences that are not pernicious to morals and public peace.'

As a boy Swift longed to be 'used like a lord'. As a man, for many years he hoped for promotion in the Church and was dissatisfied with his Dublin Deanery because it was so far from the royal corridors and the coffee-houses of London. The main reason why he was never made a bishop or an English dean was, no doubt, that the politicians – even those whom he served as a journalist – were afraid of his independence, which he often flaunted. It cannot have helped that he was the author of a violent lampoon on the Duchess of Somerset, Queen Anne's friend. But the rumour may well have been true that the Queen was scandalized by *A Tale of a Tub* because it seemed to mock all religion (or at least so seemed when interpreted to her by her favourite archbishop, Sharp). It was Swift's fate that neither his brand of intellectual high spirits nor his insistence on asking questions could fit comfortably into the Church he had chosen to serve.

There is often in his writing the sense that human nature ought to be rational but cannot bear to be, and therefore needs to control its passions by religion. For Swift acknowledged the passions: they were life-giving. Men were not rational horses. He wrote: 'In two points of the greatest moment to the being and continuance of the world, God hath intended our passions to prevail over reason. The first is, the propagation of the species, since no wise man ever married from the dictates of reason. The other is, the love of life, which, from the dictates of reason, every man would despise, and wish it at an end, or that it never had a beginning.' Yet individuals and societies must discipline this pulsing life of the instincts by the acceptance (at least in public) of the religion and morality reckoned orthodox. The passions must be censored. The central Swiftian argument about religion can be presented simply: 'We need religion as we need our dinner, wickedness makes Christianity indispensable, and there's an end of it.'[31]

The trouble about Dean Swift was, however, that he could never bring himself to believe with his whole heart that the public religion of his society, the orthodoxy of the Church of England, was entirely reasonable. In *A Tale of a Tub* Martin may be right, but he is the tale's dullest character. Swift's own religion was deliberately dull. He despised 'the art of wetting the handkerchiefs of a whole congregation' or 'drivelling to a multitude'. Partly this was due to a fear of what he and others would have found, had he bared his heart to the public. His essay on *The Mechanical Operation of the Spirit* probed the emotional (including sexual) pressures which made men get excited about religion. It was not reassuring. As John Traugott has observed, Swift 'wanted to rebuild the churches in the

---

[31] Patrick Reilly, *Jonathan Swift the Brave Desponder* (Manchester, 1982), p. 215.

decayed parishes of London, to establish bishops in the New
World, to make the Church a reality in the daily lives of his own
parishioners, and yet his obsessive probing of psychological
realities which bring assumptions of the glory of the rational
faculty into question, his hatred of man's pretensions to
spirituality, make of his religion more of an anxiety than a
faith.'[32]

What he wanted to be his innermost religion is hinted at by
odd phrases: 'God's mercy is over all his works, but divines of
all sorts lessen that mercy too much.' 'We have just enough
religion to make us hate, but not enough to make us love one
another.' But actually the religion of love was not the heart of
Swift's religion. He himself hated more successfully than he
loved. He sometimes claimed that while he hated mobs he
could love individuals, and it is true that he attracted many
friends and was kind to many sufferers. There was, however,
some blockage in him which prevented the full joy of love either
for God or for any human being. He suddenly remarked: 'Most
kinds of diversion, in men, children and other animals, are an
imitation of fighting.' He was often coarse in his writing. He
wrote perhaps the cruellest poem ever written about a woman.

We simply do not know what this ultimately isolating
blockage was, since he burned almost all his private papers.
Many biographers have attempted to trace the consequences
of an obscure birth, of the humiliation of being, in his most
formative years, a mere secretary to Sir William Temple, of the
unwillingness to marry either of the two women, Stella and
Vanessa, who came to live near him in Ireland, to whom he
wrote immortal letters, and who both adored him. Was he the
illegitimate son of Sir William Temple's father? Was Stella the
illegitimate daughter of Sir William, whom Swift could neither
marry formally nor abandon? These are improbable suggestions, but they have been made. Their possibility is a reminder
of how deep the mystery of his personality remains. All that we
know is that he was afflicted with a disease of the ears which
often made him sick, dizzy and unable to relate to the stable,
everyday world. He was afflicted, too, with a lifelong sense of

---

[32] *Focus: Swift*, ed. C. J. Rawson (London, 1971), pp. 116–17.

frustration – as well he might be, for it has been said accurately about this Englishman exiled to Dublin: 'he towers head and shoulders above all his contemporaries both as a writer and as a man.'[33]

For some reason, what Swift felt in his heart tormented him. He found relief in preaching to others, but could not accept orthodoxy. He also found relief in defending the liberty of others, but could not accept democracy. W. B. Yeats translated the famous Latin epitaph, not mentioning Christ or penitence, which this unique dean wrote to go over his grave in his cathedral:

> Swift has sailed into his rest;
> Savage indignation there
> Cannot lacerate his breast.
> Imitate him, if you dare,
> World-besotted traveller; he
> Served human liberty.

BISHOP BUTLER'S TRIUMPH

It was the achievement of Bishop Joseph Butler to answer the most important of the intellectual attacks on Christianity made by his predecessors in the English debate. We do not belittle that achievement if we also notice that his arguments became less convincing in relation to the more radical attacks made after his death in 1752.

He wrote in the plain, conversational style of his age but his thought was both original and profound, and his mind was totally free of the coarseness which infected Swift. Although at home in the age of reason, he meditated, as did Swift, on the limits of reason's power in the real world. Walking one night in his garden (as was his curious habit), he suddenly stopped and asked his chaplain: 'What security is there against the insanity of individuals? The physicians know of none . . .' After another

---

[33] Bonamy Dobrée, *English Literature in the Early Eighteenth Century* (Oxford, 1959), p. 474. The standard biography is by Irvin Ehrenpreis (2 vols, London, 1962–67).

turn in the garden, he asked a still more searching question. 'Why might not whole communities and public bodies be seized with fits of insanity, as well as individuals? . . . Nothing but this principle, that they are liable to insanity equally at least with private persons, can account for the major part of those transactions of which we read in history.'

His life had a calm which contrasts with Swift's tempestuous voyage. His parents were Presbyterians. In 1713, when he was aged twenty-one, and still a pupil in a Dissenting academy, he wrote the first of a series of modest but acute letters to the great Samuel Clarke. 'I have made it, sir, my business, ever since I first thought myself capable of such sort of reasoning, to prove to myself the being and attributes of God.' Within a little over five years he had become an Anglican, an Oxford graduate, a priest and preacher at the Rolls Chapel in London. In 1726 he published *Fifteen Sermons* on ethical topics in that chapel. He had of course delivered many more, but he offered the public only the best.

In his will he was to order 'that all my sermons, letters and papers . . . be burnt without being read by anyone.' Ten years later, in 1736, he published *The Analogy of Religion, Natural and Revealed, to the Constitution and Course of Nature*, a book written in the very quiet but also very comfortable rectory at Stanhope in the diocese of Durham. Shortly before its publication Queen Caroline summoned him to be a member of the theological discussion group which met regularly in her private rooms. The favour of the monarchy and the applause of the educated public made him Bishop of Bristol; the Deanery of St Paul's was added to supplement the meagre income. Finally, in 1750, he became Bishop of Durham and lived long enough to deliver a 'charge' to his clergy in which he urged the fulfilment of pastoral duty with detail which showed that he was no recluse – and no optimist. The surviving evidence about his daily life is not much but indicates that he lived simply as a bachelor, gave much of his large income away, and spent much of what remained on the improvement of his official houses.

Butler's talk seems to have been like his writing: always serious, commonsensical and moral but never unaware of mysteries which he could neither express nor understand. It

was the approach most likely to appeal to soberly and religiously minded readers in his age, and we can see the merit of
it if we compare him with his fellow philosopher and fellow
bishop, George Berkeley.

Berkeley was an Irishman of English descent, brilliantly
gifted and most attractive. Dean Swift was among his many
friends – and remained a friend even when his own Vanessa,
who had hoped to marry him, left her fortune to Berkeley in her
bitter disappointment. This paragon of the Irish virtues was a
devout Christian and it was his ambition to answer current
attacks on his religion by three responses: by the foundation of
a college in Bermuda to train missionaries (including Red
Indians) for the American colonies; by the writing of books
which would be as learned and as witty as any adversary's; and
by a new philosophy, better than Locke's, which would show
God among the realities. He was confident. He announced that
'those difficulties which have hitherto amused philosophers,
and blocked up the way to knowledge', were but 'dust'.
Philosophers, having raised a dust, had complained that they
could not see. However, his projects failed. The Bermuda
college never received enough support from Sir Robert Walpole's government in far off London or from the Americans
who were at least six hundred miles distant, although many
private subscribers were fired by the idea. The learning and wit
also foundered. Books in dialogue form such as *Alciphron*
(published in 1732 on his return from America) allowed a
philosophical atheist and an anticlerical rake to attack Christianity before being defeated. Although clever, the argument
offended the godly without seriously impressing the sceptics;
and rumours often surrounded Berkeley that, if not an atheist
himself, he was a facetious fool.

The philosophy did not persuade. Its essential point was
that to exist means either to be perceived or to perceive.
Material objects are known to exist only in so far as they are
perceived – either by us or by God. What most truly exists is
what perceives: 'There is not any other substance than *spirit*, or
that which perceives.' Yet the world could never be reliably
perceived by human beings with their fallible senses of sight
and touch, so that if the things of this world 'really exist, they

are necessarily perceived by an infinite mind; therefore there is an infinite mind or God.' This argument Berkeley called 'a direct and immediate demonstration of God's existence – a short method of crushing scepticism.' The philosophy of immaterialism has continued to interest philosophers, but most Englishmen reckoned that they could refute it by much the same means as Samuel Johnson employed, when he kicked a stone. Berkeley did not defend himself against his critics at any length. He concentrated on work as Bishop of Cloyne in the extreme south of Ireland, and on writing about the medical 'virtues of tar-water'. Towards the end, his mind had ceased to perceive reality.[34]

Butler knew that the English who were likely to respond to a serious argument about religion were interested in goodness more than in Berkeley-type cleverness. The first great task of his life was therefore to answer cynicism about human nature. So he advocated right conduct by arguing that virtue corresponds with our nature and vice violates it; that we have a passion for 'benevolence' as well as a passion for 'self-love'; that we have a conscience which rightly demands absolute authority over all our passions and assures us that 'self-love', properly understood, perfectly coincides with 'benevolence' and thus with virtue. All the 'passions, affections and appetites' constituting human nature should, and could, be ordered in the performance of duty. 'Duty and interest', he wrote, 'are perfectly coincident: for the most part in this world, but entirely and in every instance if we take in the future and the whole.'

Up to this point, Bishop Butler's thought was similar to the moral philosophy propounded by the third Earl of Shaftesbury. Without recourse to any appeal to a revelation in religion, the conscience could assure any man that in the long run his true self-interest would coincide with his true duty to others. Meanwhile, 'self-affection' and 'benevolence' could be held in balance without much difficulty. This tension-free

---

[34] See A. A. Luce, *The Life of George Berkeley* (London, 1949), and, for the philosophy, G. J. Warnock, *Berkeley* (revised, Harmondsworth, Middx, 1969). Edwin Gaustad studied *George Berkeley in America* (New Haven, Conn., 1979).

moral sense was to Shaftesbury akin to the aesthetic sense by which men discerned the harmony in things; the conscience saw that life itself made an orderly system. And Butler agreed with Shaftesbury that the commands of the conscience would deserve to be obeyed, even if God did not offer heaven as a reward. He agreed, too, that the various affections made a neat system. But to him religion was essential, for the hope of heaven was a part of what it meant to be human. 'There is a capacity in the nature of man,' he wrote, 'which neither riches nor honours, nor sensual gratifications, nor anything in this world can perfectly fill up or satisfy.'

Butler's writing about God was a reply to the Deists' appeal to 'natural religion' as a reality far more reliable than Christianity's ridiculous claim to be the revealed religion.

Unlike Berkeley, Butler did not feel obliged to offer a direct consideration of atheism. In his *Analogy* he took 'it for proved, that there is an intelligent Author of nature and natural Governor of the world', but little apart from the sheer existence of God could be proved; instead of proof, 'probability is the very guide of life'. The *Analogy* began strangely with a discussion of the probable effect of death; but at least this beginning showed that the author had paid some attention to the possibility that we do not survive death to enjoy future rewards for morality – a possibility which the Deists disregarded, or pretended to disregard, in order to extoll the splendid certainty of 'natural religion'. The 'proper proofs' of natural religion were, Butler held, not intellectual certainties, demonstrable however immoral a sceptic might be. They were 'the proper motives to religion, from our moral nature, from our natural apprehension of God under the character of a righteous Governor and Judge'. It is the power of the conscience that leads us 'to consider this little scene of human life, in which we are so busily engaged, as having a reference, of some sort or other, to a much larger plan of things.' But that is as far as natural religion will take us. God's 'moral government', like the rest of his government of his creation, 'must be a scheme quite beyond our comprehension'. Natural religion was as uncertain as religion based on revelation.

Since his opponents protested that Christianity contained

'many things very different from what we should have expected,' he replied that this very unexpectedness was to be expected. He was therefore not ashamed to present Christianity in an orthodox way, with miracles and Christ's mediation between God and man, but he claimed that its total effect was to satisfy the conscience and thus the reason of mankind. 'The truth of our religion, like the truth of common matters, is to be judged of by all the evidence taken together.' Those who still persisted in rejecting it were sternly reminded that Christianity did not attempt to satisfy the immoral, although it was, 'in reason, sufficient to prove and discipline that virtue, which it presupposes'. The conclusion of the *Analogy* was a solemn warning that men should not 'vilify or disregard Christianity as if they had a demonstration of its falsehood'. Scepticism need not be the most rational attitude, and 'blasphemy and profaneness' were temptations arising from 'the wantonness of vanity or mirth'.

In that society there was sufficient weight in those arguments for the book to make a material difference to the situation described in the 'Advertisement' at the beginning. 'It is come, I know not how, to be taken for granted, by many persons, that Christianity is not so much as a subject of inquiry; but that it is, now at length, discovered to be fictitious. And accordingly they treat it, as if, in the present age, this were an agreed point among all people of discernment; and nothing remained, but to set it up as a principal subject of mirth and ridicule, as it were by way of reprisals, for its having so long interrupted the pleasures of the world.' In that 'Advertisement' Butler announced his aim: not to prove the truth of Christianity, but to show that 'there is strong evidence of its truth' – and no clear case that 'there is nothing in it'. He did not appeal to the authority of the ancient Church, as did more technically learned theologians who attempted to refute the new Deists – men such as the great conservative scholar, Daniel Waterland. He would go, as his opponents did, to the tribunal of reason. He did not name a single one of his opponents; and this calm silence was perhaps his most eloquent argument. Any reply to him would have to be made at his level of seriousness, integrity and rationality – and his contemporaries produced no such reply.

In the long run, however, Bishop Butler's intellectual triumph was far from complete. A Victorian sceptic who had formerly been a clergyman, Leslie Stephen, passed a fair judgement on the whole debate in three sentences full of wisdom. 'The Deists,' he wrote, 'had triumphed so far as they had insisted upon the impossibility of reconciling the historical conception of the Christian Deity with the conceptions of metaphysical optimism. The Christians, on the other hand, had shown as triumphantly that the attempt to transfer to the pale abstraction called Nature the emotions excited by the historical religion was futile in itself, and condemned by the broad facts of experience. The result was the decline of the pale shadow of Christianity which called itself Deism, and which had never excited enthusiastic or disinterested support; and, on the other hand, the practical admission that Christianity must seek for support elsewhere than in abstract philosophy.'[35]

HANDEL'S TRIUMPH

Henry Purcell created the vacancy which George Frederick Handel filled. Purcell's father and his uncle were leading musicians at the court of Charles II and he was appointed organist at Westminster Abbey in 1679, at the age of twenty. As fertile as his contemporary Christopher Wren, he produced new music to honour many royal occasions under the later Stuarts and William and Mary. He wrote the incidental music for over forty plays; he was the father of English opera, although the infant died when he died; his songs charmed the court and were sung in taverns. In church music his was the greatest name since Orlando Gibbons, who had died in 1625,

---

[35] Leslie Stephen, *History of English Thought in the Eighteenth Century*, Vol. 1 (London, 1876), p. 271. More recent studies include E. Mossner, *Bishop Butler and the Age of Reason* (New York, 1936), and Austin Duncan-Jones, *Butler's Moral Philosophy* (Harmondsworth, Middx, 1952). James Downey studied the surviving sermons of Butler, Berkeley and some contemporaries in *The Eighteenth Century Pulpit* (Oxford, 1969).

and some of his anthems are still in the repertoire wherever this choral tradition is kept alive. The tradition had been totally silenced by the civil wars, but some of Purcell's early anthems were in the Elizabethan style of polyphony with which he had grown familiar as a chorister in the Chapel Royal. He developed as a master of the new style, introduced from Italy and France under Charles II's patronage. The 'verse anthem' now combined some choral work with declamatory solos and long passages for the violins. The noblest music of this kind was composed for the funeral of Queen Mary. It was performed again at his own funeral, only eight months later.

This master musician has been greatly and rightly honoured, but his development was cut short by his death in 1695; his achievement was the work of a mere fifteen years. John Blow had taught him, and was both his predecessor and his successor at the organ of Westminster Abbey; but when Blow died in 1708 it was seen that there was no other successor of stature. Purcell's fame has also been limited by his failure to develop music which could support popular religion. He worked for the royal court, the royal churches and the London theatre. J. A. Westrup has written that his verse anthems are 'akin to the spirit of Renaissance architecture. It is impossible to feel that they are intended solely for the glory of God. They are also to be noted and approved by man; there is an element of ostentatious magnificence that is wholly absent from the church music of the Elizabethans.'[36]

Handel made his name among the English in 1713 by the *Te Deum* which he composed for the celebration in St Paul's of the peace of Utrecht; he was much indebted to Purcell. On various other grand occasions his music was the climax of the elevating theatricality which the Church of England could still produce in order to express a nation's faith in its own power and wealth and in God, its most reliable ally. The anthems which Handel wrote for performance by voices and orchestra in the chapel of the Duke of Chandos (who had done very well out of the war, as paymaster to Marlborough's armies) were also magnificent, but the most sumptuous of this inexhaustibly fluent com-

---

[36] J. A. Westrup, *Purcell* (revised, London, 1975), pp. 207–8.

poser's church music was heard at the coronation of George II
in 1727. The ceremony in Westminster Abbey was conducted
in considerable disorder due to slackness and the new king was
well-known to be stupid, coarse and vicious. But Queen
Caroline had shown her greater intelligence by becoming
Handel's patron while he still lived in Germany; he was to
repay her by a softly elegiac anthem for her funeral. Meanwhile
the coronation anthems were admired by all. When the chorus
first exploded in 'Zadok the priest', after the mounting excitement of the introduction by the strings, men knew that a high
priest had arrived to consecrate the English Establishment.

Handel's music never voiced the self-surrender to the
Saviour, the tender gratitude for salvation and the longing for
death to be found in the Passion music or the cantatas of his
German contemporary, J. S. Bach. Bach was content to remain
within, and to perfect, the already great tradition of Lutheran
church music. Handel had his opportunity as a young man to
find security in that tradition; and he refused. His training to
write *Messiah* was far more bizarre. He went to half-Catholic,
half-pagan Italy, and dedicated himself to the opera – music
with 'a spiritual climate as remote from Christianity as it is
from Freud'.[37]

On his move to London in 1710, at the age of twenty-five, he
began a campaign to persuade the richer inhabitants of the
world's greatest city to support Italian operas, of which during
his life he composed some forty. One reason why he turned to
the 'sacred oratorio' in the 1740s was that not enough of the
English shared his own devotion to these elegant trivialities.
Samuel Johnson was to describe Italian operas as an 'exotic
and irrational entertainment'. Handel's own contemporary,
Dean Swift, denounced 'that unnatural taste for Italian music
among us which is wholly unsuitable to our northern climate
and the genius of the people, whereby we are over-run with
Italian effeminacy and Italian nonsense.' What Swift preferred
was shown by his active support of John Gay's *Beggar's Opera*, a
musical comedy which extolled in English the merits of manly
English vice; the girl who sang the leading part in that very

---

[37] Winton Dean, *Handel and the Opera Seria* (Berkeley, Cal., 1969), p. 11.

successful show found herself marrying a duke. It was noticed with disgust that, in order to sing as adults, some Italian choirboys agreed to be castrated. It did nothing to reconcile the English that this practice had begun in the papal choir.

As a young man in Rome in 1708, Handel had turned to the New Testament as a means of getting round the papal ban on operas in the holy city. In one of the noblemen's palaces, before a splendid audience of cardinals and other ornaments of a music-loving aristocracy, he had presented *La Resurrezione*, starring a *prima donna* as Mary Magdalene and adding a dramatic appearance by Lucifer to the biblical text. There were only two choruses. The sacred character of the libretto did not conceal from anyone the true purpose of *La Resurrezione*, which was to display a sumptuous union of counterpoint composition derived from Handel's own Germany with the Italian lyricism which he had acquired. The Pope rebuked those who had taken part in this blasphemy, and Handel, scenting danger, went on his way to Naples.

Messiah was an altogether more mature and serious work, composed in London in the autumn of 1741 on the basis of biblical texts selected by a rich patron of the arts, Charles Jennens. The theme unlocked all the treasure-house of the composer's genius and he wrote the music within three weeks. But this speed was possible only because *Messiah* contained so much music lifted from the secular operas; in a sense it would be true to say that it had taken Handel more than thirty years to write it. In his lifetime the work secured no great success. It received its first performance at a charity concert in Dublin in 1742; Swift was still Dean of St Patrick's and had been very reluctant to allow his cathedral's choristers to join Handel's choir. When it was performed in London, no title was given; for some years it was discreetly called 'a new sacred oratorio'. The usual setting was a charity concert, in aid of the Foundling Hospital. The score was not published until eleven years after Handel's death. The basic difficulty was that the Church of England agreed with the Pope that there must be no representation of Christ or of any other biblical personage on the stage; and even this studiously non-dramatic oratorio, a *Messiah* without a Christ, was suspect for it echoed secular operas, it was performed in theatres and it earned money for 'fiddlers' (as Swift called them). It is entirely understandable that after experiencing the Church's suspicion of *Messiah*, Handel left the New Testament alone. His only other handling of a Christian theme, *Theodora* (1750), was his own favourite among his oratorios but a commercial flop – as he complained, because rich Jews would not buy tickets for a piece which glorified a Christian martyr, and because rich ladies did not wish to see virtue praised.

His oratorios with Old Testament subjects varied in their popularity (and merits), but here was a world where the English felt at home. Handel heeded the warning given by the Bishop of London when the first of these oratorios was planned in 1732; although based on an Old Testament book which failed to mention God, *Esther* must on no account include any action on the stage. Within this limitation, the Hebrew scriptures provided many acceptable subjects. The English could recognize kings and high priests, war lords and matriarchs, and humbler heroes and lovers, who were agreeably energetic, combative and fond of food, drink and marriage. The victories and harvests which their tribal God had bestowed on the Ancient Israelites seemed to the English well-earned. The most popular of all these oratorios was *Judas Maccabeus*, composed in 1746 to celebrate the defeat of the Jacobite rebels at Culloden. The glory of the music helped the audience to forget that the event in Jewish history being celebrated was a successful rebellion.

Handel had arrived in London friendless and not knowing a word of the language. Many anecdotes were based on the fact that he never did master English – but about three thousand people insisted on attending his burial in Westminster Abbey in 1752. It is recorded that 'he would often speak of it as one of the great felicities of his life that he was settled in a country where no man suffers any molestation or inconvenience on account of his own religious principles.' That was a theologically enigmatic tribute; but the compliment was returned by the English. After a delay *Messiah* won its vast and enduring popularity. At the first London performance, George II began the practice of standing for the 'Hallelujah' chorus, and George

III continued the custom, as part of his passion for Handel's music. These Hanoverian kings did not, we may reckon, understand much; but they understood that a German composer of Italian operas had greatly helped the English to affirm their calmer creed and to celebrate the coronation of the King of kings and Lord of lords.[38]

---

[38] The best studies are Herbert Weinstook, *Handel* (revised, New York, 1959), and Paul Henry Lang, *George Frederic Handel* (London, 1967).

CHAPTER TWELVE

THIRTY YEARS OF CRISIS

THE RESTORED CHURCH
AND CHARLES II

We now turn from architecture, thought and music to church
history. Here we find that the first thirty years after 1660 were a
hectically active period, beginning with the restoration of
Charles II, continuing with the turbulent reign of James II,
and ending with the offer of the throne – or, rather, thrones – to
William and Mary. These years saw the birth of the party
system in English politics; the 'Tories' and the 'Whigs',
although later sometimes honoured as the ancestors of the
modern Conservatives and Liberals, were so named by their
enemies from words used in Catholic Ireland and Presbyterian
Scotland for despised outlaws. This fiercely quarrelsome time
also saw the birth of the denominational system in English
religion, and we shall look at the conflict from three points
of view – Anglican, Protestant Dissenting and Roman
Catholic.[1]

The Church of England became a denomination in sociolo-
gical fact, if not yet in theological theory. The word 'denomination' was an eighteenth-century word and the word 'Anglican'
did not come into general use until the nineteenth century, but
in the period 1660–90 the Church of England effectively
abandoned the attempt to be the Church of the whole English
people. It became instead a church with its own fairly systematic teaching, exchanging the dream of national unity in religion
for the possibility of becoming one day the mother of a

---

[1] The best political narrative is J. R. Jones, *Country and Court: England 1658–1714*
(London, 1978). Norman Sykes surveyed ecclesiastical history, 1660–1768, in *From
Sheldon to Secker* (Cambridge, 1959).

worldwide denomination, the Anglican Communion.[2]

The basis on which the Church of England contracted from its previous national comprehensiveness was the Act of Uniformity, to which the royal assent was given amid great ceremony on 19 May 1661. Under this act, 'every parson, vicar or other minister whatsoever' had to declare his 'unfeigned assent and consent to all and everything contained and prescribed' in the new edition of the Book of Common Prayer. He had also to declare that 'there lies no obligation upon me or on any other person, from the oath commonly called *The Solemn League and Covenant* to endeavour any change or alteration of government either in Church or State.' In particular, 'it is not lawful, upon any pretence whatsoever, to take arms against the king'. The Act, or the Prayer Book which it enforced, prescribed that it was not lawful for anyone to minister in the Church of England as a priest or a deacon without ordination by a bishop, or without the bishop's licence for a particular parish. It forbade anyone to teach in a school without the bishop's licence, or in a university without conforming to the Church of England. It also laid a new emphasis on confirmation by a bishop: 'there shall be none admitted to the Holy Communion, until such time as he be confirmed, or be ready and desirous to be confirmed'. The exceptive clause was necessary because while the layman might be willing to go to the bishop, the bishop might not be willing to hold a confirmation in the neighbourhood.

On the face of it the act applied to all Englishmen, but when it was passed everyone knew that there would be dissent from some who could plead either Protestant or Catholic scruples of conscience. This had been a deliberate decision not to include them. In effect the Act made the Church of England one religious body among others, a body united more firmly than ever before by a strict adherence to its Prayer Book, by an ardent obedience to its kings, and by the acceptance of a bishop's authority over his diocese. In Richard Hooker's time

---

[2] *Anglicanism*, ed. P. E. More and F. L. Cross (London, 1935), illustrated the thought and practice of the Church of England in the seventeenth century, but the word used in its title did not appear in any of the extracts in its 811 pages.

it had been an open question whether Queen Elizabeth's campaign against the Puritans would succeed. It had also been questionable whether episcopal ordination was necessary in order to minister in the Church of England. Some holders of distinguished offices – for example, Hadrian Saravia who ministered at Hooker's deathbed and wrote a defence of episcopal government – had never been made priests by bishops. Now the Church unambiguously adopted a church order which later generations would call 'Anglican' or (especially in the USA and in Scotland) 'Episcopal'. When Presbyterian ministers were consecrated as bishops for Scotland, they were carefully made deacons and priests first, as their predecessors had not been under James I. Only the willingness of many Anglicans to receive Holy Communion in Presbyterian or Lutheran churches when abroad remained from the old attitude.[3] When Izaak Walton, a London businessman who had retired to the bishop's palace in Winchester to pray and to fish, wrote gracious little biographies of leading Anglican divines of the previous period, he stressed their orthodoxy and if need be adjusted the facts a little.[4]

As Bishop of London and Archbishop of Canterbury, Gilbert Sheldon was the chief architect of the Church of the Restoration. He had not forgotten a vow made by Charles I that all the lands recently taken from the Church would be restored to it. He had kept this vow buried in the ground for the thirteen years of the Church's tribulations. Now the opportunity had come. Gilbert Burnet, a bishop of a later generation, deplored Sheldon's inflexibility towards the Dissenters and claimed that he did not have 'a deep sense of religion if any at all', religion being to him merely 'an engine of government and a matter of policy'. But the condemnation was unfair. Although certainly no preacher and incapable of appreciating the delicate Jeremy Taylor, Sheldon was a deeply convinced High Churchman. He was bold enough to rebuke both the King and the Lord Chancellor, Clarendon, for their indul-

---

[3] Norman Sykes, *Old Priest and New Presbyter* (Cambridge, 1956), probed the changing attitudes. See also Willem Nijenhuis, *Adrianus Saravia* (Leiden, 1980).

[4] David Novarr studied *The Making of Walton's Lives* (Ithaca, N.Y., 1950).

gence towards the Dissenters in defiance of Parliament – and to
deliver this rebuke in no uncertain terms while the aged Juxon
was still at Canterbury and it was still possible that the King
and his chief minister might appoint a less outspoken churchman as Juxon's successor. His Anglican conservatism was
sincere, had been tested in the fires of adversity, and was to
inspire a strenuous, meticulous and effective feat of administration.

Moved to the archbishopric at the age of sixty-five, Sheldon
achieved fourteen years of work. Although physically weak
towards the end, his motto was 'Do well and be merry'. He
interpreted his responsibility for the welfare of the whole
Church as strenuously as William Laud had done. He insisted
that his fellow bishops should work as hard as he did in their
dioceses – and, to prove it, should send detailed reports to him.
In practice this involved the supervision of a massive effort to
restore the pre-war routine of cathedrals, colleges and
parishes, although the buildings had been desecrated or
neglected, service books and archives had been lost, and
church life had become confused and demoralized in the
strange half-persecution under the Commonwealth. To give a
small instance: the tradition of boys singing in church choirs
had to be started again from scratch. 'A cursory survey of
Sheldon's immense correspondence', writes his modern biographer, 'can only lead the reader to conclude that never was a
church leader beset by a more stubborn, self-seeking, litigious,
insubordinate corps of clergymen.'[5] Yet this old man and his
assistants recreated a routine of church life which has not been
interrupted since his day, for all its continuing imperfections.

Sheldon understood the laity better than Laud had done.
Whereas Laud had relied on courts created by the prerogative
of the Crown, Sheldon made do with the much less alarming
diocesan courts. Whereas Laud had rejoiced to see the clergy
treated as a separate and superior caste, Sheldon agreed that
parsons should be taxed like other men and restricted to
pastoral or intellectual work. And whereas Laud had alienated
many of the richer laity (including the former spokesman of the

---

[5] V. D. Sutch, *Gilbert Sheldon* (The Hague, 1973), p. 152.

Commons who was now Earl of Clarendon and Lord Chancellor), Sheldon took infinite trouble to keep on good terms with MPs and with other gentlemen; his dinners for them were splendid and systematic. He criticized the King for not sticking closely to the wishes of the House of Commons, with the frankness which he also showed when criticizing him for his mistresses. And even the shifty and irresponsible Charles acknowledged Sheldon's invaluable strengths. Indeed, it has been suggested that the crucial decision-making event in the whole Restoration settlement was a private meeting in Canterbury on the evening of 25 May 1660 between Sheldon and the King, when Charles was making his triumphant return to his capital. Clarendon was the only other person present.

When Sheldon died in 1677, the King's chief minister was Thomas Osborne, Earl of Danby, a tough Yorkshireman. He lived to sign the invitation to William of Orange to intervene to stop the aggressive Roman Catholicism of James II. He had formed a working alliance with the old archbishop and had virtually promised the position to a close friend of his, who would carry on a policy acceptable to the Cavaliers in the House of Commons: Henry Compton, then in his mid-forties and Bishop of London.

The son of an earl killed in the civil war, Compton was one of the few clergymen of noble birth and had quickly been made a bishop and tutor to the King's two nieces, Mary and Anne, each a future queen. He was, however, much more than a careerist or a courtier. Although he had never properly functioned as a parish priest or theologian, he discharged energetically the duties of a bishop, still chiefly disciplinarian. He demanded high standards of care in the great diocese of London, holding regular conferences with his clergy; and, since the American colonies did not have their own bishop and were not likely to get one, he attempted to supervise their churches also, using previously rather vague rights as Bishop of London. He was equally self-confident when dealing with royalty and statesmen, and was a strong defender of Anglican against Roman Catholic claims. Like Danby, he signed the historic invitation to William in 1688. If he had been made Archbishop of Canterbury in 1677 he would have had at least thirty years in which to build on Gilbert Sheldon's achievement (he died in 1713).

However, he was passed over in 1677 and the leadership of the Church of England was offered to a Dean of St Paul's, William Sancroft. Compton had the same bitter experience in 1690, when he was again thought by many to be the inevitable choice for Canterbury. He had officiated at the coronation of William and Mary (introducing the ceremony of the presentation of the Bible) and had virtually taken over the duties of archbishop for more than a year. Yet once again a Dean of St Paul's was appointed – John Tillotson. Almost certainly Compton was frustrated in 1677 because King Charles was asked by his brother James not to promote a man so hostile to Roman Catholicism; and almost certainly he was frustrated in 1690 because King William was asked by his wife Mary not to appoint a man so worldly. During the excitements of 1688 he had escorted Princess Anne to safety at the head of a troop of cavalry. With reason King James had once told him that he talked like a colonel.[6]

Archbishop Sancroft was a man more delicately conscientious than Bishop Compton. By nature a scholar, he had already refused the bishopric of Chester. When Charles offered him Canterbury, he protested 'that he was very unfit for it thro' his solitary life which he had a long time led'. In saying that, he was too modest about his part in the rebuilding of St Paul's. Whilst archbishop he had the courage to take action against Bishop Wood of Lichfield, who had grossly neglected his duties and was now suspended from them for two years. But Sancroft's unhappiness in the political field became clear. He found great difficulty in dealing with the prolonged crisis created by James's conversion to the Church of Rome. While Compton was one of those who demanded James's exclusion from the succession ('the whole civil and religious constitution of the realm is in danger'), Sancroft defended the royal duke's hereditary right. When Compton refused to suspend one of his clergy for preaching against King James and was suspended himself by King James's Ecclesiastical Commission, Sancroft

---

[6] See Edward Carpenter, *The Protestant Bishop: Henry Compton* (London, 1956).

pleaded that he was too old to serve on that body. When the combative Compton leaked to the public the seven bishops' private petition against James's Declaration of Indulgence, Sancroft was uncomfortably surprised to find himself cheered by the mob and imprisoned in the Tower of London. He would not effectively defend King James against indignant Protestants such as Compton; yet he could not take the oath of allegiance to William and Mary. Suspended in 1689 and deprived of his archbishopric in 1690, he would not join in Jacobite plots to bring James back. He would have preferred William and Mary to be regents in James's absence, but put forward no workable alternative when they refused to fall in with this plan.

Activists such as Compton were insensitive when they despised this timid, good man for his agonies of conscience. No conscience as delicate as his could find it easy to know how the Church of England ought to interpret the 'divine right' of kings when the king was a Roman Catholic. Already under Charles II this had become a problem for those in the know.[7]

The year 1660 saw the restoration of a king; all else followed from that. And Charles II, a selfish sensualist, lacked any personal qualification to be Supreme Governor over a Church of England which during his reign was rich in pastors, in scholars and even in saints. The royal bedchamber was the place where he was most himself, with its unsynchronized clocks, yapping spaniels and feuding mistresses. It belonged to a universe utterly different from, say, Ralph Josselin's parsonage in Essex, where the earnest diary-keeping vicar worried endlessly over other people's problems – his wife's moods, his ten liveborn children's illnesses, his parishioners' sins and woes, his country's prosperity and its dealings with other nations – all in the faith that God could be prayed to and that he ruled over the world righteously, in small as in great matters. Charles has exercised a romantic appeal upon many generations, and in his lifetime he was often liked; he was amiable to all those who did not inconvenience him and was

---

[7] R. A. Beddard's work on the Church under Sancroft is awaited. W. G. Simon studied *The Restoration Episcopate* (New York, 1965).

admired by his people as a sportsman, wit and sexual athlete.
His court was preserved for posterity in the flattering portraits
by the Dutchman, Peter Lely, and the German, Godfrey
Kneller. But we know that Clarendon was dismayed by his
irresponsibility as a king, as was Archbishop Juxon. Those two
could be dismissed as boring and incompetent old men –
Clarendon went off into exile, to rewrite and complete his
History of the Rebellion and a sad autobiography, and to die – but
they should not be forgotten when we assess Charles II, for
they were churchmen and Royalists. In his *History*, Clarendon
pretended to have been more of a churchman and a Royalist in
the 1640s than he had been in reality.[8] Their disillusionment
was shared by every man of the age who cared seriously about
Church and State.

The 1650s had left scars on Charles's personality. Super-
ficially the 'merry monarch', he was known by shrewd people
who watched him closely to be, at heart, very sad. He had
become a total cynic about human motives because he had
been for so long surrounded by fellow exiles at each other's
throats. For some deeply resented months he had been compelled to dissemble because he had been the guest of the
Presbyterian Scots. When he became king he did not know
what it meant to be loyal or honest. In exile he had been unable
to contract a marriage thought suitable, and had worked off his
sexuality with ladies of easy virtue and in brothels. The habit
persisted through his life, so that he acknowledged fourteen
bastards but never developed a deep relationship with any
human being apart from his sister, Henrietta-Anne, who died
in 1670. He also made a habit of being foul-mouthed. He seems
to have had no overriding policy, apart from survival in order
to take his pleasures as consolations for this unease at the heart.
If religious toleration was his policy at the beginning of his
reign, it was not at the end. If he had a patriotic wish to wrest
commerce and empire from the Dutch, he did not persist in it,
and the subsidies from France, which have sometimes been justified as part of an anti-Dutch policy, were surrounded by him

---

[8] See B. H. G. Wormald, *Clarendon* (Cambridge, 1951), and H. R. Trevor-Roper,
Edward Hyde, Earl of Clarendon (Oxford, 1975).

with secrecy: he knew how his people would react if told. If he was dynastically-minded and therefore resolved to leave his throne to his brother, he must have known that he was bequeathing a disaster to the nation and did nothing at all to avert it. His apparent acceptance of the suggestion that James's powers might be limited had been no more than a temporary trick.

What his religion was anyone could guess – and many did. When he knew that he was dying he was reconciled to the Church of Rome by a simple priest, Father Huddleston, who had helped him to escape after the battle of Worcester. Possibly he reckoned that this was a 'religion for gentlemen' (as he once declared Presbyterianism was not) – or at least a religion for a gentleman to die in, if by such a conversion he could get rid of a lifetime far from virtuous. Possibly Roman Catholicism was the only faith that had ever aroused any religious feelings in him, and he had postponed his conversion simply because, unlike his brother, he did not think the loss of his throne worth a Mass. But there remains the mystery of his professed willingness, in the secret treaty of 1670, to declare himself a Roman Catholic if the French would pay him to do so and send troops to put down any rebellion. Whether or not he meant this to be more than a diplomatic bargaining counter must remain uncertain. Probably not much weight should be attached to a promise to be reconciled with the Church of Rome when the 'welfare of his kingdom' would permit it.

It was not that he was hostile to the Church of England; he could sing its praises. From a distance he admired the holiness to be found in it. When a prebendary of Winchester Cathedral, Thomas Ken, refused to house Nell Gwynne, one of the King's mistresses, Charles did not hold it against him; not long afterwards he approved his appointment as Bishop of Bath and Wells, saying: 'God's fish! The little black fellow who would not give poor Nelly a night's lodging!' But when he lay dying and the moment of truth had come, Bishop Ken bent low over the Supreme Governor and asked him if he was a member of the Church of England. Charles stared at him silently.[9]

---

[9] For a more favourable portrait see, e.g., Antonia Fraser, *King Charles II* (London, 1979).

PURITANISM BECOMES DISSENT

In the fires of the Anglican persecution which Charles II had to allow, Puritanism became 'Dissent' – a religious minority which in the end was acknowledged because respected.

The development was possible because Puritanism, however aggressive, had always been essentially a religious movement, not a programme to fulfil economic or political ambitions. A twentieth-century scholar has provided this summary of his studies of the Puritans both in England and in the new world: 'We have been told, with various degrees of crudity and subtlety, that Puritanism was the ideology of the bourgeoisie. On that subject there are two simple observations to be made. First, Puritanism never offered itself as anything but a doctrine of salvation, and it addressed itself neither directly nor indirectly to social classes but to man as man. Second, its attractions as a commitment were such that it made converts in all classes – among aristocrats, country gentry, businessmen, intellectuals, freeholders and small tradesmen.'[10] Such observations appear to be valid; and this scholar could easily have extended his list of the Puritans' secular occupations lower down the social scale. Many men without property, even 'masterless men' without regular employment, were Puritans no less than the earls so prominent in the 1640s. They had all undergone the same process of conversion. They had found the same Saviour, and essentially the same authority in some combination of the Scriptures and the Spirit without any need of a priest as mediator or interpreter.

Because its religious energy was the lifeblood of Puritanism, the movement was not destroyed when it met a political catastrophe as sudden and as total as the Norman Conquest six centuries before. It had been defeated largely because it had not agreed on how to handle power, and now when persecuted it was purified. A modern historian of the persecution has written: 'Puritanism became, for a whole generation, more a matter of life and less a subject of theological debate than it had ever been before. With humble amazement, the greatest

---

[10] Alan Simpson, *Puritanism in Old and New England* (Chicago, Ill., 1955), p. 11.

spokesmen of the persecuted groups noted that their sufferings had led to fuller life and to incalculable spiritual benefits.'[11]

It was a real persecution, far more severe than the sufferings of the Anglicans under the Commonwealth. A censorship of printed books was created by the Licensing Act of 1663 and enforced by the 'surveyor', Sir Roger L'Estrange, who held office until 1688. At the Restoration ancient laws were revived under which Puritans could be punished as traitors. The Quakers, for instance, were made guilty of treason by the mere act of refusing to swear allegiance to the king. John Bunyan was imprisoned under the Elizabethan statute of 1593, 'for retaining the Queen's subjects in their due obedience'. But other laws were added inexorably. The Corporation Act of 1661 required all mayors, aldermen, councillors and borough officials to receive 'the sacrament of the Lord's Supper according to the rules of the Church of England'. The same initiation was demanded of all its members by the House of Commons in 1661. In 1664 the First Conventicle Act, replying to feeble disorders, forbade five or more people not of the same household to meet together for worship except in accordance with the liturgy, the penalties being fines or imprisonment or (on the third offence) transportation overseas for seven years. Next year the Five Mile Act forbade ejected ministers to come within five miles of any city, chartered town or Parliamentary borough or any other place where they had exercised their ministry, unless they would take an oath never to attempt 'any alteration of government either in Church or State'. Many ministers were now driven from their homes.

In 1670 the Second Conventicle Act imposed much heavier fines on preachers or hosts who defied the law. A third of the money was to be paid to any informer who brought them to justice. The seizure and sale of a Dissenter's goods was authorized. If he had been comfortable this could reduce him to poverty, and if he was already poor this often meant depriving

---

[11] G. R. Cragg, *Puritanism in the Period of the Great Persecution, 1660–88* (Cambridge, 1957), p. 87. See also C. E. Whiting, *Studies in English Puritanism, 1660–88* (London, 1931); A. C. Underwood, *A History of the English Baptists* (London, 1947), pp. 88–115; R. Tudor Jones, *Congregationalism in England, 1662–1962* (London, 1962), pp. 33–104.

him of the tools of his trade, or of his bed. The severity of imprisonment varied with the term of the sentence and with the prison; gaolers were very much left to their own devices, some being brutal and others indulgent, particularly if paid. But many prisons were so cramped and so foul that the risk of death, or at least of the permanet ruination of one's health, was high. Many a Dissenter needed Thomas Browning's consolation, written to his people from Northampton gaol: 'Come, the worst is death, and that is the best of all.'

The first period of persecution saw far fewer surrenders than was expected. Of the Puritan clergy ejected in 1660–62, only about 210 (about a tenth) conformed, and some fifty more were willing to take the oath required under the Five Mile Act. There could be no complete evidence about the numbers of laymen attending illegal worship (often having also attended their parish churches), but many reports of arrests in many parts of the country survive, alongside many complaints by bishops and others eager to see the law enforced. Obstinately ministers persisted in preaching, although many were reduced to abject poverty; Richard Baxter would recall that 'Mr Chadwick in Somerset for a long time had little but brown rye bread and water for himself, his wife and many children, and when his wife was ready to lie in was to be turned out of door, for not paying his house-rent.' The courage shown by Dissenting ministers who remained in plague-stricken London in 1665, when many of the Anglican parish priests fled, impressed contemporaries; it was to be recalled in a vivid novel by Daniel Defoe, a boy of four at the time (*A Journal of the Plague Year*, 1722). Congregations proved ingenious in providing means for a beloved pastor to escape from his pulpit at a moment's notice, or for women, preferably pregnant, to block the entry of constables. In order to escape detection they were willing to go to fields or woods, barns or caves; to meet very early in the morning or very late at night; or to pretend to be having a party when in fact they were holding a service. They were now bound together not by any belief that they could or should regulate their neighbours but by sheer courage in holding to their own convictions in a day of darkness.

Two great men paid tributes to the quality of the church life

of the persecuted Dissenters. One was John Owen, and he paid
it by what he did as much as by what he wrote (although he
wrote many pamphlets). Appointed by Oliver Cromwell to be
the leading figure at Oxford, he had remained active in
national politics right up to the Restoration; the small congregation which he gathered in his London home, Wallingford
House, had been the centre of opposition to Richard Cromwell
and of support for General Lambert. After 1660 he could still
have led a privileged life, for he married a rich lady and
received an invitation to migrate to New England as the chief
preacher in Boston. Yet he persisted in the dangerous course of
ministering to a small Independent congregation in London,
and added to the risk by doing all he could to keep in touch with
the other Independents being persecuted. And the other
tribute was paid by Richard Baxter, whose poem, 'written
when I was silenced and cast out,' perfectly expressed the
consolation to be found in these gatherings for worship under
persecution:

> In the communion of saints
>   Is wisdom, safety and delight,
> And when my heart declines and faints
>   It's raised by their heat and light . . .
>
> Must I be driven from my books,
>   From house, and goods, and dearest friends?
> One of thy sweet and gracious looks
>   For more than this will make amends . . .
>
> The heavenly hosts world without end
>   Shall be my company above:
> And thou, my best and surest Friend,
>   Who shall divide me from thy love?

For there was a quality in the life of the small, 'gathered'
congregation seldom found in the Established Church. The
bishops' political and social duties in London took them away
from the routine of their dioceses – and that mattered, because
their pastoral duties could no longer be delegated to suffragan
bishops. Despite promises, those invaluable assistants were
not revived at the Restoration. The annual 'visitation' of the
parishes by the archdeacons depended for its vigour on the

archdeacon's personality, and in most dioceses the system by which the archdeacon was assisted by rural deans had fallen into disrepair. The conditions of the priests and the parishes seem to have varied widely. The minimum which bishops and archdeacons tried to enforce was Holy Communion at least three times a year, and Morning Prayer and Litany every Sunday. If possible other services were desirable on Sunday afternoons and on other holy days. Only in a few churches – and those mainly in London – were there daily services.

Many parish priests seem to have been quite well-off; in the 1680s Gregory King guessed that their average annual income was above £50, within the top fifth of the nation. We know that in Essex Ralph Josselin, the Puritan who had conformed, was making about £160 a year in the 1660s, £60 of this coming from his parish's tithes and the rest from land which he either leased out or farmed himself. But in 1670 John Eachard, a university don, published a widely noticed book lamenting the poverty and ignorance of the clergy in the parishes, and his charge that the clergy were held in contempt obviously did not lack all substance.

Attendance in the parish churches often fell off alarmingly as soon as Dissenters knew that they were legally free to worship elsewhere. A major cause must have been the average labourer's identification of the parson with the squire, whose local power was greatly increased by the Restoration. (It was now against the law for people to move to another parish seeking employment or better wages if they could be held likely to be charges on the rates, although the law could not be systematically enforced. Within a parish wages were supposed to be regulated by the justices of the peace, who were almost always squires and employers.) It seems a fair summary to say that the Church of England was not established in the hearts of the people as securely as it was established by the law.[12]

Being aware of the real situation in the parishes, many

---

[12] John H. Pruett, *The Parish Clergy under the Later Stuarts* (Urbana, Ill., 1978), was based on research in Leicestershire. Josselin's uniquely complete personal accounts were studied by Alan Macfarlane in *The Family Life of Ralph Josselin*.

Anglicans wanted to include at least some of the Dissenters in the National Church, despite the decisions of 1661. In 1668 Sir Orlando Bridgman led a substantial move in this direction but was defeated in the Commons. A considerable number of mayors, magistrates or juries refused to convict or punish Englishmen whose one offence seemed to be a determination to worship God in their own way. The King himself intervened to save Baptists from death in Aylesbury, to secure George Fox's release from Scarborough Castle, and on other occasions. It was clear even before the Act of Uniformity came into effect in 1662 that Charles wished to exercise his royal prerogative by allowing exemptions. Frustrated by Parliament's refusal to endorse his first Declaration of Indulgence in December 1662, he at last made the intervention he wanted by his second Declaration of Indulgence in March 1672. This allowed Protestant Dissenters to meet for worship if both the place and the preacher were licensed – and also allowing Roman Catholics to worship in private. The 'indulgence' not only confirmed widely held feelings of repugnance against the persecution, but also showed how limited its success had been. All the Quakers and some other Dissenters refused to apply for licences, but 1,610 were soon issued – 939 to Presbyterian congregations, 458 to Independents or Congregationalists, and 210 to Baptists. Almost five hundred prisoners were released. Parliament forced the King to withdraw his declaration a year after issuing it, but not before bishops had expressed alarm at the size of the Dissenting congregations – and not before the Presbyterians had seized their chance to hold fresh ordinations.

The King now abandoned the Dissenters, and under the Test Act of 1673 they (like the Roman Catholics) were excluded from office under the Crown unless they would first receive Holy Communion in the Church of England. But they could now be reasonably sure that the eventual outcome would be along the lines indicated by a bill which was passed by the Commons before being wrecked by the Lords. This allowed Protestants to meet for worship not in accordance with the Book of Common Prayer, if they took the oath of allegiance and subscribed to the doctrinal parts of the Thirty-Nine Articles. In the 1675 by-elections Dissenters began playing an active role in the Parliamentary struggle, supporting candidates thought to be sympathetic. They could not yet get to be elected themselves; of all peers and MPs in the Cavalier Parliament of 1661–79, only Lord Wharton publicly attended Dissenting worship, although a number maintained ejected ministers as their private chaplains. But Dissent was obviously going to survive, and its votes were going to count. When the Cavalier Parliament was eventually dissolved, the new House of Commons included more than twenty definite Dissenters, more than twenty close supporters; and the majority in it was commanded by the Earl of Shaftesbury. The movement he led was a definite party with a clear programme: the Whigs. Shaftesbury did not disdain help from Dissenters in his campaign to exclude the King's brother, James, from the succession to the throne as a confessed Papist. A Baptist printer, Francis Smith, was his most effective propagandist. During the struggle over 'exclusion' which ended with the dismissal of another parliament at Oxford in March 1681, Dissenters showed enough enthusiasm against James to alienate Charles permanently. They also angered the supporters of hereditary monarchy, now increasingly called 'Tories'.

The consequence was that during the period of triumph which lasted until his death, the King who had previously favoured toleration threw the Dissenters to the Anglican, Tory wolves. The renewed persecution included both the severe enforcement of the penal statutes and also some mob violence: the excitement of the 'exclusion' campaign had proved infectious. In despair an ejected Presbyterian minister and three Baptist ex-soldiers were involved in the Rye House plot to kill the King and his brother on the way back from the races in Newmarket, in 1683. Two years later many Dissenters in the south-west identified themselves with the rebellion led by the Duke of Monmouth against the new king, James II, who was at that stage still courting the Church of England; these rebels had the additional motive of despair about employment, due to the recession in the cloth trade. Both the plot and the rebellion were dismal failures, and the retribution was severe. Monmouth's defeat at the battle of Sedgemoor was followed by the 'Bloody Assize' under Judge Jeffreys, and hundreds of executions. But in March 1686 this, the severest period of the persecution of Dissent, came to an end. The King, seeing that the Church of England would never consent to the liberty he wanted for Roman Catholics, began courting the Dissenters. He issued a general pardon to those imprisoned for religious offences. Just over a year later he followed this up by his first Declaration of Indulgence, suspending both the penal laws and the Test Act.

The leading Dissenters refused to express gratitude to the King. They were well aware of the unpopularity both of James's policy to make his fellow Papists prominent in the country's government, and of his disregard of Parliament in his bid for the Protestant Dissenters' support. It needed no great political subtlety to calculate that the only assured protection for Dissent would come from the House of Commons. However, it also needed no great optimism to see that if the King's policy was to be frustrated his enemies, too, would have to bid for the Dissenters' support. The bishops, who astonished James by their petition against the reading of his second Declaration of Indulgence in church, took care to announce their 'tenderness' towards Dissent, and Lord Halifax spoke for most of the leading Anglican laity when he made handsome promises in his *Letter to a Dissenter*. From the Netherlands William made known his willingness to grant religious liberty. Plainly, a new day was coming.

In the Convention Parliament which assembled in February 1689, after James's flight to France, the leading High Anglican and High Tory statesman, the Earl of Nottingham, introduced the bill which three months later became law as the Toleration Act. Under this act Dissenters were still not allowed to enter public service; the Corporation Act and the Test Act remained on the statute book despite the new king's clumsy attempts to secure their repeal. Indeed, even the persecuting acts remained; their operation was only 'suspended' in that Dissenters could obtain licences to hold meetings for worship if they took the oaths of allegiance and left the doors unlocked, and their ministers who subscribed to the doctrinal articles (thirty-six of the thirty-nine) were exempt from the Five Mile Act. Quakers were allowed to make a declaration instead of taking an oath, but Roman Catholics were excluded from these concessions, as were Unitarians.

THE EFFECTS OF THE PERSECUTION

We do not know precisely how many Protestant Dissenters survived the great persecution with their religious loyalties intact. The general picture seems to be that many of the smaller sects which had proliferated under the Commonwealth were killed off, but that the main Dissenting denominations had kept enough members to be able to expand when the persecution ceased and public 'meeting houses' could be built. In 1676 an official census reported 108,676 Protestant Dissenters over sixteen, but the Dissenters' own counts in the 1690s showed that this was an underestimate, since the Anglicans wanted to belittle the problem. In 1715–18 a nationwide survey of Dissenting congregations was instigated by Dr John Evans on behalf of the committee of ministers of the 'three denominations' in London. At about the same time returns were made to their own central office by the Quakers. These surveys showed that in England (including Monmouthshire) there were then 638 Presbyterian, 203 Independent, 211 Particular or 'Seventh-day' Baptist, 122 General Baptist and 672 Quaker congregations. On this basis it has been calculated that those attending Dissenting places of worship then amounted to just over six per cent in the population of almost 5,500,000, nearly 180,000 of them being Presbyterians, nearly sixty thousand Independents, nearly sixty thousand Baptists and nearly forty thousand Quakers. Whether or not these figures are accurate, by 1715 Dissent was certainly a community of over a quarter of a million, mocking the Anglicans who had tried to exterminate it.[13]

The great persecution had, however, damaged Dissent in three important ways – by crippling its leadership, by narrow-

---

[13] See *Freedom after Ejection*, ed. Alexander Gordon (Manchester, 1917), and Michael Watts, *The Dissenters*, Vol. 1, pp. 267–89.

ing its appeal in society, and by destroying the Presbyterian system of synods.

Leadership was not given by martyrs of undying fame, although there were martyrs, and impressive ones. Of the Whigs who suffered after the Rye House Plot, Lord Russell, Algernon Sidney (executed because of his notes for a book he was writing) and Sir Thomas Armstrong (kidnapped back to England from Holland) had fine minds. And Abraham Annesley spoke for many when he said, before he was hanged after Monmouth's rebellion: 'As a true Englishman, I thought it my duty to venture my life in defence of the Protestant religion against Popery and arbitrary power . . . which I do not repent. For had I a thousand lives they should all have been engaged in the same cause.'[14] But such men could easily be reckoned traitors and did not make unambiguous heroes for the Dissenters to venerate. Most Dissenters would have nothing to do with rebellion.

No Dissenting minister who began his work after 1660 had the stature of Owen or Bunyan (they died in the 1680s), or Baxter or Fox (who died not long after greeting the Toleration Act). No doubt this was partly a quirk of history, but it must have been a factor that the difficulties of getting educated, encouraged, published and known were all so great. Dissent became a movement of quiet people, ministered to by steadily faithful pastors.

No Dissenter was politically prominent before John Bright, the Victorian Quaker. There were a few politicians willing to speak up loudly for Dissent, but none of them was very effective in that role in this period. The best known was the Earl of Shaftesbury, an immensely able man who had served Cromwell and Charles in his time and was always admired by his agent, the great John Locke. But Shaftesbury disliked clergymen, including Dissenting ministers, and he was called 'the greatest whoremaster in England' by Charles, an expert. His real interest came to be in limiting the powers of the monarchy. Determined to exclude James, he plunged recklessly into a

---

[14] See Iris Morley, *A Thousand Lives* (London, 1954), and Peter Earle, *Monmouth's Rebels* (London, 1977).

head-on confrontation when the predominant feeling in the country was against any risk of civil war; and he made the fatal error of backing the illegitimate and brainless Duke of Monmouth as the Protestant candidate for the throne. The reason seems to have been that Monmouth on the throne would have been under the Whigs' thumbs, whereas the more plausible candidate, James's own daughter Mary, was married to William of Orange, already a formidable ruler and to Shaftesbury an uncongenial one. This aristocrat of high ambition did not deserve the savagery of the satire heaped upon his head by John Dryden; but he also did not deserve much of the support which innocent Dissenters gave him. He gambled – and lost, dying in exile in 1683.[15]

In the House of Commons in the 1660s the totally altered position was shown when old William Prynne, who defied Laud and Cromwell alike, actually apologized for statements which were thought to encourage sedition. Later the leading Dissenter in social and political circles was William Penn, but his leadership, too, was handicapped; as we have seen, he was too involved in founding Pennsylvania and in guiding the Quakers, and then he became far too closely identified with James II. The leading MPs who represented Dissent in the 'exclusion' campaign and after were Richard and John Hampden, the son and grandson of the squire who had defied Charles I over Ship Money. The family remained very rich and could afford to pay a fine of £40,000 when the government was taking vengeance on people connected, however remotely, with the Rye House Plot. But the new John Hampden had a complex and tragic private life. During the 1680s he lost both his Christian faith and his adored wife (who died in childbirth), and was profoundly distressed; in the end his health gave way and he committed suicide, in 1696.[16]

The lack of leadership when the grand old Puritans had died off was connected with another development caused by the

[15] See K. H. D. Haley, *The First Earl of Shaftesbury* (Oxford, 1968), and J. R. Jones, *The First Whigs* (London, 1970).

[16] Douglas R. Lacey studied *Dissent and Parliamentary Politics in England, 1661–89* (New Brunswick, N.J., 1969).

persecution: the narrowing of Dissent's appeal in society. Although Puritanism had cut across the classes, that was not so true of the Dissent that emerged to enjoy toleration. There were many gentlemen still faithful to Dissent in 1700, but in the countryside the tenants or labourers of an Anglican squire often dared not offend him by forming their own chapel during the persecution, and when toleration came they did not have the energy. In the big houses or the towns everyone with social, political or intellectual ambitions was sorely tempted to forsake Dissent and many yielded to the temptation. Robert Harley, the son of a Puritan squire, would never have fulfilled his real vocation, which was to manage the House of Commons as Speaker or as Queen Anne's chief minister, if he had refused to worship with the Church of England. (Although always devious and often drunk, he seems to have remained a kind of Puritan.[17]) Bishop Joseph Butler was an example of a far more respectable man who had to abandon his parents' Presbyterian faith in order to enter his own kingdom of Oxford and philosophy. A boy who was at the same Dissenting academy as Butler, Thomas Secker, grew up to be Archbishop of Canterbury for ten years from 1758. Those left behind in Dissent were men and women whose ambitions, although still often eager, were more provincial and domestic. The backbone of Dissent came to be tradesmen in the towns, the men for whom Defoe wrote. They often prospered and the industrious thrift which they learned from parents and preachers helped mightily; but they were not going to risk spoiling good businesses.

The damage wrought by persecution also included the end of the Presbyterian system by which congregations had been linked in presbyteries and synods.

Such gatherings to discuss the problems of Church and State could not meet without arousing the fiercest wrath of the magistrates and central government; it was a time when it was officially argued that psalm-singing might conceal plotting for another civil war. Therefore they lapsed, even among those who still called themselves 'Presbyterians' – and they were not revived after 1689. The result was that the Presbyterians,

---

[17] Angus McInnes studied *Robert Harley, Puritan Politician* (London, 1970).

although they outnumbered the Independents and Baptists put together, ceased to possess their own system of church government and became virtually indistinguishable from their fellow Dissenters. The local 'meeting house' or 'chapel' was the be-all and end-all of church life – or, as it was put in the more theological terms which had been adopted by the Savoy Conference gathering representatives of more than a hundred congregations back in the still-hopeful days of autumn 1658, the Lord Jesus Christ called his followers out of the world 'to walk together in particular societies' and 'there are not instituted of Christ any stated synods in a fixed combination of churches'.[18] Of the ministers ejected from the Church of England in 1660–62, less than ten per cent are known to have accepted this Independent view of church order; yet twenty years later this view had prevailed in practice, thanks to the practical impossibility of the Presbyterian alternative. Indeed, among the Presbyterians control tended to be vested in a small group of elders or other trustees rather than in the congregation as a whole, and when the persecution was over those exercising this control tended to pride themselves on their progressiveness, success and respectability rather than on their theological orthodoxy.

The stage was now set for a theological development which would have seemed unbelievable in 1660. Presbyterian ministers were encouraged by the laymen closest to them to be progressive, and what progress meant to a minister was defined by what was taught at the best 'Dissenting Academies' where men were trained for this ministry now that the universities were closed to them. These academies often provided an education better, because wider and more modern, than the Oxford or Cambridge curriculum; it is said that some three hundred of their pupils were sufficiently distinguished to be included in the *Dictionary of National Biography*. But the academies, usually small and unstable, depended on the personalities of their staff. If the staff held unorthodox views, they could quickly and permanently influence their pupils. During

---

[18] See A. G. Matthews, *The Savoy Declaration of Faith and Order, 1658* (London, 1959).

the eighteenth century such pressures from the academies, reinforced by local trustees, inclined many, perhaps most, Presbyterian ministers towards an acceptance of current intellectual fashions, and therefore towards heresies which would have dismayed their Calvinist forefathers.[19]

THE END OF POPISH PLOTS

The third feature to be noticed in English church history 1660–90, is the end of the belief that Roman Catholics were about to impose their faith on the country by military, or at least political, action.

The end of Roman Catholicism as a political force did not mean the end of the Roman Catholic community. On the contrary, the community entered the eighteenth century as it had entered the seventeenth. On the ground it was a denomination drawing from the Mass a quiet strength which politics could neither give nor take away. Its size can be estimated with some confidence. In 1676 a census produced 11,867 names of Recusants over the age of sixteen in the Anglican province of Canterbury. In 1687 John Leyburn, the first Roman Catholic bishop to appear in the Midlands and the north for half a century, thought that he had confirmed about twenty thousand people. Although both figures were obviously rough, it seems reasonable to conclude that during the second half of the seventeenth century England included under fifty thousand Roman Catholics over sixteen. This community's priests were housed mainly in the homes of country gentlemen who had kept to the old religion, although some were in lodgings and tried to minister in towns. The papal agent,

---

[19] In *The English Presbyterians* (London, 1968), G. C. Bolam, Jeremy Goring, H. L. Short and Roger Thomas traced the evolution 'from Elizabethan Puritanism to modern Unitarianism'. Earlier studies included Olive M. Griffiths, *Religion and Learning* (Cambridge, 1935). In *English Education under the Test Acts* (London, 1931), H. J. MacLachlan studied the Dissenting academies. J. W. Ashley Smith, *The Birth of Modern Education* (London, 1954), put them in the context of the multiplication of private schools in the eighteenth century.

Agretti, estimated in 1669 that there were approximately 230 'secular' priests, 120 Jesuits, eighty Benedictine monks, fifty-five Franciscan friars and a few Dominicans and Carmelites. Other evidence suggests that this total of some five hundred clergy was about average for the period. In sum, the size of this community constituted no great threat to its fellow citizens, numbering over five millions.

Nor was there strong leadership. An old-fashioned community could be expected to look up to its aristocrats, but it so happened that at this time some leading peerages which had been identified with the old faith in the past were held by Protestants. Not a single Recusant peer or prominent gentleman of an 'old family' threw himself into supporting James II's schemes; the King had to use Anglicans, men such as Robert Spencer, Earl of Sunderland, whose conversion to the Church of Rome was manifestly political, or Irish and other strangers to London. The seventh Duke of Norfolk, who by historical precedent might have been expected to rally the old England around the old religion, announced that he was a Protestant and took himself off to Paris. Sunderland was therefore King James's closest confidant, and he was to show what he was made of by renouncing his conversion and serving King William. A compulsive gambler, he needed the money and, as has been said, 'it was a matter of indifference to him which master he cheated'.[20]

The clergy had no outstanding leader. Nominally their chief was the aristocratic Philip Howard, but he was a cardinal in Rome. Rome eventually, in January 1688, produced four bishops as 'vicars apostolic', but their powers over their four 'districts' – London, Midland, Northern and Western – were limited and none of them was of outstanding quality. The King was anxious that his favourite Jesuit, Edward Petre, should be made a bishop and a cardinal, but Innocent XI always refused. Locally the pastors were usually good priests operating in conditions which handicapped them; they could not wear cassocks in public or set up their own presbyteries. But they did

---

[20] David Ogg, *England in the Reigns of James II and William III* (Oxford, 1955), p. 193. J. P. Kenyon wrote a biography of Sunderland (London, 1958).

not include any hero of high spiritual stature. Saints such as Henry More, who had ministered year after year among the plague-stricken poor of London before being hanged in 1645, were remembered but not replaced.[21]

Few laymen were in any mood for plots or aggression. What they worried about was survival, and it was a financial worry. Often they were on reasonably good terms with their neighbours and thus escaped the full rigour of the penal laws, but Charles's grant of formal toleration to them in 1672 provoked an ominous reaction. The Pope was burned in effigy on bonfires.

The 'Popish plot' was announced in August 1678 by Titus Oates, a disgraced naval chaplain who had fled to a Jesuit college in Flanders and had been expelled from it. His patron was Israel Tonge, a beneficed Anglican clergyman and a maniac, already the author of virulent pamphlets against the menace of Popery. It was plainly implausible to claim, as Oates did, that the Jesuits were planning the murder of a king who had already risked much to get his Roman Catholic subjects tolerated. It was no more than an old wives' tale to believe that the Jesuits would also arrange another great fire in London. Even had their reports seemed more likely, it was not to be expected that a jury would hang a dog, let alone the more than thirty Englishmen who perished, on the testimony of such self-evident rogues. But a story was told by Oates and others, of sinister conversations overheard and treacherous correspondence which might still be intercepted. It stirred memories of Guy Fawkes and of the Elizabethan plots, of the horrors chronicled by John Foxe, of all the anti-papist folklore on which the bulk of England had been half-educated. Perhaps the Pope was after all Anti-Christ, although most English theologians had become embarrassed by this tradition? And the story was told at a time when the Earl of Danby was nearing the end of five years as Lord Treasurer in an atmosphere of great suspicion. He had secured Parliamentary finance for an army to intervene on the side of the Dutch

---

[21] Dom Basil Hemphill studied *The Early Vicars Apostolic of England, 1685–1750* (London, 1954).

against the French; now the Dutch and the French had made peace, yet the army was still in being and at the King's disposal. What was that army for? Although Danby made much of being a defender of the Church of England, many people were prepared to believe that he was working to make Charles an absolute king on the model of Louis XIV – and that he was himself in the pay of the French. Above all, many people were alarmed by the prospect of the succession of a Papist to the throne, now that it was clear that Charles was not going to have legitimate children. In a pamphlet published in 1678, *An Account of the Growth of Popery and Arbitrary Government*, Andrew Marvell wrote: 'Popery is such a thing as cannot, but for the want of a word to express it, be called a religion; nor is it to be mentioned with that civility which is otherwise decent to be used in speaking of the differences of human opinion about divine matters.' This abuse showed how different 'Popery' seemed in London political circles from the peaceful lives of Recusant gentlemen in the countryside, who were undeniably religious and usually on terms of civility.

So the fantastic story of the 'Popish plot' got a hearing. Then the hearing became hysteria, because of two events which Oates and Tonge cannot have anticipated. Oates repeated his story on oath before a Westminster magistrate, Sir Edmund Berry Godfrey, who was friendly to Dissenters; and after a few days, in a mystery which has never been unravelled, Sir Edmund's body was found in a ditch with a sword through it. The story included allegations against a Jesuit priest, Edward Coleman, who belonged to the household of the Duke of York; and when Coleman was arrested for investigation correspondence between him and foreign Catholics, including the French king's Jesuit confessor, was seized. Coleman had discussed the dissolution of Parliament and toleration for Roman Catholics, although the Duke was not directly implicated.

It was now inevitable that Coleman should be hanged, followed by three other priests; and that everyone afraid of James, of the Jesuits or simply of Popery should join in the agitation. The Lord Chief Justice, Scroggs, made a name for himself by the brutal energy with which he hounded the alleged perpetrators of the Popish Plot. Those put to death included Lord Stafford, condemned by the House of Lords. The victims also included (in 1681) Oliver Plunkett, the saintly Roman Catholic Archbishop of Armagh, who was falsely said to have conspired to bring a French army over to Ireland. It was the judicial murder of a pastor who had always steered clear of politics.[22]

The fact that Coleman had distributed some French subsidies to Lord Shaftesbury and to other Whigs was forgotten when, contributing to the intense excitement, it became known that the Lord Treasurer had also asked for French money. That caused Danby's fall and his imprisonment in the Tower. The threat arose that he would be impeached and that under examination he would reveal Charles's own financial dealings with the French. The Cavalier Parliament was accordingly dissolved; and in the elections the Whigs were led to victory by their leader, Shaftesbury, who had already been made Lord President of the Council. James, who had been sent into exile, believed as did many others that his brother was about to abandon him as his heir – or at the very least agree that his powers as a future monarch should be strictly limited. All Roman Catholics except James were by the Second Test Act (1678) excluded from both Houses of Parliament, and for a time the whole community lived in acute fear. About four hundred gentry and their dependents were jailed for refusing to swear the oath of allegiance of which Rome still disapproved. About a hundred priests were also arrested; twenty-three died in prison and seventeen were executed.

In the end that crisis passed. The perjuries of Oates and his collaborators became too obvious to be ignored any further, and the hysteria which they had aroused spent itself. The King displayed a tactical skill and energy which were out of keeping with his previous, and subsequent, muddled indolence. But the basic fact was that Shaftesbury's Whigs had over-reached themselves in an England without any appetite for another civil war.[23]

---

[22] See Emmanuel Curtis, *Blessed Oliver Plunkett* (Dublin, 1964), and Thomas O'Fiaich, *St Oliver of Armagh* (Dublin, 1981).

[23] The best study is J. P. Kenyon, *The Popish Plot* (London, 1972).

It was realized that it would be very difficult to exclude James from the throne of Scotland, and that the Irish Catholics would probably fight in his defence. The English, too, now inclined to accept him. Led firmly by Archbishop Sancroft, the Church rallied round the principle of the divine right of the hereditary monarchy and on the whole believed James's repeated assurances that if he became king he would do no harm to the National Church. If Anglicans were anxious at the prospect of a Papist king, they reassured themselves by the thought that no child of his present wife, Mary of Modena, had survived infancy. Since 1681 she had not conceived, with the probable result that James's throne would be inherited by his daughter from his first marriage, Mary, who in 1677 was married to the Protestant champion, William of Orange – or by her sister Anne, who was even more staunchly attached to the Church of England. And to clinch the argument in favour of the hereditary principle, in the closing stages of his reign Charles found himself able to manage without recourse to Parliament since the French were willing to send adequate subsidies. He even found himself able to pay an army, always useful to deter rebellion at home.

James II therefore in 1685 inherited a position more secure than had been the lot of any previous Stuart. He often said as much – and took pride in the fact that he had thrown it all away in order to promote the Catholic religion. After the ruin of his plans and his flight into a dozen years of exile, he of course frequently asked himself why God had not granted success as a reward for his costly devotion to the true faith. Fortunately for his faith, an explanation could come pat: he had been punished for his notorious indulgence in the sins of fornication and adultery. But we must search for a fuller answer to the questions: why did the reign of James II, which began so auspiciously, develop into being the greatest and the last of the 'Popish plots' – and why did it end as disastrously as the reign of Mary I?

THE FALL OF JAMES II

James II was genuinely religious, even while unable to live chastely, but very arrogant and obstinate, sure that God had given him authority and that he had no need to concern himself much with lesser men's reactions. The one criticism he had of his father was that he had concealed his pride too often. He himself never took any trouble to do so. To the end of his days he seems to have been unaware why he was hated and feared. When seven Anglican bishops petitioned him to withdraw his Declaration of Indulgence, he was incoherently astonished at their impertinence. As they knelt before him he could only splutter: 'This is a standard of rebellion!'

Since his life would have been so much easier had he been able to satisfy his religious instincts in his father's church and place himself at the head of the Tories, historians have often asked why he became a Roman Catholic. He knew the price to be paid. On 29 January 1669 Charles and James met Lord Arundel of Wardour (a well-known Recusant) and two other courtiers, to announce their conversions to Rome and to seek advice about 'settling the Catholic religion' in England. The courtiers were sworn to secrecy, and James attempted in vain to get permission from Rome to regard himself as a Catholic while still attending the services of the Church of England. He did not cease to receive Holy Communion with the Anglicans until 1672, and he attended other Anglican services for another four years. He claimed that he incurred these sacrifices because he had been persuaded of the truth of Catholicism by reading Richard Hooker, but the rest of his life would not support any picture of him as a calm and scholarly theologian. He never wrote down any personal apologia, and was mentally incapable of doing so; but it is possible to reconstruct his psychology. As a proud soldier-prince James believed in religious authority; as a lustful sinner he needed it, to be sure that his sins could be forgiven. He knew that the Roman Catholic Church claimed a religious authority, and a power to forgive sins, far more imposing than the Church of England's. While he was king he caused scandal by kneeling before an archbishop on a mission from the Pope. If we ask why he did not allow his

conversion to transform his sex life, we have to understand that
for Catholic princes in that age a deathbed change was usually
reckoned adequate. And if we ask why he paid no attention to
the pleas for caution which came from his co-religionists,
including the Pope, the answer seems to be that he was sure
that he understood England. He was confident that, once
Catholics were free to worship, to preach and to teach in
public, and once those who listened could see that they would
not be penalized for following their consciences, the converts
would come in a flood. He brushed aside warnings because he
was a great prince (he had defied the Pope by marrying Mary
of Modena before the Vatican had approved the arrangements) – and because he was himself a convert (as his first wife,
Clarendon's daughter Anne Hyde, had been). To his simple
mind the spiritual authority of the Roman Catholic Church was
a fact bigger than any pope's claim to advise princes about sex or
politics; and it had only to be displayed in order to be believed.

On the basis of this psychology, the pattern of James's reign
makes sense. His first aim was to persuade the Tory majority
dominating the House of Commons to tolerate Roman Catholics. To him, it seemed not an impossible aim; after all, they
were Royalists – and they were tolerating as their king one who
openly attended Mass and who refused to include an Anglican
communion in his coronation. When the Anglican Tories drew
back, he changed his tactics completely. He allied himself
instead with the Dissenters whom he had previously despised
as 'republicans' (his worst term of abuse). He issued a Declaration of Indulgence on his own authority, suspending all restrictions on worship and all tests for office-holding. He thought it
his duty to install teachers of the true faith in positions of
influence; hence his determination to see Roman Catholics
appointed as Dean of Christ Church and as President of
Magdalen College at Oxford.

As opposition to this policy hardened, so his insistence on his
authority hardened all the more. The moves which he took
showed how much authority the Crown still possessed. Personally or through agents James brought pressure on his ministers
to accept his religion; on MPs to support his programme; on
electors to vote for loyal MPs and city councils. He dismissed

his brother-in-law, Rochester, from his post as Lord Treasurer when he refused to be converted. Through the revived Ecclesiastical Commission under Judge Jeffreys he secured the suspension from office of the Bishop of London, who had refused to suspend a 'No Popery' preacher. He appointed fellow Catholics in considerable numbers to be Lord Lieutenants in the counties, justices of the peace and officers in the army. He placed Ireland under another Roman Catholic, the Earl of Tyrconnel. But he remained impervious to the popular clamour about 'Popery and arbitrary government', and it seems highly likely that one reason why he had this contempt for the clamour was that he knew that it was not his intention either to overthrow the Church of England or to abolish Parliament. He expected Anglicans soon to accept his right to govern according to his conscience and what he kept on calling 'the ancient constitution'. Surely their Tory Royalism would reassert itself? Eventually they would, he believed, accept their own moral obligation to be reconciled to the Catholic Church. He was certainly not the lackey of the French king, who offered him no help against either the Duke of Monmouth or William of Orange. Nor was he the lackey of the Pope, who at this stage was interested chiefly in his quarrel with the French king. It was very unfortunate for James that in 1685 Louis XIV began a successful police action to drive all the Protestants (the Huguenots) out of France, but there is no evidence that a similar intolerance was intended for England.

In September 1688 James began to retrace some of his steps in an effort to win back the support of the Anglican Tories. He was alarmed by the popular enthusiasm over the acquittal of the seven bishops who had petitioned him against the Declaration of Indulgence. They had been organized by Turner of Ely but had included Sancroft of Canterbury, the very embodiment of moderate Tory Royalism; and he had very foolishly put them in the Tower amid popular acclaim and had then brought them to a trial involving a jury – which had acquitted them.[21] But above all he was alarmed by evidence that Tories

---

[21] G. V. Bennett threw fresh light on this crucial incident in *Religious Motivation*, ed. Derek Baker (Oxford, 1978), pp. 267–87.

as well as Whigs had invited William of Orange to 'mediate'
between him and the nation – and William was responding
from the strength of his virtual kingship in the Netherlands.

With the advantage of hindsight we can think James idiotic
because he had not forseen the power of the opposition to his
policy, but a Stuart king was not a fool to discount the
possibility of a rebellion under Anglican and Tory auspices.
'Rebellion is as the sin of witchcraft' (1 Samuel 15:23) was a
favourite text with Anglican preachers; and in the battle which
destroyed Monmouth's sad little rebellion, the Bishop of Winchester, Peter Mews, directed the royal artillery. Had there
been more willingness to rebel effectively, there would still not
have been the ability. It needs to be remembered that 'after
1680 England seemed to be moving inexorably towards abso-
lutism and only the events of 1688 led to a change of direction,
perhaps at the last possible moment . . . Opposition to the
monarchy had been so completely crushed by 1688 that the
English and Scots were no longer able, as they had been forty
years before, to overthrow the king without foreign aid. A
foreign prince with an army had to be called in.'[25]

We should also remember how unlikely it seemed that the
very shrewd William would involve himself in such a risky
rebellion. He was married to the English king's daughter, who
always insisted that no harm should come to her father; and he
had a major European war on his hands, so that he was
unlikely to divert troops to a civil war in England. He had,
indeed, given James vital military assistance against Monmouth. He knew that James controlled a strong fleet.

What altered the whole situation was once again the unexpected. On 10 June 1688 Mary of Modena gave birth to a son,
and not even the baseless rumour that the lad had been
smuggled into the royal bedchamber in a warming pan – the
rumour that was the pretext of William's intervention – could
undo the devastating political consequences. It now seemed
certain that James's legitimate heir would be brought up a
Roman Catholic, and very possible that in due course England
would be allied with France against the alliance built up by

---

[25] J. R. Western, *Monarchy and Revolution* (London, 1972), p. 3.

William as his life's mission. The Anglican Tories had a new reason to feel desperate and William had a new reason to gamble.

The other unexpected event was that James vacated the throne. William (evading the English navy by luck or a 'Protestant wind') landed in Devon on an encouraging date for Protestants, 5 November. He received into his army many officers and gentlemen on whose loyalty James had been counting (such as John Churchill, the future Duke of Marlborough), and was even joined by the king's second daughter, Anne. And the King's nerve cracked. After that it did not matter that he had forty thousand troops while William had landed with twelve thousand. He did not stay to fight it out, as his father had done, or to argue it out, as his brother had done. He did not know how to deal with a large-scale rebellion which he had thought inconceivable. His dominant concern was, it seems, to save himself, his wife and his son from his father's fate. He fled to France – which was just what his enemies wanted, as was demonstrated when he was intercepted by fishermen and sent back to England, only to be allowed to escape again. His flight could be interpreted as an abdication; some of those with a conscience about the rights of his son could be persuaded by the tale that the infant was not his son; and those who felt that the succession ought in these circumstances to pass to Mary could be assured that as a dutiful wife Mary accepted her husband's refusal to be a mere consort. Events which could never have been anticipated led to the offer of the vacant throne by the Convention Parliament to William and Mary jointly – and to the Parliamentary provision, still unrepealed in the 1980s, that no monarch of England could be a Roman Catholic.

James reached a French port on Christmas Day 1688 and found much more happiness in exile than he or anyone else expected. His wife Mary, who previously had been forced to tolerate his attachment to his two Anglican mistresses, Arabella Churchill and Catherine Sedley, now became the dominant partner in the marriage. His sexual energies were exhausted as he grew older, while his appetite for devout practices proved insatiable. Just before he died in 1701, he said to his tearful wife: 'Consider, Madam, I am going to be happy for ever.'

What had he achieved in England for the Church in whose supposed interests he had lost his throne? It is tempting to answer: nothing. But it is better to agree with a modern historian that 'in the long run the reign perhaps did the Catholics some good. It added yet another episode to the anti-Catholic tradition but it killed, at last, the myth that there were innumerable secret Papists waiting to declare themselves. The Catholics had emerged to be counted and had been seen to be few. Their association with Jacobitism made them seem dangerous for some time more, but gradually the active animus against them died away'.[26]

ANGLICANS AS DISSENTERS

The Anglican 'nonjurors' refused to swear allegiance to William and Mary, and their story forms a touching epilogue to the story of 1660–90. In an age full of cynicism their integrity led them to renounce positions, homes and incomes rather than accept Parliament's right to dethrone James – although some of them had been foremost in the opposition to his politics. Of the seven bishops who had enraged James by their famous petition, five remained loyal to their oath to him: Sancroft of Canterbury, Ken of Bath and Wells, Lake of Chichester, Turner of Ely and White of Peterborough. Bishops Frampton of Gloucester, Lloyd of Norwich and Thomas of Worcester were also nonjurors. Bishop Cartwright of Chester had collaborated with James and now went into exile with him.

The size of this group of bishops remaining loyal to their king can be explained by the fact that almost all of them had been appointed in the 1680s specifically because they were known to

---

[26] John Miller, *Popery and Politics in England, 1660–88* (Cambridge, 1973), p. 268. Dr Miller has also written *James II: A Study in Kingship* (London, 1978), a more sympathetic portrait than F. C. Turner's *James II* (London, 1948). This was the first biography to use the exiled king's devotional papers.

be loyal; Turner, for example, had been a chaplain to James as Duke of York, then Dean of Windsor at the height of the Tory triumph under Charles. But it is still impressive that they did not desert James. Even more impressive is the fact that about four hundred clergymen in the parishes followed their example, being extolled by John Dryden:

> He join'd not in their choice; because he knew
> Worse might, and often did, from change ensue.
> Much to himself he thought; but little spoke:
> And, undepriv'd, his benefice forsook.

And distinguished clergymen who accepted William and Mary refused to fill the officially vacant sees. William Beveridge, exemplary as a parish priest and as a scholar, was unwilling to go to Bath and Wells, and John Scott the devotional writer refused Chichester. John Sharp, the Dean of Norwich who was to emerge as Archbishop of York and Queen Anne's ecclesiastical adviser, refused to take over the bishopric of Norwich from a friend. Robert South, the leading preacher of a conservative Anglicanism (who made congregations laugh), and William Wake, the future Archbishop of Canterbury then aged thirty-three, were others who refused promotion in these circumstances. No episode in the history of the Church of England does it more credit.

Although most of the nonjurors would probably have supported Sancroft's proposal to acknowledge William as regent, they would not take oaths which to them would have meant renouncing the doctrine of non-resistance to the legitimate ruler. They recalled that Christ had not resisted Pilate. That was the 'doctrine of the cross' proclaimed in Thomas Ken's will: 'I die in the Holy, Catholic and Apostolic Faith, professed by the whole Church, before the disunion of East and West; more particularly I die in the communion of the Church of England, as it stands distinguished from all Papal and Puritan innovations and as it adheres to the doctrine of the cross.' In contrast with this heroic consistency the Anglicans who accepted the new regime were bound to seem morally inferior. Of the two men who succeeded Sancroft at Canterbury, Tillotson had impressed the doctrine of non-resistance on Lord

Russell before his execution under Charles II, and Tenison had repeated precisely the same standard Anglican teaching to Monmouth before his execution under James II. William Sherlock, who succeeded Tillotson as Dean of St Paul's, had ably upheld the divine right of kings in *The Case of Resistance* (1684) – and now had to publish an equally able defence of the Revolution in *The Case of Allegiance* (1691). When a wit saw him handing Mrs Sherlock into a carriage, he declared that the Dean now had his reasons for conforming to the new government at his finger tips.

But as time went on, the nonjurors had to face their own two moral dilemmas: should a schism be perpetuated in order to preserve the sacredness of the principle that the monarchy must be strictly hereditary, and was that principle really sacred in the circumstances of the eighteenth century?

Sancroft died in 1693. He had gone back to die in the Suffolk village where he had been born, refusing to worship in his parish church because William and Mary would be named there and urging a similar constancy on others. The old man was, although shattered by his recent experiences, venerated (as Swift's *Ode to Sancroft* shows). The more forceful Bishop Lloyd, to whom he had transferred the leadership, now decided to make sure that other bishops would carry on the true Church of England. George Hickes and Thomas Wagstaffe were accordingly consecrated. The legal problems were solved – at least in the eyes of those involved in this secret ceremony – by making them suffragan bishops. They took their titles from Thetford and Ipswich, in Lloyd's own diocese of Norwich, and as authority they quoted the disused statute of 1534. They also secured the consent of the exiled James. With his usual tact, James announced that he had obtained the Pope's permission.

Wagstaffe never functioned as a bishop; although he attended the dying Sancroft as a priest, he seems to have preferred to make himself useful as a medical doctor. But Hickes, the former Dean of Worcester, was a prodigiously learned scholar (his specialisms included Anglo-Saxon literature), a prolific and formidable writer of theology, and a determined 'primus' of the faithful remnant up to his death in 1715. Before dying he arranged for two Scottish bishops to join with him in consecrating Jeremy Collier and two others. Collier, who was already conspicuous for his writing against the immorality of the London stage and for his Jacobite sympathies, became an active leader in his turn, drawing up a 'Communion Office' richer than the Prayer Book of 1662 and negotiating for reunion with Eastern Orthodox bishops on the basis of a common faith and sacramentalism. His many publications included a large *Ecclesiastical History of Great Britain*. His liturgical revision has been valued by those Anglicans who have shared his own high regard for the usages which he restored (praying for the departed; mixing water with the wine in the chalice; asking for the Holy Spirit to descend on the bread and wine; offering the bread and wine as a sacrifice or 'oblation'; anointing the sick). Nor was his death in 1726 the end of the story. One nonjuring bishop consecrated another (with or without the two co-consecrators required by canon law), and the succession lasted until Charles Booth, who earned his living as a watch and clock maker and ministered to a congregation of about thirty in his own house in Manchester, died in 1805.

The trouble about this whole tradition was that it was either illegal or, at the best, remote from the mainstream of English life in the eighteenth century. In the next century the Whig historian, Macaulay, was to declare that the nonjurors suffered 'for the sake of a superstition as stupid and degrading as the Egyptian worship of cats and onions'. Undeniably there was something odd about a tradition which had ended up as this small underground movement but which had begun when some bishops had taken their stand on the precise letter of the law. The petition which they had presented to the enraged king on 18 May 1688 had made one point only: 'that Declaration is founded upon such a dispensing power, as hath often been declared illegal in Parliament, and particularly in the years 1662 and 1672.' When summoned on 8 June after the publication of this document (publication had never been intended when it had been signed), Sancroft had declined to tell the Privy Council whether or not the handwriting was his, on the legal ground that he should not be forced to incriminate himself. The seven bishops had been sent to the Tower solely because as peers they declined to offer bail or 'recognizances' to appear in court, and when they had appeared on 29 June their counsel had entered into intricate legal arguments before the jury acquitted them of seditious libel. Yet the very bishops who had then appealed to the letter of the law had now founded a movement which could be described as treasonable.

The nonjurors' reply was that the law still favoured James II and his heirs. But it was an uncertain reply. Before James fled the country he had done his utmost to create a legal vacuum, for example by dropping the Great Seal of England into the Thames; his had not been the conduct of a monarch who upheld the law. Such was the background to the resolution adopted by a majority of 62–47 in the Convention Parliament that the King, 'having withdrawn himself out of the kingdom, had abdicated the government, and that the throne had thereby become vacant'. King William was content to leave it at that so far as the bishops were concerned, exempting them from new oath-taking unless some fresh emergency should arise. His proposal to this effect was defeated in Parliament, but even then Bishop Ken is said to have assured a friend: 'I question not but that you and several others have taken the oaths with as good a conscience as I myself shall refuse them.'

What counted decisively with the average member of the Church of England was that providence seemed to be Williamite, for events or non-events gradually invited even the devout to accept the doom of Jacobite hopes. The perpetuation of the nonjurors' schism now seemed futile, and the biggest men among them gradually acknowledged this.[27]

Bishop Ken, for example, although personally fairly content to retire to read and write as a guest in splendid Longleat House for twenty years, was always conscious of the reality with which pastors had to deal. He avoided controversy as much as possible. He even refrained from publishing most of the literary output of his prolonged retirement, although morning and evening hymns which became famous were issued in

---

[27] Gerald Straka studied *The Anglican Reaction to the Revolution of 1688* (Madison, Wisc., 1962) and edited *The Revolution of 1688 and the Birth of the English Political Nation* (Lexington, Mass., 1963).

1700 for the use of the boys of his beloved Winchester, where he had been a scholar in the college and a prebendary in the cathedral. In 1703 Queen Anne readily agreed to a reconciliation with nonjurors. One part of the plan was that Ken should be invited to resume work as Bishop of Bath and Wells. He declared himself too old, but when his friend George Hooper was appointed he surrendered his claim to the diocese and accepted a royal pension. His heart was always with those who in the parishes of the Church of England would adhere to the pastoral ideal which he had always himself obeyed. In the midst of his long poem in praise of St Edmund, the king who long ago had been martyred by the invading Danes, came these lines, unconsciously his own self-portrait:

> Give me the priest these graces shall possess;
> Of an ambassador the just address,
> A father's tenderness, a shepherd's care,
> A leader's courage, which the cross can bear,
> A ruler's arm, a watchman's wakeful eye,
> A pilot's skill the helm in storms to ply,
> A fisher's patience and a lab'rer's toil,
> A guide's dexterity to disembroil,
> A prophet's inspiration from above,
> A teacher's knowledge, and a saviour's love.
> Give me the priest, a light upon the hill,
> Whose rays his whole circumference can fill;
> In God's own word and sacred learning vers'd,
> Deep in the study of the heart immers'd . . .[28]

With motives roughly similar to Ken's, the two leading laymen among the nonjurors conformed to the Church of England. One of these was Henry Dodwell, a learned theologian; he had remained a layman because, intending to write in praise of priests and bishops, he had thought it best not to lay himself open to the charge of self-seeking. In his *Epistolary Discourse* of 1706 he went so far in the praise of bishops as to attempt to prove, in the words of his subtitle, 'that the soul is a principle naturally mortal but immortalized actually for the pleasure of

---

[28] See Hugh A. L. Rice, *Thomas Ken* (London, 1958).

God. Wherein is proved, that none have the power of giving this divine immortalizing spirit, since the apostles, but only the bishops.' Like other nonjurors (and many conforming Anglicans), Dodwell denied the validity of baptism administered by Dissenters, but in this little book of 1706 he maintained two points yet more extreme: that those who rejected confirmation by a bishop sinned against the Holy Spirit and were damned eternally, and that baptism, even when administered by a priest, was only preliminary and 'purgative' – 'beneath the dignity of an apostle to perform in person'. Now Dodwell, without acknowledging that he had ever been in schism himself, seems to have allowed an element of Church of England commonsense to enter his mind. At about the same time, Robert Nelson, a rich philanthropist, identified himself with the Established Church and was now able to be a very generous supporter and encourager of all kinds of charitable and missionary work. He was universally respected.

Towards the end of Queen Anne's reign it seemed possible that she and enough other leading figures might recognize James II's son James (usually known as 'the Old Pretender') as her heir, rather than the remote and unattractive Hanoverians. In practical terms, however, his restoration to his father's throne depended on the Old Pretender becoming an Anglican, and in 1714 he made the great refusal. After that, however unpopular the Hanoverians might be, the turning-point had been passed. The Protestant monarchy was secure and the nonjurors who refused to recognize it were living in nostalgia. The Jacobite cause became an obviously spent force after the failure of the rebellion of 1745, and 'Bonnie Prince Charlie' seemed to be acknowledging one major cause of the fiasco when in 1750, during a secret visit to London, he was received into the Church of England. But soon it was clear that the fortunes of the house of Stuart had become inseparable from those of the Church of Rome. 'James III' was buried in St Peter's, Rome, in 1766. As 'Charles III' the Young Pretender went to live in Rome and accepted its faith again, together with the consolations of the bottle. When he died in 1788 he left his English claims to his brother, Henry, a splendid and sober man. 'Henry IX' kept up all the pretence of being a king but he had been a cardinal since 1747 and when the French revolutionaries deprived him of his large income he was gracious enough to accept a pension from George III. George IV contributed to the cost of the monument to this last of the royal Stuarts. It was erected in St Peter's, Rome, when Henry was buried there in 1807.

Acknowledging reality, the Papacy had in effect recognized George III, and with him the Protestant succession in England, in 1765. By the 1790s even the Anglican bishops in Scotland, who had been nonjurors to a man, had abandoned the Jacobite cause. The few Englishmen who remained nonjurors were locked more and more into a private world. It was a little world distinguished by some fine historical scholarship (for example, by the learning of the Oxford scholar Thomas Hearne, who was willing to be excluded from the Bodleian Library rather than compromise his conscience). But the nonjurors were also divided into factions accusing each other of theological error now that it was possible to revise the Prayer Book for their own use – as was done in 1718. The dispute led to a schism between the 'Regulars' who clung to the Book of Common Prayer, and the 'Usagers' who welcomed a richer liturgical diet. And no extensive pastoral work could be attempted.[29]

However, one of the nonjurors was William Law, whose books, widely admired as elegant English prose, were also valued as a reminder of the highest standards of Christian holiness. He abandoned a Cambridge career because his conscience forbade him to swear allegiance to George I. His conscience always was active, perhaps over-active. While an undergraduate he declared that 'no condition of this life is for enjoyment, but for trial'. One of his books was on the 'absolute unlawfulness' of the theatre, and when a gift from an admirer enabled him to set up a semi-monastic establishment in his

---

[29] See L. M. Hawkins, *Allegiance in Church and State* (London, 1928); J. W. C. Wand, *The High Church Schism* (London, 1951); Sir Charles Petrie, *The Jacobite Movement* (London, 1959). More detail is in J. H. Overton, *The Nonjurors* (London, 1902), and Henry Broxap, *The Later Nonjurors* (Cambridge, 1924). There is material about Hickes, Collier and Hearne in David C. Douglas, *English Scholars 1660–1730* (revised, London, 1951).

native village (King's Cliffe in Northamptonshire) he annoyed his neighbours by giving money without discrimination to all beggars who presented themselves, deserving or undeserving. Although he refused to become a bishop he did consent to be ordained as a priest by the nonjurors (after a long delay) – and there was always in his life something of the nonjuror's lack of contact with the everyday world, even before his last phase when he had been deeply influenced by the German mystic Jacob Boehme. But he championed Christian orthodoxy against the most heretical of the Whig bishops, Hoadly; he championed God's love against the Calvinists ('God is love, yea all love, and so all love that nothing but love can come from him'); he wrote on *Christian Perfection* with a faith which stirred John Wesley; and his *Serious Call to a Devout and Holy Life* (1728) became a classic. Samuel Johnson reckoned it 'the finest piece of hortatory theology in any language'. The book was written in the Putney home of the Gibbons, to whom Law was acting as a tutor. The great historian and sceptic Edward Gibbon, who as a little boy had this contact with a saint, paid a guarded tribute: 'the philosopher must allow that he exposes, with equal severity and truth, the strange contradiction between the faith and practice of the Christian world.'

Because Law did not wish to arouse controversy by presenting any of the specific doctrines of the nonjurors, he did not include any substantial discussion of public worship in his *Serious Call*. Its concern was with how an Englishman should live when he got home from church. The omission might suggest that Law was indifferent to the Anglican forms of piety, but he made a point of attending every service in his parish church. He even insisted that the girls in the school which he ran should attend every funeral.[30]

Law's dislike of controversy was not unique at the end of the thirty years of crisis, 1660–90. Through much suffering, those years had drained away the poison of intolerance from many parts of English religion.

---

[30] See A. W. Hopkinson, *About William Law* (London, 1948), and A. K. Walker, *William Law: His Life and Thought* (London, 1973).

CHAPTER THIRTEEN

QUIETER CHURCHES

A FAILURE OF COMPREHENSION

The nonjurors were not alone in refusing to accept that the 'glorious revolution' had established a Protestant throne with an Anglican monopoly of political life but with toleration for Protestant Dissenters. There were both Presbyterian and High Anglican attempts to challenge the balanced decision.

In the crisis of 1688–89, at first it seemed likely that the Presbyterians would be able to insist on large changes in the Church of England before joining it. In Scotland the Established Church now finally threw out its bishops along with King James. The change, already probable in view of the rooted objection of the Scots to 'prelacy', was made inevitable when all but one of the bishops refused to accept King William. A Jacobite rising came to nothing and when Scotland was politically united with England in the next reign the Presbyterian character of the Church of Scotland was written into the treaty. In Ireland, too, Presbyterians gained from the defeat of James and his army. After the decisive battle of the Boyne in 1690, a Protestant ascendancy was imposed on the Catholic five-sixths of the population and it was not unreasonable to hope that this would be to the advantage of the Presbyterians. In England many wished to include the 'comprehension' of moderate Presbyterians in the Church of England. William of Orange, as he made his way to London and to the throne, showed that he expected it. He was himself a convinced Calvinist, who back in Holland had scandalized English visitors such as Thomas Ken by snubbing Anglican chaplains and never receiving communion with his Anglican wife, Mary. Mary had continued to live like a nun (that was her own phrase), but in every matter apart from her personal religion she obeyed her husband, as her religion taught her. In England William encouraged Dissenting ministers to be eloquent about the unity of the Reformed Churches, and himself addressed the Lords with this theme. To the alarmed clergy of the Church of England he often seemed to be as indifferent to their convictions as James II had been – and as late as 1775 Dr Johnson echoed the high Anglicans' prejudice when he called William 'one of the most worthless scoundrels that ever existed'.

Not only King William, who might be regarded as a latter-day conqueror of England, favoured the 'comprehension' of the moderate Presbyterians. So did William Sancroft while still functioning as Archbishop of Canterbury, together with other leading churchmen, including his two successors at Canterbury. In October 1689 a commission met to work out details such as the 'conditional' ordination of Presbyterian ministers to satisfy the bishops without claiming that Presbyterian ordination necessarily was invalid. A copy of the Book of Common Prayer survives, annotated with changes for which there would probably be agreement. At the very least, Dissenters would surely be welcome to sit in Parliament and on the towns' councils.

In the end nothing happened. The Prayer Book was not revised; the Test and Corporation Acts were not repealed; Dissent, although tolerated, was excluded as firmly from church life as it was from national and local politics. One reason was that William's speech from the throne in March 1689, about the need to admit 'all Protestants' to public offices, suggested alarmingly that many places would have to be found for other Dutchmen, whose presence in England was to be resented throughout the reign. Both Lords and Commons rejected the proposal by overwhelming majorities.

The main reason for the scheme's failure was, however, conservatism in the Church of England, voiced loudly by Bishop Compton and echoed in Parliament. Typical churchmen were in no mood to abandon their privileges, especially when they heard that some of the few clergy who supported their bishops in Scotland had been lynched or 'rabbled'. Many English parish priests were frightened that the whole Restoration settlement was about to be overthrown by another Cromwell, and many MPs prided themselves on being loyal sons of the National Church. Daniel Finch, Earl of Nottingham, made it his business to persuade William of the necessity of yielding to this Anglican conservatism if he was to have a quiet kingdom supplying money for his war against Louis XIV; and William gradually was persuaded.

His own psychology was a factor. The wishes of his wife, nominally the joint occupant of the throne until her death in 1694, do not seem to have been decisive. She remained a devout Anglican, inwardly distressed and driven to prayer by the curses of her father, James II. Mary, however, kept her distress to herself; in public she was simply the devoted wife. William – a cold man, asthmatic and it seems homosexual – never warmed to her when alive, although after her death he became devoted, and the couple's inability to have children had been established long before 1688. Essentially William had married not a wife but a cause. He was driven by the conviction that he had been predestined to save the Dutch nation from the French. He had no deep interest in England apart from the difference it could make to the nine years' war which he now conducted. His immediate problem was to hold the nation together through the military crisis of 1690. This was a serious crisis; on the day before the battle of the Boyne the Anglo-Dutch fleet was defeated off Beachy Head, and had the French army been prepared to cross the Channel it would have met with no effective resistance. Thus preoccupied, William had no energy left for English ecclesiastical problems. He permitted the Church of England to retain its exclusive privileges – just as in Ireland he permitted a system by which the well-to-do Presbyterians, no less than the miserably poor Catholics, paid tithes to the Anglican clergy, were excluded from sitting in Parliament, and until 1719 could not hold civil or military office under the Crown.[1]

---

[1] S. B. Baxter, *William III* (London, 1966), has been supplemented by Henry Harwitz, *Parliament, Policy and Politics in the Reign of William III* (Manchester, 1977). Pending the publication of his fuller study, the best guidance to the ecclesiastical history of the reign is provided by two articles by G. V. Bennett in *Essays in Modern English Church History*, ed. G. V. Bennett and J. D. Walsh (London, 1966), pp. 104–31, and *Britain after the Glorious Revolution*, ed. Geoffrey Holmes (London, 1969), pp. 155–76.

When John Tillotson became Archbishop of Canterbury in 1690 the idea of including Presbyterians in the Church over which he would be Primate was dead. And neither he nor Thomas Tenison, who followed him in 1694, was an ecclesiastical statesman. Tillotson was a preacher of everyday morality (and the first married man to occupy Lambeth Palace since Matthew Parker). Tenison was a pastor. From 1680 to 1692 he had made an admirable vicar in the crowded London parish of St Martin-in-the-Fields. A penitent Nell Gwynne had been among his grateful parishioners.[2]

A TORY FAILURE

It was now the turn of the Tories, who included the majority of the clergy, to attempt to overturn the settlement of 1688–89 by ending the toleration of Dissent.[3] To the resentment of the clergy at this toleration could now be added the resentment of the squires at the taxation of land to pay for a Dutch king's war and at the rise of 'monied' (rather than landed) men around the Bank of England as part of the stupendous effort needed to borrow money for the war on top of the taxes. Many signs pointed to a Tory reaction. One of them was the market for Clarendon's *History of the Rebellion*, brought out in the 1700s by the dead author's son, the Earl of Rochester, an active Tory politician.

At an earlier stage the Tories' natural leader would have been Henry Compton, but he was old and his disappointment at not being made Archbishop of Canterbury had bitten deep into his soul. He continued to make himself a nuisance to Archbishop Tenison when he could, but he concentrated on his work as Bishop of London and on the garden at Fulham Palace, where he collected plants from the colonies. He died in 1713, aged eighty-one. Another leading High Churchman was John Sharp, who consented to become Archbishop of York in

---

[2] See Edward Carpenter, *Thomas Tenison* (London, 1948).
[3] George Every studied *The High Church Party, 1688–1718* (London, 1956).

1694 and who under Queen Anne, when Tenison was pushed out into the cold, exercised many of the functions of an Archbishop of Canterbury. 'I hope we shall one day agree,' wrote the ever-mild Tenison to Sharp.[4]

The most highly placed leader of the High Anglicans was, however, Queen Anne herself, who had been Henry Compton's pupil. She was not a very intelligent woman, and was married to an even less intelligent man, Prince George of Denmark. From 1683 to 1700 she was pregnant every year. She had twelve miscarriages; of her six children, one was still-born and the other five died at an early age. She was sure that it was God's punishment for the treachery towards the legitimate king, although illogically she was not prepared to renounce her claim to the throne (in the fifteenth century Henry IV's attitude had been identical). When she became queen in 1702 she set herself to obliterate William's memory. She had thought it her right to succeed to the throne on her unhappy sister Mary's death. Now she would be an 'entirely English' queen, by which she meant an Anglican and a Tory sovereign. 'My own principles must always keep me entirely firm to the interests and religion of the Church of England, and will incline me to countenance those who have the truest zeal to support it.' So she said on her accession; and it was her practice. She renounced some of the taxes of the clergy ('annates' and 'tenths') which Henry VIII had secured for the Crown, and with the proceeds established Queen Anne's Bounty for the benefit of the poorer clergy. From that acorn planted in 1704 the wealth of the Church Commissioners would one day grow.[5]

The ablest spokesman of the extreme Tory attitude to the Church – so able and so extreme that he alarmed Queen Anne – was Francis Atterbury. He was also perhaps the most gifted English churchman of his generation, and one who had the additional strength of knowing that most of the parish clergy idolized him. His mind was formed by Oxford in the 1680s, the

---

[4] See A. Tindal Hart, *The Life and Times of John Sharp* (London, 1949).
[5] There are biographies of *Queen Anne* by David Green and by David Gregg (both London, 1980). See also Alan Savidge, *The Foundation and Early Years of Queen Anne's Bounty* (London, 1955).

Oxford which publicly burned the works of Thomas Hobbes and the Presbyterians' Solemn League and Covenant; the Oxford which resisted King James's attacks on the Anglican monopoly but which was very hesitant about King William and his broad-minded bishops.

Moving to London at Bishop Compton's invitation, Atterbury saw his chance: he would be a propagandist on behalf of the clergy as they were represented in the Convocation of Canterbury. That may not sound like an exciting role for a clergyman as ambitious as he was eloquent. The Convocation of Canterbury was revived in 1701 because King William had had to accept this as one of the policies of a Tory ministry, and it continued its stormy life under Anne. It usually met in Westminster Abbey. The bishops sat around the fire in the Jerusalem Chamber and the clergy in the cold chapel of Henry VII; and it was the theory of the bishops that the clergy were there to assist them when occasionally summoned into the warmth in order to answer questions. It was also the theory of the government that the meeting should confine itself strictly to the business for which the Crown had granted its licence. The reality in ecclesiastic politics was, however, that the bishops appointed by King William's government were alienated from the clergy. The quick-witted Atterbury saw that the bishops could be blamed for everything – for the withdrawal of parishioners to worship with the Dissenters, for the spread of immorality and heresy, even for the taxes. He saw, too, that it was possible to compare the House of Clergy with the House of Commons. In the 1680s the Commons had secured a settlement which prevented a king from governing without laws and taxes voted by Parliament; now in the 1700s the clergy could clip the wings of the bishops.

The higher and lower clergymen who met at the two ends of Westminster Abbey were as rude to each other as they dared to be. There was also a battle of pamphlets and books. Atterbury's writing (started by his *Letter to a Convocation Man* in 1697) was brilliantly controversial but not based on solid research into the history of the government of the Church of England. It was answered by salvoes from three big guns. Edmund Gibson, who had gone from the Lake District to become a poor but

prodigiously learned scholar at Oxford, was Archbishop Tenison's librarian at Lambeth Palace and he defended his master
against Atterbury, producing what became the standard
account of the Convocation's procedures. Some laborious
years later – years from which his health never recovered – he
published the standard work on English canon law. William
Wake, another Oxford scholar who was then rector of St
James's, Piccadilly, accompanied Gibson's really unanswerable contributions by a magisterial history of the Convocations
and other synods in England. White Kennett, almost their equal
in learning and like Wake then a London parish priest, issued
another reply to Atterbury, more readable because shorter.

In academic terms, therefore, victory went to those who
defended the bishops. Wake and Gibson went on to the highest
positions in the Church. Kennett, although not so well rewarded, became a hard-working Bishop of Peterborough and
an influential writer; his influence so annoyed the Tories that
in 1714 an altarpiece portraying him as Judas at the Last
Supper was set up in church by the rector of Whitechapel in
London.[6] Atterbury, in contrast, when he became a dean had
to accept distant Carlisle. When at last he obtained a bishopric
from the Tories in 1713, he got nothing better than poor
Rochester, to which the Westminster Deanery was annexed.

The political question was, however, whether Tory policies
which commanded the support of the Queen and the majority
in the House of Commons could prevail. Could they be forced
through the House of Lords, where the bishops' votes were
often decisive? Three bills passed the Commons, to prohibit
Dissenters from returning to their own meeting houses after
receiving the Anglican sacrament in order to qualify for office
('occasional conformity'), but were thrown out by the Lords.
Then from 1705 Whigs with little sympathy with the clergy
took over the government; their chief interest lay in the Union
Treaty with Scotland (which came into effect in 1707) and in
supporting the armies led in the European war by the Duke of
Marlborough. The Tories, who cared little for Scotland or the
Continent, accordingly set up the cry: 'The Church in danger!'

---

[6] See G. V. Bennett, *White Kennett* (London, 1957).

This cry was worked into a very widely sold sermon, originally preached before the Lord Mayor of London in St Paul's in 1709 by Henry Sacheverell, a Fellow of Magdalen College, Oxford. The sermon was so full of half-concealed insults to the bishops and the Whig ministers ('false brethren') that when the preacher went on to deny that a subject had any right to resist a monarch, thus in effect denying the validity of the removal of James II, the government seized the opportunity to impeach him before the House of Lords for sedition. But Tory-inspired riots broke out in London, and when the Lords announced their verdict they showed where their feelings lay by a light sentence: Sacheverell was not imprisoned or fined but suspended from preaching for three years. He went in victorious procession through the applause of Oxford to a rich living.[7]

The incident was the signal for Robert Harley to begin engineering in the Commons the overthrow of the government led by the Duke of Marlborough's civilian ally and financier, the Earl of Godolphin; Harley had himself been forced out of that government in 1708. And one of the first fruits of the Tory victory was the passing of the fourth Occasional Conformity Bill into law.

Step by step the Tories, controlling the Commons, now advanced in a campaign which recalled their triumph in the 1680s. The Whig majority in the Lords was broken by the creation of fresh peerages. While priority was given to ending the war by the peace of Utrecht (1713), the demands of the Anglican clergy were not forgotten. The Schism Bill was passed with enthusiasm. It closed down all the Dissenters' schools and made it necessary for all future schoolmasters to procure a bishop's licence to teach. The next step was to be a bill ending the Dissenters' right to vote in Parliamentary elections. Bishop Gilbert Burnet, who had once been secretary to William of Orange, certainly thought that the 'glorious revolution' was being undone. In a new preface written in 1712 for his *Discourse of the Pastoral Care*, he told the clergy: 'I see imminent ruin hanging over this Church.'

But by now the Tories faced problems. One was that Harley

---

[7] See Geoffrey Holmes, *The Trial of Dr Sacheverell* (London, 1973).

(now Earl of Oxford) had become an incompetent Lord Treasurer; he was habitually the worse for drink. His junior colleague, Henry St John, Viscount Bolingbroke, was only too willing to replace him but faced great dangers. Already at this stage he would probably have preferred Anne's successor to be the Old Pretender, but he acknowledged that the English would prefer a Turk to a Papist as their king. The only real alternative had been provided for in the Act of Settlement of 1701, promising the throne to the Electress Sophia of Hanover, daughter of Charles I's sister Elizabeth, and to her descendants. Almost sixty people were more closely related to Anne than the Electress Sophia was, and in any case Sophia had recently died, leaving Hanover to her unattractive son George, who had never troubled to learn English. The sole merit of this extraordinary entanglement with a German state (which was never popular) was that it, and it alone, would make sure of the Protestant succession in England. Queen Anne had shown her feelings about the prospect by forbidding Sophia to visit England or to meddle in its politics, and it had fallen to Bolingbroke to communicate one rebuke which was alleged to have killed the Electress. Her son swore vengeance.

Bolingbroke needed time, but what he would have done with it must remain a matter for speculation. On 27 July 1714 he finally prevailed on Anne to dismiss his drink-sodden senior colleague. When the Queen consented to this, she was already very ill. Even now neither she nor her council would consent to make the erratic Bolingbroke Lord Treasurer; that honour went to a duke. On 1 August she died, and the proclamation of George I went off without incident. 'What a world this is,' Bolingbroke wrote to Swift, 'and how does fortune banter us.'

The triumph of the Whigs was assured by the death of Queen Anne. By the end of the year King George had made a clean sweep of the government, and one of his proclamations had stopped the clergy preaching political (by which was meant Tory) sermons. The Earl of Oxford was sent to the Tower for two years. Bolingbroke was in deep disgrace. In 1717 the Whig government, angered by the intention of the House of Clergy to proceed against Bishop Hoadly for heresy, suspended the Convocation of Canterbury by royal writ. For a century and a half the proceedings of the Convocation were formal, apart from a session in 1741 hurriedly dissolved when the old quarrels broke out. The clergy were not allowed to complete any business until 1852. In 1719 the Occasional Conformity and Schism Acts were repealed, although a plan to repeal the Test and Corporation Acts had to be abandoned because of Anglican opposition. An Indemnity Act gave Dissenters limited protection for a year (they could not be prosecuted for nonconformity if they had survived six months in a local office without being challenged). In 1727 and in many later years this Act was renewed, but what mattered more was that the Whigs gave the cue that Dissenters were not to be troubled too zealously.

The personal ruin of Bolingbroke and of Atterbury followed. The former, believing that 'the Tory party is gone', fled to the court of the Old Pretender. Later he returned to England and tried to rebuild Toryism by his pen, now making no secret of his contempt for the clergy whose champion he had pretended to be, and his life did not flicker out until 1751. He appealed to the idea of a 'patriot king' although one did not arrive on the scene before George III in 1760. As he went home through Calais in 1723, this disillusioned gambler passed a fellow Tory going into perpetual exile: Francis Atterbury. The bishop had written a violently anti-Whig and anti-Hanoverian pamphlet, *English Advice to the Freeholders of England*, and had become persuaded that the Tories' only remaining hope was in the Jacobite cause. He refused to be bought by the Whigs with an offer of the right to be the next Bishop of Winchester. But his Jacobite plotting was exposed by Sir Robert Walpole; despite his solemn denial of the charge, he was condemned by the House of Lords; and so for a time he took Bolingbroke's place at the court of the Old Pretender. He died, very sad, in 1732.[8]

Secure in power, the Whigs were now themselves tempted to alter the settlement of 1688–89 by altering the character of the Church of England.

---

[8] Recent studies include Sheila Biddle, *Bolingbroke and Harley* (London, 1975); H. T. Dickinson, *Bolingbroke* (London, 1970); G. V. Bennett, *The Tory Crisis in Church and State, 1688–1730: The Career of Francis Atterbury, Bishop of Rochester* (Oxford, 1975).

THE CHURCH UNDER THE WHIGS

Although George I and George II had to receive Holy Communion as a condition of being monarchs under the act of 1701, they cared nothing for the Church of England and little for anything else that was English. They usually left ecclesiastical appointments (together with much other business) to their Whig ministers. For the first time the cabinet began to meet regularly without the sovereign presiding.[9]

Although the politicians in power also had to conform to the Church since the Test Act had never been repealed, few of them had much personal religion. Benjamin Hoadly, whom they had been glad to make Bishop of Bangor, expressed their conception of the Church in a sermon of 1717 on the text 'My Kingdom is not of this world'. It was a sermon as notorious as Dr Sacheverell's had been at the other extreme of ecclesiastical politics; for Hoadly virtually dissolved the Church as a structured society. It contained 'no visible, human authority . . . no judges over the conscience.' The teaching on which the Church's members agreed was there in the Bible, or in those parts of the Bible which Hoadly thought sensible, and the Church was a voluntary society of those who accept Christ as 'lawgiver and judge in all matters truly relating to conscience or eternal salvation'. But God had no special favour towards the Church; 'the favour of God follows sincerity considered as such.' Here was the 'gathered' Church advocated by the Puritans, but the basis on which it was gathered was by Puritan standards the outright denial of Christianity. If Hoadly's view had prevailed, there can be little doubt that the Church of England would have formally abandoned the old standards of belief, as well as of behaviour, as many of the Presbyterians had already done.

William Wake and Edmund Gibson had by their scholarly labours helped to prevent the clergy from endorsing the ambitions of Atterbury, and it now fell to them to persuade the Whigs to abandon the radical policy recommended by Hoadly.

---

[9] The best introduction to English politics, 1714–60, is now W. A. Speck, *Stability and Strife* (London, 1977).

They achieved this by persuading the Whigs now in power, as William of Orange had been persuaded, that it was not politically realistic to encourage the Tories to keep up their cry of 'the Church in danger!' In their own interests the triumphant Whigs must swallow, or conceal, their general contempt for religious traditions.

Wake, the obvious man to promote to Canterbury in 1716, had already shown during eleven years as Bishop of Lincoln (the largest diocese) that he insisted on high standards in church life. While archbishop he was not willing to support any radical modernization of the Church of England's doctrine or any enlargement of the liberties of the Dissenters; he even opposed the repeal of the Occasional Conformity and Schism Acts. His real interest lay in negotiations with foreign churches, and for this purpose it was all the more necessary to be able to show the Church of England's orthodoxy.

It seemed a heaven-sent moment for Christian reunion. King William and the Duke of Marlborough had made England the centre of a great, and in the end victorious, alliance against the French – and as a reward, the British empire was beginning to be worldwide. Had not the hour struck for an alliance of the Christian churches against immorality and unbelief, and as a reward might not the Church of England gain an unprecedented prestige? On the continent, a number of Roman Catholics who resented interference by Rome took an interest in the Anglican claim to be Catholic without the Pope. A number of Protestants (for example, Frederick, the first King of Prussia) believed that the old divisions between Lutherans and Calvinists were outmoded; and they observed with admiration the spectacle of a Lutheran as Supreme Governor of the Church of England, whose Articles of Belief were moderately Calvinist.[10] And to match this hopeful hour, a scholar with broad sympathies was Archbishop of Canterbury.

William Wake corresponded industriously with anti-Roman Catholics in France ('Gallicans' whose base was the Sorbonne

---

[10] Norman Sykes studied *Daniel Ernst Jablonski and the Church of England* (London, 1950).

university in Paris), with Lutherans and with Calvinists. He acknowledged the validity of the sacraments of all the Reformed Churches; he accepted the current description of England under the Hanoverians as 'the head of the Protestant interest' and found no theological reason for disrupting this alliance. But he urged the continental Protestants to get together and to recover the time-honoured system of bishops and creeds, blessings which the wise Anglicans had never forsaken. At one stage there was a Lutheran suggestion that the apostolic succession of bishops might be transmitted across the Channel by letter. Wake also urged the Frenchmen to acknowledge that the bishops of the Church of England were validly Catholic and that its orthodox creeds were sincere. There was much explanation about the consecrations of the Elizabethan bishops. In the end all this correspondence fizzled out. The various groups on the continent had no serious intention of uniting with anyone, and no serious belief that the religious arrangements of the English provided a model to be copied outside that strange island. 'We all favour too much ourselves and our own opinions' was Wake's accurate analysis. But the correspondence had the effect of suggesting that, if it had to choose, the Church of England would prefer an agreement with fellow Christians abroad to an agreement with England's own sceptics.[11]

In the end the Whigs grew bored with this archbishop who seemed to be wrapped in dreams of Christian reunion while the vital matter was to defend the Protestant succession and the Whig supremacy against any threat of a Jacobite or Tory revival. The new Whig prime minister, Sir Robert Walpole, was ruthless in getting what he wanted throughout his twenty-one years in power, the 'Robinocracy'. It was he who got the crucial evidence which ruined Francis Atterbury, and in 1723 he also got rid of William Wake as the effective chief of ecclesiastical affairs. Wake remained Archbishop of Canterbury until 1737 but was ignored in matters such as the appointment of bishops. The power was transferred to

---

[11] Norman Sykes wrote a magisterial biography of *William Wake* (2 vols, Cambridge, 1957).

Edmund Gibson, who was made Bishop of London.

He was known to be ambitious. As Walpole, ever a cynic, wrote to the Duke of Newcastle: 'He must be pope and would as willingly be our pope as anybody's.' But Gibson was also a sincere believer in the importance of the Protestant succession on the throne to English religion, and the sincerity of his attachment to the Church of England had been demonstrated by the pains he had taken to codify its canon law; his nickname was 'Dr Codex'. He set himself to reconcile the Church to the Whigs.

On the Church's side this meant erecting a barrier to the promotion of Tories; the only Tory who got past this barrier to become a bishop was Thomas Sherlock, a man of outstanding ability who was favoured by George II's clever queen and who in the end succeeded Gibson as Bishop of London.[12] But on the side of the Whigs, the reconciliation as planned by Gibson involved considering the prejudices of clergymen and cultivating their loyalties. There must be no more open contempt for the traditional standards. Young dons from Oxford and Cambridge must be flattered by being summoned to preach in London with small stipends from the government, and professorships of modern history must be established in the universities so as to explain to them what had been happening in recent centuries.

Gibson's reconciliation of the Church and the Whigs was more successful than Wake's attempt to reconcile Catholics, Lutherans and Calvinists. But the Bishop's alliance with Sir Robert Walpole, on which everything depended, could not last. Walpole grew restive under Gibson's veto of any ecclesiastical appointments which he knew would provoke the clergy. The House of Commons, on which Walpole's own power depended, grew restive under a system which perpetuated so many privileges for the Anglican clergy, while (as we have already seen) the Dissenters kept lobbying MPs for further concessions in the spirit of toleration. In the 1730s bills began appearing which dismayed Gibson – to deprive incumbents of tithes unless there was proof that they had recently

---

[12] See E. F. Carpenter, *Thomas Sherlock* (London, 1936).

been paid; to deprive churchwardens of the right to levy rates for the repair of churches (but the magistrates were still to be authorized to do this); to deprive ecclesiastical courts of jurisdiction over moral offences; to deprive the bishops of any possibility that they might be translated to richer sees; to restrict gifts to charities including churches (the Mortmain Bill). Finally the Quaker Tithes Bill proposed to transfer financial disputes between the clergy and the Quakers from the expensive and usually hostile ecclesiastical court, or the national court of the exchequer, to local magistrates. Walpole's support of this proposal so angered Gibson that the Bishop announced that he would now concentrate on the care of his diocese to the exclusion of all public business.

When Canterbury fell vacant on Wake's death, it was given to John Potter, a good scholar but a colourless ecclesiastic. Gibson had to be persuaded out of his semi-retirement to give a lead against the Jacobite rebellion in 1745. Two years later, when Potter had expired, Gibson was finally offered the archbishopric. His quarrel with Walpole no longer mattered, since the Quakers had accepted defeat and Walpole himself had fallen from power. But he was now almost eighty years old and he refused the honour. So did his Tory rival, Thomas Sherlock, who pleaded that he was afflicted with gout. So another dull appointment was made to the Primacy, to be followed by others over which we need not linger. And 'no clergyman of anything like Gibson's force and influence spoke out in public for the clergy's claims until the 1830s.'[13]

The making of bishops and deans, and of many a canon or parish priest, fell into the willing hands of Thomas Pelham-Holles, Duke of Newcastle. This duke was a great landowner who became Prime Minister, having previously been a leading minister in the government led by his brother. Yet for some thirty years he personally conducted a voluminous correspondence with clergymen who applied for jobs great or small. Always an anxious man, he was as pious as he was practical; he

---

[13] G. F. A. Best, *Temporal Pillars* (Cambridge, 1964), p. 60. Norman Sykes provided a biography of *Edmund Gibson* (Oxford, 1926). Aldren Rowden did his best for *The Primates of the Four Georges* (London, 1916).

consulted some of the clergymen he promoted about the state
of his soul. To him the labour involved in this exercise of
patronage was as necessary as was all his attention to the
details of electioneering in the parliamentary constituencies.
He was glad to be asked to carry on the good work when in 1757
William Pitt took the rest of the world off his hands. Pitt's
armies might conquer North America from Guadeloupe in the
sunshine to Quebec next to the snow, but of what use was a
transatlantic victory over the French if the Whig ascendancy
over England was not secure?[14]

This cunning political manager could appeal not only to his
correspondents' personal ambitions, but also to the fact that
most Englishmen now had an incentive to keep the peace at
home, since the nation was beginning to prosper in a modern
way. The population growth slowed down, agricultural pro-
ductivity rose and trade expanded. Capitalism had shown its
power to win King William's war, to finance the beginnings of
a great empire and to create industrial wealth. Those who
benefitted from the system, particularly the aristocracy now
building their Palladian stately homes, naturally looked in-
dulgently on any defects; these seemed like the 'Gothic' ruins
which were sometimes erected in a park. But the many hundreds of thousands of Englishmen always on the brink of
starvation also usually accepted this society with all its injus-
tice. The less privileged were encouraged to be quiet by harsh
laws; death was the penalty for many offences, including
participation in a crowd of twelve or more an hour after the
reading of the Riot Act of 1715. And the poor were also kept
quiet by the sense that the social order was secure, indeed
inevitable. There was no efficient police force and there were
no large-scale political upheavals. It is clear that 1688–89 was
generally thought to have established a society which was at its
worst tolerable.

Alexander Pope expressed the national mood of optimism
which meant all the more since he was himself a dwarf, a
lifelong invalid and, as a Roman Catholic, always in the last

---

[14] See Reed Browning, *The Duke of Newcastle* (London, 1975).

analysis an outsider. In the England of the Whigs he could profess to believe that

> All Nature is but Art, unknown to thee;
> All Chance, Direction, which thou canst not see;
> All Discord, Harmony, not understood;
> All partial Evil, universal Good.[15]

THE ALLIANCE OF CHURCH AND STATE

In his *Alliance of Church and State* (1736), William Warburton, then a country clergyman, sought to justify the establishment of the Church of England from 'the fundamental principles of the Law of Nature and of Nations'. At no point was Warburton less – or more – than complacent. He admitted that the Church had been disgraced by superstition in past ages but in a private letter he once pointed out that in Noah's ark there had been amid 'the unclean beasts and vermin that almost filled it . . . a little corner of rationality that was as much distressed by the stink within as by the tempest without'. He was sure that the Church now deserved in the main to be honoured because of this element of religious rationality; he was careful not to provoke his fellow churchmen. To him Church and State were two distinct bodies. That much he granted to the Protestant or Catholic Dissenters, abandoning Richard Hooker's attempt to reassert the total unity of England. On the other hand, it was inexpedient that an assembly of the clergy should transact any business, since no reforms were urgent; and it was wrong for the Church to excommunicate any citizen without gaining the State's approval. If there was more than one religious body within a nation, it was in accordance with 'civic utility' to choose the most numerous church and to reward it by establishment and endowment, since the welfare of society (for example, the keeping of oaths) depended on morality being

---

[15] Studies include D. H. Griffin, *Alexander Pope: The Poet in the Poems* (Princeton, N.J., 1978), and agree that religion was not decisive for him.

upheld by religion. It was also perfectly proper for the State to
exclude from the government of nation or borough any member of a church it did not favour; the Acts which gave real or
nominal Anglicans the monopoly of politics in England were
among the arrangements which could be defended from the
Law of Nature. On the other hand, the State was right to
tolerate the worship of peaceable Dissenters – and to make sure
that the Established Church's leaders were sensible, co-
operative men by appointing such men to the leadership.
Warburton was himself made Bishop of Gloucester, although
he had never been to a university. As he once wrote with
unusual candour, although miracles had been needed in the
days of the martyrs 'now the profession of the Christian faith is
attended with ease and honour; and the conviction which the
weight of human testimony and the conclusions of human
reason afford us of its truth is abundantly sufficient to support
us in our religious perseverance.'[16]

Such a defence of the Revolution Settlement applied a
coating of sweet theology to the sugar of political conservatism.
In the circumstances of the time it was not a manifestly
unreasonable argument. (The argument was at least more
reasonable than that to be found in Warburton's later and
much bigger book, *The Divine Legation of Moses*, to the effect that
the Old Testament must have been inspired by God since if it
had been merely human wisdom it would have taught more
clearly about life after death.) The Established Church of
England did seem to many to deserve its privileges because it
was the largest Church in an England which was prospering.
The literature of the period frequently showed the central
position of the parish church. Thomas Gray's meditations
amid the hallowed graves of Stoke Poges (*Elegy in a Country
Churchyard*, 1750) became immensely popular, as did Oliver
Goldsmith's novel about the fortunes of the blameless Dr
Primrose and his more human family, *The Vicar of Wakefield*,
completed in 1762. In *The Deserted Village* Goldsmith painted a
little portrait of a parish priest without blemish (so far as he
saw); it is thought to have been a portrait of his own father.

---

[16] A. W. Evans studied *Warburton and Warburtonians* (London, 1932).

Henry Fielding's Parson Thwackum would raise a smile but not total ridicule by his famous defence of the perfection of religion: 'When I mention Religion, I mean the Christian Religion; and not only the Christian Religion, but the Protestant Religion; and not only the Protestant Religion, but the Church of England.'[17]

But can the eighteenth-century bishops be defended?

Later generations have been horrified by the thought of the bishop who was in London whenever the House of Lords was sitting (usually from October or November to May or June); who voted in Parliament, and lobbied in local elections, at the bidding of his political patrons; who had little pastoral contact with ordinands, priests or people in his diocese; and whose teaching, such as it was, exuded satisfaction with the social order. These bishops, as they look out from their portraits, the faces florid under their wigs, often seem as if they have returned from a day's hunting in a vain attempt to shed the effects of the previous evening's drinking. However, in justice we ought to recall that bishops were then regarded as great officers of the State as well as of the Church, and that the prominence of twenty-six of them in the small House of Lords, holding their own with the secular aristocracy, was held to be a proof of how Christian the country was. As late as 1711 it was thought fitting for a bishop to be given high office in the government as Lord Privy Seal – John Robinson, a distinguished diplomat, who negotiated the peace of Utrecht but was less competent as Bishop first of Bristol and then of London.

Particularly in view of the veneration of this age for the rights of propertied individuals, it was not easy for an Archbishop of Canterbury or for anyone else to remove a bishop – or to rebuke him, as Archbishop Tenison found when he had to institute legal action against two exceptionally scandalous Welsh bishops. Even more difficult was it to rebuke Lancelot Blackburne, Archbishop of York 1724–43. A former naval chaplain,

---

[17] The standard modern studies are Norman Sykes, *Church and State in England in the Eighteenth Century* (Cambridge, 1934); S. C. Carpenter, *Eighteenth-century Church and People* (London, 1959); John Carswell, *From Revolution to Revolution: England 1688–1776* (London, 1973).

he was one of the worst bishops of the period, never holding a
single confirmation. But the slackness of the average eighteenth-century bishop should not be exaggerated. His conception of his duty was probably not very different from the
standard which had been normal in the Middle Ages and in
most of the post-Reformation history of the Church of
England. His essential functions in his diocese were believed to
be jurisdiction (especially through the visitation which was
supposed to be held every third year), ordaining and confirming – but no great damage was thought to be done if the
routine of the jurisdiction had to be delegated to his subordin-
ates (the chancellor, the registrar and the archdeacons); if
young men seeking Holy Orders had to travel to where he was
(perhaps in London); or if the laity seeking confirmation had to
assemble in large numbers when he appeared. This was the
system which many highly respected bishops had operated
during and since the Middle Ages. While the spiritual level of
the eighteenth-century bishops did not reach the best standards of the past, most of the new century's bishops were, it
seems, on the whole faithful to their duties as they acknowledged them. Even the hated Benjamin Hoadly (who did not
add to his attractiveness by being so crippled that he had to
preach kneeling) appears to have been faithful in this limited
sense as Bishop of Winchester.

One of the problems was the gross inequality in the incomes
of the bishops (as in the Middle Ages). In the 1760s the richest
bishoprics were worth many thousands – Canterbury 7,
Durham 6, Winchester 5, York 4½, London 4 – at a time when
Welsh bishops, or a Bishop of Bristol, Oxford or Rochester, got
under £600. The poorer bishops were still expected to live in
style and to maintain London houses, so that they had to be
financed by being deans also. Inevitably the poorer bishops
also had their eyes on succeeding their richer brethren. This
could mean that they did not dedicate themselves to their
present dioceses and that political patrons continued to have a
hold over them. And whether or not they had been lucky in
being transferred up the financial ladder, they would not
resign. There was no system of pensions for bishops, and it
seems never to have occurred to them that resignation in old

age was a moral duty – any more than this has seemed the duty of twentieth-century popes or monarchs.

It was a morally indefensible system, but it is not necessary to blame all its defects on the eighteenth century; for the system was inherited. Nathaniel Crewe, for example, was said to have paid King Charles a large sum for the benefit of his mistress Nell Gwynne in exchange for the bishopric of Durham in 1674. If he did, it turned out to be a good investment. He enjoyed the revenues of the great bishopric until his death in 1721, although he accepted a seat on the Ecclesiastical Commission which King James instituted and retained some Jacobite sympathies. The Whig bishops cold-shouldered him. The ups and downs of politics in Westminster did not really disturb the Bishop of Durham, however. He maintained a nobleman's standard of living in Durham Castle, in Auckland Castle and in the great house in Northamptonshire which he inherited with the barony of Crewe from his brother. He was not a neglectful bishop by his own standards. When he examined the fitness of candidates for the priesthood, he bade them translate into Latin the English sentence from the Prayer Book, 'I have examined them and find them so qualified'. Lord Crewe left a benefaction which still enables his happy guests in the university of Oxford to consume champagne and strawberries in his memory each year.[18]

The eighteenth-century Church of England was, however, the home of at least one saint – and he was a bishop. Thomas Wilson, chaplain to the Earl of Derby and tutor to his son, was persuaded to agree to be consecrated bishop of the Isle of Man in 1698. The stipend was small; no seat in the Lords was attached; there had been a vacancy for five years; and Wilson was appointed because the Earl of Derby was also Lord of Man. He was the pastor of his diocese until he died in 1755 at the age of ninety-two. He gave much practical help to the poor and told the farmers about new agricultural methods; he fought the smugglers; he founded schools and a public library; he learned the Manx language in order to write the first books in it. Since the Act of Uniformity did not apply to the little

---

[18] See C. E. Whiting, *Nathaniel, Lord Crewe* (London, 1940).

island in the Irish Sea, he felt able both to add to the Book of Common Prayer and to disregard any rule that communicants must kneel. He conferred with his clergy (there were about twenty-five of them) in an annual synod, and young men they agreed would be suitable as future priests were taken to live in his home for a year. He insisted on a strict discipline of sinners, excommunicating a governor's wife for making slanderous statements, suspending an archdeacon for giving communion to her, and refusing to yield although imprisoned for two months. He took an active interest in missionary work in America, writing a little book which he hoped would be of help while teaching Red Indians. He refused at least one invitation to move to a more lucrative bishopric. On the Isle of Man he had seen a vision rather like St John's on the island of Patmos.[19]

Under bishops who might be a Lord Crewe or a Thomas Wilson or something in between, the parochial clergy were a mixed lot.

One problem was that many of the medieval parishes were too small to support a full-time resident pastor at the standard which he expected now that he was probably a graduate. About half the parishes were worth less than £80 a year. Or perhaps the parsonage was reckoned uninhabitable by a gentleman's family. Because there was no machinery for merging parishes their incomes were merged, but this meant the scandal of a non-resident rector or vicar, often leaving the services to be taken by an ill-paid curate. Rowlandson's cartoons of the plump Dr Syntax with his starveling curate were fair comment. Graduates were allowed to hold two livings if not more than thirty miles apart. Non-residence was also allowed to those who taught in the universities or schools, to chaplains to the nobility, the army or the navy, to clergymen suffering from ill health or where there was no suitable house. In the diocese of Oxford in the 1780s about a hundred out of 165 incumbents

---

[19] The life and prayers of Bishop Wilson, first made widely known in a biography of 1781, were studied by H. A. L. Rice, *The Bridge Builders* (London, 1961), pp. 66–8. *The Diaries of Thomas Wilson*, the saintly bishop's far from saintly son, were edited by C. L. S. Linnell (London, 1964).

were non-resident, mainly because they lived in the university. In the diocese of York the equivalent figure was 218 out of 836; in the diocese of Exeter, 159 out of 290. On the other hand, some of the medieval parishes into which England was still divided now contained a population far too large to be cared for adequately. Manchester, for example, possessed the one medieval parish church – for a population which was at least twenty thousand by 1750. Until 1818 an Act of Parliament was required to set up a new parish, and the trouble and expense seldom seemed worthwhile. The Church's pastoral work in the increasingly industrialized Midlands and North was crippled by the attitude summed up in a remark made by Archibishop Herring of York in 1758: 'I think philosophy, Christianity and polity are all against changes.'

In the Middle Ages the defects of the ecclesiastical system and of preaching had been compensated for by popular devotion to the Mass. It had been the ambition of both Calvin and Cranmer to retain the centrality of the 'Lord's Supper', week by week, in a reformed Church; but this ambition had never been shared by the English people. With the new emphasis on the importance of spiritual preparation for the sacrament had come a new reluctance on the part of the devout to attempt a worthy preparation frequently. The exceptionally pious Queen Anne communicated once a month, but in the diocese of York in 1743 only 72 out of the 836 churches had monthly celebrations of this service. And the undevout not unnaturally found Morning Prayer tedious, as many had done in a more generally religious period. Addison depicted his beloved squire, Sir Roger, nodding off but awakening to rebuke anyone else caught asleep – and as he passed through the bowing congregation after the service, asking after absentees. They were all his tenants.

However, it would be a mistake to think that the typical parish church in the eighteenth century was totally lifeless. Archdeacons were constantly pressing for Holy Communion to be held more frequently, and Morning Prayer every Sunday and Holy Days, with the Litany on Wednesdays and Fridays – and for the churches to be kept in good repair, for which a rate could be levied on all residents in the parish. Many churches were improved, and some new churches were built. The clergy, still paid mainly by tithes, were often busy in the duties as well as in the amusements of life in the countryside. Many of them were justices of the peace; all of them, and their church-wardens, were expected to report their parishioners' moral misdemeanours each year at the archdeacon's visitation. John Wesley was one of those who bore witness to the fact that few of the parish clergy were grossly immoral. An inquiry into church life in Devon led to a conclusion which surprised the scholar who made it. It revealed 'a Church intimately involved in the life of the people, providing a great deal of their justice, acting the unenviable role of moral policeman, settling their disputes over legacies, protecting their rights, educating their children, and even pioneering much that has come to be known as social security.'[20]

A fair assessment of church life in this period must also take the work of Thomas Bray into account. In 1693 this Warwick-shire rector with humble parents were chosen by Bishop Compton of London to be his representative or 'commissary' in the American colony of Maryland. Ten years earlier the Bishop had sent a tough Scotsman, James Blair, to begin a stormy but remarkably effective attempt to build up church life in a Virginia controlled by its increasingly prosperous tobacco planters. Blair's work as commissary lasted until his death in 1743, and included the foundation of William and Mary College at Williamsburg in 1693. Probably the Bishop envis-aged that Bray would make his home in Maryland, as Blair had done in Virginia. In the end, however, Bray spent only three months in America, in 1700. He could work better for the cause from an English base.

His first concern was to recruit clergy for the colony and his second was to arm them with books, since 'none but the poorer among the clergy here could be persuaded to leave their friends and native country and go so far'. He therefore opened a public

---

[20] Arthur Warne, *Church and Society in Eighteenth-century Devon* (Newton Abbot, Devon, 1969), p. 9. See also Basil Clarke, *Church Building in the Eighteenth Century* (London, 1963). Richard Gough wrote a vivid *History of Myddle* at the beginning of the century, recounting the secrets of the parishioners who would gather Sunday by Sunday (reprinted, Harmondsworth, Middx, 1981).

appeal for parochial libraries to encourage 'religion and learning in the foreign plantations'. It was not long before he
realized that similar libraries needed to be provided to help
clergy in England and Wales – and that the need was even
greater for schools to give a rudimentary education to the
children of the poor. As the needs impressed themselves on
him, he looked with envy on the Sacred Congregation for the
Propagation (*Propaganda*) of the Faith established in Rome in
1622. He dreamed of nationwide organizations to promote his
schemes and talked to others about his hopes – with effects.
Any close imitation of Rome in the Church of England was out
of the question, but on 8 March 1699 four laymen met in
London to found a Society for Promoting Christian Knowledge, the oldest missionary society in that church. It was to
work in England as well as in the American colonies. Two
years later a Society for Propagating the Gospel in Foreign
Parts was founded with much the same support, its chief aim
being the provision of 'a sufficient maintenance . . . for an
orthodox clergy' in America. This SPG was more official as
well as more specialized than the SPCK; it was granted a royal
charter like the great trading companies, it had Archbishop
Tenison as an active leader, and it was blessed by the clergy in
their newly revived Convocation of Canterbury. For the time
being India was closed to English missionaries, since the
rapidly expanding East India Company had no wish to irritate
the 'natives'. But the SPCK and the SPG were launched on
work which would take them into all the continents. The
SPCK was especially fortunate in that an American businessman, Henry Newman, found his life's work as the society's
secretary, 1708–43 – and was extraordinarily effective.
Thomas Bray also remained busy, in the creation of libraries
and schools and in the support of the American clergy, until his
death in 1730.[21]

One of the tasks undertaken by the SPCK was 'to promote
and encourage the erection of charity schools in all parts of

---

[21] See H. P. Thompson, *Into all Lands: The History of the SPG* (London, 1951), and *Thomas Bray* (London, 1954); W. L. Cowie, *Henry Newman* (London, 1956); W. K. Lowther Clarke, *A History of the SPCK* (London, 1959).

England and Wales'. Hundreds of such schools were founded for the children of the poor by one means or another, in the century from 1690. It was a movement so notable that there was alarm in privileged circles. Were the Tory squires who were often patrons of these schools training up little Jacobites? Or were they educating the children above their station in life, giving them interests and skills which would make them discontented with their lot as servants and labourers? Bishop Gibson of London felt obliged to issue solemn instructions that in the charity schools there should be the strictest loyalty to the 'Protestant succession' on the throne and to the class system as ordained by God.[22]

Many voluntary societies for charitable work or evangelism, exhorted by preachers and strengthened by worship together in private or in church, flourished at the turn of the seventeenth and eighteenth centuries. In 1701 it was estimated that there were more than forty of them in London, where they originated (with young men as members) in the 1670s. They also existed in many provincial towns. Among them, from 1690 onwards, were 'Societies for the Reformation of Manners', in which Thomas Bray was heavily involved; *A Help to a National Reformation* (1700) was widely distributed by the SPCK. The Societies' chief aim was to prosecute offenders against the laws which still enforced morality. It is clear that with the destruction of the old Puritan censorship, drunkenness, prostitution, profanity, Sunday trading and similar behaviour flourished, and that no appeal to the law could by itself be effective in suppressing it. But it is also clear that there were many people in England who deplored the trend. After the death of Charles II a revulsion against the immorality which he had embodied was quite widespread. Even at his court there had been saints; John Evelyn wrote a biography of one of them, Mrs Godolphin, a lady-in-waiting to the Queen. The most dissolute of his courtiers, the Earl of Rochester, directed that a book should be published by Bishop Burnet recording his shame and penitence. And far away from London many people needed no persuading to criticize London's vice – men such as Sir Roger

---

[22] See Mary G. Jones, *The Charity School Movement* (Cambridge, 1938).

de Coverley, whom the devout Joseph Addison portrayed in his famous *Spectator* sketch, which was not entirely a work of the imagination. Even in the wicked city the righteous could be found. By 1720 the London societies were boasting in print that there had been 75,270 prosecutions since 1691. Within worldly London, preachers who exerted themselves could still gain a hearing. 'Orator' Henley, who offered popular journalism with an edifying tone, was so successful that admission to his congregation was by ticket only. In 1750 the Bishop of London issued a pamphlet warning his diocese that the recent earthquake had been caused by its flagrant immorality. The warning sold over a hundred thousand copies.[23]

Two very worldly earls may be cited as witnesses to the position of the Church of England in eighteenth-century society.

The Earl of Chesterfield's many letters of good advice to his illegitimate son were, immediately he was dead, sold to a publisher by the woman whom his son had married without his knowledge. In one of them mention was made of religion. The year was 1750. 'I have seldom or never written to you on the subject of Religion and Morality: your own reason, I am persuaded, has given you true notions of both; they best speak for themselves; but if they wanted assistance, you have Mr Harte at hand . . .' Chesterfield confined himself to 'the decency, the utility, and the necessity of preserving the appearances'. He hastened to assure the boy that 'I do not mean that you should talk or act like a missionary, or an enthusiast, nor that you should take up a controversial cudgel against whoever attacks the sect you are of.' He meant simply 'that you should by no means seem to approve, encourage or applaud, those libertine notions which strike at religions equally, and which are the poor threadbare topics of half wits, or minute philosophers.' 'Depend on this truth,' this earl who was an apostle of 'good-breeding' explained, 'that every man is the worse looked upon, and the less trusted, for being thought to have no religion . . . and a wise atheist (if such a thing there is) would, for his

---

[23] See D. W. R. Bahlman, *The Moral Revolution of 1688* (Princeton, N.J., 1957). Graham Midgley studied *The Life of Orator Henley* (Oxford, 1973).

own interest, and character in this world, pretend to some religion.'[24]

   Frederick Hervey was a son of the first Earl of Bristol, which explains why he was made a priest in 1755, Bishop of Cloyne in 1767 and Bishop of Derry next year. His elder brother was for a year Lord Lieutenant of Ireland, although he never set foot there. Frederick Hervey's income as Bishop of Derry was at first around £7,000 a year but it rose to near £20,000 because he was a shrewd manager of the episcopal estates. He added another £20,000 a year when he succeeded to the earldom. He was sensitive to the fact that most of those who paid tithes to the clergy of his diocese were either Roman Catholics or Presbyterians, and he supported schemes to enable Roman Catholics to swear allegiance to the Crown and to change the hated tithes into the equivalent in land to be owned by the parson; although neither of these schemes came to anything. At one stage he made himself popular (although not with other Englishmen) by demanding that Irish Catholics should be given the vote. In the two very elegant palaces which he built for himself in his diocese he was hospitable. After dinner he liked to make his clergy run races. But his real interest lay in continental travel. His journeys were so extensive and so extravagant that it is said that all Bristol Hotels are named after him; innkeepers dreamed that he would turn up. One of Hervey's motives was to collect works of art to adorn his episcopal palaces, his London house or the great house at Ickworth in Suffolk, which he rebuilt very handsomely; but his main motive in his travels seems to have been an insatiable love of amusement and adventure. After 1782 he never saw his wife again; after 1791 he never saw his diocese again; after 1792 he never saw England again. As he wandered through Europe wearing a purple cap with a golden tassel he talked about the importance of political liberty, thus alarming some of his royal and aristocratic hosts; but when war came he also appointed himself a spy on behalf of the British government, and for this reason was for a time imprisoned by the French revolutionary

---

[24] Chesterfield's *Letters*, edited by Bonamy Dobrée in 6 volumes (London, 1932), have not yet been used in a good biography.

army in Milan. He died in 1803 while on the road to Rome.

Especially after 1791 the earl-bishop gave many people the impression that he was no Christian in belief or behaviour. George III refused to speak to this 'wicked prelate'. Nelson's mistress Emma Hamilton, who knew him well, was equally shocked by him. She reported that he 'was an avowed sceptic in religion, the doctrines and institutions of which he would not scruple to ridicule in the company of women, treating even the immortality of the soul as an article of indifference.' But he did not shock all his contemporaries. Jeremy Bentham, normally no friend to parsons, found him in 1782 'a most excellent companion, pleasant, intelligent, well read and well bred, liberal-minded to the last degree'. John Wesley, who met him twice during the 1770s, noted that a sermon by the Bishop on the Holy Spirit was 'useful', that he celebrated Holy Communion 'with admirable solemnity', and that he was 'plenteous in good works'. When he died an obelisk was erected to this 'friend and protector' of all Christians in his diocese, and the subscribers included the local Roman Catholic bishop and the leading Dissenting minister.[25]

The eighteenth-century Church of England was so richly established that it seemed natural for an Earl of Chesterfield to advise his bastard son to pretend to some religious belief even if he had none – and for an Earl of Bristol to include the duties of a bishop among the many projects which for a time took a very rich man's fancy. The two earls illustrate what Bishop Warburton meant by saying that 'the profession of the Christian faith is attended with ease and honour'.

PROTESTANT DISSENT IN DECLINE
AND AT WORSHIP

One of the reasons why the Established Church was complacent in the eighteenth century was the numerical decline of its rivals.

---

[25] See Brian Fothergill, *The Mitred Earl* (London, 1974).

Among the Protestant Dissenters, the century witnessed a diminishment of the zeal for discipline which Richard Baxter had typified. Still in the 1680s it could be thought that a strict moral and theological discipline over its members, protesting against Anglican laxity, was the characteristic mark of a Dissenting congregation, just as the doctrine of the divine right of kings was characteristic of the Church of England; but during the eighteenth century it became plain that Dissenters, like Anglicans, had developed other interests.

One interest was now the basic discussion about the nature of God and the divinity of Christ. In the 1690s a fiery Welshman, Richard Davis, preached a Gospel which was enthusiastic but considerably simpler than Calvinism, and the controversy which he aroused, particularly among his fellow Congregationalists and among the Baptists, led to divisions. Almost thirty years later another dispute broke out in Exeter: a Presbyterian minister, James Pierce, was accused of not believing in the Trinity. Both sides now appealed to the Dissenting ministers in London, who argued the matter out during passionate meetings in Salters' Hall early in 1719. It was resolved by 57 votes to 53 that there was no need to insist on 'human compositions or interpretations of the doctrine of Trinity'. The defeated minority replied by subscribing publicly to a Trinitarian declaration. It did not follow that the 'non-subscribers' were all Unitarians (or even Arians), but gradually the trustees of a considerable number of Presbyterian chapels made it clear that they had no objections to up-to-date views in the pulpits. Any Calvinist in the congregation either kept quiet or walked out to the nearest Congregational chapel, and a number of Presbyterian congregations which wished to remain orthodox found it safer to become Congregational, since then the local church could be based on a covenant which all must accept.

Another interest growing among Dissenters in the eighteenth century was the feeling that there ought to be equality in all things with conforming members of the Church of England. Dissenters were tolerated, and in 1767 Lord Mansfield – the great judge who also declared that no slave could remain a slave on English soil – declared that the efforts of the corporation of the City of London to exclude occasional conformists were illegal because they amounted to 'persecution'; but there was no real equality. As late as 1770 the leading jurist of the day, Sir William Blackstone of Oxford, could assert that the laws against their worship were only 'suspended'. Dissenters were still required to take the Anglican sacrament ('occasional conformity') if they wished to hold public office; they were still unable to send their sons to Oxford, and young Dissenters could not take degrees at Cambridge; they must still be married in Anglican churches and buried in Anglican church-yards, sometimes in humiliating conditions; above all, they were still forced to pay tithes to support the Anglican clergy.

It might have been expected that the need to combine in order to exert pressure on Parliament would lead to a religious union among the Dissenters themselves, but in fact it was soon recognized that such a union was unobtainable and that what was needed was a combination for strictly practical purposes. Early in the 1690s a Common Fund to support poor ministers, and a 'Happy Union' of the ministers themselves, promised to unite Presbyterians and Congregationalists; but both joint efforts were dead by 1695 and no subsequent attempt to unite the two denominations was successful until 1972. Instead the London ministers of these denominations combined with Baptists to present various addresses to Queen Anne. The experience of being able to do this together slowly encouraged the formation of a body which would be the equivalent of the 'Meeting for Sufferings' which had organized the Quakers' approaches to the politicians ever since 1675. The Quakers were particularly active as a pressure group in the 1730s, when the other Dissenters knew that many of the Whigs would welcome their approaches; the Whigs had already set aside a thousand pounds of public money each year (the *regium donum*) to assist ministers' widows, as a token of good will. Many of the Dissenters set their heart on the complete repeal of the Test and Corporation Acts, to end the humiliation of having either to receive the Anglican sacrament or to abandon all hopes of public office; and in 1732 a committee of twenty-one laymen was established in London under the chairmanship of a wealthy banker, Samuel Holden. The Whigs were as polite to this committee as they could be without doing what was wanted. The only outcome was that a permanent and invaluable instrument of co-operation had been forged: the Protestant Dissenting Deputies.[26]

Thus the Dissenters found that the discussion of basic theology had become divisive – and that their congregations had little wish to unite as a great alternative church although it was possible to combine for the limited purpose of improving their political standing by patient lobbying. It was a situation which showed that the old fires of Puritan conviction were dying down. But just as it was inaccurate to think of the Church of England as being totally given over to worldliness, so it would be wrong to suppose that Dissent had entirely lost the Puritan heritage. Even when they prospered Dissenters could still be inspired by the Puritan spirit of self-discipline and self-sacrifice. Thus a Baptist layman who accumulated a vast fortune, Thomas Guy, used it all to build and endow Guy's Hospital in London. At a more academic level a minister, Daniel Neal, set himself the task of showing from history how it ought to have been possible to separate the Puritans' admirable piety and virtue from their less admirable intolerance. *A History of New England* (1720) was followed by *A History of the Puritans* in four volumes (1732–38). Gradually Neal's interpretation of the past won its way, constituting a fresh argument that the heirs of the English Puritans ought to be fully tolerated themselves. In 1730 a young man named Strictland Gough published *An Enquiry into the Causes of the Decay of the Dissenting Interest*, arguing that 'the spirit of the good old Puritans was nothing else but a spirit of liberty' and that the trouble was that not enough liberty had been allowed to modern theology. He was answered by a minister named Philip Doddridge. An orthodox believer although a 'non-subscriber', in Northampton he conducted the best small educational establishment in the country but was also an effective pastor of simple folk, as was shown by his book on *The Rise and Progress of Religion in the*

---

[26] See Bernard Lord Manning, *The Protestant Dissenting Deputies* (Cambridge, 1952), and N. Crowther-Hunt, *Two Early Political Associations* (Oxford, 1961). Duncan Coomer portrayed *English Dissent under the Early Hanoverians* (London, 1946).

Soul. 'Plain people of low education and vulgar taste,' he pointed out to the young modernist, 'constitute nine parts in ten of most of our congregations.' They needed a simple Gospel.[27]

This Gospel was given to Dissenters in an acceptable form by hymns. Doddridge wrote some which became much loved – by millions of Christians to come, as well as by these Dissenters – including 'O God of Jacob, by whose hand' and 'Hark the glad sound, the Saviour comes'. But the greatest work was done by Isaac Watts, who began writing hymns Sunday by Sunday for the little congregation in Southampton where his father was a deacon. He was well educated and called to be the minister of the Mark Lane congregation in London, to which the great John Owen had preached in the days of persecution, but after ten years of that he made his escape from pastoral routine, pleading that his health had broken down. He was a guest in the home of Sir Thomas Abney, a former Lord Mayor of London, for the rest of his life. The fact was that he had his own vocation, to write hymns and theology; to express the theology in the hymns. He inherited a tradition where worship was imprisoned by Calvin's insistence that only the words of Holy Scripture should be heard, apart from the exposition of Scripture in the preaching and the prayers. In practice that meant metrical psalms offensive to anyone who loved poetry and music and with little of the Gospel in them; 'of all our religious solemnities,' he wrote, 'psalmody is the most unhappily managed.' So he set himself the task of composing some seven hundred hymns, in the spirit of one of them: 'Come, let us join our cheerful songs.'

His output included *Divine Songs Attempted in Easy Language for the Use of Children* (1715). For adults or for children, his hymns all taught a theology which was orthodox but not rigid. In his prose works Watts suggested liberal compromises in the controversies over predestination and the Trinity, while his solution to the ecclesiastical problem was that there should be a National Church teaching a noncontroversial 'Natural Religion' and tolerating Dissenters and Anglicans alike. In the

---

[27] See Malcolm Deacon, *Philip Doddridge of Northampton* (Northampton, 1980).

hymns, however, his main aim was simplicity, although he acknowledged that it was 'difficult to work every line to the level of a whole congregation and yet to keep it above contempt.' Deliberately he strung plain Anglo-Saxon words together in a few well-known metres, with lines short enough to be announced before they were sung. His success was immense, preserving orthodoxy through a century when it was seldom heard so clearly from the pulpit. His *Hymns and Spiritual Songs* published in 1707 included 'When I survey the wond'rous cross'. A later collection consisted of *Psalms of David Imitated in the Language of the New Testament* (1719) and included two more hymns which became almost equally prominent features of English religion: 'O God, our help in ages past' and 'Jesus shall reign wher'er the sun'.

By the time Watts died in 1748, the use of these and other hymns had been accepted by all the Dissenters apart from Quakers and the Particular Baptists. Later in the century so stout an Anglican as Samuel Johnson admired the hymns for their purity of faith and of diction, and as the Church of England adopted the use of hymns the work of Watts became enduringly popular. There was an initial period of hesitation, when even hymns so orthodox seemed dangerous novelties to conservative Dissenters or Anglicans, who assumed that the limit of modernization had been reached with the metrical psalms. Slowly such hesitations yielded before the power of the hymns to make people love and voice a biblical faith. Watts, it has been said, 'sees the cross as Milton had seen it, planted on a globe hung in space, surrounded by the vast distances of the universe. He sees the drama in Palestine prepared before the beginning of time and still decisive when time has ceased to be.'[28] But even that tribute does not quite cover the theology which gave power to the hymns of Isaac Watts. He did not merely present the cosmic grandeur of the God revealed in Christ, as Milton had done. He expressed a warmly human

---

[28] Bernard Lord Manning, *The Hymns of Wesley and Watts* (London, 1942), p. 83. Horton Davies studied Dissenting as well as Anglican buildings and practices in *Worship and Theology in England from Watts and Wesley to Maurice* (Princeton, N.J., 1961). Other studies include Arthur P. Davis, *Isaac Watts* (London, 1948), and Harry Escott, *Isaac Watts, Hymnographer* (London, 1952).

love and gratitude towards the suffering Christ, as Milton had not done. Thus his work flowed into the hymns and into the spiritual revival led by Evangelicals such as the brothers John and Charles Wesley, who underwent their conversion experience ten years before his death. In Georgian England the religion of the Puritans seemed to be going through a depression, a winter. But here was a crocus, a herald of the Evangelical and Methodist spring, when Watts sang about the 'young prince of glory' on the cross:

> Love so amazing, so divine,
> Demands my soul, my life, my all.

CATHOLIC DISSENT IN OBSCURITY AND AT WORSHIP

Half the 'Papist' peers and hundreds of gentlemen went into exile with James II. Those remaining paid another price. In 1692 the vindictive strengthening of the penal laws included a long-lasting doubling of the land tax to pay for King William's army, and Papists were forbidden to go on any long journey without a special licence. The annual Mutiny Act claimed that the army was kept in being against militant Popery. In theory no Roman Catholic could inherit or sell land, although in practice Anglican trustees often got round the prohibition. Lower down the social scale a Roman Catholic faced prejudice and feared violence. It is not surprising that under this pressure there were many desertions from the 'old religion'. Although the general population seems to have started growing fast after about 1740 (due mainly to the conquest of smallpox and the disappearance of the rats which had carried 'the plague'), the Roman Catholic community was probably more or less static. A census of Papists conducted for Parliament in 1767 produced a figure just short of seventy thousand, and even if this was too low it seems probable that the community had grown in a hundred years by no more than twenty thousand.

The number of priests had to be reduced. Their own bishops counted fewer than four hundred of them at work in 1773, the year when the Pope suppressed the Jesuit order which had been growing increasingly unpopular. As the law stood, any Roman Catholic priest in the country could be imprisoned for life and any informer reporting the celebration of the Mass, which could be reckoned high treason, could earn £100. The last successful prosecution occurred in 1767, when John Baptist Maloney was sentenced to life imprisonment but soon released. However, the main reason why there were fewer priests was that there was less money to pay for them. In practice the authorities tolerated, although they also despised, what the priests did.

The steady pressure against Roman Catholicism was pushing its faithful adherents more and more to the margins of society. In America Maryland, which had previously been a refuge, was now made a royal colony, and the Church of England was formally established there in 1702. In England the church of James II and John Dryden was coming to seem, in John Henry Newman's words, 'no longer the Catholic Church in the country; nay, no longer, I may say, a Catholic community – but a few adherents of the Old Religion, moving silently and sorrowfully about as memorials of what had been . . . An old-fashioned house of gloomy appearance, closed in with high walls, with an iron gate and yews, and the report attaching to it that "Roman Catholics" lived there . . .' John Leyburn, who had been consecrated a bishop for the English back in 1685 when James II had been promising so much, was imprisoned after that foolish monarch's fall and, on his release, lived obscurely in London until his death in 1702. His successor, Bonaventure Giffard, led a life of equal obscurity (and, it seems, no great effectiveness) until his own death in 1734.

Yet that was not the whole picture. The political disaster of the 1680s, followed by the decline of the Roman Catholic aristocracy and gentry, ultimately liberated congregations. In the countryside and country towns, instead of being totally dependent on a patron the faithful sometimes now hired a room in an inn for Mass or built a public chapel with an unprovocative modesty; and they gradually became more prosperous themselves, as part of the general economic progress of the time. In London their numbers grew to about twenty thousand, mainly because desperately poor Irish immigrants moved there hoping to pick up a living. There was, however, a touch of Baroque splendour about some of the chapels attached to London embassies, with a considerable staff of priests and music that attracted large congregations. Other elegant chapels were to be seen in country houses. The eighteenth century also saw a modernization of medieval customs which had hitherto seemed obligatory. It was no longer thought shocking for a Roman Catholic to work on a saint's day or to take some food before working on a day which was a fast in the Church's calendar; and in 1777 Rome officially reduced the number of 'holidays of obligation' in England. Priests who had been forced to disguise themselves in public as laymen now felt more acceptable to society. It symbolized much that they tended to wear wigs and brown (not black) coats, like Dissenting ministers.

In 1715, and again in 1745, their peaceableness was tested. What had been feared since Elizabethan times came to pass: a Roman Catholic claimant to the throne aroused a rebellion. But the Jacobites were disappointed in the support they received from the priests. In 1715 some gentry in Northumberland, Durham and Lancashire joined the abortive rising but there was no widespread movement. Even less practical interest in the Jacobite cause was shown in 1745; the main reaction, it seems, was alarm about the barbarism of the Young Pretender's army of Highlanders. And another test of the new status of Roman Catholicism in the country came when in 1753 it was made a criminal offence for anyone who was not a clergyman of the Church of England to conduct a marriage, the motive being alarm at the number of clandestine marriages. In an earlier period great tension would have been created as Roman Catholic priests stopped their flocks from obeying a Protestant Parliament. Instead most of the priests behaved like the Protestant Dissenting ministers. They allowed Roman Catholics to be married in the Anglican parish churches, and blessed them afterwards.[29]

---

[29] Basil Hemphill told of 'Catholic life in the penal times' in his *The Early Vicars Apostolic of England*, up to 1750. John Bossy traced the change from 'the age of the gentry' to 'the birth of a denomination' in *The English Catholic Community, 1570–1850*. See also Hugh Aveling, *The Handle and the Axe*, pp. 238–321.

Thus in a quiet time when Roman Catholicism might seem to be dying out in England, in deepest reality it was being renewed by the transfer of its base from the houses of the rich to the hearts of the poor, from the hopes of a political conquest to the assurance of a spiritual appeal.

The new security was embodied in the self-effacing figure of Bishop Richard Challoner, who became vicar apostolic of the London district in 1741 and remained faithful to that calling as a pastor for forty years. He never compromised over faith or morals. Indeed, he did what he could to resist the 1753 Marriage Act, urging his flock to be married by one of their own priests and, if they did feel obliged to go to an Anglican church in compliance with the law, never to join in the prayers offered there. But after a time he had to admit defeat, especially when Rome refused to back him up, and he made no fuss about it. To him the incident merely illustrated the trend which he recorded in a private letter of 1769: 'Oh! 'tis a melancholy thing to see the great decay of piety and religion amongst a great part of our Catholics.' For many years he used an assumed name, 'Mr Fisher', and referred to the Pope in his letters as 'Mr Abraham'. And his pessimism about the results of any public activity by, or on behalf of, his community seemed to be justified when in 1780 there were 'No Popery' riots in London led by a lunatic peer (who later fled to France and became a Jew), Lord George Gordon.

But Richard Challoner commended his faith to the poor. The custom had been established of using aristocrats as bishops: his own predecessor in the London area was a Petre (who spent most of his time in country houses in Essex), and his most distinguished fellow bishop was Richard Stonor of Stonor Park, vicar apostolic of the Midland district (also for forty years). The theory was that such men would finance their dignity out of their own wealth and dine with the gentry on equal terms. Challoner, in contrast, lived in humble London lodgings off his own meagre stipend, and gave as much of that stipend as he could to the poor. His last word was 'charity', because he was carrying a small sum entrusted to him for the poor. Every day of his life he found time, if at all possible, to talk with the poor – the poor whose horrifying surroundings were depicted in Hogarth's cartoons. This manner of life helped him to ensure that the suppression of the Society of Jesus did little to harm the English mission, In England the Jesuits ceased to be Jesuits, because the Pope had so commanded; but many of them remained at work, for they did not cease to be priests and pastors.

Challoner was the son of a Presbyterian trader, born in 1691 in the rabidly Protestant town of Lewes. His mother, when widowed, entered domestic service and found employment in the home of the daughter of Lord Strafford, the 'Papist' peer executed at the instigation of Titus Oates. The boy was converted to this lady's religion at the age of thirteen, following his mother, and within a year had agreed to go for his education to the college at Douai. Learning or teaching he remained in Flanders until 1730, when he began half a century of missionary labours in the London slums.

Most mornings, after long prayers, were devoted to writing, and as an author he was both prolific and effective. His most used work was *The Garden of the Soul*, a manual of devotion issued anonymously in 1740. It was an unimaginative book, and those brought up on it were to be called 'Garden-of-the-Soul Catholics' in patronizing terms by later generations who preferred more emotional and flamboyant devotions. It was a book of its time, long before any liturgical movement had spread a corporate picture of the Church. It advocated communion only eight times a year; it spoke about 'hearing Mass'; it encouraged private prayers during that service; it did not translate the Latin canon (central prayer). But it was the book of a holy man, written unpretentiously in order to help laymen to be holy. Each communion was to be preceded by a week's preparation; each day was to be prayed over in self-examination; each important act was to be offered in prayer; there must be a full confession of sins to a priest when possible. It was a religion for Catholics who could not count on splendour or even regularity in their public worship. When no priest was available, the faithful could still pray in quiet groups or alone. And to show the standards at which the eighteenth century must still aim in the cultivation of the soul, this saintly bishop spent much time collecting for publication material about four hundred Elizabethan or later missionary priests (many of them martyrs) and about the medieval saints of England (whose feasts he caused to be observed again after neglect). In his controversial pamphlets he appealed to the authority of the scriptures – and for his own flock he revised the Douai Version of the Bible, producing an edition which remained standard until after the second world war.

Once, when he was reminded of the likelihood that increasing numbers of the gentry would desert a penalized religion, he replied calmly: 'There will be a new people.' It was a prophecy which began to come true even during his lifetime. An Act of Parliament in 1778, prompted on the government's side by a desire to recruit for the army among Roman Catholics in Ireland and Scotland, was the beginning of this long-suffering community's emancipation. It entitled Roman Catholic laymen to inherit or sell estates, and priests to function unharmed, if they swore an oath of loyalty to the Hanoverian dynasty. It had been negotiated by some of the remaining Roman Catholic gentry with the government. Challoner seems to have been informed, but to have agreed to leave the responsibility with the government and his own laity. This enabled him to reassure the Vatican when an inquiry arrived about the compromise involved. 'They made it a point to take no notice of us in this whole affair,' he replied to Rome on behalf of the Vicars Apostolic, 'that they might not appear, as they said, to be any ways governed in such affairs as these or influenced by their priests.' And the Vatican accepted this explanation. The contrast with the papal claim to depose Elizabeth I could scarcely be greater. On the day after the royal assent to this Act of 1778, Challoner formally required all the priests in his district to pray in public for the Hanoverian Royal Family – a touch which showed how far he was from resenting the gentry's initiative. A reaction to this compromise came with the Gordon Riots, aimed against well-to-do Roman Catholics in London; but that reaction was hysterical and violent to an extent which offended all decently-minded Englishmen. The persecution which had begun under Elizabeth I was now effectively over. By 1830 Roman Catholics would be allowed to vote in parliamentary elections. Because of further immigration from famine-stricken Ireland, by 1850 there were to be half a million Roman Catholics in England, with complete freedom to worship and with no civic disabilities imposed on them because of their faith. Challoner's prophecy about a 'new people' had been fulfilled.

When this saintly pastor died in 1781, he was buried in a friend's family vault in the Berkshire village of Milton – until in 1946 his body was brought back to London, to lie in Westminster Cathedral. So in death he received the hospitality of an Anglican parish church, whose charitable rector wrote in his register: 'Buried the Reverend Richard Challoner, a Popish Priest and Titular Bishop of London and Salisbury, a very pious and good man, of great learning and extensive abilities.'[30]

---

[30] Edwin Burton compiled *The Life and Times of Bishop Challoner* (2 vols, London, 1909). Later research was presented in *Challoner and His Church*, ed. Eamon Duffy (London, 1981). The main background to Challoner's pastoral work was depicted by George Rudée, *Paris and London in the Eighteenth Century* (London, 1969).

Outline of Events

1547   Death of Henry VIII transfers power to Protestants
       under Protector Somerset; chantries suppressed
1549   First Book of Common Prayer
1552   Second Book of Common Prayer, more Protestant,
       and Forty-Two Articles
1553   Death of Edward VI transfers power to Catholics
       under Mary I
1554   Mary I marries Philip of Spain; Cardinal Pole
       reconciles England to Papacy
1556   Burning of Archbishop Thomas Cranmer
1558   Elizabeth I succeeds Mary I as Queen of England
1559   Acts of Supremacy and Uniformity establish Church
       of England; Book of Common Prayer slightly
       revised; Matthew Parker becomes Archbishop of
       Canterbury
1562   John Jewel's *Apologia* for Church of England
1563   John Foxe's *Book of Martyrs*; Thirty-Nine Articles of
       Religion
1565   Archbishop Matthew Parker's *Advertisements* cause
       Puritan protests
1570   Pope Pius V claims to depose Queen Elizabeth I
1572   Puritan *Admonition to Parliament*
1574   English mission of Roman Catholic priests from Douai
       begins
1576   Archbishop Edmund Grindal refuses to suppress
       Puritan 'prophesyings' and is deprived of power
1581   Execution of Saint Edmund Campion, Jesuit leader
1582   *A Treatise of Reformation without Tarrying for Any* by
       Robert Browne
1583   Archbishop John Whitgift leads campaign against
       Puritans
1588   Defeat of Spanish Armada
1590   First half of Edmund Spenser's *Faerie Queene*
1593   First four books of Richard Hooker's *Of the Laws of
       Ecclesiastical Polity*

1604 James I presides over Hampton Court Conference;
Richard Bancroft as Archbishop of Canterbury
begins enforcement of new canons
1605 Gunpowder Plot ignites fresh hatred of Roman
Catholics
1606 *Macbeth* and *King Lear*
1607 Colonization of Virginia
1611 Authorized Version of Bible
1616 Death of William Shakespeare
1617 Conversion experience of John Donne
1620 *Mayflower* takes Pilgrim Fathers to Massachusetts
1625 Charles I begins reign and favours Arminians
1630 Ordination of George Herbert
1633 William Laud becomes Archbishop of Canterbury
1640 Parliament meets, including many Puritans
1642 Civil war begins
1643 Westminster Assembly begins reform of Church and
doctrine
1645 Henry Vaughan retreats to Wales; Richard Crashaw
to Italy
1647 Cromwell breaks Levellers' agitation
1649 Execution of Charles I
1650 George Fox first called 'Quaker'
1651 *Leviathan* by Thomas Hobbes
1653 Oliver Cromwell made Lord Protector
1656 *Reformed Pastor* by Richard Baxter
1660 Restoration of Charles II; first meetings of Royal
Society encourage science
1662 Act of Uniformity excludes Dissenters from Church of
England
1664 First Conventicle Act begins persecution of Dissenters
1667 *Paradise Lost* by John Milton; Thomas Traherne moves
to London
1675 Sir Christopher Wren begins rebuilding of St Paul's
Cathedral
1678 'Popish Plot'; first part of John Bunyan's *Pilgrim's
Progress*
1681 William Penn chartered to found Pennsylvania
1685 Charles II becomes Roman Catholic on deathbed

1687   *Principia Mathematica* by Isaac Newton
1688   James II flees after failure to protect Roman Catholics
1689   Act of Toleration; *Essay Concerning Human Understanding*
         by John Locke
1690   William III wins battle of Boyne
1693   Death of nonjuror ex-archbishop, William Sancroft
1702   Queen Anne begins reign, favours High Churchmen
1707   *Hymns and Spiritual Songs* by Isaac Watts
1714   Death of Queen Anne transfer power to Whigs
1719   Dissenting ministers' debate about Holy Trinity
1723   Archbishop William Wake deprived of power by Sir
         Robert Walpole
1726   *Gulliver's Travels* by Jonathan Swift
1728   *A Serious Call to a Devout and Holy Life* by William Law
1730   *Christianity as Old as the Creation* by Matthew Tindal
1736   *The Analogy of Religion* by Joseph Butler
1741   G. F. Handel composes *Messiah*; Richard Challoner
         becomes vicar apostolic of London district

INDEX

Abbot, G., 197–8
Abney, Sir T., 501
Act for Abolishing Diversity of Opinions, 34
Act of Uniformity (1559), 79, 97; (1661), 428
Addison, J., 491, 495
Admonitions, 152, 163
Advertisements, 92
Allen, W., 126–8, 137–9
Allestree, R., 307
Ames, W., 245
Anabaptists, 53, 73
Analogy of Religion, 416,419–21
Andrewes, L., 186, 195–8, 320
Anne, Queen, 446, 473–7, 491
Apocrypha, 146
Areopagitica, 331, 334
Aristotle, 99, 101
Arminians, 183, 188–9, 204, 267, 277–8, 329
Articles of Religion (1552), 52; (1563), 151
Arundel, Earl of, 228, 232
Arundel of Wardour, Lord, 455
Arundell, Sir J., 140
Ascham, R., 81
Askewe, A., 34
Atterbury, F., 473–8
Aubrey, J., 391
Aylmer, J., 160

Bach, J. S., 443
Bacon, Sir F., 95, 156, 199, 381, 393
Baltimore, Lord, 254
Bancroft, R., 85, 98, 141, 165–9, 187, 193–5, 203
Baptism, 51, 145
Baptists, 167–8, 296, 335–6, 444, 499, 502
Barclay, R., 347
Barebones Parliament, 294
Barlow, W., 90, 169
Barnes, R., 74
Barrow, H., 167
Barrow, I., 387
Baxter, R., 129, 292, 297, 301, 308, 310, 313–9, 438–9
Beard, T., 290
Becket, Sir T., 282
Bedford church, 335–6
Bedford, Earls of, 156, 158, 257, 275
Bellarmine, Cardinal, 134, 175, 233
Benet of Canfield, 236–8
Bentham, J., 497

Berkeley, G., 417–18
Bermuda college, 417
Beveridge, W., 49
Bible (Coverdale's), 41; (Bishops), 93; (Douai), 133, 508; (Geneva), 146, 186; (Authorized), 185–6
Bishop, W., 234
Bishops in Church of England, 33, 80, 83–4, 90–1, 97, 99, 149–50, 182–3, 270–5, 306–10, 429, 439, 487–9
Blackstone, Sir W., 499
Blake, R., 295
Blake, W., 327, 387
Blair, J., 492
Blow, J., 422
Bolingbroke, Lord, 477–8
Bonner, E., 37, 49, 137
Boorstin, D., 354
Booth, C., 493
Bossy, J., 143
Boston, 251
Boucher, J., 46
Bowland, T., 153
Boyle, R., 389
Boyne, battle of, 469
Bradford, J., 18
Bradford, W., 248–9
Bramhall, J., 308
Bretchgirdle, J., 109
Bridgman, Sir O., 376, 441
Bristol, Earl of, 496–7
Browne, R., 167
Browne, Sir T., 364
Browning, T., 438
Bucer, M., 39, 50
Buchanan, G., 182
Buckingham, Duke of, 189–91, 201–2, 230
Buckley, S., 228
Bull, G., 403
Bull, J., 231
Bullinger, H., 39, 160
Bunyan, J., 333–6
Burghley, Lord, 75, 78–9, 137, 143, 156, 164
Burnet, G., 373, 476, 494
Butler, J., 415–21, 447
Byrd, W., 102–4

Calamy, E., 308
Calvinism, 39, 50–2, 144–5, 174–7, 183–4, 188, 191, 277–8, 329, 405–6, 498
Cambridge Platonists, 369–72, 396

Campion, E., 21–3, 70, 73
Canons (Cranmer's), 53–4; (1604), 193; (1640), 203, 311
Carolina, 395
Caroline, Queen, 416, 423
Cartwright, T., 162–3, 166
Catesbury, Sir W., 140
Catesby, R., 228
Cavalier Parliament, 365, 442
Cecil, Lord D., 319
Cecil, R., 78, 165, 175
Cecil, W., see Burghley
Centuries of Meditation, 374–8
Challoner, R., 506–9
Chandos, Duke of, 422
Chantries, 24, 37
Charles I, 188–93, 198–200, 230–1, 256, 272–86, 429
Charles II, 292–306, 349, 433–5, 441–2, 451–4
Charles V, 58–9
Charles, the Young Pretender, 466
Cheshire, 142
Chesterfield, Earl of, 495–6
Cheynell, F., 367
Chichester diocese, 84–6
Chillingworth, W., 366–7
Choral tradition, 102–4, 147, 421–2, 430
Church courts, 84, 149, 154, 430
Churchill, A., 459
Civil War (First), 276–9; (Second), 285
Clarendon, Earl of, 263, 275, 303, 309, 431, 434, 472
Clarke, S., 387, 403–4
Clement VIII, 99
Clitherow, M., 22
Coke, Sir E., 195
Coleman, E., 452
Coleridge, S. T., 107
Collier, J., 463
Collins, A., 401
Colton, R., 22
Communion, see Eucharist
Compton, H., 431–3, 470, 472
Comprehension (1688–9), 469–71
Conduitt, J., 390
Confirmation, 41, 51, 146, 428
Congregationalists, see Independents
Connecticut, 251, 254
Contarini, Cardinal, 64
Conventicle Act, 437
Convention Parliament, 443
Convocations (1553), 67; (1563), 151–2; (1640), 273–4; (1661), 311; (1701–19), 474–8
Coriolanus, 117

Cornish rebellion, 42–3
Corporation Act, 437, 478
Corpus MSS, 34–95
Cottington, Lord, 230
Cotton, J., 108, 248–9, 251, 256
Cotton, M., 250
Council of Trent, 27, 64–5
Counter-Reformation, 26–30, 103–4, 132–8, 224–39
Courteney, E., 60–1
Coverdale, M., 40, 90, 149, 185
Cox, R., 35, 172
Cragg, G. R., 406
Cranmer, T., 19–20, 33–4, 36, 39–43, 47, 49–56, 60–1, 66–7, 74
Crashaw, R., 225–7, 320
Cressy, S., 236
Crewe, N., 489
Cromwell, O., 26, 272, 278–80, 315
Cromwell, R., 300–2, 315
Cudworth, R., 340
Curteys, R., 84

Dale, T., 241
Danby, Earl of, 431, 451–3, 470, 498–505
Dance, G., 307
Daniel, S., 242
Danvers, Lady, 207, 215
Davenport, F., 53
Davies, R., 108
Davis, R., 498
De Garcina, Friar, 68
De Soto, Friar, 68
Declaration of Independence, 353
Declaration of Indulgence, 351, 441, 443, 446
Declaration of Sports, 184, 191
Dedham, 173
Dee, J., 378
Defoe, D., 406–8, 438
Dering, E., 153
Devon, Earl of, 201
Dibdale, R., 126
Digby, Lord, 261
Diggers, 287
Directory of Public Worship, 278, 288
Dissent, 436–49, 470, 498–503
Dissenting Academies, 448–9
Dod, J., 257
Doddridge, P., 501
Dodwell, H., 465
Donne, J., 82, 128, 207–17, 231, 241
Dort, Synod of, 183, 188, 368
Douai college, 127, 235–6
Dryden, J., 398–40, 461
Duppa, B., 306

Eachard, J., 440
Edgehill, battle of, 291
Edward VI, 32, 48, 54–6
Edwards, T., 280
Edwards, J., 394
Egerton, Sir T., 211
Eikon Basilike, 99, 286
Ejection (1662), 313, 428–9
Ejectors, 297
Eliot, J., 246
Eliot, T. S., 110, 196, 209
Elizabeth I, 45, 60–1, 76–83, 91–2, 114, 124–5, 147, 152–70, 382
Elizabeth of Bohemia, 184
English College, Rome, 128–9
Erasmus, 37
Essay Concerning Human Understanding, 394
Essex, Earls of, 78, 114, 257, 279
Eucharist, 26–7, 33, 41–2, 51, 73–4, 80, 146–7, 491
Evans, J., 444
Evelyn, J., 296, 494

Faerie Queene, 105–7
Fairfax, Sir T., 279, 283, 287, 331
Falkland, Lord, 276, 367
Fawkes, G., 117, 228–9
Feckenham, J., 137–8
Fell, M., 341, 344
Felton, J., 133
Ferrar, N., 220, 242
Field, J., 151, 166, 171
Fielding, H., 487
Fielding, J., 24
Fifth Monarchy Men, 301–2
Fisher, M., 243
Five Mile Act, 437
Fleetwood, C., 304
Fletcher, J., 120, 124, 161
Fletcher, R., 160–1
Fox, G., 298, 339–48
Foxe, J., 18–19, 54, 71–5, 149, 162
Framlingham, 56, 141
Frederick of Prussia, 480

Garard, J., 131, 140
Garden of the Soul, 507
Gardiner, H., 209
Gardiner, S., 17, 24, 34–5, 37, 41, 47, 50, 61–4, 75
Gardiner, S. R., 259
Garnet, H., 131
Garnet, T., 132
Gauden, J., 99, 286
George I, 477
George II, 425

George III, 426, 467, 497
Gibbon, E., 468
Gibbons, G., 360
Gibbons, O., 421
Gibson, E., 474, 482–3, 494
Gifford, B., 504
Gifford, W., 139
Gilbert, Sir H., 241
Gilpin, B., 49
Glanvill, J., 385
Godfrey, Sir E., 452
Godolphin, Mrs, 494
Goldsmith, O., 486
Goodman, G., 83, 224–5
Goodwin, T., 257–8
Gordon riots, 506, 508
Gough, S., 500
Grace Abounding, 334
Grand Remonstrance, 267
Gray, T., 486
Greene, R., 127
Greenham, R., 171–2
Greenwich, 68, 357
Greenwood, J., 167
Gregory XIII, 134, 139
Gresham's College, 384
Grey, Lady Jane, 55–6, 61
Grindal, E., 84, 105, 147, 152–3, 160–2
Guise, Duke of, 127, 139
Gulliver's Travels, 408–10
Gunpowder plot, 117, 229
Guy, T., 500
Gwynne, N., 435, 472, 489

Hales, J., 367–8
Hall, J., 322
Hamilton, E., 497
Hamlet, 111, 114, 116
Hammond, H., 307
Hampden, J., 267, 291, 446
Hampton Court Conference, 169–70, 182
Harding, T., 96
Harley, R., 406, 447, 476
Harvard College, 246
Harvey, F., 496–7
Harvey, W., 381
Hawksmoor, N., 360
Hearne, T., 467
Heath, N., 40, 137
Helwys, T., 268
Henrietta Maria, Queen, 189, 230, 272
Henry VIII, 124–5
Henry VIII, 23, 31–5, 124–5
Henry, Prince of Wales, 182
Henry, the Pretender, 466–7
Herbert, G., 215–21, 226

Herbert, Lord, 366
Herring, T., 491
Herst, R., 232
Hickes, G., 462
Higginson, F., 244
High Commission, 154, 203, 313
Hilton, W., 235
Hind and Panther, 398–9, 401
Hoadly, B., 468, 479, 488
Hobbes, T., 390–3
Holden, S., 499
Holtby, R., 130
Hooker, R., 27, 98–102, 148, 316, 455, 485
Hooker, T., 248–51, 258
Hooper, G., 465
Hooper, J., 18, 41, 47, 56
Hopkins, M., 380
Hopton, S., 377
Howard, F., 196
Howell, J., 206
Huddleston, Father, 435
Hunt, R., 241
Hunt, S., 108
Hunt, T., 131
Hurst, J., 18
Hurstfield, J., 187
Hutchinson, A., 252
Hutchinson, J., 261
Huxley, A., 237

Indemnity Act, 478
Independents, 280, 296–7, 316, 437, 444
Inflation, 43–6, 271
Ireland, 105–6, 270, 292, 469, 471, 496, 508–9
Ireton, H., 298–9

Jacob, H., 269
Jacobites, 466, 505
James I, 169, 181–9, 212–13, 228–30, 233, 382
James II, 351, 398, 442–60, 464
James, the Old Pretender, 458, 466
Jeffreys, Judge, 442, 457
Jennens, C., 424
Jesuits, 128–33, 503, 507
Jewel, J., 94–8, 160
Jews, return of, 296
Johnson, E., 250
Johnson, F., 167–8
Johnson, S., 208–9, 418, 423, 468, 470, 502
Jones, I., 231
Jonson, B., 229, 264, 378
Joseph, Père, 237–8
Josselin, R., 304, 313
Justification, 27–9

Juxon, W., 205, 286, 307, 434

Keith, G., 347
Ken, T., 461–5, 469
Kennett, W., 475
Kett's rebellion, 45
Kidderminster, 315–18
King, G., 347
King Lear, 118–24
Knappen, M. M., 177
Knox, J., 51, 60, 77, 155, 182
Knox, R., 335, 354–5

Lambert, J., 300–2
Lancashire, 143
Lanfranc, 40
Lasco, J. à, 39
Latimer, H., 19, 44, 49, 57
Latitudinarians, 372
Laud, W., 186, 189, 198, 273, 278, 366
Law, W., 467–8
Laws of Ecclesiastical Polity, 98–102
Leaf, J., 18
Leicester, Earl of, 77–8, 105, 135, 156
Leighton, A., 204
Leishman, J. B., 212
Lely, Sir P., 434
Leo XIII, 90
L'Estrange, Sir R., 437
Letters concerning Toleration, 395
Levellers, 283–4
Leviathan, 391–2
Lewis, C. S., 106
Leyburn, J., 504
Lilburne, J., 287, 341
Litany, 33
Little Gidding, 220
Lloyd, D. and T., 350
Lloyd, W., 460, 462
Locke, J., 388, 393–7, 445
London rebuilding, 357
London revolutionaries, 268–70
Long Parliament, 267–8, 294, 303
Longleat, 32, 464
Loyola, St I., 128, 132
Luffe, J., 344
Lycidas, 321

Macaulay, T. B., 400, 463
Macbeth, 110, 117
Magic, 379–80
Malone, E., 108
Maloney, J. B., 504
Manchester, Earl of, 257, 279
Manning, B., 270
Mansfield, Lord, 498

Margaret of Navarre, 82
Marlborough, Duke of, 459, 475
Marlow, C., 25, 112, 379
Marriage of clergy, 38, 59, 91–2
Marprelate tracts, 165
Marshall, S., 264
Marston Moor, battle of, 278
Martin, G., 133
Martyr, P., 39, 50, 53
Martyrs, Catholic, 20–3, 70
Martyrs, Protestant, 17–20, 65–6, 69–70
Marvell, A., 452
Massachusetts, 243–51, 254, 257, 342
Mary I, 17, 36, 55–69
Mary II, 469–71
Mary of Modena, 454, 456, 458
Mary Queen of Scots, 32, 55, 77–8, 81, 134–5
Maryland, 255, 504
Mass, see Eucharist
Mather, I., 251
Mather, T., 183
Maximilian, Emperor, 135
Mayne, C., 20
Measure for Measure, 116, 122
Meiderlin, P., 317
Merbecke, J., 42
Meres, F., 111
Messiah, 424–5
Mews, P., 458
Mildmay, Sir W., 165
Milton, J., 188, 262, 278, 293, 301, 319–32, 502
Mollard, A., 379
Monck, G., 302–3
Monmouth, Duke of, 442, 445–6
Montague, J., 183
Montague, Lady, 136
More, H., 371, 396, 451
More, Sir T., 21, 24, 64, 210
Morley, G., 189, 309
Morley, T., 104
Mounteagle, Lord, 228
Mountjoy, Lord, 132

Naseby, battle of, 274
Naylor, J., 298, 341–2
Neal, D., 500
Neale, Sir J., 157
Neile, R., 161, 184, 204
New England, 243–55
New Model Army, 279–82, 291–2
Newcastle, Duke of, 482–3
Newman, H., 493
Newman, J. H., 53, 504
Newton, Sir I., 380, 386–90

Nonjurors, 460–8
Norden, J., 24
Norfolk, Dukes of, 35, 134, 450
Northumberland, Duke of, 45, 48–9, 54–7
Northumberland, Earls of, 134–5, 229
Norton, T., 54
Nottingham, Earl of, 471
Nowell, A., 80, 151

Oates, T., 451–3
Occasional Conformity Act, 475–8
Order of the Communion (1548), 39–40
Ordinal (1550), 49
Ormes, C., 20
Ornaments in church, 38, 48, 146
Othello, 116–17
Overall, J., 174
Owen, J., 301, 316, 439, 501
Oxford, Earl of, see Harley

Paget, Sir W., 32, 43, 61
Panzoni, G., 230
Paradise Lost, 326
Parish churches, 36–8, 85–9, 145–50, 258, 296–8, 439–40, 490–2
Parker, M., 45, 90–4
Parr, C., 35, 45, 82
Patrick, S., 373
Paul III, 64
Paul IV, 65
Paul's Cross, 25
Pearson, J., 307
Penn, Sir W., 339, 348–51
Pennsylvania, 349–53
Penry, J., 167
Pepys, S., 345
Perkins, W., 175–6, 266
Perne, A., 163
Persons, R., 108, 128–9, 139, 141, 233
Petition of Right, 267
Petre, E., 450
Petre, W., 56
Philip of Spain, 60, 62, 69, 135
Pilgrim Fathers, 243–4
Pilgrim's Progress, 334–6
Pilkington, J., 160
Pitt, W., 484
Pius IV, 135
Pius V, 133
Platonism, 366, 396
Plowden, E., 22
Plunkett, O., 453
Pocahontas, 242
Pole, Cardinal, 43, 64–9
Ponet, J., 47, 60, 71
Pope, A., 386, 484–5

Popish plot, 451–3
Portland, Earl of, 230
Potter, J., 483
Powell, M., 323
Powicke, Sir M., 23
Prayer Book (1549), 33–4, 39–42; (1552), 30; (1559), 79, 87–8, 109, 145, 158–9; (Scottish), 192; (prohibited), 296–7; (1662), 312–13, 428
Praying Indians, 246–7
Preaching, 25, 88–9, 147–8, 174–7, 373
Presbyterians, 149–50, 280–9, 296–7, 444, 447–9, 469, 498
Preston, battle of, 285
Preston, J., 255–7, 385
Pride's Purge, 285
Priest to the Temple, 219
Protestant Dissenting Deputies, 449–500
Protestantism, 26–30, 57, 72–5
Prynne, W., 204, 266, 269, 446
Pseudo-Martyrs, 128, 210
Purcell, H., 421–2
Purgatory, 37–8
Puritans (Elizabethan), 44–77; (American), 240–55; (Cromwellian), 275–336, 436–7, 500
Putney debates, 284
Pym, J., 259, 261, 272, 275–6

Quakers, 254, 298, 339–55, 444, 483, 499
Queen Anne's Bounty, 473
Quietism, 237
Quinney, T., 87
Quinones, Cardinal, 41

Rainborough, T., 284
Rainolds, J., 169, 185
Ralegh, Sir W., 24–5, 230, 241
Ranters, 288
Ratramn, 33
Ray, J., 289
Reasonableness of Christianity, 396–7
Recusants, 21–2, 126–43, 156, 183, 228–34, 296, 449–60, 503–9
Reformation of manners, 494–5
Regensburg, 28
Regnans in excelsis, 133
Religio Laici, 398–9
Religio Medici, 364–5
Religious toleration, 251–5, 395–7, 443–4
Restoration settlement, 304–13, 426–31
Rhode Island, 252, 255
Ridley, N., 19, 33, 40, 49, 51, 169
Ridolfi, R., 133–5, 139
Rigby, J., 22
Robinson Crusoe, 407–8

Robinson, J., 243
Robinson, J. (Bishop), 487
Rochester, Earls of, 457, 494
Rogers, J. (martyr), 17
Rogers, J., 298
Roman Catholicism, see Counter-Reformation, Martyrs (Catholic) and Recusants
Rowlandson, T., 490
Rowse, A. L., 109
Royal Society, 384–6
Rubens, Sir P., 231
Rudyard, Sir B., 259
Rupert, Prince, 199, 276, 278
Russell, Lord, 445
Rye House plot, 442, 445

Sabbath, 147
Sacheverell, H., 476
St John, O., 276
St Omer, 129
St Paul's Cathedral, 25, 33, 205, 358–61
Salem, 379
Sampson, T., 159
Samson Agonistes, 327, 332
Sancroft, W., 358, 432–3, 454, 457, 470
Sander, N., 156
Sanderson, R., 306
Sandys, E., 161
Sandys, Sir E., 242
Sandys, W., 84
Sarum Use, 41
Saye and Sele, Lord, 256
Schism Act, 476–8
Science, 378, 381–90
Scory, 90
Scotland, 32, 182, 192–3, 276–8, 281, 293, 469
Scrooby, 243
Scott, J., 461
Scott, M., 21
Scott, R., 379
Scroggs, Lord Chief Justice, 452
Secker, T., 447
Sedley, C., 459
Sedgmoor, battle of, 458
Seekers, 290
Selkirk, A., 407
Serious Call, 468
Seymour, T., 45, 76
Shaftesbury, Earls of, 403, 405, 408–9, 453
Shakespeare, W., 73, 87, 107–26, 146, 148
Sharp, J., 413
Sheen, 68
Sherlock, T., 402
Sherlock, W., 462

Sheldon, G., 309, 358, 362–3, 429–30
Shirley, J., 231
Ship money, 267
Shorter Catechism, 277–8
Sibbes, R., 257
Sibthorpe, R., 198
Sidney, A., 445
Sixtus V, 139
Skinner, Bishop, 307
Smeaton, M., 76
Smith, Captain J., 242
Smith, J., 370
Smith, R., 234
Smithfield, 68
Smyth, J., 168
Socinians, 368–9
Solemn League and Covenant, 276, 289, 306, 328
Somerset, Duke of, 31–3, 43–6, 48
Sophia, Electress, 477
South, R., 461
Southampton, Earl of, 112–13, 242
Southwell, St R., 21, 104, 132, 235
Southwell, Sir R., 17
SPCK, 493
Spelman, Sir H., 204
Spenser, E., 105–7, 208
Spilsbury, J., 269
SPG, 493
Stafford, Lord, 453, 507
Stapleton, T., 20, 49, 99
Star Chamber, 203, 311
Stephen, Sir L., 421
Stephenson, M., 342
Stillingfleet, E., 372, 394
Stonor, R., 506
Strafford, Earl of, 193, 273–4
Stubbe, J., 152
Sunderland, Earl of, 450
Supreme Governor, 79–80
Swift, J., 406–15, 423, 462

Tale of a Tub, 410, 413
Tallis, T., 103
Taylor, J., 361–4, 429, 465
Taylor, R., 18
Tempest, 120–2, 241
Temple, 217–20
Tenison, T., 472–3
Test Acts, 441, 453, 478
Thirlby, T., 47
Thomson, L., 166
Thorndike, H., 307
Thoughts on Religion, 411
Thynne, Sir T., 32
Tijou, J., 360

Tillotson, J., 204, 266, 372–3, 385, 406, 432, 462, 472
Timon of Athens, 117
Tindal, M., 404
Tithes, 148, 194–5, 258, 288, 296, 298
Toland, J., 402–4
Toleration Act, 395, 443–4
Topcliffe, R., 21
Tories, 427, 442, 472–8, 482
Traherne, T., 373–8
Traugott, J., 413
Travers, W., 98, 100, 166–7
Tresham, Sir T., 140
Trevelyan, G. M., 355
Troilus and Cressida, 116
Tuckney, A., 277
Tunstall, C., 47
Turner, F., 457, 460
Twelfth Night, 113–14, 157, 167, 170
Tyrconnel, Earl of, 457

Unitarians, 368–9, 498
Ussher, J., 296, 316

Van Dyck, Sir A., 231
Vanbrugh, Sir J., 360
Vane, Sir H., 276
Vaughan, H., 221–4
Vaux, Lord, 140
Verney, Sir E., 262
Vestments, 47, 51, 146, 159, 506
Vicars apostolic, 450, 506
Virginia, 241, 492–3

Wagstaffe, J., 462
Warberton, W., 485–6
Wake, W., 461, 475, 479–81
Walpole, H., 21, 70
Walpole, Sir R., 481–3
Walsingham, Sir F., 140, 156
Walton, I., 102, 306, 429
Ward, M., 238–9
Ward, S., 385
Warwick, Earls of, 156, 257, 279
Waste, J., 20
Waterland, D., 420
Watts, I., 501–3
Wentworth, P., 153–4
Wesley, J., 468, 492, 497, 503
Westcote, S., 104
Westminster Abbey, 68–9, 105, 228, 357–8
Westminster Assembly, 287–8
Westmorland, Earls of, 13, 134–5
Weston, W., 104, 131, 141
Wharton, Lord, 442
Whicote, B., 369–70

Whigs, 427, 442, 445–6, 453, 479–85

Whiston, W., 387

Whitaker, A., 242

Whitaker, W., 175

White, T., 236

Whitehead, G., 354

Whitelocke, B., 293–4

Whitgift, J., 144, 148, 154, 162–4, 167

Whittingham, W., 146

Wightman, E., 183

Willey, B., 393

William III, 454, 458–9, 469–73

William, Prince of Orange, 136

Williams, R., 251–4, 280

Windebank, Sir F., 230

Winstanley, G., 287

Winter's Tale, 120–1

Winthrop, J., 244, 247, 252–3

Wise, T., 370

Witchcraft, 184, 379–80

Woolman, J., 353

Woolston, T., 401–2

Worcester, battle of, 293

Wordsworth, W., 386–7

Wren, Sir C., 356–61, 384

Wren, M., 204, 226

Wyatt, Sir T., 60–1, 76

Yeats, W. B., 415

Young, T., 320